ACT SUCCESS
Strategies for Mastering the ACT

Academic Educational Resources

© 1993, 2007, 2008, 2009 by Academic Educational Resources.
All rights reserved. First edition 1993
Fourth Edition 2009

Printed in the United States of America

ISBN-13: 978-0-615-33547-6

All rights reserved. No part of this book may be reproduced or transmitted in any form or by any means, electronic or mechanical, including photocopying, recording, or by any information storage and retrieval system, without prior written permission of the Publisher, except where permitted by law.

Published by Academic Educational Resources, Chicago, IL

www.academiceducationalresources.com

*ACT is a registered trademark of ACT, Inc., which does not endorse this product.

TABLE OF CONTENTS

How to Use the ACT Success Textbook	IV
About the ACT	V
The Keys to Success	VIII

Chapter 1: *English Strategies and Review* — 1

Introduction and General Hints	2
English Rules	4
Skill Builders: Fragments #1 and #2	15
Skill Builders: Punctuation #1, #2, #3, and #4	22
Skill Builder: Commas	30
Skill Builders: Possessives, Apostrophe #1 and #2	32
Skill Builders: Subject/Verb and Subject/Pronoun Agreement #1 and #2	39
Skill Builders: Transitions #1 and #2	42
Skill Builders: Transitions and Modifiers #1 and #2	46
Skill Builders: Rhetorical Questions #1 and #2	50
Skill Builder: Deleting	55
Punctuation Summary Sheet	58
Skill Builders: Integrated Punctuation #1 and #2	59
English Quiz: English Made Easy	63
English Practice Passage #1	66
English Practice Passage #2	69
English Practice Passage #3	72

Chapter 2: *Math Strategies and Review* — 77

Introduction and General Hints	78
Math Rules: Formulas, Strategies, and Review	81
Skill Builder: Area Formulas	96
Skill Builder: Order of Operations	98
Skill Builder: Slope of Lines	100
Skill Builder: Midpoint Formula	102
Skill Builder: Pythagorean Theorem	104
Skill Builder: Distance Formula	106
Skill Builder: Prime Numbers	108
Skill Builder: Even and Odd Numbers	109
Skill Builder: Percents	110
Skill Builder: Greatest Common Factor	112
Skill Builder: Least Common Multiple	113
Skill Builder: Motion Problems	114
Skill Builder: Exponents	116
Skill Builder: Radicals	118
Skill Builder: Quadratics	119
Skill Builder: Circles	121
Skill Builder: Right Triangle Trig	123

TABLE OF CONTENTS
(CONTINUED)

Skill Builder: Logarithms	125
Skill Builder: Complex Numbers	127
Math Quiz: Pre-Algebra	130
Math Quiz: Algebra	132
Math Quiz: Plane Geometry	136
Math Quiz: Circle & Coordinate Geometry	140
Math Quiz: Advanced Algebra	144
Math Quiz: Trigonometry	148

Chapter 3: *Reading Strategies and Review* — **153**

Introduction, Rules, and Strategies	154
Skill Builder: Finding the Main Idea	160
Skill Builders: Determining Character & Attitude #1, #2 and #3	162
Skill Builder: Skimming for Details	165
Skill Builders: Cause and Effect #1 and #2	166
Reading Practice Passage #1: Fiction	170
Reading Practice Passage #2: Social Science	172
Reading Practice Passage #3: Humanities	174
Reading Practice Passage #4: Natural Science	176

Chapter 4: *Science Strategies and Review* — **179**

Introduction, Rules, and Strategies	180
Skill Builders: Interpreting Graphs #1, #2 and #3	186
Skill Builders: Analyzing Data #1, #2, #3, #4, #5, and #6	190
Skill Builders: Opposing Viewpoints #1, #2, and #3	202
Science Practice Passage #1	210
Science Practice Passage #2	212
Science Practice Passage #3	214

Chapter 5: *Writing Strategies and Review* — **217**

Introduction and Essay Essentials	218
Skill Builder: The Thesis Statement	219
Rules/Strategies: The Overall Approach	220
Skill Builder: Essay Planning & Organizing	222
Exercises to Improve Essay Writing Skills	224

Chapter 6: *Complete Practice Tests* — **225**

Practice Test #1	227
Practice Test #2	291
Practice Test #3	359
Practice Test #4	419
Practice Test #5	485

TABLE OF CONTENTS
(CONTINUED)

Chapter 7: *The 24 Hour Countdown* — **549**

Chapter 8: *Scantrons (Bubble Sheets)* — **551**

Chapter 9: *Answer Keys* — **569**

    English Answer Keys — **570**
    Math Answer Keys — **576**
    Reading Answer Keys — **578**
    Science Answer Keys — **580**
    Practice Test #1 Answer Key — **584**
    Practice Test #2 Answer Key — **585**
    Practice Test #3 Answer Key — **586**
    Practice Test #4 Answer Key — **587**
    Practice Test #5 Answer Key — **588**

How to use the ACT SUCCESS textbook!

We know this must be a stressful time in your life: balancing school work, family, friends, sports, jobs, AND college admission! Whew…that's a mouth full. The ACT SUCCESS textbook has been created with your busy life in mind.

The ACT is a five section test: English, math, reading, science, and writing. The ACT SUCCESS program covers all these areas. As we created this book, we made a point of reviewing and teaching only material presented on this high stakes test. We won't waste your time on skills you do not need for success! Essentially, if it's not in this book, it's not on the ACT!

The ACT is unlike any test you have ever taken. It requires a new way of thinking. Look at it this way. In your English or math class, you would need a minimum of 70% to earn the lowest possible C. However, on the ACT, 70% correct would turn into a score of about 25. (The ACT is scored 1 – 36. You will learn more about scoring in a minute.) While a 25 might or might not be a good score for you, it is far above the national average of a 21. What does all this mean? It means you can get a lot of questions wrong on the ACT and still get a good score and go to college! The key is to never give up while taking the test.

Even your teachers need to re-learn how to take the ACT and teach it effectively! In fact, there is no teacher's guide for this book because we want every student to know exactly what our teachers know! We have trained them, and now they will train you.

With that said, we would like to take this opportunity to introduce you to the layout of the ACT SUCCESS textbook. You will receive more specifics as you progress through the book but in general your ACT preparation will consist of two components: first you will learn our time-tested strategies and review important skills, and then you will work through a number of full practice tests. The book's chapters are divided by subject in the order that they will appear on the ACT. Each chapter progresses from general information and strategies to "Skill Builders" (where you will review important concepts and get comfortable with ACT-type questions), to quizzes and practices passages that will help you measure how far you have come. From there, you will be ready for the practice tests. You will have learned everything that will be covered on the ACT, and all that's left to do is practice, practice, practice!

We wish you nothing but ACT SUCCESS!

ABOUT THE ACT

FORMAT

The ACT test consists of 4 multiple choice sections plus a writing section. The sections are as follows:

English - 45 minutes/75 questions
Math - 60 minutes/60 questions
Reading - 35 minutes/40 questions
Science - 35 minutes/40 questions
Writing - 30 minutes to write an essay

SCORING

The four multiple choice sections (English, Math, Reading, and Science) are scored on a scale from 1 – 36; the more questions you answer correctly, the higher your score will be. You will receive an individual score for each subject test, as well as a *composite* score. Your composite score is found by averaging your four subject test scores – that is, adding them all together and dividing the sum by four – and rounding (round up at .5 or above).

For example, let's say a student took a practice ACT, and received the following scores:

English: 26
Math: 21
Reading: 24
Science: 24

This student's composite score would therefore be a 24.

(Added together, these scores total 95. Divide that value by four, and you get 23.75. Because 23.75 has a decimal value greater than or equal to .5, we must round up to 24).

When colleges speak of ACT scores or list the median ACT score of their student bodies, they are generally speaking in terms of composite scores.

The only aspect of the ACT not scored from 1 – 36 is the Writing section. Every essay is read by two essay graders, who each give the writing sample a score ranging from 1 – 6. These scores are added together, resulting in a Writing score ranging from 2 – 12. Students will also receive a combined English/Writing score (on a scale of 1 – 36), drawing one-third from your Writing score and two-thirds from your English score.

Neither the Writing score nor the combined English/Writing score is factored into your composite score. But keep in mind, every college that you apply to will see your Writing scores, so you must still do your best!

PRACTICE TESTS

The most important aspect of your preparation for the ACT is taking full practice tests. Once you have reviewed all of the skills presented in this book and learned our proven strategies for ACT SUCCESS, you can truly begin to measure your progress as a test-taker. Do not expect to reach your score goals on the first practice test. It takes time to master the strategies and familiarize yourself with the ACT. As you move through the various practice tests, always keep one goal in mind: **steady progress**.

Though scale scores (explained above) are certainly important, the most helpful tool to measure your progress is actually your raw score on each subject test. In other words, on each successive practice test, your goal should always be to answer more questions correctly than you did on the previous test. Always think in terms of how many questions you answer correctly, because in most cases, for every one question you get right on the Reading and Science sections, your scale scores go up by a full point; on the English and Math sections, you get about 1 scale point for every 2 questions you answer correctly. Keep track of your scores on the sheets provided after each practice tests, and push yourself to answer at least one more question correctly per section as you move through the tests. If you can reach this very modest goal, by the time you finish working through this book, **you will have raised your composite score by 3 points!**

The point is simple: you might think that one little question does not matter, but you could not be further from the truth! Getting one or two more questions right might just help you get into the college of your dreams!

MONITORING TIME

We will discuss pacing for each section in the strategies for that particular section.
To succeed on this test, both during practice and on the actual test, you need to be responsible for keeping track of time. Please practice pacing yourself so that you are not surprised during the actual ACT.

Suggestion for time keeping: Use a digital watch on both the practice tests and on the actual test. Be sure it has a stop watch feature and does not beep. If you must use a watch with a sweeping second hand, set it to noon before you begin each test. It is far easier to gauge your time from this setting.

Regardless of which type of watch you choose, the most important thing is that you do your practice tests using the watch that you will use on the actual test day.

BUILDING ENDURANCE

The ACT test is close to 4 hours in length. Your ultimate goal should be to complete a full practice test in one sitting before the actual test. You should begin to build endurance by doing at least 2 sections together (ie: English then Math or Reading then Science). Additionally, the ACT test is always given in the morning, so it is a good idea to do at least some of your practicing in the morning (especially if you are not a "morning person"!)

BUBBLE SHEET (ALSO KNOWN AS THE SCANTRON)

There is no penalty for guessing, so the most important thing is that you LEAVE NO BLANKS!

A good strategy for filling in your scantron is to "Code in Blocks": complete one full page of the test circling the answers in the book, then, before you go to the next page, fill in the circles on the scantron.

Ultimately, you should complete your scantron sheet in a way that feels comfortable, but DO NOT wait until the end of the test to fill in all of the circles as you might run out of time, resulting in blank answers and a lower score.

The Keys to Success

These are general guidelines! Through practice you will learn which strategies work best for you. However, to be successful you must remember the following:

ADAPT
Learn the format of the test.
Do not linger over difficult questions.
Do not panic if a question seems unfamiliar or more difficult. Make an educated guess and move on.
Leave no blank answers.
Take practice tests and learn from your mistakes.

CONCENTRATE
Learn how to pace yourself.
Read the questions carefully.
Practice without interruptions.
Condition your mind.

TRAIN
In order to achieve your goal, you must practice, practice, practice!
Think of preparing for the test like running a marathon: you cannot run for ten minutes a day and expect to be successful.
Increase your stamina each week by doing more.
In order to reach the finish line, you must take a full test in one sitting.

Chapter 1
English Strategies and Review

ENGLISH

The ACT English test is possibly the easiest section to make vast skill and score improvements. There are 5 passages, each with 15 questions, for a total of 75 questions.

THREE REASONS TO LOVE THE ENGLISH SECTION
(even though it seems really long!)

- It's the first section of the test, so you aren't tired (yet!)

- Many of the questions are based on just a few punctuation/grammar rules.

- Although there are 75 questions, they keep repeating ideas, so if you know the rules, it's like being asked the same question over and over again!

DO'S AND DON'TS

- **DO** approach this section as if you were reading an English paper that has to be corrected.

- **DO** pick the clearest, most concise way of stating something. SHORTEST IS BEST as long as you have a complete sentence.

- **DO** read to the end of a sentence before answering a question. This way you will be sure that you pick an answer that creates a complete sentence.

- **DO** test "OMIT the underlined portion" or "DELETE the underlined portion" first: when it is listed as an answer choice, it is the correct answer about fifty percent of the time. Remember, though, that means it is a wrong answer fifty percent of the time as well, so choose OMIT when the underlined portion is repetitive or does not fit the main idea of the passage.

- **DO** be careful when selecting an answer with the word "being" in it, as it is seldom correct.

- **DO** look for wrong answers. Wrong answers are often much easier to find than right ones. Unless the right answer comes to you immediately, **ELIMINATE WRONG ANSWERS!**

- **DON'T** jump from question to question—read the entire passage; however, you are often reading for technical issues, not content. Regarding content, you only need a very basic idea of what is going on to answer the content questions.

- **DON'T** be afraid to pick NO CHANGE. It is a correct answer as often as any other answer.

PACING AND PRACTICE

- You have 45 minutes to complete 5 passages—that's 9 minutes per passage.

- Hint for practicing your pacing: Draw a box at the end of each section. Under each box write in multiples of 9 (9, 18, 27, 36, and 45). You must be finished in 45 minutes. As you take the exam, time yourself and write in the actual time you take to finish. This will give you and your teacher a strong idea of where you need to speed up or slow down.

- The sections do not get more difficult as you go, so it is best to finish even if you have to make a few guesses along the way.

- It takes practice to get used to the English section. The good news is that if you apply the rules and strategies while taking the practice tests, you will be fully prepared for the actual test.

HOW TO USE ACT SUCCESS TO STUDY FOR THE ENGLISH SECTION

The remainder of this chapter consists of the ACT Success "English Rules," Skill Builders, the "English Made Easy" quiz, and practice passages.

The English Rules cover absolutely **everything** that the English section tests – everything you need to know is covered right here! For instance, even though there are hundreds of rules for how to use commas in the English language, the ACT will only ask you about 6 of them; and they are all listed in a few pages! Keep in mind, the English portion of the exam is the easiest section of the test on which to raise your score. However, you must master the following rules! Trust what you are learning because these rules work! It usually takes students a little while before they know how to apply the following rules and techniques. It's natural to make mistakes in the beginning; that's how we learn. Don't give up because you will master this test!

Immediately after a series of English Rules is introduced, you will be asked to complete a Skill Builder corresponding to what you have just learned. As you have just learned "The Rules," you should not expect to get every question right on the Skill Builders. Their purpose is simply to show you how a given topic is tested on the ACT and what types of questions you should expect. You will then be introduced to more material, followed by more Skill Builders.

After all of "The Rules" and Skill Builders have been introduced, you will take a short quiz called "English Made Easy". Once you have completed and corrected the quiz, it will list many of the most important rules, and the quiz will serve as a concise study guide to the ACT English Rules. At the end of the chapter, you will come to practice passages that offer you your first opportunity to work through actual test-like passages. These practice passages combine everything you have learned and covered so far, and everything you need to know to achieve ACT SUCCESS!

GOOD LUCK!

ENGLISH RULES
Strategies and Review

SENTENCE FRAGMENTS

In order to succeed on the English test, you must be able to recognize what is, and is not, a complete sentence. Every complete sentence must contain a subject, a verb, and express a **complete thought**.

- Short groups of words can be sentences:

    She likes milk.

    This is a complete sentence. "She" is the subject, "likes" is the verb, and the author's thought is complete.

- Very long groups of words might not be complete sentences:

    Although the weather was rainy and more clouds were gathering in the gray overcast sky…

    This is an example of a sentence fragment. The thought is incomplete and leaves the reader dangling. (If you are anything like me, this fragment leaves you asking the question: "Although *what*?")

- If you are unsure whether a group of words is a complete sentence, ask yourself the following series of questions:

    1) **Is it finished?**

        If not, as in the second example above, you are dealing with a fragment. If it is, move on to question 2…

    2) **Is it a complete thought?**

        Again, if the answer is no, the sentence cannot be complete. If the answer is yes, move on to question 3…

    3) **Is it a complete sentence?**

    Unless the answer to all three questions is "yes," it cannot be a complete sentence!

PUNCTUATION

Mastering these rules is one of the keys to success!

COMMA — **There are six comma rules to learn for the ACT.**

1. Commas are used to mark the end of an introductory clause or phrase and are followed by a complete sentence. Introductory clauses often begin with words such as *although, when, while, since, if, and because*. (Yes. The word *because* can start a sentence!)

    Ex: When it stops raining, Aaron is going to wash his car.

    Ex: Although I'd love to go to the movie with you, I need to study for the ACT.

Please notice that each clause is followed by a comma and then a complete sentence. Also, the subject of the sentence must be mentioned immediately after the comma in order for it to make sense.

    Ex: Feeling very sad, she felt a tear run down her cheek.

This sentence is correct because it is clear that "she" was feeling very sad. If the sentence were written, "Feeling very sad, a tear ran down her cheek" it would be incorrect. A tear cannot feel sad!

2. Commas are used to set off non-restrictive clauses/appositives (phrases that interrupt the flow of the sentence).

    Ex: David, a champion swimmer, hoped to make the Olympic team.

To check for interruptions, remove the words between the commas. If the remaining portion is a complete sentence and the meaning is not changed, then the commas are correct. If not, then test another answer. <u>Be sure to read the whole sentence!</u>

Also, words such as *however, for example, for instance*, and *though* are usually surrounded by commas.

3. Commas are used to separate two or more adjectives preceding a noun.

    Ex: The ACT is not a stressful, difficult test.

    However, do not use a comma if the first adjective describes the second.

    Ex: The man wore a bright blue sweater. (*Bright* describes the type of *blue*.)

4. Commas separate more than two words in a series.

    Ex: I bought eggs, milk, and butter at the store.

    <u>Note</u>: The last comma before the "and" (here after "milk") is optional, but the ACT tends to leave it in.

ENGLISH RULES

COMMAS (continued)

5. A comma <u>before a conjunction</u> can be used to separate two complete sentences. (Conjunction words are *and, but, or, so*.)

    Ex: The palm trees blew softly in the wind, and the hot sun beat down from the sky.

    Do NOT use a comma without the conjunction to separate two complete sentences!

    Ex: The palm trees blew softly in the wind, the sun beat down from the sky.

6. A comma can be used at the end of a sentence followed by an afterthought.

    Ex: The football game was a massacre, forty-nine to zero.

Other comma hints:

When in doubt, leave the comma out!

Just because you pause when reading a sentence does not mean the sentence requires a comma!

If all four answer choices are identically worded and three of the four answer choices contain commas in various places, the correct answer is likely to be the one that omits the commas!

DASH – There are two dash rules used on the ACT. Dashes are similar to commas in these two cases.

1. The dash, like the comma, is used to mark an interruption.

Ex: The Chicago Marathon - a race of endurance, strength, and skill – is difficult to complete.

Please note that two dashes or two commas can be used interchangeably; however, do not use one of each.

2. The dash can also be used to stress a word or phrase at the end of a sentence.

    Ex: Danny's hair is unlike anyone else's in the family - thick and dark.

SEMICOLON – There are two semicolon rules to know for the ACT.

1. The semicolon is used to separate complete sentences.

    Ex: Shannon practiced diligently for the ACT; she eventually earned a great score.

2. The semicolon is also used before a coordinating conjunction (*however, therefore*) to separate two sentences.

    Ex: I enjoy living in a small community; however, the neighbors are often too nosy.

ENGLISH RULES

COLON – There are three colon rules for the ACT. There is ALWAYS a complete sentence prior to the colon.

1. The colon is used after a complete sentence followed by a summary list.

    Ex: I have many hobbies: golfing, rock climbing, sailing, and windsurfing.

2. The colon is also used at the end of a complete sentence followed by an afterthought.

    Ex: Japan has a high literacy rate: 99 percent.

3. The colon is also used to separate two complete sentences when the second sentence explains or restates an idea in the first.

    Ex: These seat covers are the most durable kind: they are reinforced with double stitching and covered with a heavy plastic coating.

APOSTROPHE (POSSESSIVES) – An apostrophe is used to show ownership.

1. If there is one owner, use *'s*.
    Ex: Jim's car is brand new.

2. If there is more than one owner, use *s'*.
    Ex: Ten boys' bikes were stolen.

3. Words that are plural without adding the "s" form the possessive by adding *'s*.
    Ex: Women's, men's, people's, children's

    Their = more than one owner
    There = location
    They're = they are

    It's = it is
    Its = one owner
    Its' = THIS IS NOT A WORD, BUT THE ACT OFTEN GIVES IT AS AN ANSWER CHOICE — DON'T EVER CHOOSE IT!

Quiz!

You now know four ways to separate or combine complete sentences. What are they?
1.

2.

3.

4

ENGLISH RULES

GRAMMAR

SUBJECT-VERB AGREEMENT

Always check verbs for agreement! Within a sentence, a singular subject must be followed by a singular verb, and a plural subject must be followed by a plural verb.

Example: The stack of books is on the floor.
The subject here is "stack," which is singular, so the verb "is" is correct.

BE CAREFUL! Verbs are not made plural just by putting an "s" on the end. If you want a singular verb, put the word "he or she" in front of it and make sure it works. If you want a plural verb, put the word "they" in front of it and make sure it works.

Example: He sits.
They sit.

One of the ACT's most common questions begins with a singular subject and is followed by several prepositional phrases with plural nouns and then a verb. This verb MUST be singular so as to agree with the sentence's singular subject.

Example: The color of the glass in the panes of glass in the windows of the nearby houses is actually a reflection of the suns rays.

Though there are multiple nouns in the prepositional phrase above, the subject in this sentence is in fact "color." You must therefore use the singular verb "is."

SUBJECT-PRONOUN AGREEMENT

Within a sentence, a singular subject must be followed by a singular pronoun and a plural subject must be followed by a plural pronoun.

Example: Each of the boys took his seat on the bus.
Since the subject is "each of the boys," it is singular. His is a singular pronoun.

PARALLEL PHRASING

Express ideas in a consistent, grammatical way. Phrases or words in a series must be in the same form.

DO THIS: *I like to ski, sail and swim.* NOT THIS: I like to ski, sailing and swimming.

GRAMMAR

USAGE

Affect = verb. Think of it as "a" is for action, and verbs are action words.
Effect = noun.

Who = subject.   Ex: The ACT is a test for students <u>who</u> work hard.
Whom = object. Ex: The ACT is a test for students <u>whom</u> I see as hard workers.

TRANSITIONS

If all answers except one have a transition, pick the one without a transition.
- A. Consequently, the dog
- B. Therefore, the dog
- C. *The dog*
- D. For example, the dog

If all answers contain transitions…

1. Look for two transitions that have similar meanings. To help you learn which transitions are similar to one another, the chart below lists transitions by category.

2. Eliminate the two with similar meanings.

3. Look at the sentence before and after the transition to determine how the sentences should be linked. One of the 2 remaining answers should clearly be the better choice.

Transitions By Category

Comparison or Contrast		Cause and Effect	
However	Nevertheless	Thus	So
Yet	In like manner	Then	Because
Likewise	On the contrary	Therefore	On account of
Similarly	Instead	As a result	Since
Nonetheless	Conversely	Accordingly	Consequently

Addition		Emphasis	
Also	Second	Indeed	In other words
Besides	As well	In fact	Especially
Too	In addition	Even	
Moreover	Furthermore		

Examples

For instance	As an illustration	That is
Namely	Also	For example
In particular		

ENGLISH RULES

MODIFIERS

If you have an introductory phrase, the subject of the sentence must come immediately after the comma.

DO THIS: *Feeling very sad, the girl felt a tear run down her cheek.*
NOT THIS: Feeling very sad, a tear ran down her cheek.
   (The girl was feeling sad, not the tear!)

TYPES OF RHETORICAL QUESTIONS

ACT English scores are broken down into two categories: (1) usage and mechanics (previously covered in this textbook); and (2) rhetorical skills. It is imperative that you learn the seven different types of rhetorical questions that the ACT tends to ask. Be sure to look for (and underline) the clue in the question. With a little practice, you will master these question types!

DELETE

When choosing whether or not to delete a phrase, decide if the phrase contains significant details and then look at the function of the phrase in the sentence.

INTRODUCTORY PHRASES

If a question asks you to pick the sentence that best introduces a paragraph, read the next sentence or two. Think about what you would say, and then go to the answer choices. There should only be one answer choice that has anything to do with what you predicted.

Be careful to only read one or two sentences! If you read the whole paragraph, you might then pick an answer choice that has to do with a smaller detail in the paragraph, rather than the overall topic.

Example: William Shakespeare's plays have been performed all over the world.
If the sentence above is the "next" sentence that you read, then there should only be one answer choice that has to do with Shakespeare's plays.

ADD

Only add if it proves relevant to the main idea and is not redundant information.

ILLUSTRATE/SUPPORT

If a question asks which of the answers best "illustrates" or "supports" something, pick the answer that gives the most specific details/examples.

NOT/LEAST

If a question asks, "Which of the following is NOT acceptable," or "Which is LEAST acceptable," the important thing to remember is that 3 answers will be correct, so eliminate the three correct answers and pick the remaining one.

Even though the test writers capitalize the word "NOT" or "LEAST" in the question, it is often helpful to circle or underline it as you read the question to remind yourself that you need to switch gears and look for the wrong answer rather than the right one.

PARAGRAPH OR SENTENCE ORDER

If a question asks about paragraph order, it typically has to do with chronological order. Link the topic and concluding sentences of each paragraph. If a question asks about sentence order, there is typically an order of actions. For example, *you can't get up before you fall down!*

SUPPOSE THE AUTHOR...

If the last question of the passages begins with "Suppose the author..." follow these two steps:

1. Two answers will begin with "Yes" and two with "No". Ask yourself, "Is the question a one sentence summary of the passage?" If it is, pick "yes", if not, pick "no." (Remember, for it to be a one sentence summary, it must summarize the ENTIRE passage, not just be a topic that was discussed in one paragraph.)

2. Once you have done step one & are down to two answers, pick the one that has the explanation that paraphrases the question.

Additional Notes

ENGLISH SKILL BUILDERS

SENTENCE FRAGMENTS

In order to succeed on the English test, you must be able to recognize what is, and is not, a complete sentence. Every complete sentence must contain a subject, a verb, and express a **complete thought**.

- Short groups of words can be sentences:

    She likes milk.

    This is a complete sentence. "She" is the subject, "likes" is the verb, and the author's thought is complete.

- Very long groups of words might not be complete sentences:

    Although the weather was rainy and more clouds were gathering in the gray overcast sky…

    This is an example of a sentence fragment. The thought is incomplete and leaves the reader dangling. (If you are anything like me, this fragment leaves you asking the question: "Although *what*?")

- If you are unsure whether a group of words is a complete sentence, ask yourself the following series of questions:

    1) **Is it finished?**

    If not, as in the second example above, you are dealing with a fragment. If it is, move on to question 2…

    2) **Is it a complete thought?**

    Again, if the answer is no, the sentence cannot be complete. If the answer is yes, move on to question 3…

    3) **Is it a complete sentence?**

    Unless the answer to all three questions is "yes," it cannot be a complete sentence!

ACT SUCCESS
English Skill Builder – Fragments #1

Directions: In the passage below, certain words and phrases are underlined and numbered. In the right hand column, you will find alternatives for the underlined part. For each question, choose the alternative you consider best. If you think the original version is best, choose "NO CHANGE." Be sure to read the entire sentence before making a selection.

The Power of Lightning

Lightning is a powerful electrostatic discharge created during a thunderstorm. Lightning's abrupt electric discharge accompanied by the release of visible light and other forms of electromagnetic radiation. The electric current passing through the discharge channels quickly heats and expands the air into a plasma, creating acoustic shock waves (thunder) in the atmosphere.

1.
   A. NO CHANGE
   B. Lightning's abrupt electric discharged
   C. Lightning's abrupt electric discharge is accompanied by
   D. Lightning's abrupt electric discharge is accompanied

A bolt of lightning can achieve temperatures approaching 28,000 kelvins (50,000 degrees Fahrenheit) in a split second. This is about five times hotter than the surface of the sun. The heat of lightning that strikes loose soil or sandy areas of the ground may fuse the soil or sand into glass channels called fulgurites. These are sometimes found under the sandy surfaces of golf courses and beaches, or in desert regions. Evidence that lightning spreads out into branching channels when it strikes the ground.

2.
   F. NO CHANGE
   G. than the surface
   H. of the sun
   J. OMIT the underlined portion

3.
   A. NO CHANGE
   B. Fulgurites are evidence that lightning spreads out
   C. Evidence is that lightning spreads out
   D. Fulgurites are evidence that spreads out

Trees are frequent conductors of lightning to the ground. If the damage is severe, the tree may not be able to recover, and decay sets in, eventually killing the tree. Occasionally, may explode completely. It is commonly thought that a tree standing alone is more frequently struck, though in some forests, lightning scars can be seen on almost every tree.

4.
   F. NO CHANGE
   G. Occasionally, a tree may completely.
   H. Occasionally, may explode.
   J. Occasionally, a tree may explode completely.

ACT SUCCESS
English Skill Builder – Fragments #1

Almost 2000 each year are injured by lightning strikes.
          5
Between 25 and 33 percent of those struck die. Lightning injuries result from three factors: electrical damage, intense heat, and the mechanical energy that these generate. While quick death is common due to the huge voltage of a lightning strike, survivors often fare better than victims of other
                          6
electrical injuries caused by a more prolonged application of lesser voltage.

5. A. NO CHANGE
    B. People each year injured
    C. Almost 2000 people each year are injured
    D. Almost 2000 people each year injured

6. F. NO CHANGE
    G. survivors often fare better
    H. often better than victims
    J. survivors often fare better than

Copyright © 2009 by Academic Educational Resources. All rights reserved.

ACT SUCCESS
English Skill Builder—Fragments #2
Directions: Read the passage and then choose the best answer to each question.

Generation Me Vs. You Revisited

<u>Conventional wisdom that today's young people</u>[1] — schooled in the church of self-esteem, vying for spots on reality television, promoting themselves on YouTube — are more self-involved than their predecessors. Heck, they join Facebook groups like the Association for Justified Narcissism. A study released last year by the Pew Research Center for the People and the Press dubbed Americans age 18 to 25 as the "Look at Me" generation and reported that this group said that their top goals were fortune and fame.

Yet despite exhibiting some signs of self-obsession, <u>young Americans are not more self-absorbed than earlier generations</u>[2], according to new research challenging the prevailing wisdom.

<u>Point out that bemoaning the self-involvement</u>[3] of young people is a perennial adult activity. Others warn that if young people continue to be labeled selfish and narcissistic, they just might live up to that reputation.

However, recent research has shown there have been very few changes in the thoughts, feelings and behaviors of youth over the last 30 years. In other words,

1. **A.** NO CHANGE
   B. That today's young people
   C. Conventional wisdom's that today's young people
   D. Conventional wisdom maintains that today's young people

2. **F.** NO CHANGE
   G. young Americans not more self-absorbed than earlier generations
   H. not more self-absorbed than earlier generations are young Americans
   J. earlier generations are not more self-absorbed than young Americans

3. **A.** NO CHANGE
   B. Some scholars point out that bemoaning
   C. Point out that some scholars bemoaning
   D. That bemoaning

ACT SUCCESS
English Skill Builder—Fragments #2

the YouTube broadcasts of today's the new age seminars
<u>   </u>
                          4
of 1978. This challenges a 2006 study that found

narcissism is much more prevalent among people born in

the 1980s <u>than in earlier generations.</u>
                       5

    Scholars suggest several reasons why the young

may be perceived as having increased narcissistic traits.

<u>The personal biases of older adults, the news media's</u>
                                6
<u>emphasis on celebrity, and the rise of social networking</u>
                                6
<u>sites that encourage egocentricity.</u>
                   6

    "Youth bashing" has become so common that

accomplishments tend to be forgotten, like the fact that

young people today have a closer relationship with their

parents than existed between children and their parents

<u>in the 1960s. Or that they popularized the alternative</u>
                                        7
<u>spring break</u> in which a student opts to spend a vacation
        7
helping people in a third world country instead of

chugging 40s in Cancún.

4. **F.** NO CHANGE
   G. the YouTube broadcasts of today the new age seminars
   H. the YouTube broadcasts today's new age seminars
   J. the YouTube broadcasts of today are the new age seminars

5. **A.** NO CHANGE
   B. in earlier generations.
   C. than earlier.
   D. OMIT THE UNDERLINE PORTION

6. **F.** NO CHANGE
   G. The personal biases of older adults, the news media's emphasis on celebrity, and the rise of social networking sites encourage egocentricity.
   H. Including the personal biases of older adults, the news media's emphasis on celebrity, and the rise of social networking sites that encourage egocentricity.
   J. The personal biases of older adults are the news media's emphasis on celebrity and the rise of social networking sites that encourage egocentricity.

7. **A.** NO CHANGE
   B. in the 1960s, or that they popularized the alternative spring break
   C. in the 1960s. They popularized the alternative spring break
   D. in the 1960s they popularized the alternative spring break

PUNCTUATION

Mastering these rules is one of the keys to success!

COMMA — **There are six comma rules to learn for the ACT.**

1. Commas are used to mark the end of an introductory clause or phrase and are followed by a complete sentence. Introductory clauses often begin with words such as *although, when, while, since, if, and because.* (Yes. The word *because* can start a sentence!)

    Ex: When it stops raining, Aaron is going to wash his car.

    Ex: Although I'd love to go to the movie with you, I need to study for the ACT.

Please notice that each clause is followed by a comma and then a complete sentence. Also, the subject of the sentence must be mentioned immediately after the comma in order for it to make sense.

    Ex: Feeling very sad, she felt a tear run down her cheek.

This sentence is correct because it is clear that "she" was feeling very sad. If the sentence were written, "Feeling very sad, a tear ran down her cheek" it would be incorrect. A tear cannot feel sad!

2. Commas are used to set off non-restrictive clauses/appositives (phrases that interrupt the flow of the sentence).

    Ex: David, a champion swimmer, hoped to make the Olympic team.

To check for interruptions, remove the words between the commas. If the remaining portion is a complete sentence and the meaning is not changed, then the commas are correct. If not, then test another answer. <u>Be sure to read the whole sentence!</u>

Also, words such as *however, for example, for instance*, and *though* are usually surrounded by commas.

3. Commas are used to separate two or more adjectives preceding a noun.

    Ex: The ACT is not a stressful, difficult test.

    However, do not use a comma if the first adjective describes the second.

    Ex: The man wore a bright blue sweater. (*Bright* describes the type of *blue*.)

4. Commas separate more than two words in a series.

    Ex: I bought eggs, milk, and butter at the store.

    <u>Note</u>: The last comma before the "and" (here after "milk") is optional, but the ACT tends to leave it in.

ENGLISH RULES

COMMAS (continued)

5. A comma <u>before a conjunction</u> can be used to separate two complete sentences. (Conjunction words are *and, but, or, so*.)

   Ex: The palm trees blew softly in the wind, and the hot sun beat down from the sky.

   Do NOT use a comma without the conjunction to separate two complete sentences!

   Ex: The palm trees blew softly in the wind, the sun beat down from the sky.

6. A comma can be used at the end of a sentence followed by an afterthought.

   Ex: The football game was a massacre, forty-nine to zero.

Other comma hints:

When in doubt, leave the comma out!

Just because you pause when reading a sentence does not mean the sentence requires a comma!

If all four answer choices are identically worded and three of the four answer choices contain commas in various places, the correct answer is likely to be the one that omits the commas!

DASH – There are two dash rules used on the ACT. Dashes are similar to commas in these two cases.

1. The dash, like the comma, is used to mark an interruption.

Ex: The Chicago Marathon - a race of endurance, strength, and skill – is difficult to complete.

Please note that two dashes or two commas can be used interchangeably; however, do not use one of each.

2. The dash can also be used to stress a word or phrase at the end of a sentence.

   Ex: Danny's hair is unlike anyone else's in the family - thick and dark.

SEMICOLON – There are two semicolon rules to know for the ACT.

1. The semicolon is used to separate complete sentences.

   Ex: Shannon practiced diligently for the ACT; she eventually earned a great score.

2. The semicolon is also used before a coordinating conjunction (*however, therefore*) to separate two sentences.

   Ex: I enjoy living in a small community; however, the neighbors are often too nosy.

COLON – There are three colon rules for the ACT. There is ALWAYS a complete sentence prior to the colon.

1. The colon is used after a complete sentence followed by a summary list.

    Ex: I have many hobbies: golfing, rock climbing, sailing, and windsurfing.

2. The colon is also used at the end of a complete sentence followed by an afterthought.

    Ex: Japan has a high literacy rate: 99 percent.

3. The colon is also used to separate two complete sentences when the second sentence explains or restates an idea in the first.

    Ex: These seat covers are the most durable kind: they are reinforced with double stitching and covered with a heavy plastic coating.

APOSTROPHE (POSSESSIVES) – An apostrophe is used to show ownership.

1. If there is one owner, use *'s*.
    Ex: Jim's car is brand new.

2. If there is more than one owner, use *s'*.
    Ex: Ten boys' bikes were stolen.

3. Words that are plural without adding the "s" form the possessive by adding *'s*.
    Ex: Women's, men's, people's, children's

    Their = more than one owner
    There = location
    They're = they are

    It's = it is
    Its = one owner
    Its' = THIS IS NOT A WORD, BUT THE ACT OFTEN GIVES IT AS AN ANSWER CHOICE — DON'T EVER CHOOSE IT!

<u>Quiz!</u>

You now know four ways to separate or combine complete sentences. What are they?
1.

2.

3.

4

ENGLISH RULES

ACT SUCCESS
English Skill Builder – Punctuation #1

Directions: In the passage below, certain words and phrases are underlined and numbered. In the right hand column, you will find alternatives for the underlined part. For each question, choose the alternative you consider best. If you think the original version is best, choose "NO CHANGE." Be sure to read the entire sentence before making a selection.

The Space Race

The Space Race, an informal competition between the United States and the Soviet Union. Lasted roughly from 1957 to 1975. It involved the parallel efforts by each of those countries to explore outer space with artificial satellites, to send humans into space, and to land people on the moon.

1. **A.** NO CHANGE
   B. Soviet Union, lasted roughly
   C. Soviet Union lasted roughly
   D. Soviet Union; lasted roughly

Though its roots lay in early rocket technology and in the international tensions following World War II. The Space Race effectively began after the Soviet launch of Sputnik 1 on 4 October 1957. The term originated as an analogy to the arms race. The Space Race became an important part of the cultural and technological rivalry between the USSR and the U.S. during the Cold War, space technology became a particularly important arena in this conflict, both because of its military applications and its psychological benefit of raising morale.

2. **F.** NO CHANGE
   G. World War II the Space Race
   H. World War II: the Space Race
   J. World War II, the Space Race

3. **A.** NO CHANGE
   B. Cold War space technology
   C. Cold War. Space technology
   D. Cold War's space technology

While the Sputnik 1 launch can clearly be called the start of the Space Race, its end is more debatable. Most hotly contested during the 1960s, the Space Race continued apace through the Apollo moon landing of 1969. Although they followed Apollo 11 with five more lunar landings, American space scientists turned to new arenas. Skylab would gather data; and the Space Shuttle would work on returning spaceships intact from space journeys. Americans would claim that by first landing a man on the moon, they

4. **F.** NO CHANGE
   G. Space Race. Its end
   H. Space Race its end
   J. Space Race it's end

5. **A.** NO CHANGE
   B. gather data. And the
   C. gather data, the
   D. gather data, and the

ACT SUCCESS
English Skill Builder – Punctuation #1

had won this unofficial "race." Soviet scientists, meanwhile, pushed ahead with their own projects and did not concede defeat. Nevertheless, as the Cold War cooled, and as other nations began to develop their own space programs, and the notion of a continuing "race" between the two superpowers became less important.

6.
F. NO CHANGE
G. space programs; and the notion
H. space programs. The notion
J. space programs, the notion

ACT SUCCESS
English Skill Builder – Punctuation #2

Directions: In the passage below, certain words and phrases are underlined and numbered. In the right hand column, you will find alternatives for the underlined part. For each question, choose the alternative you consider best. If you think the original version is best, choose "NO CHANGE." Be sure to read the entire sentence before making a selection.

The History of the Internet

The Internet evolved from a small, clandestine study conceived by the U.S. Dept. of Defense in 1969 to test methods of enabling computer networks to survive military attacks, by means of the dynamic rerouting of messages. As the ARPAnet (Advanced Research Projects Agency network), it began by connecting three networks in California with one in Utah: these communicated with one another by a set of rules called the Internet Protocol (IP).

1. **A.** NO CHANGE
   B. military attacks. By means
   C. military attacks by means
   D. military attacks; by means

2. **F.** NO CHANGE
   G. Utah these
   H. Utah, these
   J. Utah. And these

By 1972, when the ARPAnet was revealed to the public, it had grown to include about 50 universities and research organizations with defense contracts but a year later the first international connections were established with networks in England and Norway. A decade later, the Internet Protocol was enhanced with a set of simple standard, communication protocols, the Transmission Control Program/Internet Protocol (TCP/IP) that supported both local and wide-area networks.

3. **A.** NO CHANGE
   B. contracts, a year
   C. contracts a year
   D. contracts; a year

4. **F.** NO CHANGE
   G. set of simple, standard, communication
   H. set of simple, standard communication
   J. set of simple standard communication

In the 1980s as large commercial companies began to use TCP/IP to build private internets, ARPA investigated transmission of multimedia - audio, video, and graphics - across the Internet. Other groups investigated hypertext and

5. **A.** NO CHANGE
   B. In the 1980s as large,
   C. In the 1980s, as large
   D. In the 1980s, large

ACT SUCCESS
English Skill Builder – Punctuation #2

created tools such as Gopher that allowed users to browse menus, that are lists of possible options.
                                                                6
In 1989 many of these technologies were combined to create the World Wide Web, initially designed to aid
                                                                                            7
communication among physicists who worked in widely separated locations, the Web became immensely popular and eventually replaced other tools. Also during the late 1980s, the U.S. government began to lift restrictions on who could use, the Internet and commercialization of the Internet began.
                                                                8
In the early 1990s, with users no longer restricted to the scientific or military communities, the Internet quickly expanded to include universities, companies of all sizes, libraries, public and private schools, local and state governments, individuals, and families.

By 2000 it was estimated that the number of adults using the Internet exceeded 100 million, and this was in the
                                                                                                       9
United States alone.

6. **F.** NO CHANGE
    G. menus which are lists, of possible options.
    H. menus, which are lists of possible options.
    J. menus; which are lists of possible options.

7. **A.** NO CHANGE
    B. Web. Initially designed
    C. Web initially designed
    D. Web which was initially designed

8. **F.** NO CHANGE
    G. use the Internet, and commercialization
    H. use the Internet and, commercialization
    J. use the Internet, commercialization

9. **A.** NO CHANGE
    B. million this
    C. million but this
    D. million, this

ACT SUCCESS
English Skill Builder—Punctuation #3
Directions: Read the passage and then choose the best answer to each question.

My Favorite Horrible Book

As an English teacher, people often ask me to name
                     ―――――――――――――――
                              1
my favorite book or my favorite fictional character. My

first reaction has usually been to reject the question out-

of-hand, how can someone
   ――――――――――
        2

whose read thousands of literary works covering
―――――
   3
multiple genres pick one favorite? But I

recently started considering the question more carefully.

I began to realize that; although I could not possibly pick
                     ―――――――――――
                            4

my favorite book right now. I could certainly have made
                      ――――
                        5
that decision when I was ten years old – and when I was

twelve and fourteen, too. I had comparatively few books

to pick from, so the choices were easy. At ten, for
        ―――――――――――――――
                 6

example – my favorite book was *Joe DiMaggio; Lucky*
―――――――――
    7
to Be a Yankee, an adoring pseudo-biography by a radio

announcer-turned-author named Bill Stern. It was a

horrible book, I loved it dearly. The great DiMag was
        ―――――――
           8
painted as the portrait of perfection. He was incapable of

1. **A.** NO CHANGE
    B. people often require me
    C. I am often asked
    D. students sometimes demand of me

2. Which of the following is LEAST acceptable?
    F. NO CHANGE
    G. hand; how
    H. hand. How
    J. hand; how, I ask myself,

3. **A.** NO CHANGE
    B. who'se
    C. who's
    D. whos'

4. **F.** NO CHANGE
    G. that. Although
    H. that: although
    J. that although

5. **A.** NO CHANGE
    B. now, I
    C. now; I
    D. now: I

6. Which of the following is LEAST acceptable?
    F. NO CHANGE
    G. from; the choices, therefore,
    H. from, the choices
    J. from: the choices

7. **A.** NO CHANGE
    B. example, my
    C. example my
    D. example: my

8. Which of the following is LEAST acceptable?
    F. NO CHANGE
    G. book, but I
    H. book, but for some reason I
    J. book, yet I

ACT SUCCESS
English Skill Builder—Punctuation #3

error, on or off the field; he <u>was in other words</u> not
9

human.

    That book, <u>however,</u> did have something very
10

significant in common with the best young <u>peoples'</u>
11

literature of the last thirty <u>years, it</u> quenched a young
12

person's <u>thirst; for</u> heroes.
13

9.   A. NO CHANGE
    B. was however
    C. was, however
    D. was, in other words,

10. F. NO CHANGE
    G. However,
    H. – however,
    J. , likewise,

11. A. NO CHANGE
    B. people's
    C. peoples
    D. folk's

12. F. NO CHANGE
    G. years it
    H. annual literary issues, it
    J. years; it

13. A. NO CHANGE
    B. thirst for
    C. thirst, for
    D. thirst, in need of

ACT SUCCESS
English Skill Builder—Punctuation #4

Directions: Read the passage and then choose the best answer to each question.

DiMaggio or Silvertongue?

I think that all children need to find heroes but not wooden <u>one's</u> like that iconic Joe DiMaggio who
₁

captivated me for a while. <u>Instead,</u> they need
₂

1. **A.** NO CHANGE
   B. ones
   C. ones'
   D. wons

2. **F.** NO CHANGE
   G. Likewise,
   H. Additionally,
   J. Moreover,

protagonists with whom they can <u>identify – young</u>
₃
people who are courageous but fearful, daring but conflicted, intelligent but insecure, strong in some ways but weak in others. <u>Fortunately,</u> kids today can find
₄

3. Which of the following is LEAST acceptable?
   A. NO CHANGE
   B. identify. Young
   C. identify; they need young
   D. identify. They need young

4. **F.** NO CHANGE
   G. Unluckily,
   H. Unfortunately,
   J. But on the other hand

literary <u>heroes (of both genders, incidentally)</u> who are
₅

5. Which of the following is NOT acceptable?
   A. NO CHANGE
   B. heroes – of both genders, incidentally –
   C. heroes of both genders
   D. heroes. Of both genders, incidentally,

human and <u>multi-dimensional, such</u> protagonists abound
₆

6. **F.** NO CHANGE
   G. multi-dimensional; such
   H. multi-dimensional, in fact, such
   J. multi-dimensional, without a question of a doubt, such

in many magical pieces of contemporary <u>literature.</u>
₇
<u>Pieces</u> which were written specifically for young
₇

7. **A.** NO CHANGE
   B. literature. Pieces of various types
   C. literature, pieces
   D. literature pieces

<u>reader's</u> consumption. Ironically, those very "real"
₈
characters are often found in fantasies or in novels which contain many elements of fantasy.

Harry Potter, Lyra Silvertongue (*The Golden Compass*), and Ender Wiggin (*Ender's Game*), for

8. **F.** NO CHANGE
   G. readers.
   H. readers'
   J. one's

ACT SUCCESS
English Skill Builder—Punctuation #4

example, are imperfect young heroes whose flaws and conflicts mirror those of they're readers. Potter is a horribly harried Harry whose hormones play havoc with

his heroism, in other words, he's a grouchy

kid. Just like many of his fellow adolescents. Lyra is an extraordinarily clever and courageous truth-seeker, but she is also, ironically, a stubborn, sneaky prevaricator (as her name so cleverly implies). Ender (also a thought-provoking name choice) is a surpassingly brilliant but aggressive and violent warrior who may, moreover, be a mass murderer, misguided heroic intentions notwithstanding.

All of these wonderfully drawn characters' problems profoundly reflect those of their readers, who themselve's stumble crazily along that tortuous path toward adulthood. Favorite book? Favorite hero? These may turn out to be important questions after all. An understanding of the paradoxical natures of fictional young people – mixtures of fortitude and folly, ferociousness and fragility – may help our own kids as

they dare to embark; like those flawed young heroes, on the quest for their best selves.

9. **A**. NO CHANGE
   B. there
   C. there young
   D. their

10. **F**. NO CHANGE
    G. heroism. In
    H. heroism in
    J. heroism, therefore in

11. **A**. NO CHANGE
    B. kid, just
    C. kid. Exactly
    D. kid. In countless ways just

12. **F**. NO CHANGE
    G. on the other hand
    H. all other distinctions notwithstanding
    J. all appearances undoubtedly to the contrary

13. **A**. NO CHANGE
    B. themselves'
    C. themself
    D. themselves

14. **F**. NO CHANGE
    G. kid's
    H. kids'
    J. children's

15. **A**. NO CHANGE
    B. embark, like those flawed young heroes,
    C. embark – like those flawed young hero's
    D. embark, like those deeply flawed young hero's,

ACT SUCCESS
English Skill Builder—Commas
Directions: Read the passage and then choose the best answer to each question.

Being Fair to Freud

When some friends and I got together the other
                                              _____
                                                    1
night the question of the most influential figure of the
____
  1

20th century came up. The rest of the table tossed out
                                                     ___
                                                      2
names from Einstein to Elvis Presley, and although all
_____
                    2
the suggestions were people who indeed changed our

world in profound, indelible ways to me there was only
         _____
                   3

one possible answer. But when I nominated Sigmund
                        _____
                                    4
Freud, the father of psychoanalysis my friends just
_____
                    4
groaned and rolled their eyes!

Of course, I understood why, attacked on all
_____
                          5
sides by everyone. From religious leaders to feminists,
_____
                          5
Freud is typically introduced to students these days by
_____
  5
someone complaining about the things he got wrong.

We've all heard about the embarrassing missteps, like
                                         _____
                                               6
his sexist ideas about the female psyche or the fact that,
_____
                              6
as a young man, he briefly advocated the use of certain
_____
       6
drugs later found to be dangerous. I just can't believe

that students aren't also taught about all the amazing

things which he got right.
_____
            7

1. A. NO CHANGE
   B. together, the other night
   C. together the other night,
   D. together. The other night

2. F. NO CHANGE
   G. names, from Einstein to Elvis Presley
   H. names, from Einstein to Elvis Presley,
   J. names from Einstein to Elvis Presley

3. A. NO CHANGE
   B. profound indelible ways,
   C. profound, indelible ways,
   D. profound, indelible, ways

4. F. NO CHANGE
   G. when I nominated Sigmund Freud, the father of psychoanalysis,
   H. when, I nominated Sigmund Freud the father of psychoanalysis,
   J. when I nominated, Sigmund Freud the father of psychoanalysis,

5. A. NO CHANGE
   B. Of course I understood, why attacked on all sides by everyone from religious leaders to feminists, Freud
   C. Of course, I understood why attacked on all sides by everyone, from religious leaders to feminists Freud
   D. Of course, I understood why. Attacked on all sides by everyone from religious leaders to feminists, Freud

6. F. NO CHANGE
   G. missteps like his sexist ideas about the female psyche, or the fact that as a young man
   H. missteps, like his sexist ideas about the female psyche, or the fact that as a young man,
   J. missteps like his sexist ideas about the female psyche or the fact that as a young man,

7. A. NO CHANGE
   B. things, that he got right.
   C. things which, he got right.
   D. things he got right.

ACT SUCCESS
English Skill Builder—Commas

Freud not only invented psychoanalysis, pretty much single-handedly but he also developed many of its core theories, including those of repression, transference, and the subconscious. Broadly speaking, we are indebted to him for the very idea that how we behave as adults depends on our experiences as children a notion now universally accepted. So it seems very silly indeed to dismiss him based on a few isolated paragraphs found in one or two of his sixteen major works.

And besides, even if you do think Freud was a terrible guy, this doesn't mean he wasn't influential, someone else at the table said the answer was Hitler, and no-one objected to that!

It really is curious that people are so reluctant to admit how Freud's ideas have shaped modern society. In fact I can't help but wonder, what Freud would say about it!

8. F. NO CHANGE
   G. psychoanalysis pretty much, single-handedly
   H. psychoanalysis pretty much single-handedly,
   J. psychoanalysis pretty much single-handedly

9. A. NO CHANGE
   B. theories including those of repression, transference and
   C. theories, including those of repression, transference and,
   D. theories including those of repression transference and

10. F. NO CHANGE
    G. experiences as children, a notion now
    H. experiences, as children a notion now
    J. experiences as children, a notion, now

11. A. NO CHANGE
    B. guy this doesn't mean he wasn't influential. Someone
    C. guy. This doesn't mean he wasn't influential. Someone
    D. guy, this doesn't mean he wasn't influential. Someone

12. F. NO CHANGE
    G. fact, I can't help but wonder
    H. fact I can't help, but wonder
    J. fact, I can't help but wonder,

ACT SUCCESS
English Skill Builder – Possessives

Directions: In the passage below, certain words and phrases are underlined and numbered. In the right hand column, you will find alternatives for the underlined part. For each question, choose the alternative you consider best. If you think the original version is best, choose "NO CHANGE." Be sure to read the entire sentence before making a selection.

The First American Female Pilot

After the final performance of one last practice landing, the French instructor nodded to the young African-American woman at the controls and jumped down to the ground. Bessie Coleman was on her own now. She lined up the nose of the open cockpit biplane on the runway's center mark, gave the engine full throttle, and took off into history.

1. A. NO CHANGE
   B. the runways center mark
   C. the runway's centers mark
   D. the runway center's mark

It was a long journey from the American Southwest, where she'd been born in 1893, to these French skies. Colemans future didn't look too promising then. After a year at Langston Industrial College, Coleman headed for Chicago to see what could be done to realize a dream. Ever since she had seen her first airplane when she was a little girl, Coleman had known that someday, somehow, she would fly. She hoped that her dream's would come true in Chicago.

2. F. NO CHANGE
   G. Colemans future's
   H. Coleman's future
   J. Colemans futures

3. A. NO CHANGE
   B. her dreams would
   C. her dreams' would
   D. her's dreams would

Try as she might, however, Coleman could not obtain flying lessons anywhere in the city. Then she sought aid from Robert S. Abbott, one of the *Chicago Weekly Defenders* top reporters. The newspaperman got in touch with a flight school in France that was willing to teach this determined young woman to fly.

4. F. NO CHANGE
   G. *Weekly Defenders* top reporter's
   H. *Weekly Defender's* top reporters
   J. *Weekly's Defender* top reporters

Bessie Coleman took a quick course in French, settled her affairs, and sailed for Europe. While there, she had as one of her instructors Anthony Fokker, the famous aircraft

5. A. NO CHANGE
   B. settled her affair's
   C. settled her affair
   D. settled her affairs'

ACT SUCCESS
English Skill Builder – Possessives

designer. She earned all of her instructors praise because of her hard work and dedication. Coping with a foreign language and flying daily in capricious, unstable machines held together with baling wire was daunting, but Coleman persevered.

    On June 15, 1921, Bessie Coleman earned an international pilot's license, issued by the International Aeronautical Federation. Not only was she the first black woman to win her pilots wings, she was the first American woman to hold this coveted license. By doing so, she opened the door for womens' progress in the field of aviation.

    She was ready for a triumphant return to the United States to barnstorm and lecture, proof that if the will is strong enough, ones dream can be attained.

6. **F.** NO CHANGE
   G. her instructor's praise
   H. her instructors praise's
   J. her instructors' praise

7. **A.** NO CHANGE
   B. international pilots license
   C. international pilots' license
   D. international pilot license

8. **F.** NO CHANGE
   G. win her pilot's wings
   H. win her pilots' wings
   J. win her pilot wing's

9. **A.** NO CHANGE
   B. door for womens progress
   C. door for women's progress
   D. door for women progress

10. **F.** NO CHANGE
    G. ones dream's can
    H. ones' dream can
    J. one's dream can

ACT SUCCESS
English Skill Builder—Apostrophe #1
Directions: Read the passage and then choose the best answer to each question.

Take a Bow, Loser, the Spotlight's Yours

America, a country renowned — for good or ill — as the land that enshrined success as a prize to be cherished above all others has lately evinced a sneaky fascination with failure. The biggest hit on Broadway, *Wicked*, strip-mines the escapist cheer from the *Wizard of Oz* story with determined ruthlessness, glorifying a certain once-reviled green gal in the process. The losers on *American Idol* are almost as famous as the winners — sometimes more so. Kicked off one contest show, a new-minted pseudo-celebrity becomes a star of the next. Paris Hiltons' very pointlessness constitutes the whole of her appeal; no one really wants her to acquire a talent.

1. **A.** NO CHANGE
   B. Paris Hilton
   C. Paris Hilton's
   D. Paris Hiltons's

On the surface *American Idol* may appear to be firmly in a triumphalist mode in keeping with the American idea of glorifying the victorious: its the embodiment of the conceit that you too, unprepossessing nobody from nowhere, can be an overnight sensation. And yes, the winner, chosen by fiat of the people themselves, emerges with a recording contract and a future in boldface columns.

2. **F.** NO CHANGE
   G. it's
   H. their
   J. they're

But there is a cheerfully merciless attitude pervading the long process by which a winner is selected. In it's early stages *American Idol* includes a carnival of the most deplorably deluded contestants, some of whom turn their rejection into an occasion for showboating in the media spotlight.

3. **A.** NO CHANGE
   B. its
   C. their
   D. they're

Copyright © 2009 by Academic Educational Resources. All rights reserved.

ACT SUCCESS
English Skill Builder—Apostrophe #1

More than a hint of ghoulish malice spices the frenzied attention to Britney Spears' faults. Reality TV shows like *The Surreal Life* or *Flavor of Love* invariably improve average Americans feelings about their fameless existences by exposing the pathos and desperation it often seems to leave in its wake.

It seems everywhere you look in the marketplace of popular entertainment, merit badges are now being bestowed for underachievement. Maybe this new mood enshrining failure as the new success is related to the last decade or so of dissatisfaction with the countries ostensible political winners, and the policies they've pursued. But it surely reflects a population embarking on the new century with a perhaps not unhealthy dent in its self-esteem.

4. F. NO CHANGE
   G. Britney Spears fault
   H. Britney Spears' fault
   J. Britney Spears's faults

5. A. NO CHANGE
   B. American
   C. American's
   D. Americans'

6. F. NO CHANGE
   G. country's
   H. countries'
   J. countries's

ACT SUCCESS
English Skill Builder—Apostrophe #2
Directions: Read the passage and then choose the best answer to each question.

Finding the Flexibility to Survive

Every Friday night the cashier's at a Chevron gas
                        —————
                           1
station food mart offers us a discount on all the leftover

apples and bananas. To ensure the best selection

possible, my mother and I pile into my father-in-laws'
                                      ———————————
                                           2
car and pull up to the food mart at 5 p.m. on the dot.

Before the times of the Chevron food mart, there

were the times of the calculator. My mother would

carefully prop it up in the cart's child seat and frown as
                                —————
                                  3
she entered each price. Since the first days of the

calculator's appearance, the worry lines on her childrens'
                                                —————————
                                                    4
faces have only grown deeper.

Chevron shopping started like this: One day my

mother suddenly realized that she had maxed out almost

every credit card, and we needed groceries for the week.

The only credit card she hadn't maxed out was the

Chevron card, and the companies station on Eagle Rock
                        —————————
                            5
Boulevard has a pretty big mart attached to it.

Grocery shopping at Chevron has its drawbacks.

The worst is when we have so many items that it takes

the checker what seems like hours to ring up everything.

A line inevitably forms behind us, and the customers's
                                         ——————————
                                              6
impatience is obvious. It's that line that hurts the most

the way they look at us. My mother never notices — or

maybe she pretends not to.

1. **A.** NO CHANGE
   B. cashier
   C. cashiers'
   D. cashiers's

2. **F.** NO CHANGE
   G. father-in-law
   H. father-in-law's
   J. father-in-laws',

3. **A.** NO CHANGE
   B. cart
   C. carts
   D. carts'

4. **F.** NO CHANGE
   G. child's
   H. children's
   J. childrens

5. **A.** NO CHANGE
   B. company
   C. company's
   D. companies'

6. **F.** NO CHANGE
   G. customer
   H. customer's
   J. customers'

Copyright © 2009 by Academic Educational Resources. All rights reserved.

ACT SUCCESS
English Skill Builder—Apostrophe #2

Its often difficult but I hold on to the idea of
⎯⎯
7
flexibility tightly. I believe that being flexible keeps me

going — keeps me from being ashamed of the way my

family's is different from other families. Whenever I feel
⎯⎯⎯⎯
8
the heat rise to my face, I remind myself that grocery

shopping at a gas station is just a twist on the normal

kind of grocery shopping. My belief in flexibility helps

me get through the difficult times because I know that

no matter what happens, my mother and I will always

figure out a way to survive.

7. **A.** NO CHANGE
   B. It's
   C. They're
   D. Their

8. **F.** NO CHANGE
   G. family
   H. familys'
   J. families'

GRAMMAR

SUBJECT-VERB AGREEMENT

Always check verbs for agreement! Within a sentence, a singular subject must be followed by a singular verb, and a plural subject must be followed by a plural verb.

Example: The stack of books is on the floor.
The subject here is "stack," which is singular, so the verb "is" is correct.

BE CAREFUL! Verbs are not made plural just by putting an "s" on the end. If you want a singular verb, put the word "he or she" in front of it and make sure it works. If you want a plural verb, put the word "they" in front of it and make sure it works.

Example: He sits.
They sit.

One of the ACT's most common questions begins with a singular subject and is followed by several prepositional phrases with plural nouns and then a verb. This verb MUST be singular so as to agree with the sentence's singular subject.

Example: The color of the glass in the panes of glass in the windows of the nearby houses is actually a reflection of the suns rays.

Though there are multiple nouns in the prepositional phrase above, the subject in this sentence is in fact "color." You must therefore use the singular verb "is."

SUBJECT-PRONOUN AGREEMENT

Within a sentence, a singular subject must be followed by a singular pronoun and a plural subject must be followed by a plural pronoun.

Example: Each of the boys took his seat on the bus.
Since the subject is "each of the boys," it is singular. His is a singular pronoun.

PARALLEL PHRASING

Express ideas in a consistent, grammatical way. Phrases or words in a series must be in the same form.

DO THIS: *I like to ski, sail and swim.* NOT THIS: I like to ski, sailing and swimming.

ACT SUCCESS
English Skill Builder – Subject/Verb and Subject/Pronoun Agreement #1

Directions: After reading the passage, choose the best answer to each question.

Approaching the harbor, I admire the sunlight reflecting off the clear blue water. The boats rocking against the dock glistens inviting. My father leads my siblings and me to a blue speedboat at the end of the dock. Jumping in first, he helps the rest of us into the boat.

1.
- A. NO CHANGE
- B. glistening
- C. glisten
- D. glistened

With my father as captain, we pushes off and are on our way. As we make our way through the no-wake zone, the low hum of the engine provides a taste of what is to come.

2.
- F. NO CHANGE
- G. they push
- H. he push
- J. we push

My brother and sister sits in the bow, getting a view of the lake in front of us. I take the seat next to my father and, rubbing sunscreen onto my face, prepare for the ride.

3.
- A. NO CHANGE
- B. sitting
- C. sit
- D. both sits

Soon we are out in the middle of the lake; my father opens the throttle and we start speeding through the water. We hear laughter as my brother and sister feel wind on their faces as the breeze catches their hair. Opening the cooler, I take out an apple and shiver slightly as the coldness prickles it's skin. I hand my brother and sister each a soda and then hear the fizzy sound as he unscrew the lids.

4.
- F. NO CHANGE
- G. feeling
- H. feels
- J. will feel

5.
- A. NO CHANGE
- B. my
- C. its
- D. their

6.
- F. NO CHANGE
- G. they unscrews
- H. they unscrew
- J. him unscrews

A few hours later, warmed by the sun and weary from our ride, we head back to shore. The spray from the motor splashes my siblings, who is leaning over the side of the boat. My father guides the boat alongside the dock and kills the engine. We return from our trip happy yet tired and already looked forward to next time.

7.
- A. NO CHANGE
- B. leaned
- C. leans
- D. are leaning

8.
- F. NO CHANGE
- G. looking
- H. we looks
- J. they look

Copyright © 2009 by Academic Educational Resources. All rights reserved.

ACT SUCCESS
English Skill Builder – Subject/Verb and Subject/Pronoun Agreement #2

Directions: Read the passage and then choose the best answer to each question.

A World on the Move

Virtually every aspect of global migration can be seen in Cape Verde, a tiny West African nation where the number of people who have left approach the
₁
number who remain and almost everyone have a close
₂
relative in Europe or America.

Migrant money buoys the economy. Migrant
₃
votes sway politics. Migrant departures split parents from children. Lofty talk of opportunity abroad mixes at cafe tables here with accounts of false documents and sham marriages.

The intensity of the migrant experience make
₄
this barren archipelago the Galapagos of migration, a microcosm of the forces straining American politics and remaking societies across the globe.

An estimated 200 million people lives outside
₅
the country of their birth, and they help support a swath of the developing world as big if not bigger. Migrants sent home about $300 billion last year, and those sums
₆
building houses, educating children and seeding
₆
small businesses, and they have made migration central to discussions about how to help the global poor.

1. **A.** NO CHANGE
   B. approaching
   C. approaches
   D. approached

2. **F.** NO CHANGE
   G. has
   H. had
   J. having

3. **A.** NO CHANGE
   B. buoy
   C. buoyed
   D. buoying

4. **F.** NO CHANGE
   G. made
   H. making
   J. makes

5. **A.** NO CHANGE
   B. live
   C. lived
   D. living

6. **F.** NO CHANGE
   G. those sums is building
   H. those sums are building
   J. those have building

GRAMMAR

TRANSITIONS

If all answers except one have a transition, pick the one without a transition.
- A. Consequently, the dog
- B. Therefore, the dog
- C. *The dog*
- D. For example, the dog

If all answers contain transitions…

1. Look for two transitions that have similar meanings. To help you learn which transitions are similar to one another, the chart below lists transitions by category.

2. Eliminate the two with similar meanings.

3. Look at the sentence before and after the transition to determine how the sentences should be linked. One of the 2 remaining answers should clearly be the better choice.

Transitions By Category

Comparison or Contrast		Cause and Effect	
However	Nevertheless	Thus	So
Yet	In like manner	Then	Because
Likewise	On the contrary	Therefore	On account of
Similarly	Instead	As a result	Since
Nonetheless	Conversely	Accordingly	Consequently

Addition		Emphasis	
Also	Second	Indeed	In other words
Besides	As well	In fact	Especially
Too	In addition	Even	
Moreover	Furthermore		

Examples		
For instance	As an illustration	That is
Namely	Also	For example
In particular		

MODIFIERS

If you have an introductory phrase, the subject of the sentence must come immediately after the comma.

DO THIS: *Feeling very sad, the girl felt a tear run down her cheek.*
NOT THIS: Feeling very sad, a tear ran down her cheek.
  (The girl was feeling sad, not the tear!)

ENGLISH RULES

ACT SUCCESS
English Skill Builder—Transitions #1
Directions: Read the passage and then choose the best answer to each question.

The Financial Literacy Crisis

A recent study found that most parents felt better prepared to give their teens advice on the "birds and the bees" than on investing; yet, Americans have
<u>   </u>
                 1
become alarmingly inept when it comes to making some of the most important decisions of their lives.

1. **A.** NO CHANGE
   B. for example
   C. similarly
   D. consequently

Millions of Americans accumulate unmanageable debt, fail to save for a rainy day (and retirement), and make countless other poor financial choices that eventually leave them worse off. <u>So</u> before railing
                                                                                          2
against consumer stupidity, consider this: It's not always their fault. Many of those bad decisions are caused or exacerbated by a lack of knowledge.

2. **F.** NO CHANGE
   G. That is,
   H. But
   J. Likewise

The time for claiming ignorance as an excuse, <u>furthermore</u>, may be coming to an end. Because of
   3
skyrocketing foreclose rates and credit card debt, public- and private-sector groups have launched a flurry of programs aimed at promoting financial education. But some experts suggest that even such efforts could be fruitless because they might not change consumers' behavior. They say the focus should instead be on making the financial world easier to understand.

3. **A.** NO CHANGE
   B. in fact
   C. however
   D. likewise

<u>Indeed</u>, a major part of the problem, educators
    4
say, is that the financial systems that consumers navigate have become so complex. Easy access to credit, self-directed retirement accounts, and complicated mortgage options all force Americans to make decisions they may

4. **F.** NO CHANGE
   G. On the other hand
   H. Also
   J. Accordingly

ACT SUCCESS
English Skill Builder—Transitions #1

not be prepared for.

    Most Americans have extremely low levels of financial literacy, research suggests, despite its importance. The JumpStart Coalition for Personal Financial Literacy tests 12th graders every two years by asking them practical money questions. The students consistently record an average score of 50 to 55 percent, generally considered to be a failing grade. On the other hand, research on adults shows that about 3 in 4 workers don't know how much money they need to save for a comfortable retirement. Only about half of respondents in one study were able to correctly answer two simple questions about interest rates and inflation.

    Such poor results matter, says Annamaria Lusardi, a professor of economics at Dartmouth College, because research also shows that people who understand basic financial principles are better at retirement planning, accumulating wealth, and avoiding debt. In fact, she found that people who develop financial plans accumulate from 10 to 15 percent more wealth than those who don't, even after taking into consideration income and education levels.

5. **A.** NO CHANGE
   B. On the contrary
   C. Likewise
   D. Second

6. **F.** NO CHANGE
   G. Nevertheless
   H. Also
   J. On the other hand

ACT SUCCESS
English Skill Builder—Transitions #2
Directions: Read the passage and then choose the best answer to each question.

Darwinmania!

The party is about to begin.

In a week or so, the trumpets will sound, heralding the start of 18 months of non-stop festivities in honor of Charles Darwin. July 1, 2008, is the 150th anniversary of the first announcement of his discovery of natural selection, the main driving force of evolution. Then₁ 2009 is the 200th anniversary of Darwin's birth (Feb. 12), as well as being the 150th anniversary of the publication of his masterpiece, *On the Origin of Species* (Nov. 24), the extravaganza is set to continue until the end of next year. Get ready for Darwin hats, t-shirts, action figures, naturally selected fireworks and evolving chocolates. Oh, and lots of books and speeches.

But hold on. Does he deserve all this? He wasn't, however, the first person to suggest that evolution₂ happens. As a result, his grandfather, Erasmus Darwin,₃ speculated about it towards the end of the 18th century; at the beginning of the 19th, the great French naturalist Jean-Baptiste Lamarck made a strong case for it. Lamarck, however, failed to be generally persuasive₄ because he didn't have a plausible mechanism. He could see that evolution takes place, but he didn't know how. That had to wait until the discovery of natural selection.

1. **A.** NO CHANGE
   B. On the other hand
   C. Likewise
   D. Since

2. **F.** NO CHANGE
   G. after all
   H. for instance
   J. even

3. **A.** NO CHANGE
   B. On the contrary
   C. Accordingly
   D. For example

4. **F.** NO CHANGE
   G. for instance
   H. in particular
   J. in other words

ACT SUCCESS
English Skill Builder—Transitions #2

Natural selection is what we normally think of as Darwin's big idea. Indeed, he wasn't the first to discover that, either. At least two others — a doctor called William Wells and a writer called Patrick Matthew — discovered it years before Darwin did. Wells described it (admittedly briefly) in 1818, when Darwin was just 9; Matthew did so in 1831, the year that Darwin set off on board HMS Beagle for what became a five-year voyage around the world.

5. **A.** NO CHANGE
   B. Furthermore,
   C. Yet
   D. Accordingly,

It was a few months after returning from this voyage that Darwin first began to consider seriously the possibility of evolution, or the "transmutation of species." At this time he knew nothing of Wells's and Matthew's accounts of natural selection; besides, both accounts languished in obscurity until after the "Origin" was published.

6. **F.** NO CHANGE
   G. for instance
   H. indeed
   J. in other words

ACT SUCCESS
English Skill Builder – Transitions and Modifiers #1

Directions: After reading the passage, choose the best answer to each question.

No Longer Invisible

When I started junior high, my only expectation for myself was to stay invisible. I was shy, sensitive, and intimidated by the rest of the school. Besides, it's strange how I aspired to run
                                                              1
for sixth-grade secretary. Broadcasted on the intercom, the
                                                                            2
math teacher announced that anyone interested in running for
                                 2
student council should see him. I followed the massive crowd
                 2
to the math classroom, and without even thinking twice, I filled out and turned in the forms.

   Obsessed with winning, the sixth-grade hall was adorned
                                       3
with neon posters made by students. Buttons, bookmarks and
                  3
flyers littered the hallways and cafeteria. Furthermore, my
                                                                         4
printer lazily spit out what seemed like a million bookmarks. I cut them out and brought them in to school.

   Everything went as planned until it was time for my speech. Getting ready to talk, my hands clammed up and my
                              5
sweat glands went into overdrive. My short, page-long speech
                  5
didn't take more than a minute to read, but I felt as if I had been on that musty old stage for an eternity. Then, things
                                                                                   6
happened so fast that I can't remember every detail about the election. But what I do remember so vividly is that I won!

1.
   A. NO CHANGE
   B. So,
   C. Also,
   D. In addition,

2.
   F. NO CHANGE
   G. Broadcasted on the intercom, the announcement said that anyone interested in running for student council should see the math teacher.
   H. Broadcasted on the intercom, running for student council, the math teacher announced that everyone interested should see him.
   J. Broadcasted on the intercom, announced the math teacher, everyone interested in running for student council should see him.

3.
   A. NO CHANGE
   B. Obsessed with winning, neon posters adorned with pictures of students covered the sixth-grade hall.
   C. Obsessed with winning, pictures of students covered the sixth-grade hall.
   D. Obsessed with winning, students plastered the sixth-grade hall with neon posters.

4.
   F. NO CHANGE
   G. However,
   H. Meanwhile,
   J. Instead,

5.
   A. NO CHANGE
   B. Getting ready to talk, I started to feel swe and my hands became clammy.
   C. Getting ready to talk, my sweat glands went into overdrive, and my hands clammed up.
   D. My sweat glands went into overdrive, and hands clammed up, getting ready to talk.

6.
   F. NO CHANGE
   G. Also,
   H. Besides,
   J. Nevertheless,

ACT SUCCESS
English Skill Builder – Transitions and Modifiers #2

Directions: After reading the passage, choose the best answer to each question.

To be a Shaman

What is a shaman? They have been called by many names - doctor, priest, artist, visionary, master of ecstasy. Thus, they have been branded as sorcerers, witch doctors, charlatans, and voodoo priests. With their natural cures, the methods of healing shamans remains a challenging mystery to the western world.

1.
- A. NO CHANGE
- B. In addition,
- C. Accordingly,
- D. Besides,

2.
- F. NO CHANGE
- G. To western civilization, the natural cures of healing shamans remains a mystery.
- H. Still a provocative mystery to western civilization, the healing methods of shaman's natural cures.
- J. With their natural cures, shamans and their methods of healing remain a mystery to western civilization.

Moreover, people wonder if the shaman understands some human need to embrace deep, mythic, spiritual levels within the soul.

3.
- A. NO CHANGE
- B. In fact,
- C. Furthermore,
- D. Conversely,

One difference between a shaman's view and ours is that we separate the physical and the spiritual world. They do not. Similarly, in their minds there is no barrier between dream and reality, and they move easily between one and the other.

4.
- F. NO CHANGE
- G. In addition,
- H. In fact,
- J. Likewise,

The shaman is both physician and priest, and the condition of the spirit is as important as the body's physical state. The condition of the spirit and the physical body using natural remedies are treated by the shaman. No one knows where or when this shaman's tradition began. Shamans learn from their elders: therefore, some say this tradition is passed down from ancient elders.

5.
- A. NO CHANGE
- B. Using natural remedies, both the spirit and the physical body treat the shaman.
- C. Using natural remedies, the shaman treats both the condition of the spirit as well as the body's physical state.
- D. Treated by the shaman, the condition of the spirit and physical body use natural remedies.

6.
- F. NO CHANGE
- G. yet
- H. however
- J. nevertheless

47

TYPES OF RHETORICAL QUESTIONS

ACT English scores are broken down into two categories: (1) usage and mechanics (previously covered in this textbook); and (2) rhetorical skills. It is imperative that you learn the seven different types of rhetorical questions that the ACT tends to ask. Be sure to look for (and underline) the clue in the question. With a little practice, you will master these question types!

DELETE

When choosing whether or not to delete a phrase, decide if the phrase contains significant details and then look at the function of the phrase in the sentence.

INTRODUCTORY PHRASES

If a question asks you to pick the sentence that best introduces a paragraph, read the next sentence or two. Think about what you would say, and then go to the answer choices. There should only be one answer choice that has anything to do with what you predicted.

Be careful to only read one or two sentences! If you read the whole paragraph, you might then pick an answer choice that has to do with a smaller detail in the paragraph, rather than the overall topic.

Example: William Shakespeare's plays have been performed all over the world.
If the sentence above is the "next" sentence that you read, then there should only be one answer choice that has to do with Shakespeare's plays.

ADD

Only add if it proves relevant to the main idea and is not redundant information.

ILLUSTRATE/SUPPORT

If a question asks which of the answers best "illustrates" or "supports" something, pick the answer that gives the most specific details/examples.

NOT/LEAST

If a question asks, "Which of the following is NOT acceptable," or "Which is LEAST acceptable," the important thing to remember is that 3 answers will be correct, so eliminate the three correct answers and pick the remaining one.

Even though the test writers capitalize the word "NOT" or "LEAST" in the question, it is often helpful to circle or underline it as you read the question to remind yourself that you need to switch gears and look for the wrong answer rather than the right one.

PARAGRAPH OR SENTENCE ORDER

If a question asks about paragraph order, it typically has to do with chronological order. Link the topic and concluding sentences of each paragraph. If a question asks about sentence order, there is typically an order of actions. For example, *you can't get up before you fall down!*

SUPPOSE THE AUTHOR...

If the last question of the passages begins with "Suppose the author..." follow these two steps:

1. Two answers will begin with "Yes" and two with "No". Ask yourself, "Is the question a one sentence summary of the passage?" If it is, pick "yes", if not, pick "no." (Remember, for it to be a one sentence summary, it must summarize the ENTIRE passage, not just be a topic that was discussed in one paragraph.)

2. Once you have done step one & are down to two answers, pick the one that has the explanation that paraphrases the question.

ACT SUCCESS
English Skill Builder – Rhetorical Questions #1

Directions: Read the passage and then choose the best answer to each question.

A Gift from the Grandmothers

Somehow, it just didn't feel right. Although I felt blessed and honored to have the opportunity, I just had a hard time saying aloud that I was "a graduate student at Harvard University." After all, I know good and well that I'm just a country girl from Sweetwater, Tennessee, who never saw herself as the Ivy League type.

[1] I was proud to be the first from my family to attend college. [2] Many of my black and Latino colleagues in the Graduate School of Education felt the same way. [3] It wasn't that we were embarrassed about being smart or weren't proud to be there; it was just that the perception people have of "Hah-vahd," conjured up images of privilege and snobbery. [4] Many of us were first–generation college graduates from lower to middle-class families. [5] We actually discussed whether going to Harvard was an asset or liability when our goal was to return to the neighborhoods we came from, "keep it real," and be taken seriously by regular folks. 3

Very quickly graduation day arrived. I sat dazed in my cap and gown on the same lawn where I'd seen Nelson Mandela receive an honorary degree. Hazel Trice Edney

1. Which of the following alternatives to the underlined portion would NOT be acceptable?
   A. NO CHANGE
   B. too
   C. all too well
   D. OMIT the underlined portion.

2. Which of the following choices best introduces the paragraph?
   F. NO CHANGE
   G. I preferred to tell people that I "went to school in Boston."
   H. I was not alone in this dilemma.
   J. None of my white classmates voiced a similar concern.

3. For the sake of logic and coherence of this paragraph, Sentence 5 should be placed:
   A. where it is now.
   B. before Sentence 1.
   C. after Sentence 2.
   D. after Sentence 3.

4. Which of the following options is the LEAST acceptable alternative to the underlined portion?
   F. Before I knew it, graduation day had arrived.
   G. Unfortunately, graduation day was here before I knew it.
   H. Incredibly, I made it to graduation day.
   J. I graduated on a warm sunny day in May.

ACT SUCCESS
English Skill Builder – Rhetorical Questions #1

was a friend of mine. [5] She was believed to be the first African American woman ever to give the graduate student address at a Harvard graduation. My friend rose and walked quickly to the podium. Suddenly, listening to Hazel, proudly watching her represent all of us, it hit me. This wasn't about me. I was there as a representative. I looked up into the branches of the centuries-old trees and thought about what they would have looked like back in 1636. I thought about where my ancestors would have been in 1636, 1736, 1836, even 1936, and how remote the possibility seemed that any of their daughters would ever be at Harvard.

No, this degree was not about me at all. This was about standing on the shoulders of my black grandmothers who lived in Tennessee: black women whose potential went untapped and whose intelligence was so long ignored. These women could have been idle, except they rerouted genius, pouring it into rearing the next generation. I was here because they could not be but had the self-respect and insight to pass something significant on to their offspring.

5. The writer is considering adding the following phrase to the end of the preceding sentence:

    who had won the speech contest.

    Should the writer add this phrase here?
    A. Yes, because it adds an important detail about why Hazel is giving the student address.
    B. Yes, because it provides additional information about achievements black women have made at Harvard.
    C. No, because it is redundant; the essay already mentions Hazel's achievements.
    D. No, because it is not relevant to the main idea of the essay.

6. Which of the choices best illustrates the contrast between the writer and her grandmothers?
    F. NO CHANGE
    G. could also read and write
    H. scrubbed floors and cared for babies
    J. were great teachers

Question 7 asks about the preceding passage as a whole.

7. Suppose that the writer's goal had been to write an essay describing her grandmothers' achievements. Would this essay fulfill this goal?
    A. Yes; the writer shares how thankful she was that her grandmothers did a wonderful job raising the next generation.
    B. Yes; the writer is able to achieve something that her grandmothers could not.
    C. No; the writer is mostly talking about her friend Hazel's achievements.
    D. No; the writer discusses being thankful for her grandmothers' influence, but focuses on her own accomplishments.

ACT SUCCESS
English Skill Builder – Rhetorical Questions #2

Directions: Read the passage and then choose the best answer to each question.

Where the Heck Is Iwerksland?

[1]

Everyone knows about Disneyland, but have you ever heard of Iwerksland? You probably haven't, because there is no such place. <u>Even if there were, no-one would probably go anyway.</u>
                                       1

[2]

Back in 1919, Walt Disney was a teenager working in a Kansas City art studio with his best friend, Ub Iwerks. <u>Fascinated by the new innovation of animated cartoons, the two started up their own animation company called Laugh-O-Gram.</u> Although the studio employed several individuals
                                       2
who went on to become pioneers of animation, it only managed to produce a few cartoons before going bankrupt in 1923. ⬚3

1. Which of the following choices best accomplishes the author's goal of increasing the reader's interest in the story about to be told?
   A. NO CHANGE
   B. You couldn't get there even if you had a rocketship.
   C. But there might have been, if things had worked out a little differently.
   D. But that has never stopped people before.

2. Which of the following alternatives to the underlined portion would NOT be acceptable?
   F. The two started up their own animation company called Laugh-O-Gram, which fascinated the new innovation of animated cartoons.
   G. Animated cartoons were a new innovation that fascinated the two, and so they started up their own animation company called Laugh-O-Gram
   H. The two were fascinated by the new innovation of animated cartoons, and started up their own animation company called Laugh-O-Gram.
   J. The two soon started up their own animation studio called Laugh-O-Gram, having been fascinated by the new innovation of animated cartoons.

3. At this point, the author is considering adding the following sentence:

   > One of the legends who worked at Laugh-O-Gram was Friz Freleng, who would later direct many of the most famous Bugs Bunny cartoons.

   Should the author make this addition?
   A. Yes, because it establishes that Laugh-O-Gram employed people who went on to work for Warner Bros., in addition to Disney.
   B. Yes, because it provides a better transition into the next paragraph than the previous sentence.
   C. No, because the passage does not explain what it means to "direct" a cartoon.
   D. No, because it is an unnecessary detail that distracts the reader from the main subject of the essay.

ACT SUCCESS
English Skill Builder – Rhetorical Questions #2

[3]

<u>Disney and Iwerks had both been born in 1901.</u>
            4
Their most popular creation was a now-forgotten character named "Oswald the Lucky Rabbit." Disney and Iwerks severed their ties with the studio after a budget dispute, but since Universal owned the rights to Oswald, they desperately needed to create a new character. It was then, in the spring of 1928, that Ub Iwerks remembered the pet mice that he and Disney used to keep in their Kansas City office, and was inspired to draw the first sketches of a new mouse character. Disney named him Mortimer Mouse, but his wife Lillian hated the name and suggested he change it to Mickey.

4. Which of the following choices best introduces the paragraph?
   F. NO CHANGE
   G. Disney and Iwerks then moved to Los Angeles, where they produced cartoons for Universal Studios.
   H. Many more businesses would go under a few years later, when the Great depression started.
   J. Disney and Iwerks were both big baseball fans, and in 1923 Babe Ruth had batted .393 with 41 home runs.

[4]

[1] Meanwhile, Walt Disney was becoming the premier name in animation. [2] Unfortunately, his subsequent work did not meet with much success. [3] Iwerks animated the first few Mickey Mouse cartoons entirely by himself. [4] The two had a falling-out in 1930, and Iwerks left to found his own studio. [5] While it's true that Walt Disney developed Mickey's personality, and provided his voice once it became possible to produce cartoons with sound, Iwerks was the one who had first

ACT SUCCESS
English Skill Builder – Rhetorical Questions #2

drawn the character and was doing all the laborious animation work. [5]

[5]

Iwerks eventually reconciled with his old friend and returned to Disney Studios as a special-effects wizard, developing the machinery that first enabled the mixing of animation and live action, and winning two Oscars for his innovations. <u>Unfortunately, his techniques were used to make *Song of the South*, a film that is now considered to have been in poor taste.</u> Certainly, it was Walt Disney who ultimately had more business sense, but far too few people know Ub Iwerks's name, considering that he was the man who created the mouse that started it all.

5. The most logical order for the sentences in paragraph is:
   A. The order they are in now.
   B. 1, 5, 3, 2, 4
   C. 3, 5, 4, 2, 1
   D. 5, 1, 2, 4, 3

6. The author is considering deleting the underlined sentence. Should the author make this deletion?
   F. Yes, because the content is not directly relevant to the legacy of Ub Iwerks.
   G. Yes, because the passage does not go on to explain what made *Song of the South* objectionable.
   H. No, because it provides yet another humorous example of Iwerks's bad luck.
   J. No, because it is important for readers to know that even the Disney Corporation has made films that considered offensive.

Question 7 asks about the preceding passage as a whole.

7. Suppose that the author had intended to write an essay about how unsung individuals have often made greater contributions to their fields than the famous people they worked with. Would this essay fulfill that goal?
   A. Yes, because it establishes that Walt Disney owed his eventual success to Ub Iwerks.
   B. No, because the passage discusses only Ub Iwerks and not unsung contributors in general.
   C. Yes, because it mentions two Oscars won by Ub Iwerks, but not any won by Walt Disney.
   D. No, because the conclusion admits that it was Walt Disney who had more business sense.

ACT SUCCESS
English Skill Builder – Deleting

Directions: After reading the passage, choose the best answer to each question.

[1]

Color is an important facet of nature, influencing the life of almost every creature. Color is ultimately a sensation in our minds, associated with rays of light striking our eyes. The human eye has special cells (cone cells) containing three different pigments, which respond differently to different colors [1].

[2]

In nature, animals employ colors for many purposes. The most obvious is camouflage, which allows creatures to blend into their background and avoid detection. Often the animal's color changes with the seasons to coincide with foliage changes [2]. A classic example of the selective advantage of camouflage is found in English peppered moths. Normally light in color, black specimens grew more common as 19th century industrial England burned more coal, which deposited considerable soot on buildings and trees. Of course birds would more easily see and catch lighter moths against this background. Now approximately 90 percent of the moths in industrial areas of England are dark.

[3]

Nonetheless, many animals are brightly and conspicuously colored [3]. One purpose of vivid display is warning. Poisonous and ill-tasting creatures use bright, easily recognized patterns as signals, reminding would-be predators to look but not taste. Predators avoid them, an

1. The writer is considering deleting the preceding sentence. Should the writer make this deletion?
   A. Yes, because it adds unnecessary details to the paragraph.
   B. Yes, because it contradicts the main idea of the paragraph.
   C. No, because it helps explain the previous sentence.
   D. No, because it provides a transition to the next paragraph.

2. The writer is considering deleting the phrase *to coincide with foliage changes* from the preceding sentence. Should the writer make this deletion?
   F. Yes, because it doesn't provide any helpful information.
   G. Yes, because it detracts from the writer's main point.
   H. No, because it provides a link to the next sentence.
   J. No, because it helps explain why the animal's color changes.

3. If the writer were to delete the word *nonetheless* from the preceding sentence, the paragraph would primarily lose:
   A. Evidence for why many animals are brightly colored.
   B. A sense of contrast with paragraph two.
   C. A lively introduction to the topic of the paragraph.
   D. An important supporting detail.

ACT SUCCESS
English Skill Builder – Deleting

advantage to both. And if imitation is the sincerest form of flattery, it can also be a key to survival. So effective are color patterns in protecting bad-tasting and poisonous insects that completely harmless varieties sometimes mimic these patterns. The bluffers are afforded the same protection as their undesirable relatives so long as they do not become too numerous. Certain moths and butterflies make more bizarre use of color. Large eye-like markings on their wings apparently frighten, or at least confuse, birds and other predators. Similar markings are found on some fish [4]. Some insects use color to disguise themselves as inanimate objects – imitating things ranging from leaves to bird droppings.

[4]

Color plays an important role in many animals' mating behavior. Usually, color functions either to warn off rivals or to make an individual more attractive in competition for a mate. This is especially obvious when just one sex is highly colored, as are male robins and peacocks [5].

[5]

Human use of color dates back probably 150,000 to 200,000 years when prehistoric people first used red and yellow clays to paint their bodies [6]. Early humans also burned bones and teeth to produce black pigments. Other mineral colors soon came into use, made from ores of iron, copper and lead. Organic colors were obtained from insects,

4. The writer is considering deleting the preceding sentence. Should the writer make the deletion?
   F. Yes, because the paragraph is focusing on insects use of color.
   G. Yes, because the sentence does not add any new information to the paragraph.
   H. No, because the sentence provides an important detail to the main idea of the paragraph.
   J. No, because it helps explain the use of markings.

5. If the writer were to delete paragraph 4 from passage, the passage would primarily lose:
   A. Evidence supporting the use of color as protection
   B. Support for the idea that color can be used as camouflage.
   C. Information about robins and peacocks.
   D. Details that explain an important function color plays in many animals' lives.

6. If the writer were to delete the preceding sentence, paragraph would primarily lose:
   F. Details about what colors were most important to prehistoric people.
   G. A context for the value of color to prehistoric people.
   H. A logical transition from paragraph 4.
   J. Information about how colored dyes were obtained

other animals, and plants. Chalk and lime were used for white [7]. Reds were made from the root of madder plants, the dried bodies of female cochineal insects, and cinnabar. Blue came from copper minerals and the indigo plant. Typically these substances were first washed and dried, then mixed into oils for use in crafts such as painting, pottery, and textiles.

7. Should the writer delete the preceding sentence?
   A. Yes, the information is irrelevant.
   B. Yes, the author has already explained where white dye came from.
   C. No, it explains what people used to create the color white.
   D. No, it provides an important detail about what people used white dye for.

PUNCTUATION SUMMARY SHEET

GOOD NEWS: Although you need to know many punctuation rules in order to write well, only a handful are tested on the ACT. Here is a summary of the punctuation rules that are tested most frequently on the ACT English section.

> **0 COMMAS**
> **When in doubt, leave the comma out!**
> *Then she became the first woman in Missouri history, to hold a statewide office....*
> *(The comma does not need to be in the sentence.)*

> **1 COMMA = an introductory group of words OR an afterthought**
> <u>Introductory Clause</u>: *Although it is raining, I'm going to go for a walk.*
> <u>Afterthought</u>: *They lost the football game, forty-nine to zero.*

If you see 1 comma in an answer choice, it must follow one of these formulas to be a right answer:

1) Intro phrase/clause + COMMA + complete sentence
2) Complete sentence + COMMA + afterthought.

> **2 COMMAS = an appositive (a word group that interrupts the sentence)**
> *Taste of Chicago, a festival of food, takes place every summer.*

If you see 2 commas, you need to be able to take out the word group between the commas <u>without changing the meaning of the sentence</u>.

(NOTE: Sometimes ACT uses 2 dashes instead of 2 commas. That's fine, but you may not use one of each. *Taste of Chicago – a festival of food – takes place every summer.*)

> **THAT vs. WHICH:** These words mean the same thing.
> Typically, on this test, the difference is "that" does not have a comma before it and "which" do

> **2 COMPLETE SENTENCES** - There are 4 ways to separate/combine two complete sentences
>
> **Period** -- *It is hot. The sun is shining.*
>
> **Semicolon** -- *It is hot; the sun is shining.*
>
> **Comma + Conjunction** (and, but, or, so) – *It is hot, and the sun is shining.*
>
> **Colon** -- *It is hot: the sun is shining.*

IMPORTANT: On the ACT, all four of these are considered equal. If you have 2 complete sentences, you will never have to choose one of these four techniques over another.

BUT...the COLON is the only one of the 4 listed above that does something in addition to separating two sentences. It can come before a list or an explanation.
If it is correct, it will follow this formula: Complete sentence + COLON + list or explanation.

ENGLISH RULES

ACT SUCCESS
English Skill Builder— Integrated Punctuation #1
Directions: Read the passage and then choose the best answer to each question.

One-Note Wonder

There was absolutely no reason to be <u>nervous, he</u> had performed "Carnival of Venice" many times.

<u>Nevertheless,</u> it was an easy piece to play. It sounded difficult, but that was an illusion. Actually, any piece he <u>played, on the trumpet, was</u> easy for him, if the notes flew by with blinding speed. The hard selections, those that really made him <u>sweat; was</u> the slow pieces like Aaron Copland's "Quiet City." Anyone <u>whom</u> had tried to play that <u>deceptively, difficult, devilish</u> opus had consciously courted big <u>trouble. Because</u> each note was exposed and transparent. One tiny <u>error, was</u> all that was needed to ruin the performance.

"Carnival of <u>Venice" on the other hand was</u> full of difficult-sounding fancy <u>passages; the notes</u> came and went so quickly that it would take super-human ears to

1. A. NO CHANGE
   B. nervous he
   C. nervous, like he
   D. nervous. He

2. F. NO CHANGE
   G. Besides,
   H. However
   J. On the other hand

3. A. NO CHANGE
   B. played on the trumpet was
   C. played, on the trumpet was
   D. played on the trumpet, was

4. F. NO CHANGE
   G. sweat, was
   H. sweat were
   J. sweat, were

5. A. NO CHANGE
   B. whoever
   C. whomever
   D. who

6. F. NO CHANGE
   G. deceptively, difficult, devilish,
   H. deceptively difficult, devilish,
   J. deceptively difficult, devilish

7. A. NO CHANGE
   B. trouble because
   C. trouble; because
   D. trouble, because

8. F. NO CHANGE
   G. error: was
   H. error was
   J. error. Was

9. A. NO CHANGE
   B. Venice," on the other hand—was
   C. Venice," on the other hand, was
   D. Venice"; on the other hand was

10. F. NO CHANGE
    G. passages, the notes
    H. passages. The notes,
    J. passages wherefore the notes

Copyright © 2009 by Academic Educational Resources. All rights reserved.

ACT SUCCESS
English Skill Builder— Integrated Punctuation #1

hear any mistakes. <u>Moreover, he was still shaking</u> like
                              11

crazy as he prepared to <u>play and perform</u> the crowd-
                                    12

pleasing cornet solo.

<u>He began, the first</u> note sounded very much like
     13

<u>that</u> of a sick elephant trumpeting for help. It was the
  14

correct note, but it was so out-of-tune and ugly that he

seriously considered just walking off the stage

<u>immediately,</u> he might forever be remembered as the
       15

one-note wonder.

11. Which of the following is LEAST acceptable?
    A. NO CHANGE
    B. However, he was still shaking
    C. He was still, however, shaking
    D. Regardless, he was still shaking

12. F. NO CHANGE
    G. perform
    H. perform and perhaps play
    J. perform and play

13. A. NO CHANGE
    B. began, however the first
    C. began, however, the first
    D. began. The first

14. F. NO CHANGE
    G. that
    H. something like
    J. OMIT

15. Which of the following is UNACCEPTABLE?
    A. NO CHANGE
    B. immediately. He
    C. immediately, and he
    D. immediately; he

ACT SUCCESS
English Skill Builder—Integrated Punctuation #2
Directions: Read the passage and then choose the best answer to each question.

Overcoming the "Carnival" War

Somehow though the intrepid trumpeter
<u>   </u>
    1

gathered his <u>wits'</u> and continued even though panic had
          2

stolen his very soul. The next phrase – a flock of fast,

flashy <u>flurries, actually</u> came out pretty well. Continuing
          3

to the next section despite himself, <u>the instrument</u>
                                            4
<u>seemed to return slowly to his control.</u>
               4

<u>With a sigh of relief,</u> the next passage and then the next
       5

rolled out with increasing precision and beauty. He <u>had,</u>
                                             6
<u>at least for this one performance,</u> mastered his fear.
      6

Calmly <u>now, with no nervousness,</u> he proceeded with
        7

ever-greater control and confidence. The <u>war –</u>
                                       8
<u>performer versus paranoia –</u> was won. The audience
     8

exploded into <u>loud and thunderous</u> applause at the
              9

finish, and he bowed <u>gratefully and appreciatively.</u>
                   10

1. A. NO CHANGE
    B. Somehow, though
    C. Somehow though,
    D. Somehow, though,

2. F. NO CHANGE
    G. wit's
    H. wits
    J. 'wits

3. A. NO CHANGE
    B. flurries actually
    C. flurries – actually
    D. flurries. Actually

4. F. NO CHANGE
    G. the instrument and him seemed to return slowly to control.
    H. he gradually regained control of his instrument.
    J. his instrument gradually seemed to correct himself.

5. A. NO CHANGE
    B. As he breathed a figurative sigh of relief,
    C. Relieving himself,
    D. Relieving itself,

6. F. NO CHANGE
    G. had at least for this one performance,
    H. had at least, for this one performance
    J. had at least for this one performance

7. A. NO CHANGE
    B. now with no nervousness,
    C. now, with no nervousness
    D. OMIT

8. F. NO CHANGE
    G. war – performer versus paranoia,
    H. war, performer versus paranoia--
    J. war performer versus paranoia

9. A. NO CHANGE
    B. loud and ear-splitting
    C. thunderous and loud
    D. thunderous

10. F. NO CHANGE
    G. with gratefulness and appreciation
    H. gratefully and with appreciation
    J. appreciatively

ACT SUCCESS
English Skill Builder—Integrated Punctuation#2

If only confidence had endurance. Like the Energizer Bunny.
　　　　　　　　　　　　　　11

11. Which of the following is LEAST acceptable?
    A. NO CHANGE
    B. If only confidence, like the Energizer Bunny, had endurance.
    C. If only confidence had endurance, like the Energizer Bunny
    D. If only confidence, like the Energizer Bunny, would go on and on.

　　He knew better, the apparent end of the war was
　　　　　　　　12
just a temporary cease-fire; the bullets and ballistics of flagrant fright would begin flying again all too soon – no doubt at the very next performance. Until then, he would practice "Carnival of Venice" like a madman; perhaps
　　　　　　　　　　　　　　　　　　　13
that's exactly what he was.

12. F. NO CHANGE
    G. He knew better. The
    H. He knew better the
    J. He knew better? The

13. A. NO CHANGE
    B. madman, perhaps
    C. madman, perhaps in a nutshell
    D. madman. Perhaps when

ACT SUCCESS
English Quiz: English Made Easy

Directions: Fill in the missing information in space provided below. Once it is filled out, this quiz will serve as a concise study guide to the ACT English Rules. Mastering these rules is one of the keys to success!

COMMAS – There are six comma rules to learn.
1.

2.

3.

4.

5.

6.

Other comma hints:
1.

2.

3.

DASH – There are two dash rules. Dashes are similar to commas in these two cases.
1.

2.

SEMICOLON – There is one rule to know.
1.

COLON – There are three colon rules to know.
1.

2.

3.

ACT SUCCESS
English Quiz: English Made Easy

<u>APOSTROPHE</u> – An apostrophe is used to show ownership.

1.

2.

3.

<u>SENTENCES:</u>

You now know four ways to separate or combine complete sentences. What are they?

1.

2.

3.

4.

<u>Know the correct usage of the following words.</u>

1. **Their** =   2. **There** =   3. **They're** =

4. **Its'** =   5. **It's** =   6. **Its** =

English Practice Passages

ACT SUCCESS
English Practice Passage #1

Directions: Read the passage and then choose the best answer to each question. Use a watch to time yourself, taking no longer than nine minutes per passage.

Asia's Architecture

To see <u>one of the greatest</u> examples of the maxim
"architecture is art you walk through," one should view the American embassy building in Hong Kong. If you <u>ride it's enormous</u> escalator, you immediately will be overwhelmed by the sheer spaciousness of Sir Norman Foster's larger-than-life Erector set. Completed in 1986, it was one of the first buildings in Asia to break from the glass-and-concrete standard that blots all too many urban skylines. ⟦3⟧ Asia now has its share of structures that defy the conventional, and many more are on the way.

Building-spotting is usually an urban adventure, but Japan's Miho <u>Museum lying deep</u> in the pine forest of Shigaraki, a 20-minute drive from Kyoto. Designed by I.M. Pei, the renowned Chinese-born architect, the building challenges Asia's "go-high-or-go-home" architectural motto. Where others scrape the skies, the 13-meter-tall Miho sinks <u>deep; built so that eighty</u> percent of the structure is underground. Visitors pass through a curving tunnel and across a suspension bridge before reaching the museum

1. **A.** NO CHANGE
   B. one of the most greatest
   C. the most great
   D. the greatest

2. **F.** NO CHANGE
   G. ride its enormous
   H. ride its' enormous
   J. are riding it's enormous

3. At this point, the writer is considering adding following sentence:

   It also inspired architects and builders everywhere to go against the grain.

   Given that it is true, would this be a relevant addition make here?
   A. Yes, because it provides the reader with a better understanding of Foster's building.
   B. Yes, because it helps transition from the exam building to the passage's main idea.
   C. No, because it detracts from the focus on HSBC building in Hong Kong.
   D. No, because it is inconsistent with the style of t passage to mention specific qualities of individ buildings.

4. **F.** NO CHANGE
   G. Museum which lies deep
   H. Museum lies deep
   J. Museum, lying deep

5. **A.** NO CHANGE
   B. deep; eighty
   C. deep, building eighty
   D. deep built, so that

Copyright © 2009 by Academic Educational Resources. All rights reserved.

ACT SUCCESS
English Practice Passage #1

itself. It is filled with spectacular sculptures and it is valued at $250-million.

    [1] Another gem exists in China. [2] When people talk about architecture in the People's Republic, they often focus on the buildings that line Shanghai's Bund Road. [3] And why not? [4] Across Shanghai's Huangpu River and alongside the hideous Oriental Pearl TV Tower stands the 88-story Jin Mao Tower, measuring 420 meters and it reaches toward heaven. [5] The Jin Mao hints at a pagoda style, creating a rhythmic pattern as the building rises. 9

[6] The 555-rooms that make up the Grand Hyatt Shanghai, the world's tallest hotel, fill the top floors. [7] But the most interesting structure in China is yet to be built. [8] The proposed National Theater in Beijing will be a dewdrop-shaped design, one that has been mired in controversy. [9] It clashes with both traditional values and the nearby architecture. [10] If the theater is constructed, it will liven up

6. F. NO CHANGE
   G. It being filled with spectacular sculptures
   H. Being filled with spectacular sculptures, it
   J. The museum, filled with spectacular sculptures,

7. Which of the following alternatives to the underlined portion would NOT be acceptable?
   A. they often mention
   B. they often talk of
   C. they often talk on
   D. they often direct their focus to

8. F. NO CHANGE
   G. as well reaches
   H. it being
   J. reaching

9. The writer is considering deleting the following phrase from the preceding sentence (placing a period after the word *style*):

   creating a rhythmic pattern as the building rises

   Should the writer make this deletion?
   A. Yes, because the information in unrelated to the topic addressed in this paragraph.
   B. Yes, because the information fails to describe the architectural merits of the Jin Mao Tower.
   C. No, because the information shows why the Oriental Pearl TV Tower is *hideous*.
   D. No, because the information helps define the term *pagoda style*, which might otherwise puzzle readers.

10. F. NO CHANGE
    G. make
    H. which are making
    J. OMIT the underlined portion.

11. A. NO CHANGE
    B. dewdrop-shaped design one that has been mired
    C. dewdrop-shaped design, miring
    D. dewdrop-shaped design; one mired

ACT SUCCESS
English Practice Passage #1

the capital's conventional, boring skyline. [12]

Architects have started messing with new, nonstandard
                    _____
                              13
designs throughout Asia. The variety of the continent's

cultures and landscapes inspire builders to try
                        _____
                              14
new ideas.

12. Upon reviewing this paragraph and finding that some information has been left out, the writer composes the following sentence incorporating the information:

> Most of the prominent buildings around the proposed location feature dull, straight-edged designs.

This sentence would most logically be placed after Sentence:
- **F.** 4
- **G.** 5
- **H.** 9
- **J.** 10

13.
- **A.** NO CHANGE
- **B.** have begun implementing new
- **C.** have begun to start to try new
- **D.** have really experimented with new

14.
- **F.** NO CHANGE
- **G.** make builders inspired to
- **H.** inspires builders to try
- **J.** inspire builders trying

Question 15 asks about the preceding passage as a whole.

15. Suppose the writer's goal had been to write a brief essay focusing on the history and development of Asian architecture. Would this essay successfully fulfill this goal?
- **A.** Yes, because the essay describes the origins of Asian architecture and its early builders.
- **B.** Yes, because the essay focuses on the buildings in Asia with the most historical importance.
- **C.** No, because the essay focuses on architects who were not born in Asia.
- **D.** No, because the essay focuses on recent architectural developments within Asia.

9

Copyright © 2009 by Academic Educational Resources. All rights reserved.

ACT SUCCESS
English Practice Passage #2

Directions: Read the passage and then choose the best answer to each question. Use a watch to time yourself, taking no longer than nine minutes per passage.

A Lobster Community

<u>On</u> terms of status, the lobster has come a long way. In a short one hundred years, *Homarus americanus*, or the Maine lobster, ascended from humble fare to <u>food for those whom dine royally</u>, a true success story. Prior to the nineteenth century, only widows, orphans, and servants ate lobster. And in some parts of New England, serving lobster to prison inmates more than once a week was forbidden by law; <u>breaking the law meant a fine and possible suspension.</u> Lobsters are *Arthropoda*, the phylum whose membership includes insects and spiders. Although lobsters are highly unsightly, their sweet, salty, sensual taste has been noted, and <u>their status and price have risen</u>. This more than compensates for the lobster's roach-like appearance and the work involved in extracting meat from <u>their shell</u>. However, the fishermen <u>of</u> Isle Au Haut still refer to them as "bugs."

Isle Au Haut (pronounced I-LA-HOE) is a small inhabited island off the coast of Maine in Penobscot Bay, an <u>area; that is regarded as</u> "the lobster capital of the world." In lobster fishing communities such as Isle Au Haut, the calendar year can be best described as a two-season <u>system, but</u> it includes the lobster season and the off-season.

1. A. NO CHANGE
   B. In
   C. From
   D. With

2. F. NO CHANGE
   G. food to those who
   H. food for those who
   J. those whom

3. The writer wants to continue emphasizing the early status of lobster as *humble fare*. Given that all of the choices are true, which one best accomplishes this goal?
   A. NO CHANGE
   B. doing so was considered cruel and unusual punishment
   C. inmates could not eat any seafood
   D. that law does not exist today

4. F. NO CHANGE
   G. they have rising status and price
   H. there has been a rise in their status and price
   J. their rising in status and price

5. A. NO CHANGE
   B. its shell
   C. their shells
   D. shells

6. Which of the following alternatives to the underlined portion would NOT be acceptable?
   F. from
   G. on
   H. at
   J. in

7. A. NO CHANGE
   B. area that is regarded as
   C. area that, is regarded as
   D. area, that is regarded as,

8. F. NO CHANGE
   G. system it
   H. system, it
   J. system. It

Copyright © 2009 by Academic Educational Resources. All rights reserved.

ACT SUCCESS
English Practice Passage #2

For most of us on the island, fishing season begins in early May and ends around the first of December. Because some fishermen extend or shorten on either end, we generally have a seven-month fishing season. The people on the island spend the off-season on vacation. Each lobster season is typical only in that it is different from every preceding span of seven months in which lobsters have been fished. There are trends, patterns, and habits that are observed by every generation, but each individual season has its own quirks, ebbs, and flows of cooperative crustaceans.

Although the individual members are for the most part hardy, the year-round community on the island remaining concerned and fragile. This winter's population of forty-seven people is down from seventy residents just two years ago. Ever-increasing land values, corresponding property taxes, and extremely limited employment opportunities threaten us like vultures circling prey.

If it weren't for the lobster, the buzzards may have already gotten to us. But recently our fishermen have been fortunate, enjoying a lobster population boom. Every year-round family has been affected positively by the surge in revenue generated by the fisheries. Other than the fact that we all live on this rock, our only common bond is lobster.

9. A. NO CHANGE
   B. Whereas
   C. After
   D. Although

10. Given that all of the choices are true, which one provides information most relevant to the main focus of paragraph?
    F. NO CHANGE
    G. are worried about the future of their industry.
    H. fish in other areas during the off-season.
    J. are accustomed to surprises in the regular cycle.

11. A. NO CHANGE
    B. island, which remains
    C. island remains
    D. island that remains

12. F. NO CHANGE
    G. just as
    H. as like
    J. such as

13. The writer is considering revising this sentence by omitting the underlined portion (placing a period after *fortunate*). If the writer did this, the paragraph would primarily lose:
    A. information necessary to explain why the fishermen are not facing immediate threats.
    B. details that show how the fishermen plan to compensate for rising costs.
    C. details that establish the time in which the essay was written.
    D. interesting but irrelevant information about the island.

14. F. NO CHANGE
    G. Because of
    H. Despite the
    J. In

ACT SUCCESS
English Practice Passage #2

Our own little piece of America hangs on by a thread, tied to the fates of the lobsters and our fishermen's groups.
     15

15. A. NO CHANGE
    B. groups of our fishermen.
    C. groups to which our fishermen belong.
    D. our fishermen who belong to groups.

9

ACT SUCCESS
English Practice Passage #3

Directions: After reading the passage, choose the best answer to each question. Use a watch to time yourself, taking no longer than nine minutes per passage.

A Tale of Two Wizards

Not since the Beatles ruled pop music in the 1960s has a phenomenon dominated pop culture in quite the same way as the *Harry Potter* books. With total worldwide sales of more than 30 million copies and counting, the young wizard from Hogwart's School of Witchcraft and Wizardry has ruled childrens' bestseller lists
₁

and has dwarfed the sales of adult titles as well.
₂

When the paperback edition of *Harry Potter and the Prisoner of Azkaban* was first released on June 20, 1999, it
₃
outsold all other children's books combined by a five-to-one margin. And when *Harry Potter and the Goblet of Fire* came out this year, U.S. publisher Scholastic sold more than 3 million copies during the first week alone.

In New Zealand, the release date for *Harry Potter and the Goblet of Fire* was a week later. The media frenzy was so high that the *Auckland Herald* devoted a full page to two
₄

sisters who got a copy a few days early. Their father, who
₅
had just returned from the United States and was able to
₅

1.
   A. NO CHANGE
   B. children's
   C. child's
   D. childrens

2. The writer is considering deleting the underlined portion from the preceding sentence. If the writer were to do the essay would primarily lose:
   F. a minor detail in the essay's introduction.
   G. an explanation of the *Harry Potter* plot lines.
   H. the writer's opinion about the significance of the *Harry Potter* series.
   J. a specific example of the literary worth of Rowling's novels.

3.
   A. NO CHANGE
   B. 1999; it
   C. 1999, and it
   D. 1999. It

4.
   F. NO CHANGE
   G. had been devoted
   H. will have devoted
   J. devotes

5.
   A. NO CHANGE
   B. father,
   C. father had
   D. father having

ACT SUCCESS
English Practice Passage #3

"smuggle" in a copy. More recently, Harry Potter author J K. Rowling read to an estimated 12,000 eager listeners, the largest crowd ever to hear an author read.

But even as Pottermania remains and stays at a fever
pitch, many people are celebrating the 100th anniversary of another world-famous wizard, *The Wizard of Oz*. Since it first appeared in book form in 1900, *The Wizard of Oz* has delighted millions of readers throughout the world. The 1939 MGM film version of *The Wizard of Oz* remains one of history's most popular films, and new 100th anniversary editions of the book are bringing L. Frank Baum's classic tale to a whole new generation of children. An exhibit at the Library of Congress even paid homage to the story's enduring legacy. [7]

Beyond being immensely popular and adored by many,
the *Harry Potter* books, and *The Wizard of Oz* series share
other similarities. Both were largely praised by critics.

Therefore, both have drawn criticism from some quarters for
their portrayal of magic and wizardry and their possible
affect on young people. Indeed, parents and other

6. F. NO CHANGE
   G. and keeps going
   H. by continuing
   J. OMIT the underlined portion.

7. If the writer were to delete the preceding sentence, the paragraph would primarily lose:
   A. background information about Baum's novel.
   B. a detail demonstrating the popularity of *The Wizard of Oz*.
   C. a comment by the author about a novel that is unrelated to *Harry Potter*.
   D. an essential comparison between Baum and Rowling.

8. F. NO CHANGE
   G. immensely popular – adored by
   H. adored by
   J. immensely popular from being adored by

9. A. NO CHANGE
   B. the *Harry Potter* books and *The Wizard of Oz* series
   C. the *Harry Potter* books and *The Wizard of Oz* series,
   D. the *Harry Potter* books, and *The Wizard of Oz* series,

10. F. NO CHANGE
    G. Both
    H. However, both
    J. Undoubtedly, both

11. A. NO CHANGE
    B. effect on
    C. affects on
    D. effects on

Copyright © 2009 by Academic Educational Resources. All rights reserved.

ACT SUCCESS
English Practice Passage #3

groups attacked the *Harry Potter* series, concerned about witchcraft, more than any other book in 1999.

However, many supporters of the *Harry Potter* books feel that their worthy in and of themselves. Others even

claim the attacks should come to a conclusion because the books help develop the desire to read in general.

12. F. NO CHANGE
 G. groups, attacked the *Harry Potter* series, concer about witchcraft more
 H. groups, concerned about witchcraft, attacked the *Harry Potter* series more
 J. groups, attacked the *Harry Potter* series concer about witchcraft, more

13. A. NO CHANGE
 B. they were
 C. they're
 D. there

14. Which of the following alternatives to the underli portion would be LEAST acceptable in terms of context of this sentence?
 F. should come to an end
 G. should reach completion
 H. should come to a halt
 J. should end

Question 15 asks about the preceding passage as a whole.

15. Suppose the writer had intended to write a brief es that compares and contrasts the *Harry Potter* series *The Wizard of Oz* series. Would this essay successf fulfill the writer's goal?
 A. Yes, because the essay highlights a number of similarities and differences between the two nove
 B. Yes, because the essay discusses each novel separately in order to show connections.
 C. No, because the essay focuses primarily on the *Harry Potter* series and only briefly mentions *The Wizard of Oz*.
 D. No, because the essay simply provides an overv of the sales record of each novel.

9

Additional Notes

Chapter 2
Math Strategies and Review

MATH

The ACT math test covers most areas of high school mathematics. No matter your math level or proficiency, you will score to your maximum potential by completing the review and practice items in this textbook.

HIGHLIGHTS

- 60 multiple choice questions.
- 60 minutes.
- There is no penalty for guessing, so you **must** answer every question.
- You **may** use a calculator on the ACT Math section. The TI-83 and TI-84 are allowed on the test. The TI-89 is **not** allowed.

Content Area	Percent of Test	Typical Number of Questions
Pre-Algebra	23%	14
Elementary Algebra	17%	10
Intermediate Algebra	15%	9
Coordinate Geometry	15%	9
Plane Geometry	23%	14
Trigonometry	7%	4
Total	100%	60

DO'S AND DON'TS

- **DO** use your test booklet! Often a quick sketch will help solve the problem. If a diagram is already provided, begin by marking all known information.

- **DO** work backwards. This is especially true when there are variables in the question and numbers in the answer choices. For these questions, use the "**Plug & Chug**" strategy: plug answer choices back into the problem to find the correct solution to the problem.

- **DO** utilize the "**Plug in C Strategy**" when working backwards: All ACT math answers are listed in numerical order, either smallest to largest or vice versa. Therefore, when possible, plug in choice "C" (or "H"). If it is not the right answer, it will be immediately clear whether larger or smaller answer choice would have led you to the correct answer. If you need a larger number, you can immediately eliminate choices "A" and "B"; if you need a smaller one, you can eliminate "D" and "E". By using this method, you can eliminate 3 choices by only checking one!

- **DO** assign the variable(s) a number and evaluate the problem accordingly if a question has variables in the answer choices. **Plug in an easy number** to work with, like 2 or 3. (Beware of using zero or 1; they are more trouble than they are worth!).

Copyright © 2009 Academic Educational Resources. All rights reserved.

- **DO** be sure to **answer the question being asked**! One of the most commonly made mistakes on the ACT is also one of the most avoidable. A good way to avoid this scenario is to underline the part of the question that directly poses the question (i.e. "what is the value of x?"). That way, after you finish solving the problem, you can quickly glance back at the part of the question that you have underlined and double check that you are answering the right question (i.e. circling the answer that corresponds to the value of x, rather than the value of y).

- **DO** read the question first. In other words, in long word problems, look at the question stem as a way to preview what the question really wants you to find.

- **DO** assume that diagrams are drawn to scale if you don't know where to start on a problem or cannot find the answer mathematically, and estimate lengths and angle measures from the diagram.

- **DO** look for wrong answers in addition to correct ones, and use **Process of Elimination**. Even if you do not find then answer, if you can guess after eliminating three answer choices, your probability of guessing correctly has improved from 20% to 50%!

- **DO** start the test with your calculator in degree mode. To put at TI-83 or TI-84 in degree mode, first press the "MODE" button, located directly to the right of the yellow "2nd" button. Once in the "MODE" screen, look to the third line down. It will say "Radian" and "Degree." Make sure "Degree" is highlighted. If it is not, place the cursor on "Degree" and press the "ENTER" button. "Degree" should now be highlighted, and your calculator will be in degree mode.

- **DO** be alert for charts/graphs that apply to more than one question.

- **DON'T** spend too much time on any one question.

PACING

- 60 minutes to answer 60 questions corresponds to one minute per question. However, you should target 25 minutes for the first 30 questions, which will save you extra time to work through the more difficult questions on the back half of the test.

- Remember: DO NOT leave any answers blank. However, on the practice tests it is helpful to mark which questions you guessed on, so you can see which math concepts you might need to brush up on.

INCREASING DIFFICULTY

The Math test is the only section of the ACT arranged in order of difficulty; generally speaking, you will find significantly easier questions toward the beginning of the test and more difficult questions toward the end. (This is not to say, of course, that you will never find a "tough" question on the first half or an "easy" question at the end.) Knowing that the test is laid out in this way can help you tremendously as you work through the section on test day. For instance, if one of the first questions seems extremely complicated, you are probably over-thinking it; if the answer to one of the last ten questions appears extremely obvious and straightforward, it likely is not the correct answer.

While there is no precise point where the Math section jumps from easy to difficult questions, a good rule of thumb is that typically the first 30 questions cover the more basic skill sets, whereas the last 30 questions test more advanced topics. You might find that you are entirely unfamiliar with some of the advanced topics, and that's okay! If you have never taken an advanced algebra or a trigonometry class, you are not expected to know the answers to these questions. **Remember: you can still receive an excellent score on the ACT Math without any knowledge of these advanced skills!**

HOW TO USE ACT SUCCESS TO STUDY FOR THE MATH SECTION

The remainder of the ACT Math chapter of this book is divided into three sections. First, you will come across the ACT Success "Math Rules." Think of this section as a detailed study guide for the ACT math. It lists every topic tested on the math section, as well as facts and formulas related to those topics. Every concept that is tested on the ACT is covered in "The Rules," so you never have to look anywhere else! Study the formulas (as they will not be provided on the ACT), and use it as a handy reference tool as your studying progresses.

After "The Rules" you will come to a series of Skill Builders. Generally speaking, they follow the trend of increasing difficulty: Skill Builders that come earlier correspond to more basic concepts that will tend to be tested on the first half of the ACT Math section; Skill Builders that appear later correspond to more advanced concepts, and tend to show up on the second half of an actual ACT. You probably have seen all of these topics before, and though everything might seem familiar, more than likely at some point you will not remember something that you have learned in the past. Don't worry if you do not remember a concept! That's what these Skill Builders are here for! The Skill Builders will help you to brush up on forgotten topics and put you in a mindset for success.

Following the Skill Builders, which are divided by topic, you will work through a few math quizzes. These quizzes are divided by subject (Algebra, Plane Geometry, etc.), and incorporate all of the topics you have come across on the Skill Builders and then some. Just as the Skill Builders can alert you to topics that you might need to work on, the quizzes will help you determine which subjects are your strengths and which are your weaknesses. Obviously the ACT is not divided by subject, but these quizzes will show you exactly which areas you need to review further, and should help you to focus and plan your preparation for the ACT Math section.

It might seem overwhelming now, but once you get going you will see that studying for math is like riding a bicycle, and that you are well on your way to ACT SUCCESS!

GOOD LUCK!

MATH RULES
Formulas, Strategies, and Review

Properties of Numbers

Integers are whole numbers and their opposites.
Examples: ...-6,-5,-4,-3,-2,-1,0,1,2,3,4,5,6...   (Note: 0 is neither positive nor negative)

Prime numbers are integers greater than 1 that have no factors other than 1 and the number itself.
Examples: 2,3,5,7,11,13,17,19,23,29...   (Note: 1 is not prime; 2 is the only even prime)

Greatest Common Factor (GCF)
The greatest number which divides into both numbers.
Example: The GCF of 8 and 12 is 4.

Least Common Multiple (LCM)
The lowest number which both numbers divide into.
Example: The LCM of 4 and 6 is 12.

Order of operations **PEMDAS (please excuse my dear aunt Sally)**
Parentheses
Exponentiation
Multiplication / **D**ivision
Addition / **S**ubtraction
For Absolute value problems it may help to think of parentheses right inside the absolute value bars: *Example:* $-2|4-5|-3$ *can be thought of as* $-2|(4-5)|-3$
It may also be helpful to enter the problem into your calculator.

Motion Problems

Distance = (rate)(time) $d = rt$

Also, $t = \dfrac{d}{r}$ and $r = \dfrac{d}{t}$

Percents

$\dfrac{Part}{Whole} * 100 = \%$

Example: $\dfrac{10}{25} * 100 = .4 * 100 = 40\%$

Word Problem: What number is equal to 40% of 25?

Answer: $\dfrac{x}{25} * 100 = 40\% \rightarrow \dfrac{x}{25} = \dfrac{40}{100} \rightarrow 100x = 1{,}000 \rightarrow x = \mathbf{10}$

MATH RULES   Copyright © 2009 Academic Educational Resources. All rights reserved.

Rules for Exponents

$x^a x^b = x^{(a+b)}$, $(x^a)^b = x^{ab}$, $x^0 = 1$, $x^{-a} = \dfrac{1}{x^a}$, $\dfrac{x^a}{x^b} = x^{(a-b)}$, $\sqrt[n]{x} = x^{\frac{1}{n}}$, $x^a = x^b \Rightarrow a = b$

Quadratic Equations

The **quadratic formula** for solving the equation $ax^2+bx+c=0$; $x = \dfrac{-b \pm \sqrt{b^2 - 4ac}}{2a}$

(It is strongly recommended that you have a quadratic formula program on your calculator. This can save time on the test.)

For real numbers: zeros, roots, solutions and x-intercepts are **all** the same.

Geometry Facts

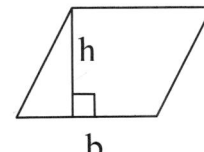

Area of a <u>Parallelogram</u> = (base)(height)
A = bh

(Note: Squares and rectangles are parallelograms.)

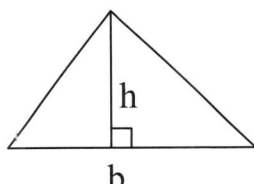

Area of a <u>Triangle</u> = ½ (base)(height)
A = ½ bh
sum of the angles = 180°

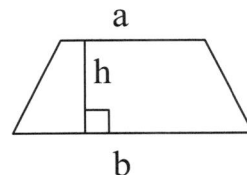

Area of a <u>Trapezoid</u> = (average of the bases)(height)
$A = \left(\dfrac{a+b}{2}\right)h$

Perimeter = the sum of the lengths of all the sides

Circle $A = \pi r^2$ $C = 2\pi r = \pi D$

MATH RULES   Copyright © 2009 Academic Educational Resources. All rights reserved.

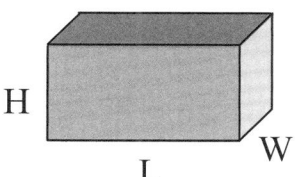

Rectangular Prism (Box)
Volume = LWH
Surface Area = 2LW+2WH+2LH

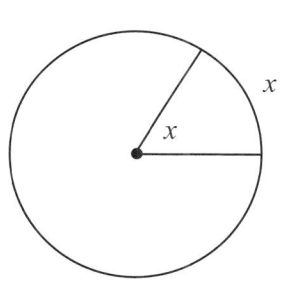

A central angle has the same measure as the intercepted arc.

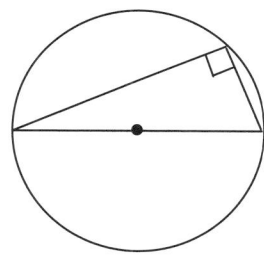

Any angle inscribed in a semi-circle is a right angle.

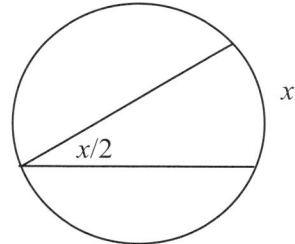

An inscribed angle is ½ the measure of the intercepted arc.

Triangles

Pythagorean Theorem

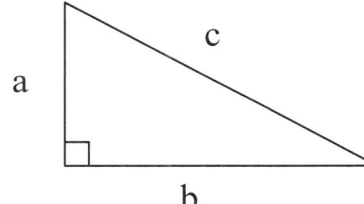

For a right triangle
$a^2 + b^2 = c^2$

Most common triples on ACT
3-4-5
6-8-10
5-12-13

Other triples
7-24-25
8-15-17

Special Right Triangles

30° - 60° - 90°

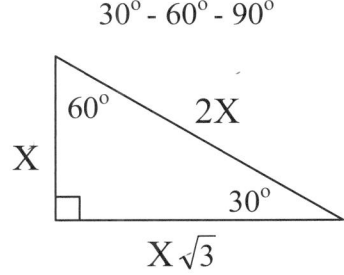

45° - 45° - 90°

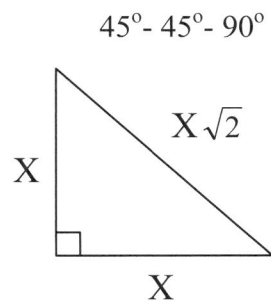

MATH RULES   Copyright © 2009 Academic Educational Resources. All rights reserved.

Triangle Inequality: The sum of the lengths of the shortest two sides of a triangle is always greater than the length of the longest side.

The largest angle is always opposite the longest side and the smallest angle is always opposite the shortest side.

Sides are congruent if and only if the opposite angles are congruent.

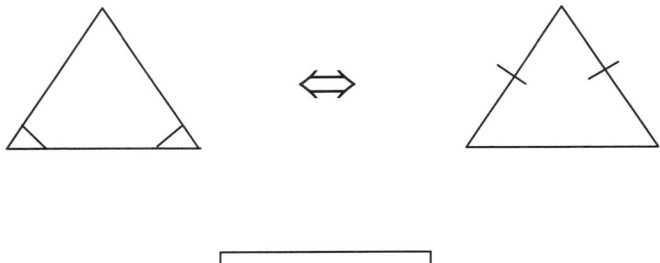

Polygons

For a polygon with N sides:
Sum of interior angles = $(N-2)180°$
Number of diagonals = $\dfrac{N(N-3)}{2}$

A **regular polygon** has equal sides and equal angles.

Congruent polygons are the same shape and size (all angles and sides are congruent).

Similar polygons are the same shape, but can be different sizes (angles are congruent and sides are proportional).

Parallel Lines & Angles

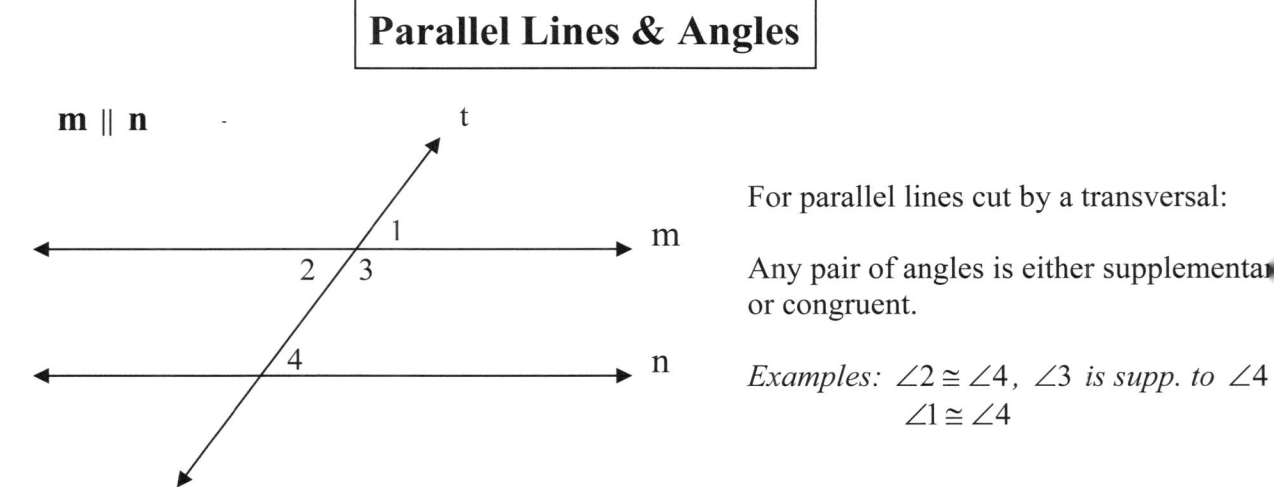

For parallel lines cut by a transversal:

Any pair of angles is either supplementary or congruent.

Examples: $\angle 2 \cong \angle 4$, $\angle 3$ *is supp. to* $\angle 4$
$\angle 1 \cong \angle 4$

MATH RULES Copyright © 2009 Academic Educational Resources. All rights reserved.

Rules for Lines

Slope-Intercept Form: $y = mx+b$, where m is the slope and b is the y-intercept.

When given a line in Standard Form ($Ax+By = C$), it is often helpful to convert to slope-intercept form by solving for y.

The slope formula for a line containing two points (x_1,y_1) and (x_2,y_2):

$$\text{Slope} = m = \frac{rise}{run} = \frac{\Delta y}{\Delta x} = \frac{(y_2 - y_1)}{(x_2 - x_1)}$$

Parallel lines have the same slope.

Perpendicular lines have slopes that are opposite reciprocals.
(or, the product of their slopes is -1)

Coordinate Geometry

The **midpoint formula** for the coordinates of the midpoint between (x_1,y_1) and (x_2,y_2):

$$\left(\frac{x_1 + x_2}{2}, \frac{y_1 + y_2}{2}\right)$$ or (average of the x-values, average of the y-values)

The **distance formula** for the distance between the two points (x_1,y_1) and (x_2,y_2):

$$D = \sqrt{(x_2 - x_1)^2 + (y_2 - y_1)^2}$$

Instead of using the distance formula, you can sketch out a right triangle and use the Pythagorean Theorem. The distance formula just does this for two general points. Use whichever method you are more comfortable with.

The **equation of a circle** with the center of (h,k) and a radius r:

MATH RULES

$$(x-h)^2 + (y-k)^2 = r^2$$

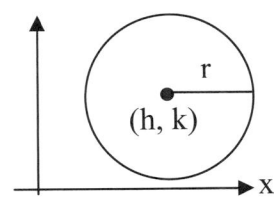

Example: The circle $(x-4)^2+(y+3)^2=25$ has center $(4,-3)$ and radius 5.

Sequences and Series

Arithmetic sequences have a common difference (add the same number to get from one term to the next).
Example: 4,7,10,13,16,19... (d=3)

Geometric sequences have a common ratio (multiply by the same number to get from one term to the next).
Example: 1,2,4,8,16,32,64... (r=2)

Statistics

Given a set of numbers:
The **mean** is the average.
The **median** is the middle number when arranged in order.
(Note: If there is an even number of numbers in the set, the median is the average of the two middle numbers.)
The **mode** is the number that occurs most often.
The **range** is the largest number minus the smallest number.

$$\text{Average} = \frac{\text{Sum of Numbers}}{\text{Number of Numbers}}$$

Sum of Numbers = (Average)(Number of numbers)

Probability / Counting Problems

For equally likely outcomes:

$$\text{Probability} = \frac{\text{Number of successful outcomes}}{\text{Total number of outcomes}}$$

Multiplication Principle:

If there are n ways to select one item and m ways to select another, then there are (n)(m) ways to select one of each type.

MATH RULES   Copyright © 2009 Academic Educational Resources. All rights reserved.

Example: If someone has 3 shirts, 4 pairs of pants and 5 shoes how many different outfits are possible? Answer (3)(4)(5) = 60 possible outfits.

There are n! ways to order n different objects.

[Note: n! = n(n-1)(n-2)…(3)(2)(1) and is read "n factorial"].

Example: How many ways can 5 different books be arranged on a bookcase?

Answer: 5! = 120

(Helpful hint: 5! can be evaluated on the TI-83/84 using Math, Prob, !)

Complex Numbers

$$i^2 = -1$$

(Helpful hint: The TI-83/84 has i above the decimal point)

Properties of Logs

For positive numbers:

$\log_b x = y$ if and only if $b^y = x$

$\log_b(xy) = \log_b x + \log_b y$

$\log_b\left(\dfrac{x}{y}\right) = \log_b x - \log_b y$

$\log_b x^n = n \log_b x$

$\log_b x = \dfrac{\log x}{\log b}$

Trigonometry

SOH-CAH-TOA

$$\sin\theta = \frac{opposite}{hypotenuse}, \quad \cos\theta = \frac{adjacent}{hypotenuse}, \quad \tan\theta = \frac{opposite}{adjacent} = \frac{\sin\theta}{\cos\theta}$$

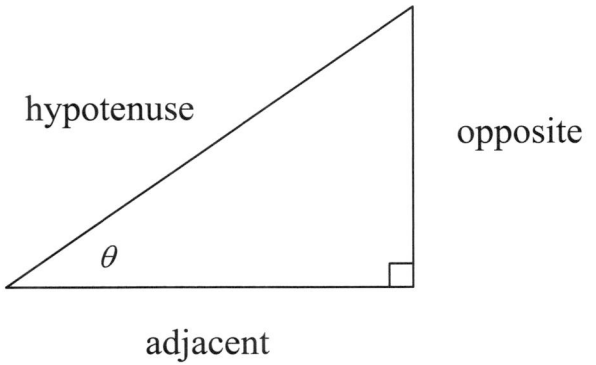

Reciprocal Identities

$$\csc\theta = \frac{1}{\sin\theta}, \quad \sec\theta = \frac{1}{\cos\theta}, \quad \cot\theta = \frac{1}{\tan\theta}$$

Pythagorean Identity

$$\sin^2\theta + \cos^2\theta = 1$$

$1 - \cos^2 = \sin^2$
$1 - \sin^2 = \cos^2$

MATH RULES

Math Example Problems

1. The price of an item is first marked down 20% and then up 20%. Express as a percentage the overall change in the price of the item.

   A) 0%
   B) +4%
   C) -4%
   D) +10%
   E) -10%

2. Find the largest angle of a triangle where the first angle is three times the second angle, and the third angle is 40° more than the first.

   F) 20°
   G) 28°
   H) 60°
   J) 84°
   K) 100°

3. If k is an integer, which of the following must be odd?

   I. $k+1$ II. $k^2 + 1$ III. $2k + 1$

   A) I only
   B) II only
   C) I and II
   D) I and III
   E) III only

4. Eva can complete a job in four hours. Jill takes ten hours, and Eric takes twenty hours. How long will it take them to do the job working together?

   F) $\frac{2}{5}$ hours
   G) $2\frac{1}{2}$ hours
   H) 4 hours
   J) $11\frac{1}{3}$ hours
   K) 34 hours

MATH RULES   Copyright © 2009 Academic Educational Resources. All rights reserved.

Additional Topics on the ACT

The following topics can and will show up on the test. However, this material is generally less likely to be on any given test than the material earlier in this packet based on prior test content. It is recommended that you have a solid understanding of earlier material before spending too much time studying this additional material.

More on Quadratic Equations

For a quadratic equation $ax^2+bx+c=0$:

$$\text{sum of the roots} = -\frac{b}{a}$$

$$\text{product of the roots} = \frac{c}{a}$$

The discriminant is b^2-4ac:

If $b^2-4ac > 0$
2 real solutions

If $b^2-4ac = 0$
1 real solution
(double zero)

If $b^2-4ac < 0$
No real solutions
2 complex solutions

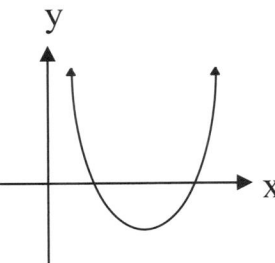
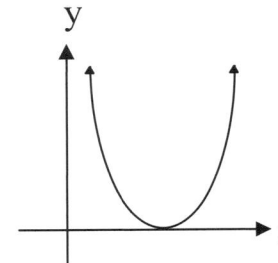
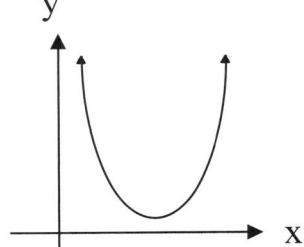

The graph of $y = ax^2+bx+c$ is a parabola.
Vertex form of a parabola is $y = a(x-h)^2 + k$.
The Vertex is (h,k)   If a >0 the parabola opens up.
                        If a<0 the parabola opens down.

Factoring Rules of Thumb

Many problems can be solved by factoring.

Don't forget to 1st take out the Greatest Common Factor (GCF).

Then look for difference of squares or try using the product sum method.

Difference of Squares: $x^2 - y^2 = (x-y)(x+y)$

Product sum method: To factor $x^2 + bx + c$ look for two numbers that add to b and multiply to c.

MATH RULES

More on Lines

Given the standard form $Ax + By = C$ Slope = $-\dfrac{A}{B}$,   y-intercept = $\dfrac{C}{B}$

To find x-intercepts set y=0 and solve for x
To find y-intercepts set x=0 and solve for y

More on Triangles

The sum of the exterior angles (1 per vertex) = 360°

An exterior angle is equal to the sum of the 2 remote interior angles.

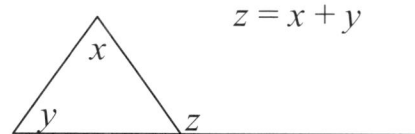

$z = x + y$

Connecting the midpoints of the three sides of a triangle forms four congruent triangles which are all similar to the original triangle.

If the endpoints of a segment are the midpoints of 2 sides of a triangle, the segment is parallel to the 3rd side and its length is ½ the length of the 3rd side.

Properties of Quadrilaterals

- Opposite sides of a parallelogram are congruent.
- Opposite angles of a parallelogram are congruent.
- Consecutive angles of a parallelogram are supplementary.
- Diagonals of a parallelogram bisect each other.
- Diagonals of a rhombus are perpendicular bisectors of each other.
- Diagonals of a rhombus are angle bisectors.
- Diagonals of a rectangle are congruent.
- Diagonals of an isosceles trapezoid are congruent.

(Note: It can be helpful to use your intuition rather than memorizing all of these rules.
For quadrilaterals, if a property seems like it is true, then it probably is.)

MATH RULES   Copyright © 2009 Academic Educational Resources. All rights reserved.

More Geometry Facts

The volume of any figure with a uniform cross section is the area of the base times the height. Two special cases of this are the cylinder and the prism.

Volume of a prism = (area of Base)(height) = Bh

Volume of a cylinder = (area of Base)(height) = $Bh = \pi r^2 h$

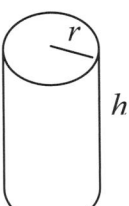

Arc length formula:

$s = \left(\dfrac{\theta}{360°}\right)(2\pi r)$ (θ in degrees)

$s = r\theta$ (θ in radians)

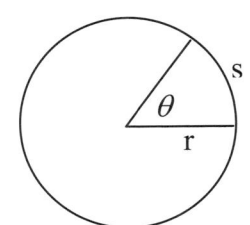

More Trig

Trig Graphs

$y = A\sin(Bx)$ or $y = A\cos(Bx)$
amplitude = $|A|$
period = $\dfrac{2\pi}{|B|}$ or $\dfrac{360°}{|B|}$

Additional pythagorean Identities

$\tan^2\theta + 1 = \sec^2\theta$, $1 + \cot^2\theta = \csc^2\theta$

To convert from degrees to radian multiply by $\dfrac{\pi}{180°}$

To convert from radians to degrees multiply by $\dfrac{180°}{\pi}$

More Sequences and Series

For Arithmetic Sequences and Series:

If a_n is the nth term and d is the common difference then:
$$a_n = a_1 + (n-1)d$$

The sum of the first n terms (S_n) is:
$$S_n = \frac{n}{2}(a_1 + a_n)$$

Inverse Functions

If f and g are inverse functions and f(c)=d, then g(d)=c.

If f and g are inverse functions then f[g(x)] = x and g[f(x)] = x.

An inverse function is the reflection over the line x=y (45° line through the origin).

To find an inverse function swap x and y then resolve for y.

Composite Functions

To evaluate f[g(x)] first find g(x) and then plug the result into f(x).

Example: $f(x) = 3x + 5$ and $g(x) = x^2$ Then $f[g(3)] = f(9) = 32$

Max/Min Problems

To maximize $X - Y$ make X as large as possible and Y as small as possible.

For $X, Y > 0$
$\frac{X}{Y}$ is maximized by making X as large as possible and Y as small as possible.

MATH RULES   Copyright © 2009 Academic Educational Resources. All rights reserved.

Additional Notes

Math Skill Builders

ACT SUCCESS
Math Skill Builder – Area Formulas

Directions: Choose the best answer to each question.

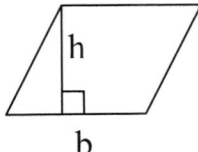

Area of a Parallelogram = (base)(height)
$$A = bh$$

(Note: Squares and rectangles are parallelograms.)

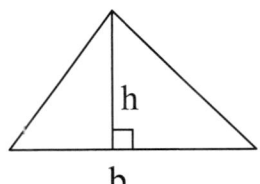

Area of a Triangle = ½ (base)(height)
$$A = \tfrac{1}{2} bh$$
sum of the angles = 180°

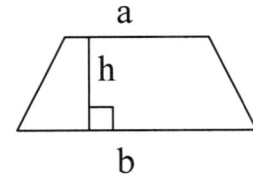

Area of a Trapezoid = (average of the bases)(height)
$$A = \left(\frac{a+b}{2}\right)h$$

Circle $\quad A = \pi r^2 \quad C = 2\pi r = \pi D$

1. What is the area of the parallelogram pictured below?

    A. 56
    B. 63
    C. 72
    D. 80
    E. 96

    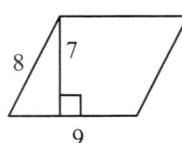

2. What is the area of the trapezoid pictured below?

    F. 65
    G. 120
    H. 125
    J. 130
    K. 168

    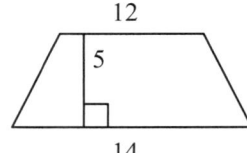

ACT SUCCESS
Math Skill Builder – Area Formulas

3. What is the area of a circle with a diameter of 12?
    A. 12π
    B. 24π
    C. 36π
    D. 48π
    E. 144π

4. What is the area of a rhombus with diagonals of lengths 6 and 8?
    F. 14
    G. 24
    H. 30
    J. 48
    K. 64

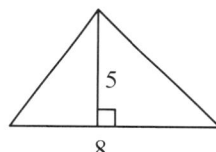

5. What is the area of the triangle pictured below?
    A. 10
    B. 15
    C. 20
    D. 25
    E. 40

6. What is the area of the following rectangle?
    F. 14
    G. 20
    H. 21
    J. 40
    K. 60

ACT SUCCESS
Math Skill Builder – Order of Operations

Directions: Choose the best answer to each question.

Order of operations **PEMDAS (please excuse my dear aunt Sally)**
Parentheses
Exponentiation
Multiplication / **D**ivision
Addition / **S**ubtraction
For Absolute value problems it may help to think of parentheses right inside the absolute value bars: *Example:* $-2|4-5|-3$ *can be thought of as* $-2|(4-5)|-3$
It may also be helpful to enter the problem into your calculator.

1. What is the value of the following expression?
   $$3 \cdot 2^2 - 3(5-1)$$
   A. 0
   B. 15
   C. 20
   D. 24
   E. 30

2. What is the value of the following expression?
   $$|5-7|-|7-5|-|9-6|$$
   F. -7
   G. -3
   H. -1
   J. 3
   K. 7

3. What is the value of the following expression?
   $$-2^2 + 4/2$$
   A. -2
   B. 0
   C. 4
   D. 6
   E. 8

4. What is the value of the following expression?
   $$4 + 6/3 - 3^2$$
   F. -6
   G. -3
   H. 3
   J. 6
   K. 15

Copyright © 2009 by Academic Educational Resources. All rights reserved.

ACT SUCCESS
Math Skill Builder – Order of Operations

5. What is the value of the following expression?

    $2|1-3|/2$

    A. -4
    B. -2
    C. 0
    D. 2
    E. 4

6. What is the value of the following expression?

    $(-3)^2 + 2^2 - 5^2$

    F. -30
    G. -12
    H. -5
    J. 20
    K. 38

ACT SUCCESS
Math Skill Builder – Slopes of Lines

Directions: Choose the best answer to each question.

Slope-Intercept Form: y = mx+b, where m is the slope and b is the y-intercept.

The slope formula for a line containing two points (x_1,y_1) and (x_2,y_2):

$$\text{Slope} = m = \frac{rise}{run} = \frac{\Delta y}{\Delta x} = \frac{(y_2 - y_1)}{(x_2 - x_1)}$$

Parallel lines have the same slope.

Perpendicular lines have slopes that are opposite reciprocals.
(or the product of their slopes is -1)

1. What is the slope of the line that passes through the points (1,2) and (7,-2)?

   A. $-\frac{3}{2}$
   B. $-\frac{2}{3}$
   C. $\frac{2}{3}$
   D. $\frac{3}{2}$
   E. 4

2. What is the slope of the line that passes through the points (2,3) and (5,9)?

   F. 1
   G. 2
   H. 3
   J. 4
   K. 5

3. What is the slope of the line with the following equation: $y = 3x + 6$?

   A. $-\frac{1}{3}$
   B. 2
   C. 3
   D. 4
   E. 5

Copyright © 2009 by Academic Educational Resources. All rights reserved.

ACT SUCCESS
Math Skill Builder – Slopes of Lines

4. What is the slope of the line parallel to the line with the following equation: $y = -\frac{1}{2}x + 5$?

   F. -2
   G. -1
   H. -0.5
   J. 1
   K. 2

5. What is the slope of the line perpendicular to the line with the following equation: $y = -\frac{1}{3}x - 4$?

   A. $-\frac{1}{3}$
   B. 1.5
   C. 2
   D. 2.5
   E. 3

ACT SUCCESS
Math Skill Builder – Midpoint Formula

Directions: Choose the best answer to each question.

The **midpoint formula** for the coordinates of the midpoint between (x_1, y_1) and (x_2, y_2):

$$\left(\frac{x_1 + x_2}{2}, \frac{y_1 + y_2}{2} \right)$$ or (average of the x-values, average of the y-values)

$$\text{Average} = \frac{\text{Sum of Numbers}}{\text{Number of Numbers}}$$

1. What is the midpoint of (3,5) and (-2,7)?
   A. (0.5, 6)
   B. (1, 7)
   C. (0, 5)
   D. (-0.5, 5)
   E. (1, 8)

2. What is the midpoint of -4 and 10 on the real number line?
   F. 1
   G. 2
   H. 3
   J. 4
   K. 5

3. What is the midpoint of (2, -4) and (4, 12)?
   A. (2, 5)
   B. (2, 7)
   C. (3.5, 3)
   D. (3, 4)
   E. (3, 5)

4. What is the y-coordinate of the midpoint of (6, -5) and (11, -11)?
   F. -5
   G. -6
   H. -7
   J. -8
   K. -9

5. What is the x-coordinate of the midpoint of (4, -3) and (-2, 11)?
   A. -1
   B. 0
   C. 1
   D. 2
   E. 3

ACT SUCCESS
Math Skill Builder – Midpoint Formula

6. The midpoint of a segment is (4, 2). One endpoint of the segment is (-1, 3). What are the coordinates of the other endpoint of the segment?
   F. (-2, 7)
   G. (1.5, 2.5)
   H. (4, -11)
   J. (8, 1)
   K. (9, 1)

7. The midpoint of a segment is (3, 7). One endpoint of the segment is (2, 5). What are the coordinates of the other endpoint of the segment?
   A. (-2, -3)
   B. (2.5, 6)
   C. (3, 7)
   D. (4, 9)
   E. (4.5, 11)

ACT SUCCESS
Math Skill Builder – Pythagorean Theorem

Directions: Choose the best answer to each question.

For a right triangle
$a^2 + b^2 = c^2$

Most common triples on ACT
3-4-5
6-8-10
5-12-13

Other triples
7-24-25
8-15-17

1. What is the length of the hypotenuse in the triangle below?

   A. $\sqrt{17}$
   B. $\sqrt{65}$
   C. 13
   D. 15
   E. 17

   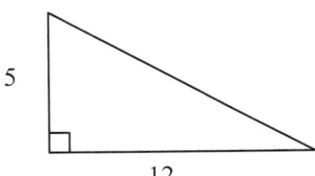

2. What is the length of the third side in the triangle below?

   F. 2
   G. $4\sqrt{2}$
   H. 8
   J. $\sqrt{71}$
   K. $\sqrt{130}$

   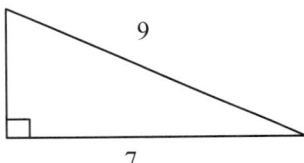

3. The legs of a right triangle are 6in and 8in long. How many inches long is the hypotenuse?

   A. $\sqrt{14}$
   B. 9
   C. 10
   D. 14
   E. 15

4. What is the length of the unknown side in the triangle below?

   F. 1
   G. 6
   H. 7
   J. 9
   K. 11

   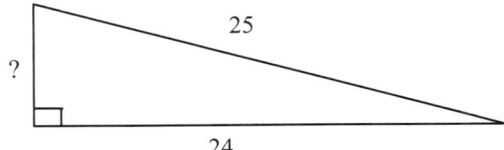

ACT SUCCESS
Math Skill Builder – Pythagorean Theorem

5. The hypotenuse of a right triangle is 17 units long. One of the legs is 8 units long. How many units long is the other leg?
   A. 11
   B. 15
   C. 17
   D. 25
   E. 31

6. Jane starts at the origin of a coordinate system. She travels 3 miles due north, and then 4 miles due east. How far is Jane from the origin?
   F. 3
   G. 4.2
   H. 4.5
   J. 4.8
   K. 5

ACT SUCCESS
Math Skill Builder – Distance Formula

Directions: Choose the best answer to each question.

The **distance formula** for the distance between the two points (x_1, y_1) and (x_2, y_2):

$$D = \sqrt{(x_2 - x_1)^2 + (y_2 - y_1)^2}$$

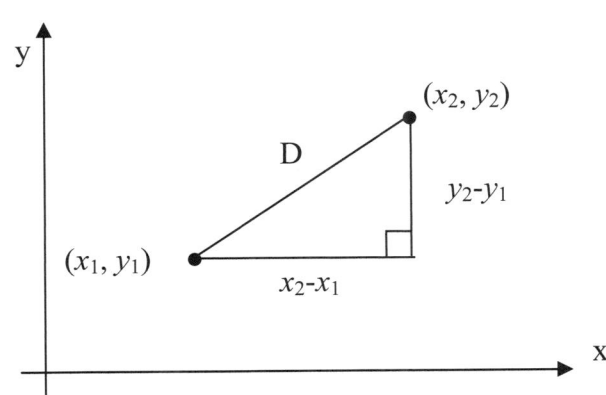

Instead of using the distance formula, you can sketch out a right triangle and use the Pythagorean Theorem. The distance formula just does this for two general points. Use whichever method you are more comfortable with.

1. What is the distance between the points (1, 2) and (6, 4)?

    A. $\sqrt{11}$
    B. $\sqrt{15}$
    C. $\sqrt{17}$
    D. $\sqrt{23}$
    E. $\sqrt{29}$

2. What is the distance between the points (2, 3) and (-1, 5)?

    F. $\sqrt{11}$
    G. $\sqrt{13}$
    H. $\sqrt{18}$
    J. $\sqrt{23}$
    K. $\sqrt{31}$

3. What is the distance between the points (6, 7) and (11, 2)?

    A. $2\sqrt{11}$
    B. $2\sqrt{13}$
    C. $5\sqrt{2}$
    D. $5\sqrt{23}$
    E. $7\sqrt{31}$

ACT SUCCESS
Math Skill Builder – Distance Formula

4. A boat leaves a dock from the origin of a coordinate system at noon. The boat travels to the point (4, 7) on the same coordinate system. How far is the boat from the origin?

    F. 8
    G. $\sqrt{65}$
    H. $\sqrt{73}$
    J. $\sqrt{93}$
    K. 11

5. A triangle has vertices at (-3, -5), (7, -5), and (2, 7). What is the perimeter of the triangle?

    A. $8\sqrt{11}$
    B. 30
    C. $8\sqrt{15}$
    D. 36
    E. 40

ACT SUCCESS
Math Skill Builder – Prime Numbers

Directions: Choose the best answer to each question.

Prime numbers are integers greater than 1 that have no factors other than 1 and the number itself.
Examples: 2,3,5,7,11,13,17,19,23,29… (Note: 1 is not prime; 2 is the only even prime)

1. How many prime numbers are there between 25 and 45?
   A. 3
   B. 4
   C. 5
   D. 6
   E. 7

   29, 31, 37, 41, 43

2. How many prime numbers are less than 10?
   F. 2
   G. 3
   H. 4
   J. 5
   K. 6

3. How many of the following 5 numbers are prime?
   1, 2, 21, 39, 49
   A. 1
   B. 2
   C. 3
   D. 4
   E. 5

4. How many of the following numbers are prime?
   -4, -3, 0, 1, 2
   F. 0
   G. 1
   H. 2
   J. 3
   K. 4

5. How many distinct prime factors does 60 have?
   A. 3
   B. 4
   C. 5
   D. 6
   E. 7

6. Twin primes are pairs of prime numbers that differ by 2. For example, 3 and 5 are twin primes. How many pairs of twin primes are there in which both numbers less than 30?
   F. 4
   G. 5
   H. 6
   J. 7
   K. 8

Copyright © 2009 by Academic Educational Resources. All rights reserved.

ACT SUCCESS
Math Skill Builder – Even & Odd Numbers

Directions: Choose the best answer to each question.

1. How many of the following numbers are even?
   $$-2, 0, 2, 6, 11$$
   A. 0
   B. 1
   C. 2
   D. 3
   E. 4

2. How many of the following numbers are odd?
   $$-4, -1, 0, 3, 8$$
   F. 0
   G. 1
   H. 2
   J. 3
   K. 4

3. Which of the following expressions can be odd for some integer x?
   A. $2x$
   B. $3x + 5x$
   C. $2x + 6x$
   D. $2x + 4x + 5x$
   E. $(2x)^2$

4. Which of the following expressions must be odd for all integer values of n?
   F. n^2
   G. $n^2 + 1$
   H. $2n^2 + 1$
   J. $3n^2 + 1$
   K. $4n^2 + 4$

5. Which of the following expressions must be even for all integer m?
   A. m^2
   B. $m^3 + 2m^2$
   C. $3m^2$
   D. $6m^3$
   E. $9m^3$

6. Which of the following expressions must be odd for all integer k?
   F. $k + k$
   G. $k + 2k$
   H. $k + (k+1)$
   J. $k^2 + k$
   K. $2k^2$

ACT SUCCESS
Math Skill Builder – Percents

Directions: Choose the best answer to each question.

$$\frac{Part}{Whole} * 100 = \%$$

Example: $\frac{10}{25} * 100 = .4 * 100 = 40\%$

Word Problem: What number is equal to 40% of 25?

Answer: $\frac{x}{25} * 100 = 40\% \rightarrow \frac{x}{25} = \frac{40}{100} \rightarrow 100x = 1,000 \rightarrow \boldsymbol{x = 10}$

1. A book normally costs $50. The book is on sale for 35% off. What is the sale price of the book?

   A. $17.50
   B. $27.50
   C. $32.50
   D. $37.50
   E. $45.00

2. 60% of a number is 30. What is the number?

   F. 18
   G. 35
   H. 40
   J. 45
   K. 50

3. A calculator normally sells for $80. The sale price is $64. What is the percent discount?

   A. 20%
   B. 25%
   C. 30%
   D. 50%
   E. 80%

4. John invests $20,000 in a savings account that pays 4.5% annual interest. How much money will John have after one year?

   F. $900
   G. $20,900
   H. $21,000
   J. $22,500
   K. $90,000

Copyright © 2009 by Academic Educational Resources. All rights reserved.

ACT SUCCESS
Math Skill Builder – Percents

5. Abby got 21 questions right on a recent algebra test. She scored 84% on the test. How many questions were on the exam?

   A. 18
   B. 23
   C. 25
   D. 28
   E. 35

6. A number is first increased by 20%. The resulting number is then decreased by 50%. What percent of the original number is the final number?

   F. 60%
   G. 65%
   H. 70%
   J. 80%
   K. 90%

ACT SUCCESS
Math Skill Builder – Greatest Common Factor

Directions: Choose the best answer to each question.

Greatest Common Factor (GCF)
The greatest number which divides into both numbers.
Example: The GCF of 8 and 12 is 4.

1. What is the greatest common factor of 24 and 36?
    A. 4
    B. 6
    C. 12
    D. 96
    E. 864

2. What is the greatest common factor of 16 and 56?
    F. 2
    G. 4
    H. 8
    J. 112
    K. 896

3. What is the greatest common factor of 7 and 14?
    A. 1
    B. 7
    C. 14
    D. 28
    E. 98

4. What is the greatest common factor of $3x^2y^3$ and $6xy^4$?
    F. $3xy^3$
    G. $3x^2y^3$
    H. $3x^2y^4$
    J. $6x^2y^3$
    K. $6x^2y^4$

5. What is the greatest common factor of $w^3x^2z^2$ and x^4z^2?
    A. x^2z^2
    B. x^4z^2
    C. $w^2x^2z^2$
    D. $w^3x^2z^2$
    E. $w^3x^4z^2$

6. What is the greatest common factor of $2xy$ and $4x$?
    F. $8x^2y$
    G. $4y$
    H. $4x$
    J. $2y$
    K. $2x$

ACT SUCCESS
Math Skill Builder – Least Common Multiple

Directions: Choose the best answer to each question.

Least Common Multiple (LCM)
The lowest number which both numbers divide into.
Example: The LCM of 4 and 6 is 12.

1. What is the least common multiple 8 and 12?
    - A. 1
    - B. 4
    - C. 24
    - D. 48
    - E. 96

2. What is the least common multiple of 6 and 21?
    - F. 1
    - G. 3
    - H. 21
    - J. 42
    - K. 126

3. What is the least common multiple of 8 and 16?
    - A. 2
    - B. 4
    - C. 8
    - D. 16
    - E. 32

4. What is the least common multiple of 4 and 5?
    - F. 1
    - G. 4
    - H. 5
    - J. 10
    - K. 20

5. One bird chirps every 6 seconds and another bird chirps every 15 seconds. If the two birds just chirped, how many seconds will it be before the two birds next chirp at the same time?
    - A. 15
    - B. 21
    - C. 24
    - D. 30
    - E. 90

6. Two lights are flashing. The first light flashes every 12 seconds, and the second light flashes every 18 seconds. If the two lights just flashed at the same time, how many seconds later will the two lights next flash together?
    - F. 12
    - G. 18
    - H. 24
    - J. 36
    - K. 216

ACT SUCCESS
Math Skill Builder – Motion Problems

Directions: Choose the best answer to each question.

Distance = (rate)(time) $d = rt$

Also, $t = \dfrac{d}{r}$ and $r = \dfrac{d}{t}$

1. A train travels at a constant rate of 50 miles per hour for 4 hours. How many miles does the train travel?
    A. 150
    B. 200
    C. 250
    D. 300
    E. 400

2. A runner takes 3 hours to run 15 miles. What is the speed of the runner in miles per hour?
    F. 3
    G. 5
    H. 15
    J. 30
    K. 45

3. A speed boat has a maximum speed of 40 miles per hour. How far will the boat travel if it goes at maximum speed for 2.5 hours?
    A. 16
    B. 20
    C. 40
    D. 80
    E. 100

4. About how long does it take a car traveling at 35 miles per hour to complete a 450 mile trip?
    F. 8
    G. 10
    H. 13
    J. 15
    K. 20

ACT SUCCESS
Math Skill Builder – Motion Problems

5. Jane goes on a trip in her car. To get to her destination, it takes Jane 6 hours traveling at a constant rate of 40 miles per hour. How many miles per hour faster would Jane have to travel in order to make the same trip in 5 hours?
   A. 6
   B. 8
   C. 10
   D. 20
   E. 50

6. Two trains are currently 600 miles apart on a straight track. The trains are traveling toward each other. The first train is traveling at 40 miles per hour, and the second train is traveling at 60 miles per hour. How long will it be before the two trains pass each other?
   F. 5
   G. 6
   H. 7
   J. 8
   K. 9

ACT SUCCESS
Math Skill Builder – Exponents

Directions: Choose the best answer to each question.

Useful **exponent** rules:

$x^a x^b = x^{(a+b)}$

$(x^a)^b = x^{ab}$

$x^0 = 1$

$x^{-a} = \dfrac{1}{x^a}$

$\dfrac{x^a}{x^b} = x^{(a-b)}$

$\sqrt[n]{x} = x^{\frac{1}{n}}$

$x^a = x^b \Rightarrow a = b$

1. Which of the following expressions is equivalent to $(2x^2 x^3)^4$?

   A. $2x^9$
   B. $2x^{10}$
   C. $16x^9$
   D. $16x^{10}$
   E. $16x^{20}$

2. Which of the following is equivalent to $x^{\frac{2}{3}} y^{\frac{1}{3}} z^{\frac{1}{2}}$?

   F. $\sqrt[6]{x^3 y^2 z^4}$
   G. $\sqrt[6]{x^4 y^2 z^3}$
   H. $\sqrt[6]{x^4 y^4 z^3}$
   J. $\sqrt[6]{x^5 y^2 z^3}$
   K. $\sqrt[6]{x^5 y^3 z^2}$

ACT SUCCESS
Math Skill Builder – Exponents

3. What is the value of x in the equation $9^x 3^2 = 27$?

    A. $\dfrac{1}{3}$

    B. $\dfrac{1}{2}$

    C. 0

    D. 1

    E. 2

4. Which of the following is equivalent to $(x^2 x^3)^4$?

    F. x^4

    G. x^9

    H. x^{10}

    J. x^{20}

    K. x^{24}

5. What is the value of w in the following expression?
$$x^{w^2} = x^{\frac{1}{25}}$$

    A. $\dfrac{1}{10}$

    B. $\dfrac{1}{5}$

    C. 5

    D. 10

    E. 25

ACT SUCCESS
Math Skill Builder – Radicals

Directions: Choose the best answer to each question.

1. Which of the following best describes an irrational number?
   A. A decimal that neither terminates nor repeats.
   B. Any expression with a radical sign.
   C. A decimal that repeats.
   D. Any complex number.
   E. Fractions that are not perfect squares.

2. How many of the following four numbers are irrational?
$$2\sqrt{3} - 2\sqrt{3}, \quad 3\sqrt{5} - 2\sqrt{5}, \quad \sqrt{9}, \quad \sqrt{38}$$
   F. 0
   G. 1
   H. 2
   J. 3
   K. 4

3. Which of the following numbers is rational?
   A. $\sqrt{\dfrac{25}{36}}$
   B. $\sqrt{3}$
   C. $\sqrt{\pi}$
   D. $\sqrt{13}\,\sqrt{3}$
   E. $\sqrt{21}$

4. Simplify the following expression: $\sqrt{48} = ?$
   F. $2\sqrt{3}$
   G. $3\sqrt{2}$
   H. $3\sqrt{4}$
   J. $4\sqrt{3}$
   K. $4\sqrt{12}$

5. In its simplest form, $\sqrt{27} = ?$
   A. $2\sqrt{3}$
   B. 3
   C. $3\sqrt{3}$
   D. $3\sqrt{9}$
   E. $9\sqrt{3}$

6. $2\sqrt{50} = ?$
   F. $4\sqrt{25}$
   G. 10
   H. $10\sqrt{2}$
   J. $50\sqrt{2}$
   K. 100

ACT SUCCESS
Math Skill Builder – Quadratics

Directions: Choose the best answer to each question.

The **quadratic formula** for solving the equation $ax^2+bx+c=0$; $x = \dfrac{-b \pm \sqrt{b^2 - 4ac}}{2a}$

(It is strongly recommended that you have a quadratic formula program on your calculator. This can save time on the test.)

For real numbers: zeros, roots, solutions and x-intercepts are **all** the same.

For a quadratic equation $ax^2+bx+c=0$:

$$\text{sum of the roots} = -\frac{b}{a}$$

$$\text{product of the roots} = \frac{c}{a}$$

Many problems can be solved by factoring.

Don't forget to 1st take out the Greatest Common Factor (GCF).

Then look for difference of squares or try using the product sum method.

Difference of Squares: $x^2 - y^2 = (x-y)(x+y)$

Product sum method: To factor $x^2 + bx + c$ look for two numbers that add to b and multiply to c.

1. What is the solution set for the following equation?
$$x^2 + 7x + 3 = 11$$
   A. $\{-8, -1\}$
   B. $\{-8, 1\}$
   C. $\{-7, 4\}$
   D. $\{-4, 7\}$
   E. $\{-1, 8\}$

2. What are the solutions to the following equation?
$$x^2 + 7x + 6 = 0$$
   F. -6
   G. -1
   H. -7, -6
   J. -7, -1
   K. -6, -1

ACT SUCCESS
Math Skill Builder – Quadratics

3. What is the sum of the roots of the following equation?
$$2x^2 - 5x - 3 = 0$$
   A. -2
   B. -1
   C. $\frac{1}{2}$
   D. $\frac{3}{2}$
   E. $\frac{5}{2}$

   $(2x+1)(x-3)$
   $x = 3, -\frac{1}{2}$

4. What are the solutions to the following equation?
$$4x^2 = 36$$
   F. ± 1
   G. ± 2
   H. ± 3
   J. ± 4
   K. ± 5

5. What is the product of the roots of following equation?
$$x^2 + 3x + 2 = 0$$
   A. 5
   B. 2
   C. 1
   D. 0
   E. -1

   $(x+2)(x+1)$
   $x = -2, -1$

ACT SUCCESS
Math Skill Builder – Circles

Directions: Choose the best answer to each question.

$A = \pi r^2 \qquad C = 2\pi r = \pi D$

The **equation of a circle** with the center of (h,k) and a radius r:

$$(x-h)^2 + (y-k)^2 = r^2$$

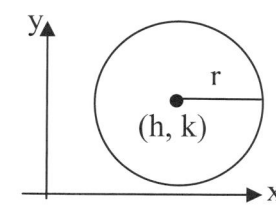

Example: The circle $(x-4)^2+(y+3)^2=25$ has center (4,-3) and radius 5.

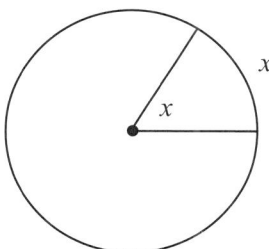 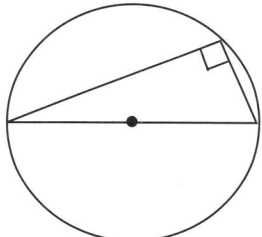 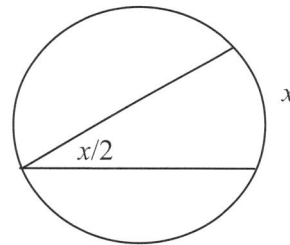

A central angle has the same measure as the intercepted arc.

Any angle inscribed in a semi-circle is a right angle.

An inscribed angle is ½ the measure of the intercepted arc.

1. What is the equation for a circle with its center located at the point (3, 5) and a radius of 4 units?

    A. $(x-3)^2 + (y-5)^2 = 16$
    B. $(x+3)^2 + (y+5)^2 = 16$
    C. $(x-3)^2 + (y-5)^2 = 4$
    D. $(x+3)^2 + (y+5)^2 = 4$
    E. $(x+3)^2 + (y+5)^2 = 2$

ACT SUCCESS
Math Skill Builder – Circles

2. What is the equation for a circle with center (-2, 4) and a radius of $\sqrt{12}$?

    F. $(x+2)^2 + (y-4)^2 = \sqrt{12}$
    G. $(x+2)^2 + (y-4)^2 = 12$
    H. $(x-2)^2 + (y+4)^2 = 12$
    J. $(x-2)^2 + (y+4)^2 = 144$
    K. $(x-2)^2 + (y-4)^2 = 144$

3. What is the area, in square inches, of a circle with a diameter of 12 inches?

    A. 6π
    B. 12π
    C. 18π
    D. 24π
    E. 36π

4. Which of the following is closest to the circumference of a circle with a radius of 7?

    F. 11
    G. 22
    H. 33
    J. 44
    K. 55

5. The circle below has a radius of 3cm. Chord $\overline{CD}$ is 1.7cm from the center of the circle. About how many centimeters long is chord $\overline{CD}$?

    A. 3.0
    B. 3.5
    C. 4.9
    D. 5.9
    E. 7.5

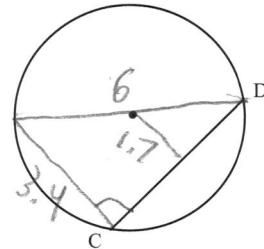

ACT SUCCESS
Math Skill Builder – Right Triangle Trigonometry

Directions: Choose the best answer to each question.

SOH–CAH–TOA:

$$\sin\theta = \frac{opposite}{hypotenuse}, \quad \cos\theta = \frac{adjacent}{hypotenuse}, \quad \tan\theta = \frac{opposite}{adjacent} = \frac{\sin\theta}{\cos\theta}$$

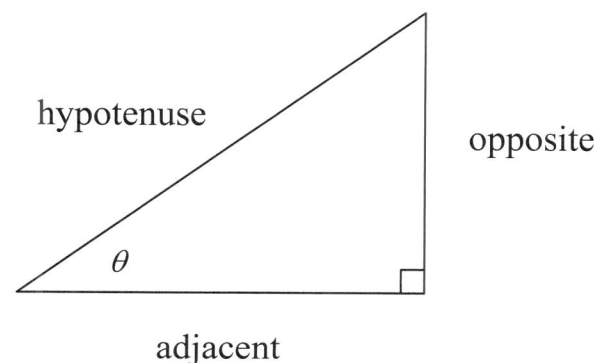

1. What is the length of the unknown side in the triangle below?

   A. 4.3
   B. 5.5
   C. 6.5
   D. 7.9
   E. 8.4

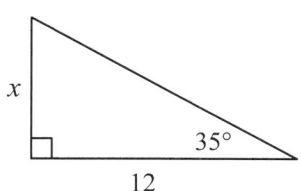

2. What is the value of *w* in the triangle below?

   F. 2.2
   G. 3.0
   H. 4.1
   J. 7.9
   K. 9.1

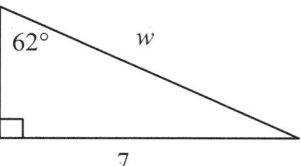

Copyright © 2009 by Academic Educational Resources. All rights reserved.

ACT SUCCESS
Math Skill Builder – Right Triangle Trigonometry

3. Sue is standing 80ft away from the base of a tree on level ground. The angle of elevation to the tree is $39°$. What is the height of the tree to the nearest foot?

   A. 65
   B. 72
   C. 81
   D. 94
   E. 105

4. Joe is flying a kite. He has let out 200 ft of string from his reel, and the angle of elevation from the ground to his kite is $53°$. Assuming the sting is taught, which of the following is the best estimate of the height of the kite?

   F. 150
   G. 160
   H. 170
   J. 180
   K. 210

5. Which of the following is closest to the length of the hypotenuse in the triangle below?

   A. 8
   B. 11
   C. 13
   D. 17
   E. 18

6. The hypotenuse of a right triangle is 19 units long. One angle of the triangle measures $40°$. What is the sum of the lengths of the legs of the triangle?

   F. 11
   G. 15
   H. 22
   J. 27
   K. 29

ACT SUCCESS
Math Skill Builder – Logarithms

Directions: Choose the best answer to each question.

Properties of **logarithms**:

For positive numbers:

$\log_b x = y$ if and only if $b^y = x$

$\log_b(xy) = \log_b x + \log_b y$

$\log_b\left(\dfrac{x}{y}\right) = \log_b x - \log_b y$

$\log_b x^n = n \log_b x$

$\log_b x = \dfrac{\log x}{\log b}$

1. What does $\log_3 27$ equal?
   A. 1
   B. 2
   C. 3
   D. 6
   E. 9

2. Which of the following is equivalent to the expression $\log_b x + \log_b y$?
   F. $\log_b(xy)$
   G. $\log_b(x+y)$
   H. $\log_b(\frac{x}{y})$
   J. $(\log_b x)(\log_b y)$
   K. xy

3. Which of the following is equivalent to $\log_a w - \log_a v^2$?
   A. $\log_a(w - v^2)$
   B. $\log_a w + 2\log_a v$
   C. $\log_a(\frac{w}{v^2})$
   D. $\log_a(\frac{w}{2v})$
   E. $2\log_a(\frac{w}{v})$

ACT SUCCESS
Math Skill Builder – Logarithms

4. What is the solution to the equation $\log x + \log x = 2$?
    - F. 1
    - G. 5
    - H. 10
    - J. 20
    - K. 100

5. What is the value of x in the equation $\log_{36} x = 0.5$?
    - A. 6
    - B. 12
    - C. 18
    - D. 72
    - E. 144

6. What is the solution to the following equation: $\log_4 16 + \log_2 8 = x$?
    - F. 2
    - G. 4
    - H. 5
    - J. 8
    - K. 16

ACT SUCCESS
Math Skill Builder – Complex Numbers

Directions: Choose the best answer to each question.

$$i^2 = -1$$

(Helpful hint: The TI-83/84 has an "*i*" above the decimal point)

1. Which of the following is equivalent to $(2+3i)^2$?
   A. 0
   B. 13
   C. $-5+12i$
   D. $4+12i$
   E. $4+9i^2$

2. Which of the following is equivalent to $(3+4i)^2$?
   F. -7
   G. $-7+12i$
   H. $-7+24i$
   J. 25
   K. 49

3. How many non-real roots does the following equation have?
   $$5x^2 - 6x + 17 = 11$$
   A. 0
   B. 1
   C. 2
   D. 3
   E. Cannot be determined

4. Which of the following expressions is equivalent to $(2+3i)-(4+7i)$?
   F. $-2-4i$
   G. $-2+10i$
   H. $2-6i$
   J. $2+4i$
   K. $2+10i$

5. $2i(2+3i)$ can be simplified to which of the following?
   A. 10
   B. 22
   C. $10i$
   D. $-6+4i$
   E. $6+4i$

Math Practice Quizzes

ACT SUCCESS
Math Quiz: Pre-Algebra

Directions: Choose the best answer to each question.

1. 35% of what number is 28?
   - A. 0.8
   - B. 8
   - C. 9.8
   - D. 80
   - E. 98

2. What is the largest factor shared by 24, 48, 60, and 78?
   - F. 2
   - G. 6
   - H. 12
   - J. 18
   - K. 78

3. Anne scored an average of 65 on her first four tests. What must she score on her fifth test in order for her average on five tests to be 70?
   - A. 80
   - B. 90
   - C. 95
   - D. 100
   - E. 110

4. Simplify the following: $3 + (2 + 5^2)/3 = ?$
   - F. 6
   - G. 8
   - H. 9
   - J. 10
   - K. 12

5. If $\frac{4}{5} + \frac{-3}{10} = x + 1\frac{1}{2}$, then x = ?
   - A. -10
   - B. -2
   - C. -1
   - D. 1
   - E. 2

6. Mrs. White's gross monthly income is $1,800. If 15% is withheld for income taxes, 7% for Social Security, and 2% for insurance, what is her net monthly income (after deducting these expenses)?
   - F. $432
   - G. $630
   - H. $1,210
   - J. $1,368
   - K. $1,530

ACT SUCCESS
Math Quiz: Pre-Algebra

7. Joe has taken four tests in his Algebra class, earning test scores of 86, 66, 78, and 81. He needs an average of 80 on 5 tests to earn a "B". What is the minimum score Joe can earn on his next test in order to have an average of at least 80 for his 5 tests?
   A. 83
   B. 85
   C. 87
   D. 89
   E. 91

8. Rewrite these fractions in order from smallest to largest: $\frac{3}{4}, \frac{2}{3}, \frac{5}{6}, \frac{4}{5}$

   F. $\frac{3}{4} < \frac{2}{3} < \frac{5}{6} < \frac{4}{5}$
   G. $\frac{4}{5} < \frac{5}{6} < \frac{2}{3} < \frac{3}{4}$
   H. $\frac{4}{5} < \frac{2}{3} < \frac{5}{6} < \frac{3}{4}$
   J. $\frac{2}{3} < \frac{3}{4} < \frac{4}{5} < \frac{5}{6}$
   K. $\frac{2}{3} < \frac{4}{5} < \frac{3}{4} < \frac{5}{6}$

9. A golf club manufacturer makes irons with 7 different shaft lengths, 3 different grips, 5 different lies, and 2 different club head materials. How many different combinations are offered?
   A. 17
   B. 76
   C. 150
   D. 210
   E. 300

10. A bag contains 6 white, 3 blue, and 7 green marbles. If one marble is chosen at random, what is the probability of picking a white marble?
    F. $\frac{1}{16}$
    G. $\frac{1}{3}$
    H. $\frac{3}{8}$
    J. $\frac{5}{8}$
    K. $\frac{6}{10}$

ACT SUCCESS
Math Quiz: Algebra

Directions: Choose the best answer to each question.

1. A student answers 8 ACT questions in 12 minutes. How long would to take to answer 20?

   A. 8
   B. 12
   C. 18
   D. 24
   E. 30

2. Which of the following are the roots of the equation $x^2 + 3x + 2 = 0$?

   F. {-2, -3}
   G. {-2, 3}
   H. {-1, -2}
   J. {-1, 2}
   K. {1, 2}

3. In a certain library, the ratio of fiction to nonfiction books is 3:5. If the library contains a total of 8,000 books, how many of the books are non-fiction?

   A. 2,400
   B. 3,000
   C. 3,600
   D. 4,800
   E. 5,000

4. What are the roots of the equation $x^2 + 5x = -6$?

   F. {-3, -4}
   G. {-3, -2}
   H. {-2, -1}
   J. {0, -2}
   K. {1, 2}

5. If $x = -2$, then $x^2 - x = ?$

   A. -6
   B. -2
   C. 0
   D. 4
   E. 6

ACT SUCCESS
Math Quiz: Algebra

6. $\frac{x^2 - x - 6}{x + 2} = ?$

   F. $x^2 - \frac{1}{2}x - 3$
   G. $x^2 - 2$
   H. $x - 2$
   J. $x - 3$
   K. x

7. If $2 + 4B > A$, which of the following is true?

   A. $B < \frac{A-2}{4}$
   B. $B > \frac{A-2}{4}$
   C. $B > 4A + 2$
   D. $B > 4A + 2$
   E. None of the above.

8. If $14 = 3x - 1$ and $B = 6x + 4$, what is the value of B?

   F. -26
   G. -5
   H. 1
   J. 5
   K. 34

9. Which of the following is the graph of the solution to $6 + 3x > x - 4$ on the real number line?

   A.
   B.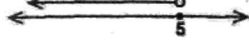
   C.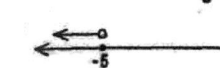
   D.
   E.

10. $(2x^2 + 5x - 3) - (3x^2 + 5x - 12) = ?$

    F. $-x^2 + 10x - 15$
    G. $x^2 + 10x - 9$
    H. $-x^2 - 9$
    J. $-x^2 - 15$
    K. $-x^2 + 9$

ACT SUCCESS
Math Quiz: Algebra

11. Find the solution set if $\dfrac{2x-1}{6} = \dfrac{3x}{8}$

    A. -4
    B. $-\dfrac{3}{2}$
    C. $-\dfrac{2}{3}$
    D. $\dfrac{2}{3}$
    E. $\dfrac{3}{2}$

12. Solve the following equation: $4(x-3) > 9(x+2)$

    F. $x < -1$
    G. $x > -1$
    H. $x > -6$
    J. $x < -6$
    K. $x > -\dfrac{6}{5}$

13. Which of the following is equal to $4x^2 - 4x - 15$?

    A. $(2x-5)(2x-3)$
    B. $(4x+5)(x-3)$
    C. $(2x+3)(2x-5)$
    D. $(2x-15)(2x+1)$
    E. $(2x-3)(2x+5)$

14. Which of the following are the solutions for x if $(x-1)(x+9) = 11$?

    F. $\{-10, 2\}$
    G. $\{-1, 9\}$
    H. $\{1, -9\}$
    J. $\{10, -2\}$
    K. $\{12, 2\}$

15. Which of the following equations could be used to solve the following problem? The sum of the squares of two consecutive whole numbers is 85. Find the number.

    A. $[x+(x+1)]^2 = 85$
    B. $x^2 + (x^2 + 1) = 85$
    C. $x^2 + (x+2)^2 = 85$
    D. $x^2 + (x+1)^2 = 85$
    E. None of these.

ACT SUCCESS
Math Quiz: Algebra

16. Which of the following inequalities corresponds to the graph?

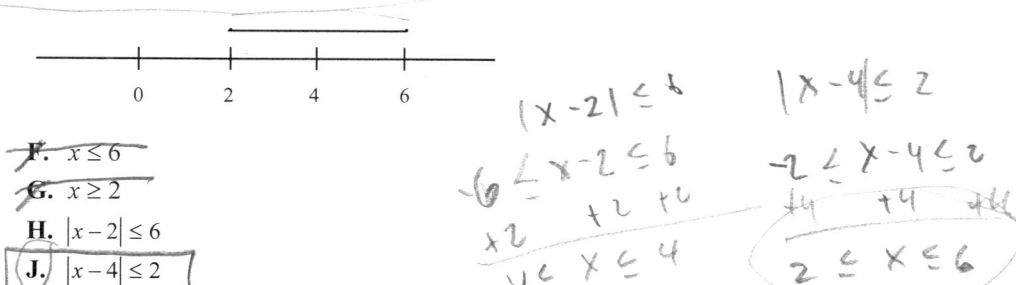

F. $x \leq 6$
G. $x \geq 2$
H. $|x - 2| \leq 6$
J. $|x - 4| \leq 2$
K. $|x - 6| \leq 2$

17. If $a = -3$ and $b = 4$, then $ab^2 - (a - b) = ?$

A. 151
B. 55
C. -41
D. -47
E. -49

18. What is the solution set for the equation $3 - (x - 5) = 2x - 3(4 - x)$?

F. $-\dfrac{3}{2}$
G. $\dfrac{3}{10}$
H. 0
J. $\dfrac{10}{3}$
K. 5

19. Which of the following expressions is equal to $x - [3x - (1 - 2x)]$?

A. $3x^2 + 2x - 1$
B. $-4x + 1$
C. $-4x - 1$
D. -1
E. 1

20. Which of the following is the simplified form of the product of the two polynomials $(x - 1)(x^2 + x + 1)$?

F. $x^3 + 1$
G. $x^3 - 1$
H. $x^3 - x - 1$
J. $x^3 + x^2 + x$
K. $x^3 + 2x^2 + 2x + 1$

ACT SUCCESS
Math Quiz: Plane Geometry

Directions: Choose the best answer to each question.

1. In the figure below, line *m* is parallel to line *n*, and line *t* is a transversal crossing both *m* and *n*. Which of the following lists contains 3 angles that are all equal in measure?

   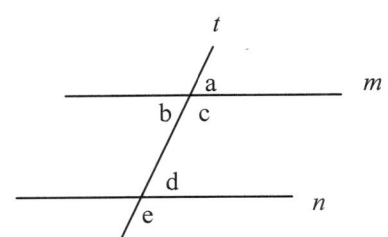

   A. ∠a, ∠b, ∠d
   B. ∠a, ∠c, ∠d
   C. ∠a, ∠c, ∠e
   D. ∠b, ∠c, ∠d
   E. ∠b, ∠c, ∠e

2. In ΔRST below, the measure of ∠S is 40°, and the measure of ∠T is twice the measure of ∠S. What is the measure of ∠R?

   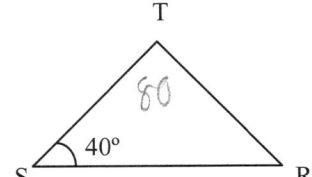

   F. 40°
   G. 60°
   H. 80°
   J. 100°
   K. 120°

3. In the figure below, $\overline{CA}$ is perpendicular to $\overline{AB}$ and $\overline{CB}$ is perpendicular to $\overline{BD}$; $\overline{AB}$ is 3 units long, $\overline{CA}$ is 4 units long, and $\overline{BD}$ is 12 units long. How many units long is $\overline{CD}$?

   A. 13
   B. 17
   C. 19
   D. 24
   E. 25

4. Jim had a rectangular-shaped garden with sides of lengths 16 feet and 9 feet. He recently remodeled his garden, converting it into a square design with the same area as the original garden. How many feet in length is each side of the new square-shaped garden?

   F. 7
   G. 9
   H. 12
   J. $5\sqrt{7}$
   K. 16

ACT SUCCESS
Math Quiz: Plane Geometry

5. The length of a rectangle is 4 more than 5 times its width. Find the dimensions of the rectangle if its perimeter is 68 meters.
   A. W = 5   L = 29
   B. W = 6.8   L = 27.2
   C. W = 9   L = 25
   D. W = 13.6   L = 54.4
   E. W = 15   L = 19

6. If ΔABC is similar to ΔDEF, and the sides of the triangles have the measures indicated in the diagram below, what is the length of $\overline{BC}$?

   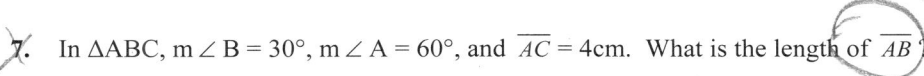

   F. $1\frac{1}{4}$
   G. 3
   H. $3\frac{1}{5}$
   J. 5
   K. 20

7. In ΔABC, m∠B = 30°, m∠A = 60°, and $\overline{AC}$ = 4cm. What is the length of $\overline{AB}$?

   A. $\frac{4\sqrt{3}}{3}$
   B. $\frac{8\sqrt{3}}{3}$
   C. $4\sqrt{2}$
   D. $4\sqrt{3}$
   E. 8

8. If ΔABC is an isosceles right triangle with base angles A and B, which of the following best describes angles B and C?
   F. B is acute, C is acute.
   G. B is acute, C is right.
   H. B is acute, C is obtuse.
   J. B is right, C is acute.
   K. B is obtuse, C is acute.

Copyright © 2009 by Academic Educational Resources. All rights reserved.

ACT SUCCESS
Math Quiz: Plane Geometry

9. △ABC is isosceles with base angles B and C. If m∠ABD = 100°, what is m∠A?

   A. 20°
   B. 30°
   C. 40°
   D. 50°
   E. 60°

   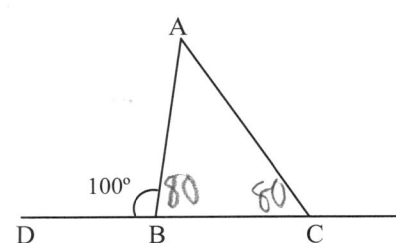

10. What is the side length of a square with the same area as a 3 - 4 - 5 right triangle?

    F. $\sqrt{6}$
    G. $2\sqrt{3}$
    H. $2\sqrt{6}$
    J. 6
    K. 12

    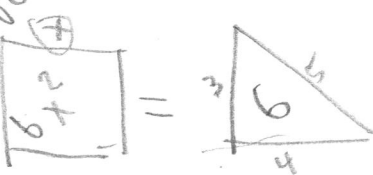

11. A box with which of the following dimensions holds exactly twice a much as a box with length 3, width 4, and height 5?

    A. L = 3, W = 8, H = 10
    B. L = 6, W = 4, H = 5
    C. L = 6, W = 4, H = 10
    D. L = 6, W = 8, H = 5
    E. L = 6, W = 8, H = 10

12.

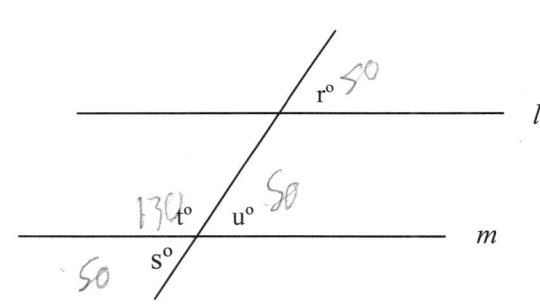

In the figure above, $l \parallel m$ and r = 50°. What is the value of s + t + u ?

   F. 230°
   G. 240°
   H. 250°
   J. 270°
   K. 310°

Copyright © 2009 by Academic Educational Resources. All rights reserved.

ACT SUCCESS
Math Quiz: Plane Geometry

13.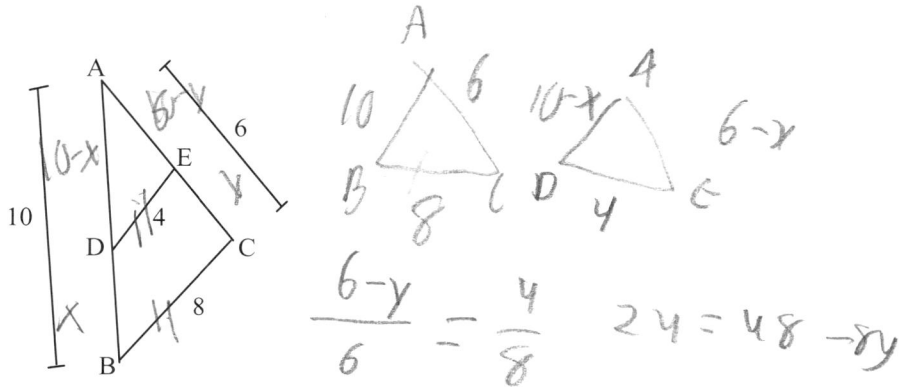

In the figure above, the lengths of line segments are given in feet. If $\overline{BC}$ is parallel to $\overline{DE}$, how many feet long is $\overline{AE}$?

A. $2\frac{2}{5}$
B. 3
C. $2\sqrt{2}$
D. $6\frac{2}{3}$
E. 12

14. The rectangle pictured below has lengths as marked. What is the area, in square units, of the shaded triangle?

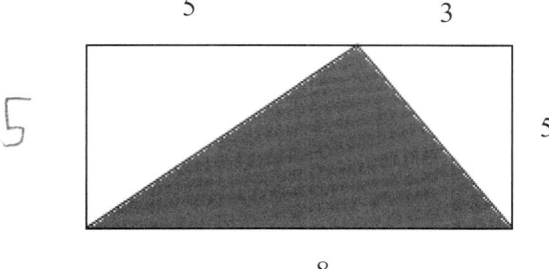

F. 16
G. 20
H. 25
J. 32
K. 40

ACT SUCCESS
Math Quiz: Circle & Coordinate Geometry

Directions: Choose the best answer to each question.

1. What is the distance between the points (-2, 1) and (5, -4)?
   - A. $3\sqrt{2}$
   - B. $2\sqrt{5}$
   - C. $2\sqrt{6}$
   - D. $\sqrt{74}$
   - E. $\sqrt{82}$

2. What is the slope of the line through the points (5, -2) and (-1, -5)?
   - F. -2
   - G. $-\dfrac{7}{4}$
   - H. $-\dfrac{1}{2}$
   - J. $\dfrac{1}{2}$
   - K. 2

3. What is the equation of a line passing through the point (4, -8) with a slope of $-\dfrac{3}{5}$?
   - A. $3x + 5y = -28$
   - B. $3x + 5y = 28$
   - C. $3x + 5y = -4$
   - D. $5x - 3y = -4$
   - E. None of these.

4. What is the center of the circle defined by the equation $(x-1)^2 + (y+2)^2 = 10$?
   - F. (-2, 1)
   - G. (-1, 2)
   - H. (1, -2)
   - J. (2, -1)
   - K. $\sqrt{10}$

5. What is the slope of the line passing through the points (2, 3) and (-6, -1)?
   - A. -1
   - B. -0.5
   - C. 0.25
   - D. 0.5
   - E. 1

ACT SUCCESS
Math Quiz: Circle & Coordinate Geometry

6. If a circle has a circumference of 5π, what is its area?

   F. 25π
   G. 20π
   H. 12.5π
   J. 10π
   K. 6.25π

7. If one endpoint of a line segment is (-2, -4) and the midpoint of the segment is (-5, -7), what is the other endpoint?

   A. (-8, -10)
   B. (-1, 1)
   C. (1, -1)
   D. (1.5, 1.5)
   E. (-3.5, -5.5)

8. What is the slope of a line parallel to the line with equation $3x + 2y = 1$?

   F. $-\frac{3}{2}$
   G. $\frac{1}{2}$
   H. $\frac{2}{3}$
   J. 1
   K. $\frac{3}{2}$

9. A, B, C, and D are points on a line, with D as the midpoint of $\overline{BC}$. The lengths of $\overline{AB}$, $\overline{AC}$, and $\overline{BC}$ are 10, 2, and 12 respectively. What is the length of $\overline{AD}$?

   A. 2
   B. 4
   C. 6
   D. 10
   E. 12

10. In the figure below, the slope of the line through points P and Q is $\frac{3}{2}$. What is the value of K?

    F. 4
    G. 5
    H. 6
    J. 7
    K. 8

Q (K, 7)
P (1, 1)

ACT SUCCESS
Math Quiz: Circle & Coordinate Geometry

11. For all nonzero a and b, $\dfrac{(10a^2b^2)(-9a^2b^3)}{6a^2b^4} = ?$

   A. $-15b$
   B. $-15a^2b$
   C. $-15a^2b^2$
   D. $\dfrac{a^2b^2}{15}$
   E. $\dfrac{12}{b}$

12. Which of the following points is NOT on the graph of $y = x^2 + 2x - 3$?

   F. $(-3, 0)$
   G. $(-1, -4)$
   H. $(0, -3)$
   J. $(1, 0)$
   K. $(8, 0)$

13. Which of the following equations defines a line perpendicular to the line with equation $5x - 2y = 20$?

   A. $5x - 2y = -20$
   B. $5x + 2y = 20$
   C. $2x + 5y = 20$
   D. $2x - 5y = 20$
   E. $5x + 20y = 2$

14. What is the equation of the circle graphed below?

   F. $x + y = 2$
   G. $x - y = 2$
   H. $x^2 + y^2 = 4$
   J. $x^2 - y^2 = 4$
   K. $y^2 - x^2 = 4$

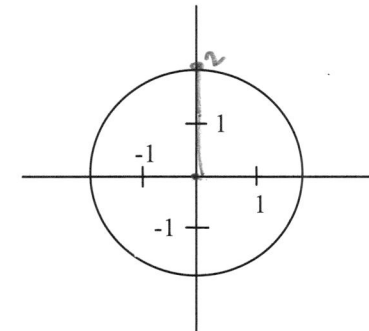

ACT SUCCESS
Math Quiz: Circle & Coordinate Geometry

15. If the area of a circle is 9π, which of the following statements must be true?
    - I. The radius of the circle is 3.
    - II. The diameter of the circle is 6.
    - III. The circumference of the circle is 6π.

    A. I only.
    B. II only.
    C. III only.
    D. I and II only.
    E. I, II, and III.

16. If the radius of circle P is 3 units, what is the length in units of arc $\overarc{AB}$?

    F. $\frac{1}{6}\pi$

    G. $\frac{1}{3}\pi$

    H. π

    J. 3π

    K. 6π

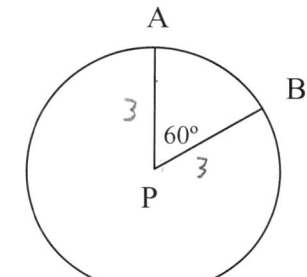

Copyright © 2009 by Academic Educational Resources. All rights reserved.

ACT SUCCESS
Math Quiz: Advanced Algebra

Directions: Choose the best answer to each question.

1. Simplify the following expression: $2\sqrt{18} - \sqrt{50} = ?$

   A. $-7\sqrt{2}$
   B. 1
   C. $\sqrt{2}$
   D. 60
   E. None of these

2. If $x^2 - 2x - 5 = 0$, then $x = ?$

   F. $\{1 \pm \sqrt{5}\}$
   G. $\{1 \pm \sqrt{6}\}$
   H. $\{3, -1\}$
   J. $\{2 \pm \sqrt{6}\}$
   K. $\{5, -3\}$

3. Simplify: $\dfrac{12x^6 y^4 z^2}{6x^2 y^4 z^8} = ?$

   A. $\dfrac{2x^4}{z^6}$
   B. $2x^8 y^8 z^{10}$
   C. $6x^4 z^{-6}$
   D. $\dfrac{2x^3}{z^4}$
   E. $\dfrac{2x^6}{z^4}$

4. What is the value of $\dfrac{(x^{2y+2})(x^{6y-1})}{x^{4y-3}}$?

   F. x^{3y-2}
   G. x^{3y+4}
   H. x^{4y-2}
   J. x^{4y+1}
   K. x^{4y+4}

5. The sum of two numbers is 25. The sum of their squares is 313. What is the value of the larger number?

   A. 10
   B. 11
   C. 12
   D. 13
   E. 14

Copyright © 2009 by Academic Educational Resources. All rights reserved.

ACT SUCCESS
Math Quiz: Advanced Algebra

6. For which of the following values of "a" would the following system of equations have an infinite number of solutions?

    $$\begin{array}{l} 2x - y = 6 \\ 8x - 4y = 3a \end{array}$$

    F. 2
    G. 6
    H. 8
    J. 18
    K. 24

7. The equation $x^2 - 10x + k = 0$ has only one solution. What is the value of k?

    A. 0
    B. 5
    C. 10
    D. 20
    E. 25

8. The price of admission for a concert was $8 for adults and $5 for children. Altogether, 1,024 tickets were sold for a total of $6,680. How many children's tickets were sold?

    F. 140
    G. 308
    H. 504
    J. 716
    K. 724

9. Which of the following expressions is equivalent to $(2x^3)^2$?

    A. $4x^5$
    B. $4x^6$
    C. $8x^5$
    D. $8x^6$
    E. $64x^6$

10. If $2a^2b^3 < 0$, then which of the following CANNOT be true?
    F. $a = b$
    G. $a < 0$
    H. $a > 0$
    J. $b < 0$
    K. $b > 0$

ACT SUCCESS
Math Quiz: Advanced Algebra

11. What is the slope of a line parallel to the line with equation $3x + 2y = 1$?

    A. $-\frac{3}{2}$

    B. $\frac{1}{2}$

    C. $\frac{2}{3}$

    D. 1

    E. $\frac{3}{2}$

12. For the complex number i such that $i^2 = -1$, what is the value of $i^4 + 2i^2$?

    F. -2
    G. -1
    H. 0
    J. 1
    K. 2

13. For which nonnegative value of x is the expression $\frac{1}{9-x^2}$ undefined?

    A. 81
    B. 18
    C. 9
    D. 3
    E. 0

14. If $\log_x 81 = 4$, then $x = ?$

    F. 3
    G. 9
    H. $\frac{81}{4}$
    J. $\frac{81}{\log 4}$
    K. 81^4

15. If $f(x) = -2x^2$, then $f(-3) = ?$

    A. -36
    B. -18
    C. 12
    D. 18
    E. 36

Copyright © 2009 by Academic Educational Resources. All rights reserved.

ACT SUCCESS
Math Quiz: Advanced Algebra

16. For all x, $\dfrac{2x}{5} + \dfrac{x}{6}$ is equivalent to:

    F. $\dfrac{3x}{11}$
    G. $\dfrac{3x}{30}$
    H. $\dfrac{7x}{30}$
    J. $\dfrac{13x}{30}$
    K. $\dfrac{17x}{30}$

17. Whenever $\dfrac{1}{x} + \dfrac{1}{x+1}$ is defined, it is equivalent to:

    A. $\dfrac{2x+1}{x(x+1)}$
    B. $\dfrac{2}{2x+1}$
    C. $\dfrac{3}{x+1}$
    D. $\dfrac{1}{x+1}$
    E. $\dfrac{2}{x}$

18. Which of the following describes the solutions(s), if any, to the system of equations below?

    $$\begin{array}{l} 2x - 4y = -20 \\ -4x + 2y = 22 \end{array}$$

    F. No solution.
    G. Infinitely many solutions.
    H. $x = -2$ and $y = 4$ only
    J. $x = -3$ and $y = 5$ only
    K. $x = -4$ and $y = 3$ only

19. If $f(x) = x - 18$, then $f(x+h) = ?$
    A. $x + h - 18$
    B. $x - 18h$
    C. $hx - 18$
    D. $hx - 18x$
    E. $hx - 18h$

20. What is the product of $(2x)^3$ and $3y^2$

    F. $6x^3y^2$
    G. $24x^3y^2$
    H. $24x^3y^5$
    J. $54x^3y^2$
    K. $72x^3y^2$

ACT SUCCESS
Math Quiz: Trigonometry

Directions: Choose the best answer to each question.

1. If $0° < x < 90°$ and $\cos x = \dfrac{1}{2}$, then $\sin x = ?$

   A. $\dfrac{1}{2}$

   B. $\dfrac{\sqrt{3}}{2}$

   C. $\dfrac{2\sqrt{3}}{3}$

   D. $\sqrt{3}$

   E. 2

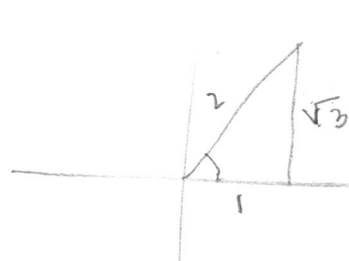

2. For the right triangle shown below, all of the following statements are true EXCEPT:

   F. $\sin \theta = \dfrac{b}{c}$

   G. $\tan \alpha = \dfrac{a}{b}$

   H. $\cos \theta = \dfrac{c}{a}$

   J. $\sin \theta = \cos \alpha$

   K. $\cot \alpha = \tan \theta$

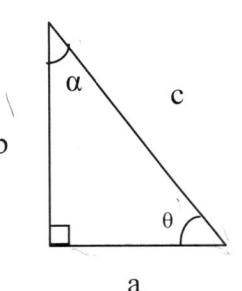

3. In the right triangle shown below, the length of $\overline{BC}$ is 5 units and $\angle A = 60°$. Approximately how many units long is $\overline{AC}$ to the nearest hundredth of a unit? (Note: $\sin 60° \approx 0.886$, $\cos 60° = 0.5$).

   A. 2.89
   B. 4.33
   C. 5.77
   D. 7.50
   E. 8.65

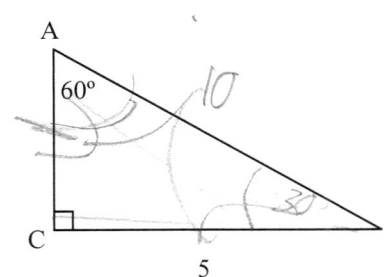

Copyright © 2009 by Academic Educational Resources. All rights reserved.

ACT SUCCESS
Math Quiz: Trigonometry

4. The radio station WEST is erecting a new tower. A support wire will be attached to the ground at point A and run to the top of the tower at point B, as shown below. The wire must be at least as long as $\overline{AB}$. Which of the following expresses the length of $\overline{AB}$ in feet?

   F. $250 \cos 70°$
   G. $250 \sin 70°$
   H. $250 \tan 70°$
   J. $\dfrac{250}{\cos 70°}$
   K. $\dfrac{250}{\sin 70°}$

   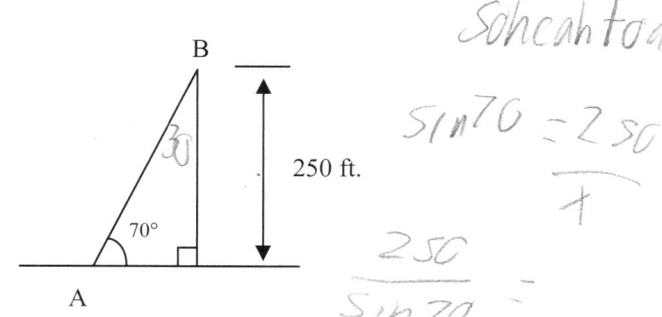

5. A lamppost casts a 10-foot-long shadow when the sun is at a 60° angle with the ground. Which of the following equations gives the height x, in feet, of the lamppost?

   A. $\cos 60° = \dfrac{x}{10}$
   B. $\cot 60° = \dfrac{x}{10}$
   C. $\sec 60° = \dfrac{x}{10}$
   D. $\sin 60° = \dfrac{x}{10}$
   E. $\tan 60° = \dfrac{x}{10}$

   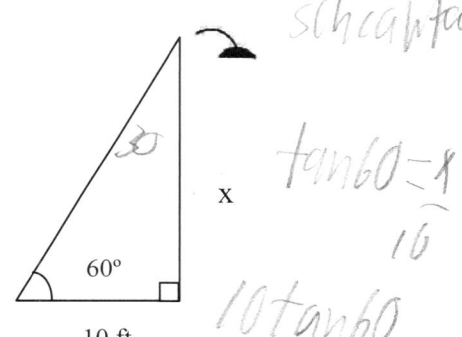

6. Two lookout towers are located about 7 miles apart at equal elevation. A fire is sighted between the two towers, at angles 37° and 42° from the towers' respective lines of sight (as indicated in the diagram below). Which of the following expressions, if any, gives the approximate distance, in miles, between the fire and Tower A?
   (Note: The "law of sines" states that the ratio between the length of the side opposite an angle and the sine of that angle is the same for all of the interior angles in a given triangle.)

   F. $\sqrt{37^2 + 42^2}$
   G. $7 \tan 42°$
   H. $\dfrac{7 \cos 42°}{\cos 101°}$
   J. $\dfrac{7 \sin 42°}{\sin 101°}$
   K. The distance cannot be approximated without more information.

ACT SUCCESS
Math Quiz: Trigonometry

7. Which of the following angles is NOT coterminal with an angle that measures 40°?

   A. −320°
   B. 400°
   C. 680°
   D. 760°
   E. 1,120°

   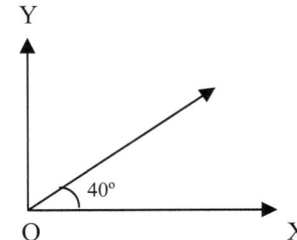

8. Whenever $\dfrac{2\cos\theta\sin\theta}{\cos^2\theta + (1-\sin^2\theta)}$ is defined, it can be simplified to:

   F. 2
   G. $\tan\theta$
   H. $\cot\theta$
   J. $\sin\theta\cos\theta$
   K. $\dfrac{2}{\cos\theta - \sin\theta}$

9. In the right triangle show below, what is the cosecant of $\angle A$?

   A. $\dfrac{5}{13}$
   B. $\dfrac{5}{12}$
   C. $\dfrac{13}{12}$
   D. $\dfrac{12}{5}$
   E. $\dfrac{13}{5}$

   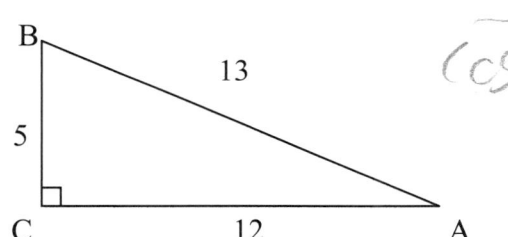

10. The secant of a 60° is 2. What is the tangent of this angle?

    F. $\dfrac{1}{2}$
    G. $\sqrt{3}$
    H. 2
    J. 3
    K. $2\sqrt{3}$

ACT SUCCESS
Math Quiz: Trigonometry

11. For values of x where sin x, cos x, and tan x are all defined, (sin x)(cos x)(tan x) = ?

    A. $\sin^2 x$
    B. $\cos^2 x$
    C. $\tan^2 x$
    D. 1
    E. -1

12. Compared to the graph of cos θ, the graph of 4 cos (2θ) has:

    F. 8 times the amplitude and the same period.
    G. 4 times the amplitude and twice the period.
    H. 4 times the amplitude and half the period.
    J. $\frac{1}{4}$ the amplitude and twice the period.
    K. $\frac{1}{4}$ the amplitude and half the period.

13. If tan A = x, then which of the following expressions MUST also equal x?

    A. cot A
    B. sec A + cos A
    C. sin A + cos A
    D. $\frac{\sin A}{\cos A}$
    E. $\frac{\cos A}{\sin A}$

Chapter 3
Reading Strategies and Review

READING

There are 4 reading passages, each with ten questions. Sound simple, right?

ACT reading passages will appear boring to most teenagers. Ok. So what? The passages are intended to be boring so that you, the test taker, will lose focus and concentration. It is your job to know this and take action. You MUST become an active, demanding reader. The very second you "space out" while reading is the very second you miss important information and get questions wrong that you deserved to get right.

Your *emotional reaction* to boring passages is to judge them and silently say, "This sucks." You MUST move beyond this immature attitude. Instead, you need to have an *intellectual reaction* to the passages and silently say, "I choose to read this. I choose to seek out the important information in the passages. I choose to improve my score. I choose to be accepted to more colleges. I choose to earn more scholarship money. I deserve this."

Becoming an active, demanding reader is not difficult, with a little practice. As you learn about the four different types of ACT reading passages and the skills needed to answer the questions, you will begin to grasp the essence of active, demanding reading. You will have a strategy for the ACT reading passage that will work for you – one that will help you attain your maximum score. No longer will your eyes aimlessly wander across the page while your brain inadvertently thinks about where you're going on Saturday night. Instead, your eyes will see while your brain digests and analyzes the information. Sure, you might not understand every single word the ACT writes, but that does not always matter. As long as you remain an active, demanding reader you will comprehend enough information to score to your maximum potential!

The Four Passage Types – In the Order They Appear on the ACT

PASSAGE 1: FICTION

- This passage is a story.
- Use *CPR* strategy by identifying *C*haracters, *P*roblem (or issue), and *R*esolution (or ending).
- Know each *Character's Personality* traits and *R*elationship to the other characters in the passage.

PASSAGE 2: SOCIAL SCIENCE

- This passage is informative.
- Read the first paragraph carefully for the author's purpose. To determine the author's purpose, ask yourself "Why did the author write this?" or "What is the one main thing the author wanted me to know after reading this passage?"

- Quickly read the body, focusing on location of details.
- Pay attention to the last paragraph and particularly the last sentence because it often restates the main idea.
- Use *TD* strategy: read for the author's **T**hesis and main **D**etails

PASSAGE 3: HUMANITIES

- This passage is often a narrative but sometimes resembles a social science passage.
- While reading, focus on the author/narrator's attitudes toward the subject of the passage.
- If it's a narrative, there will be an issue and resolution; use *CPR*.
- If it is informative, score a touchdown: use the *TD strategy*.

PASSAGE 4: NATURAL SCIENCE

- This passage is also informative.
- Read the passage for the big picture focusing on the first and last paragraphs for thesis.
- Don't spend too much time learning details; just read for location of information.
- Always use *TD* on the natural science passage.

WHAT TO LOOK FOR

- Questions about a passage usually follow <u>one main idea</u>. The author wrote the passage for a reason; once you figure out the point that the author is trying to make, you will be well on your way to answering questions correctly.

- On the Prose Fiction and (sometimes) the Humanities passages, remember to use CPR: characters, problem, resolution. There is always an issue in the passage, so identify it! Every prose fiction passage will also have a conclusion or resolution, even if it's not a final one.

- On the non-fiction passages – Social Science, Natural Science, and (sometimes) Humanities – focus on the TD: thesis and details. Be sure to read the first two paragraphs carefully, as they generally contain the author's *purpose, thesis, or main idea*. The rest of the passage contains details that support the author's main idea. You do not need to memorize them all on your initial read. If you can simply pick out the author's important supporting details (each paragraph generally corresponds to one major detail), you will be in great shape as you move on to the questions.

TYPES OF QUESTIONS

Although the content of the passages changes from test to test, the types of questions do not. If you know how to answer each type of question, you will find that the reading section is really the same from test to test.

- *Main idea or author's purpose* = look for general, vague, or broad answer.

- *Inferential* = make an assumption based on what you read; don't bother looking back.

- *Tone* = usually positive.

- *Detail* = If the question includes "the passage states" or "the passage indicates", the answer is in passage. When referring to line numbers, read before and after lines given. However, be sure to read all answer choices <u>before</u> looking back in order to save valuable time!

- *Vocabulary word* = must look back for context: read next line for clues as to meaning then plug in words.

- *"EXCEPT" or "NOT" question* = answer as if true/false question.

DO'S AND DON'TS

- **DO** read all choices and try to eliminate before looking back. It is acceptable to look back as long as you first use process of elimination! When looking back, you must do so <u>very</u> <u>quickly</u>!

- **DO** be consistent with theme; questions often repeat themselves.

- **DON'T** look back for the answer without reading all choices and eliminating wrong answers first.

- **DO** match ideas, not just words. Be sure your selection answers the question.

- **DO** be careful on questions with specific line references. When looking back in the passage, make sure to read a few lines before and after the given line reference for context.

- **DO** look at the title (located just above the beginning of the passage) for Social Science, Humanities and Science. It can often give you a clear hint as to what the passage is primarily about.

- **DO** choose moderate words such as *sometimes, tend to be, likely*.

- **DON'T** choose answers containing definitive words like *always, never, only, alone*.

YOUR PERSONAL READING STRATEGY

Each student will approach the ACT reading test slightly differently. No two brains are identical; therefore, no two strategies are identical. However, for most students there is a definitive reading strategy that produces the highest possible ACT reading score. It is extremely simple.

Step 1: Read the entire passage quickly but actively, seeking out the most important information. You are allowed to annotate or underline, but only do this if it is already one of your reading strengths. When you finish reading the passage, you should be able to mentally answer the CPR or TD questions! If you cannot do this easily, you were not actively reading! (Reading the passage should take between 4 – 5 minutes.)

Step 2: Answer the questions. Be sure to read ALL FOUR answer choices, using process of elimination, BEFORE looking back to the passage. (Answering questions should take about 4 – 5 minutes.)

No matter what, you must complete each passage in LESS THAN 9 MINUTES! In order to reach your maximum reading score, it is imperative that you get to all four passages! Remember, it is possible to get some answers wrong on the ACT and still achieve an amazing score!

An alternative strategy that works for some students is to actively read only the first and last paragraphs while skimming the body of the passage and then answering the questions as described above. This strategy should only be used if you are so instructed by your ACT teacher. (This often works for students whose maximum ACT reading score typically falls below an 18, which in most cases still meets state standards.)

No matter what, **DO NOT** waste precious time by reading the questions first! This strategy is a virtual guarantee of a low reading score. Again, DO NOT read the questions first unless specifically instructed to do so by your ACT teacher. On rare occasion, this strategy will work, but for 99% of students it turns into disaster.

PACING

You have a little less than **9 minutes** per passage.

1. Always spend more time answering questions (i.e. 5 minutes) than reading the passage (i.e. 4 minutes).

2. You can speed up your reading by using an index card or pencil to help you focus.

3. It is better to make educated guesses on a few questions throughout the test than to guess on an entire passage. Remember: each passage has both easy questions and difficult questions. If you spend too much time on the difficult questions early on, you will miss out on the last passage's easy questions!

4. Hint for practicing your pacing: Draw a box at the end of each section. Under the first box, write in 8 – 9. Under the second, write in 17 – 18. Under the third, 26 – 27, and under the fourth, write in 35. With 35 minutes to complete 4 passages, you actually get 8 minutes and 45 seconds per passage, so try you best to complete each passage in less than 9 minutes! You MUST be finished in 35 minutes. As you take the exam, time yourself and write in the actual time you take to finish. This will give you and your teacher a strong idea of where you need to speed up or slow down.

REMEMBER: To get a good score on the reading test, you must finish it—even if you have to make some guesses along the way!

HOW TO USE ACT SUCCESS TO STUDY FOR THE READING SECTION

The remainder of this chapter contains Skill Builders and practice passages. The skill builders cover topics that will help you to hone in on and practice skills and techniques that, if you master them, will help you to succeed on the reading section. Take the lessons of these skill builders to heart – the strategies work!

Following the Skill Builders are four practice passages, one of each passage type (outlined above). Taken together, the four practice passages are equal to a full reading test. Therefore, once you have worked through the practice passages, you will have seen everything that actually appears on the ACT Reading section.

REMEMBER: In every passage, don't lose sight of the main idea; always keep moving; and know when to use *CPR* and when to score a *TD*. Follow the rules, and you will be fine!

GOOD LUCK!

Reading Skill Builders

ACT SUCCESS
Reading Skill Builder – Finding the Main Idea

Directions: Read each paragraph and identify the main idea. Write a short sentence restating the main idea in your own words.

1. I never longed for piano lessons as a child. I got them because my own mother had wanted them badly, but her widowed father, who was a guard at Stateville Penitentiary in Illinois during the Depression, could not afford them. Mom was determined that her six daughters would not be thus deprived. I was in third grade when she informed me that my older sister Claire and I would begin lessons with Miss Pruessner. I was glum about this but had no choice.

   _____
   _____
   _____
   _____

2. What makes modern cosmology an empirical science is that we are literally able to peer into the past. When you look at your image reflected off a mirror one meter away, you see the way you looked six nanoseconds ago--the light's travel time to the mirror and back. Similarly, cosmologists do not need to guess how the universe evolved; we can watch its history through telescopes. Because the universe appears to be statistically identical in every direction, what we see billions of light-years away is probably a fair representation of what our own patch of space looked like billions of years ago.

   _____
   _____
   _____
   _____

3. Philosopher and historian Thomas S. Kuhn has suggested that scientific disciplines act a lot like living organisms: instead of evolving slowly but continuously, they enjoy long stretches of stability punctuated by infrequent revolutions with the appearance of a new species--or in the case of science, a new theory. This description is particularly apt for my own area of study, the causes and consequences of mass extinctions--those periodic biological upheavals when a large proportion of the planet's living creatures died off and afterward nothing was ever the same again.

   _____
   _____
   _____
   _____

4. Celebrated for his ferocity in battle, Crazy Horse was recognized among his own people as a visionary leader committed to preserving the traditions and values of the Lakota way of life. When the War Department ordered all Lakota bands onto their reservations in 1876, Crazy Horse became a leader of the resistance. Constant military harassment and the decline of the buffalo population eventually forced Crazy Horse to surrender; he was one of the last important chiefs to yield.

   _____
   _____
   _____
   _____

Copyright © 2009 by Academic Educational Resources. All rights reserved.

ACT SUCCESS
Reading Skill Builder – Finding the Main Idea

5. Most of us would find it difficult and uncomfortable to converse for any extended period without using our hands and arms. Gestures play a role whenever we attempt to explain something. At the very least, such motions are co-verbal; they accompany our speech, conveying information that is hard to get across with words. Hand movements can display complex spatial relations, directions, the shape of objects. They enable us to draw maps in the air that tell a puzzled motorist how to reach the turnpike. People who do not gesture rob themselves and their listeners of an important informational channel.

6. Sleeping until noon and general grumpiness may be a stereotype of teenagers, but since mood disorders tend to begin in the teen years it is important that sleep problems in adolescents not be summarily dismissed. Poor sleep not only has a powerful impact on daytime cognitive and social functioning, but it could also lead to major psychiatric disorders. Depression in teens may be preceded by either insomnia or its opposite, oversleeping (hypersomnia). Also, teens rarely keep to a standard routine: last minute homework, classes beginning at 8 a.m., and late nights out with friends can severely throw off their sleep schedule. In the long run, that takes its toll.

7. A recent study shows that introverts and extroverts show activity in different brain structures, which mirror the wildly opposing aspects of their personalities. Researchers used positron emission tomography (PET) to measure cerebral blood flow—an indicator of brain activity—in individuals rated on a personality test as shy or gregarious. Introverts showed increased blood flow in the frontal lobes, the anterior thalamus and other structures associated with recalling events, making plans and problem solving. Extroverts, on the other hand, displayed more activity in the posterior thalamus and posterior insula, regions involved in interpreting sensory data. These results highlight what the researchers consider the main difference between introverts and extroverts: inward and outward focus.

8. Antioxidants found in nuts and green vegetables such as spinach, broccoli and brussel sprouts are rich in vitamins C and E and may have a protective effect against Alzheimer's disease. Researchers tracked the diets of 815 people, ages 65 or older, who initially had similar symptoms of Alzheimer's. By the end of the study, those whose diets included the most vitamin E experienced 70 percent fewer symptoms of Alzheimer's than did subjects who ate foods with little or no vitamin E.

ACT SUCCESS
Reading Skill Builder – Determining Character and Attitude #1

Directions: After reading the passage, choose the best answer to each question.

In 1774, Thomas Paine was alone and poverty-stricken in England. But he had gained the friendship of Benjamin Franklin, who was then in London. Franklin advised Paine to go to America to make a fresh start. Paine arrived in Philadelphia with nothing except letters of recommendation from Franklin, which won him recognition from the publisher of a new periodical, the *Pennsylvania Magazine*. He soon became the contributing editor and wrote on a wide range of topics.

The independence movement was growing rapidly in Philadelphia, and Paine threw himself into the cause of freedom with heart and soul. He had known only hardship and discrimination in England, where he had been born and raised – a fact which helped to make him an ardent American patriot. In 1776, he published a series of pamphlets called *The Crisis*. The first of these began, "These are the times that try men's souls. The summer soldier and the sunshine patriot will, in this crisis, shrink from the service of their country… Tyranny, like hell, is not easily conquered." Washington had the pamphlet read aloud to his shivering soldiers at Valley Forge. Paine's bold, clear words encouraged the Continental Army during the darkest days of the war.

1. Thomas Paine can best be described as which of the following?
   A. A lazy peasant
   B. A wealthy aristocrat
   C. A hardworking nationalist
   D. A brave soldier

2. It can be inferred that Paine felt which way about England?
   F. He was a strong supporter of England's politics.
   G. He remained loyal to England and planned to return.
   H. He felt cheated by his upbringing in England.
   J. He disagreed with England's social policies.

3. The overall mood of the excerpt from *The Crisis* is:
   A. optimistic
   B. depressing
   C. rousing
   D. pessimistic

4. The author's tone can best be described as:
   F. informative
   G. sarcastic
   H. humorous
   J. persuasive

ACT SUCCESS
Reading Skill Builder – Determining Character and Attitude #2

Directions: After reading the passage, choose the best answer to each question.

When Julia was offered a position with a fashion magazine near the end of her senior year in college, she was pleased; yet she was not entirely sure she would accept the magazine's offer. True, the magazine was presenting her with an important opportunity; and yes, doubtless her creative abilities would be challenged when she had to keep coming up with ideas for articles. But each day she reflected upon her own strong background in history and political science as well as journalism and photography. She found herself excited by the thought of a different kind of writing: stories that would appear on the streets each day, would be read by millions, and would tell people what was happening in politics, business, and international affairs.

The magazine's offer was definite: she could have the job as long as she started working by July 1. That meant four weeks – four weeks in which to think about it – four weeks in which to look elsewhere.

1. Compared to other work she was considering, Julia felt that the fashion magazine's offer would be:
   A. less fulfilling
   B. less work
   C. more exciting
   D. more lucrative

2. Julia's decision making style regarding accepting the job offer can best be described as:
   F. impulsive
   G. indecisive
   H. lackadaisical
   J. contemplative

3. Julia would probably enjoy which of the following jobs the most?
   A. An advice columnist
   B. A television reporter
   C. A news journalist
   D. A novelist

4. Julia's mood as presented by the author in this passage can best be described as:
   F. nervous
   G. sad
   H. excited
   J. reflective

Adapted from the NASSP ACT Reading Student Workbook (1990)
Copyright © 2009 by Academic Educational Resources. All rights reserved.

ACT SUCCESS
Reading Skill Builder – Determining Character & Attitude #3

Directions: After reading the passage, choose the best answer to each question.

This passage was adapted from From Ernest Hemingway, "For Whom the Bell Tolls."© 1940 by Ernest Hemingway.

    The young man, whose name was Robert Jordan, was extremely hungry and he was worried. He was often hungry but he was not usually worried because he did not give any importance to what happened to himself and he knew from experience how simple it was to move behind the enemy lines in this country. It was as simple to move behind them as it was to cross through them, if you had a good guide. It was only giving importance to what happened to you if you were caught that made it difficult; that and deciding whom to trust. You had to trust the people you worked with completely or not at all, and you had to make decisions about the trusting. He was not worried about any of that. But there were other things.

1. Robert Jordan can best be described as:
   A. ignorant
   B. thoughtful
   C. suspicious
   D. egotistical

2. Which of the following is true about Robert Jordan?
   F. He is always hungry.
   G. He is afraid of getting caught.
   H. Something is bothering him.
   J. He is very trusting of everyone.

3. Robert Jordan's mood in this passage is which of the following?
   A. Concerned
   B. Eager
   C. Upset
   D. Elated

ACT SUCCESS
Reading Skill Builder – Skimming for Details

Directions: Read the passage quickly, skimming for the details. Then choose the best answer to each question.

Over 3,500 years ago, Rome was no more than a soggy marsh and the Acropolis was just an empty rock, but Egypt was on the brink of its greatest age - the New Kingdom. There was an explosion of creativity, wealth and power in Egypt that would make it the envy of the world. After defeating the Hyksos invaders, successive Pharaohs expanded and maintained their Empire through both force and diplomacy. In the process, they won Egypt vast amounts of gold, influence and respect.

Behind the power of the Egyptian empire lay a vast wealth of natural resources. Chief among these was the river Nile, the freeway of the ancient world, whose floodplains also provided huge expanses of fertile farming ground that kept Egypt self-sufficient and usually famine-free. Along the banks of the Nile, the humble papyrus plant was used to create a bureaucratic efficiency and cultural sophistication previously unknown to mankind. To the south, in the deserts of Nubia, gold mines gave Egypt the unimaginable wealth that formed the real power behind the throne. The same gold also saw the start of a golden age for Egyptian art and architecture, as Pharaohs built magnificent temples and tombs for themselves and their families.

The New Kingdom saw the reign of some of Ancient Egypt's most powerful and charismatic Pharaohs. The word pharaoh comes from the Egyptian 'per-aa', meaning "great house" and referred to the royal palace. Only quite late in the New Kingdom did it come to refer to the king himself.

Like other kings, the Pharaoh sat at the top of the social and political order, acted as commander-in-chief and controlled all military occupations. But the Pharaoh was much more than just the head of state. He also helped maintain 'Maat' - the divine order in the world. Without the Pharaoh, the Egyptians believed that the world would descend into chaos.

But the Pharaohs are only part of the story. Although they sat at the top of society, Egypt's success and legacy owes a great deal to those beneath them: the soldiers, craftsmen, priests and farmers.

Just as important were the women. Egyptian religion gave women a central role in the divine order and they were seen as central to their husbands' success. Although there were few women in power, all women were treated with respect and enjoyed legal rights that other women would still be waiting for, thousands of years later.

1. According to the passage, Egypt expanded their Empire after defeating which invaders?
   A. The New Kingdom
   B. The Hyksos
   C. The Pharaohs
   D. The Romans

2. The passage states that Egypt was successful because of the efforts of all of the following EXCEPT:
   F. the Pharaohs.
   G. the farmers.
   H. the priests.
   J. the astrologers.

3. Based on information in the passage, the use of which natural resource led to an unprecedented level of cultural sophistication?
   A. The Nile river
   B. The fertile farming ground
   C. The papyrus plant
   D. The gold mines

4. The passage indicates which of the following about Pharaohs?
   F. Egyptians believed that without the pharaoh, all order would cease to exist in the world.
   G. They ruled Egypt using only brute force.
   H. They are completely responsible for Egypt's rise to prominence.
   J. They built beautiful temples for all of Egypt's royalty.

5. According to the passage, the word pharaoh comes from an Egyptian word that means:
   A. royal palace.
   B. king.
   C. per-aa.
   D. great house.

6. Based on lines 43-49, women in Egypt:
   F. lived longer than the men.
   G. had less legal rights than most women today.
   H. had an important role religiously.
   J. were not allowed to hold positions of power.

ACT SUCCESS
Reading Skill Builder – Cause and Effect #1

Directions: After reading the passage, choose the best answer to each question.

In the fall of 1989, The Krenz government decided to allow East Berliners to apply for visas to travel to West Berlin. However, Günter Schabowski, the East German Minister of Propaganda had been on vacation prior to this decision and hadn't been fully updated on the decision. During a press conference on November 9, 1989, he was handed a note that he decided to read out loud. The note said that East Berliners would be allowed to cross the border with proper permission. When asked whom this would apply to etc. he couldn't answer. And he was asked when this would come into action. He didn't really know so he just assumed it would be the same day.

Tens of thousands of people immediately went to the checkpoints in the Wall and demanded entry into West Berlin. They quickly became a major crowd control problem for the surprised and overwhelmed border guards. It became clear that there was no way to hold back the huge crowd of East German citizens short of dispatching the army to kill them all. The masses could also not be convinced to turn back or calm down — they had heard of Mr. Schabowski's statement, and they wanted it to be acted upon. In face of the escalating crowd safety situation, the guards eventually just yielded, opening the access points and allowing people through with minimal identity verification checks. The ecstatic East Berliners were soon greeted by jubilant West Berliners on the other side in a celebratory, party atmosphere. November 9 is thus considered the date the Wall fell.

1. Which of the following can be blamed for causing the fall of the Berlin Wall?
   A. The West Berliners' determination.
   B. Schabowski's ignorance.
   C. The East Berlin army's violence.
   D. The Krenz government's decision to allow East Berliners to apply for visas.

2. If the guards at the Berlin Wall hadn't yielded to the masses, what would have probably happened?
   F. The East Berliners would have eventually given up and gone home.
   G. The Krenz government would have changed its mind about allowing people to apply for visas.
   H. The West Berliners would have stormed the Wall and broken through.
   J. The crowd would have erupted into violence and many people would have died.

3. Schabowski could have done all of the following to create a better outcome EXCEPT:
   A. Not gone on vacation when he did.
   B. Read the note to himself before deciding to read it out loud.
   C. Gone to the Berlin Wall himself after the press conference.
   D. Made up a future date for when the government's decision would go into effect.

Adapted from Wikipedia.org
Copyright © 2009 by Academic Educational Resources. All rights reserved.

ACT SUCCESS
Reading Skill Builder – Cause and Effect #2

Directions: After reading the passage, choose the best answer to each question.

The Underground Railroad was a large source of friction between the North and South. Many northerners empathized with those who assisted the slaves' escape to safety. For several years, southerners pushed for strong laws to force the recapture of runaway slaves. The Fugitive Slave Law of 1793 was the first law passed by the U.S. Congress to speak to the issue of escaped slaves in free states. It made it a federal crime to help an escaping slave, and created the legal mechanism by which escaped slaves could be seized (even in "free" states), brought before a magistrate, and returned to their masters. The Act made every runaway slave a fugitive-for-life, liable to recapture at any time anywhere within the territory of the United States, along with any children born of enslaved mothers.

In 1850, Congress passed the Fugitive Slave Law of 1850, which required the capture of fugitive slaves. This prohibited runaways from settling legally in free states, requiring them to escape into Canada. The law also provided momentum for the growth of Underground Railroad paths through free states such as Ohio. During the same period, a series of futile slave uprisings led to retaliatory violence against innocent slaves, which increased the numbers of runaways heading North.

1. Which of the following did NOT lead to the Underground Railroad's growth?
   A. The Fugitive Slave Law of 1793
   B. The Fugitive Slave Law of 1850
   C. Canada's willingness to turn over runaway slaves.
   D. The slave rebellions in the South.

2. If the Fugitive Slave Law of 1850 had never been passed, which of the following would probably have been true?
   F. More runaways would have settled in Northern states.
   G. More runaways would have gone to Canada.
   H. More runaway slaves would have been captured and returned to their owners.
   J. There would have been more stops along the Underground Railroad.

3. Passage of the Fugitive Slave Law of 1793 probably had what effect?
   A. Fewer runaway slaves were returned to their owners.
   B. People who aided escaped slaves had to do so secretly.
   C. Owners could capture runaway slaves and take them home.
   D. Runaway slaves were able to settle safely in free states.

Copyright © 2009 by Academic Educational Resources. All rights reserved.

Reading Practice Passages

ACT SUCCESS
Reading Practice Passage #1: Fiction

Directions: After reading the passage, choose the best answer to each question. Use a watch to time yourself, taking no longer than 8 – 9 minutes per passage.

PROSE FICTION: This passage is adapted from *Staying Fat for Sarah Byrnes*, a novel by Chris Crutcher (©1993 by Chris Crutcher).

My dad left when I still had a month to go in the darkroom, and historically when people have tried to figure me out (as in, "What went wrong?"), they usually conclude that Mom spoiled me; gave me everything I wanted because I had no pappy. Truth is, Mom thinks I'm a whole lot better off without that particular pappy and has told me a thousand times she's glad I had the good sense to stay packed away until he split. They were young. My mother was my age now when I was born, and so was my dad.

I don't know very much about Dad, really. In eighteen years he's made no effort to contact me, and all I have is a picture. He's a college professor somewhere in the midwest; Mom thinks Geology. She doesn't think Geology is in the Midwest, she thinks that's what he teaches. The fact that he's excited about rocks hasn't had much genetic influence on me as far as I can tell, but what I see in the picture of him has. My dad is a tub of lard. At least he was at eighteen. I'm not talking about a guy who should have gone light on the desserts and between-meal snacks. I'm talking about a guy who should have spread Super Glue on his lips before showing his face outside his bedroom each morning. My dad could have sold his extra chins for marble sacks.

And my mom is a fox. Really. Bona fide, hundred-thousand-dollar-silver-pelt fox. She has dark brown hair and green eyes and this slinky, long, muscular body that she keeps in perfect working order, and I know for a fact half the kids who come to my house hope to catch her in shorts and a tank top. Sheesh, she's only thirty-six years old.

"Mom," I said one morning a couple of years ago, Dad's picture clutched tight in my beefy paw, "tell me something. Tell me why somebody who looks like you would fall for someone who looks like *this*." I plopped the picture on the coffee table in front of her.

"Looks aren't everything, Eric," she said.

"His looks aren't *anything*," I said back. "And he left them for me." She looked up and smiled.

"You look a lot better than your dad," she said. "He was compulsive, ate all the time. You're big and solid. That's different."

"Big and solid as twelve pounds of mashed potato in an eight-pound bag," I said. "If you dressed me up an orange-and-red sweater, you could ride me arou the world in eighty days."

"And you have a much better sense of humor th your father," she said, probably remembering Da high regard for rocks. Mom was never one to let dwell on the parts of me I didn't like.

My name is Eric Calhoune, and though I have sp hours in the weight room since that conversation, m folks call me Moby. My English teacher, Mrs. Lem who is also my coach, sometimes calls me Eric Well-read, because I'm pretty smart. She also calls Double-E, for Eric Enigma.

"I can't figure exactly how you're put togetl inside," she says. "You're a jock who doesn't comp in his best sport, a student who doesn't excel where aptitude is highest, and you surround yourself with supporting cast straight out of 'The Far Side.'"

"Tweech his own," I said, and pirouetted tippy-to out of the room, in keeping with my image as Double-

1. This passage is written from the point of view of:
   A. a grown man reminiscing about childhood insecurities.
   B. an adolescent struggling to come to terms wi both his past and present situations.
   C. an unidentified narrator observing a mother-s relationship.
   D. a teacher attempting to help one of her studen reach his full potential.

2. Information found in lines 38-43 reveals that Eri mother:
   F. is proud of her son and hopes he will follow his father's footsteps.
   G. believes that her son is just like his father.
   H. respects her son and encourages him to feel good about himself.
   J. thinks her son is funny, but is concerned abo his weight.

ACT SUCCESS
Reading Practice Passage #1: Fiction

3. It can most reasonably be inferred from the passage that Mrs. Lemry:
   A. thinks that Eric has great potential, but is confused as to why he doesn't put forth more effort to achieve it.
   B. is not amused by Eric's antics and maintains a strong dislike for him.
   C. regards Eric as her prize student and expects him to grow up to do great things.
   D. believes Eric to be lazy and unreachable as a student.

4. Eric Calhoune can best be characterized as someone who:
   F. cautiously approaches others and is very self conscious.
   G. adamantly tries to succeed in school and extracurricular activities.
   H. is overly selfish, conceited, and self-absorbed.
   J. humorously attacks his own shortcomings.

5. Eric's description of his mother in the third paragraph (lines 26-32) reveals that:
   A. he is embarrassed and self conscious concerning his mother's appearance.
   B. he wishes that his mother looked different physically.
   C. he is proud of his mother's beauty.
   D. he believes that his mother cares too much in regards to her physical appearance.

6. Based on information provided in line 57, the word *Enigma* refers to:
   F. a riddle.
   G. an incredibly intelligent person.
   H. a slacker.
   J. a perplexing or baffling person.

7. It can most reasonably be inferred from the passage that Eric, in regards to his father, feels:
   A. insecure as to why his father left before he was born.
   B. angry and wishes that his father would take the initiative to spend time with him.
   C. happy and joyous that he reminds his mother so much of his father.
   D. aware but annoyed that he takes after his father physically.

8. Based on information given in lines 58-62, Mrs. Lemry appears to be:
   F. a very strict disciplinarian who forbids students to question her authority.
   G. an intelligent and witty teacher who expects the most out of her students.
   H. a creative yet flighty woman who very rarely has any insight as to what is going on around her.
   J. a young, inexperienced teacher who is also quite a pushover.

9. As he is revealed in the second paragraph (lines 11-25), Eric's father can best be characterized as:
   A. an active father who is greatly involved in Eric's life.
   B. a boring, overweight man who was unprepared to be a father.
   C. a kind and generous man who fell out of love with Eric's mother.
   D. a "deadbeat dad" who never had any interest in raising a child.

10. The comment, "She doesn't think Geology is in the Midwest, she thinks that's what he teaches," (lines 14-16) helps establish the narrator's:
    F. confusion and lack of knowledge concerning the whereabouts and lifestyle of his father.
    G. happiness and relief regarding the fact that his father left before he was born.
    H. sense of humor and wittiness, even in light of a difficult subject.
    J. sensitivity and sadness when faced with the topic of his father.

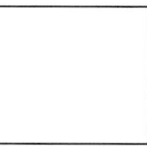

ACT SUCCESS
Reading Practice Passage #2: Social Science

Directions: After reading the passage, choose the best answer to each question. Use a watch to time yourself, taking no longer than 8 – 9 minutes per passage.

SOCIAL SCIENCE: This passage is adapted from the book *Turbulent Years: The 60s* by the editors of *Time-Life Books* (© 1998 by Time Life, Inc.).

In the furious debate over the Vietnam War that polarized the nation, each camp had its own potent symbol. A hand held aloft, fingers forming a V, was a call for peace that was often reinforced by thousands of
[5] voices chanting, "Peace now!" Antiwar protesters like those gathered in Manhattan in 1969 were denounced as traitorous "peaceniks" by their opponents, who seized on the nation's flag to express support for the war – the only position possible, they said, for a true
[10] patriot.

Peace groups began to demonstrate against the war as early as 1963, when the only Americans in Vietnam as yet were military advisers rather than combat troops, but hardly anyone noticed. As the war
[15] escalated, however, so did opposition. Unlike previous wars, this one was brought home by an uncensored flow of vivid photographic and TV images. Horrified by the carnage, college students, political radicals, and a large contingent of mainstream Americans banded
[20] together in a movement the likes of which the nation had never seen before. Calling variously for immediate peace negotiations, a bombing halt, or unilateral withdrawal, they paraded, picketed, conducted teach-ins, held candlelight vigils and staged strikes. A
[25] widening chasm separated these so-called doves from the pro-war hawks. Some of the hawks held their own pro-war protests and clamored for the doves to love their country or leave it. Even so, many hawks eventually turned against the war – not for moral
[30] reasons but simply because it seemed unwinnable.

Even before the antiwar movement emerged, there were rumblings of unrest on campus. In 1962, the manifesto for a new group called Students for a Democratic Society (SDS) described a college
[35] generation "looking uncomfortably to the world we inherit" because of racial bigotry and the Cold War. In 1964, student veterans of the civil rights movement launched the Free Speech Movement at the University of California at Berkeley to protest a campus ban on
[40] political activity. Then, soon after the first combat troops were sent to Vietnam in 1965, the nation's first teach-in was held at the University of Michigan, drawing 3,000 teachers and students to discussions about the war. Thereafter, activists at scores of colleges
[45] organized teach-ins and began staging protests against both the war and campus policies.

Although many students professed distrust anyone over 30, a wide spectrum of older protesters le credibility to the antiwar movement - clerg
[50] professional people, pacifists, housewives, antinucle activists, even members of the military.

Benjamin Spock, famed for his book on childca was co-chair of the Committee for a Sane Nucl Policy and an old hand at peace protests. In 1968,
[55] genial pediatrician was sentenced to prison conspiring to counsel draft evaders, a conviction t was later reversed. Martin Luther King Jr., the 19 Nobel Peace Prize winner, was a relative latecomer the movement. Reluctant to break with Presid
[60] Johnson because he championed civil rights legislati King finally came out against the war in 1967.

Older leaders often differed with the aims or tact of the young, frowning on extremists who deman immediate withdrawal or marched under the Vietco
[65] flag chanting "Ho, Ho, Ho Chi Minh!" Neverthele some of the most radical methods of protest w employed not by fuzzy-cheeked youths, but by a pair Roman Catholic priests.

On May 17, 1968, two Catholic priests sto
[70] outside Draft Board 33 in Catonsville, Maryland, a calmly broke the law. Father Philip Berrigan and brother, Daniel, were tossing matches into two w baskets stuffed with records they had stolen from draft board. Longtime social activists, the Berrig
[75] destroyed the files of 378 men about to be induc because, they said, they were "Christians who take faith seriously." Sentenced to prison terms, Berrigans went underground. Philip was apprehende few weeks later. Daniel, during his four months
[80] freedom, became the first priest on the FBI's m wanted list. The Berrigans' civil disobedience inspi similar draft-board actions elsewhere.

1. The passage most strongly suggests that:
   A. the conflict in Vietnam was encouraged by the American public, especially the younger citizens.
   B. the only people in the United States who were protesting were young members of the counterculture.
   C. many people in the United States were agains the war in Vietnam, old and young alike.
   D. there were almost no pro-war activists living the United States.

ACT SUCCESS
Reading Practice Passage #2: Social Science

2. The main purpose of the last paragraph (lines 69-82) is to:
   F. illustrate exactly why the clergy was protesting the Vietnam War.
   G. portray the fact that all who protested did so in a violent and angry manner.
   H. show that the Catholic religion as a whole was strongly opposed to the participation of the United States in the war.
   J. explain that there were few boundaries for those who opposed the conflict of Vietnam or for those who punished them.

3. Which of the following most accurately states the main idea of the third paragraph (lines 31-46)?
   A. College students were appalled at the idea of bans being put on their freedom to speak freely and act against politics.
   B. Colleges and universities proved to be a powerful venue for antiwar movements.
   C. Teachers and professors thought up teach-ins to help educate students about the country's political activity.
   D. The Students for a Democratic Society was formed solely to educate others on the happenings in Vietnam.

4. As it is used in line 2, the term "*potent*" means:
   F. powerful.
   G. essence.
   H. possible.
   J. ineffective.

5. The author's attitude toward the main idea of the passage can best be characterized as:
   A. one-sided and exaggerated.
   B. detached and uncaring.
   C. analytical and unbiased.
   D. open-minded and enthusiastic.

6. It can be reasonably inferred from the passage that the author believes that:
   F. Americans should have felt a patriotic responsibility to support the war.
   G. everyone in America had the right to voice his or her opinion of the war.
   H. those who believed in the war did not express themselves as adamantly as those who opposed it.
   J. people who were accepting of the war were uninformed and unintelligent.

7. The main function of the fifth paragraph (lines 52-61) in relation to the passage as a whole is most likely to provide a contrast between:
   A. protesters who were originally considered upscale members of society and those who were stereotypically thought of as college students and hippies.
   B. famous men who were indifferent and detached from the issues of the war and the youthful protesters.
   C. the antiwar doves and the pro-war hawks.
   D. people of the United States during the war who were on different socioeconomic levels.

8. The author asserts that antiwar doves and pro-war hawks:
   F. were opposites who never were going to come to a mutual agreement regarding the war in Vietnam.
   G. despised each other to the point of violently sabotaging planned responses to the war, literally causing neither voice to publicly be heard.
   H. began as the same group, but later split due to differing opinions on the war in general and ways to have their opinions heard.
   J. were more alike than they realized, eventually coming to similar conclusions only for different reasons.

9. The author indicates that the Vietnam War caused opposition unlike what America had ever seen before due to which of the following reasons?
   A. The college students who were protesting were more educated and experienced than ever before.
   B. This was the first war in U.S. history where the public was forced to see the actual damage and violence occurring through photographs and television broadcasts.
   C. The adults of the nation encouraged the youth to protest the war, convincing them that it would prove that the students were productive members of society.
   D. More American soldiers were being killed in this war than any prior war, and the parents of these soldiers initiated rallies and other such opposition to the war.

10. The main idea of the quotation from the manifesto of the Students for a Democratic Society (lines 35-36) is that members of the SDS believed that:
    F. their world was racist and in turmoil.
    G. they lived in a world full of beauty and peace.
    H. they wanted to end civil unrest because they were unhappy with the current state of the world.
    J. their world was filled with people who would never understand them.

ACT SUCCESS
Reading Practice Passage #3: Humanities

Directions: After reading the passage, choose the best answer to each question.
Use a watch to time yourself, taking no longer than 8 – 9 minutes per passage.

HUMANITIES: This passage, which describes the life of Madeline Gleason, an innovator during 1940s America, is adapted from *Women of the Beat Generation* (©1996 by Brenda Knight).

Poet, painter, and playwright Madeline Gleason played a vital role in revolutionizing modern poetry through the creation of the San Francisco poetry school of the late forties and fifties. Born in Fargo, North
[5] Dakota, in 1903 as the only child of Irish Catholic parents, she found her way to poetry early. In the late twenties, as drought turned much of the Midwest into a dust bowl, she left Fargo, settling first in Arizona and then Oregon, paying her way as a singer and comic in a
[10] traveling minstrel show.

In 1935, she came to San Francisco, where she founded the San Francisco Poetry Guild, laying the foundation for the Beat poets to come. When Allen Ginsberg, Gary Snyder, Michael McClure, and other
[15] prime movers of the Beat Generation came to San Francisco with their wild new free verse, Madeline Gleason was already there, fascinating audiences with her singular style.

A seminal historical force amongst the West
[20] Coast literati, she initiated, with Robert Duncan and James Broughton, the Festival of Contemporary Poetry reading in 1947 at the Labaudt Gallery, which brought the first widespread recognition to Bay Area poets and established San Francisco as a major center of
[25] American poetry. Madeline's first book, *Poems*, published in 1944, had a powerful effect on the emerging writing community of the time. Her musicality and mysticism caused Robert Duncan to claim that she "had a direct channel with God."

[30] Initially a member of the Kenneth Rexroth poetry circle, Madeline focused on mythical themes that stood out in sharp contrast against the freely formed poetics of her contemporaries. Her elegiac poetry was more closely aligned with poet Mary Fabilli's husband, poet-
[35] priest William Everson, than with the more modern poets that came later. Powerfully combining the strict beat of music with the lucid motion of language, her poetry is magical, heavily woven with fairy tales, children's rhymes, and powerfully haunting rhythms,
[40] presenting lively parables.

Although Madeline did not introduce free verse or end stops, she did provide one of the first forums for the modern poetry reading. In April 1947, despite warnings of failure from the naysayers, she organized
[45] the San Francisco Poetry Festival, the first such festival in the United States. Based upon the format of a music festival, readings were performed by the original authors, sometimes with the accompaniment of mu[sic]. The feedback was so tremendously favorable
[50] another festival was planned for the fall. It qui[ckly] became an institution, attracting East Coast po[ets] including early Beats. These festivals were precursors to the more popular readings of the 19[50s] and 1960s, when poetry, music, and other m[edia]
[55] combined to form a spontaneous "bop" feeling.

Immensely talented, Madeline could seemingly [do] anything she turned her hand to - painting, writ[ing,] singing. Her paintings are wildly colorful city scene[s on] backgrounds of pure black. She was fascinated by [the]
[60] chock-a-block development of San Francisco and [the] brilliant tangles of neon. North Beach, where she [had] her happiest moments, was her favorite subject for [her] paintings.

In the late 1960s, toward the end of her [life,]
[65] Madeline moved from the North Beach scene to a [far] outer district of San Francisco. As she moved away f[rom] the lively center of poetry and art she so loved, [she] became very ill and depressed. Her companion [of] twenty-five years, Mary Greer, remarked that "Made[line]
[70] died of despair, what all poets die of."

Madeline and the other leaders of the San Franc[isco] Renaissance were important precursors to the [Beat] poets. By making art and poetry the center of their li[ves,] their life's work, they started an important shif[t in]
[75] America's attitude about literature and the humani[ties.] They took poetry out of the classrooms and out into [the] streets. They brought life, energy, and music [to] writing, setting free the muse and opening up a worl[d of] possibilities.

1. It can reasonably be inferred from the passage th[at]
   A. Madeline Gleason led a difficult life, full of heartbreak and sorrow.
   B. all poets of the 1950s were musical in nature.
   C. many poets of Madeline's time focused on mythical subjects for their writing.
   D. Madeline Gleason was an innovator in the ar[t of] writing and in creating new venues for readi[ng] poetry.

ACT SUCCESS
Reading Practice Passage #3: Humanities

2. It can reasonably be inferred from the sixth paragraph (lines 56-63) that Madeline was:
   F. unhappy and bitter regarding the life that she led as a poet.
   G. a famous and inspiring actress as well as poet.
   H. as talented in other areas of the arts as she was in writing.
   J. inspired by her home in North Beach and only wrote about it.

3. In the last paragraph (lines 71-79), the author uses the word *their* many times in reference to:
   A. the leaders and innovators of the San Francisco Renaissance.
   B. the Beat poets and writers.
   C. the teachers and educators of America who chose to bring poetry outside of the classroom.
   D. the fans and readers of Beatnik poetry.

4. Lines 30-40 reveal that Madeline:
   F. was a very religious writer, who based her ideas on those in the Bible.
   G. cared deeply about her poetry and her visual art.
   H. wrote in a musical way that was packed with images of spirituality.
   J. had a very similar writing style to that of her contemporaries.

5. It can reasonably be inferred from the fifth paragraph (lines 41-55) that the San Francisco Poetry Festival:
   A. prevented famous poets from reading their own works to their fans.
   B. was successful but short-lived.
   C. was one of many such festivals occurring in the United States at that time.
   D. gained popularity due to the unique and innovative format that it adopted from music festivals.

6. The passage suggests that Madeline introduced to the world of poetry:
   F. the great poets Allen Ginsberg and Gary Snyder.
   G. a new and exciting free verse style.
   H. a form of writing filled with religious connotations.
   J. a venue allowing artists to read aloud their work to the public.

7. One of the main points of the last paragraph (lines 71-79) is that artists such as Madeline:
   A. engineered the Beat movement in 1950 and 1960 America.
   B. allowed poetry to be seen as entertainment and not just education.
   C. created a new form of poetry that is still taught in schools today.
   D. enjoyed writing because of the freedom and energy it supplied them in their daily lives.

8. According to the seventh paragraph (lines 64-70), Madeline Gleason died because:
   F. she became depressed and grief-stricken since moving away from the poetic hub of San Francisco.
   G. she was saddened at the thought of not being able to write any more.
   H. she contracted a fatal illness, thus stripping her of all will to live.
   J. she was a poet, and all poets must die in some isolated villa.

9. One of the main arguments made by the author is that:
   A. along with other people of her time, Madeline just wanted to make a living through writing.
   B. Madeline Gleason and other poets of her time helped pave the way for the Beats and other such poetry movements in America.
   C. Beat poets owe their success to people like Madeline who invented the type of poetry they became famous for.
   D. poetry must always be musical and filled with mythical themes.

10. It can most reasonably be inferred from the fourth paragraph (lines 30-40) that Madeline Gleason's writing style was:
    F. imitated from that of William Everson.
    G. inspired by stories, music, and myth.
    H. created in spite of how much she was disliked by her contemporaries.
    J. written as a way to change American poetry into a Beat style.

8 – 9

ACT SUCCESS
Reading Practice Passage #4: Natural Science

**Directions: After reading the passage, choose the best answer to each question.
Use a watch to time yourself, taking no longer than 8 – 9 minutes per passage.**

NATURAL SCIENCE: This passage is adapted from the article "Avian Flu Across the Globe" in *Dimensions* Magazine (© 2006 by John A. Molinari and Jane Halaris).

According to the World Health Organization (WHO) and Centers for Disease Control and Prevention (CDC) as of May 8, 2006, there have been 207 confirmed cases of human infection with avian influenza virus in nine countries. The lethality of this strain in comparison to those causing seasonal influenza outbreaks is evidenced by the fact that more than 55% (115) of those diagnosed with the disease have died. Other countries have reported outbreaks of the disease in poultry with possible infections in humans, but these latter cases await confirmed diagnoses. Avian influenza is spread to other animals, including humans, primarily through fecal matter, although airborne transmission can occur from the virus present in nasal and oral secretions.

The first avian influenza human cases were reported in Hong Kong in 1997, with isolation of the specific strain from 18 infected people, six of who died from the illness. This human outbreak coincided with a massive epidemic of highly pathogenic avian influenza in the region's domestic poultry population. Widespread alarm was rapidly followed by emergency destruction of the entire poultry population of Hong Kong, approximately 1.5 million birds. This drastic, yet necessary, response has been credited with delaying the progression of avian influenza in Southeast Asia. Fortunately, subsequent infections in poultry and humans in the region did not appear again until 2003. In 2003 and early 2004, however, new outbreaks among poultry in eight Asian countries signaled a precursor of the human infections to follow. Even with the destruction of more than 100 million birds in the affected countries, relief from the avian pandemic was only temporary. Reports of the avian flu currently continue with instances of infection in poultry and wild birds confirmed in Europe, Africa, and the East.

Influenza is caused by a highly infectious group of RNA viruses that are transmitted primarily via microbial-laden secretions in respiratory droplets. A sudden onset of constitutional and respiratory symptoms occurs after an incubation interval of usually 2 days, which typically are far more severe than those presented with a cold. The most common influenza symptoms include a rapidly developing fever, cough, sore throat, and muscle aches. In contrast, illness following infection with the virus can present with a wide range of symptoms ranging from those found with seasonal influenza to severe respiratory complications a worst-case scenario.

Individuals diagnosed with the current avian f have experienced high fever and an unusual progressive influenza course, characterized by extensiv fluid accumulation in the lungs with rapid deterioratic and destruction of respiratory tissues. Early symptom in a patient include diarrhea, vomiting, and chest a abdominal pain. Bleeding from the nose and gums h also been observed in some patients. The high mortali associated with avian influenza does not appear to due only to viral pathogenicity. Compelling eviden exists indicating that an over-reaction by the infecte person's immune system against a replicating virus respiratory tissues may be responsible for the massi accumulation of fluid and damage seen in many bird f cases.

While currently no commercially available huma vaccine against the avian influenza virus exist extensive and accelerated research conducted within t past few years has recently led to the development a testing of an effective possible candidate. This is purified, subvirion vaccine administered intramuscular in two relatively high doses. Analysis of antibo responses indicated that the vaccine stimulate neutralizing titers associated with protection agair influenza. Of additional importance was the fact that t vaccine was generally well tolerated by recipients. brief, despite the continuing release of alarming nev and figures, the key to responding effectively to t current adaptation and spread of avian influenza humans, may well be linked with how we prepare durir this time of advance notice before a global huma pandemic infection.

1. The primary purpose of the passage is to:
   A. discuss the symptoms and causes of avian influenza and suggest that researchers need to devise a way to prepare for the disease.
   B. compare and contrast the difference between avian influenza and seasonal influenza.
   C. explain ways in which other countries have successfully dealt with the threat of avian flu.
   D. encourage readers to keep away from potenti causes and carriers of avian influenza.

ACT SUCCESS
Reading Practice Passage #4: Natural Science

2. The passage most clearly indicates that attempts to create a vaccine have been:
   F. highly successful.
   G. completely unsuccessful.
   H. moving in the right direction, with no solid results yet.
   J. stalled due to financial issues.

3. The passage states that all of the following are symptoms of avian influenza that differ from seasonal flu symptoms EXCEPT:
   A. extensive fluid accumulation in the lungs with rapid deterioration and destruction of respiratory tissues.
   B. cough, sore throat, muscle aches.
   C. bleeding from the nose and gums.
   D. severe chest and abdominal pain.

4. Which of the following questions is NOT answered by information provided in the passage?
   F. What is the difference between seasonal and avian flu?
   G. What are the causes and methods of spreading avian flu?
   H. How are researchers looking to prevent the spread of avian influenza?
   J. Why does the avian flu primarily affect birds when it initially reaches an area?

5. The main purpose of lines 75-81 is:
   A. to warn the public that avian influenza is a serious health risk, and everyone should get inoculations immediately.
   B. that avian influenza is not a threat to Americans.
   C. to suggest to the public that if the world does not prepare for avian flu, a pandemic may occur..
   D. to discuss that there are few differences between avian and seasonal influenza.

6. According to the last paragraph (lines 65-81), avian influenza is being prepared for by:
   F. researching a possible vaccine that not only effectively cures the disease, but is also tolerable to humans.
   G. watching the bird population carefully and preparing to kill any that contract the disease.
   H. marketing an over the counter medication that will prevent humans from contracting avian influenza.
   J. providing immunization shots to any person who feels threatened by the disease.

7. It can be reasonably inferred from the passage that the people of Hong Kong reacted to the outbreak of avian influenza in the late 1990's in all of the following ways EXCEPT:
   A. breaking out into massive panic and alarm.
   B. bringing in medical specialists to help control the outbreak in animals and prevent it from spreading to people.
   C. killing and destroying the bird population of over 1.5 million.
   D. finding a way to isolate the strain of the virus that causes avian flu in humans.

8. Information in the first paragraph (lines 1-15) indicates that avian influenza can be spread through all the following EXCEPT:
   F. blood.
   G. fecal matter.
   H. air.
   J. nasal and oral secretions.

9. The author would most likely agree with which of the following statements?
   A. Avian influenza is very similar to seasonal influenza and is no real threat at this time.
   B. Avian influenza can be controlled simply by ridding the population of all infected birds.
   C. Avian influenza is quickly becoming a threat to humans, and researchers must look into preventative measures immediately.
   D. Scientists have discovered a marketable cure for avian influenza, so it is currently a very treatable disease.

10. The main idea of the second paragraph (lines 16-36) is that:
    F. eliminating inflected animals in the area is not a solution to avian influenza.
    G. Hong Kong prevented the avian flu from spreading by destroying its bird population.
    H. scientists believe that avian flu is far more deadly to humans than the seasonal flu.
    J. people should evacuate any area that contains animals possessing avian influenza.

8 – 9

Additional Notes

Chapter 4
Science Strategies and Review

SCIENCE

The ACT science reasoning test appears to be the most difficult of the four, but, with a little practice, it becomes fairly straightforward. **This is the point in the test where many students lose focus. Do not let this happen!**

GENERAL HINTS

- The Science section is really a reasoning or logic test. While it helps to be familiar with the various areas of science, you do NOT need to have prior knowledge of the subject matter to successfully answer the questions!

- Think of the Science section as a puzzle or riddle that you have to figure out.

- The focus is on interpreting data and information and making logical conclusions – NOT knowing specific scientific facts.

- With all of the information put in front of you and only 35 minutes to answer all of the questions, the science section can seem overwhelming. The most important thing you can do to conserve time is orient yourself. Think of it like shopping at a grocery store…

Let's say you are going to the supermarket and all you need to buy is milk and bread. The supermarket carries tens of thousands of items – will you need to go through each item on each aisle in order to find the two that you are looking for? Of course not! You would use the aisle signs to figure out exactly where to go, then scan the appropriate aisle until you find what you are looking for. The whole process would take you a few seconds. The science section is no different. Sure, there is a considerable amount of information provided with each passage, but don't let it slow you down. Orient yourself using the headings on charts and graphs the same way you would at the grocery store, and the ACT science reasoning can be as straightforward as buying a loaf of bread.

- It is important to be FLEXIBLE and able to SHIFT GEARS when doing this section. In other words, if one method doesn't work, try another. If looking at one piece of information doesn't help you, look in a different place.

HOW TO TAKE THE TEST

1. For most of the passages, your first step should be to inspect the charts. Look at the data, reading the labels and headings quickly. Your goal is to just get a general idea of where everything is. DO NOT WORRY IF YOU DON'T UNDERSTAND WHAT'S GOING ON. It may be confusing, but there isn't enough time to try to completely comprehend

each experiment. Plus, reading the passages **completely** is usually a waste of valuable time.

2. Your focus then becomes the questions. Read through the first question and underline key words. DO NOT go straight to the data yet.

3. Next, match the information in the question to the appropriate chart/graph(s). BE SURE THAT YOU ARE LOOKING AT THE CORRECT GRAPH OR CHART! **Then, work backwards from the answers.** Use process of elimination to help you determine the true answer.

   NOTE: Almost every question refers to a data table even though the question might not specifically mention that table. Use the answers as a guide to locate the correct table.

4. Think simply and linearly! Try not to over think – the answers are usually simpler than you realize.

5. If you are not able to find the answer using just the charts and graphs, then you may have to go to the text. Sometimes italicized words can be helpful. If the questions states "based on the information," you should look at the text. The introductory passage may have some information to help you.

DO'S AND DON'TS

- **DO** focus on the charts and graphs. The only passage that MUST involve reading is the *opposing viewpoint*.

- **DO** pretend that you are shopping at an unfamiliar grocery store: use the headings to help you!

- **DO** look for patterns, trends and directions. If there is an obvious pattern such as a column of numbers increasing or decreasing, draw an arrow to show that trend.

- **DO** write in the test booklet. Circling and underlining help prevent careless errors.

- **DO** work backwards from each answer – use process of elimination. (Treat each answer choice as a true/false question, and eliminate the false ones. There should only be one true answer.)

- **DON'T** let the wording of the questions confuse you. Break them down; translate them into basic elements, one at a time. They often put much more information in the questions that you actually need to answer them.

- **DON'T** worry about the large amount of data – test writers often provide much more information than you need.

TYPES OF QUESTIONS

In general, there are three types of questions:

- *Patterns and trends:* For this type of question, you need to find the answer based on the data. Focus on investigating the information *directionally*: does pressure increase or decrease when velocity increases? When exposed to more sunlight, do the plants flower more frequently, less frequently, or is there no relationship?

- *Hypothesis:* This question involves yes/no or true/false answers. These questions can be best tackled by a "plug and chug" method. Try each answer out as you go through them.

- *Logic*: These questions are designed to challenge your thinking. You should focus on connecting the information. If the question talks about the *design* of the experiment, you may need to read a little bit.

ACT science questions can also be thought of as either *navigation* or *manipulation* questions.

- Within each passage there are typically at least three *navigation* questions: that is, questions that you can answer simply by locating the necessary information in a chart or graph.

- The remaining questions (approximately two per passage) involve *manipulation*. These questions involve two steps: you must first *navigate* to the appropriate information, then use the data in some way to find the correct answer.

TYPES OF PASSAGES

- The Science section contains seven passages.

- Three of the passages have five questions, three have six questions, and one has seven questions. ACT calls the passages with five questions "data representation," the passages with six questions "research summary," and the passage with seven questions "conflicting viewpoints."

- The five and six question passages will all be accompanied by charts and graphs, and should be approached using the techniques detailed above.

- The seven question passage – always the *opposing viewpoints* passage – is unique.

OPPOSING VIEWPOINTS PASSAGE

There is one passage out of the seven that is not about interpreting data. It can fall anywhere in the test, but you will easily recognize it because it will consist of a brief introduction to the topic followed by 2-4 sections (ie: Scientist 1, Scientist 2…or The Dust Theory, The Dirt Theory, The Rock Theory...) written in paragraph form. It is the only science passage with seven questions, and often does not include any tables, charts, or graphs. It may look like you need to read everything but you do not!

In many ways, the opposing viewpoints passage is similar to the Reading section: it is essential that you determine the MAIN IDEA of each view.

REMEMBER: it's called the "opposing viewpoints" passage for a reason. Though they will discuss the same general topic, the views must oppose each other in some fundamental way. Once you have figured out each view's main idea and where the views disagree, you will be in great shape on the questions.

Follow these steps on the opposing viewpoints passage:

1. Skim the introductory paragraph.

2. Read enough of each viewpoint to determine their respective main ideas (usually the main idea can be found in the first two sentences).

3. Then go straight to the questions. Look back when you need to, using as much logic as possible.

4. There are two basic types of questions. The first is a simple word match – just look for the words in the passages. The second asks you to define the viewpoint. These may seem more difficult, but just think in terms of the main idea.

5. Questions often ask about one of the viewpoints but list answer choices that correspond to the other(s). Look to eliminate these extraneous answer choices first.

PACING

- With seven passages and 35 minutes, you have approximately 5 minutes per passage; however, some will take a minute less while others may take a minute more. Try to use pacing boxes during practice.

- Don't rush; just be conscious of your time from the beginning.

- If you can't figure a question out, just take your best guess and move on. You will not have enough time to dwell on questions, and it is better to guess on one or two than to not even make it to an entire passage.

- If you find yourself struggling with finishing, complete the opposing views passage last. (Be careful on your scantron sheet!)

- Don't panic as you begin to practice. It may take you longer at first! You will get the hang of it!!!

REMEMBER: The science section is not arranged in order of difficulty. The easiest passages could be anywhere in the test, so it is important to get to the end, even if you have to make a few educated guesses along the way.

HOW TO USE ACT SUCCESS TO STUDY FOR THE SCIENCE SECTION

The ensuing pages contain a number of Skill Builders and practice passages that mimic the types of passages found on the science section of the ACT. The Skill Builders are divided by passage type, in the following order: interpreting graphs, analyzing data, and opposing viewpoints. Remember, on the actual ACT, these passages will NOT necessarily pop up in this order.

You will likely notice that all three "Interpreting Graphs" Skill Builders are based upon the same two graphs. This will not be the case on the ACT; it is presented in this way to demonstrate how much information can be pulled from a given graph, and allow you to practice locating the various types of trends and information that the ACT may ask you to find in a graph.

Remember, throughout the Science section you are to choose the **BEST** answer of the four choices. There may not always be a perfect answer, or you may find two choices that appear to be decent answers. No matter what, though, there will always be one answer choice that is better than all of the others.

GOOD LUCK!

Science Skill Builders

ACT SUCCESS
Science Skill Builder – Interpreting Graphs #1

Directions: After reading the passage, choose the best answer to each question.

The growth of tumor cells in a culture depends on the amount of nutrients in the culture. Cell production can be determined by counting the number of cells. The effects of various concentrations of glucose and calcium on the growth of three different cell types were tested. Each culture dish began the test with 0.5 million cells, to which was added a solution containing known concentrations of either glucose or calcium. The results after three days are shown below.

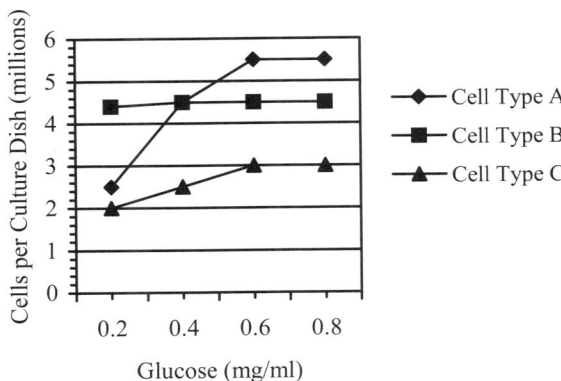

Figure 1

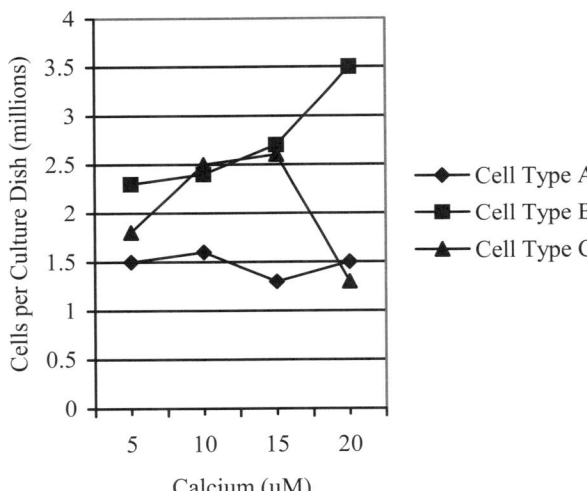

Figure 2

1. Which of the following variables is represented by the axis of the graphs?
   A. The number of cells per culture dish after three days
   B. The concentration of glucose or calcium present in the solution after three days.
   C. The number of cells added to each culture dish on the first day.
   D. The concentration of glucose or calcium present in the solution on the first day.

2. According to Figure 1, which cell type(s) produced the largest number of cells with a glucose concentration 0.4 mg/ml?
   F. Cell type A
   G. Cell type B
   H. Both cell types A & C
   J. Both cell types A & B

3. Which of the following conclusions is most consistent with the data presented in Figure 1?
   A. High concentrations of glucose can have detrimental effects on the growth of some cell types.
   B. Glucose concentrations of 0.2 to 0.6 mg/ml stimulate the growth of cell types A, B, and C.
   C. The relationship between the concentration of glucose and the number of cells per dish is the same for cell types B and C.
   D. The growth of cell type B is less affected by the concentration of glucose than is the growth of cell type A.

4. Based on the data in Figure 1, which of the following statements about the impact of glucose on cell growth most accurate?
   F. All cell types require at least 0.89 mg/ml of glucose for maximum cell growth.
   G. Type B cells need more glucose than type A cells maximum cell growth.
   H. With glucose concentrations less than 0.4 mg/ml, type A cells proliferate more than type B or C cells.
   J. All cell types will achieve maximum cell growth in solution containing 0.6 mg/ml of glucose.

5. Which of the following data support the conclusion that increasing the concentrations of nutrients does NOT necessarily increase cell growth?
   A. The growth of type C cells when the three lower concentrations of glucose were tested.
   B. The growth of type C cells when the three lower concentrations of calcium were tested.
   C. The growth of type B cells when the three higher concentrations of glucose were tested.
   D. The growth of type B cells when the three higher concentrations of calcium were tested.

ACT SUCCESS
Science Skill Builder – Interpreting Graphs #2

Directions: After reading the passage, choose the best answer to each question.

The growth of tumor cells in a culture depends on the amount of nutrients in the culture. Cell production can be determined by counting the number of cells. The effects of various concentrations of glucose and calcium on the growth of three different cell types were tested. Each culture dish began the test with 0.5 million cells, to which was added a solution containing known concentrations of either glucose or calcium. The results after three days are shown below.

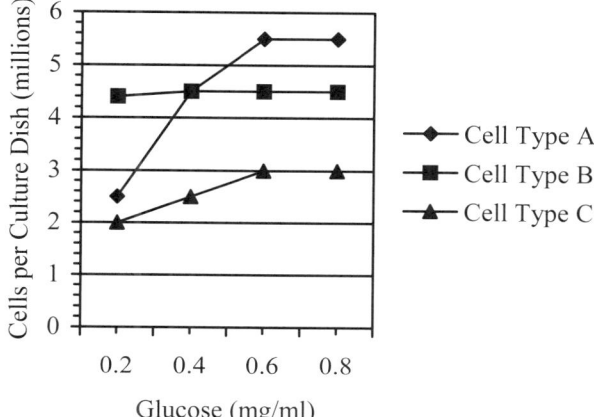

Figure 1

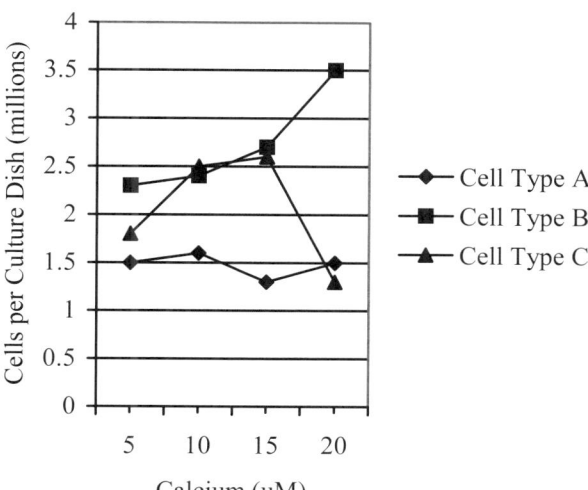

Figure 2

1. Based on the trends in Figure 2, which of the following statements about cell behavior could you predict if 25 uM of calcium were introduced?
   A. Cell type B would produce around 4 million cells.
   B. Cell type A would produce around 2 million cells.
   C. Cell type C would produce around 2.5 million cells.
   D. Cell type C would produce around 0 million cells.

2. Based on the data presented in Figure 2, about how many millions of cells did cell type C produce with a calcium concentration of 20 uM?
   F. 1.5
   G. 2.5
   H. 3.5
   J. 1.3

3. Which of the following statements regarding the relationship between calcium and cell growth is supported by the graphs?
   A. As higher concentrations of calcium are introduced, all cell types produce more cells.
   B. As higher concentrations of calcium are introduced, all cell types produce fewer cells.
   C. As higher concentrations of calcium are introduced, only cell type B consistently produces more cells.
   D. As higher concentrations of calcium are introduced, cell type C gradually produces fewer cells.

4. With a calcium concentration of 20 uM, which cell type(s) produced the fewest cells?
   F. Cell type A
   G. Cell type B
   H. Cell type C
   J. Both cell types B & C

5. Which cell type(s) saw a steady increase in the number of cells produced with increasing concentrations of the calcium solution?
   A. Cell type A
   B. Cell type B
   C. Both cell types B & C
   D. Both cell types A & C

Copyright © 2009 Academic Educational Resources. All rights reserved.

ACT SUCCESS
Science Skill Builder – Interpreting Graphs #3

Directions: After reading the passage, choose the best answer to each question.

The growth of tumor cells in a culture depends on the amount of nutrients in the culture. Cell production can be determined by counting the number of cells. The effects of various concentrations of glucose and calcium on the growth of three different cell types were tested. Each culture dish began the test with 0.5 million cells, to which was added a solution containing known concentrations of either glucose or calcium. The results after three days are shown below.

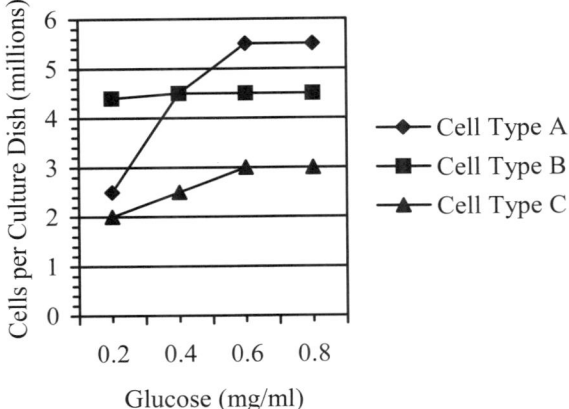

Figure 1

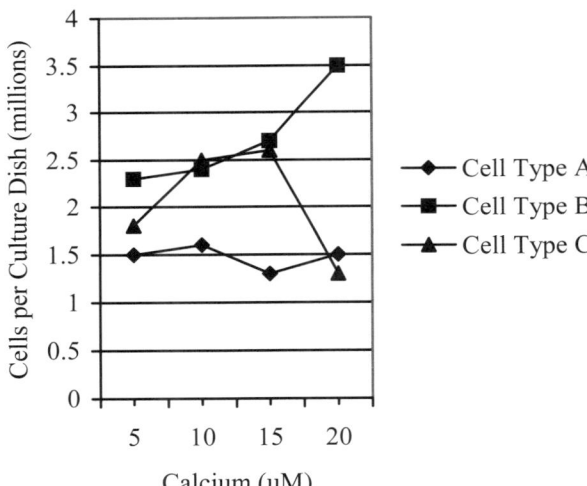

Figure 2

1. Based on the information in Figures 1 and 2, one would predict that the growth of cell type A would be greater than that of cell type C in solutions containing all of the following EXCEPT:
   A. 0.2 mg/ml of glucose and 20 uM of calcium.
   B. 0.2 mg/ml of glucose and 15 uM of calcium.
   C. 0.4 mg/ml of glucose and 10 uM of calcium.
   D. 0.6 mg/ml of glucose and 20 uM of calcium.

2. Based on the data in Figures 1 and 2, which of the following statements is most accurate?
   F. Cell type A will always produce the most new cells.
   G. Cell type C produces the least number of cells in a solution containing calcium.
   H. Cell type B steadily produces more cells as a high concentration of glucose is added.
   J. Cell type C is the only cell type to see a decline cell production as a higher calcium concentration introduced.

3. Based on the data in Figures 1 and 2, what can concluded about the effectiveness of using glucose calcium to stimulate cell growth?
   A. In all cell types, calcium is more effective than glucose at stimulating cell growth.
   B. In all cell types, glucose is more effective than calcium at stimulating cell growth.
   C. Calcium is more effective than glucose at stimulat cell growth in cell type B.
   D. Glucose is more effective than calcium at stimulat cell growth in cell types A and C.

4. Introduction of which of the following solutions resul in the greatest amount of type A cells?
   F. A glucose concentration of 0.3 mg/ml.
   G. A glucose concentration of 0.7 mg/ml.
   H. A calcium concentration of 10 uM.
   J. A calcium concentration of 20 uM.

5. If a solution of 13 uM of calcium were introduced t culture dish containing type A cells, one could expec count about how many cells in the dish after 3 days?
   A. 1.5 million
   B. 2.5 million
   C. 3 million
   D. 4.5 million

Copyright © 2009 by Academic Educational Resources. All rights reserved.

ACT SUCCESS
Science Skill Builder – Analyzing Data #1

Directions: After reading the passage, choose the best answer to each question.

Under conditions of zero gravity, such as during space travel, bones weaken because of the quick loss of bone density. This decrease in bone density is correlated with increased levels of calcium in the urine and a decrease in the mineral content of the bones. Three potential treatments were tested on rats while they were in a zero gravity orbit for five days. The amount of calcium in their urine and the mineral content of their spinal vertebrae were measured before, during, and one day after their flight.

Experiment 1

One group of rats was given a high calcium diet for one month prior to and then during the flight. Another group of rats was given a regular diet. The average urinary calcium levels and bone mineral contents of the animals are shown in Table 1.

Table 1

	Control Diet	Test Diet
Urinary Calcium (mg/mL)		
Before flight	60	89
Day 1 of flight	69	96
Day 3 of flight	83	98
Day 5 of flight	84	96
After flight	63	81
Bone Mineral Content (gm/cm^2)		
Before flight	0.327	0.332
After flight	0.198	0.209

Experiment 2

Some hormonal growth aids, such as an insulin-like growth factor (IGF), can promote bone cell replication. Rats were given various doses of IGF the day before the flight. The results are shown in Table 2.

Table 2

	IGF (mg per rat)			
	Control	5	50	500
Urinary Calcium (mg/mL)				
Day 1 of flight	69	67	68	69
Day 3 of flight	84	78	74	71
Day 5 of flight	87	86	84	71
Bone Mineral Content (gm/cm^2)				
Before flight	0.344	0.339	0.336	0.341
After flight	0.197	0.206	0.278	0.330

Experiment 3

Each day while in flight, rats were placed in activity wheels controlled by timed motors and given periods of wheel running activity. Instead of measuring urinary calcium concentrations, the muscle mass of the hind legs was measured. This value is expressed as the ratio of post-flight to pre-flight measurements. The data is shown in Table 3.

Table 3

	Wheel Running Activity per Day (hours)			
	0	2	4	6
Muscle Mass (post-flight/pre-flight)	0.90	0.95	1.00	1.0
Bone Mineral Content (gm/cm^2)				
Before flight	0.334	0.309	0.316	0.3?
After flight	0.187	0.206	0.278	0.3?

1. According to Experiment 2, which amount of IGF resulted in the lowest concentration of calcium in rats' urine after 5 days in flight?
   A. 0 mg
   B. 5 mg
   C. 50 mg
   D. 500 mg

2. The data from Experiment 3 supports which of following statements?
   F. As the muscle mass ratio increases, the bone mineral content before the flight decreases.
   G. The higher the muscle mass ratio, the greater the bone mineral content after the flight.
   H. The lower the muscle mass ratio, the greater the bone mineral content after the flight.
   J. If muscle mass ratio remains constant, the bone mineral content will increase.

3. If 25 mg of IGF were given to each rat, the urinary calcium concentration after 3 days of flight would be closest to which of the following?
   A. 71 mg/mL
   B. 73 mg/mL
   C. 76 mg/mL
   D. 85 mg/mL

4. In Experiment 1, the rats given the test diet had the highest amount of calcium in their urine how many days into the flight?
   F. 3 days
   G. 5 days
   H. 1 day
   J. After the flight

5. What can be concluded about the effects of exercise on bone mineral content from Experiment 3?
   A. More activity per day results in a greater loss of minerals from the bones during flight.
   B. More activity per day results in less of a loss of minerals from the bones during flight.
   C. More activity per day leads to a greater bone mineral content before the flight.
   D. More activity per day leads to a smaller bone mineral content after the flight.

6. Do the results of these experiments support the statement that the loss of bone density during space travel can be prevented?
   F. Yes. In Experiments 2 and 3 bone mineral content after the flight increased with the use of IGF and wheel running activity.
   G. Yes. In Experiment 1 the bone mineral content of the test group was similar to that of the control group after the flight.
   H. No. In Experiment 2 the urinary calcium levels on days 3 and 5 were greater in control rats than in the IGF-treated rats.
   J. No. In Experiment 3 wheel running activity did not increase either muscle mass or bone mineral content.

7. Which of the following factors was an experimental value in Experiment 1?
   A. The volume of urine produced.
   B. The length of time the test diet was given to the rats.
   C. The amount of calcium in the rats' diets.
   D. The time spent in zero gravity conditions.

8. Which of the following is true about the effect of a high calcium diet on the content of calcium found in the rats' urine during flight?
   F. The urinary calcium content steadily increased throughout the flight.
   G. The urinary calcium content steadily decreased throughout the flight.
   H. The urinary calcium content decreased and then increased during flight.
   J. The urinary calcium content increased and then remained the same during flight.

9. Based on the results of Experiment 2, which of the following amounts of IGF resulted in the greatest disparity in before flight and after flight bone mineral content?
   A. 0 mg
   B. 5 mg
   C. 50 mg
   D. 500 mg

10. A representation of the relationship between the amount of IGF given to each rat and the bone mineral content after the flight is best shown by which of the following graphs?

    F.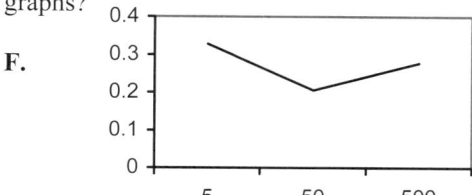

    G.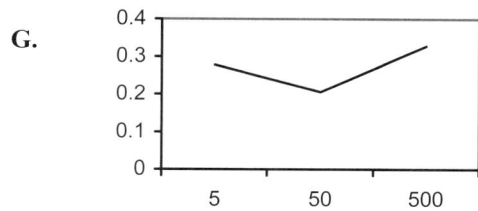

    H.
    J.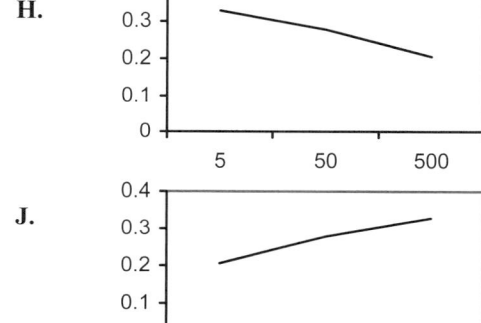

11. In Experiment 2, if 500 mg of IGF were given to each rat every day during flight, one could predict that:
    A. Bone mineral content after the flight would be much higher than the pre-flight amount.
    B. Urinary calcium concentrations might not rise between days 3 and 5 in flight.
    C. The decline in bone mineral content would happen more quickly.
    D. Urinary calcium concentrations might exceed 90 mg/mL on day 5 in flight.

12. In Experiment 3, if rats were given 5 hours of wheel running activity per day, one could predict that:
    F. Bone mineral content after the flight would be about 0.225 gm/cm^2.
    G. Muscle mass ratio would be about 1.03.
    H. Muscle mass ratio would be about 0.93.
    J. Bone mineral content before the flight would be about 0.345 gm/cm^2.

ACT SUCCESS
Science Skill Builder – Analyzing Data #2

Directions: After reading the passage, choose the best answer to each question.

Geologists classify rocks in three groups, according to the major Earth processes that formed them. The three rock groups are igneous, sedimentary, and metamorphic. Igneous rocks are formed from melted rock that has cooled and solidified. Sedimentary rocks are formed at the surface of the Earth, either in water or on land. They are layered accumulations of sediments – fragments of rocks, minerals, animals or plants. Sometimes sedimentary and igneous rocks are subjected to pressures so intense or heat so high that they change completely. They become metamorphic rocks, which form while deeply buried within the Earth's crust. Rocks can also be classified by their hardness, density, or porosity. Typical rocks along with their rock type and hardness are shown in Table 1.

Table 1		
Rock Type	Strength Range (MPa)	Example Rocks
Igneous	40 - 320	Andesiste Diorite Granite
Metamorphic	80 - 160	Gneiss Marble Quartzite
Sedimentary	10 - 80	Limestone Sandstone Shale

Study 1

A full beaker containing 1 liter of water was weighed. Next, a dry sample of sandstone was weighed and then immersed in the beaker. After the displaced water was removed, the beaker was weighed again. The *relative density* (a measure of mass per unit of volume) was calculated by dividing the dry sample weight by that of the displaced water. The procedure was repeated with samples of four different rocks. The results are shown in Table 2.

Table 2	
Rock	Relative Density (SI)
Granite	2.19
Marble	2.01
Quartzite	2.23
Sandstone	1.85
Shale	2.02

Study 2

Another sample of sandstone was tested for *fracture strength* by applying pressure to a small rock core at the rate of 0.7 MPa/s until the rock failed. Again, the procedure was repeated with samples of four different rocks. The amount of stress necessary to cause failure in each rock core was recorded (see Table 3).

Table 3	
Rock	Fracture Strength (MPa)
Granite	210
Marble	225
Quartzite	280
Sandstone	42
Shale	91

Study 3

The volumes of five samples of shale were calculated and then each sample was dumped into a beaker containing a known volume of water. The beakers were sealed and left for two hours to ensure that the samples were fully saturated. Then, the remaining water was removed from each beaker and measured. Using this data, the *porosity* (the proportion of the non-solid volume to the total volume of the material) of each sample was calculated. Once the samples had dried, their *fracture strengths* were calculated (see Table 4).

Table 4		
Shale Sample	Porosity (%)	Fracture Strength (MPa)
1	10	31
2	19	62
3	28	90
4	15	43
5	26	85

1. Rocks with a higher porosity can hold more water when saturated than those with a lower porosity. Based on this information, which of the following samples of shale from Study 3 would hold the most water when saturated?
   A. Sample 2
   B. Sample 3
   C. Sample 4
   D. Sample 5

ACT SUCCESS
Science Skill Builder – Analyzing Data #2

2. Based on the data in Table 4, if another shale sample was tested that had a porosity of 22%, it's fracture strength would be:
   F. less than 31 MPa.
   G. between 31 and 43 MPa.
   H. between 43 and 62 MPa.
   J. greater than 62 MPa.

3. In Study 1, if a rock was not weighed until after it had been immersed in water, the results would have been affected in which of the following ways?
   A. The results would have been the same.
   B. The calculated relative density would have been higher than it truly is.
   C. The calculated relative density would have been lower that it truly is.
   D. It is impossible to predict how the results would have been affected.

4. In Study 3, which of the following is the most important reason for sealing the beaker after adding the shale?
   F. To prevent foreign objects from entering the beaker.
   G. To control the temperature of the water in the beaker.
   H. To keep the water from spilling out of the beaker.
   J. To ensure that none of the water evaporates.

5. It is known that the higher the surface area of grain-to-grain contact, the harder a rock becomes. Based on this information, which rock tested in Study 2 has the highest surface area of grain-to-grain contact?
   A. Quartzite
   B. Marble
   C. Shale
   D. Sandstone

6. All of the following are true about metamorphic rocks EXCEPT?
   F. They are stronger than sedimentary rocks.
   G. They are formed out of other rocks.
   H. They are denser than other rocks.
   J. Marble and quartzite are typical rocks.

Copyright © 2009 by Academic Educational Resources. All rights reserved.

ACT SUCCESS
Science Skill Builder – Analyzing Data #3

Directions: After reading the passage, choose the best answer to each question.

Glycolysis is the term for the metabolic breakdown of glucose. The first five steps of the reaction pathway are regarded as the *preparatory phase* because they consume energy as the glucose is converted into two three-carbon sugar phosphates (G3P). The second half of glycolysis is known as the *pay-off phase*, and is characterized by a gain of energy-rich molecules. Each reaction is catalyzed by an enzyme (E1 – E8). The reaction pathway is shown in Figure 1.

$$\text{glucose} \xrightarrow{E1} \text{glucose-6-phospate} \xrightarrow{E2} \text{fructose 6-phosphate} \xrightarrow{E3} \text{fructose 1, 6-bisphosphate} \xrightarrow{E4} \text{dihydroxyacetone phosphate}$$

$$\text{Glyceraldehydes 3-phosphate} \xrightarrow{E5} \text{1,3-bisphosphoglycerate} \xrightarrow{E6} \text{3-phosphoglycerate} \xrightarrow{E7} \text{2-phosphoglycerate} \xrightarrow{E8} \text{phosphoenolpyruvate}$$

Figure 1

Table 1 lists the enzymes involved in the *glycolysis* reactions, along with their enzyme class.

Table 1	
Enzyme	Enzyme Class
E1	Transferase
E2	Isomerase
E3	Transferase
E4	Lyase
E5	Isomerase
E6	Oxidoreductase
E7	Transferase
E8	Mutase

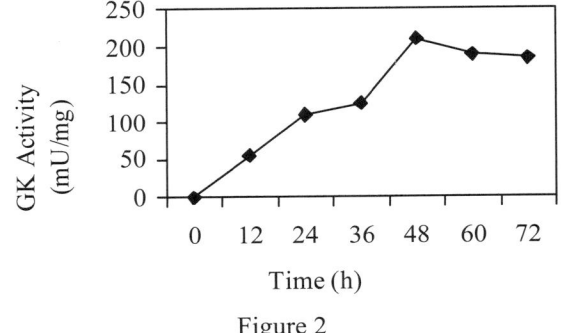

Figure 2

The endocrine β-cell of the pancreas contains glucokinase (GK), an enzyme that allows glucose to regulate its rate of metabolism. Important physiological effects, including effects on the rate of insulin secretion, are induced in the endocrine β-cell by fluctuations in the glucose concentration.

Experiment 1

Cells capable of overproducing glucokinase under the control of doxycycline were established from parental INS-1 cells. The cells were cultured in a medium containing 2.5 mM glucose and 1000 ng/ml doxycycline. They were harvested at various times to evaluate glucokinase activity (see Figure 2).

Experiment 2

The effect of increases in glucokinase activity on glucose metabolism was investigated, using the production of wa from glucose (Glc) to estimate the rate of glycolysis. C were cultured for 14 hours with doxycycline (D concentrations of 75, 150, and 500 ng/ml, as well as with the inducer. The rate of glycolysis was measured at gluc concentrations of 2.5, 6, 12, and 24 mM (see Table 2).

Table 2				
	Dxl Concentration			
Glc Concentration (mM)	0 ng/ml	75 ng/ml	150 ng/ml	500 ng/m
2.5	0.8	2.0	3.2	4.8
6	2.1	4.7	6.8	9.0
12	4.0	6.8	9.2	10.6
24	5.0	8.3	8.9	11.0

Copyright © 2009 by Academic Educational Resources. All rights reserved.

ACT SUCCESS
Science Skill Builder – Analyzing Data #3

1. For the culture with a glucose concentration of 6mM in Experiment 2, which rate of glycolysis was used as the control against which other rates were compared?
   A. 9.0
   B. 6.8
   C. 4.7
   D. 2.1

2. Based on the information presented in Table 2, which of the following combinations of glucose (Glc) concentration and doxycycline (Dxc) concentration yielded the highest rate of glycolysis?
   F. Glc 12 mM, Dxc 75 ng/ml
   G. Glc 2.5 mM, Dxc 500 ng/ml
   H. Glc 12 mM, Dxc 0 ng/ml
   J. Glc 6 mM, Dxc 75 ng/ml

3. Which of the following statements best describes the relationships between glucose-6-phospate, fructose 1, 6- bisphosphate, and fructose 6-phosphate as shown in the reaction pathway represented in Figure 1?
   A. Fructose 1, 6-bisphosphate is a precursor of glucose-6-phospate, which is a precursor of fructose 6-phosphate.
   B. Fructose 6-phosphate is a precursor of fructose 1, 6-bisphosphate, which is a precursor of glucose-6-phospate.
   C. Glucose-6-phospate is a precursor of fructose 6-phosphate, which is a precursor of fructose 1, 6-bisphosphate.
   D. Fructose 1, 6-bisphosphate is a precursor of fructose 6-phosphate, which is a precursor of glucose-6-phospate.

4. Which of the following enzyme classes are involved only in the pay- off phase of glycolysis?
   F. Isomerase, lyase, and transferase.
   G. Isomerase, transferase, oxidoreductase and mutase.
   H. Oxidoreductase and mutase.
   J. Isomerase and transferase.

5. In Experiment 1, if a cell was harvested after 30 hours, it would have glucokinase activity of around:
   A. 0 mU/mg
   B. 125 mU/mg
   C. 200 mU/mg
   D. 95 mU/mg

6. Based on the results of Experiments 1 and 2, which of the following can be reasonably deduced about the effect of doxycycline on glycolysis?
   F. As the concentration of doxycycline increases, so does the rate of glycolysis.
   G. As the concentration of doxycycline decreases, the rate of glycolysis decreases.
   H. After 72 hours, doxycycline ceases to have an effect on the rate of glycolysis.
   J. For a period of 48 hours, the rate of glycolysis will increase as the doxycycline concentration increases.

Copyright © 2009 by Academic Educational Resources. All rights reserved.

ACT SUCCESS
Science Skill Builder – Analyzing Data #4

Directions: After reading the passage, choose the best answer to each question.

To ensure tap water safety, the U.S. Environmental Protection Agency (EPA) sets limits on the amount of certain contaminants in our drinking water. Local water quality may be judged by comparing the water to the EPA benchmarks for water quality. One such benchmark is the Maximum Contaminant Level Goal (MCLG). The MCLG is the level of a contaminant in drinking water below which is there is no known or expected risk to health. Another benchmark is the Maximum Contaminant Level (MCL). An MCL is the highest level of a contaminant that is allowed in drinking water.

The Village of Grayslake, Illinois tested the local water for common contaminants in the summer and fall of 2008. The results are displayed in Table 1.

Table 1				
Compound	Average Level Detected	Range of Levels Detected	MCLG	MCL
Alpha Emitters	2.6	2.6	0	5
Beta/Photon Emitters	3.9	3.9	0	50
Bromate	2.0	0-6	0	10
Chlorine	2.0	0.5-2.0	4	4
Radium	1.6	1.6	0	5
Fluoride	1.1	0.9-1.1	4	4
Sodium	9.7	9.7	0	0
Haloacetic acids	2.0	0-4	0	60
Trihalomethanes	17.0	10-29	0	80

Dental fluorosis is a health condition caused by a child receiving too much fluoride during tooth development. Flouride consumption can exceed the tolerable upper limit when someone drinks a lot of water containing fluoride in combination with other fluoride sources. Researchers have discovered that some children may be ingesting more fluoride from toothpaste alone than is recommended as a total daily fluoride ingestion. Table 2 compares average daily fluoride ingestion from toothpaste with recommended total daily intake and Table 3 lists fluoride concentrations found in common food and beverages.

Table 2		
Age	Intake from 2 Brushings	% of Recommend Intake
2	0.66 mg	110
3	0.36 mg	50
4	0.26 mg	32
5	0.44 mg	48

Table 3			
Product	# of Samples	Mean Concentration	Range of Concentrat
Baby Food	9	4.40 ppm	1.05-8.38 p
Gatorade	13	0.85 ppm	0.02-1.04
Juice	24	0.69 ppm	0.16-1.08 p
Soda	332	0.72 ppm	0.02-1.10 p
Tea	26	2.56 ppm	0.61-6.68 p
Wine	19	1.02 ppm	0.23-2.80 p

1. Based on the information provided in Table 3, an knowledge that the maximum concentration of fluoride allowed in drinking water by the EPA is 4 ppm, which common products may contain a potentially unsafe amount of fluoride?
   A. Baby food and tea.
   B. Wine.
   C. Gatorade and Juice.
   D. Tea.

2. The average level detected was lowest for compound found in Grayslake's water?
   F. Trihalomethanes.
   G. Sodium.
   H. Fluoride.
   J. Radium.

3. Based on the information presented in Table 2, children of what age are consuming more than th recommended intake of fluoride from brushing their teeth with toothpaste containing fluoride?
   A. 5
   B. 4
   C. 3
   D. 2

ACT SUCCESS
Science Skill Builder – Analyzing Data #4

4. According to the data in Table 1, there was the greatest range of levels detected for which compound?
   F. Bromate.
   G. Trihalomethanes.
   H. Sodium.
   J. Alpha Emitters.

5. Which of the following correctly lists the ages of children who consume fluoride from 2 brushings, from the greatest intake to the least?
   A. 2, 3, 4, 5.
   B. 3, 5, 4, 2.
   C. 4, 2, 5, 3.
   D. 2, 5, 3, 4.

6. The average concentration of fluoride found in Gatorade was:
   F. 0.02 ppm.
   G. 0.85 ppm.
   H. 1.04 ppm.
   J. 2.56 ppm.

7. Based on Table 1, which compounds were detected in levels below the Maximum Contaminant Level Goals set by the EPA?
   A. Chlorine and fluoride.
   B. Chlorine and radium.
   C. Fluoride and bromate.
   D. Haloacetic acids and sodium.

8. Based on the information in Table 2, the daily recommended amount of fluoride for 2 year olds is approximately:
   F. 0.34 mg
   G. 0.46 mg
   H. 0.60 mg
   J. 0.75 mg

ACT SUCCESS
Science Skill Builder – Analyzing Data #5

Directions: After reading the passage, choose the best answer to each question.

Of the nearly 400 species of shark, only about a dozen have been involved in fatal attacks on humans, and only four are responsible for a significant number of fatal, unprovoked attacks on humans worldwide: the Bull shark, the Great White shark, the Oceanic Whitetip shark, and the Tiger shark. All four species live solely in salt water except the Bull shark, which is also capable of venturing into fresh water. The following charts present trends in fatal, unprovoked shark attacks in United States waters over the last three decades.

Table 1

Unprovoked fatal attacks in US, by species			
	1980s	1990s	2000s
Bull shark	1	1	2
Great White shark	3	2	3
Tiger shark	2	8	1
species unknown	4	1	4

Table 2

Unprovoked fatal attacks in US, by state			
	1980s	1990s	2000s
California	3	2	3
Florida	4	2	3
Hawaii	3	8	2
North Carolina	0	0	1
Virginia	0	0	1

Table 3

Unprovoked fatal attacks in US by species and state, 1980s-2000s				
	Bull shark	Great White shark	Tiger shark	species unknown
California	0	8	0	0
Florida	4	0	1	4
Hawaii	0	0	10	3
North Carolina	0	0	0	1
Virginia	0	0	0	1

1. What is the highest percentage of fatal, unprovoked attacks for which a single species is responsible in a single state?
   A. 44%
   B. 67%
   C. 77%
   D. 100%

2. In which decade did every state but one record its smallest number (ties included) of fatal, unprovoked attacks?
   F. The 1980s
   G. The 1990s
   H. The 2000s
   J. None of the above

3. Which is the only shark species responsible for fatal, unprovoked attacks in more than one state during the three decades examined?
   A. Bull shark
   B. Great White shark
   C. Oceanic Whitetip shark
   D. Tiger shark

4. Which is the only state in which an unprovoked, fatal attack could possibly have occurred in a freshwater river?
   F. California
   G. Florida
   H. Hawaii
   J. North Carolina

5. Assuming that the Oceanic Whitetip shark was responsible for every fatal, unprovoked attack by an unknown species, which species was responsible for the greatest total number of fatal, unprovoked attacks?
   A. Bull shark
   B. Great White shark
   C. Oceanic Whitetip shark
   D. Tiger shark

6. List the three charted species in order of their likelihood of responsibility for the North Carolina and Virginia attacks, in *increasing* order of likeliness.
   F. Bull shark, Tiger shark, Great White shark
   G. Tiger shark, Great White shark, Bull shark
   H. Great White shark, Tiger shark, Bull shark
   J. Bull shark, Great White shark, Tiger shark

ACT SUCCESS
Science Skill Builder – Analyzing Data #5

7. Which is the only state in which a Tiger shark could not possibly have been responsible for any of the fatal, unprovoked attacks by an unknown species?
   A. Florida
   B. North Carolina
   C. Virginia
   D. The answer cannot be determined from the given information.

8. In which decade(s) was Hawaii NOT one of the two U.S. states with the highest numbers of fatal, unprovoked shark attacks?
   F. The 2000s
   G. The 1990s
   H. The 1980s
   J. Both the 1980s and the 1990s

9. What is the most logical explanation for the fact that the Oceanic Whitetip shark is not listed as responsible for any unprovoked, fatal attacks on humans in United States waters from the 1980s to the 2000s?
   A. "Oceanic Whitetip" is just another name for the Great White shark.
   B. Oceanic Whitetip sharks leave no evidence when they attack.
   C. Oceanic Whitetip sharks are not found near the United States coastline, but rather far out in the open ocean, hence their name.
   D. Oceanic Whitetip sharks are endangered, and so when they are involved in attacks, marine biologists lie to protect them.

Copyright © 2009 by Academic Tutoring Centers. All rights reserved.

ACT SUCCESS
Science Skill Builder – Analyzing Data #6

Directions: After reading the passage, choose the best answer to each question.

A *flurm* is any type of zippenhorp that has a name beginning with a vowel. An *eklingle* is any type of zippenhorp that has a name beginning with a consonant. Some guys noticed last Thursday that the gibbousness of flurms increases with rising temperature, whereas the gibbousness of eklingles decreases with rising temperature.

A machine that measures gibbousness levels by emitting zerg pulses through a cloud of superphlogisticated plotz was invented back in the day by a wizard and a monkey on roller skates. Someone with nothing better to do recently used it to compare the gibbousness of six different zippenhorps.

Table 1

Gibbousness levels at 20°C	
Argle	63.01×10^6
Libergium	59.6×10^6
Foosins	58.0×10^6
Bip	45.2×10^6
Oprizzapam	37.8×10^6
Erfel	36.3×10^6

The principle stating that the gibbousness of a zippenhorp increasing in gibbousness doubles every 20°C and the gibbousness of a zippenhorp decreasing in gibbousness is halved every 20°C is known as *Younce's Constant*.

1. Which of the zippenhorps from the table would have the lowest gibbousness at 10°C?
   A. Erfel
   B. Argle
   C. Libergium
   D. Oprizzapam

2. At which of the following approximate temperatures would Foosins become more gibbous than Argle?
   F. 23°C
   G. 36°C
   H. 17°C
   J. 4°C

3. At which of the following temperatures would the gibbousness of Libergium NOT exceed that of Bip?
   A. 22°C
   B. 45°C
   C. -3°C
   D. None of the above

4. At what approximate temperature would Bip become the least gibbous of the six zippenhorps?
   F. 11°C
   G. 22°C
   H. 44°C
   J. 88°C

5. List the three zippenhorps that are least gibbous at 20°C in order of their gibbousness at 0°C, in *decreasing* order of gibbousness.
   A. Oprizzapam, Erfel, Bip
   B. Erfel, Oprizzapam, Bip
   C. Bip, Oprizzapam, Erfel
   D. Bip, Erfel, Oprizzapam

6. If, instead of emitting zerg pulses through a cloud of superphlogisticated plotz, the machine emitted zerg pulses through a cloud of *partially* phlogisticated plotz, how would the accuracy of the measurements be affected?
   F. The indicated gibbousness of the flurms would remain accurate, but the indicated gibbousness of the eklingles would be inaccurate.
   G. The indicated gibbousness of the eklingles would remain accurate, but the indicated gibbousness of the flurms would be inaccurate.
   H. Both the indicated gibbousness of the flurms and the indicated gibbousness of the eklingles would be inaccurate.
   J. The information provided is insufficient to determine the effect on the accuracy of the measurements.

ACT SUCCESS
Science Skill Builder – Opposing Viewpoints #1

Directions: After reading the passage, choose the best answer to each question.

Students studying circular motion were given the following information:

- An object moving in a circle experiences a *centripetal force*; that is, there must be some physical force pushing or pulling the object towards the center of the circle.

- The centripetal force for uniform circular motion alters the direction of the object without altering its speed.

- For an unbalanced force to change the speed of the object, there would have to be a component of force in the direction of (or the opposite direction of) the motion of the object.

- The *net force* (F_{net}) acting upon an object moving in circular motion is directed inwards. The net force is related to the acceleration of the object and can be calculated by multiplying the object's mass (m) by its acceleration (a). *Acceleration* is found by dividing the object's speed by the radius of the circle.

The students' teacher described the following experiment, and then asked the students to explain the results:

Suppose a car is driving on a circular racetrack. A student knows the mass of the car, and calculates the acceleration of the vehicle at two points along the track. The net force acting upon the car at the first point was greater than the net force acting upon the car at the second point.

Student 1

The car slowed down between the two points, thus lowering the car's acceleration and decreasing the net force acting upon the car.

Student 2

Although the car's speed remained constant, the path that the car took around the track was not consistent. Between the two points, the car veered outward, moving closer to the outside of the track. This increased the radius of the circle, and therefore lowered the net force acting upon the car.

Student 3

Between the two points, a piece of the car fell off, thus decreasing the net force.

1. The three explanations for the change in net force acting upon the car are similar to each other in that all explanations:
   A. contradict the explanation of centripetal force.
   B. were based on factors outside of the car's control.
   C. were based on the car changing in some way.
   D. took into account student error.

2. Based on the explanations of the 3 students, what did they all assume about what happened between the two points?
   F. That the car's acceleration decreased.
   G. That only one factor changed between the two calculations.
   H. That the car's speed decreased.
   J. That the car's mass remained constant.

3. Which of the following graphs best illustrates Student 2's description of the net force acting upon the car between the two calculations?

   A.

   B.

   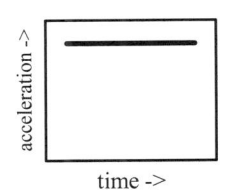

   C.

   D.

   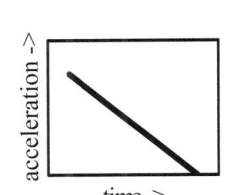
   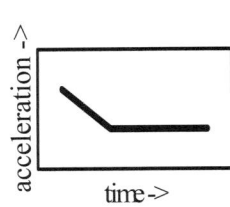

4. Based on Student 1's explanation, the car's acceleration was greatest at which of the following points?
   F. Before the first calculation.
   G. After the first calculation.
   H. Sometime between the first and second calculations.
   J. After the second calculation.

Copyright © 2009 by Academic Educational Resources. All rights reserved.

ACT SUCCESS
Science Skill Builder – Opposing Viewpoints #1

5. According to the passage, the net force acting upon the car can be determined by what operation?
   A. Multiplying the car's speed by the radius of the circle.
   B. Dividing the car's mass by its acceleration.
   C. Dividing the car's acceleration by its mass.
   D. Multiplying the car's mass by its acceleration.

6. If there was a second vehicle on the racetrack with the car, and this new vehicle pushed the car from behind between the two calculation points, could Student 1's explanation still make sense?
   F. Yes; if the second vehicle was going slower than the car originally was and the car slowed down during this time.
   G. Yes, because the vehicle would have caused the car to slow down.
   H. No; if the vehicle pushed the car it would always increase the speed of the car.
   J. No, because in order for the vehicle to catch up with the car it would have had to slow down.

7. According to the passage, centripetal force:
   A. Pushes or pulls an object toward the perimeter of a circle.
   B. Pushes and pulls an object toward the perimeter of a circle.
   C. Pushes or pulls an object toward the center of a circle.
   D. Pushes and pulls an object toward the center of a circle.

ACT SUCCESS
Science Skill Builder – Opposing Viewpoints #2

Directions: After reading the passage, choose the best answer to each question.

Students studying electric circuits were given the following information:

According to Ohm's Law, the *electric potential* difference between two points on a circuit (ΔV) is equivalent to the product of the current between those two points (I) and the total resistance of all electrical devices present between those two points (R). The equation can be written:

$$\Delta V = I * R$$

When there are two or more electrical devices present in a circuit with an energy source, they can be connected in *series* or in *parallel*. A series circuit is one that has a single path for current flow through all of its elements. A parallel circuit is one that requires more than one path for current flow in order to reach all of the circuit elements.

For series circuits, as more resistors are added, the overall current within the circuit decreases. In order for the devices in a series circuit to work, each device must work. For parallel circuits, as the number of resistors increases, the overall current also increases. Devices in a parallel circuit work independently of one other.

The students' teacher then described the following experiment:

A student created a circuit consisting of a battery and two resistors (light bulbs). The student used an ammeter to measure the current between the light bulbs, and recorded it as 8 amps. Then the student added another light bulb to the circuit. This time when the student measured the current between two of the bulbs the ammeter showed 6 amps.

Given no other information, 2 students were asked to explain the results of the experiment, and to predict how the current would be affected if one of the light bulbs burned out.

Student 1

The light bulbs were connected in a series circuit, so that as the number of light bulbs increased, the current decreased. If one of the light bulbs burned out, the circuit would no longer work and the current flowing through the circuit would be zero.

Student 2

The light bulbs were connected in a parallel circuit, so that as the number of light bulbs increased, the current decreased. If one of the light bulbs burned out, it would not affect the current.

1. Assume that Student 1's explanation is correct. Which the following is true about electric potential with tw versus three light bulbs?
   A. The electric potential is greater with two light bulbs.
   B. The electric potential is greater with three light bulbs
   C. The electric potential is the same with two or thr light bulbs.
   D. It is impossible to determine the effect of the numb of light bulbs on electric potential with the informati provided.

2. Which of the following graphs shows the relationsh between resistors and current in parallel circuits?

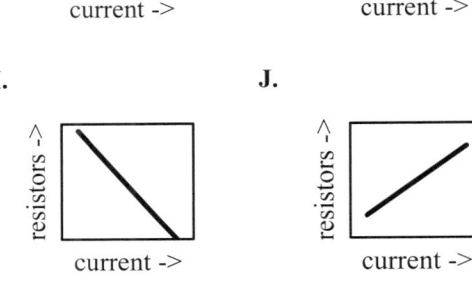

3. Did both students provide explanations that could correct?
   A. Yes; if the bulbs were connected in series, Studen would be correct, and if the bulbs were connected parallel, Student 2 would be correct.
   B. Yes; both of their explanations for the results we correct, but their predictions about the effect of a burned out light bulb were incorrect.
   C. No; Student 2's claim that an additional light bu connected in parallel would decrease the current incorrect.
   D. No; Student 1's claim that an additional light bu connected in series would decrease the current is incorrect.

4. The students' explanations for the results of experiment are similar in that they both:
   F. correctly explain the results.
   G. assume that the same battery was used during bo measurements.
   H. think that the light bulbs were connected in a ser circuit.
   J. incorrectly predict the influence of a burned out li bulb.

ACT SUCCESS
Science Skill Builder – Opposing Viewpoints #2

5. Based on the information provided and Student 1's response, which of the following would be a reasonable measurement of current if a fourth light bulb were added to the circuit?
   A. 2 amps
   B. 4 amps
   C. 6 amps
   D. 12 amps

6. According to Ohm's Law, which of the following is true about the effect of resistance and current on electric potential?
   F. As resistance increases and current decreases, electric potential increases.
   G. As resistance decreases and current increases, electric potential increases.
   H. As both resistance and current decrease, electric potential increases.
   J. As resistance and/or current increase, electric potential increases.

7. Student 1's explanation differs from Student 2's explanation because Student 1 suggests:
   A. A parallel circuit was used to connect the light bulbs.
   B. A duplex capacitor was used to connect the circuits.
   C. An Iridium transmogrifier was used to splice the circuits.
   D. A series circuit was used to connect the light bulbs.

ACT SUCCESS
Science Skill Builder – Opposing Viewpoints #3

Directions: After reading the passage, choose the best answer to each question.

Three scientists discuss various possible explanations of what causes some human beings to be considered more beautiful than others.

Scientist 1

A human face is considered attractive because it corresponds with a mathematical average of various facial features across a given gene pool. Humans have evolved to be "cognitive averagers," wary of any physical extreme because it might signal a biological disadvantage, and gravitating towards physiological "happy mediums." When photographs of many randomly selected human faces are scanned into a computer and averaged together, the resulting composite face is always judged to be extremely attractive. This phenomenon is known as *koinophilia*.

Scientist 2

The most attractive face is that which indicates the highest levels of certain hormones. The facial attributes considered most attractive in human females—full lips, wide eyes with long eyelashes, and high cheekbones—all correspond with changes in facial structure caused by heightened production of estrogen during adolescence. The higher the estrogen levels, the more extreme the effect. If the koinophilia hypothesis were correct, then people would be attracted to average hormone levels rather than high ones. But artistic representations of the most beautiful women imaginable—the Barbie doll, for example—always involve features more extreme than are found in reality, and these features are always exaggerations of the physical traits caused by an abundance of estrogen. This is called the *hyperfemininity hypothesis*.

Scientist 3

Concepts of human beauty are not inborn at all, but rather are slowly learned from society over the course of development. Humans have evolved to take cues from civilization about what attributes are socially prized, and we receive these cues from movie stars, models, and advertising. Since these industries profit when high numbers of people are dissatisfied with their appearance, the idealized traits tend to be those possessed only by a tiny minority of the population. If either of the first two hypotheses were correct, it would be impossible for the ideal body shape to have changed so drastically over the last 50 years, or for unnatural modifications like tattoos and piercings to be considered attractive. This explanation is known as *social constructionism*.

1. If an experimenter discovered that each individually tested member of a group of six-month-old babies smiled at and reached out for a picture of a traditionally attractive face over a picture of a less attractive face, this would most strongly *weaken* the viewpoint of:
   A. Scientist 1
   B. Scientist 2
   C. Scientist 3
   D. Scientists 1 and 2

2. If an experimenter discovered that primates (the order of mammals that includes humans) are always attracted to the individuals of their species that appear to be the most fertile (physically able to conceive offspring), this would most greatly *strengthen* the viewpoint of:
   F. Scientist 1
   G. Scientist 2
   H. Scientist 3
   J. Scientists 2 and 3

3. Which two scientists would agree that the physical traits considered most beautiful in humans tend to be "extreme?"
   A. Scientists 1 and 2
   B. Scientists 2 and 3
   C. Scientists 1 and 3
   D. No two scientists would agree about this.

4. If it were found that the adults found most attractive by other adults possessed facial features that were *fuller* than, but *geometrically similar* to, the facial features of the children found most attractive by other children, this discovery would be likely to *resolve* the disagreement between:
   F. Scientists 1 and 2
   G. Scientists 1 and 3
   H. Scientists 2 and 3
   J. All three scientists

5. If it were found that a randomly selected group of fashion models all experienced abnormally high levels of estrogen production during adolescence, this discovery would be likely to *resolve* the disagreement between:
   A. Scientists 1 and 2
   B. Scientists 1 and 3
   C. Scientists 2 and 3
   D. All three scientists

ACT SUCCESS
Science Skill Builder – Opposing Viewpoints #3

6. The suggestion that the ideas of Scientist 3 are not actually in opposition to the ideas of Scientists 1 and 2 is best supported by the fact that:
   F. Scientists 1 and 2 are talking about children, whereas Scientist 3 is talking about adults.
   G. Scientist 3 is only talking about what is considered attractive in women, whereas Scientists 1 and 2 discuss concepts of attractiveness in both women and men.
   H. Scientists 1 and 2 are discussing standards of attractiveness all over the world, whereas Scientist 3 discusses only the United States.
   J. Scientist 3 only uses examples about which body types and/or adornments are considered attractive, whereas Scientists 1 and 2 are concerned exclusively with the attractiveness of facial features.

7. Within which Scientist's hypothesis would a mathematical majority of people be considered exceptionally attractive?
   A. Scientist 1
   B. Scientist 2
   C. Scientist 3
   D. None of the scientists

Science Practice Passages

ACT SUCCESS
Science Practice Passage #1

Directions: After reading the passage, choose the best answer to each question.
Use a watch to time yourself, taking no longer than 5 – 6 minutes per passage.

A series of experiments were preformed to study the environmental factors affecting the growth and maturity rate of American Bullfrog (*Rana catesbeiana*) tadpoles. Maturity refers to the tadpoles' *metamorphosis* into mature bullfrogs. In all of these experiments, maturity is considered complete when a tadpole's tail is absorbed into its body.

Experiment 1

Five groups of 25 tadpoles, all 7 cm in length, were placed in separate tanks numbered 1 through 5. Each tank contained water of a different temperature. All of the groups were fed identical diets. The average maturation period and tadpole size at maturity for each group are shown in Table 1.

Table 1			
Tank No.	Water Temp. (°C)	Maturation Period (months)	Size at Maturity (cm)
1	15	36	12.8
2	20	24	14.3
3	25	20	14.9
4	30	16	16.3
5	35	30	11.1

Experiment 2

The scientists next sought to determine how food availability affects tadpole growth and maturity. Experiment 1 was repeated with 5 new groups of *Rana catesbeiana* tadpoles. This time, though, water temperature was held constant (at 25°C) in all of the tanks and the number of daily feedings given to the tadpoles was instead varied by tank (a "daily feeding" was defined as 5g of food). The average maturation period and tadpole size at maturity for each group are displayed in Table 2.

Table 2			
Tank No.	No. Daily Feedings	Maturation Period (months)	Size at Maturity (cm)
1	.25	40	9.5
2	.50	32	12.0
3	1	20	14.9
4	2	18	17.1
5	3	12	19.7

1. Which of the following conclusions can be drawn based on the results of Experiment 1?
   A. The warmer the water, the larger the tadpoles will at maturity.
   B. Generally speaking, the faster a tadpole reach metamorphosis, the smaller it will be at maturity.
   C. Generally speaking, the longer it takes a tadpole reach metamorphosis, the smaller it will be maturity.
   D. The average maturation period decreases as wa temperature increases.

2. Tadpoles given .75 daily feedings under the sa conditions as in Experiment 2 would probably ha maturation periods closest to:
   F. 16 months
   G. 19 months
   H. 26 months
   J. 31 months

3. According to the experimental results, under which the following sets of conditions would a bullfrog tadp undergo its metamorphosis the fastest?
   A. 20°C water and .50 daily feedings
   B. 20°C water and 2 daily feedings
   C. 30°C water and .50 daily feedings
   D. 30°C water and 2 daily feedings

4. Which variable remained constant throughout both the experiments?
   F. The number of tadpole groups
   G. Water temperature
   H. Maturation period
   J. Tadpole growth

ACT SUCCESS
Science Practice Passage #1

5. As a continuation of the two experiments listed, it would be most appropriate to next investigate:
   A. which species prey on *Rana catesbeiana* tadpoles.
   B. how tadpole population density affects the tadpoles' growth and maturity rate.
   C. how tadpole size at maturity affects *Rana aastesbeiana* life expectancy.
   D. how the time of day affects the quantity of food that the tadpoles consume.

6. Suppose a scientist claims that water temperature is directly releated to *Rana catesbeiana* tadpole growth. Do the results of these two experiments support his claim?
   F. Yes; according to Experiment 1, as water temperature increases, tadpole size at maturity increases.
   G. Yes; warmer water leads to shorter maturity periods, which in turn are correlated with larger average tadpole size at maturity.
   H. No; as water temperature increases, average tadpole size at maturity decreases.
   J. No; as water temperature increases, tadpole size first increases, then decreases.

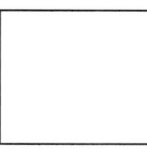

5 – 6

ACT SUCCESS
Science Practice Passage #2

**Directions: After reading the passage, choose the best answer to each question.
Use a watch to time yourself, taking no longer than 5 – 6 minutes per passage.**

Although the effective acceleration due to gravity at the earth's surface is often treated as a constant ($g = 9.80$ m/sec^2), its actual value varies from place to place because of several factors. First, a body on the surface of any rotating spheroid experiences an effective force perpendicular to the rotational axis and proportional to the speed of rotation. This *centrifugal force*, which counteracts gravity, varies with latitude, increasing from zero at the poles to a maximum at the equator. In addition, because the earth "bulges" at the equator, a body at equatorial sea level is farther from the center of the earth than is a body at polar sea level. Figure 1 shows the variation of mean values of g at sea level resulting from both effects; the contribution from "bulging" is about half that from rotation.

Figure 1

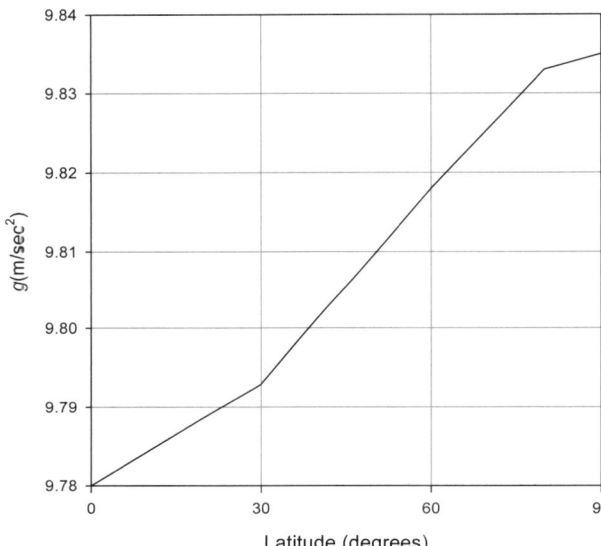

0° latitude = equator
90° latitude = pole

Measurements of g also vary depending on local rock density and altitude. Table 1 shows the effect of altitude on g at various points above sea level.

Table 1	
Change in Altitude (km)	g (m/sec^2)
1	-0.0031
5	-0.0154
10	-0.0309
25	-0.0772
30	-0.1543

1. If the earth's density was uniform, at approximately wl latitude would calculations using an estimated sea leve value of $g = 9.80$ m/sec^2 produce the least error?
   A. 0°
   B. 20°
   C. 40°
   D. 80°

2. Which of the following is true about the effect altitu has on g?
   F. Altitude has no effect on g.
   G. As the altitude decreases, g decreases.
   H. As the altitude increases, g increases.
   J. As the altitude decreases, g increases.

3. Given the information in the passage, which of following figures most closely approximates value of g at a point 10 km high along the equator?
   A. 9.75 m/sec^2
   B. 9.80 m/sec^2
   C. 9.81 m/sec^2
   D. 9.87 m/sec^2

4. Given the information provided in the passage, increase in the speed of the earth's rotation wo most likely cause which of the following results sea level?
   I. An increase in g only along the equator.
   II. A decrease in g at all non-polar points.
   III. No change in g at the poles.
   IV. An increase in g at the poles.

   F. II only
   G. I and III only
   H. II and III only
   J. II and IV only

5. Suppose that the earth stopped rotating but s "bulged". Based on information from the passa the value of g at sea level at the equator would be:
   A. exactly 9.80 m/sec^2
   B. greater than 9.78 m/sec^2
   C. exactly 9.78 m/sec^2
   D. less than 9.78 m/sec^2

Copyright © 2009 by Academic Educational Resources. All rights reserved.

6. According to the information in Figure 1, the value of g:
   F. changes by a greater average amount per degree latitude between 30° and 60° than it does near the equator or poles.
   G. changes by a greater average amount per degree latitude near the equator and the poles than it does between 30° and 60°.
   H. increases by an average of 5.8 m/sec² per degree latitude from the equator to the poles.
   J. decreases by an average of 3.1 × 10⁻³ m/sec² per degree latitude from the equator to the poles.

5 – 6

ACT SUCCESS
Science Practice Passage #3

**Directions: After reading the passage, choose the best answer to each question.
Use a watch to time yourself, taking no longer than 5 – 6 minutes per passage.**

There is a broad consensus among scientists that the Moon formed some 4.45 billion years ago, roughly 50 million years after the origin of the Solar System (including the Earth). However, there is much debate as to exactly how the Moon came into existence. Below, two scientists discuss possible explanations of the Moon's origin.

Scientist 1

The relative abundance of oxygen isotopes on the Moon is identical to the levels found on Earth. This indicates that the Moon and Earth formed at the same distance from the Sun. At the same time, the Moon's low density demonstrates that, unlike the Earth, the Moon lacks a sizeable iron core. These facts, when examined alongside the 50 million year age-gap between the two solar bodies, suggest that the Moon was once part of the Earth. In its early years, the Earth spun significantly faster than it does today. The *centrifugal force* – that is, the outward-acting force that pulls away from the axis of rotation of a spinning object – created by the rapidly-spinning Earth caused a large chunk of rock to break away from the Earth's crust. This breakage left behind a colossal basin. As the Earth evolved, this newly-formed basin flooded; it is known today as the Pacific Ocean. Lunar exploration missions have conclusively determined that the Moon's geological and chemical composition closely resembles that of the Earth's mantle, lending significant weight to the above explanation.

Scientist 2

There is no doubt that the Moon is composed at least in part of rock that originated on the mantle of the Earth. Unlike the Earth's outer layers, though, Moon rocks contain few volatile substances (like water). This means that the Moon's surface must have undergone more intense "baking," or exposure to tremendous heat, than the Earth's surface. Centrifugal force could not possibly have generated enough heat to account for the Moon's extra baking. Rather, it is clear that a giant body (a small planet roughly the size of Mars) hit the Earth, releasing an enormous amount of heat energy. This impact ejected large volumes of heated rock from the outer layers of both objects. Eventually, gravitational forces pulled together all of the ejected debris orbiting the Earth in the aftermath of the impact, forming the Earth's Moon. The giant impact theory thus accounts not only for the composition similarities between the Earth and the Moon, but also for the extra "baking" of the lunar surface.

1. Scientists 1 and 2 *disagree* on which of the following points?
   A. At least some moon rocks originated on the Earth's mantle.
   B. Oxygen isotopes are found in similar proportions on the Earth and the Moon.
   C. The Earth's rotation speed played a role in the formation of the Moon.
   D. The Moon formed 50 million years after the Earth.

2. Which of the following pieces of evidence would support Scientist 1's theory?
   F. The discovery that the Pacific Ocean basin is as old as the Earth itself.
   G. The discovery that the Earth in its infancy rotated at an even faster rate than was previously imagined.
   H. Experimental data concluding that centrifugal forces create less energy than was previously assumed.
   J. The discovery that the Moon actually materialized roughly 250 million years after the formation of the Solar System.

3. Scientist 2 dismisses which of the following aspects of Scientist 1's explanation?
   A. The Moon's low density.
   B. Centrifugal force leading directly to the formation of the Moon.
   C. The Moon's geological similarity to the Earth's mantle.
   D. The baking of the Moon's surface.

4. According to Scientist 1, the Pacific Ocean basin formed approximately how many years after the Earth?
   F. 50 million years
   G. 250 million years
   H. 4.45 billion years
   J. 50 billion years

5. To best refute Scientist 2's explanation, Scientist 1 could do which of the following?
   A. Find evidence of the Moon's iron core.
   B. Compare Moon rocks to the rocks found in the Pacific Ocean basin.
   C. Discover fossil evidence verifying that Earth's rotation speed has slowed considerably.
   D. Find evidence of water on the surface of the Moon.

ACT SUCCESS
Science Practice Passage #3

6. Scientist 2's explanation would be strengthened by evidence showing that:
   F. giant impacts occur about once every billion years.
   G. giant impacts become more prevalent as the Earth ages.
   H. giant impacts release most of their energy as light energy.
   J. giant impacts are common events in the late stages of planetary and solar system development.

7. Which of the following assumptions is implicit in Scientist 1's argument?
   A. The Moon's density is greater than the Sun's density.
   B. The rocks that constitute the lunar surface were not "baked" until after the formation of the Moon.
   C. The Earth's centrifugal force was capable of exceeding the force of the Earth's gravitational pull.
   D. The Moon's surface contains more volatile substances than the Earth's surface.

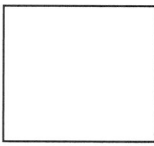

5 – 6

Additional Notes

Chapter 5
Writing Strategies and Review

WRITING

The ACT Writing section will be administered about five minutes after the end of the Science section. During the 30-minute ACT Writing, you will be asked to plan and write a persuasive essay in response to a prompt. Although there is no length requirement, higher scoring essays tend to be at least 1-1/2 pages.

THE PROMPT/ESSAY ESSENTIALS

Writing prompts from past tests have typically addressed an aspect of the high school experience.

The ACT writing prompt will look very much like this:

> Some high schools in the United States have considered dropping music and art courses. Proponents of this change believe that budget cuts demand that time, money, and resources should be directed to "core" subjects like reading and math. Others insist that music and art courses are invaluable because they instill in students a lifelong appreciation for the arts. In your opinion, should music and art courses be cut from high school programs?
>
> **In your essay, take a position on this question. You may write about either one of the two points of view given, or you may present a different point of view on this question. Use specific reasons and examples to support your position.**

The second, bold paragraph is of interest for several reasons:

- It is the universal ACT writing prompt. No matter what scenario you are asked to consider, this information will follow.

- It asks that you **TAKE A POSITION**. All too often, students think they can get by with a survey of multiple positions, or a position-less essay that omits any semblance of a thesis. No matter how completely indifferent you feel toward the issue or how reluctant you feel about taking a stand one way or another, the single most important aspect of the writing section is crafting a clear thesis statement.

- It also presents three options: side with one of the two views or take your own position. Unless you are suddenly struck by a creative alternative to the two extremes, stick with one of the two already outlined for you. This choice leaves less room for muddy thinking.

- It also calls for **SPECIFIC REASONS AND EXAMPLES**. Remember that even if your thoughts seem obvious, you need to prove them. General statements do not provide proof. For example, if you are arguing for keeping funding for the arts (based on the above prompt), you might make the statement that classes in the arts provide a much needed break in an academic day. While you would assume that any grader would know exactly what you mean, you still need to provide reasons why arts classes provide a much needed break.

ACT SUCCESS
Writing Skill Builder – The Thesis Statement

Directions: Read each prompt and take a position on the issue. Write a strong, concise thesis statement explaining your position.

1. The mayor in your city is has proposed a 9:00 pm weekday curfew for children under the age of 16. He argues that children should not be on the streets at night both to protect children from potential harm and to encourage better study habits. Opponents of the curfew ordinance argue that a legal curfew violates the rights of the children and parents alike, and that decisions regarding curfews should be made by parents alone. What is your opinion?

2. In many areas of the country, students in both private and public schools are required to wear school uniforms. The school board in your town is thinking about establishing a school uniform policy in your district that would specify exactly what can and cannot be worn by students during the school day. Should the school board institute a uniform policy?

3. Many high schools now require that students complete a given number of hours of community service in order to graduate. These schools reason that community service benefits the students as well as the community and teaches students the value of charity. Opponents of community service as a graduation requirement argue that charity is an individual matter and has no bearing on one's high school education. What do you think?

4. Your principal has decided to institute a new policy requiring every student at your high school to schedule a lunch period. He believes that a mandatory lunch break is essential in order for students to stay healthy both physically and mentally. However, many parents and teachers disagree with the principal, arguing that a mandatory lunch period will deny students the opportunity to take extra classes and potentially harm their college admissions chances. What is your opinion?

Copyright © 2009 by Academic Educational Resources. All rights reserved.

OVERALL APPROACH: TRY THE "BOW" STRATEGY

Brainstorm

Think about the question. Ask yourself about what will answer it best. Are there facts, emotions, descriptions, examples, statistics or expressions that can help you explain your ideas? Write down keywords that remind you of those ideas. This process should be completed in about one to two minutes. The target is to create a thesis.

Organize

Take the ideas in the thesis and put them in an order that is effective. Consider strength of support when ordering body paragraphs. You may want to order the body from strongest to weakest or from weakest to strongest. It depends on the impact you want to have on the reader. This process should be accomplished in approximately two to three minutes. The target is to organize thoughts into a cohesive presentation in outline form using keywords and short phrases.

Write

Write the paper. Put the ideas organized in keyword outline form onto paper in full sentences. Remember, sentences express complete thoughts. Paragraphs are composed of complete thoughts to express main ideas. Paragraphs begin with clear topic sentences, which are the building blocks of a strong thesis. The outline helps with what you want to say; punctuation and grammar help with how to say it. There should be about fifteen minutes to write the paper legibly. The target is for the reader to discern the cohesive logical expression of thought.

PLAN AHEAD: DEVELOP A TEMPLATE

For more effective time management during the test, develop a template for your essay by planning many of its components beforehand. If these decisions about structure are made in advance, you will have more time to develop your examples. The following is an example of a possible template:

First: Make a 2 column table (one column for each side) and fill in anything that you can think of that would support either side. Whichever column has more items in it after 2-3 minutes is the side you take.

Second: Write an introduction consisting of a few sentences and ending with a statement of your side. If introductions are difficult for you, use some of the opposing ideas that you listed In other words, briefly give the opposite view first; just be sure to discuss the opposite view again in your supporting paragraphs (see **below)

Third: Paragraph 1: Take the first item from your chart and support it with SPECIFIC REASONS AND EXAMPLES.

Paragraph 2: Take the first item from your chart and support it with SPECIFIC REASONS AND EXAMPLES.

**in order to get a high score, you must also incorporate the counterargument (something about the other side) in one of these paragraphs.

Fourth: Write a conclusion consisting of a few sentences that summarize your side. Do not bring up new information in the conclusion!

Another approach to the THIRD step:

Paragraph 1: Take a few of the items from your chart that support your side and support them with SPECIFIC REASONS AND EXAMPLES.

Paragraph 2: State one thing about the other side (that's your counterargument!). You can even get this from the prompt. Then write about a compromise that still supports your side. For example: If you are arguing for keeping the arts in schools, you could write "It is true that school budgets are tight, and schools need to be sure that they have enough funds to support the core curriculum, but eliminating the arts entirely is not the solution. Instead, a solution might be for schools to cut back on the variety or number of classes in the arts, but still have students take one course per semester. Additionally, schools could do fundraising events for arts classes or look for outside arts organizations that are willing to provide arts programs for the school. For example, a local artist could be asked to volunteer to spend the day speaking with students or a local dance troop could perform during an all school assembly."

ACT SUCCESS
Writing Skill Builder – Essay Planning & Organizing

Below you will find one of the prompts already introduced in the "Thesis Statement" skill builder. You should have already written a thesis statement pertaining to the topic. Now we will practice expanding a thesis statement into a useful, well-organized outline.

Directions: Expand your already composed thesis statement into a full introductory paragraph. Then outline the body of your essay by listing your three main points and supporting details in the space provided below.

> Many high schools now require that students complete a given number of hours of community service in order to graduate. These schools reason that community service benefits the students as well as the community, and teaches students the value of charity. Opponents of community service as a graduation requirement argue that charity is an individual matter, and has no bearing on one's high school education. What do you think?

USE THIS SPACE TO BRAINSTORM AND PLAN YOUR OUTLINE

ACT SUCCESS
Writing Skill Builder – Essay Planning & Organizing

Introduction:

_____
_____
_____
_____
_____
_____

I. _____

      A) _____

      B) _____

II. _____

      A) _____

      B) _____

III. _____

      A) _____

      B) _____

SCORING

Two readers will skim your essay and each person will then assign it a score from 1 to 6. If, by chance, these two scorers disagree by more than 1 point, a third reader will step in and resolve the discrepancy. Performance on the essay will not affect the English, Math, Reading, Science or composite scores. You will receive two additional scores on your score sheet—a combined English/Writing score (1-36) and a Writing test subscore (1-12). Again, neither of these scores affect your composite score in any way!

EXERCISES TO IMPROVE ESSAY WRITING SKILLS

1.) To improve "flow" from one paragraph to another, practice writing only the thesis and topic sentences for any of the prompts listed above. Give yourself five to ten minutes.

2.) To add variety to sentences, try writing a paragraph or an entire essay beginning sentences with any word but the conventional "The."

3.) To add life to a stagnant essay, change the majority of linking verbs to active verbs in a paragraph or essay draft.

4.) To work on the development of your body paragraphs, practice writing a single body paragraph with a strong topic sentence, a specific example (hypothetical examples work well when you are stuck) and references back to the thesis.

5.) To work on beginning and ending well, practice writing only introductory and concluding paragraphs.

Chapter 6
Complete Practice Tests

Practice Test #1

ENGLISH TEST

45 Minutes – 75 Questions

DIRECTIONS: In the five passages that follow, certain words and phrases are underlined and numbered. In the right-hand column, you will find alternatives for each underlined part. In most cases, you are to choose the one that best expresses the idea, makes the statement appropriate for standard written English, or is worded most consistently with the style and tone of the passage as a whole. If you think the original version is best, choose "NO CHANGE." In some cases, you will find in the right-hand column a question about the underlined part. You are to choose the best answer to the question.

You will also find questions about a section of the passage, or about the passage as a whole. These questions do not refer to an underlined portion of the passage, but rather are identified by a number or numbers in a box.

For each question, choose the alternative you consider best and fill in the corresponding oval on your answer document. Read each passage through once before you begin to answer the questions that accompany it. For many of the questions, you must read several sentences beyond the question to determine the answer. Be sure that you have read far enough ahead each time you choose an alternative.

Passage I

Cooking with Julia Child

For nearly forty years, Julia Child, the eccentric "French Chef," shared her culinary expertise with viewers of her various Public Television series and readers of her numerous cookbooks. In her unique, trilling voice, she encouraged Americans to occasionally disregard anything that might interfere with producing a wonderful meal, including waistlines, schedules, and budgets. As a cooking expert, author, and television personality, Julia Child taught us not to be afraid of food or of cooking. [2]

1.
   A. NO CHANGE
   B. Child; the
   C. Child the
   D. Child. The

2. At this point in the paragraph, the writer is considering the addition of the following sentence

   She once told an interviewer that the only food she disliked was "Food that is badly cooked."

   Would this sentence be an appropriate addition to paragraph, and why?
   F. Yes, because it supplies the crucial fact that Child did not like all food.
   G. Yes, because it adds humor and interest to the essay.
   H. No, because it interrupts the focus of introductory paragraph.
   J. No, because it contradicts information offered elsewhere in the essay.

Cooking wasn't always Julia's passion. On the other hand, she graduated from Smith College in 1934 with a degree in history; and only enough kitchen savvy to boil water. Toying with the idea of becoming a novelist or a basketball player, the CIA turned out to be the graduate's unlikely choice. During this time, while the world was in the midst of its second world war, Julia met and had married Paul Child. After the war, the two settled in Paris. Her love of French food led her to the Cordon Bleu, a premier cooking school.

In 1951, Child teamed up with two French friends, and the three founded a cooking school of their own and ten years later, the trio published *Mastering the Art of French Cooking*, one of many cookbooks Julia would publish. [9]

[1]Julias humor, enthusiasm, and strong opinions kept the audience coming back for years to hear her wish them

3. A. NO CHANGE
   B. Finally,
   C. In fact,
   D. For this reason,

4. F. NO CHANGE
   G. history and
   H. history. And
   J. history and,

5. A. NO CHANGE
   B. the unlikely choice of the graduate was the CIA.
   C. the graduate made the unlikely choice of working for the CIA.
   D. the CIA was the unlikely choice the graduate made.

6. F. NO CHANGE
   G. married
   H. was married to
   J. became married with

7. Which of the following alternatives to the underlined portion would be LEAST acceptable in terms of the context of the sentence?
   A. top ranked
   B. leading
   C. first
   D. well known

8. F. NO CHANGE
   G. own, ten
   H. own, but ten
   J. own. Ten

9. Which of the following sentences, if added here, would most effectively conclude this paragraph and introduce the topic of the next?
   A. Shortly after publishing this best-selling cookbook, the Childs moved to Massachussetts, where Julia would begin her long-running career as a televised chef.
   B. This volume, published when Child was 49, remains in print and is still considered to be a masterpiece.
   C. Julia's last published cookbook was another collaborative effort, entitled *Julia and Jacques Cooking at Home*.
   D. Simone Beck and Louisette Bertholle also founded the cooking school L'Ecole des Trois Gourmandes with Child.

10. F. NO CHANGE
    G. Julia's,
    H. Julias'
    J. Julia's

TEST 1

GO ON TO THE NEXT PAGE.

"bon appetit" at the conclusion of each show blithely.
                                                    ―――――
                                                      11
[2]They laughed with her when she fumbled a recipe, but she

accepted [12] these mistakes as a natural part of the cooking

process. [3]Until her death in 2004, at the age of 92, Julia

Child served up beautifully imagined French cuisine for an

adoring public. [4]And in the same way, her frequent
                     ―――――――――――
                          13
fumbles provided ample material for comic parody, Child

remained unflappable and completely focused on her art.

[5]Even as Americans became more and more health

conscious, they allowed themselves to splurge with Child's

encouragement. [14]

11. The best placement for the underlined portion would b[e]
    A. where it is now.
    B. after the word *years*.
    C. after the word *her*.
    D. after the word *them*.

12. At this point, the writer is considering adding [the] following clause (adding a comma after accepted):

    and encouraged her audience to accept,

    Should the writer make this addition here?
    F. Yes, because it further illustrates Child's connect[ion] to her audience.
    G. Yes, because it helps the reader better understa[nd] why Child thought mistakes were okay to make.
    H. No, because the passage is about Child and not [her] audience.
    J. No, because it does not relate to the main idea.

13. A. NO CHANGE
    B. while
    C. for instance,
    D. moreover,

14. Which of the following sequences of sentences ma[kes] this paragraph most logical?
    F. NO CHANGE
    G. 1, 3, 4, 2, 5
    H. 2, 1, 3, 5, 4
    J. 1, 5, 2, 4, 3

Question 15 asks about the preceding passage as a whole.

15. Suppose the author intended to write an essay that illustrates how popular chefs and cooking shows have impacted America's culinary choices. Would this essay successfully fulfill that goal?
    A. Yes, because the essay describes how Chi[ld's] cooking show influenced audience members to [try] French cuisine.
    B. Yes, because the author suggests that Julia Cl[ild] was the first of many popular chefs to insp[ire] Americans not to be afraid of food.
    C. No, because the focus of the essay is limited to [one] chef's character and popularity.
    D. No, because the essay states that Americans m[ake] culinary choices based more on their he[alth] concerns than on what they see on T.V.

TEST 1

GO ON TO THE NEXT PAGE

Passage II

Solicitude

I've rejected traditional roles for myself, but I allowed her to wait on me. In fact, it's one of the easiest and most natural things I have done. She bustled around that kitchen as women have done for centuries, without complaint or question, preparing every meal for her seven children and, later, for their children. Perhaps she have longed for a different kind of life; perhaps too much responsibility and a small-town husband kept her more rooted than she would have liked. [19]

As a young girl, and later a woman, in that family, I would help with the preparation and clean up, but I would serve and fetch rarely as she did. Sometimes we would half-heartedly tell her to sit down and let us wait on her. More often, for instance, we would depend on her

16. F. NO CHANGE
    G. its
    H. its'
    J. it was

17. A. NO CHANGE
    B. centuries; without
    C. centuries. Without
    D. centuries: without

18. F. NO CHANGE
    G. longed
    H. would long
    J. is longing

19. At this point, the writer is considering adding the following sentence to the end of this paragraph:

    I knew she always wanted to travel, but she made family her life.

    Should the writer make the addition here?
    A. Yes, because it provides detailed information that shows that her grandmother had her priorities in order.
    B. Yes, because it is a relevant detail at this point in the essay.
    C. No, because it contradicts information in this paragraph.
    D. No, because her love of travel has not yet been discussed.

20. The best placement for the underlined portion would be:
    F. where it is now.
    G. after the word *but*.
    H. after the word *I*.
    J. after the word *would*.

21. A. NO CHANGE
    B. as well
    C. however
    D. that is

TEST 1

GO ON TO THE NEXT PAGE.

solicitude – it was as much a part of our breakfast routine as
the runny yolks she placed before us. We'd wake to that

morning meal, roused by the smells of fresh ground coffee perking and fatty bacon sizzling, groggy from a late night of *Scrabble* and family gossip. She had already managed two loads of laundry and breakfast for grandpa by the time we'd drag ourselves, one by one, from all corners of the house and up to the breakfast bar.

"It's about time," Grandpa would say. "I've been up since 5:00." Needling late risers was one of his favorite things to do.

"Leave them alone, Charlie!" she'd say. And then to us, "Their's coffee made and juice on the table. How do you want your eggs?" And we'd glide into the adjacent dining room, to the table we had gossiped around the night before, propelled by the promise of crisp, smoky bacon and greasy fried eggs served to us as they have always been.

When she would finally sit to indulge in a cup of coffee and a slice of toast, she would sigh and listen as Grandpa would fill us in on the crops, or the pigs, or the local high school basketball team. Finishing, we'd turn to her for news of travel outside their small town. She'd speak wistfully of her visit with Auntie Babe in Canada, or with Auntie Millie, whom lived in Indiana. She'd speak hopefully of a trip to Montana, where she'd grown up. Then Grandpa would

22. Which of the following alternatives to the underlined portion is LEAST acceptable?
F. attention
G. concern
H. anxiety
J. consideration

23. If the writer were to delete the underlined portion the paragraph, the paragraph would primarily lose:
A. description that provides sensory detail.
B. evidence that the narrator enjoys breakfast.
C. detail to further the grandma's characterization.
D. a transition from the idea of the late night to the of the morning meal.

24. F. NO CHANGE
G. Causing torment to late sleepers
H. Bullyragging sleepyheads
J. Heckling those who oversleep and sleep late

25. A. NO CHANGE
B. Theres
C. They'res
D. There's

26. F. NO CHANGE
G. would always have been
H. has always been
J. had always been

27. A. NO CHANGE
B. Finished
C. After he had finished
D. Because of his finishing

28. F. NO CHANGE
G. who
H. that
J. which

mumble something about the garden or the pigs, and she'd sigh again.

Now when I think of my grandma, that's where I see her – sitting rather than serving, sighing rather than bustling. I see a woman who catered for everyone and rarely took time for herself. I see a woman rather than a wife, mother, and grandmother. Maybe I see her this way now because she isn't serving me breakfast anymore. Whatever the reason, I wish I'd seen her this way while she was still alive. I wish I'd asked her about her hopes and dreams, and her regrets. And more than anything, I wish that, just once, I'd served her breakfast. [30]

29. A. NO CHANGE
    B. to
    C. because of
    D. in regard to

Question 30 asks about the preceding passage as a whole.

30. Upon reviewing the essay, the writer is thinking about deleting the brief exchange of dialogue between her grandma and grandpa. Should the dialogue be deleted?
    F. No, because it establishes the grandfather as the antagonist.
    G. No, because it contributes to both the subject and the tone of the essay.
    H. Yes, because it shifts the focus from her grandmother to her grandfather.
    J. Yes, because the essay fails to include the dialogue in a meaningful way.

Passage III

Keiko's Legacy

[1]

Since the early 1960's, the captivity of orcas has been a billion dollar business. Audiences flock to places like Sea World to watch these magnificent creatures perform. What those eager viewers may not realize, however, is that the capture of these whales is extremely violent. <u>Teams of captors chase pods of orcas to exhaustion with speedboats, aircraft and even explosives.</u> Those that survive capture are forced into a life that is nothing like their life in the wild.

[2]

In the wild, orcas are very family-centered, living in highly organized family units called pods. <u>Since</u> they are forcibly separated, they remain with their pods until death. Orcas are social, intelligent, and have a language all their own. Orcas communicate through sound signals which <u>have been</u> different from pod to pod. Even after years in captivity<u>; and</u> as evidence of their strong family ties, orcas continue to produce the sound that is unique to their pod.

[3]

The concrete tanks that serve as the captive orca's home are <u>a far cry from</u> the massive ocean environment from which they were taken. In the wild, orcas are in constant motion, traveling up to 100 miles a day. The ocean provides them with a diverse and unrestricted environment, uniquely

31. Which of these choices, all true, would best support claim made in the preceding sentence while remain consistent with the focus of Paragraph 1?
    A. NO CHANGE
    B. Namu, the first orca successfully captured, was the first to be trained to perform.
    C. Orcas are the biggest animals to be held captive.
    D. Many orcas die from the stress of being transpo in small, concrete pens.

32. F. NO CHANGE
    G. If
    H. Before
    J. Unless

33. A. NO CHANGE
    B. is
    C. are
    D. were

34. F. NO CHANGE
    G. captivity,
    H. captivity. And
    J. captivity: and

35. Which of the choices most appropriately character the nature of the captive orca's home as compared t ocean home as it is described in Paragraph 3?
    A. NO CHANGE
    B. less practical than
    C. better than
    D. designed like

suited on their social, predatory lifestyle.
                36

So, while foraging and playing, the ocean offers orcas what
                                                37
an amusement park never could.
                37

                        [4]

In nature, orcas which lead a predatory lifestyle. They
                     38

are, meanwhile, the top predators of the oceans because of
       39

their intelligence, and their speed. In captivity,
            40

an orcas superior intelligence is wasted on crowd-pleasing
     41

tricks. [42]

                        [5]

Famous orcas, like Keiko – the whale in the movie *Free Willy* who was successfully released back into the wild –

has helped raise public awareness about the inhumane
 43
capture and treatment of these sea animals. In the past forty years, a number of organizations, including the Free Willy

36. F. NO CHANGE
    G. suited
    H. suited to
    J. suited with

37. A. NO CHANGE
    B. Thus offering what an amusement park never could, the ocean is where orcas forage and play.
    C. So, orcas, while foraging and playing, are offered by the ocean what an amusement park never could.
    D. So, unlike an amusement park, the ocean offers orcas a place to forage and play.

38. F. NO CHANGE
    G. that lead
    H. lead
    J. lead with

39. A. NO CHANGE
    B. in summary
    C. for instance
    D. in fact

40. F. NO CHANGE
    G. intelligence,
    H. intelligence and
    J. intelligence; and

41. A. NO CHANGE
    B. orcas'
    C. orcas's
    D. orca's

42. The writer is considering adding the following clause to the end of the preceding sentence:

    and he is rewarded with dead fish rather than the live prey it is used to.

    Should the writer add this clause here?
    F. Yes, because it highlights how demeaning captivity is for such superior creatures.
    G. Yes, because it illustrates how much easier it is for orcas to come by their food in captivity.
    H. No, because it provides a digression that leads the paragraph away from its focus.
    J. No, because in the wild and in captivity, whales have to eat.

43. A. NO CHANGE
    B. have
    C. had
    D. could has

TEST 1   GO ON TO THE NEXT PAGE.

Keiko Foundation and the Humane Society of the United States, have taken important steps to stop the capture of orcas in the waters surrounding the United States. Progress to stop inhuman capture and captivity throughout the world continues.

Questions 44 and 45 ask about the preceding passage as a whole.

44. The writer is considering adding the following sentence to the essay:

    The separation of a calf from its mother is especially traumatic.

    If added, this sentence would most logically be placed after the second sentence of Paragraph:
    F. 2.
    G. 3.
    H. 4.
    J. 5.

45. Suppose that the author has been asked to write an essay illustrating why the survival rate for captive orcas is so low. Would this essay successfully fulfill assignment?
    A. Yes; the essay describes the dangers orcas face during capture as well as the unhealthy life they once in captivity which leads to their early death
    B. Yes; the essay focuses on the inhumane treatment orcas; the implication of this treatment is a low survival rate.
    C. No; the essay's main focus is on the differences between an orca's life in the wild versus its life captivity rather than on is mortality rate.
    D. No; the essay portrays the life of an orca as seriously limited in captivity but emphasizes that orcas are well fed and cared for.

Passage IV

Wild Encounters

You wouldn't think I'd have much contact with wildlife, living as I do in the suburbs. I do what I can to invite birds into my yard by offering them food. The squirrels, chipmunks, and rabbits come without invitation to wreak havoc in our garden, but I don't really mind. I like having wildlife near my home – I think contact with nature is essential for our welfare and well-being.
₄₆

It is, however, the animals' welfare that worries me.
₄₇
If recent animal mishaps in our backyard are any indication, wild animals might want to steer clear of its address.
₄₈

The first mishap involved an iguana. In order to explain
₄₉
this incident, it is important to first point out that iguanas are not native to our area. Our little visitor was a Green Iguana, a reptile found throughout Central and South America where the climate is much warmer. We aren't sure how it ended up in my geraniums, but that's where I found it. Because it was camouflaged by the green leaves, it was just inches from my
₅₀
face before I discovered it. It stayed perfectly still, its eyes watching me cautiously. I ran to get my camera, snapped

46. F. NO CHANGE
    G. welfare, that is, well-being
    H. welfare, which leads to well-being
    J. well-being

47. Which of the following alternatives to the underlined portion would be LEAST acceptable?
    A. The animals' welfare is, however, what I worry about.
    B. It is the animals' welfare, however, about which I worry.
    C. However, I worry about the animals' welfare.
    D. It is, however, the animals' welfare in which I worry about.

48. F. NO CHANGE
    G. our
    H. it's
    J. their

49. A. NO CHANGE
    B. for explaining
    C. to explaining
    D. that explains

50. Which of the following alternatives to the underlined portion would be LEAST acceptable?
    F. disguised
    G. cloaked
    H. masked
    J. modified

a number of pictures as evidence that I haven't been seeing things, and then called the local Animal Rescue. They came with nets, but the frightened lizard dove out of sight and likely did not survive the cold night.

Although skunks *are* native to our area, the skunk scene that unfolded in our backyard was no less bizarre than the iguana incident. Early one morning this past spring, I saw something black and white rolling around near our swing set. A closer examination revealed that I was looking at a skunk, biting frantically at a small wire cage. I recognized it as my vacationing neighbors' catch and release cage, which he uses to rid his yard of the animals that like to nest under his deck. Inside the cage, a baby skunk had become trapped. Its mama was working to free it feverishly. My first instinct was to help her, but I caught myself before I made a foolish mistake.

In contrast, I hurried to call Animal Rescue again. This time they came with a twelve foot pole, on the end of which, was a device to trigger the lock on the cage. Determining to free her offspring: the mama skunk had, by this time, managed to drag the cage into someone else's yard. Fortunately, this mishap ended with a successful release rather than an unsuccessful capture.

51. A. NO CHANGE
    B. hasn't been
    C. hadn't been
    D. wouldn't have been

52. Given that all the choices are true, which one would introduce the new subject of this paragraph?
    F. NO CHANGE
    G. That was the last time we saw an iguana in our backyard.
    H. Skunks are generally nocturnal and we usually s one before we actually see one.
    J. More than once, our dog has surprised a skunk been sprayed.

53. A. NO CHANGE
    B. neighbor's catch and release cage,
    C. neighbors catch and release cage,
    D. neighbors' catch and release cage

54. The best placement for the underlined portion would
    F. where it is now.
    G. after the word *mama*.
    H. after the word *to*.
    J. after the word *working*.

55. A. NO CHANGE
    B. In addition,
    C. Instead,
    D. OMIT the underlined portion.

56. F. NO CHANGE
    G. pole: on the end of which was
    H. pole; on the end of which, was
    J. pole, on the end of which was

57. A. NO CHANGE
    B. Determined
    C. Determine
    D. To determine

58. F. NO CHANGE
    G. offspring;
    H. offspring,
    J. offspring

In between these two memorable incidents, we have freed one chipmunk stuck in a mouse trap and two others stuck in our window wells, helped a baby raccoon stuck in our pine tree, and caught and released a bird who was stuck in
59
our fireplace. We are now on a first-name basis with Animal Rescue. We are still nature lovers, but nature might want to keep its distance from us.

59. A. NO CHANGE
    B. whom was
    C. that was
    D. OMIT the underlined portion.

Question 60 asks about the preceding passage as a whole.

60. The writer has used first person throughout this essay. If the essay were revised so that the first person pronouns were replaced with the pronouns *one* and *one's*, the essay would primarily:
    F. gain a more polite and formal tone appropriate to the purpose of the essay.
    G. gain accessibility by speaking to a broader and more inclusive audience.
    H. lose its narrative quality and become a stilted recounting of events.
    J. lose the immediacy of its message about protecting wildlife in urban environments.

Passage V

And Then There Were Eight?

After many years of debating the issue, planetary scientists recently created quite a stir with their announcement that Pluto could be demoted from its status as one of the nine planets in our solar system. The tiny solar body that shares its name with a beloved Disney character and has been a part of our planetary vocabulary for over seventy years, is at the center of a discussion for how scientists define what a planet is.

Although there is no concrete definition on which all astronomers can agree, most believe a planet must orbit the sun and be large enough for gravity to force it into a sphere. By this definition, Pluto is a planet – the problem is, this definition also includes a multitude of other smaller bodies, like comets and asteroids, in our round solar system.

In fact, size is one of the factors since it sets Pluto apart from the other eight planets. Pluto is very small by comparison, even smaller than our moon. However, scientists do agree that size alone will not have been reason enough to re-categorize Pluto as something other than a planet. There is also the fact that its orbit around the sun is more oblong than those of the other eight planets. While the other planets orbit the sun in a common plane, forming an

61.
A. NO CHANGE
B. character, and
C. character; and
D. character. And

62.
F. NO CHANGE
G. upon
H. about
J. with

63.
A. NO CHANGE
B. which agreement from astronomers can be reached about
C. that can be reached by astronomers with agreement
D. with which all astronomers can agree about

64. Given that all of the choices are true, which description of the solar system provides the best support for the statement that precedes it?
F. NO CHANGE
G. undefined
H. debatable
J. crowded

65.
A. NO CHANGE
B. being that it
C. so that it
D. that

66.
F. NO CHANGE
G. will not be
H. is not
J. doesn't portray.

ever expanding circle, Pluto's orbit is different. Additionally, Pluto cuts across Neptune's orbit during part of its rotation, behaving more like a comet than a planet. Some astronomers speculate that Pluto, along with a number of other objects, is being held in orbit by both Neptune and the sun. The status of the other eight planets is not being questioned.

[1] More and more objects with similar orbital characteristics to Pluto's are being discovered all the time. [2] As a result, the International Astronomical Union has attempted to develop a clearer definition of what constitutes a planet. [3] The IAU have added a third criterion: it must have "cleared other objects out of the way of its orbital neighborhood." [4] It is this third criterion that would exclude Pluto from planethood. [5] Those astronomers whom favor altering Pluto's status argue that as they learn new things about the solar system, they have to reclassify accordingly. [6] Others argue that because there is no consensus on what a planet is, Pluto should maintain its status

67. Which choice best describes Pluto's orbit in relation to the other planets in a way most consistent with the preceding sentences?
    A. NO CHANGE
    B. backward
    C. elliptical
    D. flat

68. Given that all the choices are true, which one provides the most specific support for the statement in the preceding sentence?
    F. NO CHANGE
    G. Unlike Pluto, the other eight planets orbit the sun independently.
    H. Scientists refer to Pluto's moon by the name of Charon.
    J. When the very large asteroid, Ceres, was first discovered, scientists called it a planet.

69. Which of the following alternatives to the underlined portion would NOT be acceptable?
    A. NO CHANGE
    B. time; as
    C. time, and as
    D. time, as

70. F. NO CHANGE
    G. has added
    H. had added
    J. are adding

71. Which of the following alternatives to the underlined portion would be LEAST acceptable?
    A. bar
    B. eliminate
    C. rule out
    D. liquidate

72. F. NO CHANGE
    G. who
    H. which
    J. whose

as a planet owing to the fact that it has always been a
                    ―――――――――――――
                           73

planet. 74

In the scientific world, the Pluto debate continues. For the rest of the world, Pluto will likely remain that tiny little ball on the farthest outskirts of their solar system model. Pluto, however, will be Pluto, no matter how science chooses
        ―――――――
           75
to define it.

73. Which of the following alternatives to the underlined portion would NOT be acceptable?
    A. because
    B. since
    C. as
    D. notwithstanding that

74. For the sake of the logic and coherence of the preceding paragraph, Sentence 3 should be placed:
    F. where it is now.
    G. after Sentence 1.
    H. after Sentence 4.
    J. after Sentence 6.

75. A. NO CHANGE
    B. however,
    C. ; however,
    D. however

MATHEMATICS TEST
60 Minutes—60 Questions

DIRECTIONS: Solve each problem, choose the correct answer, and then fill in the corresponding oval on your answer document.

Do not linger over problems that take too much time. Solve as many as you can; then return to the others in the time you have left for this test.

You are permitted to use a calculator on this test. You may use your calculator for any problems you choose, but some of the problems may best be done without using a calculator.

Note: Unless otherwise stated, all of the following should be assumed.

1. Illustrative figures are NOT necessarily drawn to scale.
2. Geometric figures lie in a plane.
3. The word *line* indicates a straight line.
4. The word *average* indicates arithmetic mean.

---

1. If $x = 3$, then $x^2 + 2x - 12 = ?$

   A. -3
   B. 0
   C. 3
   D. 6
   E. 21

2. If $3(2x - 1) = 11x + 27$, then $x = ?$

   F. -6
   G. -2
   H. 2
   J. 6
   K. 7

3. To make space for new merchandise, a clothing store offered a 15% discount on all current stock. What was the sale price of a jacket that regularly sells for $42?

   A. $6.30
   B. $8.40
   C. $35.70
   D. $37.80
   E. $41.85

4. In the figure below, line m is parallel to line n. One angle formed with transversal line t measures 60°, as shown. What is the degree measure of $\angle a$?

   F. 30°
   G. 60°
   H. 90°
   J. 120°
   K. Cannot be determined.

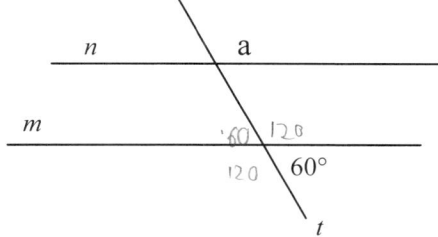

DO YOUR FIGURING HERE.

GO ON TO THE NEXT PAGE.

5. If $x = 3$, $y = 5$, and $w = 4$, what is the value of $xw^3 + \frac{3w}{2} - x^2y$?

   A. 9.0
   B. 12.0
   C. 79.5
   D. 153.0
   E. 1689.0

6. For all x, $(3x - 5)(4x + 3) = ?$

   F. $12x^2 - 15$
   G. $12x^2 + 11x - 15$
   H. $12x^2 - 11x - 15$
   J. $12x^2 + 29x - 15$
   K. $12x^2 - 29x - 15$

7. $|5 - 8| - |9 - 3| = ?$

   A. -9
   B. -3
   C. 1
   D. 3
   E. 9

8. $(5\sqrt{3})^2 = ?$

   F. 15
   G. $10\sqrt{6}$
   H. 45
   J. $34 + 10\sqrt{3}$
   K. 75

9. A carpet company uses the following formula for estimating the number of square feet, A, of carpeting needed for a room x feet by y feet, containing a stairway w feet by z feet, with n stairs:

   $$A = xy + w[z(2n - 1) + 2n]$$

   What is the company's estimate for the number of square feet of carpeting needed for a room that is 15 feet by 18 feet, containing a stairway that is 6 feet by 6 feet with 8 stairs?

   A. 826
   B. 894
   C. 906
   D. 1,086
   E. 1,636

10. An urn contains 7 blue balls, 5 white balls, and 3 red balls. What is the probability that the first ball drawn at random from the urn will NOT be red?

   F. $\frac{7}{45}$
   G. $\frac{1}{5}$
   H. $\frac{1}{3}$
   J. $\frac{7}{15}$
   K. $\frac{4}{5}$

11. A certain watch cost $100, and a certain pearl necklace costs $300. If the cost of the watch increases by 5% and the cost of the pearl necklace decreases by 10%, what will be the sum of their new costs?

   A. $375
   B. $385
   C. $395
   D. $405
   E. $415

12. In the figure below, $\overline{CA}$ is tangent to circle O at point T. If $\overline{AT} = 6$ units, $\overline{CT} = 8$ units, and $\overline{CO} = 10$ units, how many units long is the radius of the circle?

   F. 2
   G. 5
   H. 6
   J. 8
   K. 10

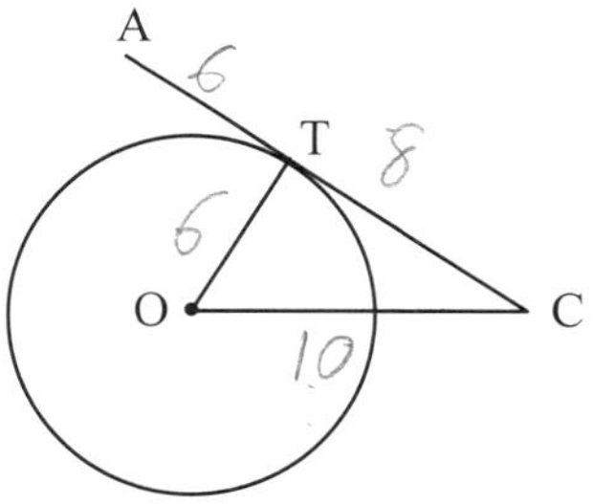

13. If A = BC, B = x, and C = yz, then AB = ?

   A. $xyzx$
   B. $yzxy$
   C. $zxyz$
   D. $xyyz$
   E. xyz

DO YOUR FIGURING HERE.

14. Which of the following inequalities specifies precisely the the real values of x that are solutions to the inequality $-5 < -3x - 7$?

F. $x < 4$
G. $x < -\frac{2}{3}$
H. $x > -\frac{2}{3}$
J. $x < \frac{2}{3}$
K. $x > 4$

15. What is the slope of the line determined by the equation $y - \frac{1}{3}x + \frac{3}{5} = 0$

A. 3
B. 1
C. $\frac{1}{3}$
D. $-\frac{3}{5}$
E. -3

16. Which of the following expresses the equation $4x - 2y = 12$ in slope-intercept form for the standard (x, y) coordinate plane?

F. $x = \frac{1}{2}y + 3$
G. $x = -\frac{1}{2}y + 3$
H. $y = 2x - 6$
J. $y = -2x + 6$
K. $y = -2x - 6$

17. Which of the following values for a in the equation $3x + 3a - 5 = 5x - a$ causes the solution for x to be 6?

A. -8.5
B. -4.25
C. 4.25
D. 8.5
E. 13.25

DO YOUR FIGURING HERE.

TEST 1

GO ON TO THE NEXT PAGE

18. The centers of 3 identically sized circles lie on the diameter of a larger circle, as shown in the figure below. Each of the 4 circles is tangent to 2 other circles, as shown. If the circumference of each small circle is 8π inches, what is the circumference of the largest circle, in inches?

F. 16π
G. 24π
H. 48π
J. 64π
K. 144π

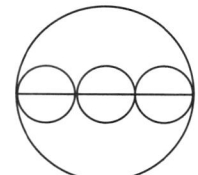

19. A recipe calls for cooking a turkey 1 hour for every 3 pounds it weighs. How long should a 19-pound turkey cook?

A. 6 hours and 15 minutes
B. 6 hours and 20 minutes
C. 6 hours and 30 minutes
D. 6 hours and $33^{1}/_{3}$ minutes
E. 6 hours and 40 minutes

20. Line t intersects parallel lines m and n. Angle measures are as shown in the figure below. What is the degree measure of $\angle a$?

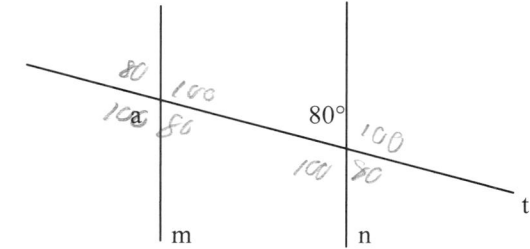

F. $10°$
G. $80°$
H. $90°$
J. $100°$
K. $110°$

21. A photocopy machine enlarges a small triangle to produce a larger, similar triangle, as shown below. If the lengths of the sides, in inches, are as marked on the figure, and the triangles are similarly oriented, what is the value of x in inches?

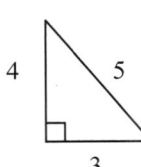
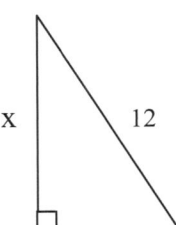

A. $7\frac{1}{5}$
B. 9
C. $9\frac{1}{2}$
D. $9\frac{3}{5}$
E. 11

22. If the lengths of adjacent sides of a rectangular playground have measures of $4x - 3$ and $2x^2 + 7$ units, respectively, then which of the following expressions represents the area, in square units, of the playground?

F. $2x^2 + 4x + 4$
G. $4x^2 + 8x + 8$
H. $8x^3 - 21$
J. $8x^3 - 6x^2 + 28x - 21$
K. $8x^3 + 6x^2 + 28x + 21$

23. Which of the following is a prime factorization of 2,100?

A. $2 \cdot 3 \cdot 5 \cdot 7$
B. $2^2 \cdot 3 \cdot 5^2 \cdot 7$
C. $2^2 \cdot 3 \cdot 5 \cdot 35$
D. $2^2 \cdot 5^2 \cdot 21$
E. $2^2 \cdot 550$

24. After Jean spent 90% of her vacation money, $100 remained. How much vacation money did she originally have?

F. $111
G. $191
H. $900
J. $1,000
K. $1,111

DO YOUR FIGURING HERE.

5. Which of the following is a simplified version of $\frac{2x+1}{x} - \frac{x-3}{5x}$, whenever $x \neq 0$?

A. $9x+2$

B. $9x^2+2x$

C. $\frac{-(x-4)}{4x}$

D. $\frac{9x+8}{5x}$

E. $\frac{9x^2+8x}{5x^2}$

6. If $2x^2 - x - 15 = 0$, what are the 2 possible values for x?

F. -5 and $\frac{3}{2}$

G. -3 and $\frac{2}{5}$

H. -3 and $\frac{5}{2}$

J. 3 and $-\frac{5}{2}$

K. 5 and $-\frac{3}{2}$

7. All angles in the figure shown below are right angles. If each side has a length of 4 centimeters, what is the area of the figure in square centimeters?

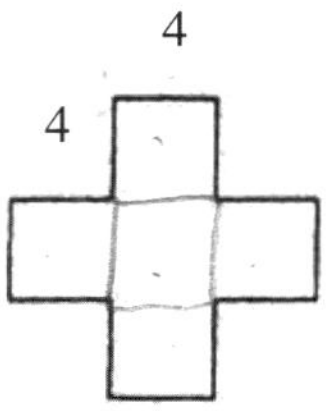

A. 32
B. 40
C. 44
D. 48
E. 80

8. If M, located at (-1, 2), is the midpoint of $\overline{AB}$, and the coordinates of A are (2, 9), what are the coordinates of B?

F. (-5, 16)
G. (-4, -5)
H. (0.5, 5.5)
J. (4, -5)
K. (5, 16)

  GO ON TO THE NEXT PAGE.

29. In the figure below, lengths in units and angles measures in Degrees are as marked. How many units long is $\overline{BC}$?

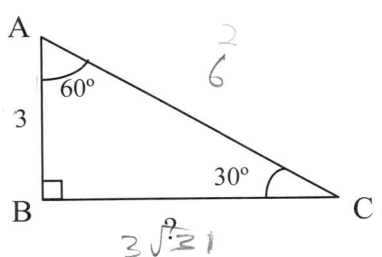

A. 3
B. $3\sqrt{2}$
C. $3\sqrt{3}$
D. 6
E. $3\sqrt{5}$

30. To increase the mean of 5 numbers by 3, by how much would the sum of the 5 numbers need to increase?

F. 3
G. 6
H. 9
J. 15
K. 18

31. Josh pounded a stake into the ground. When he attached a leash to both the stake and his dog's collar, the dog could walk 12 feet from the stake in any direction. Using 3.14 for π, what is the approximate area of the lawn, in square feet, that the dog could roam while tied to the stake?

A. 38
B. 75
C. 151
D. 377
E. 452

32. Television screen sizes are determined by the diagonal length of the rectangular screen. Chad recently changed from watching a television with a 19-inch screen to a television with a similarly shaped 32-inch screen. If a car on the 19-inch screen appeared 12 inches long, how long, to the nearest inch, would the same car appear on the 32-inch screen?

F. 16
G. 18
H. 20
J. 22
K. 24

3. In the figure below, ABCD is a square. Points are connected on each pair of adjacent sides of ABCD to form 4 congruent right triangles, as shown below. Each of these triangles has one leg that is twice as long as the other leg. If the area of the shaded region is 25 square feet, what is the area of square ABCD in square feet?

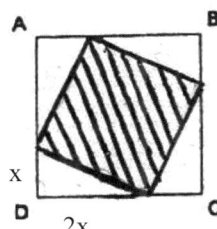

A. 225
B. 112.5
C. 56.25
D. 45
E. 27

4. A surveyor took and recorded the measurements shown in the figure below. If the surveyor wants to use these 3 measurements to calculate the length of the pond, which of the following would he find to be the most useful?

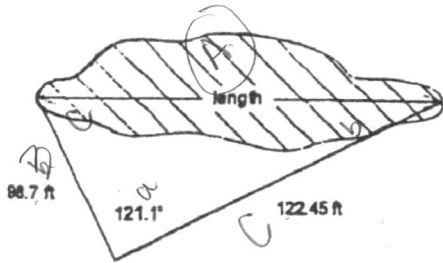

F. The Pythagorean Theorem.
G. The ratios for the side lengths of 30°-60°-90° triangles.
H. The ratios for the side lengths of 45°-45°-90° triangles.
J. The *law of cosines*, which states that for any △ABC, where a is the length of the side opposite ∠A, b is the length of the side opposite ∠B, and c is the length of the side opposite ∠C, $a^2 = b^2 + c^2 - 2bc[\cos(\angle A)]$
K. The *law of sines*, which states that the ratio between the length of the side opposite an angle and the sine of that angle is the same for all of the interior angles in the same triangle.

35. Which of the following is the graph of the equation $y = \dfrac{4x - 2x^2}{x}$ in the standard (x, y) coordinate plane?

A.
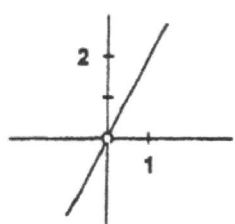

B.
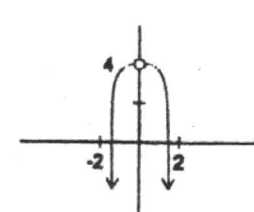

C.
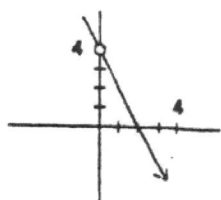

D.
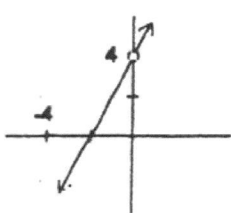

E.
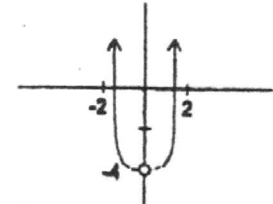

36. A line in a plane separates the plane into how many sets of points that do not contain the line?

F. 0
G. 1
H. 2
J. 3
K. Cannot be determined

37. What is the maximum number of distinct diagonals that can be drawn in the hexagon shown below?

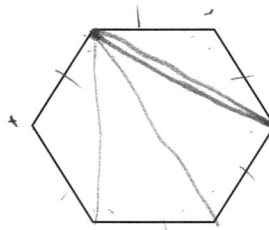

A. 12
B. 9
C. 6
D. 5
E. 4

8. In the standard (x, y) coordinate plane, the center of a circle lies in Quadrant III. If the circle is tangent to the x-axis and the y-axis, which of the following is an equation for the circle?

F. $(x+4)^2 + (y+4)^2 = 4$
G. $(x-4)^2 + (y-4)^2 = 4$
H. $x^2 + (y-4)^2 = 16$
J. $(x+4)^2 + (y+4)^2 = 16$
K. $(x+4)^2 + (y-4)^2 = 16$

9. How must be $-\frac{3}{5}$, $-\frac{4}{7}$, $-\frac{5}{6}$, and $-\frac{8}{9}$ be arranged so that they are listed in increasing order?

A. $-\frac{8}{9} < -\frac{5}{6} < -\frac{3}{5} < -\frac{4}{7}$
B. $-\frac{8}{9} < -\frac{5}{6} < -\frac{4}{7} < -\frac{3}{5}$
C. $-\frac{4}{7} < -\frac{3}{5} < -\frac{5}{6} < -\frac{8}{9}$
D. $-\frac{3}{5} < -\frac{4}{7} < -\frac{5}{6} < -\frac{8}{9}$
E. $-\frac{5}{6} < -\frac{8}{9} < -\frac{3}{5} < -\frac{4}{7}$

10. The perimeter of an elliptical billiard table is to be covered with red velvet. The perimeter of an ellipse is given by the formula: $p = \frac{\pi}{2}\sqrt{2(l^2 + w^2)}$, where l is the length and w is the width, as shown in the diagram below. If the length is 4 feet and the width is 3 feet, what is the outside perimeter of the ellipse in feet?

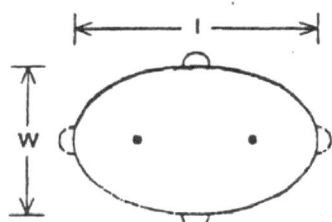

F. $\frac{5}{2}\pi\sqrt{2}$

G. $\frac{\pi}{2}(4\sqrt{2} + 3)$

H. $\frac{7}{2}\pi\sqrt{2}$

J. $(4\pi + 3)\sqrt{2}$

K. $5\pi\sqrt{2}$

DO YOUR FIGURING HERE.

253

TEST 1   Copyright © 2009 by Academic Educational Resources. All rights reserved.   **GO ON TO THE NEXT PAGE.**

41. If $\frac{A}{28}+\frac{B}{126}=\frac{9A+2B}{x}$, and A, B, and x are integers greater than 1, what must x equal?

A. 11
B. 154
C. 252
D. 1,134
E. 3,528

DO YOUR FIGURING HERE.

42. Which one of the following expresses the number of meters that a contestant must travel in a 5-lap race around a circular track with a radius of R meters?

F. $5R$
G. $5\pi R$
H. $5\pi R^2$
J. $6R$
K. $10\pi R$

43. In ΔABC, shown below, the measure of ∠B is 40°, the measure of ∠C is 35°, and $\overline{AB}$ is 27 units long. Which one of the following is an expression of the length, in units, of $\overline{BC}$?
(Note: The *law of sines* states that for any triangle, the ratio between the sine of an angle and the length of the side opposite that angle is the same for all of the interior angles in the triangle.)

A. $\frac{27(\sin 105°)}{\sin 40°}$
B. $\frac{27(\sin 105°)}{\sin 35°}$
C. $\frac{27(\sin 75°)}{\sin 40°}$
D. $\frac{27(\sin 40°)}{\sin 105°}$
E. $\frac{27(\sin 35°)}{\sin 75°}$

GO ON TO THE NEXT PAGE

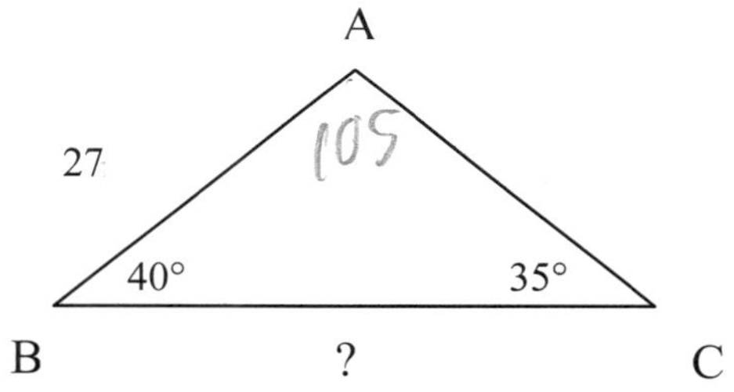

Use the following information to answer questions 44-45.

DO YOUR FIGURING HERE.

Kaylee is planning to purchase a car. She will need to borrow some of the money and has a chart, shown below, that will help her to approximate her monthly payment. The chart gives the approximate monthly payment per $1,000 borrowed.

Monthly payment per $1,000 borrowed for various annual rates and various numbers of payments.

Annual Interest rate	Number of monthly payments		
	36	48	60
5%	$29.97	$23.03	$18.87
6%	$30.42	$23.49	$19.33
8%	$31.34	$24.41	$20.28
10%	$32.27	$25.36	$21.24
12%	$33.22	$26.34	$22.24

44. Kaylee found a used car that she is thinking about purchasing. The list price is $8,785. She calculates that she will need to borrow $6,500. Approximately what would her monthly payment be if she borrowed the money for 36 months at an annual interest rate of 10%?

   F. $164.84
   G. $171.21
   H. $209.76
   J. $234.72
   K. $283.81

45. A local dealership is having an end-of-the-model-year clearance sale and is offering 5% annual interest on new-car loans for 36, 48, or 60 months. The maximum amount that Kaylee can budget for her monthly car payment is $300. Of the following loan amounts, which one represents the maximum amount that Kaylee can borrow at 5% annual interest while staying within her budget?

   A. $10,000
   B. $13,000
   C. $14,000
   D. $15,000
   E. $20,000

GO ON TO THE NEXT PAGE.

46. For $i^2 = -1$, $(5-i)^2 = ?$

   F. 24
   G. 26
   H. 24 − 5i
   J. 24 − 10i
   K. 26 + 10i

47. If x and y are integers such that $y > 12$ and $2x + y = 19$, which of the following is the solution set for x?

   A. $x \geq 4$
   B. $x \geq 3$
   C. $x \leq 4$
   D. $x \leq 3$
   E. $x \leq 0$

48. If $pq^3 t^4 > 0$, which of the following products must be positive?

   F. pq
   G. pt
   H. qt
   J. pqt
   K. pq^2

49. If $\log_3 81 = x+1$, then $x = ?$

   A. 3
   B. 4
   C. 5
   D. 6
   E. 243

0. In △RST below, ∠S is a right angle, $\overline{RT}$ = 7 units, and $\overline{TS}$ = 2 units. What does csc ∠T equal?

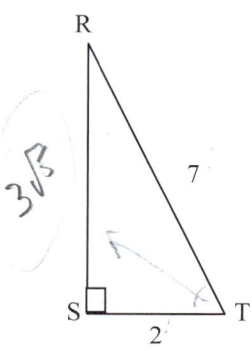

F. $\frac{2\sqrt{5}}{15}$
G. $\frac{3\sqrt{5}}{7}$
H. $\frac{7\sqrt{5}}{15}$
J. $\frac{3\sqrt{5}}{2}$
K. $\frac{7}{2}$

1. A flight instructor charges $75 per lesson, plus an additional fee for the use of his plane. The charge for the use of his plane varies directly with the cube root of the time the plane is used. If a lesson plus 27 minutes of plane usage costs $120, what is the total amount charged for a lesson involving 64 minutes of plane usage?

A. $195
B. $180
C. $157
D. $135
E. $ 60

2. In △ABD shown below, C is on $\overline{BD}$, $\overline{AC} \perp \overline{BD}$, the length of $\overline{AD}$ is 6 inches, the length of $\overline{BD}$ is 10 inches, and sin d = 0.8. What is the area of △ABD in square inches?

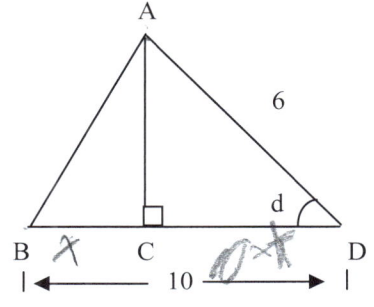

F. 6
G. 12
H. 24
J. 30
K. 60

53. For real numbers x and y, when is the equation $|2x+3y| = |2x-3y|$ true?

   A. Never
   B. Always
   C. Only when $2x = 3y$
   D. Only when $x = 0$ and $y = 0$
   E. Only when $x = 0$ or $y = 0$

54. In the figure below, all line segments that intersect are perpendicular. Using only the segments and vertices in the figure, how many distinct rectangles are there with areas less than the area of ADLI?
   (Note: If 2 rectangles have all four vertices in common, then they are not distinct.)

   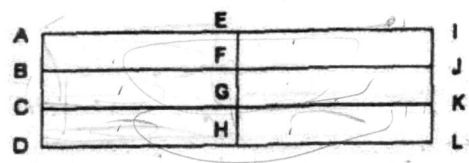

   F. 7
   G. 8
   H. 17
   J. 18
   K. 19

55. For some real number A, the graph of $y = (A+3)x + 5$ in the standard (x, y) coordinate plane passes through the point (3, 11). What is the slope of this line?

   A. -5
   B. -2
   C. -1
   D. 2
   E. $5\frac{1}{3}$

6. In the figure below, $\overline{BCF}$ is a line segment and all distances are given in inches. What is the ratio of the area of quadrilateral RBCS to the area of quadrilateral SCFT?

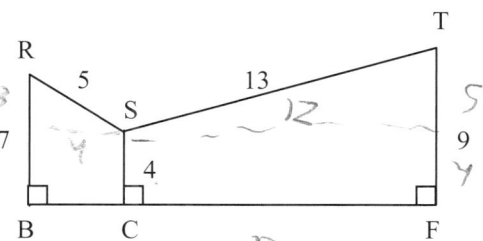

F. 9:7
G. 7:9
H. 11:13
J. 11:39
K. 11:50

7. When graphed in the standard (x, y) coordinate plane, the graphs of $y = x^2 - 5$ and $y = x + 1$ intersect at which of the following points?

A. (-3, 2) and (2, 3)
B. (-3, 4) and (2, -1)
C. (3, -4) and (-2, 1)
D. (3, 4) and (-2, -1)
E. The graphs do not intersect.

8. In septagon ABCDEFG shown below, $\angle A = 115°$ and $\angle G = 70°$. What is the sum of the measures of the other 5 interior angles?

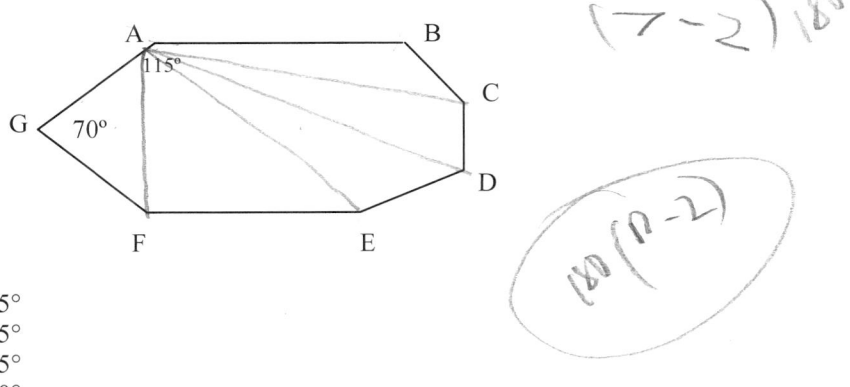

F. 585°
G. 595°
H. 655°
J. 690°
K. 715°

59. For all real numbers x and y such that the product of y and 4 is x, which of the following expressions represents the sum of y and 4 in terms of x?

A. $x + 4$
B. $4x + 4$
C. $4(x + 4)$
D. $\frac{x+4}{4}$
E. $\frac{x+16}{4}$

60. What is $\cos \frac{7\pi}{12}$ given that $\frac{7\pi}{12} = \frac{\pi}{3} + \frac{\pi}{4}$ and that $\cos(A+B) = \cos A (\cos B) - \sin A (\sin B)$?

(Note: You may use the following table of values.)

θ	sin θ	cos θ
$\frac{\pi}{6}$	$\frac{1}{2}$	$\frac{\sqrt{3}}{2}$
$\frac{\pi}{4}$	$\frac{\sqrt{2}}{2}$	$\frac{\sqrt{2}}{2}$
$\frac{\pi}{3}$	$\frac{\sqrt{3}}{2}$	$\frac{1}{2}$

F. $\frac{\sqrt{2}-\sqrt{6}}{4}$
G. $-\frac{1}{4}$
H. $\frac{\sqrt{2}-\sqrt{3}}{4}$
J. 0.999
K. $\frac{1-\sqrt{2}}{2}$

END OF TES
STOP! DO NOT TURN THE PAGE UNTIL TOLD TO DO S
DO NOT RETURN TO THE PREVIOUS TES

$$\cos \frac{7\pi}{12} = \cos\left(\overset{A+B}{\frac{\pi}{3}+\frac{\pi}{4}}\right)$$

$$(\cos A)(\cos B) - (\sin A)(\sin B)$$

$$\left(\cos \frac{\pi}{3}\right)\left(\cos \frac{\pi}{4}\right) - \left(\sin \frac{\pi}{3}\right)\left(\sin \frac{\pi}{4}\right)$$

$$\frac{1}{2}\frac{\sqrt{2}}{2} - \frac{\sqrt{3}}{2}\frac{\sqrt{2}}{2}$$

$$\frac{\sqrt{2}}{4} - \frac{\sqrt{6}}{4} \qquad \frac{\sqrt{2}-\sqrt{6}}{4}$$

NO TEST MATERIAL ON THIS PAGE.

READING TEST

35 Minutes – 40 Questions

DIRECTIONS: There are four passages in this test. Each passage is followed by several questions. After reading a passage, choose the best answer to each question and fill in the corresponding oval on your answer document. You may refer to the passages as often as necessary.

Passage I

PROSE FICTION: This passage is adapted from the short story *The First Sense* by Nadine Gordimer. (© 2006).

She has never felt any resentment that he became a musician and she didn't. Could hardly call her amateur flute playing a vocation. She sits at a computer in a city-government office earning a salary that has at least
[5] provided regularly for their basic needs.

She found when she was still an adolescent that her father, with his sports shop and the beguiling heartiness that is a qualification for that business, and her mother, with her groupies exchanging talk of female maladies,
[10] did not have in their comprehension what it was that she wanted to do.

A school outing at sixteen had taken her to a concert where she heard, coming out of a slim tube held to human lips, the call of the flute. The teacher
[15] who had arranged the cultural event was understanding enough to put the girl in touch with a musical youth group in the city. She babysat on weekends to pay for the hire of a flute, and began to attempt to learn how to produce with her own breath and fingers something of
[20] what she had heard.

He was among the Youth Players. His instrument was the very antithesis of the flute. The sounds he drew from the overgrown violin between his knees: the complaining moo of a sick cow, the rasp of a blunt
[25] saw. "Excuse me!" he would say, with a clownish lift of the eyebrows and a down-twisted mouth. Within a year, his exceptional talent had been recognized by the professional musicians who coached these young people.

[30] They played together when alone, to amuse themselves and secretly imagine that they were already in concert performance, the low, powerful cadence coming from the golden-brown body of the cello making her flute voice sound, by contrast, more like
[35] that of a squeaking mouse. In time, she reached a certa[in] level of minor accomplishment. He couldn't deceive h[er] and let her suffer the disillusions of persisting with [a] career that was not open to her level of performanc[e.] "You'll still have the pleasure of playing the instrume[nt]
[40] you love best." She would always remember what s[he] said: "The cello is the instrument I love best."

Sometimes she fell asleep to the low tender tones [of] what had become his voice, the voice of that big curv[ed] instrument, sharing the intimacy that was hers. A[t]
[45] concerts, when his solo part came, she did not reali[ze] that she was smiling in recognition, that his was a voi[ce] she would have recognized anywhere. She was awa[re] that, without a particular ability of her own, she w[as] privileged enough to have an interesting life, and [a]
[50] remarkably talented man whose milieu was also hers.

He began to absent himself from her at unexplaine[d] times or for obligations that he must have known s[he] knew didn't exist. She had suggestions for relaxation: [a] film or a dinner. He was not enthusiastic. "Next wee[k,]
[55] next week." He took the revered cello out of its solitu[de] in the case and played, to himself, to her—well, she w[as] in the room those evenings. It was his voice, th[e] glorious voice of his cello, saying something differe[nt,] speaking not to her but to some other. The voice of t[he]
[60] cello doesn't lie.

She waited for him to speak. About what ha[d] happened. To trust the long confidence between the[m.] He never did. And she did not ask, because she was al[so] afraid that what had happened, once admitted, would [be]
[65] irrevocably real.

One night, he got up in the dark, took the cel[lo] out of its bed, and played. She woke to the voice, sayi[ng] something passionately angry in its deepest bass. S[he] She knew that the affair was over. She felt a pull [of]
[70] sadness—for him. For herself, nothing. By nev[er] confronting him she had stunned herself.

1. If the fourth paragraph (lines 21-29) were omitted from the passage, the reader would not know:
   A. that he played the violin.
   B. how the couple met.
   C. that he became a famous musician.
   D. that he was an angry person.

2. Which of the following best describes what the first paragraph reveals about her character?
   F. She has a rewarding and high-paying career.
   G. She earns money playing a flute.
   H. She is generous and pragmatic.
   J. She regrets not becoming a musician.

3. Which of the following can most reasonably be inferred from the passage about her parent's feelings about music?
   A. They are accomplished musicians.
   B. They do not have a capacity for music themselves, but support her interest.
   C. They are opposed to her becoming a musician.
   D. They didn't understand why she would want to pursue a career in music.

4. In line 41, the statement *"The cello is the instrument I love best"* most nearly communicates what?
   F. She would rather play the cello than play the flute.
   G. She will stop playing the flute so that she can play the cello.
   H. She never really loved playing the flute.
   J. She loves him more than she loves playing the flute.

5. The main conflict in this passage can best be described as:
   A. Both he and she want to become famous musicians, but only one of them is able.
   B. Challenges she faces as the wife of a famous musician.
   C. Tension created when he starts distancing himself from her.
   D. Her need to choose between the flute and the cello.

6. It can reasonably be inferred from the passage that she views him as:
   F. a competent competitor.
   G. a teacher and a mentor.
   H. someone whose responsibility it is to entertain her.
   J. a talented musician whose opinion she respects.

7. In lines 59-60 the statement *"The voice of the cello doesn't lie"* mostly nearly means:
   A. that she can tell something is wrong because of the music he plays.
   B. the cello is telling her what is bothering him.
   C. he is using music to communicate his feelings to her.
   D. he is playing the cello in order to avoid talking to her.

8. Which of the following statements describing how she feels about his musical ability is most clearly supported by the passage?
   F. She respects him, but gets annoyed at how often he is out of town playing concerts.
   G. She is jealous that he is so much better than her.
   H. She loves listening to him play, and enjoys the life of a musician's partner.
   J. She is proud of his success and takes advantage of the opportunities that brings for her to play the flute.

9. The main purpose of the sixth paragraph (lines 42-50) is to:
   A. illustrate his success.
   B. show how intimate their relationship is.
   C. explain why she gets upset when he leaves her.
   D. tell the reader more about his voice.

10. Why didn't he encourage her to pursue a career as a musician?
    F. He didn't want the competition.
    G. He was jealous of her abilities.
    H. He wanted her to earn steady money for them.
    J. He didn't think she was talented enough.

TEST 1

GO ON TO THE NEXT PAGE.

Passage II

SOCIAL SCIENCE: This passage is adapted from "The Disappearing Computer" by Bill Gates, which appeared in *The World in 2003 (The Economist)*. (© 2002 by The Economist).

A few years from now, the average home entertainment system might not look much different than it does today. But it will probably have an Internet connection that enables it to download and play digital
[5] music and video, display album artwork and song titles on the television, and even interrupt your listening if an important message arrives. It will have a central processor, disk storage, graphics hardware and some kind of intuitive user interface. Add a wireless mouse
[10] and keyboard, and this home entertainment system will start looking a lot like a personal computer. Will people buy and use these systems in large numbers? Absolutely. Will they think of them as computers? Probably not.

According to Gartner Dataquest, an American
[15] research firm, the world computer industry shipped its one billionth PC in 2002, and another billion more are expected to be built in the next six years. Add to this the exploding number of embedded computers - the kind found in mobile phones, gas pumps and retail point-of-
[20] sale systems - which are fast approaching the power and complexity of desktop PCs. On one estimate, people in the United States already interact with about 150 embedded systems every day, whether they know it or not. These systems, which use up to 90 percent of the
[25] microprocessors produced today, will inevitably take on more PC-like characteristics, and will be able to communicate seamlessly with their traditional PC counterparts. They will also become amazingly ubiquitous. In 2001, according to the Semiconductor
[30] Industry Association, the world microchip industry produced around 60 million transistors for every man, woman and child on earth. That number will rise to one billion by 2010.

At the same time, the general-purpose PC as we
[35] know it today will continue to play an important, and increasingly central, role in most people's lives, but it will be at the center of a wide range of intelligent devices that most people wouldn't think of as "computers" today. This scenario is in sharp contrast to
[40] the computers of just a few years ago - back in the pre-Internet age - which were still mostly passive appliances that sat in the corner of the den or living room. Back then, people used their PCs for little more than writing letters and documents, playing games or managing their
[45] family finances.

But today we are truly in a digital decade, in wh[ich] the intelligence of the PC is finding its way into kinds of devices, transforming them from pass[ive] appliances into far more significant and indispensa[ble]
[50] tools for everyday life. Many of the core technolog[ies] of computing-processing power, storage capac[ity,] graphics capabilities and network connectivity are continuing to advance at a pace that matches or e[x]exceeds Moore's Law (which famously, and correc[tly]
[55] predicted that the number of transistors on a comp[uter] chip would double every two years).

As people find more ways to incorporate th[ese] inexpensive, flexible and infinitely customiza[ble] devices into their lives, the computers themselves
[60] gradually "disappear" into the fabric of our lives. are still a long way from a world full of disembo[died] intelligent machines, but the computing experience the coming decade will be so seamless and intui[tive] that, increasingly, we will barely notice it. At the sa[me]
[65] time, computing will become widespread enough we will take it for granted - just as most people in developed world today trust the telephone service.

The pervasiveness and near-invisibility computing will be helped along by new technolo[gies]
[70] such as cheap, flexible displays, fingernail-sized c[hips] capable of storing terabytes of data, or inducti[vely] powered computers that rely on heat and motion f[rom] their environment to run without batteries.

The economics of computing will also b[e]
[75] change. Decreasing costs will make it easy electronics manufacturers to include PC-intelligence and connectivity in even the mundane devices.

All this will lead to a fundamental change in
[80] way we perceive computers. Using one will bec[ome] like using electricity when you turn on a li[ght] Computers, like electricity, will play a role in al[most] everything you do, but computing itself will no lo[nger] be a discrete experience. We will be focused on w[hat]
[85] we can do with computers, not on the dev[ices] themselves. They will be all around us, essentia[l] almost every part of our lives, but they will effecti[vely] have "disappeared".

11. This passage is best described as being:
    A. an analysis of how computers are vanishing from everyday use in society.
    B. an argument in support of introducing more computer-friendly products.
    C. an examination of the changing roles computers have in people's lives.
    D. a thorough evaluation of the benefits and drawbacks of using computers.

12. The author uses all of the following sources of evidence to support his claims EXCEPT:
    F. research data gathered by professionals.
    G. the opinion of a scientist.
    H. statistics provided by industry experts.
    J. reference to a famous mathematical prediction.

13. The word *ubiquitous*, as used in line 29, most likely means:
    A. small.
    B. difficult to find.
    C. inexpensive.
    D. ever-present.

14. According to the passage, new technologies and decreasing costs of electronics will lead directly to an increase in all of the following EXCEPT:
    F. interconnectivity among objects.
    G. the presence of computer intelligence in everyday objects.
    H. the amount of power and batteries that will be required to run computers.
    J. computers being involved in most aspects of life.

15. Which of the following best describes how the author predicts people will perceive computers in the future?
    A. Computers will be so much a part of everyday life that people will hardly notice them.
    B. Computers will have disappeared from people's lives.
    C. People will be afraid of how invasive computers have become and will use them less.
    D. Computers will be everywhere and people will be very aware of using them constantly and will become dependent on them.

16. The word "*disappeared*" used in line 88 most likely refers to the idea that:
    F. people will no longer use computers.
    G. computers will be so imbedded in people's everyday lives that they won't even notice them anymore.
    H. computers will become invisible.
    J. computers will become so small and will be inside so many other objects that people will not be able to see them anymore.

17. All of the following are identified in the passage as parts of a future entertainment system EXCEPT:
    A. a satellite.
    B. graphics hardware.
    C. a wireless keyboard.
    D. an Internet connection.

18. The author refers to computers of the past as *"passive appliances"* (line 41) because:
    F. they were indispensable tools for everyday life.
    G. they were incapable of complex tasks.
    H. they remained in one location.
    J. people only used them occasionally for specific tasks.

19. The main point of the second paragraph (lines 14-33) can best be summarized as:
    A. There are more microchips than people.
    B. Microprocessors are being produced more quickly then we can use them.
    C. Both the number of and uses for microprocessors is rapidly increasing.
    D. There is more need for microprocessors than for personal computers.

20. In paragraph 1, the author suggests that all of the following are core technologies EXCEPT:
    F. storage capacity.
    G. power profiles.
    H. graphics capabilities.
    J. network connectivity.

Passage III

HUMANITIES: This passage is adapted from the article "The Trouble with Frida Kahlo" by Stephanie Mencimer, which appeared in *Washington Monthly* (© Washington Monthly 2002).

Never has a woman with a mustache been so revered, or so marketed, as Frida Kahlo. Like a female Che Guevara, she has become a cottage industry. Feminists might celebrate Kahlo's ascent to greatness -
5 if only her fame were related to her art. Instead, her fans are largely drawn by the story of her life, for which her paintings are often presented as simple illustration. Fridamaniacs are inspired by Kahlo's tragic tale of physical suffering - polio at six, grisly accident at 18 -
10 and fascinated with her glamorous friends and lovers. But, like a game of telephone, the more Kahlo's story has been told, the more it has been distorted, omitting uncomfortable details that show her to be a far more complex and flawed figure than the movies suggest.
15 This elevation of the artist over the art diminishes the public understanding of Kahlo's place in history and overshadows the deeper and more disturbing truths in her work.

Until the 1970s there were almost no "great" women
20 artists. As the feminist movement gathered steam, women sought to rectify that problem. Historically, women's limited opportunities meant there were few women artists to begin with, and even fewer whose work had been collected and could be definitively
25 attributed to them. Once scholars did identify significant women artists, they had to demonstrate that those artists met the male standards for admission to the canon--i.e., they had to suffer and be mostly ignored during their lifetimes. It was also helpful if the emerging female
30 artists were beautiful and had glamorous friends.

Kahlo made a perfect candidate. As if her bodily injuries weren't compelling enough, Kahlo's drama was enhanced by what she referred to as the second accident in her life: Diego Rivera, the famous Mexican muralist
35 to whom she was married for 25 years. Rivera was a notorious womanizer, a habit he did not abandon after marrying Kahlo. Both Kahlo and Rivera were active in the Communist Party and Mexican politics. Kahlo's paintings often reflect her tumultuous relationship with
40 Rivera, as well as the anguish of her ever-deteriorating health. Between the time of her accident and her death, Kahlo had more than 30 surgeries, and a gangrenous leg was eventually amputated. She dramatized the pain in her paintings, while carefully cultivating a self-image as
45 a "heroic sufferer."

While Kahlo's work never attracted the attention h[er] husband's did, it did win some critical acclai[m]. Eventually, though, her failing health left her addict[ed]
50 to painkillers and alcohol. She continued to paint, b[ut] the addiction destroyed the controlled, delica[te] brushwork that had characterized her best work. [In] 1954, suffering from pneumonia, Kahlo went to [a] Communist march. Four days later, she died in wh[at] may or may not have been a suicide.

55 If the focus of the art business must be [a] biography, that biography should at least include t[he] artists' warts. Many of Kahlo's surgeries may have be[en] unnecessary. She also made several suicide attemp[ts] and spent much of her adult life addicted to drugs a[nd]
60 alcohol. More importantly, though, Kahl[o's] Communism, now treated as somehow sort of quai[nt], led her to embrace some unforgivable politi[cal] positions. Less scandalous but worth noting is t[hat] Kahlo despised the very gringos who now champi[on]
65 her work, and her art reflects her obvious disdain for [the] United States.

Neglecting the dark side of the artist's narrati[ve] deprives the public of a full appreciation of the a[rt]. Without knowing that by 1953 Kahlo was so strung o[ut]
70 that she could barely pick up a paintbrush, how can t[he] public possibly know why some of her late work is [so] bad? Which is the really tragic part of Kahlo's sto[ry.] Because when you sweep away the sideshow, igno[re] the overwrought analysis, and take a hard look at w[hat]
75 she painted, much of it is extraordinary. Her paintin[gs] tap into sex and violence, life and death, in original a[nd] profound ways. So while women might celebr[ate] Kahlo's success, it may be that real progress has co[me] when a woman can be remembered both as a great ar[tist]
80 and as a despicable cur.

21. The author implies that Kahlo is famous primarily because of her:
    A. exceptionally liberal paintings.
    B. dramatic life full of intrigue and suffering.
    C. marriage to Diego Rivera.
    D. being one of the first female artists.

22. Frida Kahlo's story was compared to *"a game of telephone"* (line 11) because:
    F. just like a message passed over the phone, the details of her life have been told accurately.
    G. people are purposely leaving out important pieces of her history.
    H. her story has been passed on verbally from person to person.
    J. over time the story has become distorted and parts have been omitted.

23. The author states that all of the following contributed to the lack of great female artists prior to 1970 EXCEPT:
    A. the scarce number of female artists.
    B. scholars' difficulty identifying great female artists.
    C. the high standards for admission to the canon.
    D. the small amount of female artists' works that had been collected.

24. The author's tone in this passage can best be described as:
    F. persuasive.
    G. informative.
    H. sarcastic.
    J. humorous.

25. Based on the information presented in the passage, the quality of Kahlo's painting began to decline because of:
    A. her injuries.
    B. catching pneumonia.
    C. her addiction to painkillers and alcohol.
    D. her tumultuous marriage to Rivera.

26. In the context of lines 55-66, the phrase *the artists' warts* (line 57) most nearly means:
    F. Kahlo's poorer paintings.
    G. the imperfections in Kahlo's appearance.
    H. Kahlo's highest achievements.
    J. the less pleasant parts of Kahlo's life.

27. According to the passage, all of the following are true about Kahlo's paintings EXCEPT:
    A. they reflect her complicated relationship with Rivera.
    B. they dramatized the pain from her surgeries.
    C. they were all forms of self portraits.
    D. they portray concepts in unique and profound ways.

28. The author's purpose in writing this passage can best be summarized as:
    F. to discuss how the movies and Fridamaniacs are distorting the story of Kahlo's life.
    G. to convince women to embrace both the dark and light side of Kahlo's life when choosing to celebrate her success.
    H. to provide hidden details of Kahlo's life, hoping that people will realize she is not worthy of such high acclaim.
    J. to explain why some of Kahlo's later work is so bad.

29. What would the author probably say is the most tragic thing about Kahlo's story?
    A. That Rivera remained unfaithful even after their marriage.
    B. That Kahlo died so young, and wasn't able to create more paintings.
    C. The grisly accident when she was 18.
    D. That people don't realize how extraordinary her work is because they are more caught up in the sordid details of her life.

30. What is the "*sideshow*" the author refers to in line 73?
    F. the dramatic details of Kahlo's life.
    G. the critical acclaim Kahlo has received.
    H. the Fridamaniacs who idolize Kahlo.
    J. Kahlo's addictions.

Passage IV

NATURAL SCIENCE: This passage is adapted from "What Is a Planet?" by Steven Soter, which appeared in *Scientific American* (© 2006 Scientific American).

Most of us grew up with the conventional definition of a planet as a body that orbits a star, shines by reflecting the star's light and is larger than an asteroid. Although the definition may not have been very precise, it clearly categorized the bodies we knew at the time. In the 1990s, however, a remarkable series of discoveries made it untenable. Beyond the orbit of Neptune, astronomers found hundreds of icy worlds, some quite large, occupying a doughnut-shaped region called the Kuiper belt. Around scores of other stars, they found other planets, many of whose orbits look nothing like those in our solar system. They discovered brown dwarfs, which blur the distinction between planet and star. And they found planet-like objects drifting alone in the darkness of interstellar space.

These findings ignited a debate about what a planet really is and led to the decision last August by the International Astronomical Union (IAU), astronomers' main professional society, to define a planet as an object that orbits a star, is large enough to have settled into a round shape and, crucially, "has cleared the neighborhood around its orbit." Controversially, the new definition removes Pluto from the list of planets. Some astronomers said they would refuse to use it and organized a protest petition.

The new definition of a planet reflects advances in our understanding of the architecture of our solar system and others. A planet is, in effect, the end product of accretion from a disk around a star. This definition applies only to mature systems, such as ours, in which accretion has run effectively to completion. For younger systems, where accretion is still important, the largest bodies are not strictly planets but are called planetary embryos, and the smaller bodies are called planetesimals.

The IAU definition still includes roundness as a criterion for a planet, though strictly speaking, that is unnecessary. The orbital-clearance criterion already distinguishes planets from asteroids and comets. The definition also removes the need for an upper mass limit to distinguish planets from stars and brown dwarfs. The relatively rare brown dwarf companions orbiting close to stars can be classified as planets; unlike brown dwarfs in wider orbits, they are thought to have formed by disk accretion. In short, the difference between planets and non-planets is quantifiable, both in theory and by observation. All the planets in our solar system ha enough mass to have swept up or scattered away mo of the original planetesimals from their orbital zone Today each planet contains at least 5,000 times mo mass than all the debris in its vicinity. In contrast, t asteroids, comets and Kuiper belt objects, includi Pluto, live amid swarms of comparable bodies.

The historical definition of nine planets no dou retains a strong sentimental attraction. But ad h definitions devised to grandfather in Pluto tend conceal from the public the profound changes that ha occurred since the early 1990s in our understanding the origin and architecture of the solar system. For years, our schools taught that Pluto was a planet. So argue that culture and tradition are sufficient grounds leave it that way. But science cannot remain bound the misconceptions of the past. To be useful, a scienti definition should be derived from, and draw attenti to, the structure of the natural world. We can revise definitions when necessary to reflect the bet understanding that arises from new discoveries. T debate on the definition of a planet will provi educators with a textbook example to show h scientific concepts are not written in stone but contin to evolve.

31. The author of this passage would most likely ag with which of the following statements?
    A. Pluto should still be considered a planet, bas on cultural norms.
    B. We should not change scientific definitions based solely on new discoveries.
    C. Until scientists can agree unanimously, no changes should be made to scientific definitions.
    D. New scientific discoveries should be embrac and may necessitate updating old definitions.

32. The main point of the second paragraph (lines 25) is that:
    F. not all scientists agree on the definition of a planet.
    G. the IAU created a new definition of a planet.
    H. there were recently new discoveries about planets.
    J. Pluto is no longer a planet.

33. According to the passage, planetary embryos are found where?
    A. In young solar systems, where accretion is still occurring.
    B. In young solar systems, where accretion has run its course.
    C. In mature solar systems, such as our own.
    D. Wherever plants are found.

34. As it is used in line 7, the word *untenable* most nearly means:
    F. challenging.
    G. flawed.
    H. indisputable.
    J. unconditional.

35. If a new gem were discovered that would decrease the value of diamonds, how would the author most likely feel about sharing this information with the public?
    A. It is important to share this new discovery, even if it will change the way people feel about diamonds.
    B. The new gem should be kept secret. Diamonds are so important to our culture that we would not want to tarnish their reputation.
    C. It would be great to destroy the diamond's image, and therefore the new gem should be highly promoted as the new gem of choice.
    D. A team of gem experts should make a statement explaining the discovery of the new gem, but also celebrating diamonds.

36. The main purpose of the last paragraph is to:
    F. persuade the reader to use the old definition of a planet, based on the sentimental value.
    G. convince readers to accept the new definition of a planet, but to grandfather in Pluto.
    H. highlight the importance of revising definitions when necessary, based on new discoveries.
    J. encourage teachers to promote debate in their classrooms regarding the correct definition of a planet.

37. The IAU definition of a planet eliminates which criterion from the definition?
    A. roundness.
    B. orbital clearance.
    C. proximity to a star.
    D. an upper mass limit.

38. Which of the following statements about Pluto is accurate, according to information in the passage?
    F. Some historians would like to grandfather in Pluto so that it can still be considered a planet.
    G. According to the new definition, Pluto is no longer considered a planet.
    H. For over 86 years our schools have been teaching that Pluto is a planet.
    J. Pluto doesn't orbit a star, and therefore never should have been considered a planet.

39. Which of the following is true about how the scientific community is receiving the IAU's new definition of a planet?
    A. Some astronomers refuse to use the new definition.
    B. The IAU definition has been unanimously praised and accepted.
    C. The new definition has been accepted, although not everyone is happy about it.
    D. The IAU definition has been widely criticized and contradicted.

40. Which of the following did NOT precipitate scientists deciding to create a new definition of a planet?
    F. Hundreds of icy worlds were discovered.
    G. New planets whose orbits looked similar to those in our solar system were found.
    H. Brown dwarfs were discovered.
    J. Planets were found drifting alone in space.

END OF TEST

STOP! DO NOT TURN THE PAGE UNTIL TOLD TO DO SO.

DO NOT RETURN TO A PREVIOUS TEST.

SCIENCE TEST
35 Minutes — 40 Questions

DIRECTIONS: There are seven passages in this test. Each passage is followed by several questions. After reading a passage, choose the best answer to each question and fill in the corresponding oval on your answer document. You may refer to the passages as often as necessary.

You are NOT permitted to use a calculator on this test.

Passage I

So far, astronomers have found at least 161 planets orbiting other stars. The known planets have a bewildering variety of compositions, masses, and orbits. Nonetheless, the universal rules of physics and chemistry suggest that they will broadly fall into just a few types. Highlights from the Extrasolar Planet Catalog follow below. Table 1 shows the composition of the planets, while Figure 1 displays the planets' masses and orbital distances.

Table 1		
Planet Type	Composition	Stars they Orbit
Gas Giant	Hydrogen/helium Rock Metallic hydrogen	OGLE-TR-56 OGLE 2003
Carbon Orb	Silicon carbide Iron/nickel/carbon Diamond layer Carbon monoxide	PSR 1257
Water World	Silicates/water Iron/metal Water	Gliese 876
Rocky Earth	Silicate Fluid iron/nickel Solid iron/nickel Rock crust	55 Cancri Epsilon

1. The data in Table 1 and Figure 1 support which of following statements?
   A. The smaller the planet's mass, the shorter its orbi distance.
   B. The larger the planet's mass, the longer its orbital distance.
   C. The larger the planet's mass, the shorter its orb distance.
   D. The data does not support a correlation between mass and orbital distance.

2. According to Table 1 and Figure 1, which of following stars has the Gas Giant planet with the grea mass orbiting it?
   F. Gliese 876
   G. OGLE 2003
   H. 55 Cancri
   J. OGLE TR 56

3. If a new planet was discovered with a mass of 315 orbital distance of 2, and a composition of mostly r and silicate, it would probably be classified as wl type of planet?
   A. Carbon Orb
   B. Water World
   C. Rocky Earth
   D. Gas Giant

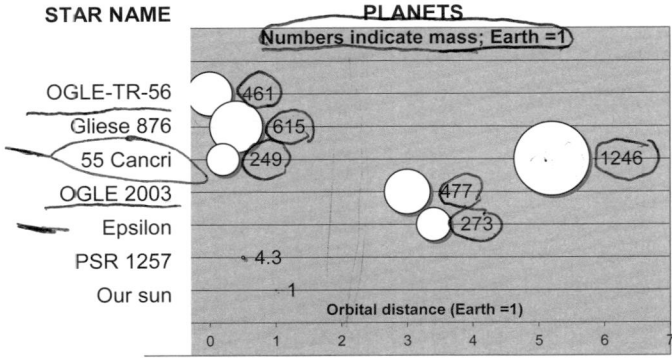

Figure 1

4. All of the following are true of the star 55 Cancri EXCEPT:
   F. 55 Cancri has the planet with the shortest orbital distance orbiting it.
   G. A planet orbiting 55 Cancri is made out of silicate, iron, and rock.
   H. There are two planets orbiting 55 Cancri.
   J. The combined mass of the planets orbiting 55 Cancri is equal to 1495.

5. Which of the following characteristics do the Rocky Earth planets have in common?
   A. They all orbit the PSR 1257 star.
   B. They all have a mass greater than 200.
   C. They are all made out of carbon and diamonds.
   D. They all have an orbital distance greater than 2.

Passage II

A group of researchers studied the greenhouse gas (GHG) and energy savings associated with using rigid plastic foam sheathing to insulate single-family housing. The results show the typical annual energy savings for a single house in the United States. Table 1 displays energy savings for various temperature zones, while Table 2 shows GHGs avoided.

Table 1				
Energy Savings (in million BTUs)	Zone 1 (colder)	Zone 3	Zone 5 (warmer)	US Average
Natural Gas	4.2	2.7	0.9	2.37
Petroleum	0.04	0.02	0.22	0.04
Coal	0.81	0.98	0.93	0.76
Hydropower	0.06	0.02	0.03	0.06
Nuclear	0.26	0.26	0.19	0.25
Other	0.03	0.02	0.23	0.03
Total Annual	5.41	4.01	2.50	3.51

Table 2				
GHGs – CO_2 (in pounds)	Zone 1 (colder)	Zone 3	Zone 5 (warmer)	US Average
Carbon Dioxide	609	608	606	599
Methane	101	101	101	101
Nitrous Oxide	4.5	4.5	4.5	4.5
HCFC-141b	588	588	588	588
HCFC-142b	1511	1511	1511	1511
Total	2813	2812	2811	2803

There is an initial use of energy and release of GHG when the insulation is installed, but over time the product will bring about a large savings. After the "payback" time expires, there is a net savings in energy and GHG emissions for as long as the insulation is in place. Figure 1 displays the payback time in years for energy and GHGs.

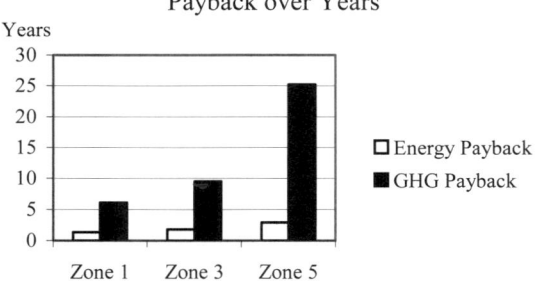

Figure 1

6. For which type of energy did foam sheathing create the highest energy savings in Zone 5?
   F. Coal.
   G. Nuclear.
   H. Natural Gas.
   J. Petroleum.

7. According to the data presented in Table 1 and Table 2, which of the following is true?
   A. Foam sheathing prevents more HCFC-141b than HCFC-142b from entering the atmosphere.
   B. Yearly energy savings vary more by zone than yearly GHGs avoided.
   C. The warmer the zone, the less the energy savings from petroleum.
   D. The US average for GHGs avoided is greatest for carbon dioxide.

8. According Figure 1, the GHG payback for Zone 3 approximately:
   F. 2 years
   G. 6 years
   H. 9 years
   J. 13 years

9. According to Table 1 and Figure 1, which of the following zone and fuel combinations yields the greatest energy savings after 1 year?
   A. Nuclear in Zone 1.
   B. HCFC-142b in Zone 3.
   C. Coal in Zone 5.
   D. Natural gas in Zone 1.

10. Ten years after installing rigid plastic foam sheathing in zone 3, which of the following is true?
    F. The customer will have a net savings in GHGs, but will still be "paying back" the energy savings.
    G. The customer will have a net savings in energy, but will still be "paying back" the GHG costs.
    H. The customer will still be "paying back" both the energy and GHG costs.
    J. The customer will be collecting net savings in both energy and GHGs.

11. Based on the data in Table 1, which of the following lists the fuels that yield the highest average energy savings, in decreasing order?
    A. Natural Gas, Coal, and Nuclear.
    B. Hydropower, Nuclear, and Other.
    C. Coal, Natural Gas, and Nuclear.
    D. Nuclear, Petroleum, and Coal.

NO TEST MATERIAL ON THIS PAGE.

GO ON TO THE NEXT PAGE.

Passage III

Ohm's law states that V = I x R and WRC/L where V = voltage, I = current, R = resistance, C = cross sectional area of the wire, W = resistivity of the wire, and L = length of the wire. Using the circuit pictured in Figure 1, a student performed two experiments.

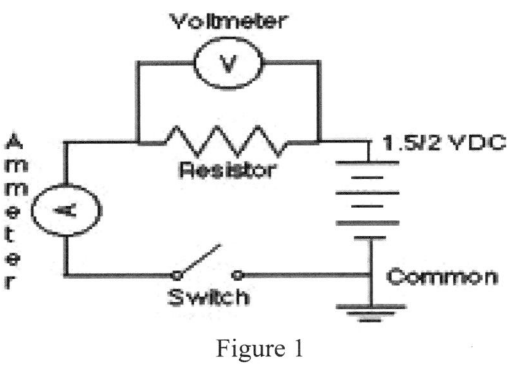

Figure 1

Experiment 1

The student used a 1.5V battery and varied the resistance to observe the effect on the current. Table 1 displays the results of the experiment.

Table 1		
Trial	Resistance (ohms)	Current (amps)
1	3	0.5
2	5	0.3
3	10	0.15
4	25	0.06

Experiment 2

The student used a constant voltage of 0.6 and three different wires to complete the circuit. Table 2 shows how the wire used affected the resistance and current. Figure 2 displays the relationship between the diameter of the wire used and the resistance measured.

Table 2			
Trial	Diameter (mm)	Resistance (ohms)	Current (amps)
1	0.28	4.29	0.14
2	0.45	1.33	0.45
3	0.71	0.81	0.74

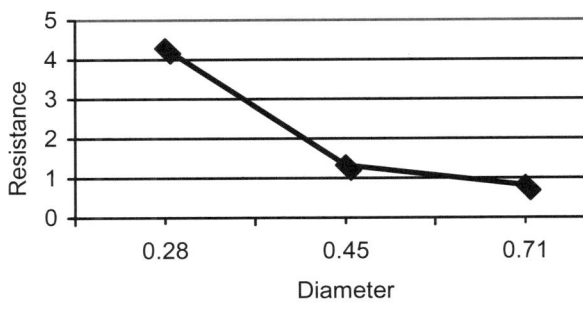

Figure 2

12. In Experiment 1, which of the following is true about the relationship between the resistance and the current?
    F. As the resistance increased, the current increased.
    G. As the resistance increased, the current decreased.
    H. As the resistance decreased, the current decreased.
    J. There was no apparent relationship between resistance and current.

13. Based on the information in Table 2 and Figure 2, can be determined that if a wire with a 0.6 mm diameter were used, the resistance would be closest to:
    A. 0.6 ohms
    B. 1.0 ohms
    C. 2.0 ohms
    D. 3.3 ohms

14. In Experiment 2, the student varied which of the following factors?
    F. The incoming voltage.
    G. The size of the wire.
    H. The length of the wire.
    J. The resistor.

15. The student hypothesized that current and resistance have an inverse relationship, meaning that an increase in one would mean a decrease in the other. Do the results of Experiments 1 and 2 support this hypothesis?
    A. No; in Experiment 1, as the resistance increases, the current increases as well.
    B. No; in Experiment 2, resistance and current are inversely related.
    C. Yes; in both experiments, as the resistance increases, the current decreases.
    D. Yes; Figure 2 displays the inverse relationship.

16. Consider a circuit like the one shown in Figure 1. Based on Experiments 1 and 2, the current will be greatest if the circuit contains which of the following resistances and wire sizes, respectively?
   F. 5 ohms, 0.45 mm
   G. 3 ohms, 0.28 mm
   H. 3 ohms, 0.45 mm
   J. 25 ohms, 0.28 mm

17. Which of the following graphs correctly demonstrates the relationship between wire size and current?

   A.
   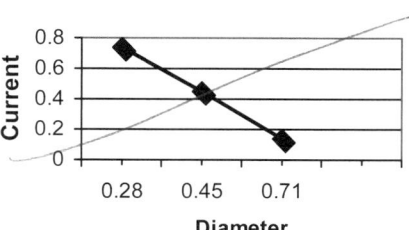

   B.
   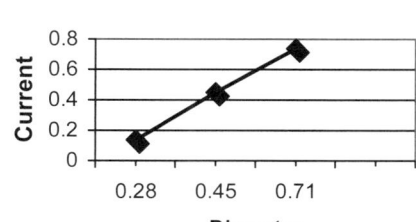

   C.
   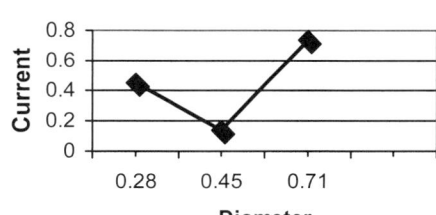

   D.
   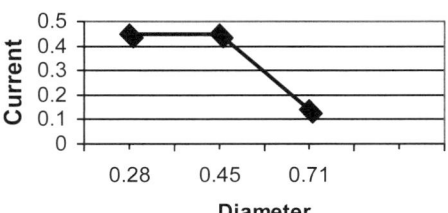

TEST 1 Copyright © 2009 by Academic Educational Resources. All rights reserved. **GO ON TO THE NEXT PAGE.**

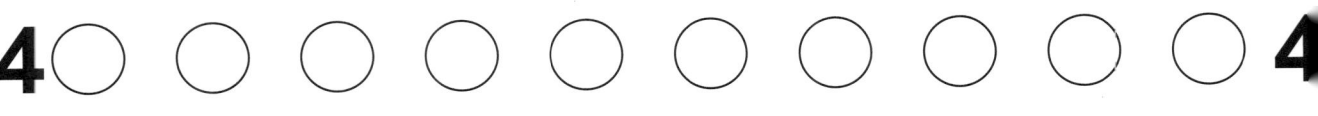

Passage IV

All hydrogens are acidic. This is true for acids such as sulfuric acid (H_2SO_4), nitric acid (HNO_3), and hydrochloric acid (HCl). Only some hydrogens within selected acid molecules may be capable of forming H+. A student conducted an experiment to determine the number of ionizable H^+ in several acids. The student started with a flask containing 0.50g of acid and a vial of 200 mL of a base solution, 0.250 M sodium hydroxide (NaOH). The student added base to the acid with constant swirling of the flask until a faint pink color persisted. The process was repeated using different acids. The data recorded from each titration is shown in Table 1.

Table 1				
Acid	Benzoic	Citric	Fumaric	Oxalic
Molecular Formula	$C_7H_6O_2$	$C_6H_8O_7$	$C_4H_4O_4$	$C_2H_6O_6$
Vol NaOH before titration (mL)	0.0	0.0	0.0	0.0
Vol of NaOH after titration (mL)	16.4	31.2	34.4	32.0

Using the results from the experiment and the molar mass of each acid, the student performed several calculations to determine the average ratio of moles of hydrogen ions to moles of acid, which is equal to the number of ionizable hydrogens in each acid molecule. The results of the calculations are displayed in Table 2.

Table 2				
Acid	Benzoic	Citric	Fumaric	Oxalic
Acid used (mol)	.0041	.0026	.0043	.0040
OH^- used (mol)	.0041	.0078	.0086	.0080
H^+ used (mol)	.0041	.0078	.0086	.0080
Ratio of hydrogen to acid	1:1	3:1	2:1	2:1

Lastly, the student rewrote the molecular formula each acid to reflect the number of ionizable hydrogens. new formulas appear in Table 3.

Table 3	
Acid	Molecular Formula
Benzoic	$HC_7H_5O_2$
Citric	$H_3C_6H_5O_7$
Fumaric	$H_2C_4H_2O_4$
Oxalic	$H_2C_2O_4 \cdot 2H_2O$

18. According to the data in Table 1 and Table 2, which required the most NaOH to complete the reaction?
    F. Benzoic
    G. Citric
    H. Fumaric
    J. Oxalic

19. Based on the information presented in Tables 2 an which acid has the most ionizable hydrogens?
    A. Benzoic
    B. Citric
    C. Fumaric
    D. Oxalic

20. Before completing the experiment, the stu hypothesized that the more NaOH the acid required, more ionizable hydrogens the acid would contain. Do results of the experiment support the hypothesis?
    F. Yes; the higher the volume of NaOH after titra the higher the number of ionizable hydrogens in acid.
    G. Yes; Table 2 shows that the acids that used more have more ionizable hydrogens.
    H. No; the acid with the most ionizable hydrogens needed the most NaOH.
    J. No; the acid that required the most NaOH does have the most ionizable hydrogens.

276
TEST 1

Copyright © 2009 by Academic Educational Resources. All rights reserved.

GO ON TO THE NEXT PAG

21. The data in Table 2 supports which of the following statements?
   A. The titration that used the most OH⁻ identified the acid with the least ionizable hydrogens.
   B. The titration that used the least H⁺ identified the acid with the most ionizable hydrogens.
   C. The titration that used the least amount of acid identified the acid with the most ionizable hydrogens.
   D. The titration that used the most acid identified the acid with the most ionizable hydrogens.

22. Which acid contains seven carbon atoms per molecule?
   F. Benzoic
   G. Citric
   H. Fumaric
   J. Oxalic

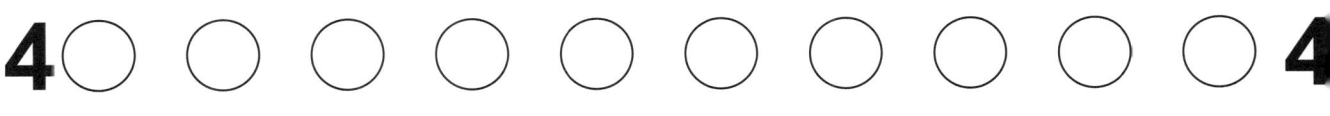

Passage V

More than 5 percent of Americans have asthma, a chronic disease that affects the airways and lungs and causes shortness of breath, wheezing, and sometimes death. In the United States, rates for asthma have steadily increased, nearly doubling during the past 20 years. There is no cure for asthma. Two researchers discuss factors that cause individuals to develop asthma.

Researcher 1

There has long been an association between the allergen *Dermatophagoides pteronyssinus* (dust mites) and asthma. Evidence for a causal relationship has been supported by bronchial challenge studies and avoidance experiments. Studies have shown that exposure in a child's own house was the primary determinant of sensitization. Research from around the world has provided evidence about other indoor allergens, specifically cats, dogs and the German cockroach. These studies showed that perennial exposure to allergens was an important cause of inflammation in the lungs and associated nonspecific bronchial hyperreactivity. Children are being exposed to more perennial allergens now than ever before. Houses are built more tightly and are better insulated, and have more furnishings and fitted carpets. In addition, children are spending more time indoors. This increased exposure to allergens, including dust mites, has led to increased sensitization, and more cases of asthma.

Since assays for total serum IgE (immunoglobulin E) became available, it has been clear that patients with asthma have, on average, higher total IgE than patients with hay fever or no allergy. Recent work on patients hospitalized for asthma has suggested that the interaction between rhinovirus and allergy occurs predominantly among patients with total IgE > 200 IU/ml. Thus, the different properties of allergens could influence both the prevalence and severity of asthma.

Researcher 2

It is widely accepted that air pollution exacerbates asthma. For example, when traffic controls were put in place during the 1996 Summer Olympic Games in Atlanta, Georgia, morning peak traffic counts declined by 23 percent This in turn lowered ozone (O3) concentrations by 13 percent, carbon monoxide (CO) by 19 percent, and nitrogen dioxide (NO2) by 7 percent. Associated with these declines in ambient air pollution were drops in Medicaid-related emergency room visits and hospitalizations for asthma (down 42 percent), asthma-related care for health maintenance organizations (down 44 percent), and citywide hospitalizations for asthma (down 19 percent). Despite such striking relationships between exposure to air pollution and asthma aggravation, air pollution has not historically been regarded as a cause of the disease. Increasingly, though, recent studies have been suggesting that air pollution may indeed be a cause of asthma.

The Children's Health Study (CHS) followed 3,5 children with no lifetime history of asthma for five year During that period 265 reported a new physician diagnosis asthma. Analysis of CHS data has shown that children livin in communities with high ozone levels developed asthm more often than those in less polluted areas. The hypothes that ozone might cause asthma is reinforced by a study 3,091 non-smoking adults aged 27 to 87 years who we followed for 15 years. The results of this study showed th 3.2 percent of the men and 4.3 percent of women report new doctor-diagnosed asthma. The researchers conclud that there was a connection between ozone concentration a development of asthma.

23. If ozone levels decrease nationwide, how wou Researcher 2 expect to see asthma rates change?
   A. An increase in prevalence of asthma.
   B. A decrease in the prevalence of asthma.
   C. No change in the prevalence of asthma.
   D. First a decrease and then an increase in the prevalence of asthma.

24. With which of the following statements wou Researcher 1 agree?
   F. Asthma rates are lower in rural areas.
   G. Men are more likely to have asthma than women.
   H. People who have pets are more likely to have asthma.
   J. Asthma rates are related to the quality of air.

25. Researcher 1 would most likely agree with which of t following statements about IgE?
   A. People who have IgE levels of 400 IU/ml have a high chance of having severe asthma.
   B. People who have IgE levels of 100 IU/ml have a high chance of having severe asthma.
   C. Most people who have asthma have low levels of IgE: less than 200 IU/ml.
   D. There has been no connection made between IgE levels and the prevalence of asthma.

26. If the prevalence of asthma in the United Stat continues to increase, Researcher 1 would likely ci which of the following as a solution to the problem?
   F. People need to spend less time outside.
   G. Houses need to be better insulated.
   H. People need to be given supplements to increase their IgE levels.
   J. Fans need to be added to houses to allow more circulation and to bring more outside air into the house.

27. If Researcher 2 is correct, which of the following graphs would best represent the relationship between CO concentrations and cases of asthma?

A.
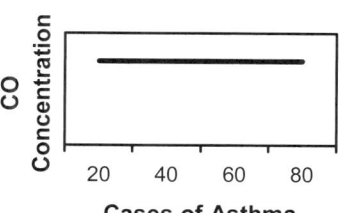

B.
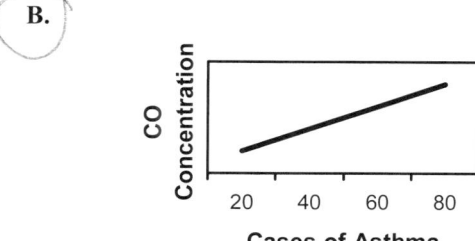

C.
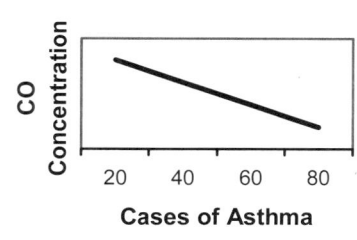

D.
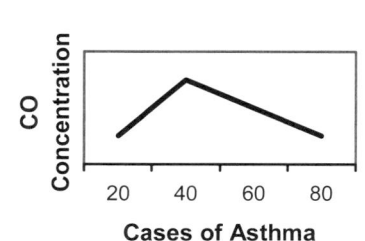

28. Researcher 2 would most likely agree with which of the following statements regarding the prevalence of asthma 20 years ago?
F. There was a higher prevalence of asthma 20 years ago because there was less pollution.
G. There was a lower prevalence of asthma 20 years ago because there were higher ozone levels and less pollution.
H. There was a lower prevalence of asthma 20 years ago because there was less pollution and lower ozone levels.
J. There was a lower prevalence of asthma 20 years ago because people spent more time outside.

29. Researchers 1 and 2 would both agree with which of the following statements?
A. Asthma rates are likely to decline over the next 20 years.
B. Air pollution and high IgE levels are the two leading causes of asthma.
C. Women are more likely to develop asthma than men.
D. Measures can be taken to lower a person's risk of developing asthma.

Passage VI

The Great Lakes Science Center (GLSC) has conducted lake-wide surveys of the fish community in Lake Michigan each fall since 1944 using standard 12m bottom trawls along contour at depths of 9 to 110m at each of seven to nine index transects. The resulting data on relative abundance, size structure, and condition of individual fishes are used to estimate various population parameters that are in turn used by state and tribal agencies in managing Lake Michigan fish stocks.

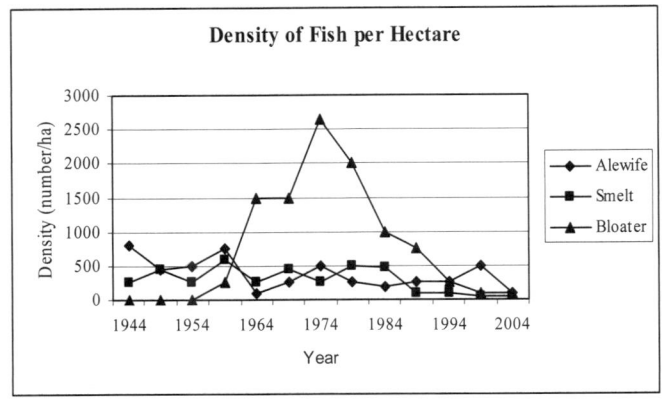

Figure 1

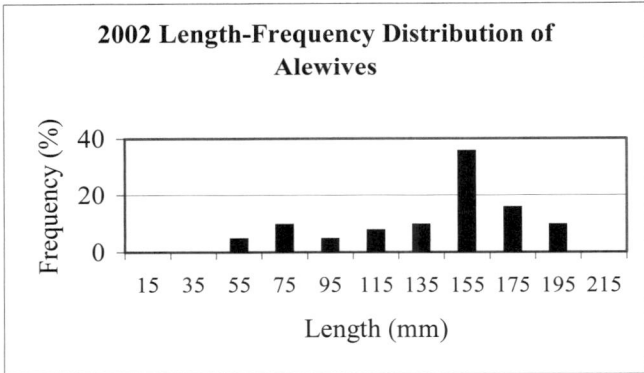

Figure 2

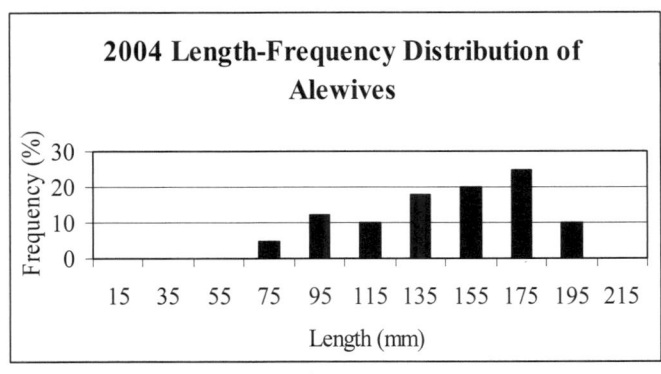

Figure 3

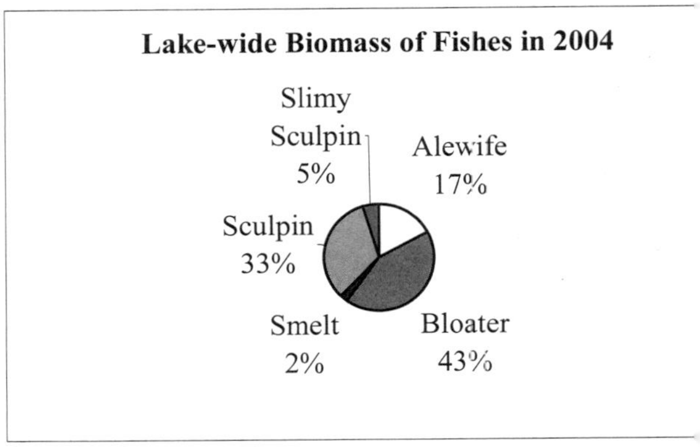

Lake-wide Biomass of Fishes in 2004
- Slimy Sculpin 5%
- Alewife 17%
- Sculpin 33%
- Smelt 2%
- Bloater 43%

Figure 4

30. According to Figure 1, which species of fish was prevalent in 1954?
F. Alewife
G. Smelt
H. Bloater
J. Smelt and Bloater

31. Based on the information in Figure 4, which of following statements is true?
A. There were more Smelt than Sculpin in 2004.
B. There were more Bloater than Sculpin in 2004.
C. There were more Alewife than Bloater in 2004.
D. There were more Slimy Sculpin than Alewife in

32. According to Figure 2 and Figure 3, which of the following is FALSE about the size of Alewives?
F. There were more 175mm Alewives in 2004 than 2002.
G. There were fewer 75mm Alewives in 2004 than 2002.
H. There were fewer 115mm Alewives in 2002 than 2004.
J. There were more 155mm Alewives in 2004 than 2002.

33. Considering the fact that the older an Alewife fish, the longer it is, and using the data in Figures 2 and 3, which of the following can be deduced about Alewife fish populations in 2002 and 2004?

A. In 2004, there were more young Alewives than in 2002.
B. In 2004, there were more adult Alewives than in 2002.
C. In 2004, the fish were, on average, younger than in 2002.
D. In 2004, the greatest percentages of fish were young.

34. Scientists at the GLSC have hypothesized that the Bloater population may be cycling in abundance, within a period of about 60 years. Does the information in Figures 1 and 4 support this hypothesis?

F. No; the population of Bloater fish has decreased since 1973.
G. No; in 2004 there were more Bloater fish than any other species.
H. Yes; the density of Bloater fish steadily increased and then decreased from 1973 to 2003.
J. Yes; in 2004 there were more Bloater fish than any other species.

Passage VII

Pertussis, commonly known as whooping cough, is a highly infectious disease of the respiratory tract caused by bacteria. The disease spreads through direct contact with secretions from the nose or throat of an infected person, or by breathing in the air when an infected person coughs. Pertussis most easily passes between people in the initial stage of illness, but it can be spread at any time during the course of the illness. Figure 1 depicts the course of Pertussis from exposure to recovery.

Incubation Period 5-21 days			Catarrhal Stage 1-2 weeks	
Weeks: -3	-2	-1	0 + 1 (onset)	2
Maximum incubation period 21 days	Average incubation period 7-10 days		*Communicability* Cold symptoms: rhinorrhea, anorexia, conjunctivitis, lacrimation, malaise, sneezing and low-grade fever	
Paroxysmal Stage 1-6 weeks					Convalescent Stage 2-3 weeks			
3	4	5	6	7	8	9	10	11	12
Paroxysmal cough, vomiting, cyanosis						Coughing			
Communicability ends after 5 days of antibiotics			Communicability usually ends 3 weeks after onset of cough if no antibiotics taken						

Figure 1

The number of reported cases of pertussis from 1974 through 2004 is depicted in Figure 2.

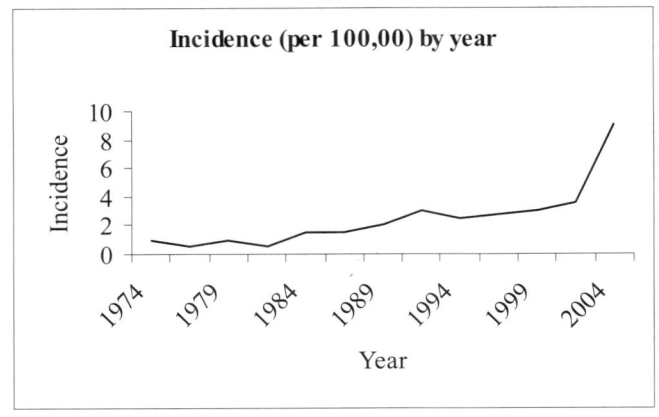

Figure 2

The number of reported cases of pertussis in 2004 age group is shown in Figure 3.

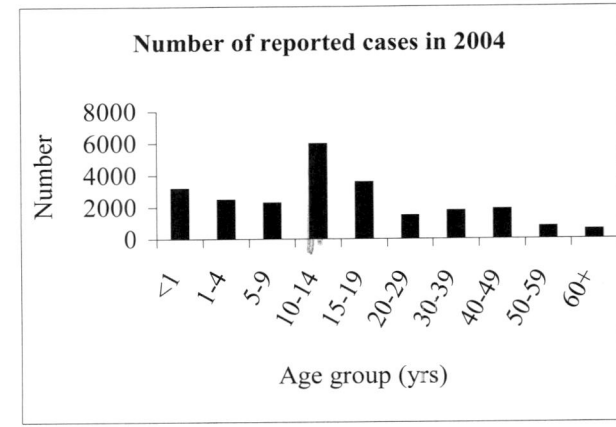

Figure 3

35. In 1991 a new vaccine for pertussis was introduced that claimed to be more effective than the previous vaccine. Does the data in Figure 2 support this claim?
    A. No; rates of pertussis increased after 1991.
    B. No; rates of pertussis remained the same after 1991.
    C. Yes; rates of pertussis decreased after 1991.
    D. Yes; rates of pertussis increased after 1991.

36. If a person was experiencing a cough, was medicated and was still contagious, he/she would be in what stage of the disease?
    F. Incubation
    G. Catarrhal
    H. Paroxysmal
    J. Convalescent

37. What is the maximum number of weeks that pertussis can be transmitted?
    A. 1
    B. 3
    C. 8
    D. 12

38. Doctors theorized that because of their immature immune systems, young children are the most susceptible to pertussis. Does the data from 2004, Figure 3, support this theory?
    F. No; pertussis mostly affected the elderly.
    G. No; teenagers were the most likely to contract pertussis.
    H. Yes; infants had the highest rate of pertussis.
    J. Yes; 7000 young children contracted pertussis.

39. Which of the following statements could be a plausible explanation for increased incidence of pertussis?
   A. Fewer infants are being vaccinated for pertussis, so more are contracting the disease.
   B. Regulations for the reporting of pertussis have loosened, so the numbers are inaccurate.
   C. The incidence of blood transfusions has risen, which has increased the risks of contracting pertussis.
   D. Vaccine immunity wanes after 5-10 years, so more young adults are succumbing to pertussis.

40. Which of the following statements about pertussis is FALSE?
   F. The disease has an incubation period ranging from 1-3 weeks.
   G. Symptoms are similar to those of a common cold.
   H. The disease is a virus that cannot be treated with antibiotics.
   J. Pertussis can be communicated via particles left in the air after a person coughs.

END OF TEST

STOP! DO NOT RETURN TO ANY OTHER TEST.

ACT SUCCESS

WRITING TEST 1 – Prompt

DIRECTIONS:

This is a test of your writing skills. You will have thirty (30) minutes to write an essay in English. Before you begin planning and writing your essay, read the writing prompt below carefully to understand exactly what you are being asked to do. Your essay will be evaluated on the evidence it provides of your ability to express judgments by taking a position on the issue in the writing prompt; to main a focus on the topic throughout the essay; to develop a position by using logical reasoning and by supporting your ideas; to organize ideas in a logical way; and to use language clearly and effectively according to the conventions of standard written English.

Your local public library has come under criticism for allowing patrons under the age of 18 to check out books that are considered unacceptable. The books are either explicit, describe graphic violence, or use questionable language. These critics argue that minors should not be given access to explicit materials. Other people think that public libraries have no business denying anyone access to any materials, and that parents should be the ones to control what books their children can and cannot read. In your opinion, should public libraries place restrictions on which books patrons under the age of 18 can check out?

In your essay, take a position on this question. You may write about either one of the two points of view given, or you may present a different point of view on this question. Use specific reasons and examples to support your position.

Use this page to *plan* your essay.

Begin WRITING TEST 1 here.

WRITING TEST 1

WRITING TEST 1

WRITING TEST 1

STOP here with the Writing Test.

Scale Scores for Practice Test 1

*These scores are based on student trials rather than national norms.

English _____
Math   _____
Reading _____
Science _____

=Total   _____

Composite = Total divided by 4 (round up at .5) _____

ACT Score*	Number Right				ACT Score*
	English	Math	Reading	Science	
36	75	60	40	40	36
35	73-74	59	39	--	35
34	72	58	38	39	34
33	71	57	37	--	33
32	70	56	36	38	32
31	69	54-55	34-35	--	31
30	68	53	33	37	30
29	67	51-52	32	36	29
28	65-66	49-50	30-31	34-35	28
27	64	46-48	29	33	27
26	62-63	44-45	28	31-32	26
25	60-61	41-43	27	30	25
24	58-59	39-40	26	28-29	24
23	55-57	37-38	24-25	27	23
22	53-54	35-36	23	25-26	22
21	50-52	33-34	22	23-24	21
20	47-49	31-32	21	21-22	20
19	44-46	28-30	19-20	19-20	19
18	42-43	25-27	18	17-18	18
17	40-41	22-24	17	15-16	17
16	37-39	19-21	16	13-14	16
15	34-36	15-17	15	12	15
14	31-33	11-14	13-14	11	14
13	29-30	09-10	12	10	13
12	27-28	07-08	10-11	09	12
11	25-26	06	08-09	08	11
10	23-24	05	07	07	10
9	21-22	04	06	06	9
8	18-20	03	05	05	8
7	15-17	--	--	04	7
6	12-14	02	04	03	6
5	09-11	--	03	02	5
4	07-08	01	02	--	4
3	05-06	--	--	01	3
2	03-04	--	01	--	2
1	00-02	00	00	00	1

Practice Test #2

ENGLISH TEST

45 Minutes – 75 Questions

DIRECTIONS: In the five passages that follow, certain words and phrases are underlined and numbered. In the right-hand column, you will find alternatives for the underlined part. In most cases, you are to choose the one that best expresses the idea, makes the statement appropriate for standard written English, or is worded most consistently with the style and tone of the passage as a whole. If you think the original version is best, choose "NO CHANGE." In some cases, you will find in the right-hand column a question about the underlined part. You are to choose the best answer to the question.

You will also find questions about a section of the passage or about the passage as a whole. These questions do refer to an underlined portion of the passage, but rather identified by a number or numbers in a box.

For each question, choose the alternative you consider b and fill in the corresponding oval on your answ document. Read each passage through once before begin to answer the questions that accompany it. For m of the questions, you must read several sentences bey the question to determine the answer. Be sure that you h read far enough ahead each time you choose an alternativ

PASSAGE I

Why I Ride a Bicycle

I waited thirty-two years before I rode a bicycle for the first time, down a tree-lined street in Toronto. I had barely sat on one before, so there were a few false starts as my boyfriend Stephen called out instructions beside me. But then I found I was moving. And since I, more than most objects, seem to obey Newton's first law of motion—an object in motion will remain in motion until acted upon by an external force—off I went, whizzing downhill, weaving like a drunk, and smiled idiotically. I didn't stop until three blocks later; where a car was speeding toward the intersection. I'd not yet learned to brake, so I just dropped both feet to the ground inelegantly. Then I got back on the bicycle and did the whole thing again.

I don't know why I'd never learned to ride before, a rite

1. **A.** NO CHANGE
   B. boyfriend, Stephen called
   C. boyfriend Stephen, called
   D. boyfriend, called

2. **F.** NO CHANGE
   G. smiling
   H. had been smiling
   J. smiles

3. **A.** NO CHANGE
   B. later. Where
   C. later, where
   D. later, and – when

of passage that most people understand somewhere around age six. Clearly, not all middle-class parents in India teach they're children to ride bicycles. Mine certainly didn't. I had singing lessons and, briefly, dancing lessons. I had math tutors and physics tutors. I even had swimming lessons but no bicycles.

It's strange to come to this mysterious activity as an adult. Most people my age are riding for so long they give little thought to an act that is nothing short of miraculous. But getting on a bike for the first time at thirty-three reveals the triumph of physics and human will that is cycling. Five hundred years ago, someone (the tireless Leonardo da Vinci, it was thought) drew a sketch of what was meant to be the worlds first bicycle, though both sketch and artist are now disputed. [8] Since then we've had the "walking machine" (Baron von Drais of Sauerbrun's wooden two-wheeled contraption without pedals, designed to aid walkers—a bicycle even I could have ridden), velocipedes, ordinaries, and high-wheel tricycles. They are all results of engineering and machine-age design, but also of something more intangible.

4. F. NO CHANGE
   G. experience
   H. practice
   J. need

5. A. NO CHANGE
   B. there
   C. their
   D. one's

6. F. NO CHANGE
   G. rode
   H. had ridden
   J. have been riding

7. A. NO CHANGE
   B. worlds first bicycle
   C. world's first bicycle
   D. world's first bicycle,

8. The writer is considering adding the following true statement:

   The sketch was done in pencil and charcoal.

   Should the writer make this addition here?
   F. Yes, because it helps support the idea that bicycles have an important place in history.
   G. Yes, because it provides necessary insight into the variety of bicycles that exist.
   H. No, because it is not relevant to the narrative at this point in the essay.
   J. No, because this information has already been presented elsewhere in the essay.

9. Given that all of the choices are true, which one most strongly reinforces the writer's attitude that bicycles are amazing inventions?
   A. Each is a marvel
   B. They are debacles
   C. Each is a creation
   D. Each is a product

The saying that to ride on a bicycle is to balance
                        10

upon two tubes of rubber and wire, connected by a frame,
  11
and to propel them forward with no more than a little foot

power and the conviction that you can. We think bicycles

carry us forward, but they don't, we carry them. It is largely
                                  12

human will that keep bicycle and rider in motion, as well as
                   13

that law of Newton's, that it can be adapted into an
                              14
exhortation: move, because if you are moving, you will keep

moving. [15]

10. Which choice provides the most concise and stylistically effective wording here?
    F. NO CHANGE
    G. Operating a bicycle one can say
    H. A person riding a bicycle
    J. To operate a bicycle

11. Which of the following alternatives to the underlined portion would be LEAST acceptable?
    A. NO CHANGE
    B. on top of
    C. atop
    D. on which

12. F. NO CHANGE
    G. don't we must carry
    H. don't: we carry
    J. don't, we are carrying

13. A. NO CHANGE
    B. by keeping
    C. keeps
    D. kept

14. F. NO CHANGE
    G. Newton's Law, which can
    H. Newton's Law which is
    J. Newton's Law and that can

15. The writer is considering concluding the essay with the following statement:

    How much of our lives are lived like this.

    Should the writer end the essay with this statement?
    A. Yes, because it adds to the writer's persuasive goal of convincing the reader to learn to ride a bicycle.
    B. Yes, because it sums up the main points of the essay in a memorable way.
    C. No, because it does not have a meaningful connection to the topic of this essay.
    D. No, because it conflicts with the overall tone and message of this essay.

PASSAGE II

The Nuclear Option

Two-thirds of Americans, unfortunately, support the use of nuclear power. [17] The technology suffered growing pains, seared into the publics mind by the Chernobyl and Three Mile Island accidents, but plants have demonstrated remarkable reliability and efficiency recently. The world's ample supply of uranium could fuel a much larger fleet of reactors than exists today.

With growing worries about global warming and the associated likelihood that greenhouse gas emissions will be regulated in some fashion. It is not surprising that governments and power providers in the U.S. and elsewhere are increasingly considering building a substantial number

16. Given that all choices are true, which one most effectively introduces the topic of nuclear power without providing a hint as to the writer's position on the topic?
   F. NO CHANGE
   G. Nuclear power supplies a sixth of the world's electricity.
   H. Nuclear power is a health and environmental threat.
   J. Nuclear power is generated at too many plants in the United States.

17. At this point, the writer is considering adding the following true statement:

   > Along with hydropower, it is the major source of carbon-free energy today.

   Should the writer make this addition here?
   A. Yes, because it adds an important detail about why nuclear power is dangerous.
   B. Yes, because it provides evidence to support the writer's statement about the popularity of nuclear power.
   C. No, because it contradicts the previous sentence.
   D. No, because this would place too much factual information at the beginning.

18. F. NO CHANGE
    G. publics minds
    H. publics' minds
    J. public's mind

19. A. NO CHANGE
    B. had demonstrated
    C. will demonstrate
    D. is demonstrating

20. F. NO CHANGE
    G. some fashion, it is
    H. some fashion; it is
    J. some fashion and it is

of additional nuclear power plants. However, more than
20,000 megawatts of nuclear capacity have come online
globally since 2000, mostly in the Far East. Yet despite the
evident interest among major nuclear operators, no firm
orders have been placed in the United States. Key
impediments to new nuclear construction are high capital
costs and the uncertainty surrounding nuclear waste
management.

    Because they are many years since construction of a
nuclear plant was embarked on in the U.S., the companies
that build the first few new plants will face extra expenses
that subsequent operators will not have to bear along with
additional risk in working through a new licensing process.

    Another costly issue that a nuclear renaissance faces is
the problem of waste management no country in the world
has yet implemented a system for permanently disposing of
the spent fuel and other radioactive waste produced by
nuclear power plants.

    The future of nuclear power in the U.S. remains in
question. The credibility of such a scenario will be largely
determined by the capability of the government coming
to pass to start moving spent fuel from reactor

21. A. NO CHANGE
    B. Nevertheless,
    C. Conversely,
    D. Indeed,

22. All of the following work as effective transition EXCEPT FOR:
    F. NO CHANGE
    G. Still,
    H. Therefore
    J. OMIT the underlined portion.

23. A. NO CHANGE
    B. it has been
    C. it was
    D. it will be

24. F. NO CHANGE
    G. bear, along
    H. bear. Along
    J. bear, and along

25. Which phrase provides the most effective and stylistically consistent transition from the previous paragraph to this one?
    A. NO CHANGE
    B. An irritating thing
    C. About the millionth problem
    D. A totally impossible problem

26. F. NO CHANGE
    G. management and there is no
    H. management, no
    J. management. No

27. A. NO CHANGE
    B. remained a question.
    C. remain in question.
    D. will remain questions.

28. The best placement for the underlined portion would be
    F. where it is now.
    G. after the word *emissions*.
    H. after the word *sites*.
    J. after the word *scenario*.

sites and by whether the American political process results in a climate change policy which might significantly limit carbon dioxide emissions.
                                                29

29. **A.** NO CHANGE
    B. that just might begin to
    C. that will
    D. which, will

Question 30 asks about the preceding passage as a whole.

30. Suppose the writer's goal had been to write a brief essay about how dangerous nuclear power is and to convince readers that the U.S. should not build new nuclear plants. Would this essay successfully fulfill that goal?
    F. Yes, because the author cited numerous examples of the tragic consequences of building nuclear power plants.
    G. Yes, because the author explains how difficult it will be for the U.S. to build new nuclear power plants.
    H. No, because the author explains how beneficial nuclear power is and addresses the difficulties the U.S. faces in trying to build new plants.
    J. No, because the author doesn't present an opinion on whether or not the nuclear power plants are dangerous.

PASSAGE III

The Rodeo

I could hear their whispers as we <u>begun</u> cantering
                                      31
around the rodeo grounds after our number was called. "I
can't believe she's riding that horse in this competition. Look
at him!" Monte snorted as if he heard their collective voices
in the wind. Yet his head was <u>up, proud as ever and</u> so was
                                   32
mine, hearing a stronger, unwavering voice.

If the truth <u>were told; he</u> wasn't the most beautiful horse
                  33
in the world. 34

<u>Naturally,</u> Monte had learned a grace that could only have
  35
come from sheer spirit and determination.

[1]"No way! No way!" [2] My butt firmly in the
saddle, my back straight, and the reins held just right, we
smoothly turned into the barrels. [3] Western equitation <u>had</u>
                                                             36
<u>been</u> as unfamiliar to Monte and me as five forks in a place
  36
setting at an upscale restaurant. [4] The voices in the wind
followed us as Monte galloped faster around the ring. [5] Far
from the bareback rides across the desert we had cherished

31. **A.** NO CHANGE
    B. beginning
    C. begin
    D. began

32. **F.** NO CHANGE
    G. up, proud as ever, and
    H. up proud as ever, and
    J. up proud as ever and

33. **A.** NO CHANGE
    B. were, told he
    C. were told, he
    D. were told he,

34. At this point, the writer is considering adding following sentence:

    His huge workhorse body and thoroughbred legs made him appear clumsy and out of proportion.

    Would this be a relevant addition to make here?
    F. Yes, because it provides clarity about why Monte is so graceful.
    G. Yes, because it adds details relevant to the focus of the paragraph.
    H. No, because it provides a digression that leads the paragraph away from its primary focus.
    J. No, because the information is already provided elsewhere in the passage.

35. **A.** NO CHANGE
    B. In fact,
    C. Meanwhile,
    D. Yet

36. **F.** NO CHANGE
    G. is
    H. will be
    J. has been

over the years, we had learned the rules and were making
                                37
believers out of the crowd. [6] Monte, now almost on his

side, was racing around the barrels as gracefully as if he had

wings touched by angels, not grazing even one barrel. 39
                        38

I patted Monte's neck as we cantered out of the ring
              40

and suddenly I didn't see or hear anyone accepting my
                                              41
family. "No one will hurt your spirit but you," my

grandfathers voice
    42

echoes in the gentle wind that kissed my cheeks and my
  43

spirit. Monte looked so proud when he and me won first
                                       44
place.

37. Which of the following alternatives to the underlined portion would be LEAST acceptable?
   A. NO CHANGE
   B. beat
   C. mastered
   D. grasped

38. If the writer were to delete the underlined portion, placing a period after the word *angels*, the paragraph would primarily lose:
   F. an emphasis on how quickly Monte raced.
   G. information about how Monte was judged.
   H. an explanation for how Monte raced gracefully.
   J. an unnecessary detail.

39. For the sake of the logic and coherence of this paragraph, Sentence 4 should be placed:
   A. where it is now.
   B. before Sentence 2.
   C. after Sentence 2.
   D. after Sentence 6.

40. Given that all of the choices are true, which one most effectively introduces the action in this paragraph while suggesting the writer's nervousness?
   F. NO CHANGE
   G. I proudly held up my head
   H. I dropped the reins
   J. I glanced anxiously at the crowd

41. A. NO CHANGE
    B. accept for
    C. except for
    D. excepting

42. F. NO CHANGE
    G. grandfather's
    H. grandfathers'
    J. grandfather

43. A. NO CHANGE
    B. will echo
    C. echoing
    D. echoed

44. F. NO CHANGE
    G. he and I
    H. him and me
    J. him and I

TEST 2

GO ON TO THE NEXT PAGE.

Question 45 asks about the preceding passage as a whole.

45. Suppose that one of the writer's goals had been illustrate that spirit and determination is just important as inborn ability. Would this essay ful this goal?
    A. Yes, because Monte was a beautiful racehorse who helped the writer overcome her challenges.
    B. Yes, because the writer was able to win the race riding Monte, even though Monte wasn't born with grace.
    C. No, because the essay doesn't address inborn abilities.
    D. No, because neither Monte nor the writer demonstrated spirit and determination.

PASSAGE IV

The Dark Ages of the Universe

Cosmologists will address some of the fundamental
questions that people attempted to resolve over the centuries through philosophical thinking, but they are doing so based on systematic observation and a quantitative methodology. Perhaps the greatest triumph of the past centuries has been a model of the universe that is supported by a large body of data. [48]

As citizens of the universe they cannot help but wonder how the first sources of light formed, how life came into existence and whether we are alone as intelligent beings in this vast space. Astronomers in the 21st century are not able to answer these questions.

First and foremost, the ultimate goal of observational cosmology is to capture the entire history of the universe, providing a seamless picture of our descent from a shapeless

46. F. NO CHANGE
 G. Cosmologists have only recently begun to address
 H. Cosmologists are addressing
 J. Cosmologists have spent many years trying to address

47. A. NO CHANGE
 B. will be
 C. is
 D. has become

48. At this point, the writer is considering adding the following sentence:

 The value of such a model to our society is sometimes underappreciated.

 Should the writer add this sentence here?
 F. Yes, because it provides an effective transition between sentences.
 G. Yes, because it explains why the writer went into so much detail describing the model.
 H. No, because the passage states elsewhere that the model is highly valued by society.
 J. No, because it changes the subject to one that is not subsequently developed.

49. A. NO CHANGE
 B. we
 C. one
 D. he

50. Which choice would best conclude this paragraph by providing insight into the main idea of the essay?
 F. NO CHANGE
 G. Astronomers now have the technology and knowledge to answer these questions and many more.
 H. Astronomers in the 21st century are uniquely positioned to answer these big questions.
 J. Astronomers are lucky to have new equipment that will help them answer these puzzles.

51. A. NO CHANGE
 B. The ultimate goal
 C. Increasingly, the ultimate goal
 D. Most importantly, the goal

gas of subatomic particles. We have a snapshot of the universe as it was 400,000 years after the big bang <u>- the cosmic microwave background radiation -</u> as well as pictures
52
of individual galaxies a billion years later.

<u>Cosmologists are currently observing this period of time, known as the Dark Ages.</u> In between the release of the
53
microwave background and the first rays of starlight was a period when the universe was dark and the microwave background no longer traced the distribution of matter. It might sound like a <u>languid gloomy</u> time, a boring interlude
54
between the immediate aftermath of the big bang and the bustling cosmos of the present day. <u>Indeed,</u> a great deal
55
happened in these <u>Dark Ages the</u> primordial soup evolved
56
into the rich zoo of celestial bodies we now see. <u>Within the inky blackness, the cosmos assembled objects with gravitational forces.</u>
57

Astronomers are currently searching for the missing pages of the cosmic photo album, which will show how the

52. The writer is considering deleting the underlined portion. Should the underlined portion be kept or deleted?
   F. Kept, because it introduces the reader to an important concept.
   G. Kept, because without it the sentence would be grammatically incorrect.
   H. Deleted, because the information is not relevant.
   J. Deleted, because it confuses the reader by introducing new terms that are never explained or discussed again.

53. Which sentence provides the best transition between paragraphs?
   A. NO CHANGE
   B. However, the time between those two periods is even more important.
   C. These snapshots tell us a lot about how the universe has evolved over time.
   D. However that still leaves a tremendous gap.

54. F. NO CHANGE
   G. languid; gloomy
   H. languid, gloomy
   J. languid gloomier

55. A. NO CHANGE
   B. But in fact,
   C. On the other hand,
   D. Besides,

56. F. NO CHANGE
   G. Dark Ages: the
   H. Dark Ages, the
   J. Dark Ages, but the

57. A. NO CHANGE
   B. Assembling objects in the cosmos, inky blackness, the gravitational forces.
   C. In the inky blackness, objects assembled the gravitational forces.
   D. In the inky blackness, gravitational forces assembled objects in the cosmos.

universe evolved during its' infancy and made the building
blocks of galaxies like our own Milky Way. This work
motivated a major fraction of future observational projects
and promises to be one of the most exciting frontiers in
cosmology over the next decade. 60

58. F. NO CHANGE
G. it's
H. its
J. her

59. A. NO CHANGE
B. will motivate
C. has been motivating
D. motivate

60. The writer is considering concluding the essay with the following statement:

> As cosmologists fill in the missing snapshots of the cosmos, they will be closer to answering the age-old questions that puzzle us all.

Should the writer end the essay with this statement?
F. Yes, because it reassures the reader that the work is not dangerous.
G. Yes, because it supports the essay's main idea and emphasizes the importance of the questions asked.
H. No, because the preceding sentence contains the same information expressed in a different way.
J. No, because it does not have a meaningful connection to the topic of this essay.

PASSAGE V

Gut Feelings

Intuitions or gut feelings, are sudden, strong judgments
              61
whose origin they can't immediately explain. Although they
                  62
seem to emerge from an obscure inner force, they actually
begin with a perception of something outside—a facial
expression, a tone of voice, or a visual inconsistency so
fleeting you're not even aware you had noticed it.
                                    63

Think of them as rapid cognition or condensed
    64
reasoning that takes advantage of the brain's built-in
shortcuts. Or think of intuition as an unconscious associative
process. 65

The best explanation psychologists now offer is
              66
that intuition is a mental matching game. The brain takes in a
                                                  67
situation, doing a very quick search of its files, and then finds
         67

61. A. NO CHANGE
   B. Intuitions, or gut feelings
   C. Intuitions, or gut feelings,
   D. Intuitions or gut feelings

62. F. NO CHANGE
   G. you can't
   H. people won't
   J. one doesn't

63. A. NO CHANGE
   B. notice
   C. felt
   D. feel

64. F. NO CHANGE
   G. Think of intuition
   H. Think on it
   J. Thinking of them

65. At this point, the writer is considering adding the following sentence:

   Long dismissed as magical or beneath the dignity of science, intuition appears to consist of fast mental operations.

   Would this be a relevant addition to make here?
   A. Yes, because it provides a needed transition between sentences.
   B. Yes, because it finally provides the official definition of "intuition."
   C. No, because it contradicts the idea expressed in the following sentence.
   D. No, because it provides a digression that leads the paragraph away from its primary focus.

66. Which phrase best introduces the sentence?
   F. NO CHANGE
   G. The only thing we know for sure is
   H. The only possible explanation is
   J. Psychologists now believe

67. A. NO CHANGE
   B. takes in a situation, does a very quick search
   C. took in a situation, doing a very quick search
   D. take in a situation, does a very quick search

GO ON TO THE NEXT PAGE.

its best analogy among the stored sprawl of memories and knowledge. Based on that analogy – you ascribe meaning to the situation in front of you. A doctor might simply glance at a pallid young woman complaining of fatigue and shortness of breath and immediately intuit one suffers from anemia.

Experience is encoded in our brains as a web of fact and feeling. When a new experience calls up a similar pattern, it doesn't unleash just stored knowledge but also an emotional state of mind and a predisposition to respond by it in a certain way.

While endless reasoning in the absence of intuitions is unproductive, some people champion the other extreme—"going with the gut" at all times.

Accordingly, intuition is best used as the first step in solving a problem or deciding what to do. The more experience you have in a particular domain, the more reliable your intuitions, because they haven't been used many times before. But even in your area of expertise, it's wisest to test out your hunches—you could easily have latched on to the wrong detail and pulled up the wrong web of associations in your brain.

68. F. NO CHANGE
    G. analogy: you
    H. analogy, you
    J. analogy; you

69. A. NO CHANGE
    B. she
    C. he
    D. her

70. Which choice best illustrates how information is stored in our brains?
    F. NO CHANGE
    G. Everything we do is stored in our brain.
    H. Experience is processed by our brains.
    J. Our brain remembers all of our experiences.

71. A. NO CHANGE
    B. respond
    C. have responded
    D. be responding

72. The writer is considering deleting this sentence. Should the sentence be kept or deleted?
    F. Kept, because it is relevant to the discussion of where intuitions come from.
    G. Kept, because it provides a useful introduction to the paragraph.
    H. Deleted, because it contradicts the idea that people should pay attention to their intuitions.
    J. Deleted, because it is stylistically inconsistent with the rest of the essay.

73. A. NO CHANGE
    B. Also,
    C. For instance,
    D. But

74. Which phrase best supports the idea presented in this sentence?
    F. NO CHANGE
    G. because you haven't formed many situational analogies.
    H. because they arise out of the richest array of collected patterns of experience.
    J. because you should trust your unconscious mind.

TEST 2

GO ON TO THE NEXT PAGE.

So pay attention to your intuition, because the

information you received is valid. But it's important to
balance this with reason so that you don't make an error of

judgment in an impulsive moment.

75. **A.** NO CHANGE
    B. have received
    C. will be receiving
    D. receive

MATHEMATICS TEST
60 Minutes—60 Questions

DIRECTIONS: Solve each problem, choose the correct answer, and then fill in the corresponding oval on your answer document.

Do not linger over problems that take too much time. Solve as many as you can; then return to the others in the time you have left for this test.

You are permitted to use a calculator on this test. You may use your calculator for any problems you choose, but some of the problems may best be done without using a calculator.

Note: Unless otherwise stated, all of the following should be assumed.

1. Illustrative figures are NOT necessarily drawn to scale.
2. Geometric figures lie in a plane.
3. The word *line* indicates a straight line.
4. The word *average* indicates arithmetic mean.

---

1. What is the value of the expression $(y - x)^3$ when $x = 5$ and $y = 1$?

    A. -64
    B. -4
    C. 4
    D. 16
    E. 64

2. What is the smallest positive integer that is divisible by 3, divisible by 5, and divisible by 6 (with no remainders)?

    F. 15
    G. 30
    H. 60
    J. 90
    K. 180

3. If $[-s + h(t \cdot 3 - w)]r = 1,$ then which of the following variables CANNOT equal 0?

    A. h
    B. r
    C. s
    D. t
    E. w

4. In a certain school district, exactly 30% of the students come from families that have only 1 child. If there are 7,340 students in the district, how many do NOT come from families with only 1 child?

    F. 220
    G. 514
    H. 2,202
    J. 5,138
    K. 7,120

DO YOUR FIGURING HERE.

GO ON TO THE NEXT PAGE.

DO YOUR FIGURING HERE.

5. For all $x < 3$, $(3-2x)^2 = ?$

A. x^2
B. $9 - x^2$
C. $9 + x^2$
D. $9 - 10x - 4x^2$
E. $9 - 12x + 4x^2$

6. What is the slope-intercept form of the equation $3y + 2x = 24$?

F. $y = -\frac{2x}{3} + 8$
G. $y = -\frac{3x}{2} + 12$
H. $3 = 2m + b$
J. $m = 2b + 24$
K. $y = 2x + 24$

7. What is the slope of a line perpendicular to the line $3x + 2y = 19$?

A. $-\frac{3}{2}$
B. $-\frac{2}{3}$
C. $\frac{2}{3}$
D. $\frac{3}{2}$
E. 3

GO ON TO THE NEXT PAG

8. The volume of cone is given by the formula $V = \frac{\pi}{3}r^2h$, where r is the radius of the base of the cone and h is the height of the cone. What is the volume, in cubic centimeters, of a cone with a height of 8cm that has a base with a radius of 3cm?

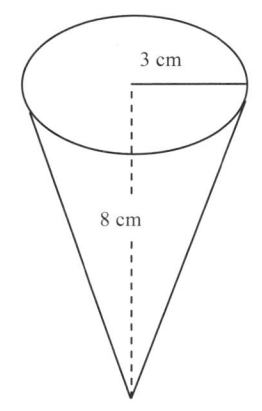

F. 72π
G. 48π
H. 24π
J. 12π
K. 8π

9. Given that m and n are parallel lines, t is a transversal crossing both m and n, and m $\angle b = 100°$, what is the measure of $\angle e$?

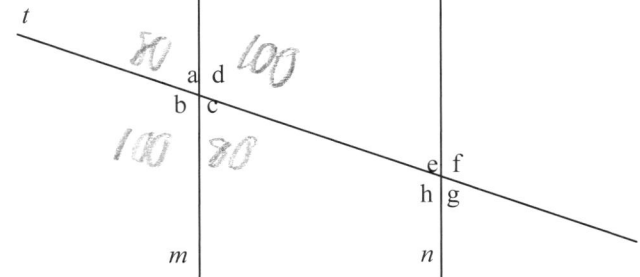

A. 40°
B. 50°
C. 80°
D. 100°
E. 120°

10. In the figure below, 3 lines intersect at the indicated angles. What is the degree measure of ∠x ?

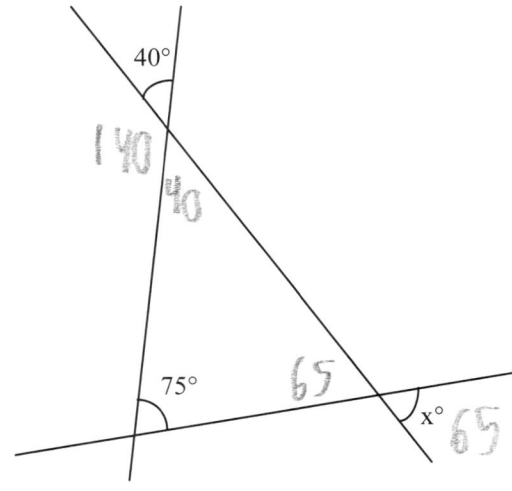

F. 35°
G. 52.5°
H. 65°
J. 70°
K. 75°

11. Find two arithmetic means between 11 and 26 such that the difference between consecutive numbers is the same:

11, _____ , _____ , 26

A. 14, 18
B. 15, 20
C. 16, 21
D. 17, 23
E. 18, 24

12. For all real numbers x and y, $(2x+3y)^2 = ?$

F. $6x^2y^2$
G. $4x^2+6y^2$
H. $4x^2+9y^2$
J. $4x^2+6xy+6y^2$
K. $4x^2+12xy+9y^2$

13. In a certain town in New Hampshire, there are 7,695 registered voters, 60% of whom are Democrats. How many of the town's registered voters are Democrats?

A. 513
B. 2,565
C. 3,078
D. 4,617
E. 7,695

4. Which of the following lines has the same graph as the line $2x - y = 12$?

   F. $6x + 3y = 36$
   G. $4x + 2y = 24$
   H. $4x - 2y = 12$
   J. $4x - 4y = 24$
   K. $-6x + 3y = -36$

5. When $\frac{1}{3}w + \frac{2}{5}w = 1$, what is the value of w?

   A. $\frac{1}{11}$
   B. $\frac{3}{8}$
   C. $\frac{11}{15}$
   D. $\frac{15}{11}$
   E. $\frac{8}{3}$

6. In the figure below, $\overline{AB}$ and $\overline{CD}$ bisect each other at E. The measure of $\angle CAE$ is 80° and the measure of $\angle BDE$ is 60°. What is the measure of $\angle CEA$?

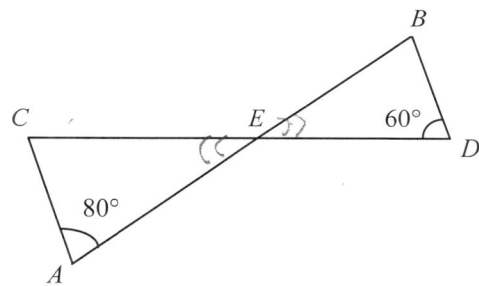

   F. 10°
   G. 30°
   H. 40°
   J. 60°
   K. Cannot be determined.

7. Given that $A = (3, 2)$ and $B = (15, 8)$ in the standard (x, y) coordinate plane, what is the distance from A to B?

   A. $5\sqrt{2}$
   B. 8
   C. $4\sqrt{10}$
   D. $6\sqrt{5}$
   E. 18

18. For all real numbers a, b, and c such that $a < b$ and $c > 0$, which of the following inequalities, if any, must be true?

   F. $a < c$
   G. $b < c$
   H. $a > c$
   J. $b > c$
   K. None of the above inequalities must be true.

19. A deli offers 4 types of sandwich meat, 3 kinds of cheese, and 5 bread varieties. When you order a sandwich at the deli, you are allowed to choose 1 meat, 1 cheese, and 1 type of bread. How many different sandwich combinations are possible at the deli?

   A. 3
   B. 12
   C. 15
   D. 30
   E. 60

20. At a certain company, 240 of the employees are women and the remaining 160 are men. What percentage of the company's workers are women?

   F. 25%
   G. $33\frac{1}{3}\%$
   H. 40%
   J. 60%
   K. $66\frac{2}{3}\%$

21. Alana leaves home to drive to college. She drives 200 miles in 4 hours before stopping for gas. She then drives 10 miles per hour faster than she did on the first part of her trip, and arrives at her dorm in 3 hours. How many miles did she drive in total?

   A. 200
   B. 300
   C. 350
   D. 380
   E. 430

2. If the monthly payment, M dollars, on a house that costs P dollars is given by the formula $M = \dfrac{P}{200} - .0008P + 40$, what is the monthly payment, to the nearest dollar, on a house that costs \$200,000?

F. \$868
G. \$880
H. \$960
J. \$1,060
K. \$1,200

3. What is the sum of the prime factors of the number 330?

A. 6
B. 19
C. 21
D. 22
E. 43

4. In the standard (x, y) coordinate plane, a line passes through the points $(1, -2)$ and $(5, 10)$. At which of the following points does the line cross the y-axis?

F. $(-8, 0)$
G. $(-5, 0)$
H. $(0, 0)$
J. $(0, -5)$
K. $(0, -8)$

5. For all positive a, b, and c, $\dfrac{2^{-1}a^{-3}b^7c^2}{(5a)^2 b^{-1} c^7} = ?$

A. $\dfrac{2b^6}{5a^2c^5}$
B. $\dfrac{2b^8c^9}{2a^5}$
C. $\dfrac{2b^8c^9}{25a^5}$
D. $\dfrac{b^8}{10a^5c^5}$
E. $\dfrac{b^8}{50a^5c^5}$

26. One endpoint of a diameter of a circle with center (2, -3) has coordinates at (5, -2) in the standard (x, y) plane. What are the coordinates of the other endpoint of the diameter?

   F. $(2-\sqrt{10},\ -3-\sqrt{10})$
   G. (-1, -4)
   H. (0, -4)
   J. $(2+\sqrt{10},\ -3+\sqrt{10})$
   K. (8, -1)

27. Payton ran $1\frac{2}{3}$ miles on Monday, $2\frac{1}{5}$ miles on Tuesday, and $1\frac{7}{8}$ miles on Wednesday. What is the median distance that he ran?

   A. 7.200 miles
   B. 5.742 miles
   C. 1.914 miles
   D. 1.875 miles
   E. None of these.

28. If $6x^2 + x - c = (cx - 1)(3x + 2)$, what is the value of c?

   F. -2
   G. -1
   H. 2
   J. 3
   K. 6

29. What is the y-coordinate of the point of intersection of the lines $y = 3x - 7$ and $y = 5x + 5$ in the standard (x, y) coordinate plane?

   A. -25
   B. -11
   C. -6
   D. 6
   E. 11

30. What is the area, in square inches, of the figure shown below?

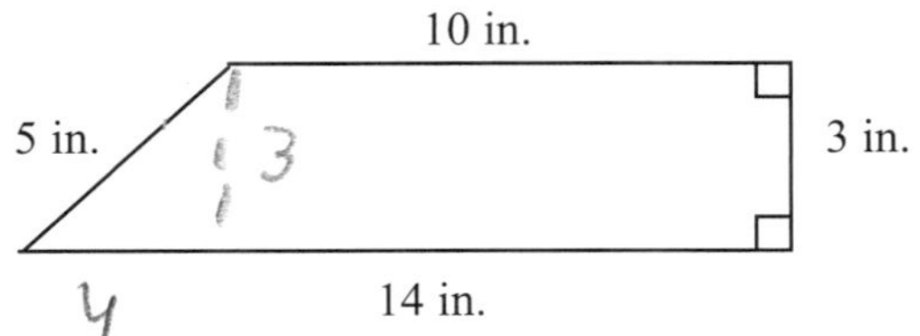

   F. 24
   G. 32
   H. 36
   J. 42
   K. 72

1. What is the solution set for the inequality $6 - 4(x - 2) > 4x + 5$?

   A. $x < -\frac{7}{8}$
   B. $x < -\frac{1}{4}$
   C. $x < \frac{9}{8}$
   D. $x > -\frac{7}{8}$
   E. $x > \frac{9}{8}$

2. For the circle whose standard equation is $(x - 1)^2 + (y + 2)^2 = 8$, the center and radius are:

   F. Center = (-1, 2) ; Radius = $2\sqrt{2}$
   G. Center = (-1, 2) ; Radius = 4
   H. Center = (0, 0) ; Radius = 4
   J. Center = (1, -2) ; Radius = $2\sqrt{2}$
   K. Center = (1, -2) ; Radius = 4

3. Parallelogram RSTU is shown below, with $\overline{UA}$ = 4 inches, $\overline{AS}$ = 7 inches, and $\overline{ST}$ = 5 inches. What is the area of RSTU in square inches?

   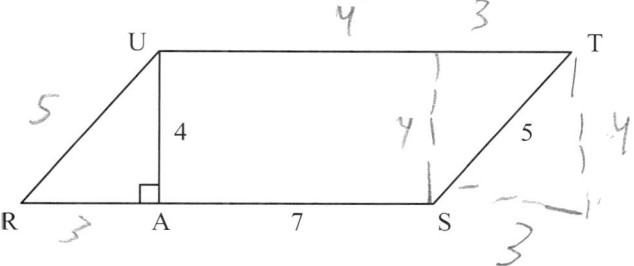

   A. 16
   B. 20
   C. 28
   D. 35
   E. 40

34. If the lengths of the sides of the triangle below are shown in inches, how many inches long is side $\overline{AB}$?

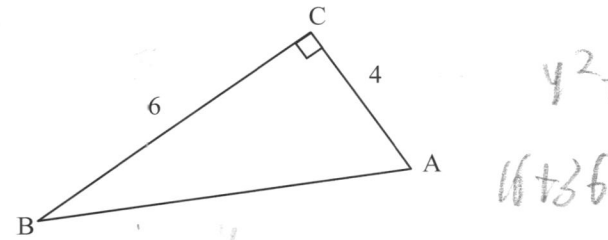

DO YOUR FIGURING HERE.

F. $2\sqrt{13}$
G. 10
H. $4\sqrt{13}$
J. 26
K. 42

35. Which of the following is the equation for a circle with diameter $\overline{AB}$, given that $A = (4, 2)$ and $B = (8, -4)$?

A. $x^2 + y^2 = 13$
B. $x^2 + y^2 = 26$
C. $(x-6)^2 + (y+1)^2 = 13$
D. $(x+6)^2 + (y-1)^2 = 13$
E. $(x-6)^2 + (y+1)^2 = 26$

36. Which of the following comprises all of the values of x for which $\frac{2}{3}x - \frac{1}{2} < \frac{1}{2}x + \frac{2}{3}$?

F. $x < 1$
G. $x < \frac{7}{6}$
H. $x < 7$
J. $x > \frac{7}{3}$
K. $x > 7$

A guide wire for a telephone tower makes an angle of 50° with the level ground and is 14 meters from the base of the tower. How many meters long in the guide wire?

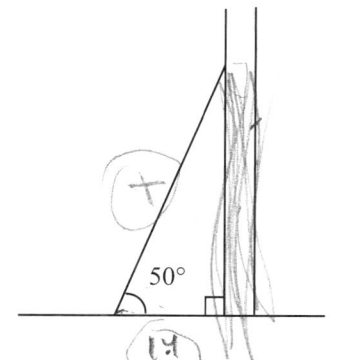

A. 3.80
B. 13.50
C. 16.68
D. 21.78
E. 22.58

For all $x^2 \neq 9$, $\dfrac{(x-3)^2}{x^2-9}$ is equivalent to:

F. -1
G. $\dfrac{1}{2}$
H. 1
J. $\dfrac{1}{x+3}$
K. $\dfrac{x-3}{x+3}$

In the standard (x, y) coordinate plane, the midpoint of $\overline{AB}$ is $(5, 7)$ and A is located at $(2, 3)$. If the coordinates of B are (x, y), what is the value of $(x + y)$?

A. 19
B. 17
C. 11
D. 8.5
E. 8

If the solutions to the equation $(x+a)(x+b) = 0$ are $x = 8$ and $x = -\dfrac{3}{2}$, then $a + b = ?$

F. -13
G. -12
H. -6.5
J. 6.5
K. 12

41. In the figure below, all line segments intersect at right angles, and all measurements are given in inches. What is the perimeter of the figure in inches?

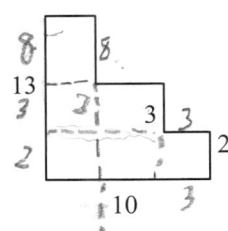

A. 23
B. 28
C. 46
D. 130
E. Cannot be determined

42. If $\cot \theta = P$, which of the following expressions must also equal P?

F. $\tan \theta$

G. $\csc \theta - 1$

H. $\sin \theta - \cos \theta$

J. $\dfrac{\sin \theta}{\cos \theta}$

K. $\dfrac{\cos \theta}{\sin \theta}$

43. A line in the standard (x, y) coordinate plane contains the points $(5, 9)$ and $(8, 3)$. What is the x-intercept of this line?

A. 19
B. $\dfrac{19}{2}$
C. 0
D. -2
E. $-\dfrac{19}{2}$

44. Each side of a given cube is a square with an area of 729 square inches. What is the volume of the cube in cubic inches?

F. 3^3
G. 3^9
H. 3^{12}
J. 3^{18}
K. 3^{64}

318
TEST 2

5. If p and q are positive integers, and $6pq^4$ and $12p^2q^2$ have a greatest common factor of 1,050, then which of the following is a possible value for the sum of p and q ?

A. 6
B. 8
C. 12
D. 35
E. 42

6. In the figure shown below, ΔABC is a right triangle, $\overline{AB}$ is 8 inches long, and $\overline{BC}$ is 10 inches long. What is the area, in square inches, of square ACDE?

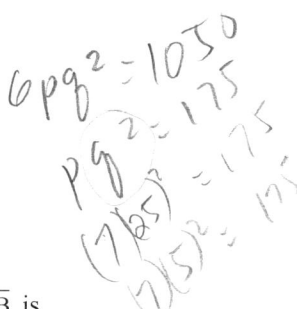

F. $2\sqrt{41}$
G. $\sqrt{164}$
H. 36
J. $8\sqrt{41}$
K. 164

7. In the standard coordinate plane, what is the distance between the points (5, 7) and (13, 11)?

A. 80
B. 12
C. $\sqrt{80}$
D. 8
E. $\sqrt{8}$

8. What value must be added to $9x^2 - 30x$ in order to *complete the square* (that is, make it a perfect square trinomial)?

F. -5
G. 5
H. 9
J. 25
K. 45

GO ON TO THE NEXT PAGE.

49. A circle in the standard (x, y) coordinate plane is tangent to the x-axis at $-a$, and tangent to the y-axis at a, with $a > 0$. The radius of the circle is 4 units. What is the equation of the circle?

A. $x^2 - y^2 = 4$
B. $x^2 + y^2 = 16$
C. $(x-4)^2 + (y-4)^2 = 4$
D. $(x+4)^2 + (y+4)^2 = 16$
E. $(x+4)^2 + (y-4)^2 = 16$

50. Compared to the graph of $y = \sin x$, the graph of $y = 2 \sin(4x)$ has:

F. 8 times the amplitude and the same period.
G. 2 times the amplitude and 4 times the period.
H. 2 times the amplitude and ¼ the period.
J. ½ the amplitude and 4 times the period.
K. ½ the amplitude and ¼ the period.

51. Which of the following is the solution set for x such that $3x - 9 \geq -3(9 - x)$?

A. The empty set.
B. The set containing only zero.
C. The set of negative numbers.
D. The set of positive numbers.
E. The set of real numbers.

52. In the figure below, square ABCD has a side length of 6 inches, and squares AEFG and CHIJ each have a side length of 1 inch. What is the area, in square inches, of the shaded pentagon DGFIJ?

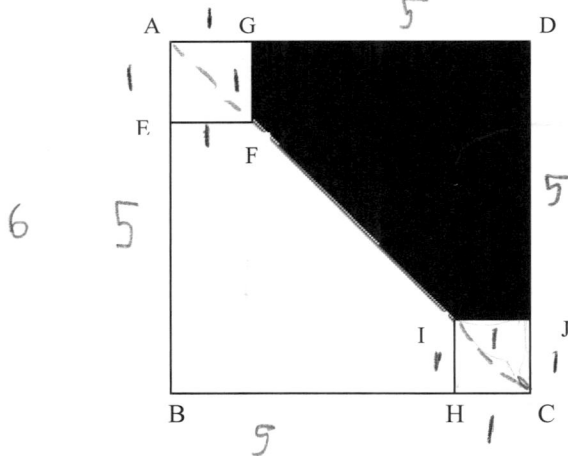

F. 9
G. 12.5
H. 17
J. 18
K. 20.5

3. Let the operation # be defined for the set of real numbers by:
$$x \# y = \frac{x+y}{3}.$$
Which of the following statements are true for all real numbers x, y, and z?

  I. $x \# y = y \# x$
  II. $(x \# y) \# z = x \# (y \# z)$
  III. $0 \# x = 0$

A. I only.
B. II only.
C. III only.
D. I and III only.
E. II and III only.

4. If $x^2 - 36a^2 = 5ax$, what are the two solutions for x in terms of a?

F. $-4a$ and $-9a$
G. $-4a$ and $9a$
H. $-3a$ and $12a$
J. $3a$ and $-12a$
K. $4a$ and $-9a$

5. For all values of θ over which $\sin\theta$ and $\cos\theta$ are non-zero,
$$\frac{\sqrt{1-\cos^2\theta}}{\sin^2\theta} \cdot \cos\theta = ?$$

A. 1
B. $\tan\theta$
C. $\cot\theta$
D. $\sec\theta$
E. $\csc\theta$

6. For values of x where $\csc x$, $\sec x$, and $\tan x$ are all defined, $(\csc x) \cdot (\sec x) \cdot (\tan x) = ?$

F. $\sec^2 x$
G. $\csc^2 x$
H. $\tan^2 x$
J. 1
K. -1

57. What is the solution set for the equation $|-x| = x$?

   A. All real numbers.
   B. $x \geq 0$
   C. $x \leq 0$
   D. Only $x = 0$.
   E. Only $x = -1$.

58. For which of the following values of a will there be exactly one real solution to the equation $2x^2 - ax + 8 = 0$?

   F. $2\sqrt{3}$
   G. 4
   H. $4\sqrt{3}$
   J. 6
   K. 8

59. If $x = 3t + 4$ and $y = 5 - t$, then which of the following equations expresses y in terms of x?

   A. $y = \dfrac{19 - x}{3}$
   B. $y = \dfrac{1 - x}{3}$
   C. $y = 9 - x$
   D. $y = x + 9$
   E. $y = x - 1$

In the circle below, radius $\overline{OA}$ has a length of 10 meters, and central angle $\angle AOB$ measures 30°. What is the area, in square meters, of shaded sector AOB?

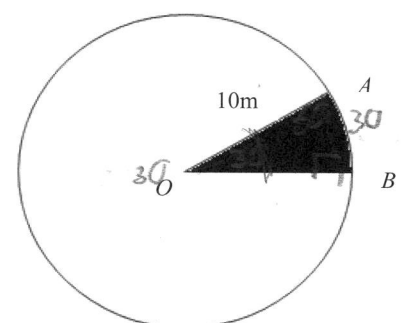

F. $\dfrac{5\pi}{6}$

G. $\dfrac{5\pi}{3}$

H. $\dfrac{10\pi}{3}$

J. $\dfrac{25\pi}{6}$

K. $\dfrac{25\pi}{3}$

DO YOUR FIGURING HERE.

END OF TEST
STOP! DO NOT TURN THE PAGE UNTIL TOLD TO DO SO.
DO NOT RETURN TO THE PREVIOUS TEST.

3

READING TEST

35 Minutes – 40 Questions

DIRECTIONS: There are four passages in this test. Each passage is followed by several questions. After reading a passage, choose the best answer to each question and fill in the corresponding oval on your answer document. You may refer to the passages as often as necessary.

Passage I

PROSE FICTION: This passage is adapted from the short story "State Champions" by Bobbie Ann Mason (1989 by Harper & Row, Publishers)

The gymnasium where the Cuba Cubs practiced was the hub of the school. Their trophies gleamed in a glass display case near the entrance, between the principal's office and the gymnasium, and the enormous
5 coal furnace that heated the gym hunched in a corner near the bleachers. Several classrooms opened onto the gym floor, with the study hall at the end. The lower grades occupied a separate building, and in those grades we used an outhouse. But in junior high we had the
10 privilege of using the indoor rest rooms, which also opened onto the gym. (The boys' room included a locker room for the team, but like the outhouses, the girls' room didn't even have private compartments.) The route from the study hall to the girls' room was
15 dangerous. We had to walk through the gym, along the sidelines, under some basketball hoops. There were several baskets, so many players could practice their shots simultaneously. At recess and lunch, in addition to the Cuba Cubs, all the junior high boys used the gym,
20 too, in frantic emulation of their heroes. On the way to the rest room you had to calculate quickly and carefully when you could run beneath a basket. The players pretended that they were oblivious of you, but just when you thought you were safe and could dash under the
25 basket, they would hurl a ball out of nowhere, and the ball would fall on your head as you streaked by. Even though I was sort of a tomboy and liked to run—back in the fifth grade I could run as fast as most boys—I had no desire to play basketball. It was too violent.

30 Doodle Floyd himself bopped me on the head once, but I doubt if he remembers it.

The year of the championship was the year I got in trouble for running in the study hall. At lunch hour one day, Judy Howell and I decided to run the length of the
35 gym as fast as we could, daring ourselves to run through the hailstorm of basketballs flying at us. We ra[n] through the gym and kept running, unable to s[top] down, finally skidding to a stop in the study hall. [We] were giggling because we caught a glimpse of what [one]
40 of the senior players was wearing under his gr[ay] practice shorts (different from the satin show sh[orts] they wore at the games), when Mr. Gilhorn, the hist[ory] teacher, big as a buffalo, appeared before us [and] growled, "What do you young ladies think yo[u're]
45 doing?"

I had on the tightest Levi's I owned. When t[hey] were newly washed and ironed, they fit snug. [My] mother had ironed a crease in them. I had on a cow[boy] shirt and a bandana. Mr. Gilhorn went on, "Now, g[irls,]
50 do we run in our own living rooms? Peggy, does y[our] mama let you run in the house?"

"Yes," I said, staring at him confidently. "[My] mama always lets me run in the house." It was a lie[, of] course, but it was my habit to contradict whate[ver]
55 anybody assumed. If I was supposed to be lady, th[en I] would be a cowboy. The truth in this instance was [that] it had never occurred to me to run in our house. It [was] too small, and the floorboards were shaky. Therefo[re, I] reasoned, my mother had never laid down the law ab[out]
60 not running in the house.

Judy said, "We won't do it again." But I woul[dn't] promise.

"I know what would be good for you girls," [said] Mr. Gilhorn in a kindly, thoughtful tone, as if he [had]
65 just had a great idea.

That meant the duckwalk. As punishment, J[udy] and I had to squat, grabbing our ankles, and duckw[alk] around the gym. We waddled, humiliated, with basketballs beating on our heads and the pla[yers]
70 following our progress with loud quacks of derision.

324
TEST 2   GO ON TO THE NEXT PAG[E]

Copyright © 2009 Academic Educational Resources. All rights reserved.

"This is your fault," Judy claimed. She stopped speaking to me, which disappointed me because we had been playmates since the second grade. I admired her short blond curls and color-coordinated outfits. She had been to Detroit one summer.

During study-hall periods, we could hear the basketballs pounding on the floor. We could tell when a player made a basket—that pause after the ball hit the backboard and sank luxuriously into the net before hitting the floor. I visited the library more than necessary just to get a glimpse of the Cubs practicing as I passed the door to the gym. The library was a shelf at one end of the study hall, and it had a couple of hundred old books—mostly hand-me-downs from the Graves County Library, including outdated textbooks and even annuals from Kentucky colleges. That year I read some old American histories, and a biography of Benjamin Franklin, and the "Junior Miss" books. On the wainscoted walls of the study hall were gigantic framed pictures, four feet high, each composed of inset portraits of all the faculty members and the seniors of a specific year. They gazed down at us like kings and queens on playing cards. There was a year for each frame, and they dated all the way back to the early forties.

1. The main conflict in this passage can best be described as the:
   A. discrepancy between the treatment of boys and the treatment of girls at the narrator's school.
   B. tension created by the dangerous route through the gym the narrator had to follow in order to use the restroom.
   C. challenges the narrator faces as a headstrong seventh grader.
   D. hostility Judy Howell expresses toward the narrator following the duckwalk incident.

2. It can reasonably be inferred from the passage that the narrator views Mr. Gilhorn as:
   F. a powerful figure determined to make her experience in junior high miserable.
   G. someone whose assumptions had to be challenged despite his position of authority.
   H. a history teacher who enjoys humiliating students, especially girls.
   J. a generally kind and thoughtful teacher with a notorious sense of humor.

3. Details in paragraph 4 (lines 46-51) most strongly suggest that in junior high the narrator:
   A. was vain about her appearance.
   B. dressed in a way that made her stand out.
   C. would rather have been riding a horse than attending school.
   D. made the best of her few clothing options.

4. The detailed description throughout the passage of the gymnasium where the Cuba Cubs practiced most strongly suggests that:
   F. basketball serves as a backdrop for the narrator's memories of her 7th grade experience.
   G. the narrator was preoccupied with basketball because, as a girl, she was not allowed to participate.
   H. the narrator is unable to forget the location of her most humiliating experience as a junior high student.
   J. because of its position in relation to other rooms at her school, the gymnasium stands out in the narrator's memory.

5. As it is depicted in the 9th paragraph (lines 71-75), the relationship between the narrator and Judy Howell is best described by which of the following statements?
   A. The two are long-time friends who look and act alike.
   B. The two are long-time friends with a history of causing trouble.
   C. The two are envious of and easily angered by each other.
   D. The two share a long-standing friendship but differ in their attitude toward authority.

6. It can reasonably be inferred from the passage that which of the following events happened first in the narrator's life?
   F. She witnessed the Cuba Cubs win the state championship in basketball.
   G. She was bopped on the head with a basketball by Doodle Floyd.
   H. She earned the privilege of using an indoor restroom rather than an outhouse during school.
   J. She got in trouble for running in study hall.

7. In line 20, the narrator's description of the junior high boys playing basketball "*in frantic emulation of their heroes*" most nearly means that these boys:
   A. anxiously attempted to imitate the players on the high school basketball team.
   B. nervously dodged the basketballs being thrown at them by the older students.
   C. secretly played basketball when members of the Cuba Cubs were otherwise occupied.
   D. awkwardly retrieved the basketballs thrown by the Cubs during practice.

8. As she is revealed in the passage, the narrator is best described as:
   F. dishonest, disrespectful, and easily distracted.
   G. fearful, contradictory, and playfully irresponsible.
   H. athletic, shallow, and overly proud.
   J. observant, strong-willed and youthfully impulsive.

9. It can reasonably be inferred from the passage that Doodle Floyd:
   A. is the narrator's boyfriend the year the Cubs won the state championship.
   B. is the senior player whom the narrator regar as a significant member of the team.
   C. is one of the players credited with making t Cuba Cubs' state championship possible.
   D. is the student who informed Mr. Gilhorn that the narrator and Judy Howell were running study hall.

10. Which of the following statements about why t narrator visited the library so often while she w in seventh grade is most clearly supported by t passage?
    F. She was an avid reader, especially of American history.
    G. She was fascinated by the pictures of faculty and seniors that lined the library walls.
    H. She was distracted by the sounds of basketballs on the gymnasium floor and co not concentrate during study hall.
    J. She was eager to pass the gym door on the way to the library to get a quick look at the Cubs practicing basketball.

NO TEST MATERIAL ON THIS PAGE.

GO ON TO THE NEXT PAGE.

Passage II

SOCIAL SCIENCE: This passage is adapted from "The Real History of Reality TV Or, How Alan Funt Won the Cold War" written by Charles B. Slocum, WGAw Assistant Executive Director.

The manifest destiny of television technology is real-time viewing of all the places the audience is not. It's the ultimate peek into the neighbor's kitchen window. The entertainment conglomerates found a way
[5] to make televised life a business, so now there is a lot of it.

Reality-based television is not new, of course. Alan Funt, with his 1948 TV series *Candid Camera* is often credited as reality TV's first practitioner. In fact,
[10] he started a year earlier with *Candid Microphone* on radio. *Truth or Consequences* started in 1950 and frequently used secret cameras. Both of these two pioneering series created artificial realities to see how ordinary people would respond.

[15] The reality series of today borrow a lot from these precedents and differ mostly in scope and locale. A number of "who am I?" game shows accommodated the clunky nature of early TV technology by bringing real people into the studio. *What's My Line* premiered in
[20] 1950; *I've Got a Secret* in 1952; *To Tell the Truth* in 1956. These shows seem tame by today's standards, but were certainly cutting a new edge in the 1950s. The judge who married Marilyn Monroe and Arthur Miller appeared live on *What's My Line* within a week of
[25] performing the wedding. Even in the earliest days, the camera roamed out of the studio occasionally with film technology. *You Asked For It* took the viewer to amazing sights and spectacular phenomena as early as 1950.

[30] Perhaps ahead of its time was *An American Family* on PBS in 1973. It was unusual in its focus on a seemingly mundane family named the Louds, who harbored sensational secrets. This series pushed the documentary genre beyond its traditional bounds. The
[35] daily lives of the Loud family were on display. Sociologist Margaret Mead noted to TV Guide that this no longer fit the documentary category and that we needed a new name for this type of television. We now call it reality TV.

[40] In the commercial environment that governs almost all our television, the economics are too attractive to ignore. Reality makes for cheap entertainment. In virtually every line of the production budget, reality-based programming is cheaper than
[45] traditional programming. Not as much equipment is needed, and it's cheaper. There is a smaller crew. There are fewer paid performers. There are fewer sets. The economic role of reality-based programming is to permit a network to cost-average down the price of
[50] programming across the entire primetime schedule. A network can spend only about half of what it receives in ad revenue on the programming in which the ads run. The more it pays for *ER* and *Friends*, the less it can afford.

[55] Reality television may not be the sociological trifle many assume it is. The late Alan Funt asserted that his *Candid Camera* taught a subversive lesson: to resist unjust or ridiculous authority. Did three decades of *Candid Camera* help us questions authority during the
[60] Watergate era? Did exporting it contribute to the fall of Communism?

There are other signs of positive contribution to the social landscape from reality television. *Extreme Makeover: Home Edition* has as much or more heart as
[65] *Truth or Consequences'* military reunions did decades earlier. *America's Most Wanted* has helped catch actual criminals. Can reality television actually contribute as well as tear down?

These are questions for sociologists and historians.
[70] Economics, not ideology, drove the decisions to schedule reality television. At the start of television, now in its relative maturity, television networks need lower-cost programs to balance higher cost drama and comedy. Reality-based programs marry low-cost
[75] production techniques from news with narrative storylines from drama and comedy.

The live remote can take us to Baghdad or to the *Big Brother* house. We can watch Geraldo blow open Al Capone's vault or we can wait to see if O.J., Martha,
[80] Scott or Michael will be found guilty. The ambush has lived on from *Candid Camera, 60 Minutes*, and *This Is Your Life* to *Punk'd*. The supernatural dimension that ripped into this plane through *Crossing Over with Jonathan Edwards* and the *Pet Psychic*. Animals
[85] grounded in this world are featured in *Animal Precinct* and *Emergency Vet*.

In all this diversity, reality TV has one appeal which it shares with fiction—we as viewers hope, desperately, to find something relevant to our own lives.
[90] We seek any small hint about how to live our own lives just a bit better, to justify our hope, or to see that we are not alone in what we face in our life. The possibility

that reality-based stories will reveal something real is so enticing that the televised society is just fine with us. Turn the camera on.

11. The passage most strongly suggests that reality TV was created primarily to:
  A. balance network programming costs.
  B. replace documentaries.
  C. question unjust authority.
  D. contribute to the social landscape.

12. When the author describes real-time viewing as "*the ultimate peek into the neighbor's kitchen window*" in the first paragraph (line 3), he most nearly means which of the following?
  F. Reality TV crosses the line of decency.
  G. Networks are allowed to break the law.
  H. Private lives become public entertainment.
  J. Anyone can become a star.

13. The primary function of the last paragraph is to:
  A. imply that the viewing public is desperate to escape the reality of their own lives.
  B. explain why the viewer response to reality TV has been so favorable.
  C. illustrate the diversity of programming available because of reality-based stories.
  D. summarize the details about reality programming presented in the passage.

14. According to the passage, what is the primary difference between the reality series of today and the pioneering series of the 40s and 50s?
  F. In the reality series of today there are fewer game shows and more secret camera shows.
  G. In the early days of TV the emphasis was on the real world rather that artificial realities.
  H. In the early series there were fewer surprises because of the limitations of the studio setting.
  J. In modern reality series there is a broader range of programming and it is frequently filmed outside a studio setting.

15. Based on paragraph 6 (lines 55-61), Alan Funt would most likely agree with which of the following statements?
  A. Today's reality-based TV contributes little to society.
  B. Cameras have no business outside the television studio.
  C. The primary goal of television should be diversity.
  D. Reality TV should do more than simply entertain.

16. The discussion in the 5th paragraph (lines 40-54) about the governing principal behind reality TV appears most to undermine the idea that:
  F. economics determines television programming.
  G. ideology drives scheduling decisions.
  H. reality TV is a sociological trifle.
  J. primetime programs bring in the greatest revenue.

17. According to the 9th paragraph (lines 77-86), *Punk'd* is similar to Candid Camera in that:
  A. it depends upon a live remote.
  B. it has a game show format.
  C. it pushes the documentary genre beyond traditional boundaries.
  D. it employs secret cameras to ambush unsuspecting victims.

18. The passage implies that *An American Family* did not fit the documentary genre because of its emphasis on:
  F. drama.
  G. fact.
  H. a single object.
  J. artistic form.

19. The passage implies that which of these is most responsible for the appeal of reality TV programming?
  A. technology.
  B. economics.
  C. relevancy.
  D. ideology.

20. In the first paragraph (line 4), the phrase "*entertainment conglomerates*" can best be defined as:
  F. those controlling the economics of entertainment.
  G. those monitoring the secret cameras.
  H. those responsible for a show's popularity.
  J. those determining how a series should be categorized.

Passage III

HUMANITIES: This passage is adapted from the article "The Global Hierarchy of Race," by Martin Jacques (2003 by Guardian).

I always found race difficult to understand. It was never intuitive. And the reason was simple. Like every other white person, I had never experienced it myself: the meaning of color was something I had to learn. The
5 turning point was falling in love with my wife, an Indian-Malaysian, and her coming to live in England. Then, over time, I came to see my own country in a completely different way, through her eyes, her background. Color is something white people never
10 have to think about because for them it is never a handicap, never a source of prejudice or discrimination, but rather the opposite, a source of privilege. However liberal and enlightened I tried to be, I still had a white outlook on the world. My wife was the beginning of my
15 education.

But it was not until we went to live in Hong Kong that my view of the world, and the place that race occupies within it, was to be utterly transformed. Rather than seeing race through the prism of my own society, I
20 learned to see it globally. When we left these shores, it felt as if we were moving closer to my wife's world: this was east Asia and she was Malaysian. And she, unlike me, had the benefit of speaking Cantonese. So my expectation was that she would feel more
25 comfortable in this environment than I would. I was wrong. As a white, I found myself treated with respect and deference; my wife, notwithstanding her knowledge of the language and her intimacy with Chinese culture, was the object of an in-your-face racism.

30 In our 14 months in Hong Kong, I learned some brutal lessons about racism. First, it is not the preserve of whites. Second, some form of racism exists in every ethnic group. Every race displays racial prejudice, is capable of racism, and carries assumptions about its
35 own virtue and superiority. Each aspect of racism, furthermore, is subtly different, reflecting the specificity of its own culture and history.

Second, there is a global racial hierarchy that helps to shape the power and the prejudices of each race. At
40 the top of this hierarchy are whites. The reasons are deep-rooted and profound. White societies have been the global top dogs for half a millennium, ever since Chinese civilization went into decline. With global hegemony, first with Europe and then the US, whites
45 have long commanded respect, as well as arousing fear and resentment, among other races. Powerfully vested common privilege, a special kind of deference throughout the world, be it Kingston, Hong Kong,
50 Delhi, Lagos - or even, despite the way it is portrayed in Britain. Whites are the only race that never suffer any kind of systemic racism anywhere in the world. And the impact of white racism has been far more profound and baneful than any other: it remains the only
55 racism with global reach.

Being top of the pile means that whites are peculiarly and uniquely insensitive to race and racism, and the power relations this involves. We are invariably the beneficiaries, never the victims. Even when well-
60 meaning, we remain strangely ignorant. The club enjoyed by whites does not reside simply in the abstraction - western societies - but in the skin of each and every one of us. Whether we like it or not, in every corner of the planet we enjoy an extraordinary personal
65 power bestowed by our color. It is something we are largely oblivious of, and consequently take for granted, irrespective of whether we are liberal or reactionary, backpackers, tourists or expatriate businessmen.

The existence of a de facto global racial hierarchy
70 helps to shape the nature of racial prejudice exhibited by other races. Whites are universally respected, even when that respect is combined with strong resentment. A race generally defers to those above it in the hierarchy and is contemptuous of those below it. The
75 Chinese - like the Japanese - widely consider themselves to be number two in the pecking order and look down upon all other races as inferior. Their respect for whites is also grudging - many Chinese believe that western hegemony is, in effect, held on no more than
80 prolonged leasehold. Those below the Chinese and Japanese in the hierarchy are invariably people of color (both Chinese and Japanese often like to see themselves as white, or nearly white). At the bottom of the pile, virtually everywhere it would seem, are those of
85 African descent, the only exception in certain cases being the indigenous peoples.

We can only understand - and tackle racism - if we are honest about it. And when it comes to race - more than any other issue - honesty is in desperately short
90 supply.

The dominant race in a society, whether white or otherwise, rarely admits to its own racism. Denial is nearly universal. The reasons are manifold. It has

white individuals see attitudes as nothing more than a
its own prejudices. It will regard its racist sense, having
the force and justification of nature. Only when
challenged by those on the receiving end is racism
outed, and attitudes begin to change.

Martin Jacques is a visiting fellow at the London School of Economics. The death of his wife, Harinder Veriah, in 2000 in a Hong Kong hospital triggered an outcry, which culminated in this summer's announcement by the Hong Kong government that it would introduce anti-racist legislation for the first time.

21. The main point of this passage is that:
    A. Racial prejudice is a global problem.
    B. White is the dominant race in every society.
    C. White racism has a greater global impact than other forms of racism.
    D. Most people are oblivious to their own racism.

22. Based on its use in lines 44 and 79, the word "*hegemony*" means:
    F. racial prejudice within a society.
    G. grudging deference toward superior races.
    H. authority of one nation over another.
    J. universal denial regarding prejudice.

23. According to the author, a significant difference between being white and being any other race is that:
    A. whites rarely admit to their racism.
    B. whites are never the victims of systematic racism.
    C. whites carry assumptions about their superiority.
    D. whites are contemptuous of those below them on the racial hierarchy.

24. It can be inferred that the primary purpose of this passage is to:
    F. inform readers about the author's experience with racial prejudice.
    G. persuade readers to travel outside their country to better understand global racism.
    H. present a viewpoint to readers on why racism exists in order to encourage attitude change.
    J. educate readers about the Harinder Veriah's experiences with racism.

25. The author states all of the following reasons why the dominant race in a society denies it own racism EXCEPT:
    A. it regards racism as part of the natural order of things.
    B. it is often unaware of its prejudice.
    C. it wants to maintain its privileged rank.
    D. it would encourage further resentment within the hierarchy.

26. What, according to the author, was the cause of the racism directed toward the author's wife in Hong Kong?
    F. She was married to a white man.
    G. Malaysians are below the Chinese on the hierarchy of race.
    H. The Chinese like to see themselves as white.
    J. She was unable to speak the language.

27. When the author says in the first paragraph (line 2) that race was "*never intuitive*," he most nearly means that:
    A. he had to be taught about racism.
    B. he believes racism can't be understood.
    C. he understood racism without having to experience it.
    D. he learned to see racism globally.

28. According to the passage, racist attitudes will exist as long as:
    F. white societies remain at the top of the hierarchy.
    G. they go unchallenged by victims of racism.
    H. people of different races exist.
    J. global governments refuse to pass anti-racist legislation.

29. The author would most likely agree with which of the following statements?
    A. Color is a minor factor in determining position on the global hierarchy.
    B. Intermixing of colors will eventually end racism.
    C. The prevalence of racism is both underestimated and underplayed.
    D. White societies have the moral authority to change racist attitudes.

30. When the author refers to a "*de facto global racial hierarchy*" in line 69, he is referring to:
    F. the order of the hierarchy as determined by people's intuition.
    G. the existence of racial prejudice despite attempts to end it.
    H. the public acceptance of the global hierarchy.
    J. the unofficial but nonetheless actual existence of the racial hierarchy.

NO TEST MATERIAL ON THIS PAGE.

GO ON TO THE NEXT PAGE.

Passage IV

NATURAL SCIENCE: This passage is adapted from Rebecca Lindsey's article "Smoke's Surprising Secret" featured in January 2004 on the NASA Earth Observatory Website: http://earthobservatory.nasa.gov/Study/SmokeSecret/

When crops, rangeland, and managed forests come down with diseases, farmers and ranchers all over the world sometimes choose to burn the diseased fields in an attempt to sterilize the area, giving little thought to
5 the smoke that can spread hundreds of miles away. A high school student working on a back yard science project now has pretty clear evidence that such fires may not kill everything we thought. In samples of the smoke from massive fires in Central America that
10 reached Texas in the spring of 2002, she found living fungal spores that were perfectly able to start new colonies. This surprising discovery from a young, amateur scientist has the potential to change the prevailing wisdom on the benefits of burning diseased
15 crops and timber.

When Sarah Mims discovered that smoke drifting across the Gulf of Mexico from fires in Central America was bringing fungal spores to the air around her home in Seguin, Texas, she was definitely surprised. When
20 Mims set out microscope slides and a continuous-operation air filter on a deer stand in her family's yard, she expected to get a collection of dust samples that she could check for the presence of fungus and bacteria.

Mims had read that dust from the Sahara Desert,
25 more than 4,000 kilometers away in North Africa, could be blown all the way over the Atlantic Ocean to North and South America. In the summer of 2001 numerous dust events in Florida and Texas created colorful sunsets and layered a thin blanket of dust on car
30 windshields. Of course, Texas itself can be a dusty place. "I wanted to find out whether the dust was local, or whether some of it could be coming from the Sahara," says Mims.

Mims analyzed the particles caught on her
35 microscope slides using a cross-polarized light source that makes dust particles made out of quartz—a characteristic of Saharan dust— glitter with all the colors of the rainbow. Since the local dust, from a kind of soil called caliche that is common in South Texas,
40 doesn't change color under polarized light, Mims knew that the sparkling, shimmering dust she had collected wasn't from Texas.

"I counted the number of spores and the number of carbon particles on the slides," explains Mims. "If
45 spores were coming from fungus that lived in our a[rea] then there shouldn't be any relationship between amount of black carbon soot and the number of fu[ngal] spores."

Instead what Mims found was that when
50 number of carbon particles went up, the number certain kinds of spores—but not all of them—went too. This is exactly what you would expect to se[e] some of the spores came from local sources and s[ome] came along with the smoke. It certainly seemed that
55 airborne fungus was related to the Central Amer[ican] smoke.

As her final piece of evidence, Mims used sate[llite] observations of aerosols from the Sea-viewing W[ide] Field-of-View Sensor (SeaWiFS), the Total O[zone]
60 Mapping Spectrometer (TOMS), and the Adva[nced] Very High Resolution Radiometer (AVH[RR]) combined with models of the atmosphere from National Oceanic and Atmospheric Administration showed the "back trajectory" of the air that was si[tting]
65 over Texas on the days her samples and the sate[llite] images were captured. On the days when her fi[lters] were dirtiest and her microscope slides were cov[ered] with the most particles, the satellite images showed of aerosols over the region, and the back traje[ctory]
70 maps showed the air was coming from North Africa.

Disease-causing bacteria and fungi have known to hitch a ride across the Atlantic on Sah[aran] Dust particles (they have probably played a role i[n the] decline of Caribbean coral reefs over the past
75 decades). For this reason, Mims decided to see whe[ther] she might be able to find bacteria or fungal spore[s in] the Asian dust that sometimes reaches Texas in spring. In the spring of 2002, she set out her micros[cope] slides along with Petrifilms—strips of gel and nutri[ents]
80 that can be used to grow microorganisms like bac[teria] and mold.

"The technique was a success. Within a few d[ays] Mims' gel strips were practically a jungle of diffe[rent] colored splotches, each one a separate fungal col[ony.]
85 Large numbers of spores were also visible on microscope slides she had exposed to the air al[most] every day between April 25 and May 17.

"There were a lot of fungal spores that I c[ould] identify on the slides," says Mims, "even at the

90 beginning of the period. But there really wasn't much dust." What she did see on the slides was a lot of black carbon particles, in other words, soot. To help solve the puzzle, Mims turned to satellite images. Observations from the Sea-viewing Wide Field-of-View Sensor
95 (SeaWiFS) during that time showed huge plumes of smoke from forest fires in southern Mexico and Central America crossing the Gulf of Mexico and blowing over Texas.

31. The primary purpose of this passage is to:
   A. explain one student's discovery about disease-carrying spores spread by drifting smoke.
   B. encourage the efforts of young scientists interested in fungal spores.
   C. describe the techniques required to trace airborne fungus from Central America.
   D. take a stand against the practice of burning diseased fields because of the likelihood of spreading fungus.

32. The passage mentions Sarah Mims using all of the following methods to analyze the source of the dust she had collected EXCEPT:
   F. cross-polarization
   G. satellite observations
   H. atmospheric models
   J. cell aggregation.

33. According to the passage, what was the last step Mims took to determine if some of the fungal spores on the gel strips came from Central America?
   A. She compared the number of carbon particles with the number of fungal spores.
   B. She analyzed dust particles with polarized light.
   C. She used a High Resolution Radiometer to check for the presence of aerosols
   D. She examined satellite images to determine the source of the black particles on her gel strips.

34. According to paragraph 6, one purpose of looking at a "back trajectory map" is to:
   F. pinpoint the direction air particles would likely travel.
   G. distinguish between paths taken by aerosols versus those taken by fungal spores.
   H. trace the path of air particles to their source
   J. identify trends in air particle movement.

35. According to paragraph 4 (lines 34-42), the cause of the rainbow-colored dust on Mims' microscope slides was:
   A. caliche soil common in South Texas.
   B. a Florida dust event in the summer of 2001.
   C. quartz from the Sahara Desert.
   D. smoke from fires in Central America.

36. The passage most clearly suggests that bacteria and fungi on Saharan dust particles are responsible, in part, for the:
   F. increase in respiratory problems among Texas residents.
   G. suspension of aerosols over Florida and Texas.
   H. reduction in the protective ozone layer.
   J. decline in the Caribbean coral reefs.

37. It may be reasonably inferred from the passage that since the airborne fungus on Mims' gel strips came from the Central American fires, then:
   A. the Mexican authorities have been negligent in allowing such fires as a means of sterilization.
   B. the diseases the fires were meant to eliminate could spread to Texas crops and timber.
   C. the fungal spores have the potential to travel as far north as Canada.
   D. the methods currently used to identify fungal spores will have to be changed.

38. Which of the following questions is not answered by the information given in the passage?
   F. What techniques can scientists use to observe the presence of aerosols over a given region?
   G. What is the significance of Mims' discovery about airborne fungal spores?
   H. How are fungal colonies distinguished on Petrifilm?
   J. Why is quartz absent from caliche soil?

39. As it is used in line 14, the phrase *prevailing wisdom* most likely refers to:
   A. the discovery that living fungal spores can start new colonies.
   B. the respect Mims has earned from veteran because of her discovery.
   C. the belief that burning diseased fields is the best way to eliminate disease.
   D. the idea that an amateur scientist could disprove current thinking.

40. In the context of the 5th paragraph, lines 43-48 primarily serve to emphasize:
F. the movement of air particles over North Africa.
G. the correlation between dust particles and aerosols.
H. the difference between methods used to observe air movement.
J. the benefits of using satellite images to observe Aerosols.

NO TEST MATERIAL ON THIS PAGE.

SCIENCE TEST
35 Minutes – 40 Questions

DIRECTIONS: There are seven passages in this test. Each passage is followed by several questions. After reading a passage, choose the best answer to each question and fill in the corresponding oval on your answer document. You may refer to the passages as often as necessary.

You are NOT permitted to use a calculator on this test.

Passage I

Scientists examined several ingredients commonly used as active agents in sunscreen. The goal of the study was to determine which ingredients are most effective at blocking harmful UV rays.

Scientists used PABA, oxybenzone, octyl salicylate, and a broad-spectrum commercial sunscreen (SPF 45). The samples were exposed to sunlight with wavelengths ranging from 240 to 440 nm. The percent transmittance of UV rays at each wavelength was recorded. The data was collected manually using a spectrophotometer. The results, in 20 nm increments, are shown in Table 1.

Figure 1 displays the intensity of sunlight across spectrum.

Table 1				
nm	PABA	oxybenzone	octyl salicylate	commercial sunscreen
240	38.2	15.7	12.7	15.2
260	2.9	19.2	83.5	24.5
280	1.7	3.2	33.1	4.2
300	9	4.2	3	1.5
320	82.9	6	10.8	2.5
340	99.2	9.7	93.5	25.5
360	100	45.3	100	67.6
380	100	92.6	100	96.8
400	100	100	100	99.8
420	100	100	100	100
440	100	100	100	100

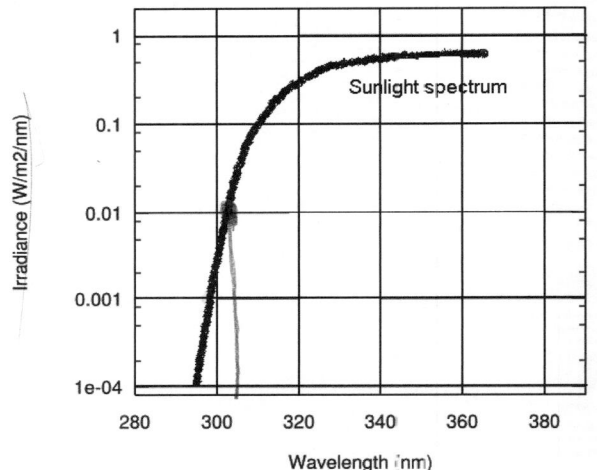

Figure 1

In 1975, Thomas B. Fitzpatrick, MD, PhD, of Harvard Medical School, developed a classification system for skin type. This system was based on a person's complexion and responses to sun exposure. Table 2 lists the skin types and their characteristics.

		Table 2	
Skin Type	Color	Reaction to UVA	Reaction to Sun
Type I	Very fair skin tone	Very Sensitive	Always burns easily, never tans
Type II	Fair skin tone	Very Sensitive	Usually burns easily, tans with difficulty
Type III	Fair to medium skin tone	Sensitive	Burns moderately, tans gradually
Type IV	Medium skin tone	Moderately Sensitive	Rarely burns, always tans well
Type V	Olive or dark skin tone	Minimally Sensitive	Very rarely burns, tans very easily
Type VI	Very dark skin tone	Least Sensitive	Never burns, deeply pigmented

1. According to Table 1, which substance had the highest percent transmittance of UV rays for sunlight with a wavelength of 260 nm?
   A. Octyl salicylate
   B. PABA
   C. Oxybenzone
   D. Commercial sunscreen

2. Based on the information in Figure 1, sunlight is most intense at which of the following wavelengths?
   F. 290 nm
   G. 300 nm
   H. 320 nm
   J. 340 nm

3. A person with fair skin tone, whose skin burns but also tans slowly, likely has which of the following skin types?
   A. Type I
   B. Type II
   C. Type III
   D. Type IV

4. Experts state that anyone whose skin is sensitive or very sensitive to UVA should always wear sunscreen. According to Table 2, people with which skin types should always wear sunscreen?
   F. Types I and II
   G. Types I, II, and III
   H. Types II, III, and IV
   J. Types V and VI

5. In sunlight with an irradiance of 0.01 W/m2/nm, oxybenzone would be expected to have a UV ray percent transmittance of:
   A. 3.8 %
   B. 5 %
   C. 9.7 %
   D. 100 %

Passage II

The most common type of red-green color perception defect is caused by a mutation on the X-chromosome. X-linked red-color blindness is a recessive trait. The eggs of the mother will contain either a normal X chromosome (X^R) or an X chromosome with the mutation (X^r) causing red-green color blindness. The sperm of the father will contain the normal X chromosome, the X chromosome with the mutation, or the Y chromosome. Females *heterozygous* (one normal gene, one mutated gene) for this trait have normal vision. The color perception defect manifests itself in females only when it is inherited from both parents. By contrast, males inherit their sole X-chromosome from their mothers, and become red-green color blind when this one X-chromosome has the color perception defect.

Genotype refers to the combination of alleles that an individual has for a gene. Table 1 lists the possible genotypes for red-green color perception and their corresponding effects on vision.

Table 1	
Female Genotype	Vision
$X^R X^R$	normal
$X^R X^r$	normal, carrier
$X^r X^r$	red-green color blind
Male Genotype	Vision
$X^R Y$	normal
$X^r Y$	red-green color blind

Students interviewed members of the Allen family to investigate the inheritance of red-green color blindness. Figure 1 displays the family tree of the Allen family.

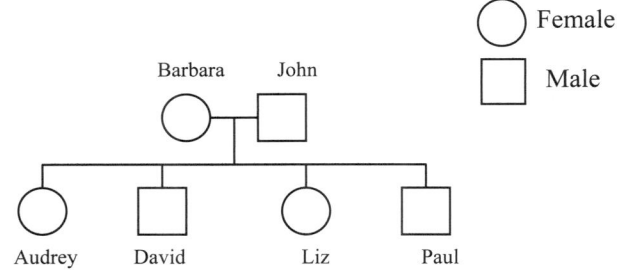

Figure 1

Study 1

Students interviewed Barbara and John and learn that Barbara is red-green color blind, while John is n Based on this information, the students deduced that th four children have the following genotypes:

Females:	$X^R X^r$
Males:	$X^r Y$

Figure 2

Study 2

Students assumed that Liz would have children w a man who has normal vision, and using a Pundit squ calculated all of the possible genotypes for their childre

$X^R X^R$	$X^R Y$
$X^R X^r$	$X^r Y$

Figure 3

Study 3

Students assumed that David would have child with a woman who has red-green color blindness, using a Pundit square calculated all of the poss genotypes for their children:

$X^r X^r$	$X^r Y$

Figure 4

6. A female who has normal vision but is a carrier red-green color blindness must have which of following genotypes?
   F. $X^R X^R$
   G. $X^R X^r$
   H. $X^r X^r$
   J. $X^R Y$

7. For a couple to produce only red-green colorbl children, regardless of the child's sex, they would n to have which of the following pairs of genotypes?
   A. $X^R X^R$ and $X^r Y$
   B. $X^r X^r$ and $X^R Y$
   C. $X^R X^r$ and $X^r Y$
   D. $X^r X^r$ and $X^r Y$

8. All of the male offspring exhibited red-green color blindness in Studies:
   F. 1 and 3.
   G. 1, 2, and 3.
   H. 2 and 3.
   J. 1 and 2.

9. Suppose that the students who worked on Study 2 are correct, and that Liz has children with a man who has normal vision. If they have 8 children, how many of them would be expected to have red-green colorblindness?
   A. 1
   B. 2
   C. 4
   D. 8

10. The ratio of Barbara and John's offspring with normal vision to offspring with red-green colorblindness is:
    F. 1:2
    G. 2:1
    H. 1:1
    J. 3:1

11. Barbara's parents could have had which of the following pairs of genotypes?
    A. $X^r X^r$ and $X^R Y$
    B. $X^R X^r$ and $X^r Y$
    C. $X^R X^R$ and $X^r Y$
    D. $X^R X^R$ and $X^R Y$

Passage III

Crude oil contains many different types of carbons. Different carbon chain lengths have different boiling points, so they can be separated using *distillation* – the process of boiling and then condensing a liquid in order to separate and purify its components (see Figure 1).

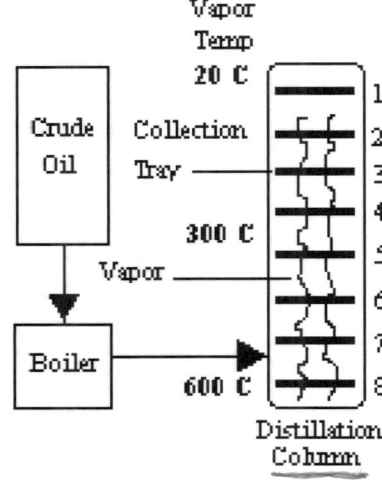

Figure 1

Crude oil is put into a boiler. The boiler is connected to a distillation column filled with collection trays. As the heated oil boils, the vapors released enter the distillation column and rise to the top. When a substance in the vapor reaches a height where the temperature of the column is equal to that substance's boiling point, it will condense to form a liquid. The liquid is gathered on the collection trays.

Experiment 1

Students determined the boiling points of various components of crude oil by recording the temperature of the vapor at various heights in the distillation column, then determining which component was collected in each of the 8 collection trays. See Table 1 and Table 2.

Table 1	
Boiling Point	Tray #
20° C	1
40° C	2
120° C	3
200° C	4
350° C	5
400° C	6
500° C	7
600° C	8

Table 2	
Crude Oil Component	Tray #
Gas	1
Naptha	2
Gasoline	3
Kerosene	4
Diesel	5
Lubricating Oil	6
Heavy Gas Oil	7
Residual Oil	8

The students distilled one barrel of crude oil. Figure 2 shows the breakdown of that barrel, in terms of which components were collected.

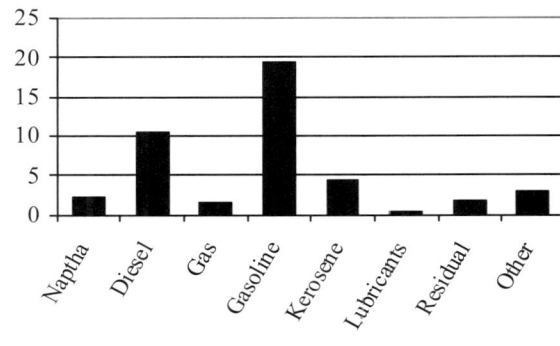

Gallons/barrel of crude oil

Figure 2

Experiment 2

Students determined the number of carbons in each component of crude oil and recorded the data in Table 3.

Table 3	
Crude Oil Component	# of Carbons
Diesel	12+
Gas	1-4
Gasoline	5-12
Heavy Gas Oil	20-70
Kerosene	10-18
Lubricating Oil	20 - 50
Naptha	5-9
Residual Oil	70 +

12. Based on the results of Experiment 1, the boiling temperature of Naptha is:
    F. 20°
    G. 40°
    H. 120°
    J. 200°

13. According to the results of Experiment 1, one barrel of crude oil contains about how many gallons of diesel?
    A. 2
    B. 6
    C. 11
    D. 29

14. One of the students hypothesized that the components of crude oil with the highest boiling points would be collected at the top of the distillation column. Do the results of Experiment 1 support the student's claim?
    F. No; as the vapor rose in the distillation column, the temperature cooled, so the components with the lowest boiling points were collected at the top of the column.
    G. No; there was no correlation between boiling point and location in the distillation column.
    H. Yes; gasoline and diesel had the highest boiling points, and they were collected in the top two trays.
    J. Yes; the lower the collection tray was in the distillation column, the lower the component's boiling point.

15. A scientist claimed that the more carbons a substance has, the higher its boiling point will be. Do the results of Experiment 1 and Experiment 2 support this claim?
    A. No; there is no relationship between the number of carbons and the boiling point.
    B. No; diesel has more carbons than gasoline, yet its boiling point is lower.
    C. Yes; residual oil has the most carbons and the lowest boiling point, while gas has the fewest carbons and the highest boiling point.
    D. Yes; residual oil has the most carbons and the highest boiling point, while gas has the fewest carbons and the lowest boiling point.

16. Which of the following components of crude oil has the highest boiling point?
    F. Naptha
    G. Kerosene
    H. Heavy gas oil
    D. Diesel

Passage IV

Solubility refers to the ability of a one substance, the *solute*, to dissolve in another (the *solvent*). The balance of molecules between the solvent and the solute determines the solubility of one substance in another. Factors such as temperature and pressure will alter this balance, thus changing the solubility.

Experiments to determine the solubility of methane and carbon dioxide in polyamide (PA-11) were performed in the temperature range 50 – 90° C, and the pressure range 50-150 atm for methane and 20-40 atm for carbon dioxide. Table 1 displays the solubility (sol) of methane in PA-11. Table 2 shows the solubility (sol) of carbon dioxide in PA-11.

Solubility = (g gas/g PA-11) x 10^3

Figure 1 shows the pressurization cycle for methane at 100 atm and 50° C. The mass gain divided by the polyamide mass determines the solubility of the gas.

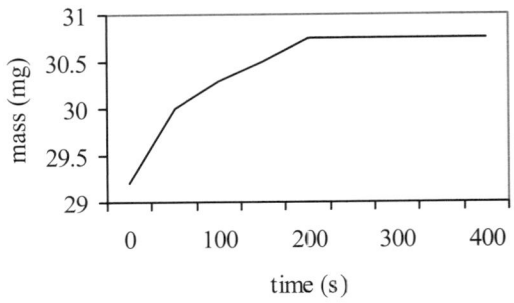

Figure 1

Table 1 - Methane					
T = 50° C		T = 70° C		T = 90° C	
Pressure (atm)	Sol	Pressure (atm)	Sol	Pressure (atm)	Sol
51.2	3.18	55.3	2.61	53.1	2.38
107.2	4.51	104.0	4.97	106.5	5.14
156.6	3.45	158.1	5.33	144.4	6.52

Table 2 – Carbon Dioxide					
T = 50° C		T = 70° C		T = 90° C	
Pressure (atm)	Sol	Pressure (atm)	Sol	Pressure (atm)	Sol
22.1	12.8	20.3	11.8	20	6.93
31.1	18.9	26.4	14.3	30.4	12.0
39.8	23.1	37.5	18.7	42.4	14.0

17. Which of the following substances did NOT become more soluble as pressure increased?
  A. Methane at 70° C
  B. Methane at 50° C
  C. Carbon dioxide at 50° C
  D. Carbon dioxide at 90° C

18. According to Table 2, at which temperature carbon dioxide the most soluble under pressure 31.1 atm?
  F. 50° C
  G. 70° C
  H. 90° C
  J. 100° C

19. Figure 1 supports which of the following claims about polyamide mass gain over time?
  A. The polyamide steadily gained mass.
  B. The polyamide lost mass over time.
  C. The polyamide gained mass at first, and then lost mass.
  D. The polyamide quickly gained mass and then leveled off.

20. If the experiment was repeated at a temperature 90° C and a pressure of 80 atm, the solubility methane would be closest to:
  F. 2.5 atm
  G. 3.75 atm
  H. 5.08 atm
  J. 5.50 atm

21. Based on the results shown in Table 2, which of the following conclusions can be drawn regarding the relationship between pressure and solubility?
    A. Solubility increases with pressure only above 70° C.
    B. As pressure increases, solubility decreases.
    C. As pressure increases, so does solubility.
    D. There is no correlation between pressure and solubility.

22. In this experiment, which substance functioned as the *solvent*?
    F. Methane
    G. Carbon dioxide
    H. Mass
    J. Polyamide

Passage V

As shown in Figures 1 & 2, the composition of soil varies by Zone. Scientists wanted to determine which types of prairie plants grew best in which Zones. To accomplish this, they visited prairies in Zone 3 and in Zone 4 and determined average plant height and root depth (see Table 1). They also looked at several 1-acre plots in both Zone 3 and Zone 4, and recorded the average number of each type of plant found (see Figure 3).

Table 1		
Plant name	Root depth (m)	Plant height (m)
Aster	2.4	0.5
Big Blue Stem	3.0	2.1
Compass Plant	5.0	2.4
Goldenrod	2.2	1.0
Indian Grass	2.8	2.3
Kentucky Blue Grass	0.1	0.1
Lead Plant	4.5	-0.8
Purple Coneflower	1.8	1.5

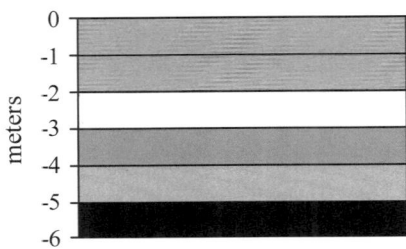

Figure 1

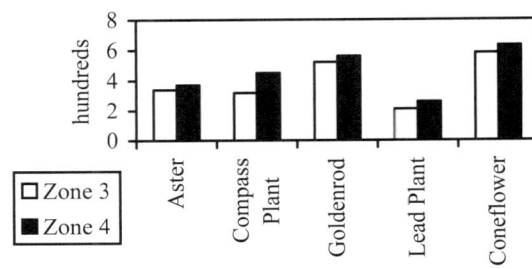

Figure 3

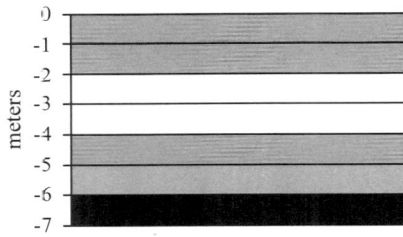

Figure 2

Legend	
Sandy clay	
Clay	
Nodular clay	
Gravel	
Bedrock	

23. In which Zone is clay found at a depth of –3.5m?
    A. Zone 3
    B. Zone 4
    C. Zones 3 & 4
    D. Neither Zone 3 or 4

24. Of the prairie plants studied, which had the tallest average plant height?
    F. Aster
    G. Kentucky Blue Grass
    H. Indian Grass
    J. Compass Plant

25. Based on the data in Figure 3, which of the following can be concluded about the prevalence of plants per Zone?
    A. The prairie plants studied grow more easily Zone 4.
    B. The prairie plants studied grow more easily in Zone 3.
    C. The prairie plants studied grow equally well Zone 3 as they do in Zone 4.
    D. No conclusion can be drawn about the prevalence plant growth per Zone.

26. A plant growing in which Zone would have roots that reach clay first?
   F. Zone 3.
   G. Zone 4.
   H. None of the plants studied have roots that would reach clay.
   J. Plants in Zone 3 and Zone 4 would reach clay at the same depth.

27. The average Lead Plant growing in Zone 3 would have roots that, at their deepest point, reach down to which of the following soil layers?
   A. Sandy clay
   B. Clay
   C. Gravel
   D. Bedrock

Passage VI

According to new research, changes to agricultural practice and forestry management could cut greenhouse gas (GHG) emissions and slow climate change. Each year, nearly 33 million acres of forestland around the world are cut down, according to the Food and Agriculture Organization of the United Nations. Tropical felling alone contributes 1.5 billion metric tons of carbon - some 20 percent of all man-made GHG emissions - to the atmosphere annually. If such losses were cut in half, it could save 500 million metric tons of carbon annually and contribute 12 percent of the total reductions in GHG emissions required to avoid unpleasant global warming, researchers reported.

Two proposed changes to agricultural practice and forestry management are described:

No-till Farming

Bruce McCarl, an agricultural economist at Texas A&M University, advocates more widespread adoption of no-till farming, a practice that involves leaving unharvested crop stalks and other plant matter behind in the field undisturbed by plows and other soil-agitating instruments.

Basically, the carbon stored inside the remains sinks into the soil instead of being stirred up and sent into the atmosphere when the soil is prepared for planting using conventional means. Such no-till farming provides a double benefit for farmers: improved soils and reduced fuel use, because it negates the need to harvest the stalks with tractors and other equipment. The opportunity to pour carbon back into the soil exists because farming over the past century has depleted its levels of organic carbon, but, as with water, the soil can only hold so much carbon before it is saturated. This would work for the next 30 to 50 years, before the soil will reach its limit and other actions will be needed.

Biofuels

Growing biofuels – crops used as fuel – represents another potential way of cutting GHGs by replacing fossil fuels. According to Stephen Ogle, an ecosystem research scientist at Colorado State University, biofuel production represents a direct reduction in GHG emissions, because crops dedicated to energy will reassimilate some of the carbon dioxide emitted by energy use.

This change, however, is not without peril. If a permanent shift does not occur, it could lead to higher food prices as well as to the conversion of marginal lands back into crop production, which would, in turn, lead to GHG emissions.

28. Both proposals describe methods that will reduce GHG emissions by:
   F. increasing the amount of carbon that will be released into the atmosphere.
   G. decreasing the amount of carbon that will be released into the atmosphere.
   H. allowing plants to absorb and store more carbon than they currently do.
   J. growing more plants in order to create more oxygen.

29. According to the passage, what causes 20% of all man-made GHG emissions?
   A. No-till farming
   B. Biofuel production
   C. Forestland being cut down
   D. Tropical felling

30. The no-till farming approach offers which of the following benefits to farmers?
   F. Less water usage and better soil.
   G. Better soil and less fuel usage.
   H. Less fuel usage and less fertilizer needed.
   J. Less strain put on the tractors and shorter growing time for crops.

31. Which of the following is an example of a biofuel?
   A. Ethanol made from sugar cane used as fuel in a petrol engine.
   B. Coal being used to create electricity.
   C. Grapes being grown and turned into wine.
   D. Wind power being harnessed and used to create electricity.

32. Bruce McCarl would most strongly *disagree* with which of the following statements about no-till farming?
   F. All other factors remaining constant, a farm that adopts no-till farming will see a net reduction in its GHG emissions.
   G. No-till farming is not a permanent solution toward curbing agricultural GHG emissions.
   H. Though the stalks left in the fields after crops are harvested will reduce GHG emissions, they might also have an adverse effect on future crop yields.
   J. The carbon stored inside the unharvested crop stalks left in no-till fields will be reassimilated by the soil.

33. Stephen Ogle would probably agree most with which of the following statements?
    A. If farmers want to lessen their contribution to GHG emissions, they should plant more trees every year.
    B. Growing corn to convert into ethanol is one of the best ways farmers can decrease their GHG emissions.
    C. By not tilling their crops, farmers will be releasing fewer GHGs into the atmosphere.
    D. Farmers should convert all marginal land they own back into crop production and grow biofuels.

34. Which proposal has the most potential for long-term success?
    F. No-till farming, because it will be effective for the next 30 to 50 years.
    G. No-till farming, because it can make the largest contribution toward decreasing GHG emissions.
    H. Biofuels, because if a permanent shift occurs, GHG emissions will be reduced indefinitely.
    J. Biofuels, because once we run out of fossil fuels, we will have to use biofuels.

Passage VII

Figure 1 shows the average sleep pattern of a child, Figure 2 shows the average sleep pattern of a young adult, and Figure 3 shows the average sleep pattern of an elderly person. At Stage 0, the person is awake. As sleep moves from Stage 1 to Stage 4, it grows progressively deeper. REM sleep, commonly associated with dreaming, is predominant in the final third of a sleep cycle.

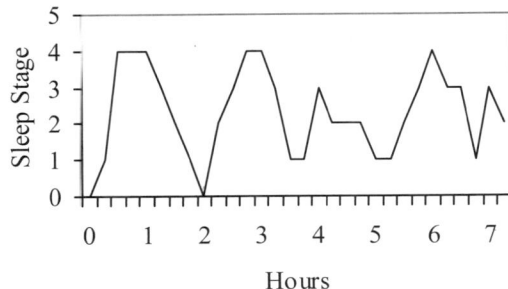

Figure 1

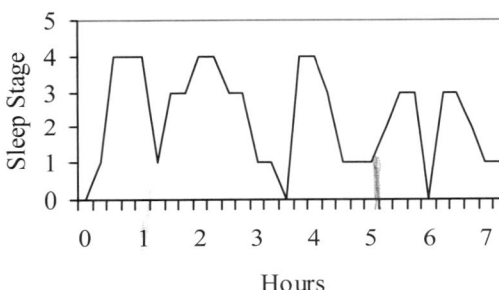

Figure 2

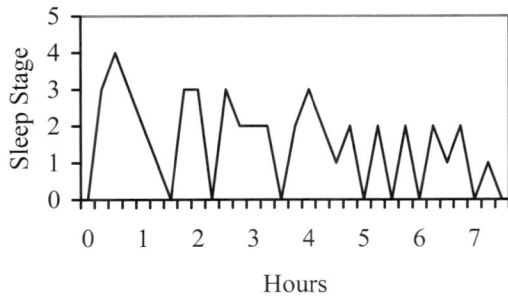

Figure 3

35. According to Figure 2, a young adult who has been asleep for 5 hours will most likely be in which sleep stage?
    A. Stage 0
    B. Stage 1
    C. Stage 3
    D. Stage 5

36. Based on the information in the passage, a child will wake up how many times during a 7-hour stretch of sleep?
    F. 7
    G. 2
    H. 1
    J. 0

37. According to Figure 3, an elderly person can be predicted to be in which sleep stage after 8 hours?
    A. 0
    B. 2
    C. 3
    D. The sleep stage cannot be determined from the data.

38. Based on the data presented in Figures 1, 2 and 3, which of the following conclusions can be properly drawn?
    F. As people age, they wake up more frequently during the night.
    G. As people age, they wake up less frequently during the night.
    H. As people age, they spend more time in deep sleep.
    J. As people age, they spend more consecutive time in each sleep stage.

39. Based on the information in the passage and in Figure 2, at which of the following hours into a sleep interval would a young adult be most likely to experience REM sleep?
    A. 0
    B. 1
    C. 2
    D. 7

40. At which of the following hours of sleep will a child most likely be in the deepest sleep?
    F. 2
    G. 3
    H. 5
    J. 7

END OF TEST
STOP! DO NOT RETURN TO ANY OTHER TEST

ACT SUCCESS

WRITING TEST 2 – Prompt

DIRECTIONS:

This is a test of your writing skills. You will have thirty (30) minutes to write an essay in English. Before you begin planning and writing your essay, read the writing prompt below carefully to understand exactly what you are being asked to do. Your essay will be evaluated on the evidence it provides of your ability to express judgments by taking a position on the issue in the writing prompt; to main a focus on the topic throughout the essay; to develop a position by using logical reasoning and by supporting your ideas; to organize ideas in a logical way; and to use language clearly and effectively according to the conventions of standard written English.

The need for a long summer vacation has been questioned by a group of parents. These parents would like students to attend school all year long, with several short vacation breaks at different times during the year. This group believes that children forget too much of what they have learned over the long summer break. Other people think that students need the long summer vacation to decompress from the school year and to participate in various extra-curricular activities. In your opinion, should schools abandon long summer vacations and adopt a year-round calendar?

In your essay, take a position on this question. You may write about either one of the two points of view given, or you may present a different point of view on this question. Use specific reasons and examples to support your position.

Use this page to *plan* your essay.

Begin WRITING TEST 2 here.

WRITING TEST 2

WRITING TEST 2

WRITING TEST 2

STOP here with the Writing Test.

Scale Scores for Practice Test 2

*These scores are based on student trials rather than national norms.

English _____
Math   _____
Reading _____
Science _____

=Total   _____

Composite = Total divided by 4 (round up at .5) _____

ACT Score*	Number Right				ACT Score*
	English	Math	Reading	Science	
36	75	60	40	40	36
35	73-74	59	39	--	35
34	72	58	38	39	34
33	71	57	37	--	33
32	70	56	36	38	32
31	69	54-55	34-35	--	31
30	68	53	33	37	30
29	67	51-52	32	36	29
28	65-66	49-50	30-31	34-35	28
27	64	46-48	29	33	27
26	62-63	44-45	28	31-32	26
25	60-61	41-43	27	30	25
24	58-59	39-40	26	28-29	24
23	55-57	37-38	24-25	27	23
22	53-54	35-36	23	25-26	22
21	50-52	33-34	22	23-24	21
20	47-49	31-32	21	21-22	20
19	44-46	28-30	19-20	19-20	19
18	42-43	25-27	18	17-18	18
17	40-41	22-24	17	15-16	17
16	37-39	19-21	16	13-14	16
15	34-36	15-17	15	12	15
14	31-33	11-14	13-14	11	14
13	29-30	09-10	12	10	13
12	27-28	07-08	10-11	09	12
11	25-26	06	08-09	08	11
10	23-24	05	07	07	10
9	21-22	04	06	06	9
8	18-20	03	05	05	8
7	15-17	--	--	04	7
6	12-14	02	04	03	6
5	09-11	--	03	02	5
4	07-08	01	02	--	4
3	05-06	--	--	01	3
2	03-04	--	01	--	2
1	00-02	00	00	00	1

Copyright © 2009 by Academic Educational Resources. All rights reserved.

Practice Test #3

1

ENGLISH TEST

45 Minutes – 75 Questions

DIRECTIONS: In the five passages that follow, certain words and phrases are underlined and numbered. In the right-hand column, you will find alternatives for the underlined part. In most cases, you are to choose the one that best expresses the idea, makes the statement appropriate for standard written English, or is worded most consistently with the style and tone of the passage as a whole. If you think the original version is best, choose "NO CHANGE." In some cases, you will find in the right-hand column a question about the underlined part. You are to choose the best answer to the question.

You will also find questions about a section of the passage or about the passage as a whole. These questions do refer to an underlined portion of the passage, but rather identified by a number or numbers in a box.

For each question, choose the alternative you consider and fill in the corresponding oval on your answer document. Read each passage through once before begin to answer the questions that accompany it. For many of the questions, you must read several sentences beyond the question to determine the answer. Be sure that you have read far enough ahead each time you choose an alternative.

PASSAGE I

Regret

Edith Simpson had never thought of marrying. She had never been in love. At the age of twenty she had received a proposal, which she had promptly <u>declined</u>, and
₁

at the age of fifty she had not <u>completely</u> lived to regret it. So
₂
she was quite alone in the world, except for her dog Ponto.

One morning Edith stood on her porch contemplating a band of very <u>small children who to all</u>
₃
<u>intents and purposes,</u> might have fallen from the clouds, so
₃
unexpected and bewildering was their coming, and so unwelcome. They were the children of <u>their</u> nearest
₄
neighbor, Margaret.

The young woman had appeared but five minutes before, accompanied by these four children. Her face was red and disfigured from tears and excitement. She had been

1. Which of the following alternatives to the underlined portion would NOT be acceptable?
   A. refused
   B. rejected
   C. turning down
   D. dismissed

2. F. NO CHANGE
   G. only
   H. happily
   J. DELETE the underlined portion.

3. A. NO CHANGE
   B. small children who, to all intents and purposes,
   C. small children who to all intents and purposes
   D. small children, who to all intents and purposes,

4. F. NO CHANGE
   G. her friend, the
   H. my
   J. her

360
TEST 3

GO ON TO THE NEXT PAGE

Copyright © 2009 Academic Educational Resources. All rights reserved.

summoned to a neighboring parish by the dangerous illness of her mother. "It's no question, Ms. Simpson; you just got to keep those youngsters for me until I come back!" She left them crowded into the narrow strip of shade that had began to cover the porch of the long, low house. [6]

5. A. NO CHANGE
   B. is beginning
   C. had begun
   D. begun

6. The writer is considering deleting the preceding sentence from the story. Should the sentence be kept or deleted?
   F. Kept, because it provides a relevant transition to the following paragraph.
   G. Kept, because it tells the reader that Edith agreed to keep the children.
   H. Deleted, because it does not sufficiently establish the time of day.
   J. Deleted, because the house has already been described elsewhere.

Edith stood, and contemplated, the children. She began by feeding them. If her responsibilities had begun and ended there, they could easily have been fulfilled, but little little children are not little pigs: they require and demand attentions that were wholly unexpected by Edith, and which she was ill prepared to give.

7. A. NO CHANGE
   B. and began contemplating
   C. as she contemplated
   D. contemplating

8. F. NO CHANGE
   G. little pigs they
   H. little pigs, they
   J. little pigs however they

She was, indeed, very inept in her management of Margaret's children during the first few days. How could she know that Timmy always wept when yelled in a loud and commanding tone of voice? At night, when she ordered them one and all to bed, firmly yet gently, they stayed uncomprehending before her. But at the end of two weeks,

9. A. NO CHANGE
   B. chastised
   C. shouted to
   D. scolded at

10. Which of the following choices best provides specific insight into Edith's normal daily life?
    F. NO CHANGE
    G. as she would have shooed the chickens into the hen house,
    H. with a stern face and commanding voice,
    J. after they changed into their pajamas,

Edith had grown quite used to these things; and she no
                                    11

longer complained. Also at the end of two weeks that
                 12

Edith, one evening– looked up to see Margaret
       13

approaching. [14] How still it was when they were gone!

Edith stood upon the gallery, looking and listening. She

turned into the house. She gave one slow glance through

the room, it's shadows creeping and deepening around her
              15

solitary figure. She let her head fall down upon her bended

arm, and began to cry.

11. A. NO CHANGE
   B. these things. And she
   C. these things, and she
   D. these things, she

12. F. NO CHANGE
   G. (Do NOT begin new paragraph) It was
   H. (Begin new paragraph) OMIT the underlined portion
   J. (Begin new paragraph) It was also

13. A. NO CHANGE
   B. one evening
   C. one evening;
   D. OMIT the underlined portion.

14. At this point, the author is considering adding following sentence:

   After a tearful reunion, and the loud bustling of packing, the children and Margaret were off.

   Should the writer make this addition here?
   F. Yes, because it provides a transition between preceding and following sentences.
   G. Yes, because it explains why the children leave.
   H. No, because contains unnecessary details.
   J. No, because it is not relevant to the narrative at point in the story.

15. A. NO CHANGE
   B. its
   C. her
   D. their

PASSAGE II

Standing Up to Dance and Sing

Early hominids largely looked and acted like apes. There was, however, one key difference, but they stood and walked upright.

This change in posture and mobility has profound implications for our evolution and "may have initiated the greatest musical revolution in human history." That is the conclusion of Reading University archaeologist Steven Mithen, continuing his search for the essence of human behavior.

Particularly within the past two million years it was that early humans refined the ability to walk, run and jump. With their big brains and bottoms, spring-loaded legs, and sophisticated sensorimotor control, they could also dance, Mithen argues, if not sing. Darwin also touched on the topic, positing that unable to woo with words, our ancestors "endeavored to charm each other with musical notes and rhythm." [21]

Essential to both bipedal locomotion and music, rhythm plays a pivotal role as well in language. Music and

16. F. NO CHANGE
    G. difference, they
    H. difference they
    J. difference: they

17. A. NO CHANGE
    B. had profound
    C. may have had profound
    D. gives profound

18. F. NO CHANGE
    G. whom continued searching
    H. who continues his search
    J. who has continued his tireless efforts searching

19. A. NO CHANGE
    B. years,
    C. years. It was that early
    D. years; early humans

20. F. NO CHANGE
    G. there
    H. they're
    J. its

21. The writer is considering deleting the preceding sentence from the essay. Should the sentence be removed?
    A. Yes, because the addition of another expert's opinion clouds Mithen's ideas.
    B. Yes, because it provides a poor transition to the next paragraph.
    C. No, because Darwin is the main topic of the paragraph.
    D. No, because it provides support for Mithen's theory.

language share other similarities. Both can move or
                          22
manipulate us. Both can be spoken, written or gestured.

Both possess hierarchical structure. And both seem to

activate multiple regions of our brains.

    Yes, language ultimately supplanted music's role in
    23
emotional expression and became our means of conveying

ideas and information. Music, however, still stirs our most

basic emotions. Until the relatively recent advent of
                            24
syntactic language in modern humans, Mithen maintains, it

was music that helped hominids find a mate, soothe a child,

or cheer a companion, and provided a groups social glue.
                                       25

    Like language, much of music does not fossilize.

We have elegant bird-bone flutes from sites in Germany and

France as old as 36,000 years - unequivocal musical
             26
instruments. Beyond that, one is hard-pressed to display

tangible evidence of music's role in pre-human society.

Mithen must speculate that Neanderthals, for instance,

were strumming on stalactites, drumming on mammoth
                            27
skulls or otherwise made music without leaving a trace. Just

step inside a cave used by prehistoric people, and it is easy
            28
to appreciate its acoustic potential. By drawing data from a

diverse range of disciplines, Mithen made a persuasive
                                       29

22. Which choice provides the most concise and stylistically effective wording here?
    F. commonalities important to human evolution
    G. interesting facts discovered by Mithen
    H. intriguing attributes
    J. uses to early humans

23. Which of the following alternatives to the underlined portion would be LEAST acceptable?
    A. Although,
    B. Indeed,
    C. True,
    D. OMIT the underlined portion.

24. F. NO CHANGE
    G. unusually delayed
    H. untimely
    J. much needed

25. A. NO CHANGE
    B. groups'
    C. group's
    D. groups,

26. The best placement for the underlined portion would be:
    F. where it is now.
    G. after the word *have*.
    H. after the word *bird-bone*.
    J. after the word *flutes*.

27. A. NO CHANGE
    B. strumming stalactites and drummed
    C. had been strumming stalactites, or drumming
    D. strummed stalactites, drummed

28. Given that all the choices are true, which one would appeal to the reader's sense of sound?
    F. NO CHANGE
    G. a reverberating cave
    H. an empty cave
    J. a cool cave

29. A. NO CHANGE
    B. is making
    C. makes
    D. also made

case that our ancestors walked upright and brings to
                        ―――――――――
                            30
prehistory a sense of sound.

30. Given that all the choices are true, which one would best conclude this essay by summarizing one of its main points?
F. NO CHANGE
G. used rhythm
H. eventually developed language
J. played complex musical instruments

PASSAGE III

Shopping for Dancing Shoes

Mom sits on the slightly worn floral sofa in the
           ―――
            31
reception room of the nursing home, watching the door like

a sentinel standing guard. She was going shopping. Her

silver-white hair was set off by a pretty lavender pantsuit,

and on her feet she wore a slightly worn pair of athletic
                   ―――――――――――
                         32
shoes.

I smiled and kissed her on the cheek. "Come on –
                                          ―――――――
                                              33
Mom, we're going to the May Company to buy you a new
―――
 33
pair of shoes. Then we'll stop and get some of that Chinese

food you love. Okay?"

She stood up and smoothed her outfit. "New shoes.

Oh, boy." Then she looked at me with confusion mirrored in

her soft, hazel, eyes. "By the way, you're a pretty young
    ―――――――――
         34
lady. Do I know you?"

She clutched a small leather handbag, which
                                ―――――――――――――
                                       35
contained Grandma's External Hard
―――――――――
    35
Drive, a book my sister and I created to help her remember
―――――――――
    36
who people were and why she lived at the nursing home.

[1] Her attention span was growing very short these

days, so I knew it had to be a quick excursion. [2] She

settled into the car, and we drove the short distance to the

31. A. NO CHANGE
    B. had been setting
    C. was sitting
    D. sat reclining

32. F. NO CHANGE
    G. feet, she wore: a
    H. feet; she wore a
    J. feet she wore a,

33. A. NO CHANGE
    B. "Come on, Mom,
    C. "Come on Mom
    D. "Come on Mom:

34. F. NO CHANGE
    G. hazel soft
    H. soft hazel,
    J. soft hazel

35. A. NO CHANGE
    B. handbag, that contained
    C. handbag. That contained
    D. handbag, which containing

36. F. NO CHANGE
    G. Drive. A book
    H. Drive a book
    J. Drive; a book

shopping center. [3] It was not like in the old days when she would spend a whole day looking for great bargains, trying on clothes and shoes for hours, and then packing up our purchases and headed for the Chinese restaurant. [4] I felt a little catch in my throat. [39]

Once I settled her into a chair in the shoe department, she chatted away with the clerk, since he didn't know her, he had to discover that she loved to dance. He was very gentle as he slipped various styles of shoes on her fragile feet. She would stand for a moment, walk around a bit and try on the next pair, and thank him each time for being so helpful.

"She's such a sweet lady," he said to me. "How old is your mom?"

"She'll be ninety next month," I said taking her hand in mine and patting it.

"Young man," she said in a voice that belied her age, "I like these shoes, but how am I going to dance in them? When they play that rock and roll music, I just have to dance."

He smiled broadly and took her around in a dance position. "Let's just try them out, okay?"

37. A. NO CHANGE
B. they
C. I
D. we

38. F. NO CHANGE
G. heading
H. head
J. and heading

39. For the sake of the logic and coherence of this paragraph, Sentence 1 should be placed:
A. where it is now.
B. after sentence 2.
C. after sentence 3.
D. after sentence 4.

40. F. NO CHANGE
G. clerk. Since he
H. clerk: since he
J. clerk, he

41. Given that all of the choices are true, which one provides the most insight into the mother's behavior?
A. NO CHANGE
B. he was surprised at how friendly she was.
C. he asked her a lot of questions.
D. he had no idea that mini strokes had robbed this charming woman of her memory.

42. F. NO CHANGE
G. thanking him
H. and then sincerely thank him
J. all the while thanking him

43. A. NO CHANGE
B. month," I said, taking
C. month," I said taking,
D. month," I said and taking

So Mom and the young man walked up and down
the aisles of the shoe department. She smiled up at
him. "Thank you, young man. These will do just fine."

I could feel tears which welled up in my eyes as
I said, "Are you ready for that Chinese food?"

"I sure am. You're a pretty young lady. Do I know you?"

44. F. NO CHANGE
G. listened wistfully to the music coming over the mall sound system.
H. danced to silent music as he carefully led her throug some simple steps in the shoe department of the Ma Company.
J. spun around the hardwood dance floor in the center of the mall.

45. A. NO CHANGE
B. tears welling up
C. tears begin to well up quickly
D. the threat of tears beginning to well

PASSAGE IV

Food for Thought

For the first million years of their existence, the early members of our genus, *Homo*, shared the African landscape with another group of hominids, the *robust australopithecines*. Although the two groups were closely related, there seem to be striking differences between them. Perhaps most notably, the robusts had giant molars, thick tooth enamel and a bony crest on top of the skull that anchored huge chewing muscles.

Sacred ecological wisdom holds that two closely related species cannot live side by side unless they differ significantly in the way they use local resources. To explain how early Homo coexisted with the robusts for so long, experts concluded that whereas Homo developed a large brain and tool-making capabilities that enabled it to pursue a diet rich in meat, the robusts became dedicated vegetarians, evolving the anatomical equivalent of a mouth full of teeth to process nuts, fruits, seeds or tubers, or some combination thereof.

But in recent years the various vegetarian scenarios have come under fire, in large part due to the results of findings from studies of carbon isotopes. These isotopes derive from the food an animal eats and become

46. F. NO CHANGE
    G. were
    H. are
    J. is

47. Which of the following alternatives to the underlined portion would NOT be acceptable?
    A. near
    B. along
    C. atop
    D. on

48. F. NO CHANGE
    G. Acknowledging
    H. Accepted
    J. Controversial

49. A. NO CHANGE
    B. so long experts
    C. so long. Experts
    D. so long; experts

50. Which of the following choices best serves the purpose of creating a metaphorical image to further describe the robusts?
    F. NO CHANGE
    G. drill
    H. saw
    J. pepper grinder

51. A. NO CHANGE
    B. because
    C. based solely on
    D. OMIT the underlined portion.

incorporated into its tissues over time. [52] In the case of the robusts, the ratio of carbon 13 to carbon 12 in their teeth is higher than would be expected of animals that ate mostly fruit and nuts but lower than that of creatures that subsisted on grass seeds.

Graduate student Alan B. Shabel of the University of California, Berkeley, offering up a possible solution to the
                                                    53
riddle of the robusts. He proposed that they were built for eating not tough plant stuffs but hard-shelled invertebrates. Shabel noted that throughout eastern and southern Africa,
                                                                              54
wetlands then abounded, as they do today. And like modern
─────
   54
wetlands, these ancient lakes, rivers and marshes would have been rich in crabs and mollusks, such as giant land
─────────────
        55
snails.

[56] [1] According to Shabel, that makes his theory of what the robusts were dining on the only one that is consistent with all the available data. [2] Looking at the contemporary African animals that specialize in eating this prey, Shabel finds that they have the same peculiar
              ─────
                57
skull features seen in the robusts. [3] They use they're
                                              ───────
                                                 58
powerful chewing apparatus to crunch through the shells.

52. If the writer were to delete the phrase "and beco incorporated into its tissues over time" from preceding sentence (placing a period after the w eats), the paragraph would primarily lose:
 F. a description of how carbon isotopes are stored in animal.
 G. an explanation of how carbon isotopes are formed.
 H. information that helps readers understand how carbon isotopes were collected.
 J. an unnecessary detail.

53. A. NO CHANGE
 B. will offer
 C. offered
 D. is offering

54. F. NO CHANGE
 G. Africa
 H. Africa. Wetlands
 J. Africa; wetlands

55. A. NO CHANGE
 B. most likely have been fairly rich
 C. in all probability been rich
 D. definitely have been very rich

56. For the sake of the logic and coherence of paragraph, Sentence 1 should be placed:
 F. where it is now.
 G. before Sentence 3.
 H. after Sentence 3.
 J. after Sentence 4.

57. A. NO CHANGE
 B. found
 C. will find
 D. is finding

58. F. NO CHANGE
 G. their
 H. there
 J. its

[4] Although, as current evidence indicates, the robusts lived
       ___
        59
in wetland areas, perhaps they, too, evolved to exploit these

armored invertebrates.

59. **A.** NO CHANGE
    B. However,
    C. Still,
    D. If,

> Question 60 asks about the preceding passage as a whole.

60. Suppose the writer's goal had been to write a brief essay exemplifying how new studies and theories can emerge that contradict accepted scientific wisdom. Would this essay successfully fulfill that goal?
    F. Yes, because it describes how Shabel developed a theory to explain a hole in conventional beliefs regarding the diets of the robusts.
    G. Yes, because it explains the new technology of calculating carbon isotopes.
    H. No, because the essay focuses on the genus *Homo* instead of on new theories.
    J. No, because Shabel's theory has not been proven yet.

PASSAGE V

Is Being Right-Handed All for the Greater Good?

Ask why most people are right-handed, and the answer might fall along the same lines as why fish school. Neuroscientists suggest that social pressures drive individuals to coordinate their behaviors so that they get an evolutionary edge.
<u>61</u>

Approximately 85 percent of people prefer their right hand, which is controlled by the left hemisphere of the
<u>62</u>
brain. One theorized benefit of locating a particular function in one hemisphere is that it frees the other to deal with different tasks. But that idea does not explain why population-wide trends for handedness in the first place exist.
<u>63</u>
Moreover, evidence gleaned in recent years has overturned the long-held belief that human handedness is a unique by-product of brain specialization attributable to language. [64]

[1] The presence of lateralization throughout the animal kingdom suggests some benefit from it, contend neuroscientists. [2] Lateralization <u>seem to</u> confer an
<u>65</u>
advantage for some fish as well – in certain species, the majority tends to swim left when a predator attacks, whereas other species head right. [3] The potential benefits

61. Which choice would most effectively conclude sentence in a way that demonstrates group benefit as important as individual benefit?
   A. they are similar to everyone else's behaviors.
   B. everyone in the group gets an evolutionary edge.
   C. they are unique.
   D. other members of the group gain an evolution edge.

62. F. NO CHANGE
   G. right hand that is
   H. right hand, that is
   J. right hand which, is

63. A. NO CHANGE
   B. for handedness exist in the first place.
   C. exists in the first place for handedness.
   D. in the first place for handedness exists.

64. The writer is considering deleting the prece sentence from the paragraph. Should the sentence kept or deleted?
   F. Kept, because it reassures the reader that a controversial idea is not true.
   G. Kept, because it provides additional evidence for people prefer one hand over the other.
   H. Deleted, because it provides a digression that le the paragraph away from its primary focus.
   J. Deleted, because it contradicts the main idea presented in the paragraph.

65. A. NO CHANGE
   B. is seeming to
   C. seemed to
   D. seems to

of such patterns may not seem intuitive, a predator could
learn that attacking a fish on one particular side is more
effective. [4] When threatened, fish turned in the same
direction have a greater chance of survival than if they
scatter to become a darting swarm of head-butting fish.
[5] But this idea fits with the conventional explanation of
why fish school at all. 68

In addition, the fish data does not explain human
handedness. One neuroscientist theorized that mammals
are lateralized as they are in the brain simply because their
ancestors were; going back to the process's origins in fish.
Research on chimpanzees supports that idea. Researchers
recently published data showing that wild chimpanzees
display heritable population-wide hand preferences in
certain tool-aided tasks. 71

Given fanciful theories of lateralization, what
about the lefties, the outliers, those who zig when all
others zag? Safety from predators increases

66. F. NO CHANGE
G. intuitive, but a predator
H. intuitive a predator
J. intuitive: a predator

67. A. NO CHANGE
B. had turned
C. turning
D. were turning

68. For the sake of the logic and coherence of this paragraph, Sentence 5 should be placed:
F. where it is now.
G. after sentence 2.
H. before sentence 4.
J. after sentence 1.

69. A. NO CHANGE
B. Therefore,
C. Nevertheless,
D. In fact,

70. F. NO CHANGE
G. were, going
H. were and going
J. were going

71. At this point, the writer is considering adding the following sentence:

The chimpanzee findings fill in what had been a troublesome missing link between lower vertebrates and humans.

Would this be a relevant addition to make here?
A. Yes, because it connects the previous sentences to the main idea of the paragraph.
B. Yes, because it explains why the fish data is important.
C. No, because it contradicts the idea expressed in the preceding sentence.
D. No, because the information it contains is redundant.

72. F. NO CHANGE
G. the only scientific explanations
H. possible and probable evolutionary theories
J. evolutionary theories

with group size: but so does competition, making different
behavior beneficial. Studies of left-handedness in some
  ―――――
      73

one-on-one sports such as boxing, suggest the same. So
―――――――――――――――――――――――――――
                    74
relax, all you nonconformists.

73. A. NO CHANGE
    B. size but so does competition, making
    C. size, but so does competition making
    D. size but so does competition making

74. F. NO CHANGE
    G. sports such as boxing suggest
    H. sports, such as boxing, suggest
    J. sports such as, boxing suggest

Question 75 asks about the preceding passage as a whole.

75. Suppose the writer had been asked to write a persuasive essay convincing the reader that it is more beneficial to be right-handed than left-handed. Did the writer accomplish the task?
    A. Yes; the writer describes many ways in which being right-handed aids in survival of the species.
    B. Yes; the writer explains why more people are right-handed than left-handed.
    C. No; the writer makes a case that it is more beneficial to be left-handed than right-handed.
    D. No; this is an informative essay that focuses on why lateralization occurs.

MATHEMATICS TEST
60 Minutes—60 Questions

DIRECTIONS: Solve each problem, choose the correct answer, and then fill in the corresponding oval on your answer document.

Do not linger over problems that take too much time. Solve as many as you can; then return to the others in the time you have left for this test.

You are permitted to use a calculator on this test. You may use your calculator for any problems you choose, but some of the problems may best be done without using a calculator.

Note: Unless otherwise stated, all of the following should be assumed.

1. Illustrative figures are NOT necessarily drawn to scale.
2. Geometric figures lie in a plane.
3. The word *line* indicates a straight line.
4. The word *average* indicates arithmetic mean.

$|8-5|-|5-8| = ?$

A. -6
B. -4
C. -2
D. 0
E. 6

DO YOUR FIGURING HERE.

A clown charges $15 for scheduling plus $20 per hour worked. The total owed to the clown is $75. How many hours did the clown work?

F. $2\frac{1}{2}$
G. 3
H. $3\frac{3}{4}$
J. 5
K. 6

A truck averages 20 miles per gallon. The price of gas is $3 per gallon. How much will it cost for the truck to make a 160 mile trip?

A. $6.66
B. $8.00
C. $24.00
D. $53.33
E. $183.00

$v^2 - 28u + 60 - 25u^2 + 8u$ is equivalent to:

F. $16u^2$
G. $16u^6$
H. $-24u^4 - 20u^2 + 60$
J. $-24u^2 - 20u + 60$
K. $-25u^2 - 20u + 60$

GO ON TO THE NEXT PAGE.

5. The following figure is a 5-pointed star. Each of the sides of the star is 4 cm. What is the perimeter of the figure?

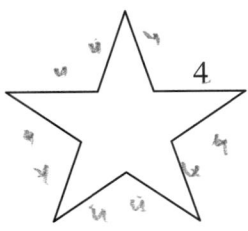

A. 12
B. 20
C. 32
D. 36
E. 40

6. The expression $(5y+2)(y-3)$ is equivalent to:

F. $5y^2 - 5$
G. $5y^2 - 6$
H. $5y^2 - 13y + 6$
J. $5y^2 - 13y - 6$
K. $5y^2 + 2y - 6$

7. If 60% of a given number is 18, then what is 15% of the given number?

A. 1.2
B. 2.4
C. 3.6
D. 4.5
E. 6.0

8. The following 5 consecutive integers add up to 225.

$x-3, \ x-2, \ x-1, \ x, \ x+1$

What is the value of x?

F. 43
G. 44
H. 45
J. 46
K. 47

9. In the standard (x,y) coordinate plane, point M with coordinates (2,3) is the midpoint of $\overline{AB}$, and B has coordinates (6,1). What are the coordinates of A?

A. (8,4)
B. (4,2)
C. (2,4)
D. (-2,5)
E. (-6,11)

376
TEST 3

0. The figure below is drawn accurately in the standard (x,y) plane. Which of the following is the best estimate of the measure of angle θ?

   F. 100°
   G. 120°
   H. 150°
   J. 180°
   K. 220°

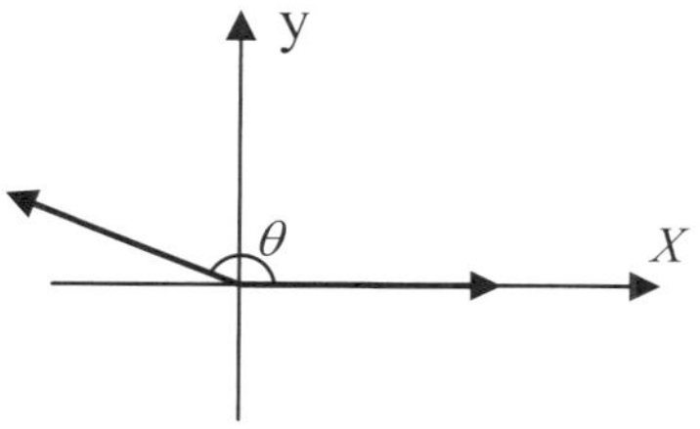

DO YOUR FIGURING HERE.

1. If $ax + b = d$ and $a \neq 0$, then $x = ?$

   A. $\frac{b-d}{a}$
   B. $\frac{b+d}{a}$
   C. $\frac{d-b}{a}$
   D. $\frac{d}{a-b}$
   E. $-\frac{db}{a}$

2. For all x, $\frac{3x}{4} + \frac{x}{3}$ is equivalent to:

   F. $\frac{4x}{7}$
   G. $\frac{4x}{12}$
   H. $\frac{7x}{12}$
   J. $\frac{9x}{12}$
   K. $\frac{13x}{12}$

3. What is the number of degrees the *hour* hand of a clock moves in 8 hours?

   A. 240°
   B. 270°
   C. 720°
   D. 1440°
   E. 2880°

Use the following information to answer questions 14-16.

300 students voted in a recent student council election at National High School. The results for student council president are given in the table below.

Candidate	Number of votes
John	60
Lisa	120
Aaron	90
Angela	30

14. What percent of the vote did Lisa receive in the election?

   F. 20%
   G. 30%
   H. 40%
   J. 80%
   K. 120%

15. The total student population at National High School is 500. Assume that the election results accurately represent the views of the entire student population. How many votes would John likely have received if everyone voted?

   A. 80
   B. 100
   C. 120
   D. 150
   E. 200

16. If the information in the table were converted into a pie chart, then the central angle of the sector for Aaron would be how many degrees?

   F. 72°
   G. 90°
   H. 108°
   J. 120°
   K. 144°

378
TEST 3

7. In square ABCD shown below, E is the midpoint of $\overline{AB}$. What is the ratio of the area of $\triangle AED$ to the area of the square.

   A. 1:2
   B. 1:3
   C. 1:4
   D. 3:1
   E. 4:1

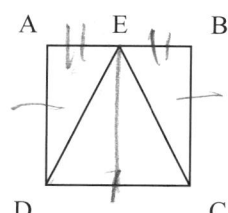

8. What is the slope of a line parallel to the line $y = \frac{2}{5}x - 5$ in the standard (x,y) coordinate plane?

   F. -5
   G. $-\frac{5}{2}$
   H. $\frac{2}{5}$
   J. 2
   K. $\frac{8}{3}$

9. Larry cut a 50 foot long board into 2 pieces. The ratio of the lengths of the 2 pieces is 3:7. What is the length, to the nearest foot, of the longer piece?

   A. 15
   B. 20
   C. 25
   D. 30
   E. 35

10. What is the smallest integer greater than $\sqrt{71}$?

    F. 5
    G. 7
    H. 8
    J. 9
    K. 72

11. Cathy is planning to tile her bathroom floor. Each tile Cathy will use is 4 inches by 6 inches. The bathroom floor is a rectangle measuring 6 feet by 8 feet. What is the minimum number of tiles that Cathy will need?

    A. 100
    B. 144
    C. 288
    D. 300
    E. 526

DO YOUR FIGURING HERE.

GO ON TO THE NEXT PAGE.

22. For right $\triangle ABC$ below, what is $\tan \angle C$?

F. $\frac{6}{10}$
G. $\frac{6}{8}$
H. $\frac{8}{10}$
J. $\frac{10}{8}$
K. $\frac{8}{6}$

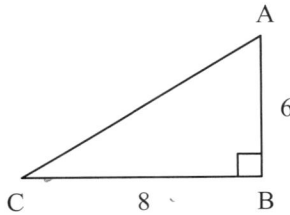

23. What is the solution set for $x^2 + 6x = -5$?

A. $\{\}$
B. $\{-5, 6\}$
C. $\{-5, -1\}$
D. $\{-3, 6\}$
E. $\{6\}$

24. For all $b > 1$, the expression 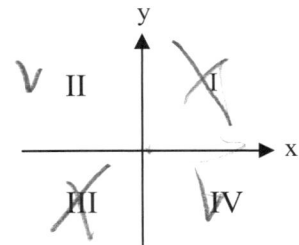 equals:

F. $\frac{5}{2}$
G. $-b^2$
H. b^2
J. $-\frac{1}{b^2}$
K. $\frac{1}{b^2}$

25. If a point Q has coordinates that are opposite in sign then which quadrant could it be located in?

A. I only
B. III only
C. I or III only
D. I or II only
E. II or IV only

The fixed costs of manufacturing clocks in a factory are $1,700.00 per day. The variable costs are $12.50 per clock. What is the cost of producing c clocks in 1 day?

F. $1712.50c
G. $12.50c - $1700.00
H. $1,700.00c + 12.50
J. $1700.00 – 12.50c
K. $1700.00 + $12.50c

△ABC is similar to △DEF. Select side lengths are indicated in the diagram below. What is the perimeter of △DEF?

A. 10.5
B. 22.5
C. 25.5
D. 35.5
E. 55.5

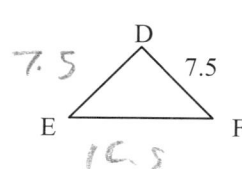

If $\frac{5\sqrt{11}}{a\sqrt{11}} = \frac{5\sqrt{11}}{11}$, then a = ?

F. 1
G. $\sqrt{5}$
H. $\sqrt{11}$
J. 55
K. 121

Train A leaves Chicago on its way to Washington D.C. at the same time that train B leaves Washington D.C. on its way to Chicago. Train A is traveling at 50 mph while train B is traveling at 60 mph. Assume the distance between Chicago and Washington D.C. is 1210 miles along the track and the trains make no stops. How many hours will it be before the two trains pass each other moving in opposite directions?

A. 11
B. 12
C. 15
D. 22
E. 23

Eric is looking to choose an outfit to wear. Eric has five shirts, four pairs of pants and three pairs of shoes. If Eric chooses one of each for his outfit, how many different outfits are possible?

F. 12
G. 20
H. 30
J. 48
K. 60

31. What is the area, in square units, of parallelogram ABCD?

   A. 24
   B. 54
   C. 56
   D. 63
   E. 72

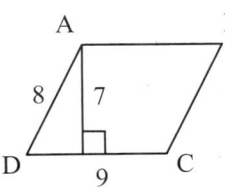

32. Given $f(x) = 5x + 2$ and $g(x) = 3x^2 - 1$, which of the following is an expression for $f(g(x))$?

   F. $3x^2 + 5x + 1$
   G. $3x^2 + 5x - 1$
   H. $15x^2 - 3$
   J. $15x^2 + 1$
   K. $15x^2 + 5x - 1$

33. A formula used to calculate the distance traveled for an object in free fall starting at rest is $d = \frac{1}{2}gt^2$, where d is the distance traveled, in meters; g is the acceleration due to gravity; and t is the time the object has fallen, in seconds. An object is dropped from rest and falls for 3 seconds. Given that $g = 9.8$ meters per second squared, what is the best estimate for the distance, in meters, the object falls?

   A. 10
   B. 20
   C. 45
   D. 60
   E. 90

34. A right circular cylindrical container is used to store strawberry ice cream at a local ice cream shop. The container has a diameter of 10 inches and a height of 12 inches. The volume of a right circular cylinder is given by the formula $V = \pi r^2 h$. If each customer eats an average of 6 cubic inches of strawberry ice cream, what is the approximate number of customers a full container of ice cream will serve?

   F. 10
   G. 50
   H. 160
   J. 200
   K. 940

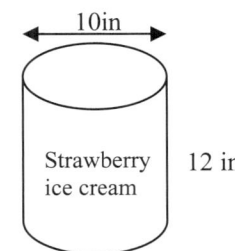

5. $(2x \cdot x^3)^4$ is equivalent to:

   A. $2x^7$
   B. $2x^{16}$
   C. $8x^7$
   D. $16x^7$
   E. $16x^{16}$

6. Air is composed of approximately 80% nitrogen. There are 1.2×10^{23} nitrogen molecules in a 6 liter sample of air. The rest of the air is composed of mostly oxygen. What is the average number of nitrogen molecules per liter in the given sample?

   F. 7.2×10^2
   G. 7.2×10^4
   H. 2×10^{12}
   J. 2×10^{22}
   K. 7.2×10^{22}

7. Which of the following is equivalent to the inequality $5x - 10 \geq 10x + 15$?

   A. $x \leq -5$
   B. $x \geq -5$
   C. $x \leq 10$
   D. $x \geq 10$
   E. $x \leq -15$

8. The table below shows the number of goals scored by the American High School water polo team in each of the 20 games during the past season. What is the average number of goals per game scored by the team during the season?

Number of goals scored in the game	Number of games with this many goals scored
5	1
6	4
7	9
8	4
9	2

   F. 5.2
   G. 6.9
   H. 7.1
   J. 7.5
   K. 8.6

39. Ann is standing on the ground 120 feet away from the base of a tree. The angle of elevation to the top of the tree from Ann's position is 40°. Which of the following is closest to the height of the tree, expressed in feet?

   A. 50
   B. 77
   C. 92
   D. 100
   E. 144

40. A box has a length of 8 cm, a width of 4 cm and a height of 4 cm. What is the total surface area of the box in square centimeters?

   F. 32
   G. 64
   H. 84
   J. 128
   K. 160

41. John can walk 3 miles in m minutes. At that rate, how many minutes will it take him to walk 8 miles?

   A. $8m$
   B. $\frac{3}{8m}$
   C. $\frac{8}{3m}$
   D. $\frac{3m}{8}$
   E. $\frac{8m}{3}$

42. What is the area, in square units, of trapezoid DEFG?

   F. 31
   G. 60
   H. 72
   J. 90
   K. 135

43. Which of the following expressions must be odd for any positive integer value of n?

   A. n^2
   B. $2n^2$
   C. $2n^2 + 1$
   D. $3n^2 + 1$
   E. $4n^2$

4. Which of the following is a rational number?

   F. $\sqrt{5}$
   G. $\sqrt{e}$
   H. $\sqrt{11}$
   J. $\sqrt{\frac{6}{36}}$
   K. $\sqrt{\frac{25}{81}}$

5. Jane's math grade after taking 4 of 5 equally weighted tests is exactly 89%. Jane needs a grade of at least 90% in order to receive an A in the class. What is the minimum grade that Jane must receive on the 5th test in order to receive an A in the class?

   A. 90%
   B. 92%
   C. 94%
   D. 96%
   E. 98%

6. The figure below consists of a large equilateral triangle divided into smaller triangles by connecting trisection points of adjacent sides. What fraction of the large triangle is shaded?

   F. $\frac{2}{5}$
   G. $\frac{1}{2}$
   H. $\frac{5}{9}$
   J. $\frac{2}{3}$
   K. $\frac{7}{9}$

47. $f(x) = 5\sin x + 2$ and $g(x) = |f(x)| - 2$. Which of the following values is NOT part of the range of $g(x)$?

A. -3
B. -2
C. -1
D. 2
E. 4

48. Which of the following is a solution to the equation $3^{3x+2} = 9^{x-1}$?

F. -10
G. -4
H. 0
J. 1
K. 3

49. What is the sum of the interior angles of pentagon ABCDE?

A. 360°
B. 450°
C. 540°
D. 630°
E. 720°

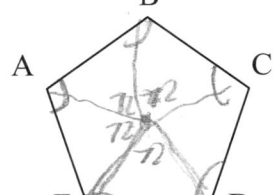

50. If $3x^2 y^2 z^3 < 0$, then which of the following must be true?

F. $x > 0$
G. $x < 0$
H. $y < 0$
J. $z > 0$
K. $z < 0$

51. In the circle below, chord $\overline{AB}$ is 12 units long and 4.6 units from the center of the circle. To the nearest tenth, what is the radius of the circle?

A. 7.6
B. 8.5
C. 9.1
D. 11.3
E. 13.4

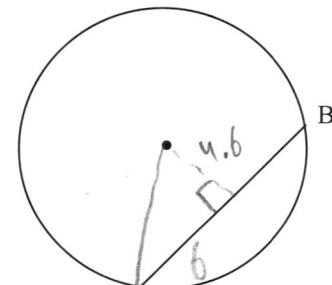

2. What is the sum of the first 60 even integers?

DO YOUR FIGURING HERE.

F. 3660
G. 4110
H. 5250
J. 5500
K. 6740

3. If $\log 2x + \log 50 = 2$ and $x > 0$ then what must x equal?

A. -48
B. 0
C. 0.5
D. 1
E. 20

4. In the figure below, line m is parallel to line n. What is the measure of angle α?

F. 35°
G. 50°
H. 70°
J. 80°
K. 145°

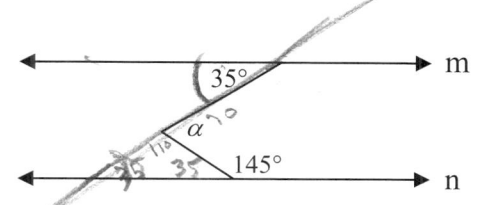

5. A circle has a radius of 10 inches. An arc of the circle is intercepted by a central angle of 60°. What is the length, in inches, of the arc?

A. π
B. $\frac{3\pi}{2}$
C. 2π
D. $\frac{10\pi}{3}$
E. 4π

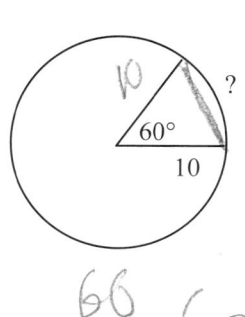

GO ON TO THE NEXT PAGE.

56. In a game, 20 balls are each labeled with one number. The balls are labeled with the integers from 1 to 20. A game is played by randomly choosing two balls without replacement from a bag containing the 20 balls. A player wins the game if either two odd numbers or two even numbers are chosen. What is the probability that if Joe plays the game once he will win?

F. $\frac{9}{19}$
G. $\frac{1}{2}$
H. $\frac{11}{19}$
J. $\frac{3}{5}$
K. $\frac{3}{4}$

57. If $0 \leq x \leq \frac{\pi}{2}$ and $\sin x = \frac{20}{29}$, then $\cos x + \tan x = ?$

A. $\frac{1211}{382}$
B. $\frac{1021}{609}$
C. $\frac{20}{21}$
D. $\frac{21}{29}$
E. $\frac{\sqrt{13}}{11}$

58. If $-5 \leq x \leq 3$ and $-4 \leq y \leq 1$, then what is the minimum value of $x - y$?

F. -6
G. -1
H. 1
J. 2
K. 7

388
TEST 3

59. In the triangle below, what is $\cot \beta$?

   A. $\frac{\sqrt{21}}{11}$
   B. $\frac{\sqrt{21}}{10}$
   C. $\frac{100}{121}$
   D. $\frac{11}{10}$
   E. $\frac{10}{\sqrt{21}}$

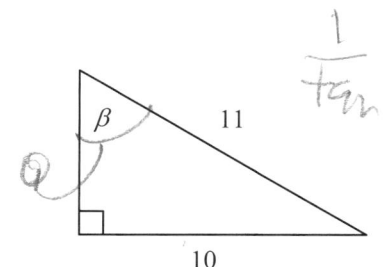

60. What is the equation of a circle with center (4, -3) and radius 5?

   F. $x^2 + y^2 - 8x + 6y = 25$
   G. $x^2 + y^2 - 8x + 6y = 5$
   H. $x^2 + y^2 - 8x + 6y = 4$
   J. $x^2 + y^2 - 8x + 6y = 0$
   K. $x^2 + y^2 - 8x + 6y = -3$

END OF TEST

STOP! DO NOT TURN THE PAGE UNTIL TOLD TO DO SO.

DO NOT RETURN TO THE PREVIOUS TEST.

READING TEST

35 Minutes – 40 Questions

DIRECTIONS: There are four passages in this test. Each passage is followed by several questions. After reading a passage, choose the best answer to each question and fill in the corresponding oval on your answer document. You may refer to the passages as often as necessary.

Passage I

PROSE FICTION: This passage is adapted from the short story "Winter Worm, Summer Weed" by Xiaolu Guo (© 2007).

A young Tibetan sits in the sand by Zha Ling Lake. He is skinny and about eighteen. The throbbing sun scorches his thick dark hair. The Kunlun Mountains reach up beyond the lake, iced snow coating
[5] the tops, peak after high peak. The boy is from Maduo County in Qing Hai province. His name is Guo Luo. Every summer Guo Luo climbs the mountains to harvest the famous herb known as Winter Worm Summer Weed. Well-known for its nourishing,
[10] beneficial properties, the herb actually comes from an insect. In winter, it is a caterpillar, a Winter Worm. Come summer, the caterpillar dies and is absorbed by the ground. There it looks like a strange weed, a worm-like herb. The Winter Worm Summer Weed is ground
[15] up and used in medicinal soups and tonics.

Tibetan is Guo Luo's native tongue. He has learned Mandarin and even picked up some English from tourists who travel to the lake, famous for its beautiful mountain landscape. When he climbs the
[20] mountains with the others, it is always Guo Luo who returns with the most herbs. It is as though the weeds offer themselves up to him. His reputation means that when Guo Luo descends the mountain, buyers will be waiting on the sand by the lake to ask his prices.

[25] In his hands are three bunches of herbs. Guo Luo's eyes are on the faraway mountaintops, covered with the eternal solid snow. He feels as though it has never melted in the eighteen years of his life. He stands still, empty yet drifting in the afternoon. Every
[30] afternoon is like this—the same clouds, same lake, same mountains. He pulls his eyes back from the mountain to the road below. He can make out rows of white hats, a green flag flapping at the lead. A tour group is coming.

[35] At the head of the group is the female tour gu[ide] from Maduo Tourism Bureau. She is already thirty [and] wears her hair as if she were younger, in a girl[ish] ponytail. She knows Guo Luo and likes to tease h[im.] But she is always good to him. Each time she lets h[im]
[40] know what to expect from her tourists at the lake. G[uo] Luo watches her usher the white hats toward him. T[he] herbs feel warm in his hand. The tourists are midd[le] aged women with money: the typically nervous ki[nd] carrying their money in cheap leather wallets arou[nd]
[45] their necks, silver and gold chains shining. On t[his] occasion, Guo Luo does very well.

One day the female guide appears, though this [is] nowhere near tourist season. She is excited; her chee[ks] are rosy. "Guo Luo! I have good news! I'm be[ing]
[50] transferred to the Tourism Bureau in the city, and [the] Bureau said I could have an assistant. Do you want [to] come and be my assistant?" Guo Luo is slow to rea[ct.] He tightens his hat, as if to help him gather his thoug[hts.] The guide stands on the parched and shriveled forr[mer]
[55] grasslands, her heart full of expectation, like a lone t[hin] cloud hoping for rain. "Guo Luo, don't you want to l[ive] in the city? You could work as a guide in the Tour[ism] Bureau there. You could drive the minibus for us." G[uo] Luo says nothing. He cannot even imagine what s[he]
[60] describes. Guo Luo doesn't answer. "If it's girls, I co[uld] introduce you to one or two." "It would have to be a c[ity] girl, to pay the right price for my herbs," Guo L[uo] finally says.

The female guide keeps still but is suddenly lik[e a]
[65] bloom that's lost its freshness. Her eyes reflect the la[nd] around them, the grassland without any grass. Guo L[uo] looks back at the mountain, its sides already closed in [by] the snow. He wishes he could be on the mountain ri[ght] now, gathering his herbs. The female guide mov[es]
[70] away, disappearing into the sandy landscape. Guo L[uo] watches her go. "Cities, girls, what does it matter," [he] mutters to himself and turns back to the mountain. T[he] Winter Worm Summer Weed lives on these mountain[s...]

1. The narrator most nearly portrays the tour guide's career ambitions as:
   A. wanting to work in rural areas.
   B. hoping to move out of the tourism industry.
   C. eager to move up in the Tourism Bureau.
   D. cautious about accepting promotions.

2. As revealed in the passage, Guo Luo is best described as:
   F. solitary; he enjoys spending time alone in nature and has no desire to go to the city.
   G. ambitious; he works hard at collecting Winter Worm Summer Weed so that he can make a lot of money selling it to the tourists and hopefully soon get a better job.
   H. impulsive; he often makes quick decisions without thinking about the consequences.
   J. lazy; he would rather sit by the lake and wait for tourists to come find him than work at promoting the Winter Worm Summer Weed.

3. The author implies the emotional state of the characters mainly through:
   A. extensive dialogue shared between the characters.
   B. physical descriptions of the characters and what they are doing.
   C. characters' thoughts and dreams that are described.
   D. elaborate images of the environment and locations where events take place.

4. It can reasonably be inferred from the last paragraph (lines 64 – 73) that the tour guide feels which way about Guo Luo's reaction to her job offer?
   F. understanding about his desire to keep gathering the Winter Worm Summer Weed.
   G. happy that she was able to convince him to take the job by offering to introduce him to women.
   H. disappointed that he didn't want the job.
   J. indifferent about his decision.

5. According to the passage, which of the following is true about the Winter Worm Summer Weed?
   A. The herb is created when a worm turns into a weed.
   B. It is well known for its pain-killing properties.
   C. It is found only on the Kunlun Mountains.
   D. The herb is actually a decaying caterpillar.

6. The relationship between Guo Luo and the tour guide can best be described as:
   F. a warm acquaintanceship that has been nurtured over time and is mutually beneficial.
   G. a friendship that was once close but has recently become tense and strained.
   H. an exclusively professional arrangement in which each person helps the other, but they are not friendly or even courteous.
   J. an easy friendship that is slowly developing into a witty flirtation.

7. The main purpose of the second paragraph (lines 16 – 24) is to provide:
   A. a detailed description of the Zha Ling Lake and its importance in Guo Luo's life.
   B. background information on Guo Luo that helps the reader understand how he came to gather Winter Worm Summer Weed.
   C. insight into Guo Luo's connection with the Winter Worm Summer Weed.
   D. a sense of Guo Luo's culture and education, which explains why he feels most at home on the mountain.

8. It can be inferred from this passage that Guo Luo's favorite place to be is where?
   F. Standing beside the road selling the Winter Worm Summer Weed and watching clouds.
   G. In the city.
   H. Sitting by Zha Ling Lake.
   J. On the mountain gathering herbs.

9. As it is used in line 29, the word *drifting* most nearly means:
   A. bored.
   B. lethargic.
   C. sporadic.
   D. content.

10. Which of the following best describes what the fourth paragraph (lines 35 – 46) reveals about the tour guide's character?
    F. She is a young girl who is flirtatious, and also an excellent tour guide.
    G. She is easygoing, fun and helpful, and enjoys joking with Guo Luo.
    H. She is flippant and rude and takes advantage of the tourists.
    J. She is professional and courteous, but mostly concerned with getting big tips from the tourists.

TEST 3

GO ON TO THE NEXT PAGE.

Passage II

SOCIAL SCIENCE: This passage is adapted from Wikipedia.com.

Margaret Thatcher was the leader of the Conservative Party from 1975 to 1990, Prime Minister of the United Kingdom throughout the 1980s and has been the only woman to hold either post. Undoubtedly one of the most significant British politicians in recent political history, she was also a polarizing figure, who brought out strong reactions from people. Likewise, her legacy is highly disputed.

Some people credit her microeconomic reforms with rescuing the British economy from the stagnation of the 1970s and admire her committed radicalism on social issues. Others see her as authoritarian and egotistical. She is accused of dismantling the Welfare State and of destroying much of the UK's manufacturing base.

The first charge reflects her government's rhetoric more than its actions, as it actually did little to reduce welfare expenditure, despite its desire to do so. The second charge may be credible in that there was a major fall in manufacturing employment, and some industries almost disappeared. The UK was widely seen as the "sick man of Europe" in the 1970s, and some argued that it would be the first developed nation to return to the status of a developing country. Instead, the UK emerged as one of the most successful economies in modern Europe. Her supporters claim that this was due to Margaret Thatcher's policies.

Critics of this view believe that the economic problems of the 1970s were exaggerated, and were caused largely by factors outside any UK government's control. Accordingly, they also argue that the economic downturn was not the result of socialism and trade unions, as Thatcher supporters claim. Critics also argue that the Thatcher period in government coincided with a general improvement in the world economy, and the buoyant tax revenues from North Sea oil, and that these were the real cause of the improved economic environment of the 1980s rather than Margaret Thatcher's policies.

Many on both the right and left agree that Thatcher had a transformative effect on the British political spectrum and that her tenure had the effect of moving the major political parties rightward. New Labour and Blairism have incorporated much of the economic, social and political tenets of "Thatcherism." The curtailing and large scale dismantling of elements of the welfare state under Thatcher have largely remained. As well, Thatcher's program of privati[zing] state-owned enterprises has not been reversed. Inde[ed] successive Tory and Labour governments have fur[ther] curtailed the involvement of the state in the econ[omy] and have further dismantled public ownership.

For good or ill, Thatcher's impact on the tr[ade] union movement in Britain has been lasting with [the] breaking of the miner's strike of 1984-1985 seen a[s a] watershed moment, or even a breaking point, for a u[nion] movement which has been unable to regain the de[gree] of power it exercised up to the 1970s. Unionization r[ates] in Britain declined under Thatcher and have [not] recovered and the legislative instruments introduce[d to] curtail the impact of strikes have not been reversed.

Thatcher's legacy has continued to stro[ngly] influence the Conservative Party itself. Success[ive] leaders have struggled with real or imagined faction[s in] the Parliamentary and national party to determine [which] parts of her heritage should be retained or jettisoned.

Margaret Thatcher and her policies were, [and] remain, highly controversial and polarizing. One t[hing] that cannot be argued, however, is that "Thatcheri[sm"] has left an indelible impression on the Un[ited] Kingdom's political scene, and her ideologies [and] actions will not soon be forgotten.

11. According to the passage, Margaret Thatch[er's] policies were all of the following, EXCEPT:
    A. divisive
    B. influential
    C. widely approved of
    D. long-lasting

12. Based on the first paragraph, which of the follo[wing] statements would the author make about Marg[aret] Thatcher's political career?
    F. As a popular Prime Minister, Thatcher made changes that will be remembered fondly for decades.
    G. Thatcher did not make significant contribu[tions] to the UK during her term as Prime Minister.
    H. Thatcher's divisive actions continue to in[spire] debate to this day.
    J. Even though she was a remarkable Prime Minister, little that she accomplished rem[ains] evident today.

13. In the 1970s, the UK was most likely referred to as the *sick man of Europe* (line 22) because:
    A. of its poor economic status.
    B. the health care system was so inefficient.
    C. Thatcher's policies were making people dependent on the welfare system.
    D. of the plague that swept the country.

14. Based on the information in this passage, which of the following can be inferred about the future of trade unions in Britain?
    F. Unionization rates will continue to rise until they exceed the level they were at during Thatcher's period in government.
    G. Because there is no penalty for striking, unions will continue to gain power.
    H. Unionization rates will continue to fall.
    J. Unless new legislation is passed, the unionization rates will remain low.

15. The author's tone in this passage can best be described as:
    A. informative.
    B. sarcastic.
    C. inquisitive.
    D. ironic.

16. According to the passage, Thatcher's legacy remains in all the following ways EXCEPT for:
    F. the cut backs to the welfare system.
    G. the privatization of state-owned enterprises.
    H. the leftist leaning of the major political parties.
    J. her controversial and polarizing affect.

17. Thatcher's critics argue that the real cause of the economic boom seen in the UK in the 1980s was what?
    A. The tax proceeds from North Sea oil.
    B. The overall improvement in the economy across Europe.
    C. The result of socialism and trade unions.
    D. The tax breaks given to the manufacturing industry.

18. The phrase *this view,* used in line 28, refers to what?
    F. The claim that Thatcher had nothing to do with the economic situation in the UK.
    G. The belief that Thatcher's policies led to the UK's economy flourishing.
    H. The idea that Thatcher influenced the decline of the UK's economy.
    J. The belief that the UK would be the first developed nation to return to the status of a developing country.

19. According to the passage, what effect did Thatcher's policies have on the manufacturing industry in the UK?
    A. Her policies had little to no affect on the industry.
    B. Because of her policies, there was a huge boom in the manufacturing industry across the UK.
    C. Thatcher's stance on trade unions created difficulties for the manufacturing industry, resulting in lower pay for the employees and higher costs to the consumers.
    D. There was a huge decline in manufacturing employment and some industries almost vanished.

20. The main idea of the passage is that:
    F. Thatcher was one of the most loved and well respected British politicians in recent history.
    G. Thatcher was one of the most significant British politicians, and although she was controversial and polarizing, she will be remembered for quite some time.
    H. Thatcher's policies had an enormous impact on Britain in the 1970s and 80s.
    J. Thatcher's authoritarian style wasn't appreciated by all, but the benefits her policies brought to Britain cannot be disputed.

Passage III

HUMANITIES: This passage is adapted from Wikipedia.com and Ikebanahq.org.

Ikebana is the Japanese art of flower arrangement. It has gained widespread international fame for its focus on harmony, color use, rhythm, and elegantly simple design. It is steeped in the philosophy
5 of developing a closeness with nature. It is centered greatly on expressing the seasons, and is meant to act as a symbol of something greater than the flower itself. As is true of all other arts, Ikebana is creative expression within certain rules of construction. Its
10 materials are living branches, leaves, grasses, and blossoms. Its heart is the beauty resulting from color combinations, natural shapes, graceful lines, and the meaning latent in the total form of the arrangement. Ikebana is, therefore, much more than mere floral
15 decoration.

The remarkably high development of floral art in Japan can be attributed to the Japanese love of nature. The Japanese have always felt a strong bond of intimacy with their natural surroundings, and even in
20 contemporary concrete-and-asphalt urban complexes, they display a remarkably strong desire to have a bit of nature near them. The Japanese house that does not at all times contain some sort of floral arrangement is rare indeed. Nature is always changing. Plants grow and put
25 forth leaves, flowers bloom, and berries are borne regularly and repeatedly throughout the seasons. Nature has its own rhythm and order. The awareness of this is the first step in involving oneself in Ikebana.

In principle, Ikebana aims not at bringing a finite
30 piece of nature into the house, but rather at suggesting the whole of nature, by creating a link between the indoors and the outdoors. This is why arrangers are likely to use several different types of plants in a single arrangement, and to give prominence to leaves and
35 flowerless branches as well as blossoms.

Many practitioners of Ikebana feel that the spiritual aspect of Ikebana is very important. One becomes quiet when one practices Ikebana. It helps you to live in the moment and to appreciate things in nature
40 that previously had seemed insignificant. One becomes more patient and tolerant of differences, not only in nature, but also in other people. Ikebana can inspire you to identify with beauty in all art forms - painting, music, etc., and to always see the best in yourself.

45 Ikebana roots can be traced to a kind of ritual flower offering made in Buddhist temples in Japan during the 6th century. Tatebana (vertical flower) in the Muromachi era (14-16th century) was regarded as first style that could be called Ikebana. It was arrang
50 in a high narrow vase. A more sophisticated style flower arrangement, called Rikka (standing flowe appeared in the 15th century. The Rikka style refl the magnificence of nature and its display. For exam pine branches symbolize rocks and stones, and w
55 chrysanthemums symbolize a river or small stream.

The most significant changes in the history Ikebana took place during the 15th century, when Muromachi ruled Japan. The large buildings and s houses that Yoshimasa had built expressed his love
60 simplicity. These small houses contained Tokono where people could place objects of art and flo arrangements. It was during this period that the rule Ikebana were simplified so that people of all cla could enjoy the art.

65 Another major development took place in the 16th century. A more simple style of flo arrangement called Nageire (meaning to fling appeared as part of the Japanese tea cerem According to this style, flowers are arranged in a vas
70 naturally as possible, no matter what materials are u Because of its association with the tea ceremony, style is also called Cha bana (tea flowers).

In the 1890s, shortly after the Meiji Restoratio period of modernization and westernization in Jap
75 there developed a new style of Ikebana called Morib or "piled-up flowers." This style appeared partly du the introduction of western flowers and partly due to westernization of Japanese living. The Moribana s which created a new freedom in flower arrangin
80 used for a landscape or garden scene. It is a style can be enjoyed wherever it is displayed and can adapted to both formal and informal situations.

Modern Ikebana dates from 1930 and goes by transliteration "'Zen'ei Ikebana'" or "'Zen'eibana'".
85 form of Ikebana is more expressive than the cla style. Along with Japanese tea ceremony calligraphy, Ikebana was one of the arts in w women were traditionally schooled in preparation marriage. Today, flower arrangement is venerate
90 one of the traditional arts in Japan. It is practice many occasions like ceremonies and parties, and mo people are still choosing to study the art.

21. It can most reasonably be inferred from the passage that compared with classic Ikebana, the modern form would feature:
    A. less dramatic composures.
    B. less representations of the seasons.
    C. more colors and types of materials.
    D. more references to the culture.

22. The passage suggests that Yoshimasa valued Ikebana because:
    F. he wanted to demonstrate his power over the lower classes.
    G. it made him feel relaxed and happy.
    H. it looked nice in the buildings and houses he built.
    J. it reflected his love of simplicity.

23. The word *steeped* used in line 4 most nearly means:
    A. brewed.
    B. soaked.
    C. immersed.
    D. inclined.

24. This passage is best described as an essay in which the author:
    F. presents a detailed explanation of how to create Ikebana arrangements.
    G. discusses the history of Ikebana and its relation to contemporary political ideas.
    H. explains why Ikebana has become famous internationally.
    J. provides an introduction to what Ikebana is and an overview of how it changed over the years.

25. The main reason the author mentioned the Japanese house (lines 22 – 24) was to emphasize:
    A. the pervasiveness of Ikebana in modern culture.
    B. the Japanese desire to be surrounded by nature.
    C. the ease with which Ikebana can be created.
    D. the fact that Japanese hold nature as sacred.

26. According to the passage, the evolution of styles of Ikebana occurred in what order?
    F. Tatebana, Rikka, Nageire, Moribana, Zen'eibana
    G. Rikka, Tatebana, Moribana, Zen'eibana, Nageire
    H. Moribana, Zen'eibana, Nageire, Rikka, Tatebana
    J. Tatebana, Nageire, Rikka, Moribana, Zen'eibana

27. Based on the information in the passage, what is the main difference between the different styles of Ikebana?
    A. The type of vase used.
    B. The symbolism of the flowers.
    C. The way the flowers are arranged.
    D. The degree of formality.

28. It can be inferred from the passage that it would be reasonable to see Ikebana arrangements in Japan at all of the following places EXCEPT:
    F. A person's backyard garden.
    G. An art gallery opening.
    H. A wedding.
    J. A courthouse.

29. The main purpose of paragraph 4 (lines 36 – 44) is to:
    A. explain how Ikebana helps practitioners see the best in themselves.
    B. share why many feel the spiritual component to Ikebana is crucial.
    C. clarify why Ikebana helps practitioners appreciate nature more.
    D. help the reader understand why people practice Ikebana.

30. Which of the following options is the best example of Ikebana that is "*creating a link between the indoors and the outdoors*" (lines 31 – 32)?
    F. A bowl with water, rocks and lilies in it.
    G. An arrangement made completely of roses.
    H. A vase containing long sticks, green leaves, and several types of flowers.
    J. A miniature garden scene that is placed indoors.

Passage IV

NATURAL SCIENCE: This passage is adapted from the article "The Promise of Plasmonics" by Harry A. Atwater, which appeared in *Scientific American* (© April 2007).

Light is a wonderful medium for carrying information. Optical fibers now span the globe, guiding light signals that convey voluminous streams of voice communications and vast amounts of data. This gargantuan capacity has led some researchers to prophesy that photonic devices - which channel and manipulate visible light and other electromagnetic waves - could someday replace electronic circuits in microprocessors and other computer chips. Unfortunately, the size and performance of photonic devices are constrained by the diffraction limit; because of interference between closely spaced light waves, the width of an optical fiber carrying them must be at least half the light's wavelength inside the material. For chip-based optical signals, which will most likely employ near-infrared wavelengths of about 1,500 nanometers, the minimum width is much larger than the smallest electronic devices currently in use. Some transistors in silicon integrated circuits, for instance, have features smaller than 100 nanometers.

Recently, however, scientists have been working on a new technique for transmitting optical signals through minuscule nanoscale structures. In the 1980s researchers experimentally confirmed that directing light waves at the interface between a metal and a dielectric (a nonconductive material such as air or glass) can, under the right circumstances, induce a resonant interaction between the waves and the mobile electrons at the surface of the metal. In other words, the oscillations of electrons at the surface match those of the electromagnetic field outside the metal. The result is the generation of surface plasmons - density waves of electrons that propagate along the interface like the ripples that spread across the surface of a pond after you throw a stone into the water.

Over the past decade investigators have found that by creatively designing the metal-dielectric interface they can generate surface plasmons with the same frequency as the outside electromagnetic waves but with a much shorter wavelength. This phenomenon could allow the plasmons to travel along nanoscale wires called interconnects, carrying information from one part of a microprocessor to another. Plasmonic interconnects would be a great boon for chip designers, who have been able to develop ever smaller and faster transistors but have had a harder time building minute electronic circuits that can move data quickly across the chip.

Plasmonic circuits would be even faster and m useful if researchers could devise a "plasmons switch - a three-terminal plasmonic device v transistor-like properties. Research groups have rece developed low-power versions of such a switch scientists can produce plasmonsters with be performance, the devices could serve as the core o ultra fast signal-processing system, an advance could revolutionize computing 10 to 20 years from n

In 2000 the name "plasmonics" was given to emerging discipline. Ultimately it may be possible employ plasmonic components in a wide variety instruments, using them to improve the resolution microscopes, the efficiency of light-emitting di (LEDs) and the sensitivity of chemical and biolog detectors. Scientists are also considering med applications, designing tiny particles that could plasmon resonance absorption to kill cancerous tiss for example. And some researchers have even theor that certain plasmonic materials could alter electromagnetic field around an object to such an ex that it would become invisible. Although not all t potential applications may prove feasible, investiga are eagerly studying plasmonics because the new promises to literally shine a light on the mysteries o nanoworld.

By studying the elaborate interplay betw electromagnetic waves and free electrons, investiga have identified new possibilities for transmitting da our integrated circuits, illuminating our homes fighting cancer. Further exploration of these intrig plasmonic phenomena may yield even more exc discoveries and inventions.

31. Which of the following questions is NOT answ by the passage?
   A. When was the term "plasmonics" coined?
   B. What are some applications for plasmonics other than computers?
   C. In what year was the first plasmonic device created?
   D. What constrains the size and performance of photonic devices?

32. The word *medium* as it is used in line 1 most ne means:
   F. channel
   G. standard
   H. average
   J. forecast

33. According to the passage, plasmonic interconnects would be helpful to chip designers because they:
    A. enable circuits to be as small as 100 nanometers.
    B. slow the rate at which data can move across the chip.
    C. would enable them to create smaller and faster transistors.
    D. would allow them to build small electronic circuits that can quickly move data across the chip.

34. Which of the following best describes how the phrase "*like the ripples that spread across the surface of a pond*" (lines 33 – 34) functions in the passage?
    F. As an example of what plasmons look like to an untrained eye.
    G. As an analogy for how the electrons in plasmons spread along the interface.
    H. As an image of the effect plasmons have on metal.
    J. As an example of what it would look like for light waves to interact with mobile electrons.

35. The author would most likely agree with which of the following statements?
    A. Light is not a good medium for transmitting data because its capacity is so limited.
    B. The study of plasmonics holds much promise for future discoveries and has many applications.
    C. Plasmonics have contributed much to the fields of computing and medicine.
    D. Plasmonics are not worth studying further, because the possible applications are not realistic.

36. The main point of the second paragraph (lines 21-35) is that:
    F. decades ago scientists proved that light waves can induce an interaction between the waves and electrons at the surface of metal.
    G. a new technique is being developed to allow optical signals to be transmitted through nanoscale structures.
    H. a new generation of surface plasmons has been created.
    J. electrons move across metal like ripples across a pond.

37. The passage indicates that in order for an optical fiber to carry light waves, its width must be:
    A. twice the light's wavelength.
    B. double the light's frequency.
    C. half the light's wavelength.
    D. one third the light's frequency.

38. According to the passage, scientists have generated surface plasmons with a shorter wavelength as the outside electromagnetic waves and with:
    F. a faster frequency.
    G. the same frequency.
    H. a slower frequency.
    J. a smaller mass.

39. With regard to the possibility of photonic devices someday replacing electronic circuits in computer chips, the information presented in this passage makes it clear that the author is:
    A. hopeful yet realistic.
    B. intrigued but cynical.
    C. optimistic but impatient.
    D. frustrated but determined.

40. The fourth paragraph (lines 49-57) establishes a cause-effect connection between:
    F. the number of terminals in the plasmonic device and the speed with which it operates.
    G. the creation of a fast signal-processing system and the power it generates.
    H. the development of a "plasmonster" switch and the creation of an ultra fast signal-processing system.
    J. plasmonic circuits and transistor effectiveness.

TEST 3

END OF TEST

STOP! DO NOT TURN THE PAGE UNTIL TOLD TO DO SO.

DO NOT RETURN TO A PREVIOUS TEST.

Copyright © 2009 Academic Educational Resources. All rights reserved.

SCIENCE TEST
35 Minutes – 40 Questions

DIRECTIONS: There are seven passages in this test. Each passage is followed by several questions. After reading a passage, choose the best answer to each question and fill in the corresponding oval on your answer document. You may refer to the passages as often as necessary.

You are NOT permitted to use a calculator on this test.

Passage I

Tornado intensity is commonly estimated by analyzing damage to structures and then correlating it with the wind speed requ to produce such destruction. This method is essential to assigning tornadoes specific values on the *Fujita Scale* (F-Scale) of torn intensity (see Figure 1).

Damage f scale		Little Damage	Minor Damage	Roof Gone	Walls Collapse	Blown Down	Blown Away	
		f0	f1	f2	f3	f4	f5	
Windspeed F scale		17 m/s 32	50	70	92	116	142	
		F0	F1	F2	F3	F4	F5	
		40 mph 73	113	158	207	261	319	
		To convert f scale into F scale, add the appropriate number						
Weak Outbuilding	−3	f3	f4	f5	f5	f5	f5	
Strong Outbuilding	−2	f2	f3	f4	f5	f5	f5	
Weak Framehouse	−1	f1	f2	f3	f4	f5	f5	
Strong Framehouse	0	F0	F1	F2	F3	F4	F5	
Brick Structure	+1	−	f0	f1	f2	f3	f4	
Concrete Building	+2	−	−	f0	f1	f2	f3	

Figure 1

A tornado is formed when the following occurs: (1) Warm, moist air rises into cool, dry air; (2) when the barrier is breached, a bulge of warm, moist air expands and condenses to form a cloud; (3) as air moves upward, the resulting instability creates a spiral of air called a *mesocyclone*; (4) cold air moves downward and rain falls as the cloud becomes a *supercell*; (5) cool, moist air from rain cycles back into a cloud, forming a spinning wall-cloud; (6) horizontal spiraling wind "tubes" are pushed upward by warm, moist air, forming a tornado. (See Figure 2).

The United States has the most tornadoes of any count and most of these tornados form in an area of the central Uni States known as "Tornado Alley." Figure 3 displays geographical (state-by-state) breakdown of the occurrence tornadoes in the US in 2005.

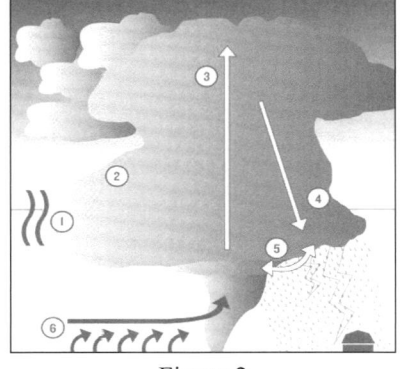

Figure 2

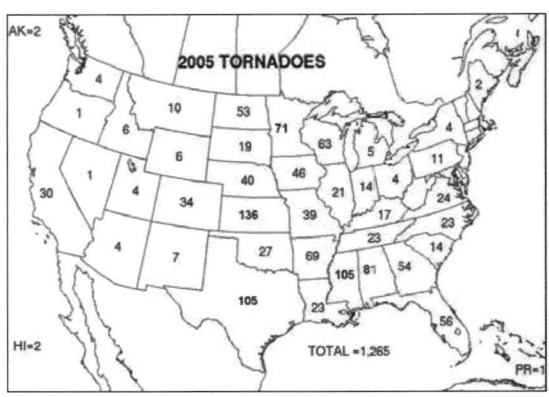

Figure 3

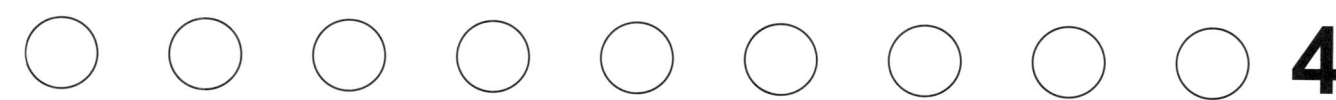

In Figure 2, the tornado is labeled with which number?
A. 1
B. 3
C. 5
D. 6

A tornado with an intensity of F4 on the Fujita Scale could have winds of which of the following speeds?
F. 70 mph
G. 155 mph
H. 190 mph
J. 210 mph

Which of the following does NOT precede the formation of a mesocyclone?
A. Warm air flowing upward
B. Cool air forming a spinning wall-cloud
C. Cloud formation
D. Moist air condensing

4. Based on the data provided in Figure 3, which of the following states can be inferred to be part of "Tornado Alley?"
F. Texas
G. Florida
H. Michigan
J. Washington

5. If the wind speed of a tornado was unknown, but it was observed that several brick buildings in the area sustained minor damage, what value would the tornado be assigned on the F-Scale?
A. F0
B. F1
C. F2
D. F3

GO ON TO THE NEXT PAGE.

Passage II

Acid deposition delivers acids and acidifying compounds to the Earth's surface. Once on the surface, they move through soil, vegetation, and surface waters and, in turn, set off a cascade of adverse ecological effects. Acid deposition occurs in three forms: wet deposition, which falls as rain, snow, sleet and hail; dry deposition, which includes particles, gases, and vapor; and cloud or fog deposition, which occurs at high altitudes and in coastal areas. Acid deposition is comprised of sulfuric acid, nitric acid, and ammonium derived from sulfur dioxide (SO_2), nitrogen oxides (NO_x), and ammonia (NH_3). Sulfuric and nitric acid lower the pH of rain, snow, soil, lakes, and streams.

Table 1
pH scale: 1 Lemon Juice, 2, 3 ← All fish die, 4 ← Trout die, 5 ← Frogs & crayfish die, 6 ← Snails die, 7–8 Neutral, Milk, 9, 10, 11 Basic, 12 Lye, 13, 14

Acidic (1–6), Neutral (7–8), Basic (9–14)

Study 1

A specially designed collection bucket was used to gather rain samples. The collector opened automatically during wet weather, allowing the precipitation to fall into the collection bucket, and then closed as soon as the precipitation stopped. The sample was then taken to a laboratory, where it was weighed and its acidity was measured. Finally, the concentrations of important inorganic chemicals found in the precipitation were analyzed. The results are shown in Table 2.

Table 2					
Sample	pH	Cl (mg/L)	Mg (mg/L)	Na (mg/L)	NH$_3$ (mg/L)
1	5.41	0.02	0.002	0.010	0.01
2	5.28	0.09	0.009	0.029	0.05
3	5.43	0.15	0.008	0.084	0.03
4	5.16	0.08	0.006	0.038	0.01
5	5.45	0.00	0.002	0.003	0.00

Study 2

Another study was done to compare the average pH precipitation across various months. The same procedure was used as in Study 1, and the results are shown in Table 3.

Table 3		
Month	Average pH	Precipitation (cm)
Jan	4.58	8.45
Feb	4.77	8.20
Mar	4.90	7.01
Apr	5.16	17.12
May	4.81	11.48
Jun	4.68	51.67
Jul	4.79	9.24
Aug	4.18	23.52
Sep	4.92	42.26
Oct	4.34	9.74
Nov	4.89	11.76
Dec	4.91	4.67

6. It is known that precipitation with a high concentration of chlorine (Cl) does more damage bodies of water than precipitation with a low concentration of Cl. Based on this information, which sample tested in Study 1 would cause the most harm rivers?
   F. Sample 1
   G. Sample 2
   H. Sample 3
   J. Sample 4

7. Based on the results of Study 2, it can be concluded that the deposition is least acidic during which season?
   A. Spring
   B. Summer
   C. Fall
   D. Winter

8. Based on the results of Study 1, which of the following be concluded about the relationship between Sodium (Na) concentration and the acidity of deposition?
   F. The lower the concentration of Na, the more basic the precipitation.
   G. The higher the concentration of Na, the more basic the precipitation.
   H. The higher the concentration of Na, the more acidic the precipitation.
   J. There is no correlation between the concentration of Na and acidity of the precipitation.

During which of the following months was there concern for the health of frogs?
A. January
B. April
C. August
D. November

The precipitation collected in Study 1 is an example of which type of acid deposition?
F. Wet deposition.
G. Dry deposition.
H. Cloud deposition.
J. Fog deposition.

11. If the collection bucket used in Study 1 had been rinsed with sulfuric acid before collecting sample number 2, the resulting pH measurement would have been:
A. It is impossible to determine.
B. Exactly 5.28.
C. Lower than 5.28.
D. Higher than 5.28.

Passage III

Students crystallized an impure, solid compound. First, they added just enough hot solvent to dissolve the compound. They then allowed the hot solution to cool, whereupon crystals began to form. Finally, the solution was placed in an ice bath to complete the crystallization process (see Figures 1 and 2). Figure 3 illustrates the progression of crystallization.

Solubility (the amount of solute that will dissolve in a specific solvent) and crystallization are directly related. Since crystallization cannot begin until the solution becomes saturated, the faster a compound dissolves, the more quickly it can begin to form into crystals.

Study 1

Students tested the solubility of four different substances. The temperature was measured in °C, and water was used as the solvent. The results of the study are displayed in Figure 4.

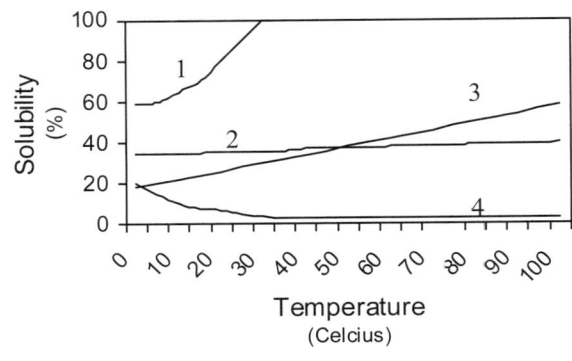

Figure 4

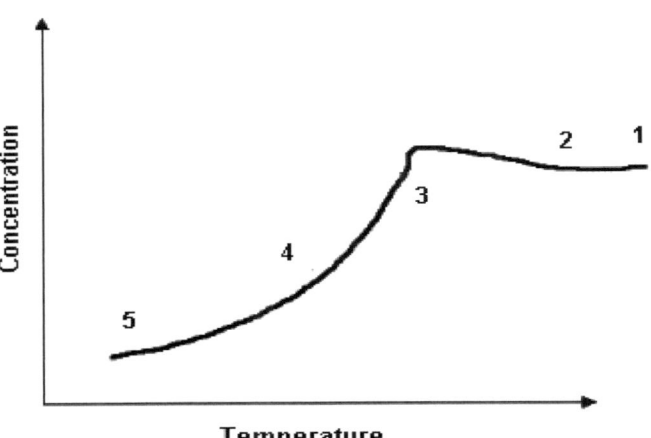

1 Solution added, undersaturated
2 Solution cools to saturation
3 Concentration decreases with crystal growth
4 Crystal growth during main cooling cycle
5 Supersaturated

Figure 3

12. In a solution of 60° C water, which sample from Study 1 would begin the crystallization process first?
    F. Sample 1
    G. Sample 2
    H. Sample 3
    J. Sample 4

13. A fifth sample was tested for solubility under the same conditions as in Study 1. The solubility at 30° was 20%. How did the solubility of Sample 5 compare with that of Samples 1–4?
    A. It was lower than Samples 1–4.
    B. It was higher than Samples 1-4.
    C. It was lower than Samples 3 and 4 but higher than Samples 1 and 2.
    D. It was lower than Samples 1-3 but higher than Sample 4.

14. According to Figure 4, the solubility of Sample 1 at a water temperature of 30° C was closest to which of the following?
    F. 20%
    G. 60%
    H. 80%
    J. 95%

15. Based on the information in the passage and Figure 3, the solution was most likely placed in an ice bath at which of the following points?
    A. 1
    B. 2
    C. 4
    D. 5

16. Based on Figure 3, which of the following best explains the relationship between temperature and crystallization?
    F. As temperature decreases, crystallization increases.
    G. As temperature increases, crystallization increases.
    H. As temperature decreases, crystallization decreases.
    J. Temperature and crystallization do not affect one another.

Passage IV

A person's blood type is determined before birth, by specific genes inherited from one's parents. One gene is inherited from the mother and one from the father; these two genes combine to establish a person's blood type. The most common blood type classification system is the ABO system, in which there are four types of blood: A, B, AB, and O. The combination of genes received from parents creates a person's *genotype*, which in turn determines that person's blood type (see Table 1).

Table 1

		Father's Blood Type			
		A	B	AB	O
Mother's Blood Type	A	A or O	A, B, AB, or O	A, B, or AB	A or O
	B	A, B, AB, or O	B or O	A, B, or AB	B or O
	AB	A, B, or AB	A, B, or AB	A, B, or AB	A, B, or AB
	O	A or O	B or O	A or B	O

The Rh (+/-) factor is inherited separately from the ABO blood types. The Rh negative gene is recessive to the dominant Rh positive gene. Therefore, it is possible to have an Rh + blood genotype and still have an Rh - gene in your genetic makeup (see Table 2).

Table 2

Genotype (DNA)	Blood Type
(+, -) or (+, +)	Rh +
(-, -)	Rh -

The genes that determine blood type cause proteins to exist on the surface of all red blood cells. These genes also ensure that only the blood cells of the proper blood type remain in the body. Because of this, not all blood is compatible (see Table 3).

Table 3

Type	Can Donate Blood To	Can Receive Blood From
A+	A+ AB+	A+ A- O+ O-
O+	O+ A+ B+ AB+	O+ O-
B+	B+ AB+	B+ B- O+ O-
AB+	AB+	Everyone
A-	A+ A- AB+ AB-	A- O-
O-	Everyone	O-
B-	B+ B- AB+ AB-	B- O-
AB-	AB+ AB-	AB- B- O-

17. According to Table 1, parents with blood types AB and CANNOT produce a child with which blood type?
    A. A
    B. B
    C. AB
    D. O

18. A child with blood type AB+ could have parents with whi of the following blood types?
    F. O+ and A-
    G. A- and B+
    H. AB- and AB-
    J. B+ and B+

19. A child who can donate blood to everyone could ha parents with which of the following blood types?
    A. A+ and AB-
    B. AB- and AB-
    C. B- and B-
    D. AB+ and AB+

20. Parents with blood types A- and A+ could produ children with which of the following blood types?
    F. A+, O+
    G. A+, A-, O+
    H. O-, O+
    J. AB+, A-, O-

The genes that determine blood type are also responsible for:
A. Determining blood Rh.
B. Controlling the types of cells in the blood.
C. Controlling blood volume.
D. Creating proteins on the white blood cells.

22. Parents with which of the following blood type pairs would produce children who can accept blood from the fewest number of donors?
F. AB+ and B+
G. A- and AB-
H. AB+ and O-
J. O- and O-

Passage V

In a study of the effects of Ritalin and Adderall on children with ADHD, subjects were given one of four possible doses of medication. Their behavior in social and academic settings was then monitored and rated. The four possible doses were: placebo (P), Ritalin given once in the morning (R1), Ritalin given twice daily (R2), or Adderall given once in the morning (A1).

The results for each group were averaged. Figure 1 shows the average behavioral rating (on a scale of 0-15, with 0 meaning no undesirable behavior) at various time periods throughout the day. Figure 2 shows the percentage of children who demonstrated side effects at a moderate or severe level on at least one day.

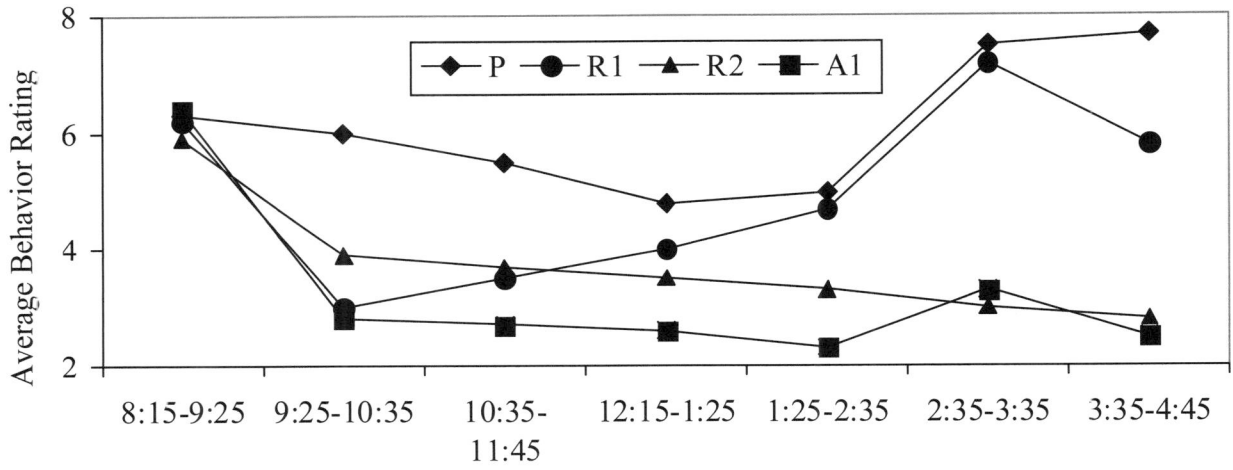

Figure 1

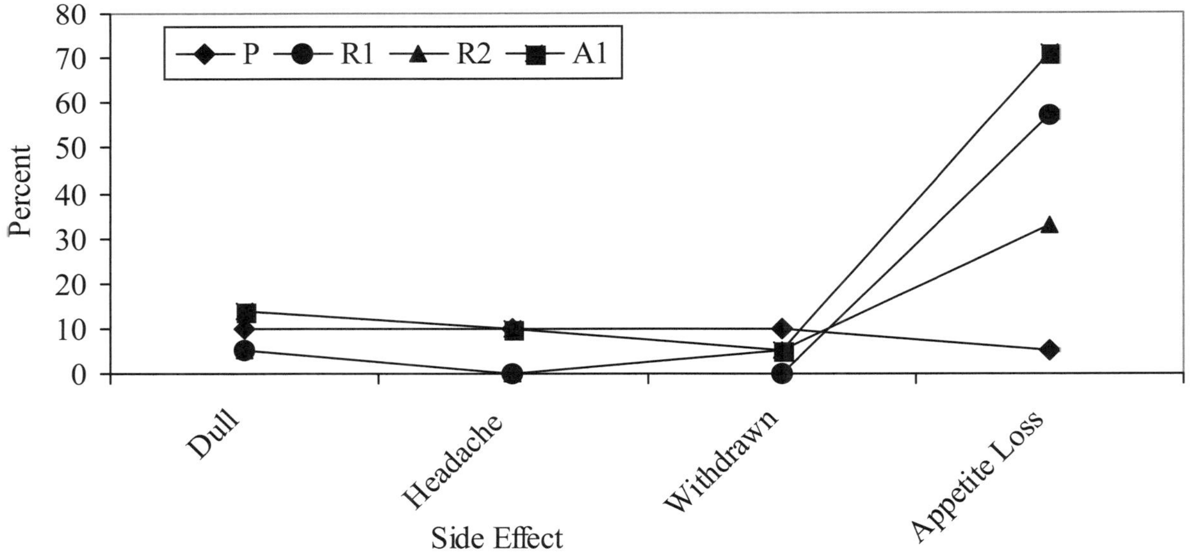

Figure 2

Based on Figure 1, during which of the following time periods was the average behavior rating most similar for the 4 groups of children?
A. 8:15-9:25
B. 9:25-10:35
C. 10:35-11:45
D. 3:35-4:45

A scientist claimed that children given one dose of Adderall daily would exhibit fewer behavior problems than children given either one or two doses of Ritalin daily. During which of the following time periods shown in Figure 1 are the results *inconsistent* with this claim?
F. 9:25-10:35
G. 10:35-11:45
H. 2:35-3:35
J. 3:35-4:45

According to Figure 2, for the group given Ritalin twice daily, the percentage of children who experienced an adverse side effect was greatest for which side effect?
A. Dull
B. Headache
C. Withdrawn
D. Appetite loss

26. According to Figure 1, which dose of medication was the least successful in controlling children's behavior problems from 3:35-4:45?
F. P
G. R1
H. R2
J. A1

27. Suppose that there were 4 children given each possible dose of medication, and that for one of the groups the behavior ratings from 12:15-1:25 for the 4 children were 2, 3, 5, and 6. Based on Figure 1, which dose of medication were these 4 children most likely given?
A. P
B. R1
C. R2
D. A1

28. Assume that an ideal medication is one that has the least side effects, yet is most effective. Based on the data provided, which dose of medication is the most ideal?
F. P
G. R1
H. R2
J. A1

GO ON TO THE NEXT PAGE.

Passage VI

Osmosis is the net movement of solvent molecules through a semipermeable membrane from pure solvent or more dilute solution to more concentrated solution. The pressure required to stop osmosis is referred to as *osmotic pressure*. This process can be observed using saltwater and a curved tube. In a U-shaped tube, saltwater is separated from pure water by a semipermeable membrane. As water passes through the membrane from dilute to more concentrated, it rises in the tube and creates pressure. Eventually this pressure prevents further passage of water through the membrane. (See Figure 1).

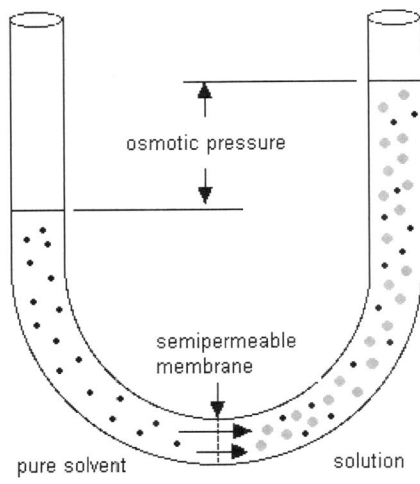

Figure 1

The following experiments were carried out to study how varying the molecular weight percentage of solvents and the temperature of solutions affects osmotic pressure. Table 1 shows the molecular weight percentages of the different solvents studied and Table 2 displays the temperatures of the various solutions used.

Table 1	
Solvent	% Weight
1	10
2	15
3	20
4	25

Table 2	
Solution	Temperature (°C)
1	10
2	20
3	30
4	35

Experiment 1

A 1000 ml glass U-shaped tube was fitted with a piece dialysis tubing (a semipermeable membrane.) Then, 600 ml 30°C mixture of water and Solvent 1 was added to the tube. solvent/water mixture was allowed to flow through the dial tubing and, for a total of 30 seconds, the amount of solution had passed through the tubing was measured every 5 seco This process was repeated using Solvents 2, 3, and 4 (see Fig 2).

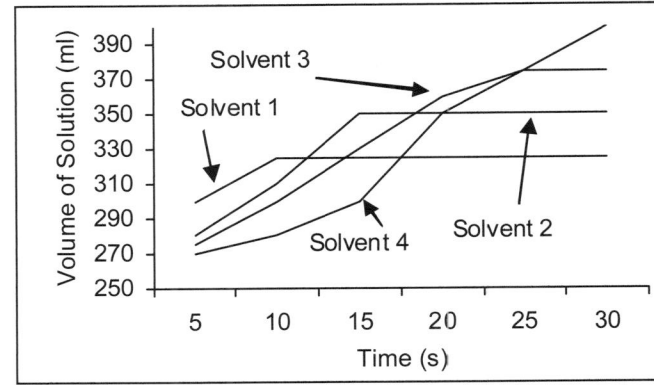

Figure 2

Experiment 2

Experiment 1 was repeated, except now Solvent 1 was for each trial and the temperature of the water was varied inst This time the solvent was allowed to flow until osmotic pres could be calculated (see Figure 3). The process was repeated solutions of three different temperatures.

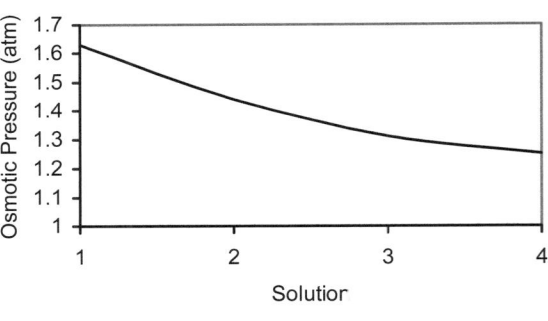

Figure 3

29. Based on Figure 2, which solvent resulted in the solution having passed through the semiperme membrane after 30 seconds?
    A. Solvent 1
    B. Solvent 2
    C. Solvent 3
    D. Solvent 4

Which of the following is true about the relationship between osmotic pressure and water temperature?
F. As temperature decreases, osmotic pressure decreases.
G. As temperature increases, osmotic pressure increases.
H. As temperature increases, osmotic pressure decreases.
J. Temperature has no effect on osmotic pressure.

Based on the information in Table 1 and Figure 2, which of the following can be inferred about the affect of a solvent's molecular weight percentage on the rate that solution passes through the semipermeable membrane?
A. The lower the % weight of the solvent, the more quickly the solution passes through the membrane.
B. The lower the % weight of the solvent, the more slowly the solution passes through the membrane.
C. The % weight has no effect on the rate that the solution passes through the membrane.
D. The hotter the water and higher the % weight of the solvent, the faster the solution passes through the membrane.

32. Was Experiment 1 successful in determining osmotic pressure for each solvent?
F. No; it is impossible to determine osmotic pressure for any of the solvents.
G. No; it is impossible to determine osmotic pressure for Solvent 4.
H. Yes; the osmotic pressure for each solvent is equal to the volume of solution that has passed through the semipermeable membrane after 30 seconds.
J. Yes; osmotic pressure is highest for Solvent 2 and lowest for Solvent 1.

33. If enough pressure is exerted, it is possible to make water molecules move from solution to pure water. This process is called *reverse osmosis*. Assume that the amount of pressure necessary for reverse osmosis is roughly twice the osmotic pressure. Using the data in Table 2 and Figure 3, one could predict that about how much pressure would be needed to perform reverse osmosis in the 30°C solution?
A. 0.7 atm
B. 1.2 atm
C. 2.8 atm
D. 3.2 atm

Passage VII

Students studying mirrors and reflection were given the following information:

There is a definite relationship between image characteristics and the distance an object is placed with regard to a concave mirror (See Figure 1). If an object is located beyond the center of curvature (C), its reflected image will be inverted (upside down) and smaller than the object itself. If an object is located precisely at C, the image will also be located at C; it will appear inverted and true to the object's actual size. When the object is placed between C and the focal length (F), the image will be inverted and larger than the object. When the object is located precisely at F, no image is formed whatsoever. Lastly, if an object is placed between F and the mirror, its image will appear upright and larger than the object.

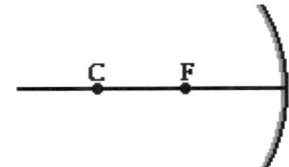

Figure 1

Given no further information, the students were asked to explain how the following magic trick is performed:

The famous Chinese magician, Foo Ling Yu, conducts a classic magic trick utilizing a concave mirror with a focal length (F) of 1.6m and a center of curvature (C) of 2.2m. Foo Ling Yu is able to utilize the mirror in such a manner as to produce an image of a light bulb at the same location and of the same size as the actual light bulb itself.

Student 1

The light bulb must have been placed exactly 1.6m in front of the mirror, creating a perfect reflection. The image would thus be in the same location as the light bulb, have the same dimensions as the light bulb, and be an upright image.

Student 2

The light bulb must have been placed exactly 2.2m in front of the mirror. The image would then be in the same location and have the same dimensions as the actual light bulb, although it would be inverted.

34. The students disagreed about which aspect of the light bulb's image?
F. Its size.
G. Its location.
H. Its orientation.
J. Its shape.

35. The two explanations were similar to each other in that both explanations:
A. Assumed that the image was upright.
B. Assumed that the exact positioning of the light bulb was important.
C. Correctly interpreted the information provided by the teacher.
D. Incorrectly interpreted the information provided by the teacher.

36. Placing the light bulb in front of the mirror at which of the following distances would have resulted in an upright image?
F. 1.0m
G. 1.6m
H. 2.2m
J. 2.6m

37. Did Student 2 provide an adequate explanation of the magic trick?
A. No; Student 2's explanation included an image that was upside down.
B. No; if the light bulb were placed at 2.2m, it would not have produced an image.
C. Yes; 2.2m is the center of curvature. Placing an object at C results in an image of the same size in the same place.
D. Yes; the magician specified that the image was inverted and Student 2 was the only student to account for this.

38. All of the following statements concerning concave mirror reflections are true EXCEPT:
F. An object placed anywhere in front of C (closer to the mirror) will produce a reflected image that is larger than the actual object.
G. An object placed anywhere in front of F (closer to the mirror) will produce an upright reflection.
H. An object placed anywhere beyond F (farther from the mirror) will produce an inverted reflection.
J. The only possible way to produce a reflected image equal in size to the actual object is to place the object precisely at C.

The teacher posed another question to the students. The students were told that the magician performed another trick in which he relocated the light bulb so as to create the illusion that it had disappeared completely. How far in front of the mirror must the light bulb have been placed in order to not produce a reflection?
A. 1.3m
B. 1.6m
C. 2.0m
D. 2.2m

40. Assume that Student 2's explanation is correct. If the magician wanted to create an image of the light bulb that was smaller than the light bulb itself, at which of the following distances in front of the mirror could he place the light bulb?
F. 1.6m
G. 2.0m
H. 2.2m
J. 2.5m

END OF TEST
STOP! DO NOT RETURN TO ANY OTHER TEST.

ACT SUCCESS

WRITING TEST 3 – Prompt

DIRECTIONS:

This is a test of your writing skills. You will have thirty (30) minutes to write an essay in English. Before you begin planning and writing your essay, read the writing prompt below carefully to understand exactly what you are being asked to do. Your essay will be evaluated on the evidence it provides of your ability to express judgments by taking a position on the issue in the writing prompt; to main a focus on the topic throughout the essay; to develop a position by using logical reasoning and by supporting your ideas; to organize ideas in a logical way; and to use language clearly and effectively according to the conventions of standard written English.

Childhood obesity is on the rise. In an effort to promote healthier eating habits, a number of schools have chosen to remove candy and soda from vending machines and to ban bake sales during school hours. Many oppose this ban because the money from the machines and from bake sales had been used to fund extracurricular activities. In your opinion, should schools take these measures to promote healthier eating habits?

In your essay, take a position on this question. You may write about either one of the two points of view given, or you may present a different point of view on this question. Use specific reasons and examples to support your position.

Use this page to *plan* your essay.

Begin **WRITING TEST 3** here.

WRITING TEST 3

WRITING TEST 3

WRITING TEST 3

STOP here with the Writing Test.

Scale Scores for Practice Test 3

* These scores are based on student trials rather than national norms.

English _____
Math _____
Reading _____
Science _____

=Total _____

Composite = Total divided by 4 (round up at .5) _____

ACT Score*	Number Right				ACT Score*
	English	Math	Reading	Science	
36	75	60	40	40	36
35	73-74	59	39	--	35
34	72	58	38	39	34
33	71	57	37	--	33
32	70	56	36	38	32
31	69	54-55	34-35	--	31
30	68	53	33	37	30
29	67	51-52	32	36	29
28	65-66	49-50	30-31	34-35	28
27	64	46-48	29	33	27
26	62-63	44-45	28	31-32	26
25	60-61	41-43	27	30	25
24	58-59	39-40	26	28-29	24
23	55-57	37-38	24-25	27	23
22	53-54	35-36	23	25-26	22
21	50-52	33-34	22	23-24	21
20	47-49	31-32	21	21-22	20
19	44-46	28-30	19-20	19-20	19
18	42-43	25-27	18	17-18	18
17	40-41	22-24	17	15-16	17
16	37-39	19-21	16	13-14	16
15	34-36	15-17	15	12	15
14	31-33	11-14	13-14	11	14
13	29-30	09-10	12	10	13
12	27-28	07-08	10-11	09	12
11	25-26	06	08-09	08	11
10	23-24	05	07	07	10
9	21-22	04	06	06	9
8	18-20	03	05	05	8
7	15-17	--	--	04	7
6	12-14	02	04	03	6
5	09-11	--	03	02	5
4	07-08	01	02	--	4
3	05-06	--	--	01	3
2	03-04	--	01	--	2
1	00-02	00	00	00	1

Practice Test #4

ENGLISH TEST

45 Minutes – 75 Questions

DIRECTIONS: In the five passages that follow, certain words and phrases are underlined and numbered. In the right-hand column, you will find alternatives for the underlined part. In most cases, you are to choose the one that best expresses the idea, makes the statement appropriate for standard written English, or is worded most consistently with the style and tone of the passage as a whole. If you think the original version is best, choose "NO CHANGE." In some cases, you will find in the right-hand column a question about the underlined part. You are to choose the best answer to the question.

You will also find questions about a section of the passage or about the passage as a whole. These questions do refer to an underlined portion of the passage, but rather identified by a number or numbers in a box.

For each question, choose the alternative you consider and fill in the corresponding oval on your ans document. Read each passage through once before begin to answer the questions that accompany it. For n of the questions, you must read several sentences bey the question to determine the answer. Be sure that you read far enough ahead each time you choose an alternati

---

PASSAGE I

No Place I'd Rather Be

[1]

I started taking group skating lessons when I was four. I progressed through various levels rapidly and gave my first ice performance at age seven, soon I started winning local and regional competitions. I began seriously training when I was nine years old. Mom and I would wake up at four o'clock in the morning, six days a week. I'd skate for five hours. Then I'd go to school.

1. **A.** NO CHANGE
   B. seven. Soon I started
   C. seven, soon I was
   D. seven. Soon I had

[2]

Saying good-bye to my family, and friends made me homesick before I even left, but I knew deep down that I had to leave and train full-time in Canada to give my dreams a chance at reality. I went to compete in the Olympic Games in 1992. No one, not my coach or even my family, ever talked to

2. **F.** NO CHANGE
   G. family, and, friends
   H. family and friends,
   J. family and friends

3. Which of the following alternatives to the under portion would NOT be acceptable?
   A. even left yet I knew
   B. even left. I knew
   C. even left; I knew
   D. even left; however, I knew

420
TEST 4

me about giving up. In fact, I wouldn't even allow myself to
                    4

think about it. I thought my thoughts would jinx me. Yet, I
                                                         5
went with the attitude that I wanted to enjoy the Olympic

spirit. 6

[3]

My practice sessions felt great leading up to the

competition. Finally, the day arrived. I remember stepping

onto the ice and thinking, I can't do this. How am I going to

keep myself from freaking out? I took a deep breath and

begun a solid performance that placed me first going into the
  7
finals.

[4]

When medals were awarded, I found myself on the top
                                                                8
step, the gold hanging around my neck and
       8

Americas national anthem playing. Words can't describe the
          9
overwhelming mixture of emotions I felt.

[5]

[1] Two days later, I was the first of the final six skaters

on the cold, but shimmering ice. [2] My long performance
          10
started well, but I slipped while completing one of my easiest

triple jumps, and my hand touched the ice. [3] I didn't want

to make two mistakes in a row, so next I did a jump with just

4. Given that all of the choices are true, which one provides information that is most relevant at this point in the essay?
   F. NO CHANGE
   G. all the hard work required
   H. the joy of competing in the Olympics
   J. winning a gold medal

5. A. NO CHANGE
   B. Nevertheless, I
   C. However, I
   D. I

6. Which of the following statements, if added at the beginning of this paragraph, would most effectively introduce readers to the information presented in the paragraph?
   F. I had always wanted to move away from home, so when the opportunity presented itself, I jumped.
   G. Eagerly I followed my coach's advice and moved to Canada where I left quickly left my childhood behind.
   H. Twenty-four hours after graduating from high school, I moved to Canada.
   J. There was only one road to success and hanging around my hometown waiting to be discovered wasn't it.

7. A. NO CHANGE
   B. begin
   C. began
   D. had begun

8. F. NO CHANGE
   G. top step the gold, hanging
   H. top, step the gold hanging
   J. top step the gold hanging

9. A. NO CHANGE
   B. Americas national anthem's
   C. Americas' national anthem
   D. America's national anthem

10. F. NO CHANGE
    G. cold yet shimmering, ice
    H. cold, shimmering, ice
    J. cold, shimmering ice

two spins to play it safe. [4] Usually jumps have three spins. [5] As I neared the end, I had one more jump, the triple Lutz. [6] Okay, this is it. [7] You have to do this, I told myself. [8] I landed perfectly. |11|

[6]

Why is ice so popular? Frozen water can be so painfully
   12
hard and oh so cold - just as life can be. Ice doesn't care who skates across its surface. It doesn't care who loses balance and falls on it's slippery back. Still, when the lights go on and
              13
the crowd roars its welcome, there's no place I'd rather be.

11. Which of the following sentences in this paragraph LEAST relevant to the purpose of describing narrator's actions, and therefore, could be deleted?
    A. Sentence 3.
    B. Sentence 4.
    C. Sentence 5.
    D. Sentence 7.

12. Which of the following choices best introduces paragraph?
    F. NO CHANGE
    G. There are so many reasons to love ice.
    H. How can anyone love ice?
    J. Ice has been around forever.

13. A. NO CHANGE
    B. its
    C. her
    D. there

Questions 14 and 15 ask about the preceding passage as a whole.

14. For the sake of the logic and coherence of this essay Paragraph 5 should be placed:
    F. where it is now.
    G. after Paragraph 3.
    H. before Paragraph 1.
    J. after Paragraph 6.

15. Suppose the writer's goal had been to write a brief essay about a significant event in his/her life. Would this essay successfully accomplish that goal?
    A. Yes, because it focuses on a specific time in the narrator's life and goes into detail about winning Olympic gold medal.
    B. Yes, because it details many events leading up to an important achievement in the narrator's life.
    C. No, because it is more of persuasive essay motivating the readers to pursue their dreams, even if it means personal sacrifice.
    D. No, because the narrator mentions several events didn't go into much detail about any one event.

PASSAGE II

A Journey on Cane River

Growing up, I knew for an absolute fact that no one on the planet was stronger than my mother. So when she told me stories of people she admired growing up, I paid attention. She was clearly in awe of her grandmother, Emily. Describing her grandmother as iron-willed and devilish,
<u>16</u>
physically beautiful and demanding of beauty from others, determined to make her farmhouse in central Louisiana a fun place to be on Sundays when family gathered, and fanatical and unforgiving about the responsibilities generated from family ties. On one hand, <u>Emily was, refined, graceful,</u>
<u>17</u>
<u>elegant</u>, soft-spoken, and classy. On the other, she was a
<u>17</u>
woman from the backwoods of Louisiana, possibly born a slave, unapologetic about dipping snuff, who buzzed on her homemade muscadine wine each and every day.

Emily <u>intrigued me, and the</u> puzzle of this woman
<u>18</u>
simmered on the back burner of my conscious mind for decades, undoubtedly <u>activating</u> questions about who I was as
<u>19</u>
well.

Hooked, I traced my mother's line to a place in Louisiana called Cane River, <u>a unique area that before the</u>
<u>20</u>
<u>Civil War housed one of the largest and wealthiest collections</u>
<u>20</u>
<u>of free people of color in the United States.</u> I decided to hire a
<u>20</u>

16. F. NO CHANGE
    G. She describes
    H. She described
    J. Because she described

17. A. NO CHANGE
    B. Emily was refined, graceful, elegant,
    C. Emily was refined, and graceful and elegant
    D. Emily was; refined, graceful, elegant,

18. F. NO CHANGE
    G. intrigued me, and, the puzzle
    H. intrigued me and, the puzzle
    J. intrigued me and the puzzle,

19. Which of the following choices is LEAST acceptable?
    A. NO CHANGE
    B. halting
    C. stirring
    D. triggering

20. If the writer were to delete the underlined portion from the sentence, the paragraph would primarily lose:
    F. details that emphasize the historical importance of the geographical location.
    G. a comparison of this location with the rest of the state of Louisiana.
    H. information that explains the narrator's reasons for searching for ancestors in Cane River.
    J. nothing at all, since these geographical details are irrelevant to the paragraph.

TEST 4

GO ON TO THE NEXT PAGE.

specialist on Cane River culture; a genealogist to find my
great-grandmother Emily's grandmother.

In a collection of ten thousand unindexed local records written in poor preserved Creole French, she found the bill of sale for my great-great-great-great-grandmother Elisabeth,

whom was sold in 1850 in Cane River, Louisiana, for eight hundred dollars.

One day, I had no choice. I had to write their story and document their lives – my history. They are, after all, real flesh-and-blood people. I pieced their lives the best I could, re-creating what life must have been like for them during the 1800s and 1900s. [26]

Resulting with *Cane River*, a novelized account covering one hundred years in America's history and following four

21. **A.** NO CHANGE
    B. culture a genealogist,
    C. culture, a genealogist,
    D. culture a genealogist

22. **F.** NO CHANGE
    G. poorly preserved
    H. preserved poorly
    J. preserved poor

23. **A.** NO CHANGE
    B. whom
    C. who have
    D. who was

24. Given that all choices are true, which one provides best transition between paragraphs?
    F. NO CHANGE
    G. Sooner or later,
    H. At this point,
    J. However,

25. **A.** NO CHANGE
    B. They were,
    C. I am,
    D. We be,

26. The writer is considering adding the following phrase the preceding sentence, after the word *could*:

    from over a thousand documents uncovered in my years of research

    Should the writer make this addition?
    F. Yes, because it emphasizes how much work the had to do in order to complete the book.
    G. Yes, because it provides details that prove that *River* is a fictional novel.
    H. No, because the information is unnecessary and away from the main idea of the sentence.
    J. No, because the information is too hard to believe

27. **A.** NO CHANGE
    B. The result was
    C. Having the result of
    D. Results were

generations of Creole slave women in Cane River, Louisiana. As they struggled to keep their families intact through the dark days of slavery, the Civil War, Reconstruction, and the pre-civil rights era of Jim Crow South. The book ended up on Oprah's book list and made the *New York Times* Bestseller list.

28. **F.** NO CHANGE
    G. Louisiana when they
    H. Louisiana, they
    J. Louisiana, who

29. Given that all of the choices are true, which one best concludes this essay by tying this paragraph to the essay's introduction?
    A. NO CHANGE
    B. I had always wanted to write a book, and was proud of my accomplishment.
    C. Finally I, along with the rest of the world, had an idea of who Emily really was.
    D. This was the first book published about Creole slave women.

    Question 30 asks about the preceding passage as a whole.

30. Suppose the writer's goal had been to describe the personal benefits of writing a book. Does this essay successfully accomplish that goal?
    F. Yes, the author explains how writing *Cane River* made her a better person.
    G. Yes, the author discusses why she wanted to write a book and then details the many steps involved.
    H. No, because it focuses instead on biographical information about the author's family.
    J. No, the essay fails to provide enough information about what the author gained from the experience of writing the book.

PASSAGE III

Illinois Prairies

There are different kinds of prairie in Illinois depending on the moisture gradient and soil type. The different kinds of prairie wildflowers, are often associated with these different
<u>   </u>
      31
moisture gradients and soil types. As an ecological habitat, grasses and herbaceous wildflowers, rather than trees and shrubs, or areas with more or less permanent water, <u>dominated</u> prairies.
      32

[33] High quality prairies are interesting

and colorful places to visit during the growing season, <u>because they demonstrate high biodiversity.</u>
                           34
Black soil prairie was the dominant type of prairie in

central and northern Illinois, <u>until</u> it was almost totally
                                    35
destroyed by agricultural development during the 19th century. The landscape of such prairies is rather flat. A high

31. A. NO CHANGE
　　B. wildflowers are often
　　C. wildflowers often
　　D. wildflowers: often

32. F. NO CHANGE
　　G. dominates
　　H. dominating
　　J. dominate

33. At this point, the writer is considering adding the following true statement:

　　　In Iowa, 6 different types of coneflowers sway in summer breezes.

　　Should the writer make this addition here?
　　A. Yes, because it helps establish that the essay is set the Midwest.
　　B. Yes, because it helps reinforce the main idea of the paragraph.
　　C. No, because it does not make clear whether coneflowers grow in every state.
　　D. No, because it takes away from the main focus of paragraph.

34. The writer is considering deleting the underlined port from the sentence. Should the phrase be kept or delete
　　F. Kept, because it provides supporting details that reinforce the main idea of the sentence.
　　G. Kept, because it establishes that prairies contain m biodiversity than any other habitat.
　　H. Deleted, because it has already been established e in the paragraph that prairies have low biodiversity
　　J. Deleted, because it draws attention away from the different types of prairies.

35. A. NO CHANGE
　　B. Illinois,
　　C. Illinois: until
　　D. Illinois. Until

quality black soil prairie has lots of wildflowers in bloom from late spring until the middle of fall. Today, small remnants of original black soil prairie can be found in pioneer cemeteries, or at construction sites.
                                    36

[1] Gravel and dolomite prairies were never very common in Illinois, and can be found primarily in northern Illinois. [2] Gravel and dolomite prairies can be rather flat, or slightly hilly. [3] Yet, the original gravel and dolomite
          37
prairies have been largely destroyed by modern development. [4] They tend to be rather dry and well drained. [5] More recently, such prairies can be found along the gravelly ballast of railroads, where they did not formerly exist. 38 [6] In this case, they are degraded and often contain flora from Western
                          39
states. 40

Hill prairies occur primarily along the Illinois and Mississippi Rivers, hill prairies are very dry and exposed to
                  41
prevailing winds from the south or west. The wildflowers of

36. Given that all choices are grammatically correct, which one best establishes that black soil prairies are difficult to find today?
  F. NO CHANGE
  G. or along old railroads.
  H. in state parks, and surrounding farmland.
  J. and in many neighborhoods.

37. A. NO CHANGE
  B. However,
  C. Unfortunately,
  D. Accordingly,

38. The writer is considering deleting the phrase "where they did not formerly exist" from the preceding sentence (and placing a period after the word *railroads*). Should the phrase be kept or deleted?
  F. Kept, because the information helps to establish the rampant proliferation of gravel and dolomite prairies in Illinois.
  G. Kept, because it strengthens the paragraph's focus on the unchanging landscape of prairies.
  H. Deleted, because it is not relevant to the description of gravel and dolomite prairies found in Illinois.
  J. Deleted, because the information detracts from the point made earlier in the paragraph that the prairies have been largely destroyed.

39. A. NO CHANGE
  B. and many bird species migrate to them
  C. consisting of a mix of native grasses and flowers and flora
  D. and are of particular interest to tourists

40. For the sake of the logic and coherence of this paragraph, Sentence 4 should be placed:
  F. Where it is now.
  G. before Sentence 1.
  H. before Sentence 3.
  J. before Sentence 6.

41. A. NO CHANGE
  B. Rivers. Hill
  C. Rivers hill
  D. Rivers; hill,

TEST 4   GO ON TO THE NEXT PAGE.

hill prairies are similar to those who are found in the drier
                                      —————————
                                           42
areas of gravel and dolomite prairies. Some species that are

found in hill prairies is typical of western areas.
                            ———————
                                43

  Sand prairies can be moist mesic or dry and their
                        ——————————————————
                                 44
landscape is either flat or slightly hilly. They usually occur

near current or former bodies of water. Their vegetation is
                                        ———————————————
                                              45
sparser than black soil prairies.
————————————————————————————
              45

42. F. NO CHANGE
    G. which are finding
    H. if found
    J. that can be found

43. A. NO CHANGE
    B. are more typical
    C. typify
    D. are more usual

44. F. NO CHANGE
    G. moist mesic, or dry; and
    H. moist: mesic or dry, and
    J. moist, mesic, or dry, and

45. Given that all of the choices are true, which best
    concludes the paragraph with a colorful image that rel
    to the description of a sand prairie?
    A. NO CHANGE
    B. Vegetation includes woody shrubs, wildflowers, a
       native prairie grasses.
    C. The spectacular vegetation includes the vibrant hu
       purple spiderwort, orange butterfly weed, and yell
       goldenrod.
    D. More than 60 colorful species of wildflowers have
       been identified as being native to sand prairies.

PASSAGE IV

Is This Guy Nuts?

On a muggy April morning Sean D. Tucker was making a practice run over Red River Parish, Louisiana in his crimson biplane. But as he begun to climb, he heard a bam from somewhere near it's tail. Part of the elevator control system had snapped, making normal steering impossible.

[1] The plane bucking wildly, hurtling 15 feet above the ground at 225 mph. [2] He wrestled the craft to an altitude of 5,000 feet, where he tried some maneuvers to gauge whether he could land safely. [3] To keep it from hitting the tarmac, Tucker performed a frantic dance - feet pumping the rudder pedals, left hand shuttling between the throttle and a lever for pitch adjustment. [4] He couldn't. [5] He said a prayer. [6] Then he prepared to abandon the machine he'd spent 11 years and a million dollars honing to perfection. 49

That day in 2006 wasn't the first time Tucker had been forced to part with a plane mid-solo. It was in fact, the third.

Such persistence in the face of near disaster accounting for why he'll be inducted into the National Aviation Hall of Fame, alongside such paragons as the Wright brothers. His

46. F. NO CHANGE
 G. began
 H. is beginning
 J. begins

47. A. NO CHANGE
 B. its'
 C. his
 D. its

48. F. NO CHANGE
 G. bucked
 H. bucks
 J. had been bucking

49. For the sake of the logic and coherence of this paragraph, Sentence 2 should be placed:
 A. where it is now.
 B. before Sentence 1.
 C. before Sentence 4.
 D. before Sentence 6.

50. F. NO CHANGE
 G. was, in fact the
 H. was, in fact: the
 J. was, in fact, the

51. A. NO CHANGE
 B. helps explain
 C. being
 D. the only reason

TEST 4

GO ON TO THE NEXT PAGE.

will to push the envelope comes from a boyhood
[52]

revelation: the greatest beauty often lies on the other side of
[53]
fear.

Today the software company Oracle sponsors Tucker to the tune of $2.1 million a year. He employs several
[54]
individual mechanics and rehearses his moves three times
[54]
a day. Besides, disaster is never more than a glitch
[55]
away, that is how he found himself about to leap from
[56]
a plane again that morning in Louisiana.

Tucker was directed to a cotton field where he could ditch the plane without endangering others. Then he jumped. "See you later, girl," he murmured looking away as he
[57]
floated down. He heard the crash, but he couldn't bear to watch.

Tucker flew at an air show in Florida two days later, but had doubts he did for months. The following October,
[58]
though, during a show in San Diego, he had what he

52. Which of the following alternatives to the underlined portion would be LEAST acceptable?
    F. desire
    G. inspiration
    H. resolve
    J. obsession

53. A. NO CHANGE
    B. revelation, the greatest
    C. revelation which was that the greatest
    D. revelation the greatest

54. F. NO CHANGE
    G. numerous mechanics
    H. several of whom are mechanics
    J. numerous particular individuals

55. A. NO CHANGE
    B. Moreover,
    C. Yet
    D. Indeed,

56. F. NO CHANGE
    G. away, which
    H. away which
    J. away; that

57. A. NO CHANGE
    B. later girl," he murmured,
    C. later girl", he murmured
    D. later, girl" he murmured,

58. F. NO CHANGE
    G. bothering himself with doubts for months.
    H. and racked by doubts he was for months.
    J. but for months he was racked by doubts.

430
TEST 4

GO ON TO THE NEXT PAGE

considered to be the first perfect flight of his career - a run so graceful that the plane seemed to pilot itself. He decided
<u>59</u>

soon afterward that retirement was not an option. [60]

59. If the writer were to delete the underlined portion, the sentence would primarily lose:
   A. a suggestion that Tucker was considering using autopilot to fly his plane.
   B. information that proves how lucky Tucker is as a pilot.
   C. a detail that helps explain why Tucker thought the flight was perfect.
   D. an irrelevant description of his flight.

60. At this point, the writer is considering adding the following true statement:

   "I'm still learning," Tucker says. "And I'm still getting better."

   Should the writer make this addition here?
   F. Yes, because it provides information that explains why Tucker decided not to retire.
   G. Yes, because it is important for the reader to know that Tucker thinks he can still improve his skills.
   H. No, because the information is irrelevant to the paragraph.
   J. No, because it contradicts the statement made earlier in the paragraph that Tucker already flies perfectly.

PASSAGE V

The Birth of Surrealism

Joan Miró was a Catalan painter, sculptor, and ceramicist born in Barcelona, Spain, in 1893. His work has been interpreted with international acclaim, earning a reputation as Surrealism, a sandbox for the subconscious mind, a re-creation of the childlike, and a manifestation of Catalan pride. In numerous interviews dating from the 1930s onwards, Miró expressing contempt for conventional painting methods as a way of supporting bourgeoise society, and famously declared an "assassination of painting" in favor of utilizing common traditional methods of blending colors.

Born to the family of a goldsmith and watchmaker, the young Miró was drawn towards the arts community that was gathering in Montparnasse and in 1920 moved to Paris.

There, under the influence of the poets and writers, developing his unique style: organic forms and flattened picture planes drawn with a sharp line. Generally thought of as a Surrealist because of his interest in automatism and the use of sexual symbols, Miró's style was influenced in variety degrees by Surrealism and Dada, yet he rejected membership

---

61. A. NO CHANGE
  B. He has earned international acclaim, his work
  C. Interpreted as having earned international acclaim, his work is seen
  D. Earning international acclaim, his work has been interpreted

62. F. NO CHANGE
  G. expressed
  H. had express
  J. were to express

63. Which choice best illustrates Miró's contempt conventional painting and helps explain "assassination of painting" mentioned earlier in sentence?
  A. NO CHANGE
  B. applying works of art by famous renaissance painters.
  C. boycotting painting as an art form and turning to sculpting instead.
  D. rejecting the visual elements of established paintin

64. F. NO CHANGE
  G. Miró was drawn to the arts community, born to th family of a goldsmith and watchmaker
  H. The arts community, born to the family of a goldsmith and watchmaker, the young Miró was drawn to
  J. The young Miró was drawn to the family of a goldsmith and watchmaker, born to the arts community

65. A. NO CHANGE
  B. writers. He developed
  C. writers, he developed
  D. writers develops

66. F. NO CHANGE
  G. varying
  H. different and varying

in any artistic movement in the interwar European years.

Andre <u>Breton, the founder of Surrealism described</u> him as
                        67
"the most Surrealist of us all."

   <u>Miró often received inspiration for his paintings in</u>
                        68
<u>visions</u>, and thus, with Andre Masson, represented the
68

beginning of Surrealism as an art movement. <u>However,</u> Miró
                                              69
chose not to become an official member of the Surrealists in

order to be free to experiment with other artistic styles

without compromising his position within the group. He

pursued his own interests in the art <u>world, ranges</u> from
                                        70
automatic drawing and Surrealism, to Expressionism and

Color Field painting.

   In his final decades Miró <u>were to accelerate</u> his work in
                              71
different media and produced hundreds of ceramics, including

the *Wall of the Moon* and *Wall of the Sun*. He also made

temporary window paintings (on glass) for an exhibit. In the

last years of his life Miró wrote his most radical and least

<u>known ideas: explored</u> the possibilities of gas sculpture and
         72
four-dimensional painting.

   He died bedridden, at his home in Palma, Mallorca on

December 25, 1983. He suffered from heart disease, and

   J. various, multiple

67. A. NO CHANGE
    B. Breton the founder of Surrealism, described
    C. Breton: the founder of Surrealism, describe
    D. Breton, the founder of Surrealism, described

68. At this point in the essay, the writer wants to highlight the significance that Miró had on painting as an art form. Given that all of the choices are true, which one would best accomplish that purpose?
    F. NO CHANGE
    G. Miró greatly disliked all bourgeoise art, especially Cubism,
    H. Miró was the first artist to develop automatic drawing as a way to undo previous established techniques in painting,
    J. Four-dimensional painting is a theoretical type of painting Miró proposed,

69. A. NO CHANGE
    B. Consequently,
    C. Furthermore,
    D. Thus,

70. F. NO CHANGE
    G. world, ranging
    H. world which ranges
    J. world and range

71. A. NO CHANGE
    B. is accelerating
    C. accelerates
    D. accelerated

72. F. NO CHANGE
    G. known ideas exploring -
    H. known ideas. He explored
    J. known ideas, he explored

visits a clinic for respiratory problems two weeks before his
death. Many of his pieces are exhibited today in the Fundació
Joan Miró in Barcelona and the U.S. National Gallery in
Washington, D.C. he is buried nearby at the Montjuïc
cemetery. Today, his paintings sell for between $250,000 and
$17 million, that was the auction price for the *La
Caresse des Etoiles* on May 6, 2008 and is the highest
amount paid for one of Miró's works to date.

73. **A.** NO CHANGE
   B. had visited
   C. visiting
   D. was to visit

74. **F.** NO CHANGE
   G. Washington D.C. he is buried nearby,
   H. Washington, D.C., he is buried, nearby
   J. Washington, D.C.; he is buried nearby

75. **A.** NO CHANGE
   B. million and that
   C. million, which
   D. million which

MATHEMATICS TEST
60 Minutes—60 Questions

DIRECTIONS: Solve each problem, choose the correct answer, and then fill in the corresponding oval on your answer document.

Do not linger over problems that take too much time. Solve as many as you can; then return to the others in the time you have left for this test.

You are permitted to use a calculator on this test. You may use your calculator for any problems you choose, but some of the problems may best be done without using a calculator.

Note: Unless otherwise stated, all of the following should be assumed.

1. Illustrative figures are NOT necessarily drawn to scale.
2. Geometric figures lie in a plane.
3. The word *line* indicates a straight line.
4. The word *average* indicates arithmetic mean.

A rectangle is four times as long as it is wide. If the width of the rectangle is 4.5cm, what is the rectangle's area, in square centimeters?

A. 17
B. 18
C. 45
D. 72
E. 81

DO YOUR FIGURING HERE.

A bubble gum machine has 120 red, blue, yellow, and green gumballs in it. If 30 are yellow, 32 are red, and 28 are green, what is the probability that the next gumball out of the machine is not blue?

F. $\frac{1}{4}$
G. $\frac{3}{4}$
H. 25%
J. 1 : 4
K. 2 : 1

Which of the following is equivalent to 4×10^{-5}?

A. -2,000,000
B. -400,000
C. 0.00002
D. 0.00004
E. 0.000004

GO ON TO THE NEXT PAGE.

4. If a 25-foot ladder leans against a building and the base of the ladder is 15 feet from the bottom of the building, at what height does the top of the ladder touch the building?

   F. 10 ft.
   G. 18 ft.
   H. 20 ft.
   J. 30 ft.
   K. 40 ft.

5. Which of the following is equivalent to $\sqrt{96}$?

   A. $4\sqrt{6}$
   B. $6\sqrt{4}$
   C. $8\sqrt{6}$
   D. $8\sqrt{12}$
   E. $16\sqrt{6}$

6. What is the perimeter of a square with an area of 49?

   F. 7
   G. 14
   H. 20
   J. 28
   K. 49

7. What is the slope of the line $4y = -2x + 4$?

   A. -2
   B. $-\frac{1}{2}$
   C. 1
   D. 2
   E. 4

8. What is the slope of any line perpendicular to the line $5x - 4y = -12$ in the standard (x,y) coordinate plane?

   F. -4
   G. $-\frac{5}{4}$
   H. $-\frac{4}{5}$
   J. $\frac{4}{5}$
   K. $\frac{5}{4}$

9. Given △XYZ with the angle measures shown below, and that point P lies on $\overrightarrow{XZ}$, what is m∠XYZ?

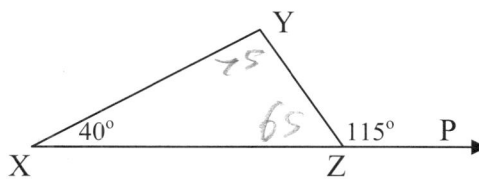

A. 25°
B. 65°
C. 75°
D. 85°
E. 140°

10. What is the area of a circle with a radius of 6?

F. 8π
G. 12π
H. 16π
J. 32π
K. 36π

11. Bette's two pieces of bacon and one egg cost $2.10. Jed's 3 pieces of bacon and two eggs cost $3.45. How much does one egg cost?

A. 45 cents
B. 50 cents
C. 60 cents
D. 70 cents
E. 75 cents

12. M, N, and x are all integers greater than 1. Given that $\frac{M}{24} + \frac{N}{108} = \frac{9M + 2N}{x}$, what must x equal?

F. 11
G. 12
H. 132
J. 216
K. 2,592

13. If ∠Y is the vertex of isosceles △XYZ (shown below), what is the value of a?

    A. 16°
    B. 17°
    C. 34°
    D. 36°
    E. 39°

    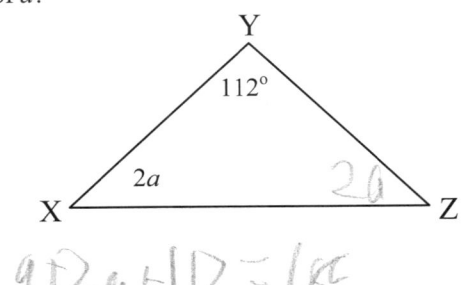

14. A function f is defined by $f(x) = -3x^2 + 4x$. What is the value of $f(4)$?

    F. −40
    G. −32
    H. 32
    J. 52
    K. 136

15. In the figure below, $\overline{MQ}$ intersects $\overline{PS}$ at point R, m∠TRS = 25°, and ∠QRT is a right angle. What is the measure of ∠MRP?

    A. 75°
    B. 90°
    C. 105°
    D. 115°
    E. 165°

    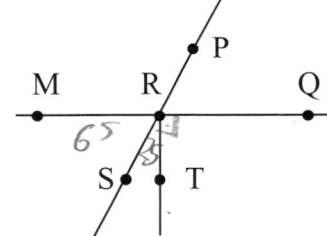

16. In △ABC below, what is tan ∠A?

    F. $\frac{5}{13}$
    G. $\frac{5}{12}$
    H. $\frac{12}{13}$
    J. $\frac{12}{5}$
    K. $\frac{13}{5}$

    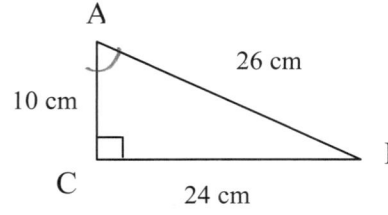

438
TEST 4

7. Jenna wants to serve a large pot of soup to 25 people by 1:15pm. If it takes her 7 minutes to assemble the ingredients, 20 minutes to cut up the vegetables, and two and a half hours to cook the soup on the stove, what is the latest time that Jenna could begin her meal preparation?

A. 9:53 am
B. 9:58 am
C. 10:18 am
D. 10:21 am
E. 10:28 am

8. Hiram's garden contains 45 tomato plants, 15 watermelon Plants, and 120 lettuce plants. Approximately what percent of the garden is occupied by watermelon plants?

F. 0.12%
G. 8.3%
H. 12%
J. 15%
K. 83%

9. What is the additive inverse of the polynomial $5x^3 - 4x^2 + 6x - 9$?

A. $-5x^3 + 4x^2 - 6x - 9$
B. $-5x^3 + 4x^2 - 6x + 9$
C. $5x^3 - 4x^2 + 6x - 9$
D. $-9 + 6x - 4x^2 + 5x^3$
E. $9 - 6x - 4x^2 + 5x^3$

10. In the standard (x, y) coordinate plane, if $\overline{AB}$ has endpoint A at (-2, 4) and midpoint M at (3, 9), where is endpoint B located?

F. (0.5, 6.5)
G. (6.5, 0.5)
H. (7, 1)
J. (8, 14)
K. (14, 8)

11. Which of the following, if any, is equivalent to the inequality $|x| - 4 < -7$?

A. $x < -3$ and $x > 3$
B. $x > -3$ and $x < 3$
C. $-3 < x < 3$
D. $-3 > x$ and $3 < x$
E. None of these.

DO YOUR FIGURING HERE.

150+7+20 = 177

1:15 10:45 10:25 10:18

439
GO ON TO THE NEXT PAGE.

22. What is the sum of the interior angles of pentagon ⬠LMNPR?

F. 180°
G. 540°
H. 600°
J. 720°
K. 900°

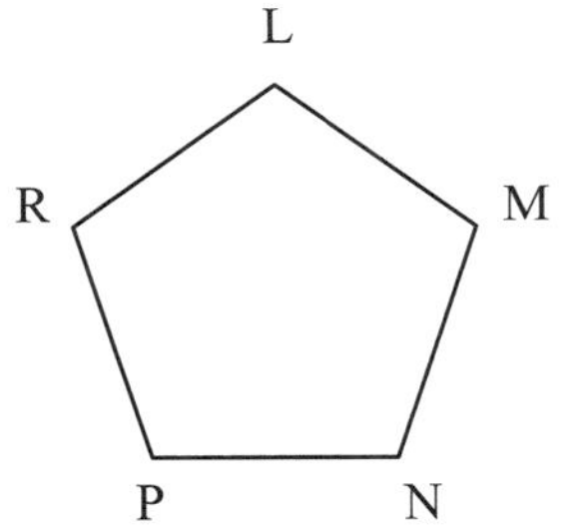

23. Which of the following values of n makes the statement $n^{1/2} = 4$ true?

A. 16
B. 8
C. 4
D. 2
E. $\frac{1}{8}$

24. If a and b can be any two real numbers such that $b < -6$ and $3a - b = 21$, which of the following is a solution set for a?

F. $a \leq 9$
G. $a \leq 5$
H. $a < 5$
J. $a \geq 9$
K. $a \geq -5$

25. Darcy used a 12m piece of rope to tie her dog to a tree while she mowed her front yard. The dog could only walk in a semi-circle because the tree was located directly next to the house (see diagram below). Assuming 3.14 for π, how much area, in square meters, could the dog cover?

A. 57
B. 75
C. 113
D. 226
E. 452

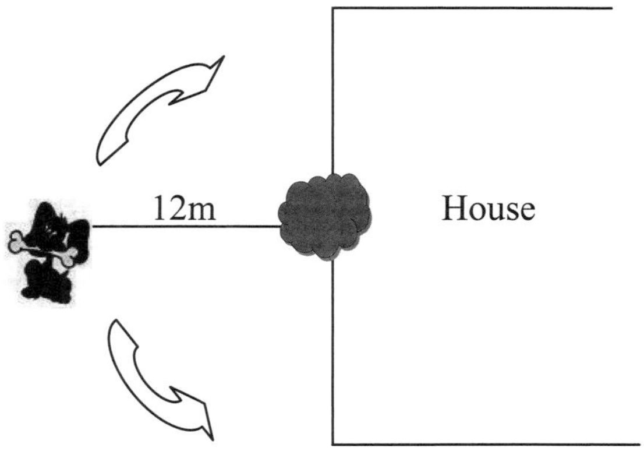

DO YOUR FIGURING HERE.

6. For $3x \neq 2y$, the polynomial expression $\dfrac{24x^2 - 7xy - 6y^2}{3x - 2y}$ is equivalent to which of the following?

   F. $2x - 3y$
   G. $2x - 12y$
   H. $3x - 2y$
   J. $8x - 3y$
   K. $8x + 3y$

7. Jose recently opened a new business. He projects that his profit will be $25,000 for the first year, and will increase by 7% over the next 8 years. Which of the following best describes the sequence formed by his annual profits?

   A. Geometric with a common ratio of 0.07
   B. Geometric with a common ratio of 1.07
   C. Geometric with a common ratio of 1.7
   D. Arithmetic with a common difference of 25.07
   E. Arithmetic with a common difference of 25,000

8. The trapezoid shown below in the standard (x, y) coordinate plane has vertices as marked. What is the area of the trapezoid in square units?

   F. 49.5
   G. 59.5
   H. 66
   J. 99
   K. 119

   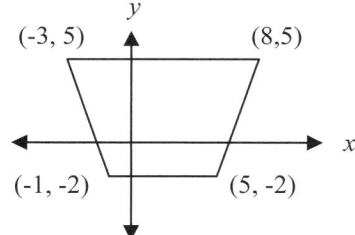

9. What is the greatest common factor of the terms $12x^4y^2$ and $6xy^3$?

   A. $6xy^2$
   B. $6x^4y^2$
   C. $6x^4y^3$
   D. $12xy^2$
   E. $12x^4y^3$

DO YOUR FIGURING HERE.

30. In the figure below, M is the midpoint of $\overline{NP}$ and △LMP is equilateral. If $\overline{NP} = 8$, what is the length of $\overline{LN}$?

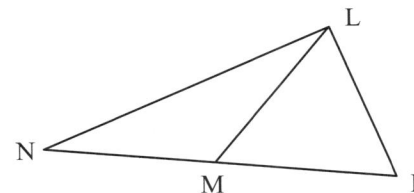

- F. 4
- G. $4\sqrt{2}$
- H. $4\sqrt{3}$
- J. 8
- K. $8\sqrt{3}$

31. The formula for converting Celsius temperature to Fahrenheit temperature is $F = \frac{9}{5}C + 32$. If the current temperature is 122° Fahrenheit, what is the temperature in Celsius?

- A. 50°
- B. 59.7°
- C. 65.5°
- D. 162°
- E. 277.2°

32. If a ratio is selected at random from the set $\{\frac{1}{3}, \frac{3}{5}, \frac{3}{7}, \frac{5}{7}, \frac{5}{9}\}$, what is the probability that the ratio is greater than $\frac{1}{2}$?

- F. $\frac{1}{5}$
- G. $\frac{2}{5}$
- H. $\frac{3}{5}$
- J. $\frac{2}{3}$
- K. $\frac{4}{5}$

33. Gertrude's Diner offers three different types of salads, two soups, four vegetable sides, five main dishes, and three desserts. If a customer can choose a salad or a soup along with one main dish, one vegetable side, and one dessert, how many different meal combinations are possible?

- A. 17
- B. 19
- C. 300
- D. 360
- E. 21,600

4. As shown below, △ABC has vertices at points A (1, 1), B (7, 2), and C (3, 4). If △ABC was reflected about the origin to form a new triangle, △ A′B′C′, which of the following correctly lists the coordinates of points A′, B′, and C′, respectively?

DO YOUR FIGURING HERE.

F. (1, 1); (2, 7); (4, 3)

G. (-1, 1); (-7, 2); (-4, 3)

H. (-1, -1); (-7, -2); (-3, -4)

J. (-1, -1); (-2, -7); (-3, -4)

K. (1, -1); (7, -2); (3, -4)

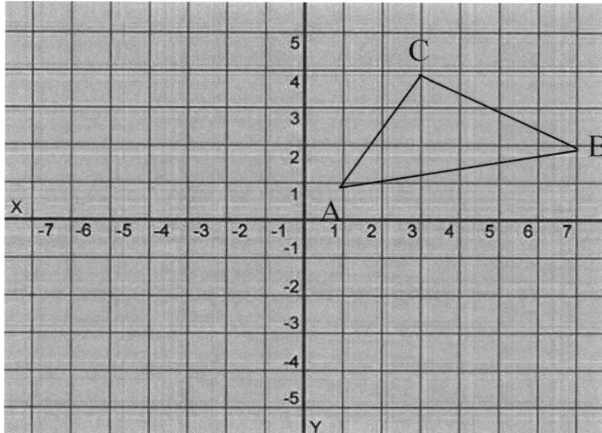

5. A military tank is 228 meters due north of its target. The commander's jeep is due west of the tank and 247 meters north/northwest of its target. Which of the following gives the distance, in meters, between the tank and the jeep?

A. 19
B. 95
C. 190
D. 475
E. 9,025

6. What is the matrix product of $[x \ 2x \ 3x] \cdot \begin{bmatrix} 6 \\ 0 \\ -2 \end{bmatrix}$?

F. $[6x \ 0 \ -6x]$

G. $[-6x \ 0 \ 6x]$

H. $\begin{bmatrix} 6x & 12x & 18x \\ 0 & 0 & 0 \\ -2x & -4x & -6x \end{bmatrix}$

J. $[0]$

K. $\begin{bmatrix} 6x & 0 & -2x \\ 12x & 0 & -4x \\ 18x & 0 & -6x \end{bmatrix}$

GO ON TO THE NEXT PAGE.

37. Which of the following expresses the number of meters an athlete must travel in a 6 lap race around a circular track with a diameter of X meters?

A. $6\pi X^2$
B. $3\pi X^2$
C. $\frac{3}{2}\pi X^2$
D. $6\pi X$
E. $3\pi X$

38. For all real numbers m and n such that the product of m and 4 is n, which of the following expressions represents the sum of m and 4 in terms of n?

F. $n + 4$
G. $4n + 4$
H. $4(n+4)$
J. $\frac{n+4}{4}$
K. $\frac{n}{4} + 4$

39. A shown below, rectangle KLMN is divided into three large squares (each labeled R) that measure x centimeters on a side, twelve small squares (each labeled S) that measure y centimeters on a side, and 12 rectangles (each labeled P). What is the total area, in square centimeters, of rectangle KLMN?

K							L
R	R	R	P	P	P	P	
P	P	P	S	S	S	S	
P	P	P	S	S	S	S	
P	P	P	S	S	S	S	
N							M

A. $3x + 4xy + 9yx + 12y$
B. $12x + 4xy + 9yx + 3y$
C. $3x^2 + 13xy + 12y^2$
D. $12x^2 + 13xy + 3y^2$
E. $3x^3 + 13xy + 12y^{12}$

444
TEST 4

For some real number D, the graph of the line $y = (D-3)x + 7$ in the standard (x, y) coordinate plane passes through the point (-5, 2). What is the slope of this line?

F. -3
G. -2
H. 0
J. 1
K. 4

When graphed in the standard (x, y) coordinate plane, the lines $x = -6$ and $y = 2x - 4$ intersect at what point?

A. (-16, -6)
B. (-6, -16)
C. (-6, 8)
D. (-6, 16)
E. (8, -6)

In △LMP, shown below, $\overline{LN}$ is the perpendicular bisector of $\overline{PM}$, cos ∠LMP = 0.4, and $\overline{PM}$ = 24 inches. How many inches long is $\overline{LM}$?

F. 9.6
G. 30
H. 40
J. 48
K. 60

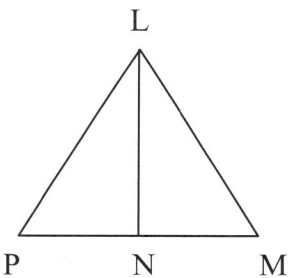

A music instructor charges $30 per lesson, plus an additional fee for violin rental. The charge for the violin varies directly with the square root of the time the violin is used. If a lesson plus 25 minutes of violin rental costs $65, how much would it cost for a lesson plus 81 minutes of violin rental?

A. $ 93
B. $105
C. $111
D. $141
E. $146

44. The figure below shows a small square inside of a larger square. The smaller square has sides 3 inches long, and the area of the shaded region is 16 square inches. What is the length, in inches, of one side of the larger square?

   F. 4
   G. $\sqrt{19}$
   H. 5
   J. $\sqrt{28}$
   K. 25

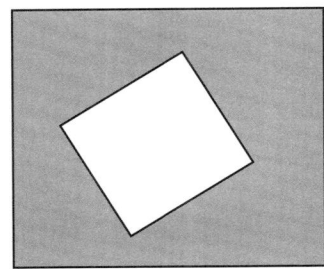

45. The quadrants of the standard (x, y) coordinate plane are labeled in the figure below. For each value of θ, let $x = \cos\theta$ and $y = \sin\theta$. Whenever $(\sin\theta)(\frac{1}{\cos\theta}) < 0$, the points (x, y) on the unit circle can lie in which of the following quadrants?

   A. III only
   B. IV only
   C. I and III only
   D. II and III only
   E. II and IV only

46. For $i^2 = -1$, $(3 - i)^2 = ?$

   F. 16
   G. $2i$
   H. $4i$
   J. $10 - 6i$
   K. $8 - 6i$

7. The volume of a sphere is determined by the equation $\frac{4}{3}\pi r^3$, where r is the radius of the sphere. In a given model of the Solar System, all of the planets are perfect spheres. If the radius of Mars is exactly 4 times greater than the radius of Venus, how many times the volume Venus is the volume of Mars?

   A. 81
   B. 64
   C. 16
   D. 12
   E. 4

8. Which of the following is equivalent to $\sqrt[2]{16r^6}$?

   F. $4r^3$
   G. $4r^4$
   H. $8r^3$
   J. $8r^4$
   K. $32r^{12}$

9. If 2 is a solution of the equation $x^2 + kx + 12 = 0$, what does k equal?

   A. -12
   B. -8
   C. -2
   D. 6
   E. 8

10. In the standard (x, y) coordinate plane, the center of the circle shown below lies on the y-axis at $y = 3$. If the circle is also tangent to the x-axis, then what is the equation of the circle?

    F. $x^2 + (y-3)^2 = 6$
    G. $x^2 + (y-3)^2 = 9$
    H. $x^2 + (y+3)^2 = 9$
    J. $(x-3)^2 + y^2 = 6$
    K. $(x+3)^2 + y^2 = 9$

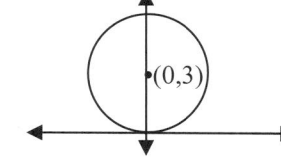

DO YOUR FIGURING HERE.

447

GO ON TO THE NEXT PAGE.

51. Which of the following equations summarizes the data listed below?

x	-2	-1	0	1	2
y	-8	-5	-2	1	4

A. $y = -2x - 2$
B. $y = 2x - 4$
C. $y = 2x + 3$
D. $y = 3x - 2$
E. $y = 3x + 2$

52. The law of sines states that for any triangle, the ratio between the sine of an angle and the length of the side opposite that angle is the same for all of the interior angles in the triangle. In $\triangle XYZ$ shown below, $\overline{ZX} = 22$ cm, $\angle Z = 32°$, and $\angle Y = 44°$. What is the length of $\overline{ZY}$?

F. $\dfrac{22(\sin 104°)}{\sin 32°}$

G. $\dfrac{\sin 32°(\sin 104°)}{\sin 44°}$

H. $\dfrac{22(\sin 32°)}{\sin 104°}$

J. $\dfrac{22(\sin 104°)}{\sin 44°}$

K. $\dfrac{22(\sin 44°)}{\sin 104°}$

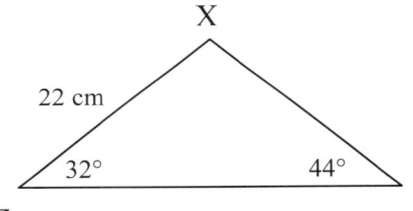

Which of the following is the graph of the equation $3x - 2y = 6$?

DO YOUR FIGURING HERE.

A.
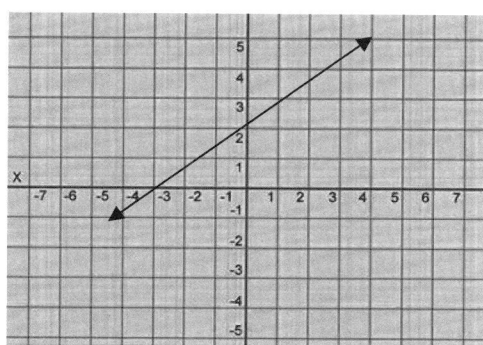

B.
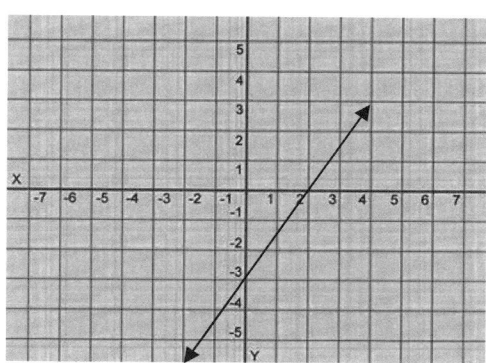

C.
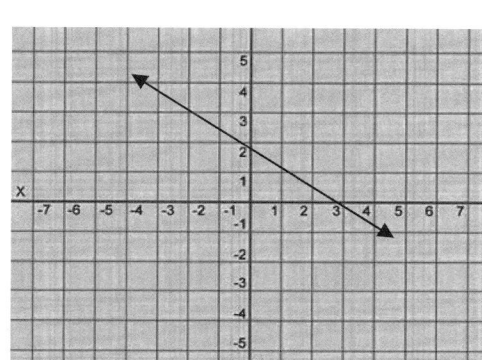

D.
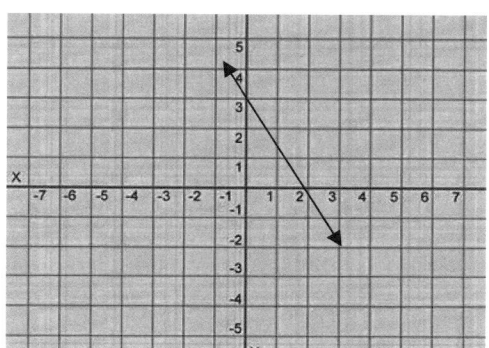

E.
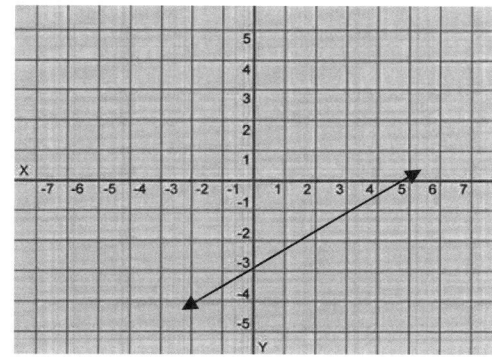

For $\sqrt{(3)(7)} \cdot \sqrt{(m)(n)} \cdot \sqrt{(7)(5)}$ to be an integer, with m and n representing positive prime numbers, the sum of $m + n$ must equal which of the following?

F. 8
G. 10
H. 12
J. 15
K. 21

449

GO ON TO THE NEXT PAGE.

55. Cam is going into business selling umbrellas. He pays $25,000 for a building and machinery, and each umbrella costs $4.00 to manufacture. If Cam sells x umbrellas for $6.50 each, which of the following equations best represents his net profit in dollars?

A. $10.50x - 25,000$
B. $6.50x - 25,000$
C. $4.00x + 25,000$
D. $4.00x - 25,000$
E. $2.50x - 25,000$

56. In the circle shown below, O lies on the center of the circle and on chords $\overline{LN}$ and $\overline{MP}$. The measure of $\overset{\frown}{PN} = 100°$. Which of the following statements is FALSE?

F. $m\angle PLN = 50°$
G. $m\angle POL = 80°$
H. $\angle PON \cong \angle NOM$
J. $\angle POL \cong \angle NOM$
K. $\overline{LP} \parallel \overline{MN}$

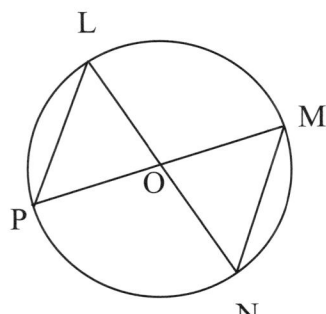

57. For all real numbers m and n, when is the equation $|m - n| = |m + n|$ true?

A. Never.
B. Always.
C. Only when $m = n$
D. Only when $m = 0$ and $n = 0$
E. Only when $m = 0$ or $n = 0$

58. What is the value of $\log_4 16$?

F. 2
G. 4
H. 12
J. 20
K. 64

Television screen sizes are measured on the diagonal. Joshua bought a new television with a 24-inch screen and gave his old 21-inch television to his younger brother. If Joshua is watching a soccer ball that appears to be 4 inches in diameter on his new screen, how long does the diameter of the same ball, to the nearest tenth of an inch, appear to his brother watching on the smaller screen?

A. 3
B. 3.5
C. 4.6
D. 3π
E. 3.5π

When $0° < x < 90°$, which of the following is NOT equal to $\tan x$?

F. $\dfrac{\sin x}{\cos x}$

G. $(\sin^2 x + \cos^2 x)(\tan x)$

H. $\dfrac{\sec x}{\csc x}$

J. $\dfrac{(\sin^2 x + \cos^2 x)}{\cot x}$

K. $\dfrac{\cos x}{\sin x}$

DO YOUR FIGURING HERE.

END OF TEST
STOP! DO NOT TURN THE PAGE UNTIL TOLD TO DO SO.
DO NOT RETURN TO THE PREVIOUS TEST.

3

READING TEST

35 Minutes – 40 Questions

DIRECTIONS: There are four passages in this test. Each passage is followed by several questions. After reading a passage, choose the best answer to each question and fill in the corresponding oval on your answer document. You may refer to the passages as often as necessary.

Passage I

PROSE FICTION: This passage is adapted from the short story "Interpreter of Maladies" by Jhumpa Lahiri. (© 2000). The story is set in India, where the Das family is visiting from America; Mr. Kapasi is their driver and tour guide.

He looked at Mrs. Das, in her red plaid skirt and strawberry t-shirt, a woman not yet thirty, who loved neither her husband nor her children, who had already fallen out of love with life. Her confession depressed
5 him, depressed him all the more when he thought of Mr. Das at the top of the path, their daughter Tina clinging to his shoulders, taking pictures of ancient ruins to show his students in America, unsuspecting and unaware that one of his sons was not his own. Mr. Kapasi felt insulted
10 that Mrs. Das should ask him to interpret her common, trivial little secret. She did not resemble the patients in the doctor's office, those who came glassy-eyed and desperate, unable to sleep or breathe or urinate with ease, unable, above all, to give words to their pains.
15 Still, Mr. Kapasi believed it was his duty to assist Mrs. Das. Perhaps he ought to tell her to confess the truth to Mr. Das. He would explain that honesty was the best policy. Honest, surely, would help her feel better. Perhaps he would offer to preside over the discussion, as
20 a mediator. He decided to begin with the most obvious question, to get to the heart of the matter, and so he asked, "Is it really pain you feel, Mrs. Das, or is it guilt?"

She turned to him and glared, mustard oil thick on
25 her frosty pink lips. She opened her mouth to say something, but as she glared at Mr. Kapasi some certain knowledge seemed to pass before her eyes, and she stopped. It crushed him; he knew at that moment that he was not even important enough to be properly insulted.
30 She opened the car door and began walking up the path, wobbling a little on her square wooden heels, reaching into her straw bag to eat handfuls of puffed rice. It fell through her fingers, leaving a zigzagging trail, causing monkeys to leap down from a tree and devour the little
35 white grains. In search of more, the monkeys began to follow Mrs. Das.

Mr. Kapasi stepped out of the car. He wanted holler, to alert her in some way, but he was worried
40 if she knew the monkeys were behind her, she w grow nervous. Perhaps she would lose her bala Perhaps they would pull at her bag or her hair. Das continued walking, oblivious, trailing grain puffed rice. Near the top of the incline, Mr. Das
45 kneeling on the ground, focusing the lens of his cam The children stood under the arcade, now hiding, emerging from view.

"Wait for me," Mrs. Das called out. "I'm coming.

Tina jumped up and down. "Here comes Mommy

"Great," Mr. Das said without looking up. "Ju
50 time. We'll get Mr. Kapasi to take a picture of the of us."

Mr. Kapasi quickened his pace, waving a branc that the monkeys scampered away, distracted another direction.

55 "Where's Bobby?" Mrs. Das asked when stopped. "Where is he?" She repeated sharply. "W wrong with all of you?"

When they found him, a little farther down the under a tree, he was surrounded by a group
60 monkeys, over a dozen of them, pulling at his T- with their long black fingers. The puffed rice Mrs. had spilled was scattered at his feet, raked over b monkeys' hands. The boy was silent, his body fro swift tears running down his startled face. His bare
65 were dusty and red with welts.

"Mr. Kapasi," Mrs. Das shrieked, noticing standing to one side. "Do something, for God's sak do something!"

Mr. Kapasi took his branch and shooed them away.
The animals retreated slowly, obedient but
unintimidated. Mr. Kapasi gathered Bobby in his arms
and brought him back to where his parents and siblings
were standing. As he carried him, he was tempted to
whisper a secret into the boy's ear. When Mr. Kapasi
delivered him to his parents, Mr. Das brushed some dirt
off the boy's t-shirt and put a visor on him right away.
"He's fine. Just a little scared, right, Bobby?" Mr. Das
said, patting the top of his head.

"God, let's get out of here," Mrs. Das said. She
folded her arms across the strawberry on her chest. "This
place gives me the creeps."

"Yeah. Back to the hotel, definitely," Mr. Das agreed.

"Poor Bobby," Mrs. Das said. "Come here a second.
Let Mommy fix your hair." When she whipped out the
hairbrush, the slip of paper with Mr. Kapasi's address
on it fluttered away in the wind. No one but Mr. Kapasi
noticed. He watched as it rose, carried higher and higher
by the breeze, into the trees where the monkeys now sat,
solemnly observing the scene below. Mr. Kapasi
observed it too, knowing that this was the picture of the
Das family he would preserve forever in his mind.

1. It can reasonably be inferred from the passage that Mr. Kapasi:
   A. was reluctant but felt an obligation to advise Mrs. Das.
   B. loathed having to spend time with the Das family.
   C. pitied the family for the physical and emotional pain they suffered on their daytrip.
   D. was envious of the family's material success and stability.

2. According to the passage, the "secret" (line 11) that Mrs. Das admits to Mr. Kapasi is:
   F. She despises the ancient ruins the family is visiting.
   G. The father of her son Bobby is not Mr. Das.
   H. She despises her children.
   J. She does not love her husband.

3. In the context of the first two paragraphs of the passage, the word "*interpret*" (line 10) most likely means?
   A. To translate.
   B. To repair.
   C. To assume.
   D. To read.

4. According to the passage, Mrs. Das does not respond to Mr. Kapasi's question of whether she feels pain or guilt because:
   F. She was in a hurry to catch up to her family.
   G. She hadn't asked him for his advice.
   H. She was speechless.
   J. She regarded him as inferior.

5. It can be reasonably inferred from the passage that Mr. Das:
   A. is equally unhappy with his marriage to Mrs. Das.
   B. is oblivious to his wife's unhappiness.
   C. is aware of his wife's secret.
   D. is remote and distant with his children.

6. Which of the following statements most accurately expresses Mr. Kapasi's feelings upon hearing Mrs. Das's confession?
   F. He is touched that she has chosen to share an intimate, private moment with him.
   G. He is hurt that she is using him to purge her guilt for past mistakes.
   H. He is concerned for Mr. Das and their children.
   J. He feels inspired and motivated to devise a solution to her problem.

7. The cause of the monkeys' aggressive behavior against Bobby is most likely the result of:
   A. Mr. Kapasi not warning Mrs. Das that the monkeys were following her.
   B. Mr. Das's photography, which incited their frenzy.
   C. Mrs. Das dropping food on the ground.
   D. Mr. Kapasi waving a stick at the monkeys.

8. The conclusion about Mrs. Das that Mr Kapasi will "preserve forever in his mind" (line 91) is most likely to be that she:
   F. is a careless, selfish woman.
   G. is trapped and needs to fully articulate her inner struggles.
   H. has undergone a transformation and will focus more attention on her family.
   J. favors her son Bobby at the expense of the rest of her family.

9. Which of the following is NOT an action Mr. Kapasi debates taking during the course of the passage?
   A. Whether to encourage Mrs. Das to be honest with her husband.
   B. Whether to reveal Mrs. Das's confession to Bobby.
   C. Whether to alert Mrs. Das that the monkeys were following her.
   D. Whether to talk to Mr. Das about his wife.

10. Which of the following statements most likely explains why the author chose to mention the monkeys "solemnly observing" (line 89) the Das family at the end of the passage?
    F. To indicate that the threat posed by the monkeys remains.
    G. To reveal Mr. Kapasi's disappointment that he will never see or communicate with Mrs. Das again.
    H. To convey Mr. Kapasi's own distance from the Das family and his new sense of clarity about who these people are.
    J. To foreshadow Mr. Kapasi's likely revelation to the Das family of Mrs. Das's behavior.

TEST 4

GO ON TO THE NEXT PAGE.

Copyright © 2009 Academic Educational Resources. All rights reserved.

NO TEST MATERIAL ON THIS PAGE.

GO ON TO THE NEXT PAGE.

Passage II

SOCIAL SCIENCE: This passage is adapted from *Sprawl: A Compact History* by Robert Bruegmann. (© 2005 by The University of Chicago).

Once an arcane term used primarily by city planners and academics, "sprawl" has recently emerged as a part of everyday speech. Most often described as unplanned, scattered, low-density, automobile-dependent development at the urban periphery, sprawl now shares space on the covers of national news magazines with perennial "big" issues like health care and race relations, and it has become a prominent issue on talk shows and campaign trails. From every direction, Americans are bombarded by the message of anti-sprawl reformers. They are told that sprawl threatens to destroy open space, consume agricultural land, drive up utility costs, undermine urban social life, heighten inequalities, deplete natural resources, and damage the environment. And, by the way, it is ugly.

Sprawl, according to these critics, represents an expensive and unsustainable pattern of development. The widely dispersed nature of this development makes everyone dependent on the automobile, which in turn, uses excessive amounts of energy, creates pollution, and contributes to global warming. Moreover, anti-sprawl activists claim, the sprawl being built today is responsible for the deterioration of many older communities that once flourished. According to its critics, sprawl hurts everyone and must be stopped. Instead of the unplanned, wasteful patterns visible at the edge of an urban area, they advocate new, carefully planned "smart growth," including denser urban infill and, where green-field construction is necessary, more compact sustainable communities, less dependent on automobiles, and more in tune with traditional urban patterns.

Most of what has been written about sprawl to date has been devoted to complaints. The usual questions asked are exactly how damaging sprawl is and what are the most appropriate ways to stop it. But sprawl should be looked at from a historic perspective, examining the way the concept of sprawl was invented and how it has been used over time. After all, sprawl, like "urban blight," the "slum," or many other terms connected with urban development, is not so much an objective reality as a cultural concept, a term born at a specific time and place and used over the years by a wide range of individuals and groups for specific purposes. In the process, it has accumulated around it an entire body of ideas and assumptions.

One of the most striking things revealed by even most cursory study of the way sprawl has been used the years is the difficulty of pinning down a com definition or linking it to realities on the ground. Is sp the area best described as "exurbia," the very low-de urban penumbra that lies beyond the regularly bui suburbs and their urban services? Or is it the n emerging suburban band of conventional subdivis golf courses, schools, and strip malls located clos toward the city? Certainly at one time even communities, even in the most densely packed neighborhoods, like Brooklyn or Manhattan in New City, were themselves relatively low in density suburban in character compared to what was then the of the city. Why wouldn't they be considered his sprawl?

In short, I believe that the individuals groups usin word "sprawl" have actually been describing se different landscapes.

Sprawl cannot be adequately explained as a si result of specific government policies, economic sys or technological advances. Notions that sprawl was ca by the widespread use of the automobile, or by anti-u attitudes, or racism are clearly inadequate. In fact, sp predates the automobile and has happened in a way t basically similar in cities with large minority popula and in cities with hardly any minority residents. It has been visible in affluent cities worldwide, even those policies very different from those in the United Stat is perhaps not inevitable, but it does seem to have be logical and perhaps even predictable result of incre wealth and the democratization of society. In this pro many more citizens have obtained the ability to exe the choices that once were the sole prerogative o wealthy and powerful.

11. This passage is best described as being:
   A. a criticism of the anti-sprawl movement and t misrepresentations of suburban communities.
   A. an argument intended to persuade suburban residents to move back into urban areas.
   C. an examination of how is a sprawl is a comple topic that resists simple definitions or opinio
   D. an analysis of the cause and effect relationshi between the automobile and sprawl.

12. All of the following are identified in the passage as common arguments critics offer against the spread of sprawl EXCEPT:
    F. increased pollution and reliance on fossil fuels.
    G. further decline and deterioration of older urban areas.
    H. greater affluence of suburban residents.
    J. poor usage and destruction of open space.

13. The main point of the third paragraph (lines 34-48) can best be summarized as:
    A. The current judgment on sprawl has been too harsh; there are many positive elements of suburban development that can and should be emphasized.
    B. Sprawl is an abstract concept that does not yet have a single shared definition; there are several conflicting interpretations of what it is.
    C. Most people interested in sprawl today are focused on how to mitigate its negative effects.
    D. Discussion on sprawl requires greater insight into the values and human relationships that have led to its development, rather than merely evaluating its strengths and weaknesses.

14. According to the passage, the preferred vision of anti-sprawl activists for the development of communities is best described as:
    F. urban, with greater reliance on mass transportation and more park space.
    G. suburban, with subdivisions and strip malls and greater emphasis on the automobile.
    H. rural, with large open spaces and a return to older communities.
    J. exurban, with great distance separating the community from a large urban area.

15. Which of the following article titles on sprawl would most likely examine sprawl as a "cultural concept?" (lines 43-44)
    A. "How Environmentalists Redefined 'Sprawl' and Changed Americans' Feelings about the Suburbs."
    B. "The Negative Impact of Sprawl on the Air Quality of Los Angeles County."
    C. "Is the Automobile to Blame for Sprawl?"
    D. "The Future of Sprawl: Projections of Growth in Suburban Chicago."

16. The author's purpose in comparing the word "sprawl" to "urban blight" and "slum" (line 41) is to:
    F. show how anti-sprawl activists use propaganda to influence public opinion.
    G. draw parallels between the decline of urban areas and the deterioration of suburbs due to mismanaged growth.
    H. explain how the meaning of and attitudes towards a concept are shaped by history and societal values.
    J. indicate the source of the word and how the term "sprawl" came to be invented.

17. It can be reasonably inferred that the author believes a major benefit of sprawl has been:
    A. the emerging band of golf courses in suburbs.
    B. its increasing importance as a prominent, national issue
    C. its relatively consistent pattern across history
    D. the greater mobility and choice it has offered to people.

18. The author refers to sprawl as *"not inevitable, but…a logical and predictable result"* (lines 76-77) because:
    F. sprawl is the natural outcome of the development and expansion of society, not the result of a single discrete cause.
    G. sprawl is a force beyond people's control and cannot be planned or accounted for.
    H. sprawl is what always happens when the wealthy flee cities and take up residence in the suburbs.
    J. sprawl is typically the result of racist attitudes or concerns.

19. The word *"inadequate"* used in line 71 most likely means:
    A. poor
    B. insufficient
    C. ridiculous
    D. simple

20. The author's tone can best be described as:
    F. sarcastic and mocking
    G. positive and idealistic
    H. angry and confused
    J. scholarly and analytical

Passage III

HUMANITIES: This passage is adapted from the article "Wild Things" by Naomi Wolf, which appeared in *The New York Times* (© New York Times 2006).

These books look cute. They come in matched paperback sets with catchy titles, and stay for weeks on the children's books best-seller list. They carry no rating or recommended age range on the cover, but their intended audience — teenage girls — can't be in doubt. They feature sleek, conventionally beautiful girls lounging, getting in or out of limos, laughing and striking poses. Any parent — including me — might put them in the Barnes & Noble basket without a second glance.

Yet if that parent opened one, he or she might be in for a surprise. *The Gossip Girl*, *A-List* and *Clique* series — the most successful in a crowded field of *Au Pairs*, *It Girls* and other copycat series — represent a new kind of young adult fiction, and feature a different kind of heroine. In these novels, which have dominated the field of popular girls' fiction in recent years, Carol Gilligan's question about whether girls can have "a different voice" has been answered — in a scary way.

In Lisi Harrison's *Clique* novels, set in suburban New York, the characters are 12 and 13 years old, but there are no girlish identity crises, no submissiveness to parents or anyone else. These girls are empowered. But they are empowered to hire party planners, humiliate other girls in their classes and draw up a petition calling for the cafeteria ladies serving their lunch to get manicures.

These novels are all about status. They promote a value system in which meanness rules, parents check out, conformity is everything and stressed-out adult values are presumed to be meaningful to teenagers. In these novels, the world of wealthy parents is characteristically seen as corrupt and opportunistic — but the kids have no problem with that.

The books have a kitsch quality — they package corruption with a cute overlay. In the world of the *A-List* or *Clique* girl, inverting Jane Austen (and Louise Alcott), the rich are right and good simply by virtue of their wealth. Seventh graders have expensive handbags and cellphones; their credit cards have no spending limits. Success and failure are entirely signaled by material possessions — specifically, by brands. You know the new girl in the *Clique* novel "Best Friends for Never" is living in social limbo when she shops at the mall, and her mother drives a dreaded sedan rather than a luxury vehicle.

In the classic tradition of young adult fiction, rich and popular girl would be the villain, and intelligent newcomer would be the heroine: she is one girl with spunk, curiosity and age-appropr[iate] preoccupations. Sara Crewe in Frances Hodg[son] Burnett's *Little Princess* loses her social standing an[d is] tormented by the school's alpha girls, but by the en[d of] the story we see them get what they deserve. In Lo[uisa] Alcott's *Little Women*, Jo March's criticism [of] "ladylike" social norms is challenged by an invita[tion] to a ball; while Meg, the eldest girl, is taken in by [the] wealthy daughters of the house and given a make[over] — which is meant to reveal not her victory a[nd] character but her weakness.

This tradition carried on powerfully through [the] 20th century. Even modern remakes, like the m[ovie] *Clueless*, show the popular, superficial girl underg[o] a humbling and an awakening as she begins to ques[tion] her allegiance to conformity and status.

In the *Clique* and *Gossip Girl* novels, meanw[hile,] every day is Freaky Friday. The girls try on a[dult] values and customs as though they were going to [wear] them forever. The narratives offer the perks of the a[dult] world not as escapist fantasy but in a cree[py,] photorealistic way, just as the book jackets show [the] girls polished to an unreal gloss. It's not surprising [that] Cecily von Ziegesar, author of the *Gossip Girl* no[vels,] matter-of-factly told an interviewer that she sees [her] books as "aspirational" (which she seemed to think [was] a good thing).

The great reads of adolescence have classi[cally] been critiques of the corrupt or banal adult world [and] should encourage our daughters to explore t[hose] themes, even if they call into question some of our [own] behaviors and values. It's sad if the point of readin[g for] many girls now is no longer to take the adult w[orld] apart but to squeeze into it all the more complia[ntly.] Sex and shopping take their places on a barren stag[e,] though, even for teenagers, these are the only dra[mas] left.

21. The main purpose of the opening paragraph is to:
    A. Describe how the books in question appear harmless and appeal to potential buyers.
    B. Persuade the reader not to purchase *Clique* or *A-List* books the next time he/she is at a bookstore.
    C. Explain how the book covers reveal the content of these novels.
    D. Draw a personal connection with other parents who purchased these or other similar titles.

22. In the context of line 23, the word *empowered* most nearly means:
    F. immature
    G. rich
    H. enabled
    J. strong

23. The author states that all of the following are true of novel series like *Gossip Girl* and *Clique* EXCEPT:
    A. The novels tell their readers that wealth defines the value of people.
    B. The teenage characters in these novels are admirable for how mature and adult-like they act.
    C. The novels encourage young girls not to defy the conventional adult world but to conform to it.
    D. The female characters in these novels are mean, superficial, and materialistic.

24. Based on information in the passage, the most likely determiner in these novels of a character's popularity is:
    F. the cost and status of the character's clothing.
    G. the maturity level of that character.
    H. the size of the character's house or the prestige of the community in which he/she lives.
    J. the intelligence of the character.

25. The author's tone in this passage can best be described as:
    A. sarcastic
    B. concerned
    C. angered
    D. bitter.

26. It can be reasonably inferred from the passage that the term "*aspirational*" (line 75) most likely reflects:
    F. an optimistic hope for the future.
    G. the desire of young readers for greater material or social success.
    H. the goal of the novels to inspire and improve future generations of women.
    J. the fantasies and escapist pleasures the novels offer.

27. The purpose of paragraph 6 (lines 47-60) is to:
    A. show how the ideas in women's literature of the 19th and 20th century are still prominent in contemporary novels aimed at adolescent girls.
    B. expose classical young adult literature for the same flaws as its contemporary brethren: appearing harmless, yet harboring dubious themes and messages.
    C. contrast the characterization and themes of many of the great works of literature by women and those of the new novels discussed in the article.
    D. relate how popular and timeless new young adult novels have become by comparing them to classic works of literature.

28. According to the passage, an important message of classic novels like *Little Women* with which the author approves is:
    F. that children need to be submissive to their parents.
    G. that young girls should learn adult behaviors and values at an early age
    H. that social standing is important determiner of a person's worth.
    J. that strong, intelligent young women should oppose the shallow or corrupting behaviors and values of the adult world.

29. With which of the following solutions would the author most likely support in combating the negative influence of novel series like *Gossip Girl*?
    A. Censor young-adult novels that promote shallow or sexist values.
    B. Encourage parents and book publishers to promote young adult fiction with female characters who defy—rather than conform to—social status and stereotypes.
    C. Promote adult novels to adolescent females since they're already being exposed to the corrupted values of the adult world.
    D. Teach these kinds of novels in schools to expose the values they portray and let adolescents debate the merits of the texts.

30. Who is the most likely audience of this passage?
    F. Parents of young adolescents who may not know what the books are really about.
    G. Fans of these or other novel series who want their lives to be like the characters in the books.
    H. The writers of these series who profit off their popularity.
    J. Younger readers who may soon be interested in these series.

Passage IV

NATURAL SCIENCE: This passage is adapted from "Lots of Animals Learn, but Smarter Isn't Always Better" by Carl Zimmer, which appeared in *The New York Times* (© 2008 New York Times).

"Why are humans so smart?" is a question that fascinates scientists. Tadeusz Kawecki, an evolutionary biologist at the University of Fribourg, likes to turn around the question: "If it's so great to be smart," Dr. Kawecki asks,
[5] "why have most animals remained dumb?" Dr. Kawecki and like-minded scientists are trying to figure out why animals learn and why some have evolved to be better at learning than others. One reason for the difference, their research finds, is that being smart can be bad for an
[10] animal's health.

Learning is remarkably widespread in the animal kingdom. Even the microscopic vinegar worm can learn, despite having just 302 neurons. It feeds on bacteria. But if it eats a disease-causing strain, it can become sick. The
[15] worms are not born with an innate aversion to the dangerous bacteria. They need time to learn to tell the difference and avoid becoming sick.

Many insects are also good at learning. "People thought insects were little robots doing everything by
[20] instinct," said Reuven Dukas, a biologist at McMaster University. Research by Dr. Dukas and others has shown that insects deserve more respect. Dr. Dukas has found that the larvae of one of the all-time favorite lab animals, the fruit fly, could learn to associate certain odors with
[25] food and other odors with predators. Dr. Dukas hypothesizes that any animal with a nervous system can learn.

But being smart does not ensure survival. The very act of learning takes a toll. The scientists trained some
[30] fast-learning flies to associate an odor with powerful vibrations. "These flies died about 20 percent faster than flies with the same genes, but which were not forced to learn," he said. Forming neuron connections may cause harmful side effects. It is also possible that genes that
[35] allow learning to develop faster and last longer may cause other changes.

"We use computers with memory that's almost free, but biological information is costly," Dr. Dukas said. He added that the costs Dr. Kawecki documented were not
[40] smart animals' only penalties. "It means you start out in life being inexperienced," Dr. Dukas said. When birds leave the nest, they need time to learn to find food and avoid predators. As a result, they are more likely to starve or be killed.

[45] Dr. Dukas argues that learning evolves to hig[h] levels only when it is a better way to respond to environment than relying on automatic responses. " good when you want to rely on information th[at is] unique to a time and place," Dr. Dukas said. Some
[50] species, for example, feed on a single flower spec[ies]. They can find plenty of nectar using automatic c[ues]. Other bees are adapted to many different flowers, e[ach] with a different shape and a different flowering ti[me]. Learning may be a better strategy in such cases.

[55] Dr. Kawecki suspects that each species evolves unt[il it] reaches an equilibrium between the costs and bene[fits] of learning. His experiments demonstrate that [flies] have the genetic potential to become significa[ntly] smarter in the wild. But only under his lab conditi[ons]
[60] does evolution actually move in that direction. [In] nature, any improvement in learning would cost [too] much.

Dr. Kawecki and Dr. Dukas agree that scientists [need] to pinpoint the tradeoffs, and they will have to ga[uge]
[65] the role of learning in the lives of many species. [As] their own knowledge increases, they will underst[and] more about humans' gift for learning.

"Humans have gone to the extreme," said Dr. Du[kas,] both in the ability of our species to learn and in [the]
[70] cost for that ability.

Humans' oversize brains require 20 percent of all [the] calories burned at rest. A newborn's brain is so big [that] it can create serious risks for mother and child at b[irth]. Yet newborns know so little that they are enti[rely]
[75] helpless. It takes many years for humans to l[earn] enough to live on their own.

Dr. Kawecki says it is worth investigating whe[ther] humans also pay hidden costs for extreme learn[ing]. "We could speculate that some diseases ar[e a]
[80] byproduct of intelligence," he said. The benefit[s of] learning must have been enormous for evolutio[n to] have overcome those costs, Dr. Kawecki argues. [For] many animals, learning mainly offers a benefi[t in] finding food or a mate.

31. The doctors quoted in this passage would most likely agree with which of the following statements?
    A. The benefits of learning are always so enormous that they outweigh the biological costs.
    B. Intelligent creatures are at greater risk for serious illness.
    C. Insects and other small animals deserve greater respect for their ability to learn and the improvements these species have made because of it.
    D. For certain species, it's often in their best interest to remain dumb.

32. What does the passage offer as evidence that insects are good learners?
    F. Some bees can pollinate many different flowers.
    G. Flies become significantly smarter in laboratory settings.
    H. Young birds are more likely to be killed or starve to death than older, more experienced birds.
    J. Fruit flies can distinguish between beneficial and harmful odors.

33. As it is used in line 15, the phrase "innate aversion" most likely means:
    A. An instinctive dislike
    B. A negative attitude
    C. A strong predilection
    D. A weakness

34. The passage suggests that the state of research on studying the learning habits of animals and insects can best be described as:
    F. Extensive, with considerable information available on many species.
    G. An ongoing debate that has fascinated and puzzled scientists for decades.
    H. Obscure, with very little interest from or relevance to the scientific community.
    J. A fairly new area that is just starting to develop hypotheses.

35. The passage mentions all of the following as potential negative consequences of increased learning EXCEPT?
    A. shorter lifespan
    B. inexperience
    C. poor health
    D. productivity

36. The statement that "[Humans] use computers with memory that's almost free, but biological information is costly" (lines 37-38) is included to make the point that:
    F. Research labs that study the learning of fruit flies and other insects are very expensive to maintain.
    G. The brains of animal and insect species are too complex to be compared to a computer chip.
    H. A species' process of acquiring new knowledge and skills is time-consuming and draining.
    J. Animals can learn and increase their intelligence, but doing so involves tradeoffs that may affect the species' ability to survive.

37. The main idea of the sixth paragraph is that:
    A. For many species, learning is most useful when it helps a life form adapt to a changing environment.
    B. Applying knowledge is more effective than relying on instinct.
    C. The ability of all bees, whether thinking or acting automatically, to find an abundance of nectar suggests learning may not have many tangible benefits for some species.
    D. Learning is only effective in certain situations.

38. According to the passage, one potential benefit of studying the role of learning in the lives of other species is that scientists can:
    F. Reduce the number of smart but helpless species killed by predators.
    G. Develop a greater understanding about humans' own gift for learning.
    H. Reach an equilibrium between the costs and benefits of learning.
    J. Help teach insects and animals better ways of adapting and responding to the environment.

39. The purpose of discussing humans' ability to learn in paragraphs 9-11 is most likely to:
    A. To explain how big newborns' brains are and how much they know from an early age.
    B. To compare the helplessness and weakness of newborn humans and animals.
    C. To show how evolutionary tradeoffs also apply to intelligent life forms.
    D. To argue that the costs of learning outweigh its benefits in society as well as nature.

40. Which of the following questions is NOT answered by the passage?
   F. How can intelligence lead to negative consequences?
   G. What are some surprising or unexpected ways in which tiny insects demonstrate an ability to learn?
   H. What tradeoffs of learning are shared by all species capable of learning?
   J. In what ways or situations does learning benefit animals and insects?

NO TEST MATERIAL ON THIS PAGE.

SCIENCE TEST
35 Minutes – 40 Questions

DIRECTIONS: There are seven passages in this test. Each passage is followed by several questions. After reading a passage, choose the best answer to each question and fill in the corresponding oval on your answer document. You may refer to the passages as often as necessary.

You are NOT permitted to use a calculator on this test.

Passage I

Friction is the force resisting the motion of two surfaces in contact or a surface in contact with a fluid. The *coefficient of friction* (COF) is a quantity symbolized by the Greek letter μ and is used to calculate the force of friction (static or kinetic.)

> The coefficient of fraction is defined as the ratio of the maximum static friction force (F) between the surfaces in contact to the normal force (N).
> $$\mu = F / N$$

Figure 1 is a diagram of a block resting on a rough inclined plane, with its weight (W), normal force (N) and friction (F) shown.

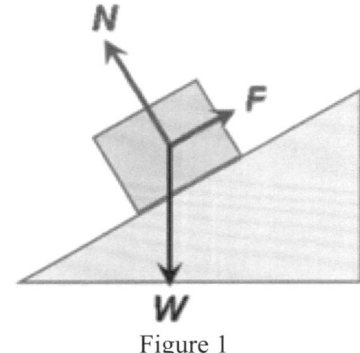

Figure 1

Scientists performed an experiment using several different materials to determine their coefficients of both static and kinetic friction. Figures 2 and 3 display the results.

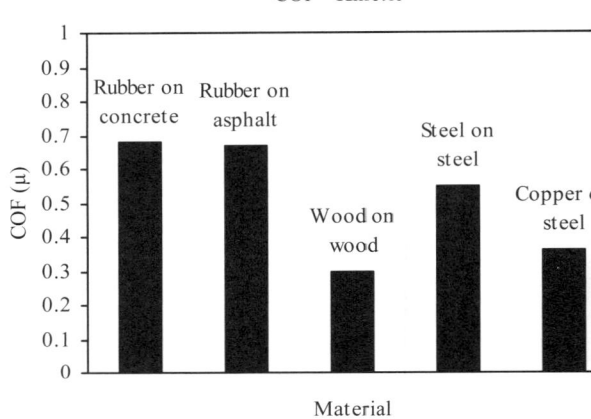

Figure 2

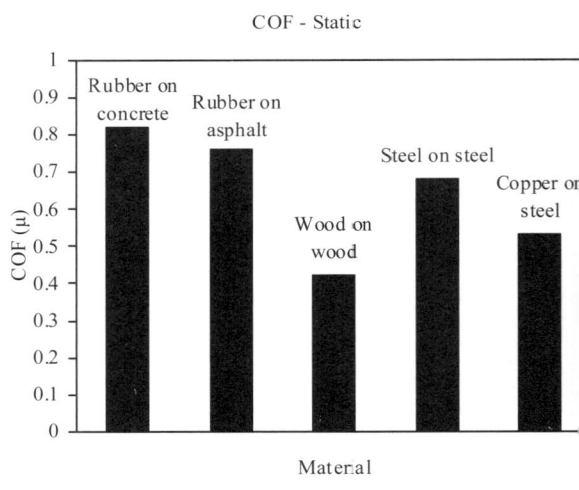

Figure 3

1. Based on the results of the experiment, which combination of materials has the largest static COF?
   A. Wood on wood
   B. Copper on steel
   C. Rubber on concrete
   D. Rubber on asphalt

2. A comparison of the COFs given in Figure 2 shows that, relative to the COF for rubber on concrete, the COF for wood on wood is approximately:
   F. 1/100 as high.
   G. 1/2 as high.
   H. 2 times as high.
   J. 10 times as high.

3. Which of the following ranks the materials used in the experiment from lowest static COF to highest static COF?
   A. Wood on wood, steel on steel, copper on steel, rubber on asphalt, rubber on concrete.
   B. Rubber on concrete, rubber on asphalt, steel on steel, copper on steel, wood on wood.
   C. Copper on steel, wood on wood, rubber on asphalt, rubber on concrete, steel on steel.
   D. Wood on wood, copper on steel, steel on steel, rubber on asphalt, rubber on concrete.

4. A student theorized that the higher the static COF for a material, the higher the kinetic COF would be. Do the results of the experiment support this theory?
   F. Yes, the materials with the highest static COF also had the highest kinetic COF.
   G. Yes, copper on steel had both the highest static COF and the highest kinetic COF.
   H. No, wood on wood had both the lowest static COF and the lowest kinetic COF.
   J. No, there is no relationship between static COF and kinetic COF for any of the materials.

5. According to Figures 1 and 2, which block would most likely slide down the incline the fastest?
   A. A steel block on a steel incline.
   B. A wood block on a wood incline.
   C. A rubber block on a concrete incline.
   D. A copper block on a steel incline.

Passage II

The main source of the world's energy for the last century has been fossil fuels. To use fossil fuels, we must be able to locate and recover them at affordable costs, convert them to usable forms, and use them without wasting them or harming the environment.

Experiment 1

Scientists set out to determine the energy potential of various fossil fuels. They burned 1 ton of each of 5 different fuel varieties, and measured the energy produced. Table 1 shows the energy content of various fossil fuels.

Table 1	
FUEL	ENERGY CONTENT (Btu/Ton)
Coal	25,000,000
Crude Oil	37,000,000
Gasoline	38,000,000
Natural Gas	47,000,000
Peat	3,500,000

Experiment 2

Students completed an experiment to measure the heat energy obtained from natural gas, using water, a Fahrenheit thermometer, and a Bunsen burner. (See Figure 1) They filled a beaker with enough water to weigh one pound (approximately 450mL). They recorded the temperature of the water, then lit the Bunsen burner and stirred the water continuously. They took several measurements of the water's temperature, at 5-minute intervals. The results of the experiment are displayed in Table 2.

Table 2	
Time (m)	Water Temperature (°F)
0	67°
5	92°
10	117°
15	142°

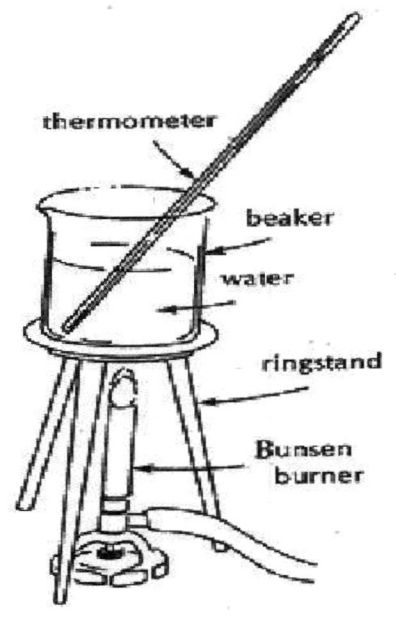

Figure 1

Each type of fossil fuel releases a different amount of energy. This energy is measured in a variety of units. Table 3 provides a conversion chart for energy units.

Table 3	
1 Btu =	.252 kilocalorie
	.000293 kilowatt-hour
1 kilocalorie =	3.97 Btu
	.0012 kilowatt-hour
1 kilowatt-hour =	3,413 Btu
	860 kilocalories
1 barrel of oil =	5,600,000 Btu
	1,410,579 kilocalories
	1,640.8 kilowatt-hours

6. According to the results of Experiment 1, which of the following ranks the different types of fossil fuels in order of energy potential, from the most Btus/Ton to the least?
   F. Peat, coal, crude oil, gasoline, natural gas.
   G. Natural gas, gasoline, crude oil, coal, peat.
   H. Gasoline, crude oil, peat, coal, natural gas.
   J. Natural gas, crude oil, peat, gasoline, coal.

7. If one Btu is the amount of heat needed to raise the temperature of one pound of water one degree Fahrenheit, then how many Btus of natural gas were used during the first 5 minutes of Experiment 2?
   A. 92
   B. 67
   C. 50
   D. 25

8. The main purpose of Experiment 2 was to:
   F. Determine the amount of energy natural gas creates.
   G. Compare various fossil fuels to see which one produces the most energy.
   H. See how long it would take to heat water to 100° F.
   J. Calculate how much water is necessary to burn 25 Btus of natural gas.

9. If Experiment 2 had been repeated using gasoline to heat the water instead of natural gas, the temperature of the water after 10 minutes would most likely have been closest to which of the following?
   A. 40° F
   B. 99° F
   C. 117° F
   D. 180° F

10. According to the data in Table 3, which unit of energy is equivalent to the most Btus?
    F. 1 kilowatt-hour
    G. 1 kilocalorie
    H. 1 barrel of oil
    J. 10,000 Btus

11. Based on the results of Experiment 2, if temperature had continued to be measured for 5 more minutes, what would the temperature of the water have most likely been at the next measurement?
    A. 85° F
    B. 142° F
    C. 167° F
    D. 200° F

Passage III

Animal waste in the form of raw manure or composted manure is routinely applied to the land as a crop fertilizer and/or soil amendment. Compost is also used as a growth medium in home gardening, ornamental nurseries, and greenhouses. A potential risk arising from the disposal of animal waste of fecal origin is the spread of pathogens, including *Escherichia coli* (*E. coli*). Scientists conducted a study to determine the fate of *E. coli* cells in cow manure applied to soil at different manure application rates and held at different temperatures.

Manure inoculated with *E. coli* was mixed with soil at a ratio of 1 part manure to 10, 25, 50, or 100 parts soil. The manure-amended soil was then held inside a polyethylene plastic box with lid at 21°, 15°, and 5° C. Soil samples were taken daily to track the survival of *E. coli* in each situation (See Figures 1-3). Table 1 shows the number of days that the pathogen survived at each application rate and at each storage temperature.

Table 1			
Ratio of Sample	5° C	15° C	21° C
1:10	42	54	103
1:25	42	152	193
1:50	56	109	174
1:100	49	109	131

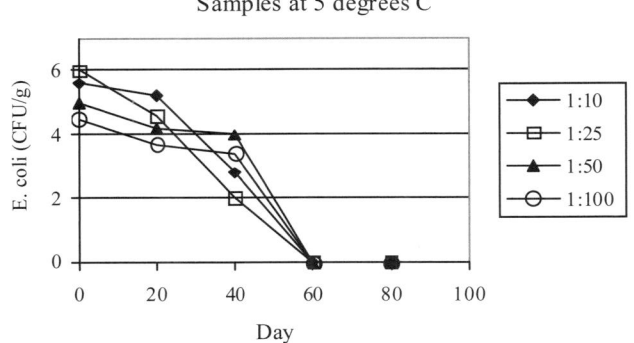

Figure 1

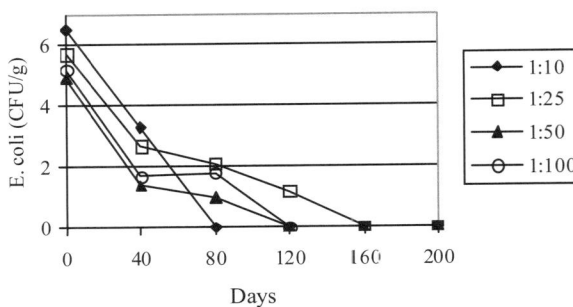

Figure 2

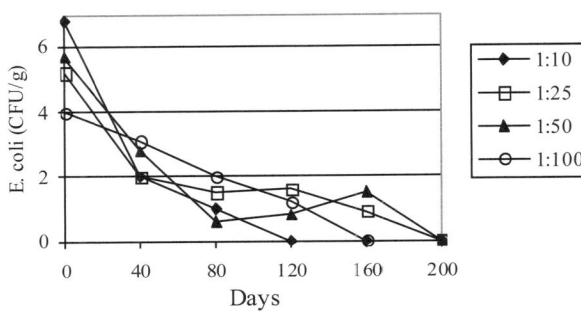

Figure 3

12. According to Table 1, the data supports which of following conclusions about the effect of tempera on survival rates of *E. coli*?
    F. The cooler the temperature, the longer the *E. coli* will survive.
    G. The hotter the temperature, the longer the *E. coli* will survive.
    H. *E. coli* will survive the longest at a temperature of 15° C.
    J. There is no correlation between temperature and survival rates of *E. coli*.

13. Based on Figure 1, after 30 days the amount of *E.* in the soil mixed at a ratio of 1:25 was at approxima which of the following levels?
    A. 1.7 CFU/g
    B. 3.1 CFU/g
    C. 4.0 CFU/g
    D. 6.2 CFU/g

14. A scientist claimed that the more soil present per part manure inoculated with *E. coli*, the shorter the *E. coli* would survive. Do the results of the study support this claim?
   F. Yes; for all ratios of soil mixture, the hotter the temperature, the longer the *E. coli* survived.
   G. Yes; at all temperatures the *E. coli* in the soil mixed at a rate of 1:25 survived longer than the *E. coli* in the soil mixed at a rate of 1:50.
   H. No; the hotter the temperature, the longer the *E. coli* survived for all ratios of soil mixture.
   J. No, at all temperatures the *E. coli* in the soil mixed at a rate of 1:100 survived longer than the *E. coli* in the soil mixed at a rate of 1:10.

15. Figure 3 indicates that, compared with the soil samples taken after 80 days, the samples collected after 160 days had higher levels of *E. coli* present in soil mixed at which of the following ratios?
   A. 1:10 only.
   B. 1:50 only.
   C. 1:50 and 1:100 only.
   D. None, *E. coli* decreased in every soil mixture.

16. Suppose a sample mixed at the ratio of 1:25 was stored at a temperature of 10° C. Based on the data in Table 1, for how many days would the *E. coli* most likely survive?
   F. 33 days.
   G. 97 days.
   H. 164 days.
   J. 210 days.

Passage IV

A science class studied the pH strength of acids and bases. The terms *strong* and *weak* indicate the ability of acid and base solutions to conduct electricity. Figure 1 displays the pH scale used to rank solutions as acidic or basic, and Table 1 provides an overview of what pH levels are considered *strong* and *weak* solutions.

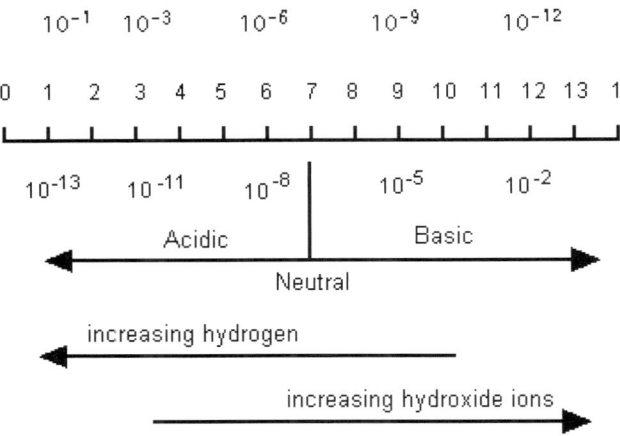

Figure 1

Table 1	
Solution	pH
Strong Acid	0 – 3
Weak Acid	4 – 6
Neutral	7
Weak Base	8 – 10
Strong Base	11 - 14

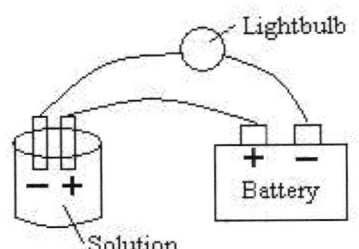

Figure 2

Table 2		
Solution	Acid or Base	Light Bulb
H_2O	Neutral	No light
HCl	Acid	Bright
$HC_2H_3O_2$	Acid	Dim
H_2SO_4	Acid	Bright
H_2CO_3	Acid	Dim
NaOH	Base	Bright
KOH	Base	Bright
NH_4OH	Base	Dim

Experiment 1

Students conducted an experiment to determine the conductivity of acid and base solutions, using a light bulb apparatus (see Figure 2). The light bulb circuit was incomplete. If the circuit is completed by a solution containing a large number of ions, the light bulb will glow brightly indicating a strong ability to conduct electricity. If the circuit is completed by a solution containing a large number of molecules and either no ions or few ions, the solution does not conduct electricity or conducts it very weakly. Students tested the conductivity of several solutions; the results are reported in Table 2.

Experiment 2

Students mixed 50 mL of each chemical wi[th] liter of water and then tested the pH of the solution. T[able] 3 displays the pH found for each chemical.

Table 3	
Chemical	pH
HCL	0.86
$HC_2H_3O_2$	2.92
H_2SO_4	1.29
H_2CO_3	3.73
NaOH	13.1
KOH	11.2
NH_4OH	9.2

17. Based on the information presented in Figure 1 and Table 1, a solution with which pH would be the strongest base?
    A. 12.5
    B. 9.7
    C. 7
    D. 0.2

18. According to the results of Experiments 1 and 2, which of the following is true?
    F. The weaker the acid or base, the brighter the light bulb glowed.
    G. The lower the pH of the solution, the brighter the light bulb glowed.
    H. The stronger the acid or base, the brighter the light bulb glowed.
    J. The higher the pH of the solution, the brighter the light bulb glowed.

19. Based on the results of Experiment 2, KOH would be classified as a:
    A. Strong acid.
    B. Neutral.
    C. Strong base.
    D. Weak base.

20. According to the information presented in Figure 1 and Table 3, it can be concluded that which of the following acids contains the most hydrogen?
    F. H_2CO_3
    G. H_2SO_4
    H. HC_2H3O_2
    J. HCL

21. Suppose the students decided to test the conductivity of an additional solution according to the procedures outlined in Experiment 1. They tested a solution of NaOCl, and they found that the solution caused the lightbulb to glow brightly. The students would be correct in classifying the NaOCl solution as which of the following?
    A. A strong base.
    B. A weak base.
    C. A weak acid.
    D. Cannot be determined from the given information.

22. Based on Table 3, which of the following figures best represents the pH values for the 3 bases tested?

F.
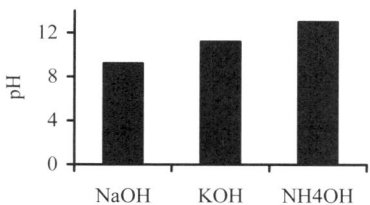

G.
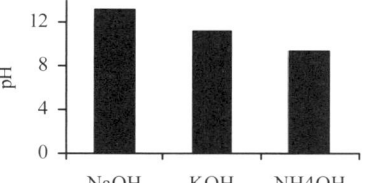

H.
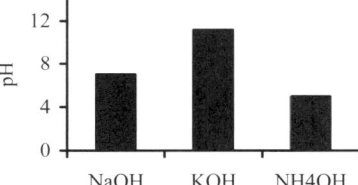

J.
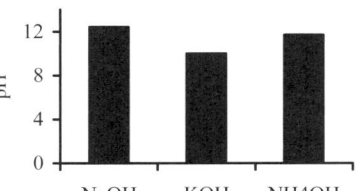

Passage V

Ethanol (ethyl alcohol, grain alcohol) is a very high-octane fuel, replacing lead as an octane enhancer in gasoline. It is a clear, colorless liquid with a characteristic, pleasant odor. Ethanol and ETBE oxygenator, made from ethanol, are much safer than the toxic and polluting MTBE fossil-fuel-derived oxygenator used by oil companies.

Ethanol production has shown to be very energy efficient, with a positive energy balance of 125%, compared to 85% for gasoline. This makes ethanol production one of the most efficient methods of producing liquid transportation fuels. Scientists have found ways to produce ethanol using the fermentation process from three basic types of raw materials, called feedstock. Figure 1 shows the fuel yields for various ethanol feedstocks, and Figure 2 compares the production costs of the various feedstock types.

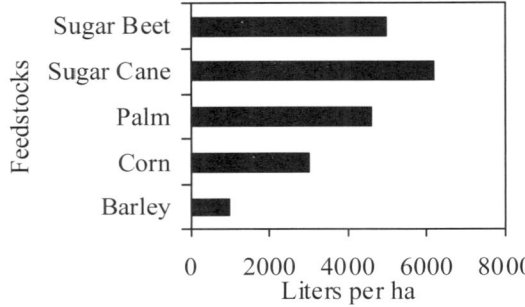

Figure 1

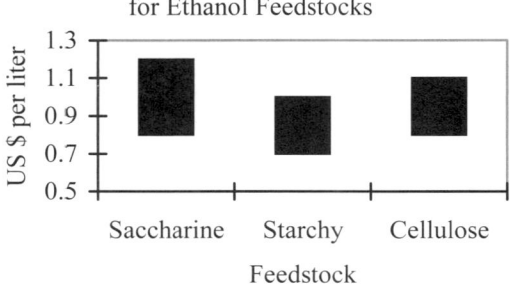

Figure 2

Scientist 1

Ethanol can be produced from *saccharine* (su containing) materials including sugar cane, sugar beets, fr whey and skim milk. Saccharine materials are preferable all others on account of their tremendous fuel yi Manufacturing ethanol from saccharine feedstocks gener requires: (1) extraction or crushing to make the sug available to the yeast enzymes during fermentation; dilution, which is only required with certain materials; fermentation; and (4) distillation.

Scientist 2

Production of ethanol is possible using *star* materials such as corn, barley, wheat, potatoes arrowroot. Though starchy materials do not yield as m ethanol per hectare as other feedstocks do, their production costs nonetheless make starchy raw materials ideal feedstocks. Converting starchy materials to eth: requires the steps of: (1) milling to free the starchy mate (2) dilution; (3) cooking to dissolve and "gelatinize" starch; (4) conversion of the starch to fermentable sugar: malting, enzymes, or acid hydrolysis; (5) fermentation; (6) distillation.

Scientist 3

Ethanol can also be produced from *cellu* materials including wood, palm, straw, corn stalks, cotton. Cellulose materials are the optimal feedstock opt as they offer a lower production cost than saccha materials and a higher fuel yield than starchy mater Manufacturing ethanol from cellulose materials requires using enzymes or acid hydrolysis to dissolve the lignin substance that gives wood strength) and expose the cellul (2) dilution; (3) fermentation; and (4) distillation.

23. According to all three scientists, what is the secon last step in the process of manufacturing ethanol?
    A. Extraction
    B. Dilution
    C. Fermentation
    D. Distillation

24. If Scientist 3 were given cellulose that had already separated from the lignin, which step could be skippe the process of creating ethanol?
    F. Step 1
    G. Step 2
    H. Step 3
    J. Step 4

25. Based on the information provided, which of the following is true about the production of ethanol?
   A. Ethanol produced from *saccharine* materials requires the least amount of time.
   B. Manufacturing ethanol from *starchy* materials contains the most processing steps.
   C. It is most cost effective to produce ethanol from *saccharine* materials.
   D. Producing ethanol from *cellulose* materials requires the most processing steps.

26. Scientist 1 would probably agree with which of the following statements?
   F. Producing ethanol from saccharine materials is most beneficial because of the ease of manufacture and the high fuel yields of the feedstocks.
   G. Producing ethanol from saccharine materials is not feasible at this point because of the high production costs and unreasonable number of steps involved in manufacturing.
   H. Saccharine materials are the most cost efficient of all ethanol feedstocks available.
   J. Saccharine materials require less processing steps than any other feedstock, and therefore are the easiest to convert into ethanol.

27. Besides the feedstock used, the three scientists' methods for manufacturing ethanol differ in which way?
   A. They do not all require a fermentation step.
   B. They do not all require a cooking step.
   C. They do not all require a dilution step.
   D. They do not all require a step to free the raw material in the feedstock (sugar, starch or cellulose).

28. This figure is a plausible representation of the process for manufacturing ethanol according to which scientist?

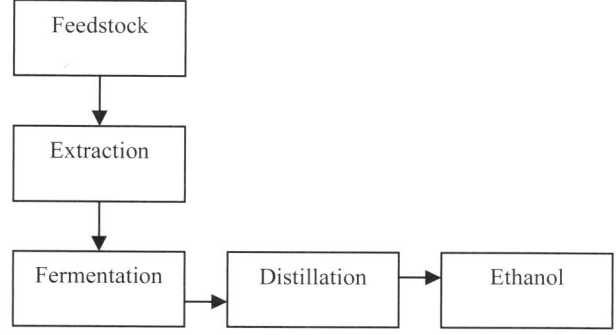

   F. Scientist 1.
   G. Scientist 2.
   H. Scientist 3.
   J. None of the scientists.

29. Ethanol produced from which of the following feedstocks would offer the best compromise between high fuel yield and low production cost?
   A. Sugar cane
   B. Barley
   C. Saccharine
   D. Palm

Passage VI

The melting point of a solid is the temperature range at which it changes from solid to liquid. When a substance melts, some of the attractive forces holding the particles together are broken or loosened so that the particles can move freely around each other but are still close together. The stronger these forces are, the more energy is required to overcome them and the higher the melting temperature.

The boiling point of a liquid is the temperature at which the vapor pressure of the liquid equals the environmental pressure surrounding the liquid. When a substance boils, most of the remaining attractive forces are broken so the particles can move freely and far apart. The stronger the attractive forces are, the more energy is needed to overcome them and the higher the boiling temperature.

The melting and boiling points of various elements, as well as background information on these elements, are given in Table 1 and Figure 1 below.

Table 1

	Element	Proton Number	Symbol
Metals	sodium	11	Na
	magnesium	12	Mg
	aluminum	13	Al
Metalloid	silicon	14	Si
Non-Metals	phosphorus	15	P
	sulphur	16	S
	chlorine	17	Cl

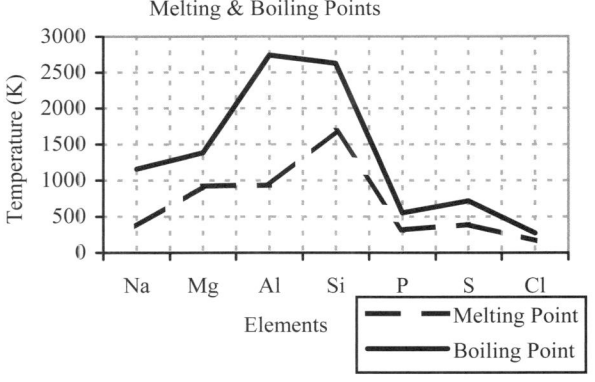

Figure 1

30. The melting point of magnesium is closest to which the following?
    F. 500 K
    G. 980 K
    H. 1,400 K
    J. 2,000 K

31. Based on the information presented in Table 1 Figure 1, it can be assumed that:
    A. As the number of protons in an element incre both the melting point and boiling point increa well.
    B. As the number of protons in an element incre the melting point decreases.
    C. As the number of protons in an element incre the melting point increases while the boiling decreases.
    D. There is no relationship between the numb protons in an element and its melting and bo points.

32. Based on Figure 1, as the melting point of an ele increases, the boiling point of the element will:
    F. decrease linearly.
    G. decrease, but not linearly.
    H. increase linearly.
    J. increase, but not linearly.

33. Which element changes from a solid to a liquid state at 1700 K?
    A. Aluminum
    B. Silicon
    C. Sulphur
    D. Chlorine

34. A student claimed that non-metals would have melting and boiling points that were closer in temperature than other elements. Does the data in Table 1 and Figure 1 support this claim?
    F. No; Aluminum is the element with the greatest difference between melting and boiling points.
    G. No; the boiling and melting points are closer in temperature for the metals than for the non-metals.
    H. Yes; Chlorine is the element with the greatest difference between melting and boiling points.
    J. Yes; the boiling and melting points are closer in temperature for the non-metals than for the metals.

Passage VII

From 1971 to 2006, there was a dramatic reduction in the number of feral honeybees in the US, and a significant, though somewhat gradual, decline in the number of colonies maintained by beekeepers. In early 2007 the rate of attrition reached new proportions, and the term *Colony Collapse Disorder (CCD)* was coined to describe this sudden decline. CCD is said to have occurred when a bee colony abruptly disappears, with little or no build-up of dead bees in or around the colonies. The cause or causes of the syndrome are not yet well understood. Proposed causes include environmental change related stress, malnutrition, disease, and pests.

Study 1

In an attempt to quantify the degree and extent of losses experienced in the US, scientists tracked beekeeping operations with various numbers of colonies between September 2006 and March 2007. For the sake of this study, a colony has encountered CCD when it loses at least 90% of its population in a period of 30 days. This loss must be accompanied by little or no trace of dead bees in or around the hive. Figure 1 displays the total losses experienced by all beekeeping operations.

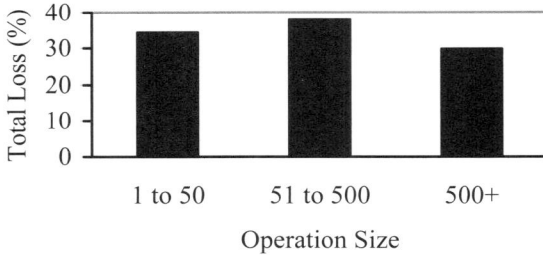

Figure 1

Table 1			
		Size:	
Cause:	1 to 50	51 to 500	500+
Starvation	40%	35%	7%
Weak in Fall	16%	30%	0%
Weather	6%	15%	7%
Pests	8%	10%	43%
Queen Death	12%	15%	7%

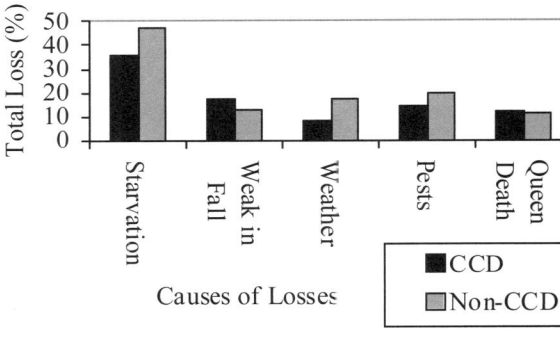

Figure 2

Study 2

Scientists studying CCD surveyed beekeepers whose hives have been affected by the disorder. The beekeepers were asked what they believe caused the CCD in their colonies. Table 1 displays the five most commonly suspected causes of CCD losses and the average percentage of loss experienced by operations of varying sizes due to each suspected cause. The scientists then surveyed beekeepers whose hives had collapsed for reasons unrelated to CCD, asking them the same question. Figure 2 compares the results from the scientists' two surveys, displaying the total loss experienced due to suspected causes of CCD and non-CCD losses, averaged for operations of all sizes.

35. Beekeepers from operations of which size experienced the lowest total losses by percentage?
 A. 1 to 50
 B. 51 to 500
 C. 500+
 D. It cannot be determined from the data provided.

36. Based on the data in Figure 2, it can be determined the least common suspected cause of CCD losses was
 F. Starvation.
 G. Weak in Fall.
 H. Weather.
 J. Queen Death.

37. According to Study 2, for operations with between 1 to 50 colonies, what was the most common suspected cause of CCD losses?
    A. Starvation
    B. Weak in Fall
    C. Weather
    D. Queen Death

38. Prior to conducting the research, 4 scientists each proposed 1 of the following hypotheses. Which hypothesis is best supported by the results?
    F. Environmental changes, including shifts in weather patterns, are the predominant causes of CCD related loss.
    G. An increase in pesticide-resistant pests is the main contributing factor to CCD loss at small beekeeping operations.
    H. The larger a beekeeping operation is, the higher the overall CCD loss will be.
    J. A shortage of food sources, especially at smaller beekeeping operations, is leading to an increase in CCD loss.

39. Figure 2 indicates that, compared with the total loss for non-CCD, the total loss for CCD was higher for which of the following causes?
    A. Starvation, Weather, and Pests.
    B. Weak in Fall and Queen Death.
    C. Weak in Fall and Weather.
    D. Starvation and Pests.

40. A scientist theorized that the number of CCD losses would be higher than non-CCD losses for beekeeping operations of all sizes. Does the data support this theory?
    F. Yes; for all causes the total loss was higher for CCD than for non-CCD losses.
    G. Yes; starvation was the most common cause of loss regardless of operation size.
    H. No; for many of the causes there were more non-CCD losses than CCD losses.
    J. No; operations with 51 to 500 colonies experienced the greatest total loss.

END OF TEST

STOP! DO NOT RETURN TO ANY OTHER TEST.

ACT SUCCESS

WRITING TEST 4 – Prompt

DIRECTIONS:

This is a test of your writing skills. You will have thirty (30) minutes to write an essay in English. Before you begin planning and writing your essay, read the writing prompt below carefully to understand exactly what you are being asked to do. Your essay will be evaluated on the evidence it provides of your ability to express judgments by taking a position on the issue in the writing prompt; to main a focus on the topic throughout the essay; to develop a position by using logical reasoning and by supporting your ideas; to organize ideas in a logical way; and to use language clearly and effectively according to the conventions of standard written English.

Many schools have instituted a policy requiring high school students to take at least one fine arts class (music, theatre, dance, visual arts, etc.) in order to graduate. Some people think that this is a good rule because high school students would benefit from exposure to the fine arts. Other people think such a policy would not be appropriate because graduation requirements should only reflect core academic subjects, and this policy would punish students who are interested in subjects other than the fine arts. In your opinion, should high schools require that students take at least one fine arts class in order to graduate?

In your essay, take a position on this question. You may write about either one of the two points of view given, or you may present a different point of view on this question. Use specific reasons and examples to support your position.

Use this page to *plan* your essay.

Begin WRITING TEST 4 here.

WRITING TEST 4

WRITING TEST 4

WRITING TEST 4

STOP here with the Writing Test.

Scale Scores for Practice Test 4

* These scores are based on student trials rather than national norms.

English   _____
Math   _____
Reading   _____
Science   _____

=Total   _____

Composite = Total divided by 4 (round up at .5) _____

ACT Score*	Number Right				ACT Score*
	English	Math	Reading	Science	
36	75	60	40	40	36
35	73-74	59	39	--	35
34	72	58	38	39	34
33	71	57	37	--	33
32	70	56	36	38	32
31	69	54-55	34-35	--	31
30	68	53	33	37	30
29	67	51-52	32	36	29
28	65-66	49-50	30-31	34-35	28
27	64	46-48	29	33	27
26	62-63	44-45	28	31-32	26
25	60-61	41-43	27	30	25
24	58-59	39-40	26	28-29	24
23	55-57	37-38	24-25	27	23
22	53-54	35-36	23	25-26	22
21	50-52	33-34	22	23-24	21
20	47-49	31-32	21	21-22	20
19	44-46	28-30	19-20	19-20	19
18	42-43	25-27	18	17-18	18
17	40-41	22-24	17	15-16	17
16	37-39	19-21	16	13-14	16
15	34-36	15-17	15	12	15
14	31-33	11-14	13-14	11	14
13	29-30	09-10	12	10	13
12	27-28	07-08	10-11	09	12
11	25-26	06	08-09	08	11
10	23-24	05	07	07	10
9	21-22	04	06	06	9
8	18-20	03	05	05	8
7	15-17	--	--	04	7
6	12-14	02	04	03	6
5	09-11	--	03	02	5
4	07-08	01	02	--	4
3	05-06	--	--	01	3
2	03-04	--	01	--	2
1	00-02	00	00	00	1

Copyright © 2009 Academic Educational Resources. All rights reserved.

Practice Test #5

ENGLISH TEST

45 Minutes – 75 Questions

DIRECTIONS: In the five passages that follow, certain words and phrases are underlined and numbered. In the right-hand column, you will find alternatives for each underlined part. In most cases, you are to choose the one that best expresses the idea, makes the statement appropriate for standard written English, or is worded most consistently with the style and tone of the passage as a whole. If you think the original version is best, choose "NO CHANGE." In some cases, you will find in the right-hand column a question about the underlined part. You are to choose the best answer to the question.

You will also find questions about a section of the pass or about the passage as a whole. These questions do refer to an underlined portion of the passage, but rather identified by a number or numbers in a box.

For each question, choose the alternative you consider and fill in the corresponding oval on your ans document. Read each passage through once before begin to answer the questions that accompany it. For m of the questions, you must read several sentences bey the question to determine the answer. Be sure that you h read far enough ahead each time you choose an alternati

Passage I

A Never-Ending Battle

Not many people know it, but the character was originally a villain. Intending it as an allegory for the growing Nazi menace in Europe, in 1933 two teenage, Jewish-American science-fiction fans—Jerry Siegel and Joe Shuster—concocted a story for a pulp magazine about an evil figure with strange mind-control powers bent on world domination. No-one took much notice.

As the political situation in Europe and the Great Depression in America both worsened, and after Siegel's father died during a robbery of his New York City clothing store; the two boys became disenchanted with writing about a villain. They decided that what the world needed were uplifting stories about a hero who used his abilities to protect societies' downtrodden and defenseless, rather than

1. A. NO CHANGE
   B. two, teenage Jewish-American, science-fiction
   C. two teenage, Jewish-American, science-fiction,
   D. two teenage Jewish-American science-fiction

2. F. NO CHANGE
   G. powers being bent
   H. powers, which bent
   J. powers were bent

3. A. NO CHANGE
   B. store, the
   C. store. The
   D. store, therefore the

4. F. NO CHANGE
   G. societys
   H. society's
   J. societies

by exploiting them.
　　　　　5

Over the next few years they revamped their creation along
　　　　　　　　　　　　　　　6
these lines altering his appearance and attributes but retaining
　　　　　　　　6
the original name: Superman.

　　　An instant success from his first appearance in 1938, when Superman gave rise to the concept of the super-hero,
　　　　　　　　7
which quickly became the dominant genre of the comic-book medium. Today, everyone knows that a super-hero is someone with special powers and a flashy costume involving shorts over tights, a cape and a logo, on the chest. But few
　　　　　　　　　　　　8
stop to consider the complex and moving psychological underpinnings of this cultural phenomenon. [9]

Although he became a powerful symbol of "the American way," Superman is, like Siegel and Shuster's parents, an immigrant: the last survivor of his doomed home
　　　　　　　　　　　　　　10
planet of Krypton. In addition to his refugee status, some of Superman's other distinguishing characteristics also reflect his creators heritage. His Kryptonian name, Kal-El, is similar
　　11
to the Hebrew for "voice of God," and there has even been speculation that the famous "S" insignia on Superman's chest is a subtle portrayal by the yellow badges that Jews were
　　　　　　12
forced to wear in Nazi Germany.

5. A. NO CHANGE
　　B. from exploiting
　　C. was exploiting
　　D. to exploit

6. F. NO CHANGE
　　G. Over the next few years, they revamped their creation along these lines, altering his appearance
　　H. Over the next few years they revamped their creation along these lines, altering his appearance,
　　J. Over the next few years, they revamped their creation, along these lines altering his appearance

7. A. NO CHANGE
　　B. however
　　C. after which
　　D. DELETE the underlined portion

8. F. NO CHANGE
　　G. shorts, over tights, a cape and a logo
　　H. shorts over tights, a cape, and a logo
　　J. shorts over tights a cape and a logo

9. If the writer were to delete the preceding sentence, the passage would primarily lose:
　　A. a logical transition into the following paragraph.
　　B. details supporting the claim that the story of the creation of Superman is a moving one.
　　C. insight into why so few people stop to consider the ideas concerned.
　　D. an explanation of the psychological underpinnings of the creation of super-heroes.

10. F. NO CHANGE
　　G. parents an immigrant, the last survivor of
　　H. parents, an immigrant, the last survivor: of
　　J. parents, an immigrant—the last survivor—of

11. A. NO CHANGE
　　B. his creators'
　　C. Superman's creators
　　D. Supermans creators'

12. F. NO CHANGE
　　G. reference to
　　H. definition of
　　J. symbol within

TEST 5　　　　　　　　　　　　　　　　　　　　　　　　　**GO ON TO THE NEXT PAGE.**

The "Man of Steel" himself is invulnerable, but the story of his creation involves a great deal of suffering: a boy's mourning for his father, a people fleeing murderous oppression, and the struggle of immigrant groups became
"more American than the Americans." Now and for all time, Superman symbolizes humanity's hope that the great power possessed by some will use for the benefit of all. [15]

13. A. NO CHANGE
    B. becoming
    C. to become
    D. had become

14. F. NO CHANGE
    G. some use
    H. some have used
    J. some will be used

Question 15 asks about the preceding passage as a whole.

15. Suppose the author had intended to write an essay about the ways in which popular entertainment has been inspired by tragedy. Would this essay fulfill that goal?
    A. Yes, because it explains how suffering, on both personal and grand scales, led inevitably to the popularity of superhero comics.
    B. No, because the essay deals primarily with one specific character.
    C. Yes, because Superman has appeared in a wide variety of media besides comic books.
    D. No, because superhero comics are a niche medium that is only popular with a select audience.

Passage II

Splat, You're Out

I'm not sure whose idea it was, but around the end of ninth grade, a bunch of guys from my class, myself included: started playing paintball.

If your not familiar, its that game where two teams run around shooting at each other with gas-powered guns that fire little pellets of brightly colored paint: get hit with a pellet, and you're out.

[1] The first thing I learned about paintball is that it's quite an investment. A decent gun at the time costs about seventy-five dollars, but that wasn't the end of it. [2] Pads aren't necessary, because getting shot in the arm or leg doesn't hurt much, but you'd be a fool to play without a facemask, throatguard, and a other piece of athletic equipment specific to male players. [3] You'll be sufficiently sick, after your first day too, to shell out for a suit of camouflage after—the odds are—getting spotted a mile away and immediately peppered. [4] And of course, paintball means regular bike rides to the sporting-goods store to buy more ammunition and get your gas canister refilled. [5] A bunch of protective gear is required too. [21]

16. F. NO CHANGE
    G. class, myself included started
    H. class—myself included—started
    J. class. Myself included, started

17. A. NO CHANGE
    B. you're not familiar, it's
    C. your not familiar, it's
    D. you're not familiar, its

18. Which of the following alternatives to the underlined portion would NOT be acceptable?
    F. getting hit with a pellet means you're out.
    G. when a player is hit, they're out.
    H. a direct hit means that a player is out.
    J. you're out once you get hit, but only until the next game.

19. A. NO CHANGE
    B. having cost
    C. costing
    D. cost

20. F. NO CHANGE
    G. The odds are, to shell out for a suit of camouflage, you'll be sufficiently sick after your first day of getting spotted, a mile away too, and immediately peppered.
    H. To shell out for a suit of camouflage after your first day, the odds are you'll be sufficiently sick of getting spotted a mile away and immediately peppered too.
    J. After your first day, the odds are you'll be sufficiently sick of getting spotted a mile away and immediately peppered to shell out for a suit of camouflage too.

21. For the sake of logic and coherence, sentence 5 should be placed:
    A. where it is now
    B. before sentence 4
    C. after sentence 1
    D. after sentence 2

TEST 5   GO ON TO THE NEXT PAGE.

Nowadays, there are official paintball ranges you can pay to play on, but we just played in the woods behind Bobby's house. It was the only location where we could be sure not to hit any homes, cars, or innocent bystanders, that surely would have brought our paintball days to an abrupt end. We cleared brush to make paths, and dug pits and erected walls to make two opposing forts. This was more yardwork than we would have done even if our parents had paid us, but no hardship was going to stand between the thrill of sneaking up on a friend and shooting him in the butt with exploding pellets of neon goo.

Now and then, the memories of my heroism that summer still bring a smile to my face. There was the time I discovered a secret trail up a hillside full of prickerbushes and picked off three guys without their having any idea where I was. Then there was the time I snuck a giant sheet of clear plexiglass into Bobby's woods, put it up between two trees, and tauntingly danced safely behind it while opponents wasted their ammo. Sure, it was cheating, but it was also hilarious.

[1] I guess, one by one, everyone got a girlfriend and stopped coming out to the games. [2] After a year or two, he probably did the same. [3] I ended up selling my gun and all

22. Which of the following choices best introduces the paragraph?
   F. NO CHANGE
   G. There weren't any official paintball ranges near (at least, not that we knew of).
   H. There were a few different guys in our crew whose houses had back woods big enough to play in.
   J. What we needed now was a safe place to play.

23. A. NO CHANGE
    B. bystanders
    C. bystanders, whom
    D. bystanders; any such occurrence

24. F. NO CHANGE
    G. our thrill
    H. us and the thrill
    J. ourselves, and the thrill

25. A. NO CHANGE
    B. brings
    C. brought
    D. have brought

26. F. NO CHANGE
    G. having
    H. him having
    J. DELETE the underlined portion

27. The author is considering deleting the underlined sentence. Should the author make this deletion?
    A. Yes, because such specific information about the rules of paintball is unnecessary in this brief essay.
    B. Yes, because it contradicts information presented elsewhere in the essay.
    C. No, because it is a humorous way of establishing that the author and his friends did not take the game too seriously.
    D. No, because it is important for the reader to know that the author is someone who once cheated at paintball.

my gear to a kid a couple of grades younger. [4] I didn't exactly remember why we stopped playing. [5] And I'd like to believe that, even now, that same equipment is still being used by some ninth-grader he is discovering the joy of squeezing the trigger on a paintball gun and hearing his shot followed by a loud pop and a swear word from his friend echoing through the woods. [30]

28. F. NO CHANGE
    G. don't exactly remember
    H. hadn't exactly remembered
    J. wouldn't remember exactly

29. A. NO CHANGE
    B. just
    C. and
    D. whose

30. The most logical order for the sentences in the final paragraph would be:
    F. NO CHANGE
    G. 4, 3, 5, 1, 2
    H. 4, 1, 3, 2, 5
    J. 3, 5, 4, 2, 1

Passage III

> The following paragraphs may or may not be in the most logical order. Each paragraph is numbered in brackets, and Question 45 will ask you to choose where Paragraph 3 should most logically be placed.

On the Borderline of History

[1]

The now-familiar story of King Arthur, complete with with Merlin the wizard, and the magic sword Excalibur first appeared in a fanciful history of England composed in the 12th century by a monk named Geoffrey of Monmouth. Since today we know that there are no such things as wizards or magic swords, and discount this version of events, but there are earlier works that mention Arthur as well. His first appearance in a surviving text is in the *Historia Brittonum*, composed by a Welsh monk around the year 830. Since Arthur's famous victory's are all supposed to have taken place over three hundred years prior, the fact that no source in all those intervening years mentions him is suspicious. On the other hand, this was not a terribly literate age, and of the few histories that were composed we know, of which many have been simply lost.

31. A. NO CHANGE
    B. story, of King Arthur complete with Merlin the wizard and the magic sword Excalibur first appeared
    C. story of King Arthur, complete with Merlin the wizard and the magic sword Excalibur, first appeared
    D. story of King Arthur complete with Merlin the wizard and the magic sword Excalibur first app

32. F. NO CHANGE
    G. swords discounted
    H. swords, we had discounted
    J. swords, we must discount

33. A. NO CHANGE
    B. Arthur's famous victories
    C. Arthurs famous victories'
    D. Arthur's famous victories'

34. F. NO CHANGE
    G. mention
    H. have mentioned
    J. were mentioning

35. A. NO CHANGE
    B. composed, but
    C. composed, we know that
    D. composed. Unfortunately,

[2]

Most of the battles and people mentioned in the *Historia* can be historically verified, which seems to support

the historicity of Arthur. [36] And yet, the earlier texts that corroborate the accounts of the battles make no mention of him. Therefore, the *Historia* does not even call Arthur a king
37
at all, but only a "war leader" who succeeding commands the
                                                  38
Britons in several battles against the invading Saxons. This would seem an account sufficiently humble at least to persuade us that *someone* named "Arthur" was involved in British history at this time, if not for the fact that the deeds attributed to him are so obviously exaggerated, such as the
                                                        39
claim that he killed 960 men single-handedly at the Battle
                                                  39
of Badon.
39

[3]

Most of us can't even remember being young enough
  40
not to have heard of him. His name is inseparable from all our romantic ideas about knights and chivalry. A majority of people think of him as an actual historical figure. But did King Arthur really exist? It's possible, but there is less

36. The author is considering adding the following sentence at the point indicated:

> Vortigern, for example, was widely written about prior to the 9th century.

Should the author make this addition?
F. Yes, because without it the essay would contain no proof that the author has actually read any earlier texts.
G. No, because it is information that most people already possess.
H. Yes, because otherwise readers might assume that the author knows only about Arthur and no other famous kings.
J. No, because it is a minor fact that interrupts the flow of the paragraph.

37. A. NO CHANGE
B. Although
C. Meanwhile
D. Curiously

38. F. NO CHANGE
G. successfully commanded
H. successful command
J. succeed commanding

39. The author is considering deleting the underlined portion and ending the sentence after the word "exaggerated." Should the author make this deletion?
A. Yes, because there is no point in including a claim that we know can't possibly be true.
B. Yes, because the essay fails to explain the significance of the Battle of Badon.
C. No, because it provides support for the claim that Arthur's deeds are clearly unrealistic.
D. No, because it establishes that even battles this long ago had high casualty rates.

40. Which of the following alternatives to the underlined portion would NOT be acceptable?
F. Many of them
G. You probably
H. The odds are that anyone you might ask
J. Even today, people

TEST 5   GO ON TO THE NEXT PAGE.

evidence to support this claim than most realize.
                                    41

[4]

Every such early reference to Arthur seeming strongly
                                           42
like an insertion of popular legend into an otherwise historical
42
text. The two most reliable accounts of first-millennium

England are the *Anglo-Saxon Chronicle* and Bede's
              43
Ecclesiastical History—make no mention of Arthur, though

they do include accounts of the battles with which he was

allegedly involved. Countless scholars have labored for

year's hope of proving Arthur's existence, only to meet with
  44

the frustration that caused archaeologist Nowell Myres to

remark that "no figure on the borderline of history and

mythology has wasted more of the historian's time." 45

41. A. NO CHANGE
    B. claim then you might think
    C. claim then there used to be
    D. claim, and than most realize

42. F. NO CHANGE
    G. seems strongly to be
    H. seemed strong until
    J. seems strong, but

43. A. NO CHANGE
    B. England, the
    C. England except for the
    D. England—the

44. F. NO CHANGE
    G. years hoped
    H. years in the hopes
    J. years and hoping

Question 45 asks about the preceding passage as a whole.

45. For the sake of logic and coherence, Paragraph 3 should be placed:
    A. where it is now
    B. before Paragraph 1
    C. after Paragraph 1
    D. after Paragraph 4

Passage IV

A Van Full of Nerds

They say boys won't dance <u>unless their lives depend on it</u>, but in my case all it took was for this girl I had a major crush on to start a ballroom dance club near the end of our sophomore year in <u>college, where we'd been for almost two years.</u> Since I'd been hearing for years about how impossible it is to get boys to <u>dance, I</u> hypothesized that no guys would show up except total nerds who couldn't find any other way to interact with girls. <u>Afterwards,</u> this category included me as well, but I figured that maybe out of all the nerds I'd be the coolest one.

<u>I made sure to wear comfortable shoes to the first meeting.</u> So did lots of cool kids, and lots of people in between. Pretty much half the school showed up, actually. I wasn't the only one who had a crush on Emily, so I guess lots of other guys had the same idea. And as for the girls, well, they never need an excuse to dance. Guys and girls switched partners every few minutes <u>until the instructor finally started to lead us</u> through the basics of several dances that I'd heard of, but knew nothing about, like the foxtrot, rhumba, and cha-cha. Emily was way up at the front of the banquet hall somewhere, <u>but the place was so packed that I would've needed a stepladder and binoculars to see her.</u>

46. Which of the following alternatives to the underlined portion would NOT be acceptable?
    F. until pigs fly
    G. like the deserts miss the rain
    H. for all the tea in China
    J. even if you pay them

47. A. NO CHANGE
    B. college, which was almost halfway over.
    C. college, which we had just gotten used to.
    D. college.

48. F. NO CHANGE
    G. dance, and
    H. dance, so
    J. dance. I

49. A. NO CHANGE
    B. Allegorically,
    C. Apparently,
    D. Although

50. Which of the following sentences best introduces the paragraph?
    F. NO CHANGE
    G. Sure enough, lots of nerds showed up to the first meeting.
    H. The first meeting was held in a banquet hall on the north end of campus.
    J. I had so much going on that week that I nearly spaced on attending the first meeting.

51. A. NO CHANGE
    B. when an instructor appeared and guided us
    C. as the instructor the club had hired led us
    D. and, meanwhile, the instructor put us

52. Given that all the choices are true, which one best expresses the author's feelings of distance from Emily?
    F. NO CHANGE
    G. in that vintage maroon dress that flared out whenever she spun around.
    H. with that friend of hers who always pulled her away whenever I tried to talk to her.
    J. probably dancing with that jerk who always wore soccer shorts, even in the winter.

For some reason, I bothered attending the next few meetings, and I noticed an odd insight: there were fewer popular kids there each time. The funny thing about popular kids are terrified of doing anything that isn't popular. So when they noticed that there were also nerds at the meetings, they figured "Better safe than sorry" and stopped coming. Since I wasn't cool enough to have a reputation to worry about, I stuck things out, and after a few weeks I was practically the most popular guy there (or at least, the least unpopular).

My plan to get closer to Emily would have worked perfectly if not for two things, like the fact that sophomore year ended and I had to wait out the summer, and the fact that Emily had decided to take her junior year abroad and wasn't there anymore in the fall. But this disappointing turn of events weren't my only problems: by this time, the club was ready to start attending ballroom dance competitions, and somehow, I was one of the best dancers and felt too guilty to quit!

For the rest of college, I spent one weekend a month driving to some stupid dance competition in a van full of nerds. If you're about to enter college yourself, heed my advice: never join a club for a girl, or at least make sure that she first isn't about to disappear to France for a year.

53. A. NO CHANGE
    B. portrayal
    C. aspect
    D. phenomenon

54. F. NO CHANGE
    G. kids is
    H. kids, who are
    J. kids is that they're

55. Which of the following alternatives to the underlined portion would NOT be acceptable?
    A. out, after
    B. out; after
    C. out: after
    D. out. After

56. F. NO CHANGE
    G. things, and the
    H. things: the
    J. things. Like the

57. A. NO CHANGE
    B. was suddenly the least of my problems
    C. were surpassed by a bigger problem
    D. is my only problem

58. The best placement in the sentence for the underlined portion would be:
    F. where it is now
    G. after the word "sure"
    H. after the word "disappear"
    J. after the word "France"

Anyway, at least now, when my friend got married, I'm the
only guy at the wedding who knows how to dance. And I
also know a lot of knock-knock jokes about math!

59.
A. NO CHANGE
B. our friends got married, I was
C. my friends were married, I was
D. a friend gets married, I'm

60. The author is considering deleting this sentence and ending the essay with the previous one. Should the author make this deletion?
F. Yes, because the sentence is sarcastic, and so far the essay has been utterly free of sarcasm.
G. Yes, because it is unrelated to dance, and the essay is primarily a sociological one about ballroom dancing's recent resurgence in popularity.
H. No, because it provides humorous insight into the author's experience of having to hang out with nerds.
J. No, because the sentence is useless without specific examples of these jokes.

Passage V

The Greatest

[1]

In Louisville Kentucky, in 1954 12-year-old Cassius
     _____
                    61

Clay's bike was stolen. Devastated, he vowed to beat up the
                       _____
                              62
thief if he ever found him, and someone suggested that

Cassius had taken boxing lessons before making such boasts.
        _____
           63

[2]

[1] It would not be the last time he would prove

Everyone wrong, but even bigger, greater struggles lay ahead.
                         _____
                                   64

[2] After winning a gold medal at the 1960 Olympics he
    _____
                           65
turned pro, and stunned the sporting world, by defeating
_____
                           65
Sonny Liston for the heavyweight championship. [3] He
_____
                     65
turned out to be a very gifted boxer, and decided to stick with

the sport, working his way up through the amateur ranks.

[4] Liston had been heavily favored, and Cassius's brashness;
                                                   _____
                                                       66
prior to the fight he'd called himself "too fast" and "too
_____
           66
pretty" to lose—had made people think he was in for a rude

awakening. 67

---

61. A. NO CHANGE
B. Louisville Kentucky, in 1954, 12-year old
C. Louisville, Kentucky in 1954, 12-year old
D. Louisville, Kentucky, in 1954, 12-year old

62. F. NO CHANGE
G. Devastation vows
H. Devastatedly vowing
J. Devastated, and he vowed

63. A. NO CHANGE
B. took
C. would take
D. had better take

64. F. NO CHANGE
G. bigger struggles
H. greater, more challenging struggles
J. more challenges to overcome

65. A. NO CHANGE
B. After winning a gold medal, at the 1960 Olympics he turned pro and stunned the sporting world, defeating Sonny Liston for the heavyweight championship.
C. After winning a gold medal at the 1960 Olympics he turned pro and stunned the sporting world by defeating Sonny Liston, for the heavyweight championship.
D. After winning a gold medal at the 1960 Olympics he turned pro and stunned the sporting world by defeating Sonny Liston for the heavyweight championship.

66. F. NO CHANGE
G. brashness prior to the fight, and
H. brashness prior to the fight—he'd
J. brashness: prior to the fight he'd

67. The most logical order for the sentences in Paragraph would be:
A. NO CHANGE
B. 1, 3, 2, 4
C. 3, 2, 4, 1
D. 3, 1, 4, 2

[3]

After the victory, Clay announced that he had converted to Islam, and changed his name to the one by which we know him today: Muhammad Ali. In addition to defeating one challenger after another, Ali became active in the Black civil-rights movement, which upset many conservative boxing fans. In 1966, the U.S. government tried to draft Ali into service in the Vietnam War. Unsurprisingly, on religious grounds, he refused to go, and was stripped of his title and imprisoned.

[4]

Released in 1970, another shot at the championship was soon in the works for Ali, against the undefeated George Foreman. Foreman seemed invincible, and fans feared that Ali might be seriously hurt or even killed. Ali spent the beginning of the fight on the ropes, and seemed to be losing badly, but then his strategy became clear: after Foreman exhausted him, Ali sprang to life, knocking out the younger fighter in the 8th round.

[5]

Ali retired in 1981, and was eventually diagnosed with Parkinson's Disease, but the sporting world he'd once shocked now revered him. He lit the Olympic flame before an adoring crowd in 1996, and Sports Illustrated magazine

68. F. NO CHANGE
    G. one, which we know
    H. one in which we know
    J. one that we know of him

69. Which of the following alternatives to the underlined portion would be LEAST acceptable?
    A. movement; this upset
    B. movement, having upset
    C. movement, thereby upsetting
    D. movement, a decision that upset

70. F. NO CHANGE
    G. Therefore, on
    H. Although on
    J. On

71. A. NO CHANGE
    B. the championship would be Ali's again if he managed to win his bout
    C. the boxing commission eventually granted Ali a chance to regain the championship: a match
    D. Ali worked his way up to another shot at the championship,

72. F. NO CHANGE
    G. exhausted,
    H. when Foreman had exhausted himself,
    J. quickly, before Foreman was exhausted,

73. A. NO CHANGE
    B. finally shocking the sporting world into revering him
    C. both shocking and revering the sporting world
    D. which the sporting world first shocked, but then revered

TEST 5   GO ON TO THE NEXT PAGE.

later named him "Sportsman of the Century," for his combination of skill, bravery and magnetism. Ali himself

still prefers the familiar title he correctly predicted he would hold: "The Greatest of All Time." 75

74. F. NO CHANGE
G. Century" for his combination of skill, bravery, and magnetism
H. Century" for his combination, of skill, bravery and magnetism
J. Century" for his combination of skill bravery and magnetism

Question 75 asks about the preceding passage as a whole.

75. Suppose the author had intended to write an essay for boxing fans about what made Muhammad Ali such a successful boxer. Did this essay achieve that goal?
A. Yes, because it makes very clear that Ali is widely considered the greatest boxer of all time.
B. No, because it is more an essay for a general audience about Ali's cultural importance.
C. Yes, because the essay describes the strategy Ali used to win one very famous fight.
D. No, because the essay's style is much too flowery and verbose to appeal to boxing fans.

END OF TEST
STOP! DO NOT TURN THE PAGE UNTIL TOLD TO DO SO

MATHEMATICS TEST
60 Minutes—60 Questions

DIRECTIONS: Solve each problem, choose the correct answer, and then fill in the corresponding oval on your answer document.

Do not linger over problems that take too much time. Solve as many as you can; then return to the others in the time you have left for this test.

You are permitted to use a calculator on this test. You may use your calculator for any problems you choose, but some of the problems may best be done without using a calculator.

Note: Unless otherwise stated, all of the following should be assumed.

1. Illustrative figures are NOT necessarily drawn to scale.
2. Geometric figures lie in a plane.
3. The word *line* indicates a straight line.
4. The word *average* indicates arithmetic mean.

If $\frac{5x}{3} + 6 = 4$, then x = ?

A. 6
B. $\frac{6}{5}$
C. 0
D. $-\frac{6}{5}$
E. -4

DO YOUR FIGURING HERE.

A Fahrenheit temperature F can be approximated by doubling the Celsius temperature C and adding 32. If the temperature outside is 18° C, what is the approximate temperature in Fahrenheit?

F. 25°
G. 41°
H. 50°
J. 68°
K. 100°

Carol worked one summer and earned money that she spent on new clothes. After spending 65% of her money, Carol had $875 left. How much money did Carol earn for the summer?

A. $1625
B. $2500
C. $3375
D. $4125
E. $7375

501

GO ON TO THE NEXT PAGE.

4. $\left(x^4\right)^{15}$ is equivalent to:

   F. $60x$
   G. $15x^4$
   H. $15x^{11}$
   J. x^{19}
   K. x^{60}

5. Doris and Clyde volunteered to help paint their friend's apartment. Doris used $1\frac{3}{4}$ gallons of paint and Clyde used $2\frac{1}{2}$ gallons. If 5 gallons of paint were purchased, how many gallons were left?

   A. $\frac{3}{4}$
   B. $1\frac{3}{4}$
   C. $3\frac{1}{4}$
   D. $4\frac{1}{4}$
   E. $4\frac{1}{2}$

6. The expression $(3p+4)(5p-6)$ is equivalent to:

   F. $8p^2 - 24$
   G. $8p^2 + 2p - 24$
   H. $15p^2 - 24$
   J. $15p^2 - 4p - 24$
   K. $15p^2 + 2p - 24$

7. What is a possible equation for a line that is parallel to $4x - 3y = 6$?

   A. $y = -\frac{4}{3}x + 2$
   B. $y = \frac{3}{4}x - 2$
   C. $y = -4x + 6$
   D. $y = \frac{4}{3}x + 2$
   E. $y = -\frac{3}{4}x - 2$

DO YOUR FIGURING HERE.

In an isosceles triangle, the measure of each of the base angles is one-third the measure of the vertex angle. What is the measure, in degrees of each of the base angles?

F. 36°
G. 60°
H. 72°
J. 108°
K. 216°

DO YOUR FIGURING HERE.

What is the length, in feet, of the hypotenuse of a right triangle with legs that are 8 feet long and 9 feet long, respectively?

A. $\sqrt{17}$
B. $\sqrt{145}$
C. 17
D. 36
E. 72

The lengths of the corresponding sides of 2 similar right triangles are in the ratio of 3:4. If the hypotenuse of the larger triangle is 6 inches long, how many inches long is the hypotenuse of the smaller triangle?

F. 3.5
G. 4
H. 4.5
J. 8
K. 18

When Sara bought gas for her car 30 years ago, the price was 20% of today's price. If today's price is $3.25, which of the following is closest to the price of a gallon of gas 30 years ago?

A. $3.05
B. $2.60
C. $1.30
D. $0.65
E. $0.60

To the nearest foot, what is the length of a diagonal of the top of a rectangular platform that is 14 feet wide and 15 feet long?

F. 16
G. 19
H. 20
J. 22
K. 29

ST 5

Copyright © 2009 Academic Educational Resources. All rights reserved.

GO ON TO THE NEXT PAGE.

13. Which real number satisfies $(3^x)(9) = 27^2$?

    A. 1
    B. 3
    C. 4
    D. 4.5
    E. 8

14. A rectangular room that is 3 feet longer than it is wide has an area of 54 square feet. How many feet long is the room?

    F. 6
    G. 9
    H. 15
    J. 18
    K. 27

15. The perimeter of a parallelogram is 36 inches, and one side measures 6 inches. What are the lengths, in inches, of the other 3 sides?

    A. 6,6,18
    B. 6,9,9
    C. 6,12,12
    D. 6,15,15
    E. Cannot be determined from the given information.

16. The average of 5 numbers is 7. If each of the numbers is decreased by 4, what is the average of the 5 new numbers?

    F. 0.0
    G. 1.0
    H. 2.0
    J. 3.0
    K. 7.0

17. Julie works in a clothing store and gets a base salary of $48.00 plus a fixed amount for each item she sells per day. Yesterday she earned $68.00 because she sold 4 items. If Julie sells 3 more items today than yesterday, what will she earn for the day?

    A. $51.00
    B. $55.00
    C. $63.00
    D. $78.00
    E. $83.00

DO YOUR FIGURING HERE.

If $\frac{6}{x} \geq \frac{1}{4}$, what is the largest possible value for x?

F. $\frac{2}{3}$
G. 1.5
H. 10
J. 24
K. 36

Starting at midnight, how many degrees has the hour hand of a clock moved when it gets to 8:00 AM?

A. 80°
B. 100°
C. 120°
D. 240°
E. 270°

An airplane has r rows of seats with $(s+d)$ seats in each row. Which of the following is an expression for the number of seats in the entire theater?

F. $(r \cdot s) + d$
G. $(r \cdot s) + (r \cdot d)$
H. $s + (r \cdot d)$
J. $r \cdot s \cdot d$
K. $r + s + d$

Which nonnegative value of x makes the expression $\frac{1}{16-x^2}$ undefined?

A. 256
B. 32
C. 16
D. 8
E. 4

A punch recipe calls for 3 parts fruit juice to 2 parts soda. In order to make 20 quarts of punch, how many quarts of fruit juice should be used?

F. 12
G. 9
H. 8
J. 6
K. 4

DO YOUR FIGURING HERE.

GO ON TO THE NEXT PAGE.

23. A line contains the points E, F, G, and H. Point F is between points E and G. Point H is between points G and F. Which of the following inequalities MUST be true about the lengths of these segments?

    A. FG < EF
    B. GH < FG
    C. FH < GH
    D. GH < EF
    E. FH < EF

24. What is the volume, in cubic centimeters, of a cone with a height of 9 centimeters and a base with a radius of 4 centimeters? (The volume of a cone is $\frac{\pi}{3}r^2h$, where r is the radius of the base of the cone and h is the height of the cone.)

    F. 144π
    G. 72π
    H. 48π
    J. 16π
    K. 9π

25. One endpoint of a diameter of a circle with center (3, -4) has coordinates (5, -3) in the standard (x,y) plane. What are the coordinates of the other endpoint of that diameter?

    A. (1, -5)
    B. (1, 2)
    C. (-1, 5)
    D. $\left(3+\sqrt{5}, -3+\sqrt{5}\right)$
    E. $\left(3-\sqrt{5}, -3-\sqrt{5}\right)$

26. At an airport, the planes take off from two airfields. One of the fields is capable of sending up a plane every 4 minutes. The other field is capable of sending up 3 planes every 10 minutes. At these rates, which of the following is the best estimate of the total number of minutes the two airfields would need to send up 15 planes?

    F. 10
    G. 12
    H. 15
    J. 18
    K. 20

DO YOUR FIGURING HERE.

7. Which of the following expressions represents the product xy, if $x = 4a^3$ and $y = -3a^5 + b$?

A. $a^3 + b$
B. $a^5 + b$
C. $-12a^8 + 4a^3b$
D. $-12a^{15} + 4a^3b$
E. $-243a^{15} + 4a^3b$

8. Ann is wrapping a gift for her friend's shower. She wants to cut ribbon so that she can place it on the gift like the picture below. What is the minimum length of the ribbon, in centimeters, that Ann would need to cut in order to wrap the box, assuming no overlap?

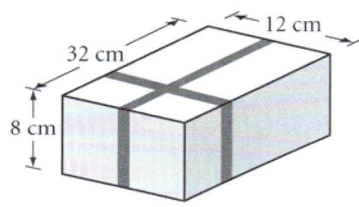

F. 52
G. 104
H. 120
J. 128
K. 3072

9. For all nonzero x and y, $\dfrac{(9x^{-2}y^2)(-8x^2y^3)}{(4x^2y^4)} =$

A. $\dfrac{-9x^6y}{4}$
B. $\dfrac{x^2y^2}{18}$
C. $-18x^{-2}$
D. $-18x^{-2}y$
E. $-18x^2y^2$

DO YOUR FIGURING HERE.

30. What is the area in centimeters of the polygon below?

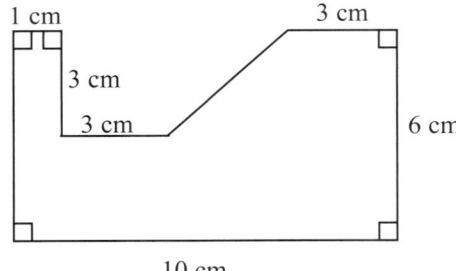

- F. 30
- G. 32.5
- H. 35
- J. 42
- K. 46.5

Use the figure below to answer questions 31 - 32.

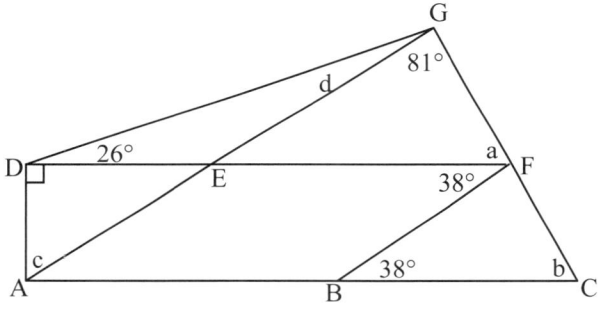

31. In the quadrilateral ACGD, DF ∥ AC and AG ∥ BF. What is the value of ∠d ?

- A. 9
- B. 12
- C. 21
- D. 26
- D. 38

32. For triangle EFG, what is the value of ∠a ?

- F. 52
- G. 58
- H. 61
- J. 71
- K. 73

A boat is anchored in a small lake with a rope that is 34 feet long. A wind blows the boat until the rope is taut and the water is 16 feet deep. Measuring across the bottom of the lake, how far has the boat moved from the anchor?

A. 30
B. 50
C. 60
D. 80
E. 120

If a and b are real numbers and $\sqrt{3\left(\frac{a^2}{b}\right)} = 1$, then what MUST be true of the value of b?

F. b must be positive
G. b must be negative
H. b must equal $\frac{1}{3}$
J. b must equal 3
K. b may have any value

In the figure below, l_1 is parallel to l_2, and l_3 is parallel to l_4. What is the value of $\angle b$?

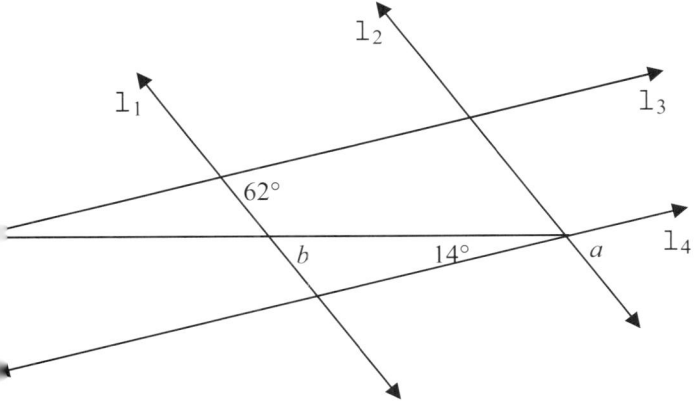

A. 44
B. 46
C. 48
D. 62
E. 132

DO YOUR FIGURING HERE.

36. If $0° \leq x \leq 90°$ and $\cos x = \frac{8}{17}$, then $\tan x = ?$

   F. $\frac{8}{15}$
   G. $\frac{15}{17}$
   H. $\frac{17}{15}$
   J. $\frac{15}{8}$
   K. $\frac{17}{8}$

37. In the figure, AD is a diameter of the circle with center O and AO = 5. What is the measure of arc BCD?

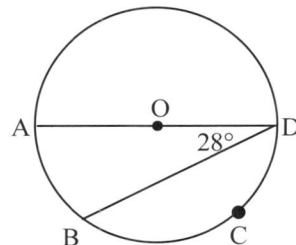

   A. 56°
   B. 116°
   C. 120°
   D. 124°
   E. 128°

38. If $\sin \theta = \frac{1}{2}$ and $\cos \theta = \frac{\sqrt{3}}{2}$, then $\csc \theta$ is?

   F. 2
   G. $\sqrt{3}$
   H. $\frac{2\sqrt{3}}{3}$
   J. $\frac{2}{3}$
   K. $\frac{\sqrt{3}}{3}$

Triangle PQR is equilateral. Find the sum of $a + b + c + d$.

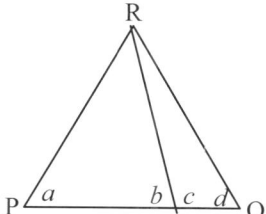

A. 180°
B. 210°
C. 240°
D. 270°
E. 300°

If $\oplus$ is defined for all positive numbers a and b by $a \oplus b = \dfrac{ab}{a+b}$, then $8 \oplus 2 =$

F. $\frac{1}{2}$
G. $\frac{2}{3}$
H. $\frac{8}{9}$
J. 1
K. $\frac{8}{5}$

The measures of the lengths of the 3 sides of a triangle are prime numbers. If two of the sides are 5 and 23, how many different lengths are possible for the third side?

A. 1
B. 2
C. 9
D. more than 18 but less than 29
E. an infinite number

If a wheel on a stationary bike is 26 inches in diameter, and Mike pedals to make the wheel revolve 50 times, what would be the total distance that the wheel would travel if it weren't stationary?

F. 169π
G. 1300
H. 676π
J. 1300π
K. 2600π

DO YOUR FIGURING HERE.

GO ON TO THE NEXT PAGE.

43. What is the equivalent of $(3i+4)^2$?

   A. $12i^2$
   B. $9i^2 + 16$
   C. $3i^2 + 24i + 16$
   D. $7 + 24i$
   E. $13 + 24i$

44. Maureen wants to put an exercise wheel in her hamster's cage. The height of the cage is 22 inches, but there must be a 1 inch space above and below the wheel to allow for the wheel frame. What is the radius of the largest wheel that Maureen can place in the cage?

   F. 5
   G. $2\sqrt{5}$
   H. 10
   J. 11
   K. 20

45. What is the sum of the first 15 multiples of 5?

   A. 375
   B. 560
   C. 600
   D. 750
   E. 1200

46. If $\frac{n!}{(n-1)!} = 5$, then $(n-2)! = ?$

   F. 6
   G. 20
   H. 30
   J. 60
   K. 120

47. At a local restaurant a customer can order a lunch special with the following choices: a salad or 2 kinds of soup and a sandwich with 4 types of meat, 2 types of bread, and 3 types of cheese. How many different combinations could be made for the lunch special?

   A. 11
   B. 12
   C. 48
   D. 72
   E. 96

What is the distance, in coordinate units, between the points $S(-\sqrt{2}, 7)$ and $T(-3\sqrt{2}, 9)$ in the standard (x,y) coordinate plane?

F. 2
G. 3
H. $2\sqrt{3}$
J. $4\sqrt{2}$
K. 6

Which of the following expressions is equivalent to $\frac{a}{b}$ if all integers a, b, and c, are positive?

A. $\frac{a \cdot c}{b \cdot c}$
B. $\frac{b \cdot a}{a \cdot b}$
C. $\frac{a \cdot a}{b \cdot b}$
D. $\frac{a+c}{b+c}$
E. $\frac{a-c}{b-c}$

The sum of twice a smaller number and three times a larger number is 49. The larger of the two numbers exceeds four times the smaller number by 7. If n is the smaller number, which equation below determines the correct value of n?

F. $2(4x+7)+3x = 49$
G. $2(4x-7)+3x = 49$
H. $(12x+7)+2x = 49$
J. $3(4x+7)+2x = 49$
K. $3(4x-7)+2x = 49$

If $x = 3t - 7$ and $y = 4 - t$, which of the following expresses y in terms of x?

A. $y = 5 - x$
B. $y = \frac{5-x}{3}$
C. $y = 4 - x$
D. $y = 11 - 3x$
E. $y = \frac{19-x}{3}$

DO YOUR FIGURING HERE

GO ON TO THE NEXT PAGE.

52. Which of the following is an equation of the line that passes through the points (2,4) and (-2, -12) in the standard (x,y) coordinate plane?

   F. $y = 8$
   G. $4x - y = 4$
   H. $4x + y = -4$
   J. $7x - 3y = 2$
   K. $8x - 2y = 7$

53. If $f(x) = 7x^2 - 4x - 10$, then $f(-3) = ?$

   A. 85
   B. 65
   C. 41
   D. -1
   E. -61

54. How much larger, in degrees, is the measure of one angle in a regular 8-sided polygon than the measure of one angle in a regular 6-sided polygon? (The measure of each interior angle of a regular n-sided polygon is $\dfrac{(n-2)180}{n}$).

   F. 15°
   G. 27°
   H. 108°
   J. 120°
   K. 135°

55. Which of the following expressions is equivalent to $3 \log_2 x + \tfrac{1}{3} \log_4 y - \log_2 z$ when x, y, and z are positive real numbers?

   A. $\log_2 \dfrac{x^3 y}{z}$
   B. $\log_2 \dfrac{z}{x^3} + \log_4 \left(\dfrac{y}{3}\right)$
   C. $\log_2 \left(\dfrac{x^3}{z}\right) + \log_4 \left(\sqrt[3]{y}\right)$
   D. $\log_2 (x - z) + \log_4 \left(\sqrt[3]{y}\right)$
   E. $3 \log_2 (x - z) + \log_4 \left(\dfrac{y}{3}\right)$

For all $x > 10$, $\dfrac{(x^2+8x+15)(x-2)}{(x^2+3x-10)(x+3)} = ?$

F. $\dfrac{3}{2}$

G. $\dfrac{(x-2)}{(x+2)}$

H. $\dfrac{2(x-2)}{x+3}$

J. 1

K. $-\dfrac{3(x-2)}{x+3}$

DO YOUR FIGURING HERE

If the amplitude of a trigonometric function is $\dfrac{1}{2}$ the nonnegative difference between the maximum and minimum values of the function, which of the following trigonometric functions has an amplitude of 3?

A. $\dfrac{1}{3}\cos x$

B. $\cos 3x$

C. $\sin \dfrac{1}{3} x$

D. $3\tan x$

E. $3\sin x$

If $90° < x < 180°$, which of the following equals $\sin x$, if $\tan x = -\dfrac{24}{7}$

F. $\dfrac{-24}{25}$

G. $\dfrac{-7}{25}$

H. $\dfrac{7}{25}$

J. $\dfrac{7}{24}$

K. $\dfrac{24}{25}$

Which of the following is the factored form of the expression $12x^2 - x - 6$?

A. $(3x+2)(4x-3)$

B. $(3x-2)(4x+3)$

C. $(4x+2)(3x-3)$

D. $(6x+1)(2x-6)$

E. $(x-2)(12x+3)$

GO ON TO THE NEXT PAGE.

60. Harry has a bag containing jelly beans: 7 pink, 8 blue, and 9 orange. How many additional pink beans must be added to the 24 jelly beans already in the bag so that the probability of randomly drawing a pink jelly bean is $\frac{1}{2}$?

F. 1
G. 5
H. 7
J. 9
K. 10

NO TEST MATERIAL ON THIS PAGE.

3

READING TEST

35 Minutes – 40 Questions

DIRECTIONS: There are four passages in this test. Each passage is followed by several questions. After reading a passage, choose the best answer to each question and fill in the corresponding oval on your answer document. You may refer to the passages as often as necessary.

Passage I

PROSE FICTION: This passage is adapted from the novel *Septembers of Shiraz* by Dalia Sofer. (© 2006). The setting is Iran in the early 1980s, after a political overthrow. The Amin family, including Shirin, were supporters of the previous government and face strife at the time of this excerpt.

Absence, Shirin thinks, is death's cousin. One day something is there, the next day it isn't. Abracadabra.

What happens to a house full of nonbeings? What if, like her father, she and her mother would one day
[5] disappear also? The house, of course, would not know it. That would be the sad part. The house would continue to exist. Its walls would remain in the same place, the doors ready to be opened and closed. The clocks' needles would continue moving forward, and at
[10] midnight starting all over again, as though the day that had just ended had never been.

This morning she stays in bed and looks out her window, at the wind dusting the sky with the trees' dry leaves. She looks at the branches, pities their nakedness
[15] and envies their patience. She watches the pale sunlight trying to break through the clouds and failing. She wonders what is the point of it all, this endless cycle.

She gets out of bed and walks through the house. She sees that the door to her father's study is closed.
[20] Resting her ear against it she hears the shuffling of papers. She opens the door without knocking. Her mother, behind the desk piled high with files, books, and photographs, looks up. "You scared me, Shirin!"

"What are you doing?"

[25] "You see all this?" her mother says. "It has to go." Her hands hover above the desk, palms up, indicating the mess below them. Normally her mother would have yelled at her for walking into a room without knocking. Today it doesn't seem to matter. "Go where?" Shirin
[30] says.

"It has to disappear. You see, people from the regime may come to search our house. We have to rid of things anything that may look suspic[ious].
[35] Remember how last year you had to tear off the [pages] with the Shah's photo from all your books? We ha[ve to] do the same thing throughout the house—make sure we have nothing that would prove that we like the regime."

"Can I help you? I can shred."

[40] "You?" She smiles. "Well, yes, why not? There [is so] much…" The circles under her mother's eyes are da[rk] today. "Oh, your breakfast!" she s[ays.]

"Are you hungry, Shirin?"

"No, I ate," Shirin lies. She sits next to her mo[ther]
[45] and rips. They tear up account balances, names [and] telephone numbers of her father's friends, ho[liday] greeting cards, and photographs—mostly of peopl[e she] doesn't recognize, or recognizes only after lookin[g at] them for a long time. Her father was young once,
[50] thinks, even handsome.

A photograph of herself on the ice-skating rink m[akes] her stop. Where would she begin ripping, in [the] middle—first tearing it in half and then into piec[es, a] lock of hair here, a squinting eye there? She leans [back]
[55] and examines the room: the open drawers, [the] overflowing desk, heaps of paper on the floor. Ha[s her] mother gone mad? What will her father think [if he] returns home and finds his life torn up?

"Are you sure we should do this?" she says.

[60] Her mother drops a paper on the desk. She rea[ches] for a cigarette and brings it to her mouth. "No, I'm [not] sure," she says.

The cigarettes appear, Shirin knows, whe[n] things are going badly.

"I'm not sure what's right anymore," Shirin," she says as she exhales, looking out the window and quietly crying. Shirin notices that her mother is still in her pajamas. The polish on her toenails has chipped. Why had she questioned her mother's judgment, like that? She takes that photograph of herself and rips.

1. The point of view from which the passage is told suggests that Shirin is most likely a/an:
   A. child confused and hurt by the absence of parental involvement in her life.
   B. teenager rebelling against strict rules and laws.
   C. college student reminiscing about childhood.
   D. adult facing the challenge of raising children of her own.

2. According to the passage, the reason why Shirin and her mother are destroying their family's personal files and photographs is because:
   F. They are planning to move to a new house soon.
   G. Possession of some of their belongings may risk punishment or retribution from those currently in power in Iran.
   H. Shirin's parents are getting a divorce.
   J. The family is trying to sell their belongings in order to buy something to eat.

3. The passage does NOT mention which of the following as something about which Shirin expresses concern?
   A. Political issues Iran is facing at the time of the passage.
   B. The health and decision-making of her mother.
   C. The disappearance of her father.
   D. The meaning of life.

4. It can reasonably be inferred from details in the passage that Shirin's mother:
   F. Is generally an optimistic and idealistic person.
   G. Is taking great pains to appear calm and collected in the wake of her husband's disappearance.
   H. Has been more protective and mothering of Shirin recently.
   J. Displays particular emotional and psychological stress due to recent events.

5. Shirin is at first reluctant to destroy a photograph of herself because:
   A. The image in the photo reminds her of a happier moment in her life.
   B. She fears she will get in trouble or hurt her family if she rips it up now.
   C. She is angry that her mother forgot to make her breakfast.
   D. She is concerned that she is erasing her family's past and her father's memories.

6. As it used in paragraph 7 (lines 31-38), the word "*regime*" refers to:
   F. states
   G. government
   H. ruler
   J. dictatorship

7. The reader can infer from details in the passage that Shirin is:
   A. silly and foolish, who is likely often yelled at by her mother.
   B. needy and demanding of other people's attention.
   C. wiser and more reflective than her age would suggest.
   D. angry and critical toward the way her parents have raised her.

8. Paragraphs two and three of the passage are significant to the reader's understanding of Shirin because they reveal the impact that:
   F. her strained relationship with her mother has had in making her cynical and mean.
   G. the silence of the house has had on her fear of aging and dying
   H. her father's absence has had on her views and attitudes towards the world.
   J. the weather has on her sense of self and her well being.

9. Which of the following would best describe the relationship between Shirin and her mother?
   A. detached
   B. maternal
   C. stressful
   D. hostile

10. Shirin's change in attitude at the end of the passage toward the destruction of family photographs is most likely the result of:
    F. her resentment toward her father because of his absence.
    G. a lack of concern toward the strict policies of the new regime.
    H. a desire to remove bad childhood memories and start over.
    J. a heightened awareness of her mother's suffering.

Passage II

SOCIAL SCIENCE: This passage is adapted from *The Post-American World* by Fareed Zakaria. (© 2008 by Fareed Zakaria).

Americans are glum at the moment, really glum. A new poll revealed that 81 percent of the American people believe that the country is on the "wrong track." In the 25 years that pollsters have asked this question, this latest response was by far the most negative. Other polls, asking similar questions, found levels of gloom that were even more alarming, often at 30- and 40-year highs. There are reasons to be pessimistic—a financial panic, a seemingly endless war in Iraq, and the ongoing threat of terrorism—but the facts on the ground are simply not dire enough to explain the present atmosphere of malaise.

American anxiety springs from something much deeper, a sense that large and disruptive forces are coursing through the world. In almost every industry, in every aspect of life, it feels like the patterns of the past are being scrambled. For the first time in living memory, the United States does not seem to be leading the charge. Americans see that a new world is coming into being, but fear it is one being shaped in distant lands and by foreign people.

Look around. The world's tallest building is in Taipei, and will soon be in Dubai. Its biggest refinery is being constructed in India. The biggest movie industry is Bollywood, not Hollywood. America no longer dominates even its favorite sport, shopping. The Mall of America in Minnesota once boasted that it was the largest shopping mall in the world. Today it wouldn't make the top ten. These lists are arbitrary and a bit silly, but consider that only ten years ago, the United States would have topped almost every one of these categories.

During the 1980s, when I would visit India—where I grew up—most Indians were fascinated by the United States. People would often ask me about Donald Trump. He was the very symbol of the United States— brassy, rich, and modern. He symbolized the feeling that if you wanted to find the biggest and largest anything, you had to look to America. Today, outside of entertainment figures, there is no comparable interest in American personalities. Now there are dozens of Indian businessmen who are now wealthier than the Donald. And that newfound interest in *their own* story is being replicated across much of the world.

For the last 20 years, America's superpower status in every realm has been largely unchalleng[ed], something that's never happened before in history[, at] least since the Roman Empire dominated the kn[own] world 2000 years ago. During this Pax Americana, [the] global economy has accelerated dramatically. And [that] expansion is the driver behind the third great power s[hift] of the modern age—the rise of the rest.

At the military and political level, we still live i[n an] American-dominated world. But along every o[ther] dimension—industrial, financial, social, cultural— distribution of power is shifting, moving away f[rom] American dominance. This will not be a world def[ined] by the decline of America but rather the rise of every[one] else.

As other nations rise, they will seek greater free[dom] of action. This necessarily means that Amer[ica's] unimpeded influence will decline. But if the world t[hat] being created has more power centers, nearly al[l are] invested in order, stability and progress. Rather [than] narrowly obsessing about our own short-term inte[rests] and interest groups, our chief priority should be to b[ring] these rising forces into the global system, to inte[grate] them so that they in turn broaden and deepen g[lobal] economic, political, and cultural ties.

Americans have not really understood the rise o[f the] rest. This is one of the most thrilling stories in his[tory.] Billions of people are escaping from abject poverty. [The] world will be enriched and ennobled as they bec[ome] consumers, producers, inventors, thinkers, dream[ers] and doers. This is all happening because of Ame[rican] ideas and actions. For 60 years, the United State[s has] pushed countries to open their markets, free up [their] politics, and embrace trade and technology. Ame[rican] diplomats, businessmen, and intellectuals have u[rged] people in distant lands to be unafraid of change, to [join] the advanced world, to learn the secrets of our suc[cess.] Yet just as they are beginning to do so, we are l[osing] faith in such ideas. We have become suspicious of t[hese] openness, immigration, and investment because no[w it's] not Americans going abroad but foreigners comi[ng to] America. Just as the world is opening up, we are cl[osing] down.

Generations from now, when historians write a[bout] these times, they might note that by the turn of the [21st] century, the United States had succeeded in its g[reat] historical mission—globalizing the world. We [don't] want them to write that along the way, we forg[ot to] globalize ourselves.

11. This passage is best described as being:
    A. An attack on American attitudes and policies.
    B. A plea to developing nations to challenge American dominance.
    C. An analysis of changing attitudes and behaviors in world affairs.
    D. A parody of Americans' pessimism in response to the ascent of other nations.

12. The passage indicates that the "acceleration of the global economy" has led to all of the following EXCEPT:
    F. The substantial decrease in poverty worldwide.
    G. The spread of American values and technologies.
    H. The increasing influence and leadership of developing nations.
    J. The embrace by many Americans of the United States' revised standing in the world.

13. The main function of the third paragraph is to:
    A. Provide evidence of America's decline by showing how much more ambitious many other countries are
    B. Show how foolish it is to compare a country's power and prosperity by the size of its shopping malls or other buildings.
    C. Argue why America needs to return to developing big and bold projects that reflect the image many foreigners used to have of the United States.
    D. Confirm that much of the prestige and extravagance once principally exclusive to the United States is now a characteristic of many other countries.

14. The word "*malaise*" (line 12) most likely means:
    F. satisfaction
    G. melancholy
    H. ambivalence
    J. frustration

15. According to the passage, many foreign countries no longer praise celebrated or powerful American figures of power because:
    A. American power has been unchallenged for more than two decades.
    B. These countries now have their own important, larger-than-life figures.
    C. The current mood in America depresses citizens from other nations.
    D. They, like the author, are supporting the rise of other countries, not America.

16. The author has most likely titled his book The *Post-American World* to make the point that:
    F. America is no longer a superpower; it is a nation in decline.
    G. Anti-Americanism is on the rise and threatens the security of the United States.
    H. The economic and cultural powers once dominated by America are now being shared among many of the world's countries.
    J. Like the ancient Roman empire, American society will vanish, necessitating "the rise of the rest" in order

17. The author's attitude toward globalization may be best characterized as:
    A. enthusiastic
    B. skeptical
    C. ambivalent
    D. distrustful

18. Why is the author critical of America's reaction to "the rise of the rest" (line 52)?
    F. America is aggressively using its military might to maintain its status as a global superpower.
    G. Many Americans have become critical of the very ideals that helped America, and now the rest of the world, prosper.
    H. Americans are too focused on the movement of many jobs to foreign countries.
    J. Americans arrogantly believed that their influence over other countries would never diminish.

19. As it is used in the passage, the word *brassy* (line 37) most nearly means:
    A. shiny
    B. subtle
    C. metallic
    D. flashy

20. Which of the following foreign policy strategies would the author most likely support America taking?
    F. American military and political power should be used to maintain its standing as the world's superpower.
    G. America should isolate itself from the rest of the world and protect its own industries and cultures.
    H. America should continue to mentor and encourage developing nations.
    J. America should work with only a select few nations it can benefit most from and ignore other less developed nations.

Passage III

HUMANITIES: This passage is adapted from "Meet Mario's Papa," an interview with Shigeru Miyamoto conducted by Kenji Hall that appeared in the November 7, 2005, edition of Business Week (© 2005 by McGraw-Hill).

As the brains behind the video games at Nintendo, Shigeru Miyamoto has shown a knack for inventing games that kids would get hooked on. In 1985, his *Super Mario Bros.* –the world's hottest-selling game ever—was the first with a scrolling screen, which expanded the playing space vertically, not just horizontally. The next year, he came up with the labyrinthine fantasy world called *The Legend of Zelda*, which could take skilled gamers hours, and sometimes weeks, to complete. And in the 1990s, his *Super Mario 64* was the first console title with 3D graphics. It even forced him to tweak the standard joystick to handle more complex commands.

Q. *What's the secret to creating a hit game?*

A. Whether it's a new game or a sequel, we want anyone to be able to play right away. That's why I think Rubik's Cube was so brilliant. I saw it for the first time at a toy convention in Japan in the early 1980s. The moment you see a Rubik's Cube, you know you're supposed to twist the pieces. And it's beautifully designed. Even if you've never handled one, you want to pick it up and try it. And once you do that, it's hard to walk away until you've solved it.

Q. *Supercomputing power has improved game graphics to the point where characters can be made to appear almost lifelike. But the characters in your games are mostly cartoons. Why?*

A. Nowadays, software makers want games to be so realistic, but first and foremost games should evoke emotions. When I made *Pikmin*, I wanted people to feel a mix of sadness and happiness. The Japanese word *itoshii* is used when you think fondly of someone. You wouldn't normally feel that when playing games, but that's what I was striving for. Games aren't just about recreation and getting to the next stage. People often tell me nobody would play a game that isn't that way -- it would be too boring. But I don't agree with them.

Q. *What's the most important ingredient in your games?*

A. The most basic element is fun. Games are interactive. They must challenge you, and reward you when you when you rise to the challenge. In my view, the game begins the moment a person touches a console—everything builds from that. When I first started creating games, I mainly wanted to make something that would surprise people. Actually, I never imagined I would be making video games. I thought I would be designing toys, like Rubik of the Rubik's Cube.

Q. *Where do you get ideas for your games?*

A. Sometimes I rely on childhood experiences. F instance, what did I find scary? Some ideas are spontaneous, some come from notes I've kept. I u to write down things I saw or heard on a Post-it, which I would stick in my scheduling book. It co be a game or something funny on TV I saw, or a story I heard someone tell.

But I would say that over the last five years o the types of games I create has changed somev Whereas before I could kind of use my imagination to create these worlds or create t games, I would say that over the last five years had more of a tendency to take interests or topi my life and try to draw the entertainment out of t

Q. *What, then, was the thinking behind your development of Miis, player-created images that gamers can customize to represent their—or anybody else's—likeness?*

A. I see the Miis as a means of and beyond char creation. What's interesting is that regardless o user's age, if they're looking at a Mii, it's their Before, when you're playing as another chara it's typical of more passive entertainment, an creating a Mii you're becoming more a part o entertainment experience.

Q. *In the future, what do you think video games be like?*

A. It's convenient to make games that are playe TVs. But I always wanted to have a custom-size screen that wasn't the typical four-cornered cath ray-tube TV. I've always thought that games wo eventually break free of the confines of a TV sc to fill an entire room.

Q. *You've been called the Steven Spielberg of v games. Recently, some gamers have been makin movies using game software. Are games and mo converging?*

A. It's a common comparison, but I don't think an appropriate one because movies aren't intera the way games are. Even so, I've learned a lot fr movies. For instance, I pay attention to how mo use music to create a mood, how many camera angles there are, or how the director sets up a scary scene.

90 *Q. Do you think violent or explicit games can negatively influence young children?*

A. The obvious objective of video games is to entertain people by surprising them with new experiences. Violence is one means of doing that, [though] I look to make people
95 laugh or smile. But the more we have parents playing video games themselves, the more they will understand the interactive world and how to deal with games that have a tremendous amount of violence.

21. This passage is best described as an interview in which the person asking the questions:
    A. concentrates mainly on Miyamoto's personal life and history.
    B. dwells on the technical demands of current video game technology and Miyamoto's role in developing this hardware.
    C. examines how videos games compare to other popular media, such as music and film.
    D. focuses on Miyamoto's video game design philosophy and development process.

22. Miyamoto most likely draws a connection between his games and the Rubik's Cube in lines 15-21 to:
    F. reiterate his early desire to design a popular toy like those he was smitten with as a young boy.
    G. support his belief that games should be designed to appeal to a player's reason, not his/her emotion.
    H. convey his desire to create games that are readily accessible to all but which also offer an elegant yet pleasurable challenge.
    J. offer an example of the kind of source material that provides plot and character ideas for a new game.

23. When Miyamoto suggests that games "aren't just about recreation and getting to the next stage" (lines 32-33), he is likely describing:
    A. his belief that video games are underappreciated works of creativity that should not be seen as mere entertainment but as serious works of art.
    B. his belief that video games can provoke and satisfy emotions like happiness and sadness, not just a desire to win or conquer.
    C. the pressure he feels to create new games that conform to what is currently popular, such as shooters and other violent games.
    D. the philosophy he has maintained throughout his design career: design games that are simple and fun for all people.

24. Miyamoto notes all of the following as sources of ideas for his video games EXCEPT:
    F. the way movie scenes are filmed and directed in order to create a mood
    G. personal experiences from childhood that left a distinct impression or convey emotion.
    H. everyday anecdotes and overheard sayings.
    J. the violent video games many parents who grew up on video games now play.

25. In the context of the interview as a whole, Miyamoto's use of the phrase "passive entertainment" (line 69) most likely refers to:
    A. media experiences that lack emotional attachment or interactivity.
    B. those video games where you cannot create your own characters.
    C. movies and other media forms that compete with video games.
    D. his goal of creating games that revel in simple pleasures.

26. Miyamoto's likely intent in referring to the Japanese concept of *itoshii* is to:
    F. critique the established belief that video games should be designed solely for the purposes of winning.
    G. connect the importance of his childhood memories to the kinds of game experiences he seeks to create.
    H. express his belief that the true mark of a great game is not great graphics but the game's ability to leave a lasting impression on the player.
    J. make clear that few, if any, games make a real emotional connection with the player.

27. It can reasonably be inferred from the passage that Miyamoto's view on the role and value of video games has:
    A. not changed, for he still maintains the same objective he held early in his career, to surprise the player.
    B. diminished, as the emphasis on realism, violence, and success has demeaned a medium he once perceived to be an art form.
    C. grown more complex, in that he seeks to craft games that engage and affect gamers' feelings.
    D. simplified, in that he now firmly believes games should be made so that no player feels frustrated or tested.

28. According to the passage, Miyamoto hopes in the near-future to:
    F. make a toy as well-regarded as the Rubik's cube.
    G. find new and exciting ways beyond conventional television screens to present and display video games.
    H. collaborate with filmmakers to make the movie-going experience more interactive.
    J. explore how his personal interests and hobbies might make for exciting new game experiences.

29. Based on his response in the passage, Miyamoto's views on violent video games can most accurately be characterized as:
    A. critical: Miyamoto believes video games should delight and uplift, not encourage hostility.
    B. enthusiastic: he appreciates the goal his and other violent video games share in their desire to surprise gamers.
    C. envious: Miyamoto has long sought to make realistic games based on contemporary issues.
    D. ambivalent: he doesn't oppose their popularity, but feels their negative effects must be dealt with or mitigated.

30. In the passage, Miyamoto makes the statement "the game begins the moment a person touches a console, everything builds from that" (lines 39-41) primarily suggest that:
    F. video games have to tantalize and excite from the very outset in order to sustain the interest of the gamer.
    G. game designers should consider the emotional excitement of the gaming experience when creating their vision.
    H. merely turning on a video game console is a more interactive experience than, say, a movie.
    J. real challenge of designing a game is just getting players to turn it on in the first place.

NO TEST MATERIAL ON THIS PAGE.

GO ON TO THE NEXT PAGE.

Passage IV

NATURAL SCIENCE: This passage is adapted from "The Running Man, Revisited" by Mayawa Montenegro, which appeared in *Seed Magazine* (© 2009 Seed Media Group LLC).

Proponents of the endurance running hypothesis (ER) believe that being able to run for extended lengths of time is an adapted trait, most likely for obtaining food, and was the catalyst that forced *Homo erectus* to evolve from its apelike ancestors. Over time, the survival of the swift-footed shaped the anatomy of modern humans, giving us a body suggestive of a marathoning past.

Our toes, for instance, are shorter and stubbier than those of nearly all other primates, including chimpanzees, a trait that has long been attributed to our committed bipedalism. But a study by anthropologists Daniel Lieberman and Campbell Rolian provides evidence that short toes make human feet exquisitely suited to substantial amounts of running. In tests where 15 subjects ran and walked on pressure-sensitive treadmills, Lieberman and Rolian found that toe length had no effect on walking. Yet when the subjects were running, an increase in toe length of just 20 percent doubled the amount of mechanical work, meaning that the longer-toed subjects required more metabolic energy, and each footfall produced more shock.

Over the years, Lieberman's team at Harvard has amassed a small ream of anatomical evidence that they believe points to a distance-running legacy. In 2004 the groups co-published a list of 26 such markers on the human body, including short toes, a hefty *gluteus maximus*, springy tendon-loaded legs, and the little-known *nuchal ligament* that stabilizes the head when it's in rapid motion.

We know that roughly 2 million years ago, *Australopithecus*, with its tiny brain, hefty jaw and diet of rough, fibrous plants, evolved into *Homo erectus*, our slim, long-legged ancestor with a big brain and small teeth suited for tearing into animal and fruit flesh. Such a transformation almost certainly involved a reliable supply of calorie-laden meat, yet according to the fossil record, spear points have been in use for 200,000 years at most, and the bow and arrow for only 50,000 years, leaving an enormous stretch of time when early humans were consuming meat without the use of tools. Lieberman believes they ran their prey to death, often called "persistence hunting."

So how long would it take to actually run an animal to death? Drawing on Harvard's extant cache of locomotion data, Lieberman began crunching numbers comparing speed, body temperature, and body weight humans and various conceivable prey. A deer and a decently fit man, Lieberman discovered, trot at almost identical pace, but in order to accelerate, a deer goes anaerobic, while the man remains in an oxygenated jogging zone. The same is true for horses, antelopes, a slew of other four-legged creatures. Since animals run anaerobically only in short bursts before they must slow down to recover, a human in pursuit may have final advantage. And because quadrupeds can't pant while they run, they also quickly overheat. To run do dinner, Lieberman realized, might simply have been matter of spurring the poor beast into a sprint enough times to make it collapse from hyperthermia.

But plenty of skeptics remain. University of Wisconsin paleoanthropologist John Hawks, who ha researched the acceleration of human evolution since advent of agriculture, questions how a trait that is supposedly specific to endurance running could pers today, when tools and farming have long since repla the old selective pressures of hunting. "If these featu really were distinctive to long-distance running, shouldn't they have disappeared?" he asks. Hawks a thinks that Lieberman and Rolian's short-toe finding essentially more evidence that humans are optimally designed for walking.

Still, persistence hunting can be found in cultures over the globe: The Kalahari Bushmen of Botswana Aborigines of Australia, and the Masai of Kenya are a few examples of tribes. Hawks would argue this is sophisticated cultural adaptation, but it could also m that we have a common, fleet-footed ancestor.

31. According to the passage, the main argument a the endurance running hypothesis is that:
    A. The development of farming made an endura running gene irrelevant; it would have been out thousands of years ago.
    B. *Homo erectus* and other early hominids bea little physical or genetic resemblance to mo humans.
    C. Persistence hunting is still a prevalent featu many contemporary nomadic, tribal societie
    D. Increased toe length over millennia present clear evidence that man is optimally design for walking, not running.

32. Adapted (line 3) most nearly means:
    F. changed
    G. inherited
    H. flexible
    J. artificial

33. Which of the following statements best summarizes the theory presented by Lieberman in the passage?
    A. How early man was able to hunt animals for hundreds of thousands of years without weapons remains beyond the knowledge of contemporary scientists.
    B. The evolution of man as a natural runner was largely a result of environment, not genetics.
    C. Bipedal creatures have a number of evolutionary advantages over animals.
    D. The survival of early humans who used endurance running to hunt for food greatly influenced modern humans.

34. The author includes paragraph four (lines 32-44) to:
    F. explain in detail how "persistence hunting" works.
    G. explain the evidence against Lieberman's research.
    H. provide a historical context that lends credibility to the endurance running hypothesis.
    J. provide a brief overview of the history of human evolution.

35. According to the passage, early humans were able to successfully persistence hunt primarily because:
    A. they were able to move faster than their prey, thereby allowing them to outrun the animal.
    B. they were able to maintain an consistent pace, while their prey could not run great distances without slowing down or suffering ill health.
    C. their short toes allowed them to run very fast with little effort.
    D. they carried over many of the strategic traits of their apelike ancestors.

36. The findings reported in the passage challenge commonly held notions of evolution by suggesting that:
    F. endurance may be a more highly prized evolutionary trait than speed.
    G. our hominid ancestors bore very little physical or genetic resemblance to our present state.
    H. the evolution of walking was unquestionably fundamental to becoming human.
    J. farming and tool invention made humans a sedentary, lazy species.

37. Which of the following is NOT evidence cited by the passage to support the endurance running hypothesis?
    A. The continued use of persistence hunting in present day societies.
    B. The dozens of unique features on the human body that lend themselves naturally to running.
    C. The longer-sized toes of the earliest hominids.
    D. The lengthy history of human meat consumption prior to the invention of hunting tools.

38. It can be reasonably inferred from the passage that the scientific community would most likely react to the hypothesis presented in the passage with:
    F. unbridled enthusiasm, as a "missing link" to understanding early man.
    G. severe skepticism, given the credibility of long held beliefs on human evolution.
    H. some concern, as Lieberman has collected little scientific evidence to support his theory.
    J. intrigue, though with a desire for additional research on the subject before accepting the theory.

39. The tone of the passage is:
    A. excited
    B. biased
    C. skeptical
    D. objective

40. With which of the following details, if added to the passage, would scientists supportive of the endurance running hypothesis most likely agree?
    F. If lined up to race, humans would outrun most animals in a short sprint.
    G. Controlling body heat is of little importance to fast animals because they quickly catch their prey or escape from a predator.
    H. Sweat glands were a key evolutionary advantage for early humans, as they allowed humans to shed heat quickly when chasing animals.
    J. The development of muscles like tendons and the *gluteus maximus* was necessary to stand up and forage for fruits and vegetables.

END OF TEST

STOP! DO NOT TURN THE PAGE UNTIL TOLD TO DO SO.

DO NOT RETURN TO A PREVIOUS TEST.

SCIENCE TEST
35 Minutes – 40 Questions

DIRECTIONS: There are seven passages in this test. Each passage is followed by several questions. After reading a passage, choose the best answer to each question and fill in the corresponding oval on your answer document. You may refer to the passages as often as necessary.

You are NOT permitted to use a calculator on this test.

Passage I

Radium-226 (^{226}Ra) activity is often elevated in bodies of water that have been augmented with ground water. Samples were collected over a two-year period in order to study ^{226}Ra activity in Florida Marsh and Cypress wetlands. Figure 1 shows the average ^{226}Ra activity from surface sediment samples collected in 2002 and 2004. Cores were taken from shallow sediment (0 to 4cm) in the wetlands and analyzed for ^{226}Ra activity. The activity, in disintegration per minute per gram (dpm/g), found in the Marsh and Cypress wetlands is displayed in Figures 2 and 3.

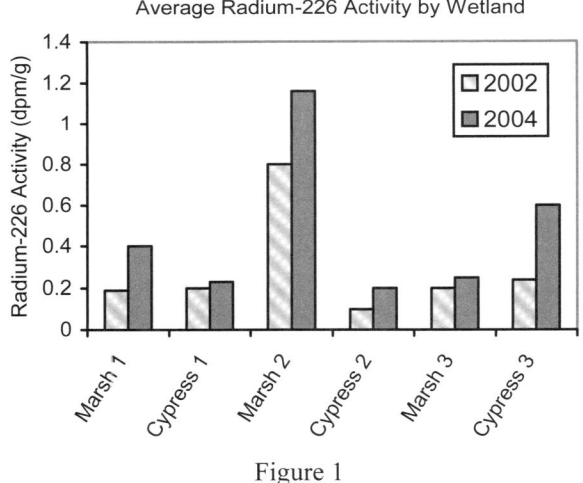

Figure 1

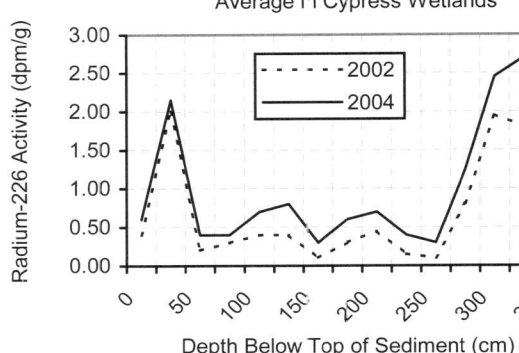

Figure 2

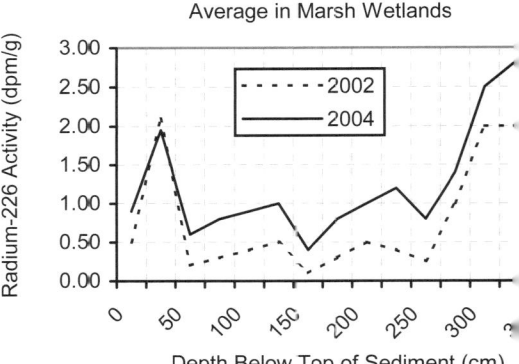

Figure 3

GO ON TO THE NEXT PAGE.

1. According to Figure 2, the average radium-226 activity in Cypress wetlands in 2004 at a depth of 200cm was closest to which of the following?
   A. 0.30 dpm/g
   B. 0.70 dpm/g
   C. 1.00 dpm/g
   D. 2.50 dpm/g

2. Based on the information in Figure 3, if the average radium-226 activity had been measured in Marsh wetlands at the depth of 400 cm in 2002, it most likely would have been closest to which of the following?
   F. 2.75 dpm/g
   G. 2.50 dpm/g
   H. 2.00 dpm/g
   J. 1.80 dpm/g

3. Which of the following is the most likely explanation for the difference in the average ^{226}Ra activity between 2002 and 2004?
   A. In 2004 the wetlands were augmented with ground water, which caused an increase in ^{226}Ra activity.
   B. In 2002 the wetlands were augmented with ground water, and in 2004 they were not. This resulted in more ^{226}Ra activity in 2004.
   C. The amount of ground water the wetlands were augmented with was higher in 2002 than in 2004.
   D. In 2004 there was more rainfall than in 2002, which created a decrease in ^{226}Ra activity.

4. If the data in Figures 2 and 3 are typical of Cypress and Marsh wetlands, one would most likely make which of the following conclusions about the ^{226}Ra activity in a wetland?
   F. ^{226}Ra activity is highest in wetlands in the top 50 cm of the sediment layer.
   G. ^{226}Ra activity gets higher as the sediment gets deeper.
   H. ^{226}Ra activity is highest in wetlands at around 325cm below the top of the sediment.
   J. Each year, the ^{226}Ra activity in wetlands will become less.

5. According to Figures 2 and 3, the ^{226}Ra activity increased between the depths of 200 and 250cm for which wetlands?
   A. Cypress wetlands in 2002.
   B. Cypress wetlands in 2004.
   C. Marsh wetlands in 2002.
   D. Marsh wetlands in 2004.

Passage II

The decomposition-extraction method for replacing an acidic anion in salt with bicarbonate ion HCO_3 is a process with the mass transfer and reaction among gas-liquid-liquid-solid phases. The profile of the concentration of the decomposition-extraction process is shown in Figure 1.

Figure 1

Experiment 1

Scientists studied the reaction of aqueous solution of sodium formate reacted with carbon dioxide in the presence of extractant tertiary amine; the acidic anion HCOO in sodium formate was replaced by HCO_3 to form sodium bicarbonate. Produced HCl was extracted by tertiary amine into the organic phase.

$$HCOONa(w) + CO_2(g) + H_2O(w) + NR_3(o) = NaHCO_3(s, w) + HCOOHNR_3(o)$$

Carbon dioxide can be absorbed into the liquid phase in three ways: (1) carbon dioxide was absorbed by the organic phase; (2) carbon dioxide was absorbed by the aqueous phase; and (3) carbon dioxide was absorbed by both the organic and aqueous phases. The CO_2 absorption rate by the aqueous and organic phases was measured individually at the same experimental conditions such as temperature, pressure, agitation speed, and liquid volume. The results are shown in Figure 2.

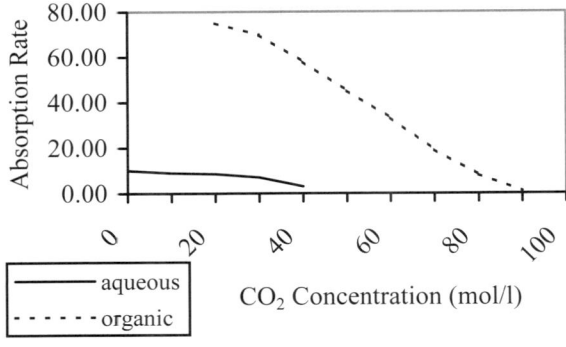

Figure 2

Experiment 2

To test the mass transfer rate of carbon dioxide from gas phase to the aqueous phase through the organic phase, following experiment was conducted. 280 mL of sodium formate solution (400 g/L) and 20 mL of organic phase was added into an agitating cell. The organic phase existed on top layer. Liquid was agitated gently. Carbon dioxide, the gas phase, to react with sodium formate in aqueous phase, would have to pass through the organic phase.

Experiment 3

To determine the mass transfer rate of carbon dioxide transferred from the gas phase into the aqueous phase directly the following experiment was conducted. 200 mL sodium formate solution (400 g/L) was placed into agitating cell and the liquid was agitated gently.

Experiments 2 & 3 were conducted under the experimental conditions. Figure 3 displays the results.

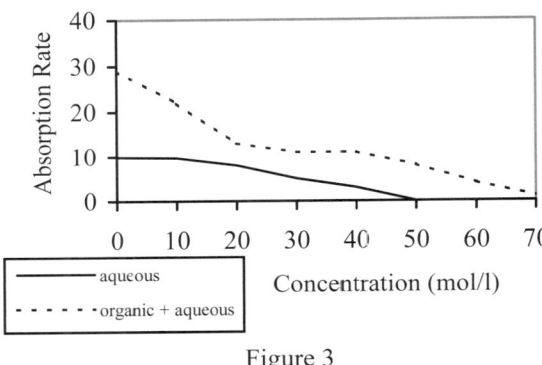

Figure 3

6. According to Figure 2, the absorption rate of carbon dioxide at a concentration of 30 mol/l in the aqueous phase was closest to which of the following?
   F. 0
   G. 5
   H. 10
   J. 70

7. Based on Figure 2, if the absorption rate of carbon dioxide had been measured in the organic phase at concentration of 20 mol/l, it would most likely been closest to which of the following?
   A. 0
   B. 10
   C. 15
   D. 80

8. Based on the information in Figure 3, which of the following is the most accurate comparison of the mass transfer of carbon dioxide in the aqueous phase versus the organic plus aqueous phase?
   F. At all levels of CO_2 concentration, the absorption rate is highest in the organic + aqueous phase.
   G. At lower levels of CO_2 concentration, the absorption rate is higher in the aqueous phase.
   H. At all levels of CO_2 concentration, the absorption rate is higher in the aqueous phase.
   J. At higher levels of CO_2 concentration, the absorption rate is lower in the organic + aqueous phase.

9. If Figures 2 and 3 show typical results for absorption rates in various phases during a decomposition-extraction process, one would most likely make which of the following conclusions about the organic phase?
   A. The organic phase is not necessary because it has the lowest capacity for absorption.
   B. The organic phase is only useful when combined with the aqueous phase.
   C. The organic phase is only beneficial at high levels of CO_2 concentration.
   D. The organic phase is crucial because it has the highest capacity for absorption.

10. According to Figure 1, during the decomposition-extraction process, the concentration of $NaHCO_3$ was highest during which phase?
    F. Gas
    G. Organic
    H. Solid
    J. Aqueous

11. All of the following statements are true about the relationship between the mass transfer of carbon dioxide and the absorption rate of the aqueous and organic + aqueous phases EXCEPT:
    A. The aqueous phase displays a lower rate of absorption.
    B. The absorption rate for organic + aqueous phase is higher than the aqueous phase.
    C. The aqueous phase exceeds a concentration of 60 mol/l.
    D. The organic + aqueous phase absorption rate declines as concentration in mol/l increases.

Passage III

Air permeability is defined as the ability of soil to transmit air through interconnected air-filled pores under an imposed air pressure gradient. Air permeability is a function of volumetric water content, porosity, pore size distribution, and pore geometry. Scientists used a soil corer air permeameter (SCAP) to digitally measure the *flow rates* of air through desert soil under low-pressure gradients. The SCAP measured air permeability both *in situ*, with the instrument inserted in the soil and *ex situ*, after the soil corer had been removed from the soil. Figures 1 and 2 display the results of field-testing conducted at two of the four sites in Arizona, over the course of three months. The porosity of the soil at each site is displayed in Figure 3. Figure 4 shows the relationship between the air pressure used and the flowrate of the air for each site.

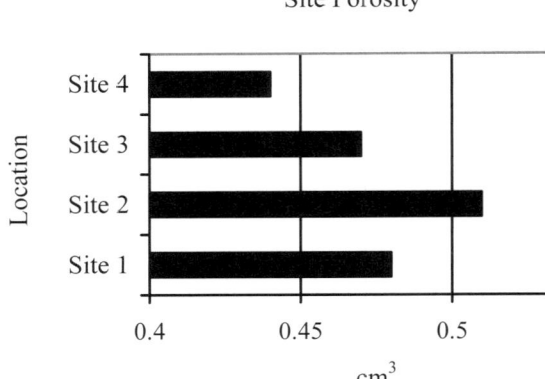

Figure 3

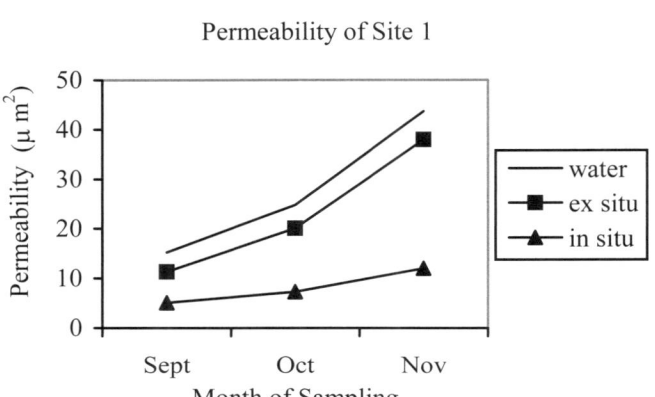

Figure 1

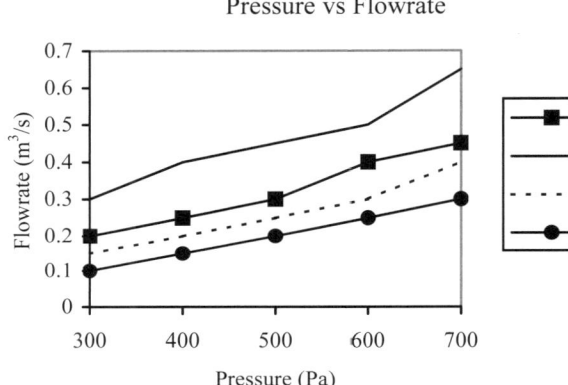

Figure 4

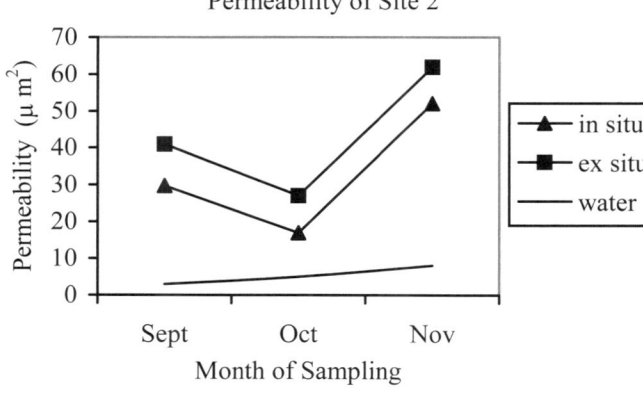

Figure 2

12. According to Figure 2, the air permeability measured in October was closest to which of the following?
   F. 5 µm²
   G. 15 µm²
   H. 20 µm²
   J. 30 µm²

13. Based on Figure 4, if the air permeability had been site 1 using 800 Pa, the flowrate would most likely been closest to which of the following?
   A. 0.5 m³/s
   B. 0.6 m³/s
   C. 0.4 m³/s
   D. 0.3 m³/s

14. Which of the following is the most likely explanation for the difference in air permeability at site 1 versus site 2?
    F. The overall air permeability is higher at site 1 due to the lower porosity of the soil.
    G. The overall air permeability is higher at site 2 due to the higher porosity of the soil.
    H. The overall air permeability at site 2 is higher because less pressure was used when testing the soil.
    J. The overall air permeability at site 2 is higher because more pressure was used when testing the soil.

15. If the data in Figures 1 and 2 is typical of air permeability measurements, one would most likely make which of the following conclusions about air permeability in situ versus ex situ?
    A. The permeability will always be higher ex situ than in situ.
    B. The permeability will always be lower ex situ than in situ.
    C. Water permeability is higher than air permeability in situ and ex situ.
    D. At high pressures, air permeability is greater in situ than ex situ.

16. According to Figure 1, which of the following statements is most accurate regarding permeability during the month of November?
    F. Permeability was lower than in previous months.
    G. Permeability was highest for air measured while the SCAP was still inserted in the ground.
    H. Permeability was highest for air measured after the SCAP had removed a core from the soil.
    J. Permeability was highest for water.

TEST 5 **GO ON TO THE NEXT PAGE.** 533

Passage IV

Scientists studying sucrose examined oranges and lemons to determine how the two fruits form and synthesize sucrose. Studies were conducted both on extractions from the fruits, and on small, intact fruits.

Study 1

Mature lemon and orange fruits were obtained and then juiced by hand. Formation of fructose was determined using two portions of the fruits: the juice, and the particulate sediment. The results are shown in Table 1.

Table 1 Formation of Sucrose by Fructose Reaction	
Preparation	Sucrose Synthesized (μmoles)
Oranges	
Juice	0.12
Particulate sediment	0.9
Lemons	
Juice	0.4
Particulate sediment	0.17

Study 2

Scientists found lemons of varying ages from the same fruit grove. Each piece of fruit was cut into sections, and various tissue samples were isolated for testing. The three tissue types tested were the *flavedo* (colored, outer layer of the peel), the *albedo* (white peel layer), and the *vesicle* (fleshy part of the fruit). The results of the formation of sucrose in lemons are shown in Figure 1.

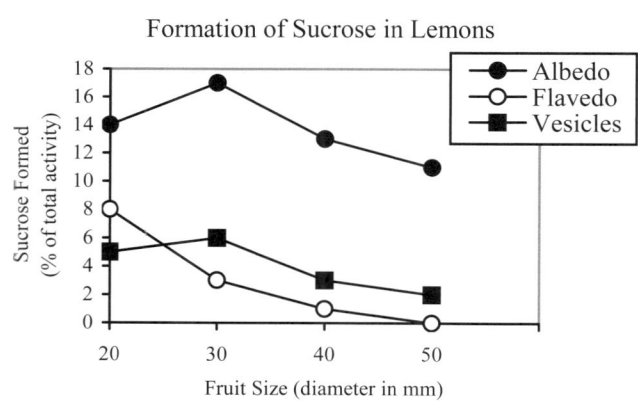

Figure 1

Study 3

Whole fruits (each weighing approximately 5g) were tested and then cut into sections to measure sucrose activity in the various tissues. Figure 2 displays the results.

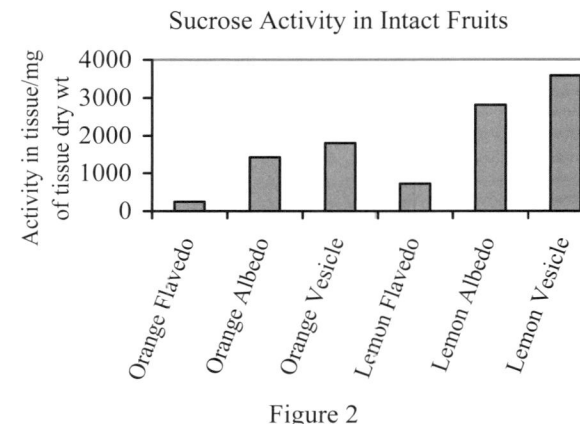

Figure 2

17. Based on Figure 1, which type of lemon tissue forms most sucrose?
 A. The albedo tissue in a large lemon.
 B. The albedo tissue in a small lemon.
 C. The flavedo tissue in a large lemon.
 D. The vesicles in a small lemon.

18. According to the results of Study 2, as fruit increased, the sucrose found in the vesicles:
 F. increased only.
 G. increased, then decreased.
 H. decreased only.
 J. decreased, then increased.

19. Based on the results of Study 3, the largest difference in sucrose activity was found in:
 A. oranges; between the flavedo tissue and the albedo tissue.
 B. oranges; between the albedo tissue and the vesicle tissue.
 C. lemons; between the flavedo tissue and the vesicle tissue.
 D. lemons; between the flavedo tissue and the albedo tissue.

20. Based on the results of Study 1, which of the following is most accurate about the formation of sucrose?
    F. Orange juice is more effective at forming sucrose than lemon juice.
    G. Orange juice is less effective at forming sucrose than lemon juice.
    H. Lemon juice and orange juice are equally effective at forming sucrose.
    J. Orange particulate sediment forms more sucrose than lemon particulate sediment.

21. Assume Study 2 was repeated using oranges instead of lemons. Based on the information presented in Figures 1 and 2, and assuming that the fruits used in Study 3 were 30mm in diameter, which of the following would most likely be the sucrose formation (as a % of total activity) in the albedo tissue of the oranges?
    A. 0
    B. 3
    C. 9
    D. 20

22. Based on the results of Study 2, which statement most accurately summarizes the formation of sucrose in lemons?
    F. The fleshy part of the lemon formed the majority of the sucrose.
    G. The colored outer layer of the peel does not form any sucrose.
    H. The part of the lemon that forms the most sucrose is dependent on the size of the lemon.
    J. More sucrose is formed in the white peel layer of a lemon than anywhere else.

Passage V

Students studying Newton's laws of motion conducted experiments to measure the change in velocities when two objects interact.

Experiment 1

Students put two identical air track gliders on an air track. (See Figure 1). The gliders were held together, with springs in contact and compressed, by a loop of thread. The thread was burned and the gliders pushed apart, according to Newton's third law of motion. As the gliders were separating, the students recorded data for each glider's position as a function of time. Using this information the students were able to calculate each glider's velocity. Table 1 lists the positions of representative points, one point on each glider, as the position of the glider changes with time.

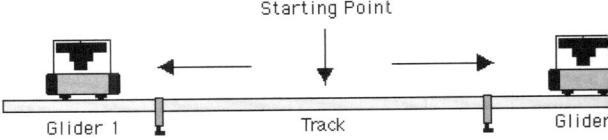

Figure 1

Figure 2 shows the ratio of velocity plotted versus ratio of the number of gliders. Figure 3 displays the distance each glider traveled, for both experiments.

Table 1		
	Glider A	Glider B
Time (s)	Position (m)	Position (m)
0	0.6882	0.6412
0.2	0.6882	0.6423
0.4	0.6974	0.6354
0.6	0.7134	0.6171
0.8	0.7295	0.6033
1	0.7478	0.5874

Experiment 2

Experiment 1 was repeated, but modified to test the effect of multiple gliders interacting with a single glider. On one side of the track was a single glider (glider A) and on the other side was a pair of gliders held together with a paper clip (glider B). Then the procedure was repeated using 3 gliders on one side. Table 2 displays the data gathered.

Table 2				
	2 Gliders		3 Gliders	
	Glider A	Glider B	Glider A	Glider B
Time (s)	Position (m)	Position (m)	Position (m)	Position (m)
0	0.5418	0.5871	0.4181	0.4571
0.2	0.5304	0.5916	0.4051	0.4636
0.4	0.5123	0.5984	0.3835	0.4680
0.6	0.4919	0.6120	0.3618	0.4766
0.8	0.4715	0.6256	0.3401	0.4853
1	0.4534	0.6302	0.3141	0.4940

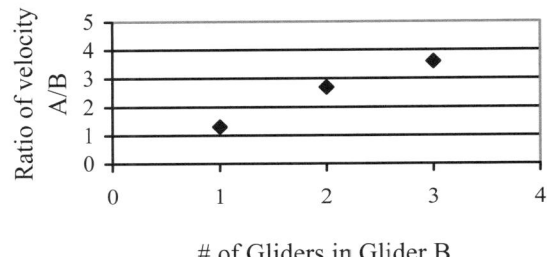

Figure 2

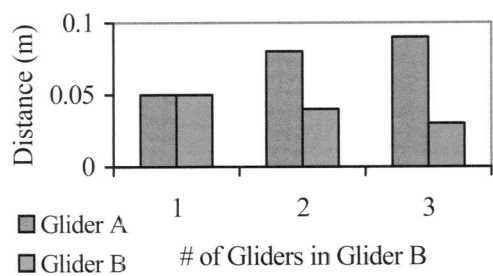

Figure 3

23. Suppose an air track was set up with glider A consisting of 1 glider and glider B consisting of 4 gliders (attached to each other). Based on Figure 2, the ratio of velocity for glider A to glider B would be closest to what number?
    A. 1
    B. 3
    C. 4
    D. 5

24. During Experiment 1, while the gliders were in motion, how frequently did the students record the position of the gliders?
    F. Three times per second
    G. Four times per second
    H. Five times per second
    J. Six times per second

25. Based on Figure 3, as the number of gliders in glider B increased, how did the distance traveled by glider A and B vary?
	A	B
A.	increased	increased
B.	increased	decreased
C.	decreased	increased
D.	decreased	decreased

26. Based on Table 2, when glider B consisted of 3 gliders, how far did glider B travel after 0.4 s?
    F. 0.0109 m
    G. 0.0113 m
    H. 0.4853 m
    J. 0.3835 m

27. According to the information presented in Figure 1 and Tables 1 and 2, gliders A and B were approximately what distance from one another before the loop of thread was burned?
    A. 0.04 m
    B. 0.40 m
    C. 0 m
    D. It cannot be determined.

Passage VI

The eukaryotic cell cycle consists of 4 major phases (see Figure 1). The S phase is when DNA synthesis occurs to replicate the chromosomes. The period between S phase and the beginning of mitosis is a growth period, called the G2 phase. Another growth period, called the G1 phase, happens between mitosis and the S phase, to complete the cycle.

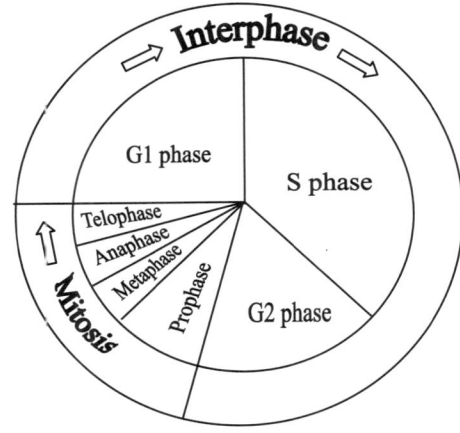

Figure 1

Study 1

Scientists studying eukaryotic cell cycles conducted experiments using a bacterium named Caulobacter crescentus, or C.crescentus. It was hypothesized that the C.crescentus clpP and clpX genes were essential for growth and a series of experiments were conducted. Biomass accumulations (monitored as optical density at 660 nm) and viable cell counts (measured as colony forming units per ml) were determined. The results are shown in Figures 2 and 3.

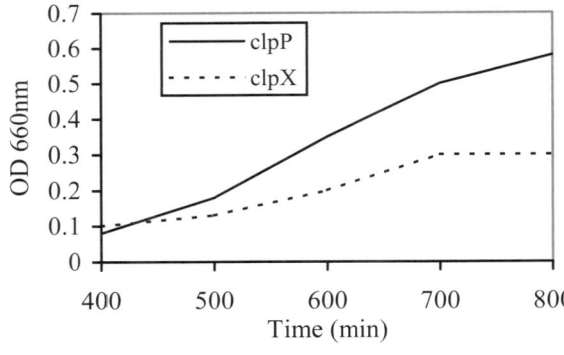

Figure 2

Figure 3

Study 2

Scientists studied the affect removing genes had o chromosome replication process. G1 cells contai chromosome, G2 cells contain 2 chromosomes, and act replicating S phase cells contain between 1 ar chromosomes. Figure 4 shows the control sample, and chromosome replication is affected by deleting eithe clpP or clpX gene from the culture.

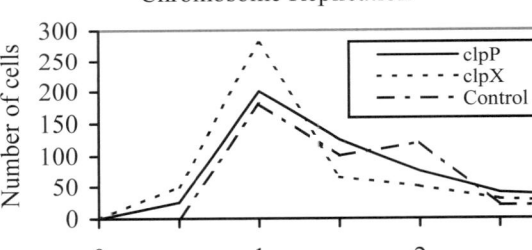

Figure 4

28. According to the results of Study 1, as the time incr from 500 to 700 minutes, the number of viable ce the clpP gene:
F. increased only.
G. increased, then decreased.
H. decreased only.
J. decreased, then increased.

29. Based on the results of Study 1, the bi accumulation for the clpX gene increased most r over which of the following time ranges?
A. 400 to 500 minutes.
B. 500 to 550 minutes.
C. 600 to 700 minutes.
D. 700 to 800 minutes.

30. According to Figure 1, which of the following phases of the eukaryotic cell cycle occurs during mitosis?
    F. G1 phase
    G. G2 phase
    H. S phase
    J. Metaphase

31. Suppose that during Study 1, the scientists had continued recording the biomass accumulation of the samples for a longer period of time. Based on the results, it is most reasonable to expect that the biomass accumulation for the clpP gene would be closest to which of the following after 1000 minutes?
    A. 0.8
    B. 0.25
    C. 0
    D. 6

32. According to the results of Study 2, which of the samples studied contained the most G1 cells?
    F. clpP.
    G. clpX.
    H. The control sample.
    J. It cannot be determined.

33. Assume that for optimal chromosome replication, it is important for the culture to have roughly the same number of cells with 1 chromosome per cell as with 2 chromosomes per cell. Based on the results of Study 2, it can most reasonably be concluded that which culture is the best for chromosome replication?
    A. The culture with either the clpP or clpX gene.
    B. The culture with the clpP gene.
    C. The culture with the clpX gene.
    D. The control sample.

TEST 5   GO ON TO THE NEXT PAGE.

Passage VII

Three substances have been shown to inhibit respiration in various organisms: hydrocyanic acid, hydrogen sulfite, and carbon monoxide. An experiment was conducted to determine the effect that each of these substances has on the respiration of the green alga *Chlorella*. Figure 1 shows the results.

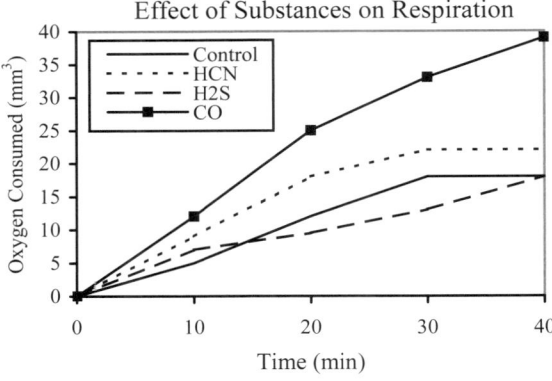

Figure 1

Researcher 1 argued that glucose would have a contradictory effect on the alga, so that if the *Chlorella* were suspended in a solution containing 1 percent glucose, there would be less of an effect on respiration. Figure 2 displays the results of the experiment.

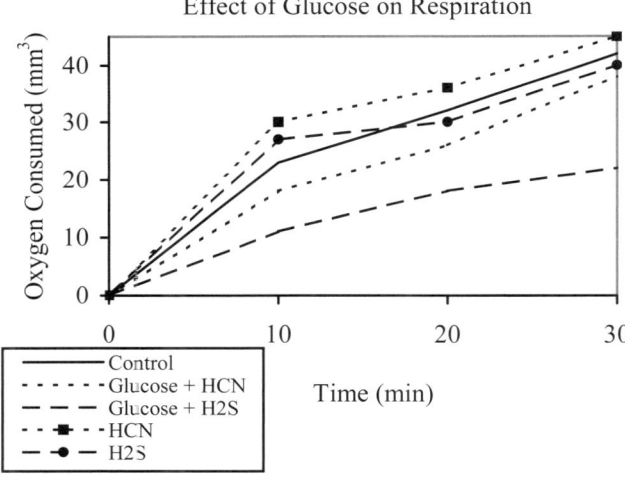

Figure 2

Researcher 2 hypothesized that light may play an active part in respiration of *Chlorella*, so an experiment was done to measure the effect of successive periods of light and darkness on the respiration of cells suspended in carbon monoxide and in nitrogen. The results are shown in Figure 3.

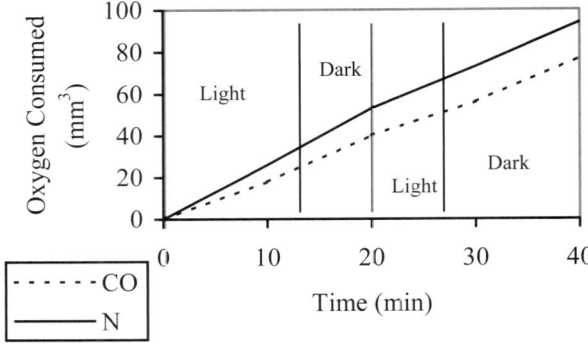

Figure 3

34. The theories of the two researchers are similar in both researchers believe:
    F. that glucose will increase the respiration of *Chlorella*.
    G. that HCN and H2S have no effect on the respir of *Chlorella*.
    H. that an additional factor will have an effect on t respiration of *Chlorella*.
    J. that CO and N also effect the respiratio *Chlorella*.

35. According to Figure 1, *Chlorella* would typi consume about how much oxygen after half an hour
    A. 10 mm^3
    B. 18 mm^3
    C. 22 mm^3
    D. 35 mm^3

36. If Researcher 1 was correct about the effect of gl on the respiration of *Chlorella*, then based o information in Figure 2, Researcher 1 would most predict that *Chlorella* suspended in a solution conta 2 percent glucose and HCN would consume how oxygen after 20 minutes?
    F. 15 mm^3
    G. 25 mm^3
    H. 30 mm^3
    J. 40 mm^3

37. Does the data in Figure 3 support Researcher 2's hypothesis?
    A. Yes; it shows that light is necessary for the respiration of *Chlorella*.
    B. Yes, it shows that equal respiration occurs in the darkness and in light.
    C. No; more respiration of *Chlorella* occurred in the darkness.
    D. No; varying the amount of light did not yield significantly different rates of respiration.

38. Suppose a third researcher studied the effect of glucose and CO on the respiration of *Chlorella*, using the same conditions and methods as Researcher 1. After 20 minutes the results showed that the sample suspended in CO had consumed 50 mm^3 of oxygen, while the sample suspended in a mixture of CO and glucose had consumed 60 mm^3 of oxygen. How would this experiment most likely affect the researchers' viewpoints?
    F. It would weaken Researcher 2's viewpoint only.
    G. It would weaken Researcher 1's viewpoint only.
    H. It would strengthen both researchers viewpoints.
    J. It would have no effect on either researcher's viewpoint.

39. According to Figure 2, which substance had the least effect on respiration of *Chlorella* after 30 minutes?
    A. HCN
    B. H2S
    C. Glucose + HCN
    D. Glucose + H2S

40. According to Researcher 2, experiment findings indicate the following is FALSE regarding the relationship between cells suspended in carbon monoxide and cells suspended in nitrogen EXCEPT:
    F. Cells suspended in carbon monoxide consume more oxygen.
    G. Cells suspended in nitrogen consume less oxygen.
    H. Cells suspended in carbon monoxide and nitrogen consume the same amount of oxygen.
    J. Cells suspended in nitrogen consume more oxygen.

END OF TEST
STOP! DO NOT RETURN TO ANY OTHER TEST.

ACT SUCCESS

WRITING TEST 5 – Prompt

DIRECTIONS:

This is a test of your writing skills. You will have thirty (30) minutes to write an essay in English. Before you begin planning and writing your essay, read the writing prompt below carefully to understand exactly what you are being asked to do. Your essay will be evaluated on the evidence it provides of your ability to express judgments by taking a position on the issue in the writing prompt; to main a focus on the topic throughout the essay; to develop a position by using logical reasoning and by supporting your ideas; to organize ideas in a logical way; and to use language clearly and effectively according to the conventions of standard written English.

Some college admissions offices no longer require students to take standardized tests like the ACT. These colleges believe that standardized tests do not accurately or effectively measure a student's ability to succeed in college. Other colleges maintain that standardized tests are necessary, as they provide the only realistic way to directly compare students who attended different high schools. In your opinion, should colleges consider standardized test scores when reviewing students' applications for admission?

In your essay, take a position on this question. You may write about either one of the two points of view given, or you may present a different point of view on this question. Use specific reasons and examples to support your position.

Use this page to *plan* your essay.

Begin WRITING TEST 5 here.

WRITING TEST 5

WRITING TEST 5

STOP here with the Writing Test.

Scale Scores for Practice Test 5

* These scores are based on student trials rather than national norms.

English _____
Math   _____
Reading _____
Science _____

=Total   _____

Composite = Total divided by 4 (round up at .5) _____

| ACT Score* | Number Right | | | | ACT Score* |
	English	Math	Reading	Science	
36	75	60	40	40	36
35	73-74	59	39	--	35
34	72	58	38	39	34
33	71	57	37	--	33
32	70	56	36	38	32
31	69	54-55	34-35	--	31
30	68	53	33	37	30
29	67	51-52	32	36	29
28	65-66	49-50	30-31	34-35	28
27	64	46-48	29	33	27
26	62-63	44-45	28	31-32	26
25	60-61	41-43	27	30	25
24	58-59	39-40	26	28-29	24
23	55-57	37-38	24-25	27	23
22	53-54	35-36	23	25-26	22
21	50-52	33-34	22	23-24	21
20	47-49	31-32	21	21-22	20
19	44-46	28-30	19-20	19-20	19
18	42-43	25-27	18	17-18	18
17	40-41	22-24	17	15-16	17
16	37-39	19-21	16	13-14	16
15	34-36	15-17	15	12	15
14	31-33	11-14	13-14	11	14
13	29-30	09-10	12	10	13
12	27-28	07-08	10-11	09	12
11	25-26	06	08-09	08	11
10	23-24	05	07	07	10
9	21-22	04	06	06	9
8	18-20	03	05	05	8
7	15-17	--	--	04	7
6	12-14	02	04	03	6
5	09-11	--	03	02	5
4	07-08	01	02	--	4
3	05-06	--	--	01	3
2	03-04	--	01	--	2
1	00-02	00	00	00	1

Chapter 7
The 24 Hour Countdown

THE 24 HOUR COUNTDOWN – AVOIDING ANXIETY

THE NIGHT BEFORE

- Gather supplies such as ID, ACT confirmation slip, sharpened pencils, erasers, watch, and calculator. **Be sure to check the ACT web site for info on approved calculators, time keeping devices, IDs, etc**

- Check the batteries in your calculator to be sure that they are new enough that they don't run out during the test.

- If you are taking the test at a location other than your school, be sure that you know how to get there.

- Do not do a new practice test: if you are having an "off night", it may affect your confidence.

- If you feel the need to study, review rules and strategies as well as any notes you may have taken and any errors from your practice tests.

- Do not drastically alter your habits. For example, do not force yourself to go to bed at 8:30pm when you usually don't go to bed until 11pm. If you do, you will likely just lie awake, and it will cause anxiety rather than leaving you well rested.

- If you choose to go out, take responsibility for your own transportation home. If your friends want to stay our later than you do, and you are depending on one of them for a ride, it will cause unnecessary stress.

TEST DAY

- Dress comfortably.

- Eat your usual breakfast. If you are not typically a breakfast eater, just remember that you will have only one 10 minute break approximately 2 hours after the test begins.

- Leave in plenty of time to arrive at the test site early. You may run into unexpected travel delays or have to find a room in an unknown location.

- During the test, if you feel as if you have done poorly on a section, *put it behind you and move on confidently!* You composite score is determined by taking an average of all four multiple choice sections. A lower score on one section can be balanced out by higher scores on the other sections.

- **REMEMBER: Because you have prepared, you know how to take this test and can adapt to any questions asked. When you open your test booklet, it may seem as if the questions are more difficult than those you have practiced. Just start using your strategies and you will soon realize that you have all of the tools that you need to succeed on the ACT.**

CHAPTER 8
SCANTRONS
(BUBBLE SHEETS TO USE WITH PRACTICE TESTS)

ACT·PLAN·EXPLORE Diagnostic Test

Student Information

Please bubble in the appropriate box: PRE-TEST | MID-TERM | POST-TEST

LAST NAME | **FIRST NAME** | **SITE** | **CLASS** | **ZIP CODE** | **RACE/ETHNICITY**

- White, Non-Hispanic
- American Indian or Alaskan Native
- Hispanic or Latino
- Black or African American
- Asian
- Native Hawaiian or Pacific Islander
- Other

GENDER
- MALE
- FEMALE

GRADE
- 7th Grade
- 8th Grade
- 9th Grade
- 10th Grade
- 11th Grade
- 12th Grade
- Other

STUDENT ID

NCLB Administrative Use
- IEP
- LEP
- SES

TEST & FORM CODE
- ACT
- PLAN
- EXPLORE

FORM

Please Enter Your Mailing Address

Name
Address
City   State   Zip
School   Date

PLEASE USE A NO. 2 PENCIL

RIGHT ■ ● | WRONG ✗ ⊖

Using a number 2 pencil completely fill in the bubble. If you make an error, carefully erase and re-bubble your new choice. This will insure optimum scanning results.

CAUTION

THE FOLLOWING SECTION IS USED FOR OPTIONAL QUESTIONING, IT IS NOT PART OF YOUR TEST! SECTION 1 OF THE TEST BEGINS ON THE BACK OF THIS FORM.

1–102 (answer bubbles 1–5)

Copyright © 2009 Academic Educational Resources. All rights reserved.

ACT·PLAN·EXPLORE Diagnostic Test

ENGLISH
EXPLORE 1-40 • PLAN 1-50 • ACT 1-75

MATH
EXPLORE 1-30 • PLAN 1-40 • ACT 1-60

READING
EXPLORE 1-30 • PLAN 1-25 • ACT 1-40

SCIENCE
EXPLORE 1-28 • PLAN 1-30 • ACT 1-40

THE AREA BELOW IS FOR OFFICIAL USE ONLY. DO NOT MARK.

1 READER NO.

2 READER NO.

3 READER NO.

Copyright © 2009 Academic Educational Resources. All rights reserved.

ACT·PLAN·EXPLORE Diagnostic Test

Student Information

Please bubble in the appropriate box: PRE-TEST / MID-TERM / POST-TEST

LAST NAME | FIRST NAME | SITE | CLASS | ZIP CODE | RACE/ETHNICITY

RACE/ETHNICITY:
- White, Non-Hispanic
- American Indian or Alaskan Native
- Hispanic or Latino
- Black or African American
- Asian
- Native Hawaiian or Pacific Islander
- Other

GENDER
- MALE
- FEMALE

GRADE
- 7th Grade
- 8th Grade
- 9th Grade
- 10th Grade
- 11th Grade
- 12th Grade
- Other

STUDENT ID

NCLB Administrative Use
- IEP
- LEP
- SES

TEST & FORM CODE
- ACT
- PLAN
- EXPLORE

FORM

Please Enter Your Mailing Address

Name
Address
City   State   Zip
School   Date

PLEASE USE A NO. 2 PENCIL

RIGHT | WRONG

Using a number 2 pencil completely fill in the bubble. If you make an error, carefully erase and re-bubble your new choice. This will insure optimum scanning results.

CAUTION

THE FOLLOWING SECTION IS USED FOR OPTIONAL QUESTIONING, IT IS NOT PART OF YOUR TEST! SECTION 1 OF THE TEST BEGINS ON THE BACK OF THIS FORM.

Questions 1–102, each with answer choices ① ② ③ ④ ⑤

Copyright © 2009 Academic Educational Resources. All rights reserved.

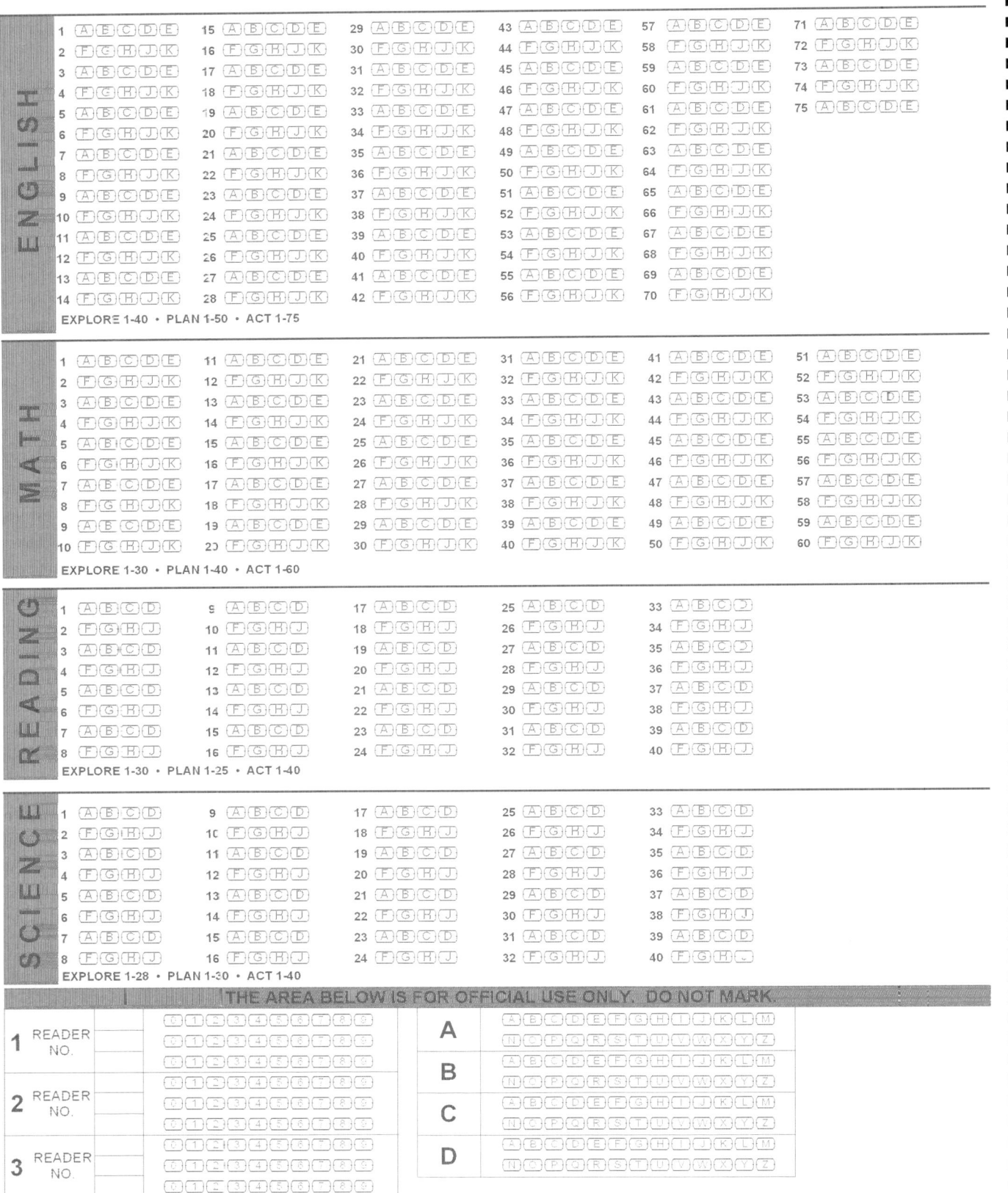

ACT·PLAN·EXPLORE Diagnostic Test

Student Information

Please bubble in the appropriate box: PRE-TEST / MID-TERM / POST-TEST

LAST NAME | FIRST NAME | SITE | CLASS | ZIP CODE | RACE/ETHNICITY

RACE/ETHNICITY
- White, Non-Hispanic
- American Indian or Alaskan Native
- Hispanic or Latino
- Black or African American
- Asian
- Native Hawaiian or Pacific Islander
- Other

GENDER
- MALE
- FEMALE

GRADE
- 7th Grade
- 8th Grade
- 9th Grade
- 10th Grade
- 11th Grade
- 12th Grade
- Other

STUDENT ID

NCLB Administrative Use
- IEP
- LEP
- SES

TEST & FORM CODE
- ACT
- PLAN
- EXPLORE

FORM

Please Enter Your Mailing Address

Name
Address
City   State   Zip
School   Date

PLEASE USE A NO. 2 PENCIL

RIGHT ■ ● | WRONG ⊠ ⊟

Using a number 2 pencil completely fill in the bubble. If you make an error, carefully erase and re-bubble your new choice. This will insure optimum scanning results.

CAUTION

THE FOLLOWING SECTION IS USED FOR OPTIONAL QUESTIONING, IT IS NOT PART OF YOUR TEST! SECTION 1 OF THE TEST BEGINS ON THE BACK OF THIS FORM.

1–102 answer bubbles (1 2 3 4 5)

Copyright © 2009 Academic Educational Resources. All rights reserved.

ACT·PLAN·EXPLORE Diagnostic Test

ENGLISH
EXPLORE 1-40 • PLAN 1-50 • ACT 1-75

MATH
EXPLORE 1-30 • PLAN 1-40 • ACT 1-60

READING
EXPLORE 1-30 • PLAN 1-25 • ACT 1-40

SCIENCE
EXPLORE 1-28 • PLAN 1-30 • ACT 1-40

THE AREA BELOW IS FOR OFFICIAL USE ONLY. DO NOT MARK.

1 READER NO.
2 READER NO.
3 READER NO.

A
B
C
D

Copyright © 2009 Academic Educational Resources. All rights reserved.

ACT·PLAN·EXPLORE Diagnostic Test

Student Information

Please bubble in the appropriate box: PRE-TEST / MID-TERM / POST-TEST

LAST NAME | FIRST NAME | SITE | CLASS | ZIP CODE | RACE/ETHNICITY

RACE/ETHNICITY:
- White, Non-Hispanic
- American Indian or Alaskan Native
- Hispanic or Latino
- Black or African American
- Asian
- Native Hawaiian or Pacific Islander
- Other

GENDER
- MALE
- FEMALE

GRADE
- 7th Grade
- 8th Grade
- 9th Grade
- 10th Grade
- 11th Grade
- 12th Grade
- Other

STUDENT ID

NCLB Administrative Use
- IEP
- LEP
- SES

TEST & FORM CODE
- ACT
- PLAN   FORM
- EXPLORE

Please Enter Your Mailing Address
Name
Address
City   State   Zip
School   Date

PLEASE USE A NO. 2 PENCIL
RIGHT   WRONG

Using a number 2 pencil completely fill in the bubble. If you make an error, carefully erase and re-bubble your new choice. This will insure optimum scanning results.

CAUTION
THE FOLLOWING SECTION IS USED FOR OPTIONAL QUESTIONING, IT IS NOT PART OF YOUR TEST! SECTION 1 OF THE TEST BEGINS ON THE BACK OF THIS FORM.

Answer bubbles 1–102, each with options 1 2 3 4 5.

Copyright © 2009 Academic Educational Resources. All rights reserved.

ACT·PLAN·EXPLORE Diagnostic Test

ENGLISH

EXPLORE 1-40 • PLAN 1-50 • ACT 1-75

MATH

EXPLORE 1-30 • PLAN 1-40 • ACT 1-60

READING

EXPLORE 1-30 • PLAN 1-25 • ACT 1-40

SCIENCE

EXPLORE 1-28 • PLAN 1-30 • ACT 1-40

THE AREA BELOW IS FOR OFFICIAL USE ONLY. DO NOT MARK.

1 READER NO.

2 READER NO.

3 READER NO.

Copyright © 2009 Academic Educational Resources. All rights reserved.

ACT·PLAN·EXPLORE Diagnostic Test

Student Information

Please bubble in the appropriate box: PRE-TEST | MID-TERM | POST-TEST

LAST NAME | FIRST NAME | SITE | CLASS | ZIP CODE | RACE/ETHNICITY

RACE/ETHNICITY:
- White, Non-Hispanic
- American Indian or Alaskan Native
- Hispanic or Latino
- Black or African American
- Asian
- Native Hawaiian or Pacific Islander
- Other

GENDER:
- MALE
- FEMALE

GRADE:
- 7th Grade
- 8th Grade
- 9th Grade
- 10th Grade
- 11th Grade
- 12th Grade
- Other

STUDENT ID

NCLB Administrative Use:
- IEP
- LEP
- SES

TEST & FORM CODE:
- ACT
- PLAN
- EXPLORE

FORM

Please Enter Your Mailing Address

Name
Address
City   State   Zip
School   Date

PLEASE USE A NO. 2 PENCIL

RIGHT   WRONG

Using a number 2 pencil completely fill in the bubble. If you make an error, carefully erase and re-bubble your new choice. This will insure optimum scanning results.

CAUTION

THE FOLLOWING SECTION IS USED FOR OPTIONAL QUESTIONING, IT IS NOT PART OF YOUR TEST! SECTION 1 OF THE TEST BEGINS ON THE BACK OF THIS FORM.

Questions 1–102, each with answer bubbles 1 2 3 4 5.

Copyright © 2009 Academic Educational Resources. All rights reserved.

ACT·PLAN·EXPLORE Diagnostic Test

ENGLISH
EXPLORE 1-40 • PLAN 1-50 • ACT 1-75

MATH
EXPLORE 1-30 • PLAN 1-40 • ACT 1-60

READING
EXPLORE 1-30 • PLAN 1-25 • ACT 1-40

SCIENCE
EXPLORE 1-28 • PLAN 1-30 • ACT 1-40

THE AREA BELOW IS FOR OFFICIAL USE ONLY. DO NOT MARK.

1 READER NO.
2 READER NO.
3 READER NO.

A
B
C
D

Copyright © 2009 Academic Educational Resources. All rights reserved.

ACT·PLAN·EXPLORE Diagnostic Test

Student Information

Please bubble in the appropriate box:
- [ ] PRE-TEST
- [ ] MID-TERM
- [ ] POST-TEST

LAST NAME | **FIRST NAME** | **SITE** | **CLASS** | **ZIP CODE**

RACE/ETHNICITY
- [ ] White, Non-Hispanic
- [ ] American Indian or Alaskan Native
- [ ] Hispanic or Latino
- [ ] Black or African American
- [ ] Asian
- [ ] Native Hawaiian or Pacific Islander
- [ ] Other

GENDER
- [ ] MALE
- [ ] FEMALE

GRADE
- [ ] 7th Grade
- [ ] 8th Grade
- [ ] 9th Grade
- [ ] 10th Grade
- [ ] 11th Grade
- [ ] 12th Grade
- [ ] Other

STUDENT ID

NCLB Administrative Use
- [ ] IEP
- [ ] LEP
- [ ] SES

TEST & FORM CODE
- [ ] ACT
- [ ] PLAN
- [ ] EXPLORE

FORM: _____

Please Enter Your Mailing Address

Name: _____
Address: _____
City: _____ State: _____ Zip: _____
School: _____ Date: _____

PLEASE USE A NO. 2 PENCIL

RIGHT	WRONG
■ ●	X ⊖

Using a number 2 pencil completely fill in the bubble. If you make an error, carefully erase and re-bubble your new choice. This will insure optimum scanning results.

CAUTION

THE FOLLOWING SECTION IS USED FOR OPTIONAL QUESTIONING, IT IS NOT PART OF YOUR TEST! SECTION 1 OF THE TEST BEGINS ON THE BACK OF THIS FORM.

(Questions 1–102, each with answer bubbles 1 2 3 4 5)

Copyright © 2009 Academic Educational Resources. All rights reserved.

ACT·PLAN·EXPLORE Diagnostic Test

ENGLISH
EXPLORE 1-40 • PLAN 1-50 • ACT 1-75

MATH
EXPLORE 1-30 • PLAN 1-40 • ACT 1-60

READING
EXPLORE 1-30 • PLAN 1-25 • ACT 1-40

SCIENCE
EXPLORE 1-28 • PLAN 1-30 • ACT 1-40

THE AREA BELOW IS FOR OFFICIAL USE ONLY. DO NOT MARK.

1 READER NO.
2 READER NO.
3 READER NO.

A
B
C
D

Copyright © 2009 Academic Educational Resources. All rights reserved.

ACT·PLAN·EXPLORE Diagnostic Test

Student Information

Please bubble in the appropriate box: PRE-TEST | MID-TERM | POST-TEST

LAST NAME | FIRST NAME | SITE | CLASS | ZIP CODE | RACE/ETHNICITY

RACE/ETHNICITY:
- White, Non-Hispanic
- American Indian or Alaskan Native
- Hispanic or Latino
- Black or African American
- Asian
- Native Hawaiian or Pacific Islander
- Other

GENDER:
- MALE
- FEMALE

GRADE:
- 7th Grade
- 8th Grade
- 9th Grade
- 10th Grade
- 11th Grade
- 12th Grade
- Other

STUDENT ID

NCLB Administrative Use:
- IEP
- LEP
- SES

TEST & FORM CODE:
- ACT
- PLAN   FORM
- EXPLORE

Please Enter Your Mailing Address

Name
Address
City   State   Zip
School   Date

PLEASE USE A NO. 2 PENCIL

RIGHT | WRONG

Using a number 2 pencil completely fill in the bubble. If you make an error, carefully erase and re-bubble your new choice. This will insure optimum scanning results.

CAUTION

THE FOLLOWING SECTION IS USED FOR OPTIONAL QUESTIONING, IT IS NOT PART OF YOUR TEST! SECTION 1 OF THE TEST BEGINS ON THE BACK OF THIS FORM.

Questions 1–102, each with answer choices 1 2 3 4 5.

Copyright © 2009 Academic Educational Resources. All rights reserved.

ACT·PLAN·EXPLORE Diagnostic Test

ACT·PLAN·EXPLORE Diagnostic Test

Student Information

Please bubble in the appropriate box: PRE-TEST / MID-TERM / POST-TEST

LAST NAME | FIRST NAME | SITE | CLASS | ZIP CODE | RACE/ETHNICITY

RACE/ETHNICITY:
- White, Non-Hispanic
- American Indian or Alaskan Native
- Hispanic or Latino
- Black or African American
- Asian
- Native Hawaiian or Pacific Islander
- Other

GENDER
- MALE
- FEMALE

GRADE
- 7th Grade
- 8th Grade
- 9th Grade
- 10th Grade
- 11th Grade
- 12th Grade
- Other

STUDENT ID

NCLB Administrative Use
- IEP
- LEP
- SES

TEST & FORM CODE
- ACT
- PLAN
- EXPLORE
- FORM

Please Enter Your Mailing Address

Name
Address
City State Zip
School Date

PLEASE USE A NO. 2 PENCIL

RIGHT WRONG

Using a number 2 pencil completely fill in the bubble. If you make an error, carefully erase and re-bubble your new choice. This will insure optimum scanning results.

CAUTION

THE FOLLOWING SECTION IS USED FOR OPTIONAL QUESTIONING, IT IS NOT PART OF YOUR TEST! SECTION 1 OF THE TEST BEGINS ON THE BACK OF THIS FORM.

Questions 1–102, each with answer choices 1 2 3 4 5.

Copyright © 2009 Academic Educational Resources. All rights reserved.

ACT·PLAN·EXPLORE Diagnostic Test

ENGLISH
EXPLORE 1-40 • PLAN 1-50 • ACT 1-75

MATH
EXPLORE 1-30 • PLAN 1-40 • ACT 1-60

READING
EXPLORE 1-30 • PLAN 1-25 • ACT 1-40

SCIENCE
EXPLORE 1-28 • PLAN 1-30 • ACT 1-40

THE AREA BELOW IS FOR OFFICIAL USE ONLY. DO NOT MARK.

1 READER NO.
2 READER NO.
3 READER NO.

Copyright © 2009 Academic Educational Resources. All rights reserved.

CHAPTER 9
ANSWER KEYS

ACT SUCCESS
English Skill Builders
Answer Key

Fragments #1

1. C
2. F
3. B
4. J
5. C
6. F

Fragments #2

1. D
2. F
3. B
4. J
5. A
6. G
7. B

Punctuation #1

1. B
2. J
3. C
4. F
5. D
6. J

Punctuation #2

1. C
2. F
3. D
4. H
5. C
6. H
7. B
8. G
9. A

Punctuation #3

1. C
2. F
3. C
4. J
5. B
6. H
7. B
8. F
9. D
10. F
11. B
12. J
13. B

Punctuation #4

1. B
2. F
3. B
4. F
5. D
6. G
7. C
8. H
9. D
10. G
11. B
12. F
13. D
14. F
15. B

ACT SUCCESS
English Skill Builders
Answer Key

Commas

7. C
8. F
9. C
10. G
11. D
12. F
13. D
14. H
15. A
16. G
17. D
18. G

Possessives

1. A
2. H
3. B
4. H
5. A
6. J
7. A
8. G
9. C
10. J

Apostrophe #1

1. C
2. G
3. B
4. F
5. D
6. G

Apostrophe #2

1. B
2. H
3. A
4. H
5. C
6. J
7. B
8. G

Subject/Verb and Subject/Pronoun Agreement #1

1. C
2. J
3. C
4. F
5. B
6. H
7. D
8. G

Subject/Verb and Subject/Pronoun Agreement #2

1. C
2. G
3. A
4. J
5. B
6. H

Transitions #1

1. D
2. H
3. C
4. A
5. C
6. A

ACT SUCCESS
English Skill Builders
Answer Key

Transitions #2

1. D
2. G
3. D
4. F
5. C
6. H

Transitions and Modifiers #1

1. B
2. G
3. D
4. H
5. B
6. F

Transitions and Modifiers #2

1. B
2. J
3. B
4. H
5. C
6. F

Rhetorical Questions #1

1. B
2. H
3. A
4. G
5. D
6. H
7. D

Rhetorical Questions #2

1. C
2. F
3. D
4. G
5. C
6. F
7. B

Deleting

1. C
2. J
3. B
4. F
5. D
6. G
7. C

Integrated Punctuation #1

1. D
2. G
3. B
4. J
5. D
6. J
7. B
8. H
9. C
10. F
11. A
12. G
13. D
14. J
15. A

ACT SUCCESS
English Skill Builders
Answer Key

Integrated Punctuation #2

1. D
2. H
3. C
4. H
5. B
6. F
7. D
8. F
9. D
10. J
11. A
12. G
13. A

ACT SUCCESS
English Quiz: English Made Easy
Answer Key

Commas

1. Introductory clause
2. Non-restrictive clause/appositive/interruption
3. Two or more adjectives preceding a noun
4. More than two items in a series
5. Comma + conjunction to combine two complete sentences
6. Afterthought

Comma Hints

1. When in doubt, leave the comma out
2. Just because you pause when reading does not mean a comma is required
3. If all answer choices are identically worded with commas in different places, correct answer is likely the one that omits the comma altogether.

Dash

1. Interruption
2. Afterthought

Semicolon

1. Separate two complete sentences

Colon

1. After a complete sentence followed by a summary list
2. After a complete sentence followed by an afterthought
3. Between two complete sentences when the second explains or restates an idea in the first

Apostrophe

1. 's for one owner
2. s' for more than one owner
3. 's for plural words that do not end in "s"

Sentences

1. Comma + conjunction
2. Semicolon
3. Colon
4. Period

Usage

1. Possession
2. Direction
3. They are
4. Not a word
5. It is
6. Possession

ACT SUCCESS
English Practice Passages

Answer Key

Practice Passage #1	Practice Passage #2	Practice Passage #3
1. A	1. B	1. B
2. G	2. H	2. H
3. B	3. B	3. A
4. H	4. F	4. F
5. B	5. B	5. C
6. J	6. H	6. J
7. C	7. B	7. B
8. J	8. J	8. H
9. D	9. D	9. B
10. F	10. J	10. H
11. A	11. C	11. B
12. H	12. F	12. H
13. B	13. A	13. C
14. H	14. F	14. H
15. D	15. B	15. C

Copyright © 2009 by Academic Educational Resources. All rights reserved.

ACT SUCCESS
Math Skill Builders
Answer Key

Area Formulas
1. B
2. F
3. C
4. G
5. C
6. H

Order of Operations
1. A
2. G
3. A
4. G
5. D
6. G

Slopes of Lines
1. B
2. G
3. C
4. H
5. E

Midpoint Formula
1. A
2. H
3. D
4. J
5. C
6. K
7. D

Pythagorean Theorem
1. C
2. G
3. C
4. H
5. B
6. K

Distance Formula
1. E
2. G
3. C
4. G
5. D

Prime Numbers
1. C
2. H
3. A
4. G
5. A
6. F

Even & Odd Numbers
1. E
2. H
3. D
4. H
5. D
6. H

Percents
1. C
2. K
3. A
4. G
5. C
6. F

Greatest Common Factor
1. C
2. H
3. B
4. F
5. A
6. K

Least Common Multiple
1. C
2. J
3. D
4. K
5. D
6. J

Motion Problems
1. B
2. G
3. E
4. H
5. B
6. G

Exponents
1. E
2. G
3. B
4. J
5. B

Radicals
1. A
2. H
3. A
4. J
5. C
6. H

Quadratics
1. B
2. K
3. E
4. H
5. B

Circles
1. A
2. G
3. E
4. J
5. C

Right Triangle Trig
1. E
2. J
3. A
4. G
5. E
6. J

Logs
1. C
2. F
3. C
4. H
5. A
6. H

Complex Numbers
1. C
2. H
3. C
4. F
5. D

ACT SUCCESS
Math Quizzes

Answer Key

Quiz I Pre-Algebra	Quiz II Algebra	Quiz III Plane Geometry	Quiz IV Circles	Quiz V Advanced Algebra	Quiz VI Trigonometry
1. D	1. E	1. A	1. D	1. C	1. B
2. G	2. H	2. G	2. J	2. G	2. H
3. B	3. E	3. A	3. A	3. A	3. A
4. K	4. G	4. H	4. H	4. K	4. K
5. C	5. E	5. A	5. D	5. D	5. E
6. J	6. J	6. H	6. K	6. H	6. J
7. D	7. B	7. E	7. A	7. E	7. C
8. J	8. K	8. G	8. F	8. H	8. G
9. D	9. D	9. A	9. B	9. B	9. E
10. H	10. K	10. F	10. G	10. K	10. G
	11. A	11. B	11. B	11. A	11. A
	12. J	12. F	12. K	12. G	12. H
	13. C	13. B	13. C	13. D	13. D
	14. F	14. G	14. H	14. F	
	15. D		15. E	15. B	
	16. J		16. H	16. K	
	17. C			17. A	
	18. J			18. K	
	19. B			19. A	
	20. G			20. G	

ACT SUCCESS
Reading Skill Builders
Answer Key

Finding the Main Idea
NOTE: Your answers do not need to match these exactly, but they should follow the same idea.

1. I was forced to take piano lessons because my mother wanted me to.
2. Cosmology is scientific, not guesswork.
3. Mass extinctions happen when long periods of stability are disrupted by an infrequent occurrence.
4. Crazy Horse was a legendary warrior and leader of the Lakota people who did not give up easily.
5. Gestures are an important part of any communication.
6. Poor sleep habits have a negative effect on teenager's moods and behaviors.
7. An introvert's and an extrovert's brains work differently, with introverts focusing inward and extroverts focusing outward.
8. Vitamin E has been shown to decrease the frequency of Alzheimer's symptoms

Determining Character and Attitude #1
1. C
2. J
3. C
4. F

Determining Character and Attitude #2
1. A
2. J
3. C
4. J

Determining Character and Attitude #3
1. B
2. H
3. A

Skimming for Details
1. B
2. J
3. C
4. F
5. D
6. H

Cause and Effect #1
1. B
2. J
3. C

Cause and Effect #2
1. C
2. F
3. B

ACT SUCCESS
Reading Practice Passages

Answer Key

Fiction	Humanities
1. B	1. D
2. H	2. H
3. A	3. A
4. J	4. H
5. C	5. D
6. J	6. J
7. D	7. B
8. G	8. F
9. B	9. C
10. H	10. G
Social Science	**Natural Science**
1. C	1. A
2. J	2. H
3. B	3. B
4. F	4. J
5. C	5. C
6. G	6. F
7. A	7. B
8. J	8. J
9. B	9. C
10. F	10. G

ACT SUCCESS
Science Skill Builders
Answer Key

Interpreting Graphs #1

1. A
2. J
3. D
4. J
5. C

Interpreting Graphs #2

1. A
2. J
3. C
4. H
5. B

Interpreting Graphs #3

1. B
2. G
3. C
4. G
5. A

Analyzing Data #1

1. D
2. G
3. C
4. F
5. B
6. F
7. C
8. J
9. A
10. J
11. B
12. G

Analyzing Data #2

1. B
2. J
3. B
4. J
5. A
6. H

ACT SUCCESS
Science Skill Builders
Answer Key

Analyzing Data #3

1. D
2. F
3. C
4. H
5. B
6. J

Analyzing Data #4

1. A
2. H
3. D
4. G
5. D
6. G
7. A
8. H

Analyzing Data #5

1. D
2. G
3. D
4. G
5. D
6. H
7. D
8. F
9. C

Analyzing Data #6

1. A
2. H
3. D
4. G
5. C
6. J

Opposing Viewpoints #1

1. C
2. G
3. D
4. F
5. D
6. F
7. C

Opposing Viewpoints #2

1. D
2. J
3. C
4. G
5. B
6. J
7. D

ACT SUCCESS
Science Skill Builders
Answer Key

Opposing Viewpoints #3

1. C
2. G
3. B
4. F
5. C
6. J
7. D

ACT SUCCESS
Science Practice Passages

Answer Key

Practice Passage #1	Practice Passage #2	Practice Passage #3
1. C	1. C	1. C
2. H	2. J	2. G
3. D	3. A	3. B
4. F	4. H	4. F
5. B	5. B	5. D
6. J	6. F	6. J
		7. C

TEST 1
Answer Key

English

1.	A	31.	A	61.	B
2.	H	32.	J	62.	H
3.	C	33.	C	63.	A
4.	G	34.	G	64.	J
5.	C	35.	A	65.	D
6.	G	36.	H	66.	H
7.	C	37.	D	67.	C
8.	J	38.	H	68.	G
9.	A	39.	D	69.	D
10.	J	40.	H	70.	G
11.	C	41.	D	71.	D
12.	F	42.	F	72.	G
13.	B	43.	B	73.	D
14.	J	44.	F	74.	F
15.	C	45.	C	75.	A
16.	J	46.	J		
17.	A	47.	D		
18.	G	48.	G		
19.	B	49.	A		
20.	J	50.	J		
21.	C	51.	C		
22.	H	52.	F		
23.	A	53.	B		
24.	F	54.	J		
25.	D	55.	C		
26.	J	56.	J		
27.	C	57.	B		
28.	G	58.	H		
29.	B	59.	D		
30.	G	60.	H		

Math

1.	C	31.	E
2.	F	32.	H
3.	C	33.	D
4.	J	34.	J
5.	D	35.	C
6.	H	36.	H
7.	B	37.	B
8.	K	38.	J
9.	C	39.	A
10.	K	40.	F
11.	A	41.	C
12.	H	42.	K
13.	A	43.	B
14.	G	44.	H
15.	C	45.	D
16.	H	46.	J
17.	C	47.	D
18.	G	48.	F
19.	B	49.	A
20.	J	50.	H
21.	D	51.	D
22.	J	52.	H
23.	B	53.	E
24.	J	54.	H
25.	D	55.	D
26.	J	56.	J
27.	E	57.	D
28.	G	58.	K
29.	C	59.	E
30.	J	60.	F

Reading

1.	B	31.	D
2.	H	32.	G
3.	D	33.	A
4.	J	34.	G
5.	C	35.	A
6.	J	36.	H
7.	A	37.	D
8.	H	38.	G
9.	B	39.	A
10.	J	40.	G
11.	C		
12.	G		
13.	D		
14.	H		
15.	A		
16.	G		
17.	A		
18.	J		
19.	C		
20.	G		
21.	B		
22.	J		
23.	C		
24.	F		
25.	C		
26.	J		
27.	C		
28.	G		
29.	D		
30.	F		

Science

1.	D	31.	B
2.	G	32.	J
3.	C	33.	B
4.	F	34.	H
5.	B	35.	A
6.	F	36.	H
7.	B	37.	D
8.	H	38.	G
9.	D	39.	D
10.	J	40.	H
11.	A		
12.	G		
13.	B		
14.	G		
15.	C		
16.	H		
17.	B		
18.	H		
19.	B		
20.	J		
21.	C		
22.	F		
23.	B		
24.	H		
25.	A		
26.	J		
27.	B		
28.	H		
29.	D		
30.	F		

TEST 2
Answer Key

English

1.	A	31.	D	61.	C
2.	G	32.	G	62.	G
3.	C	33.	C	63.	B
4.	G	34.	G	64.	G
5.	C	35.	D	65.	A
6.	J	36.	F	66.	J
7.	D	37.	B	67.	B
8.	H	38.	H	68.	H
9.	A	39.	B	69.	B
10.	J	40.	J	70.	F
11.	D	41.	C	71.	B
12.	H	42.	G	72.	G
13.	C	43.	D	73.	D
14.	G	44.	G	74.	H
15.	C	45.	B	75.	D
16.	G	46.	H		
17.	B	47.	A		
18.	J	48.	J		
19.	A	49.	B		
20.	G	50.	H		
21.	D	51.	B		
22.	H	52.	F		
23.	B	53.	D		
24.	G	54.	H		
25.	A	55.	B		
26.	J	56.	G		
27.	A	57.	D		
28.	J	58.	H		
29.	C	59.	B		
30.	H	60.	G		

Math

1.	A	31.	C	
2.	G	32.	J	
3.	B	33.	E	
4.	J	34.	F	
5.	E	35.	C	
6.	F	36.	H	
7.	C	37.	D	
8.	H	38.	K	
9.	C	39.	A	
10.	H	40.	H	
11.	C	41.	C	
12.	K	42.	K	
13.	D	43.	B	
14.	K	44.	G	
15.	D	45.	C	
16.	H	46.	K	
17.	D	47.	C	
18.	K	48.	J	
19.	E	49.	E	
20.	J	50.	H	
21.	D	51.	E	
22.	G	52.	H	
23.	C	53.	A	
24.	J	54.	G	
25.	E	55.	C	
26.	G	56.	F	
27.	D	57.	B	
28.	H	58.	K	
29.	A	59.	A	
30.	H	60.	K	

Reading

1.	C	31.	A
2.	G	32.	J
3.	B	33.	A
4.	F	34.	H
5.	D	35.	C
6.	H	36.	J
7.	A	37.	B
8.	J	38.	J
9.	C	39.	C
10.	J	40.	G
11.	A		
12.	H		
13.	B		
14.	J		
15.	D		
16.	G		
17.	D		
18.	F		
19.	C		
20.	F		
21.	A		
22.	H		
23.	B		
24.	H		
25.	D		
26.	G		
27.	A		
28.	G		
29.	C		
30.	J		

Science

1.	A	31.	A
2.	J	32.	H
3.	C	33.	B
4.	G	34.	H
5.	B	35.	B
6.	G	36.	H
7.	D	37.	D
8.	F	38.	F
9.	B	39.	D
10.	H	40.	G
11.	B		
12.	G		
13.	C		
14.	F		
15.	D		
16.	H		
17.	B		
18.	F		
19.	D		
20.	G		
21.	C		
22.	J		
23.	B		
24.	J		
25.	A		
26.	J		
27.	C		
28.	H		
29.	D		
30.	G		

TEST 3
Answer Key

English

1.	C	31.	C	61.	B
2.	J	32.	F	62.	F
3.	B	33.	B	63.	B
4.	J	34.	J	64.	H
5.	C	35.	A	65.	D
6.	F	36.	F	66.	J
7.	D	37.	D	67.	C
8.	F	38.	J	68.	H
9.	B	39.	B	69.	C
10.	G	40.	G	70.	G
11.	C	41.	D	71.	A
12.	J	42.	F	72.	J
13.	D	43.	B	73.	B
14.	F	44.	H	74.	H
15.	B	45.	B	75.	D
16.	J	46.	G		
17.	B	47.	A		
18.	H	48.	H		
19.	B	49.	A		
20.	F	50.	J		
21.	D	51.	B		
22.	H	52.	F		
23.	A	53.	C		
24.	F	54.	F		
25.	C	55.	A		
26.	J	56.	J		
27.	D	57.	B		
28.	G	58.	G		
29.	C	59.	D		
30.	G	60.	F		

Math

1.	D	31.	D	
2.	G	32.	H	
3.	C	33.	C	
4.	J	34.	H	
5.	E	35.	E	
6.	J	36.	J	
7.	D	37.	A	
8.	J	38.	H	
9.	D	39.	D	
10.	H	40.	K	
11.	C	41.	E	
12.	K	42.	H	
13.	A	43.	C	
14.	H	44.	K	
15.	B	45.	C	
16.	H	46.	J	
17.	C	47.	A	
18.	H	48.	G	
19.	E	49.	C	
20.	J	50.	K	
21.	C	51.	A	
22.	G	52.	F	
23.	C	53.	D	
24.	H	54.	H	
25.	E	55.	D	
26.	K	56.	F	
27.	C	57.	B	
28.	H	58.	F	
29.	A	59.	B	
30.	K	60.	J	

Reading

1.	C	31.	C	
2.	F	32.	F	
3.	B	33.	D	
4.	H	34.	G	
5.	D	35.	B	
6.	F	36.	G	
7.	C	37.	C	
8.	J	38.	G	
9.	D	39.	A	
10.	G	40.	H	
11.	C			
12.	H			
13.	A			
14.	J			
15.	A			
16.	H			
17.	A			
18.	G			
19.	D			
20.	G			
21.	B			
22.	J			
23.	C			
24.	J			
25.	B			
26.	F			
27.	C			
28.	J			
29.	B			
30.	H			

Science

1.	D	31.	A	
2.	J	32.	G	
3.	B	33.	C	
4.	F	34.	H	
5.	B	35.	B	
6.	H	36.	F	
7.	A	37.	C	
8.	J	38.	F	
9.	B	39.	B	
10.	F	40.	J	
11.	C			
12.	F			
13.	D			
14.	J			
15.	C			
16.	F			
17.	D			
18.	G			
19.	C			
20.	F			
21.	B			
22.	J			
23.	A			
24.	H			
25.	D			
26.	F			
27.	B			
28.	H			
29.	D			
30.	H			

TEST 4
Answer Key

English

1. B	31. B	61. D	
2. J	32. J	62. G	
3. A	33. D	63. D	
4. J	34. F	64. F	
5. D	35. A	65. C	
6. H	36. G	66. G	
7. C	37. C	67. D	
8. F	38. J	68. H	
9. D	39. A	69. A	
10. J	40. H	70. G	
11. B	41. B	71. D	
12. H	42. J	72. H	
13. B	43. B	73. B	
14. G	44. J	74. J	
15. A	45. C	75. C	
16. H	46. G		
17. B	47. D		
18. F	48. G		
19. B	49. C		
20. F	50. J		
21. C	51. B		
22. G	52. J		
23. D	53. A		
24. H	54. G		
25. B	55. C		
26. F	56. G		
27. B	57. B		
28. J	58. J		
29. C	59. C		
30. J	60. F		

Math

1. E	31. A
2. G	32. H
3. D	33. C
4. H	34. H
5. A	35. B
6. J	36. J
7. B	37. D
8. H	38. K
9. C	39. C
10. K	40. J
11. C	41. B
12. J	42. G
13. B	43. A
14. G	44. H
15. D	45. E
16. J	46. K
17. C	47. B
18. G	48. F
19. B	49. B
20. J	50. G
21. E	51. D
22. G	52. J
23. A	53. B
24. H	54. F
25. D	55. E
26. K	56. H
27. B	57. E
28. G	58. F
29. A	59. B
30. H	60. K

Reading

1. A	31. D
2. G	32. J
3. B	33. A
4. J	34. J
5. B	35. D
6. G	36. J
7. C	37. A
8. F	38. G
9. D	39. C
10. H	40. H
11. C	
12. H	
13. B	
14. F	
15. A	
16. H	
17. D	
18. F	
19. B	
20. J	
21. A	
22. H	
23. B	
24. F	
25. B	
26. G	
27. C	
28. J	
29. B	
30. F	

Science

1. C	31. D
2. G	32. J
3. D	33. B
4. F	34. J
5. B	35. C
6. G	36. H
7. D	37. A
8. F	38. J
9. B	39. B
10. H	40. H
11. C	
12. G	
13. B	
14. J	
15. B	
16. G	
17. A	
18. H	
19. C	
20. J	
21. D	
22. G	
23. C	
24. F	
25. B	
26. F	
27. B	
28. F	
29. D	
30. G	

TEST 5
Answer Key

English

1.	D	31.	C	61.	C
2.	F	32.	J	62.	F
3.	B	33.	B	63.	D
4.	H	34.	F	64.	G
5.	D	35.	C	65.	D
6.	G	36.	J	66.	H
7.	D	37.	D	67.	C
8.	H	38.	G	68.	F
9.	A	39.	C	69.	B
10.	F	40.	F	70.	J
11.	B	41.	A	71.	D
12.	G	42.	G	72.	H
13.	C	43.	D	73.	A
14.	J	44.	H	74.	G
15.	B	45.	B	75.	B
16.	H	46.	G		
17.	B	47.	D		
18.	G	48.	F		
19.	D	49.	C		
20.	J	50.	G		
21.	C	51.	C		
22.	F	52.	F		
23.	D	53.	D		
24.	H	54.	J		
25.	A	55.	A		
26.	F	56.	H		
27.	C	57.	B		
28.	G	58.	G		
29.	B	59.	D		
30.	H	60.	H		

Math

1.	A	31.	G	
2.	J	32.	C	
3.	B	33.	F	
4.	K	34.	A	
5.	A	35.	C	
6.	K	36.	F	
7.	D	37.	D	
8.	F	38.	F	
9.	B	39.	E	
10.	H	40.	K	
11.	D	41.	B	
12.	H	42.	J	
13.	C	43.	D	
14.	G	44.	H	
15.	C	45.	C	
16.	J	46.	F	
17.	F	47.	D	
18.	J	48.	H	
19.	D	49.	A	
20.	G	50.	J	
21.	E	51.	B	
22.	F	52.	G	
23.	B	53.	B	
24.	H	54.	F	
25.	A	55.	C	
26.	K	56.	J	
27.	C	57.	E	
28.	H	58.	K	
29.	J	59.	A	
30.	E	60.	J	

Reading

1.	A	31.	A	
2.	G	32.	G	
3.	A	33.	D	
4.	J	34.	H	
5.	D	35.	B	
6.	G	36.	F	
7.	C	37.	C	
8.	H	38.	J	
9.	A	39.	D	
10.	J	40.	H	
11.	C			
12.	J			
13.	D			
14.	G			
15.	B			
16.	H			
17.	A			
18.	G			
19.	D			
20.	H			
21.	D			
22.	H			
23.	B			
24.	J			
25.	A			
26.	H			
27.	C			
28.	G			
29.	D			
30.	G			

Science

1.	B	31.	A	
2.	H	32.	G	
3.	A	33.	D	
4.	H	34.	H	
5.	D	35.	B	
6.	H	36.	F	
7.	D	37.	D	
8.	F	38.	G	
9.	D	39.	B	
10.	H	40.	D	
11.	C			
12.	J			
13.	A			
14.	G			
15.	A			
16.	J			
17.	B			
18.	G			
19.	C			
20.	F			
21.	C			
22.	J			
23.	D			
24.	H			
25.	B			
26.	F			
27.	A			
28.	H			
29.	C			
30.	J			